THE COMMUNIST PARTY OF CHINA
A CONCISE HISTORY

ALAIN CHARLES ASIA PUBLISHING

Published by
ACA Publishing Ltd.
University House
11 13 Lower Grosvenor Place
London SW1W 0EX, UK
Tel: +44 (0)20 3289 3885
E mail: info@alaincharlesasia.com
Web: www.alaincharlesasia.com

Beijing Office
Tel: +86 (0)10 8472 1250

Translators (in order of appearance): Hui Cooper & Dennis Cooper, Haiwang Yuan, Martin Ward, James Trapp, Jiang Lin

Published by ACA Publishing Ltd in association with People's Publishing House, Beijing, China

Chinese language copyright © 中国共产党简史 *(Zhong Guo Gong Chan Dang Jian Shi)* 2021, by People's Publishing House and the Party History Press of the CPC

English translation text © 2022, ACA Publishing Ltd, London, UK

ALL RIGHTS RESERVED. NO PART OF THIS PUBLICATION MAY BE REPRODUCED IN MATERIAL FORM, BY ANY MEANS, WHETHER GRAPHIC, ELECTRONIC, MECHANICAL OR OTHER, INCLUDING PHOTOCOPYING OR INFORMATION STORAGE, IN WHOLE OR IN PART, AND MAY NOT BE USED TO PREPARE OTHER PUBLICATIONS WITHOUT WRITTEN PERMISSION FROM THE PUBLISHER.

The greatest care has been taken to ensure accuracy but the publisher can accept no responsibility for errors or omissions, or for any liability occasioned by relying on its content.

Paperback ISBN: 978-1-83890-009-0
eBook ISBN: 978-1-83890-010-6

A catalogue record for *The Communist Party of China: A Concise History* is available from the National Bibliographic Service of the British Library.

Mao Zedong solemnly proclaims the founding of the PRC's Central People's Government on the Tiananmen Gate Tower on 1 October 1949

Deng Xiaoping makes an important speech to celebrate the 35th anniversary of the founding of the PRC on 1 October 1984

Jiang Zemin waves on the Tiananmen Gate Tower to acknowledge a mass parade of troops taking part in a general assembly to celebrate the 50th anniversary of the founding of the PRC on 1 October 1999

Hu Jintao makes an important speech to celebrate the 60th anniversary of the founding of the PRC on 1 October 2009

Xi Jinping makes an important speech to celebrate the 70th anniversary of the founding of the PRC on 1 October 2019

CONTENTS

CHAPTER 1 - THE FOUNDING OF THE COMMUNIST PARTY OF CHINA AND HOW IT THREW ITSELF INTO THE POWERFUL CURRENT OF THE GREAT REVOLUTION

1. The historical mission of national rejuvenation and the difficult task of exploring every source of power — 3
2. The May Fourth Movement and the spread of Marxism in China — 7
3. The founding of the Communist Party of China and the formulation of the democratic revolutionary programme — 13
4. The First KMT-CPC Cooperation and the rise of the high tide of the Great Revolution — 21
5. The Northern Expedition and the Worker-Peasant Movement — 27
6. The breakdown of KMT-CPC Cooperation and the failure of the Great Revolution — 31

CHAPTER 2 - SETTING OFF A STORM OF AGRARIAN REVOLUTION

1. Resisting KMT reactionary rule by armed struggle — 39
2. Mao Zedong and the opening up of a new path for the Chinese revolution — 44
3. The Red Army's victory in its struggle against 'encirclement and suppression' and building revolutionary bases in rural areas — 50
4. The situation after the Mukden Incident and the start of the Central Red Army's Long March — 57
5. The Zunyi Conference and success of the Red Army's Long March — 64
6. Strive for the establishment of a national anti-Japanese united front — 74

CHAPTER 3 - THE MAINSTAY OF THE NATIONAL WAR OF RESISTANCE AGAINST JAPANESE AGGRESSION

1. The party's line of all-out resistance and formulation of protracted war policy — 81
2. Waging anti-Japanese guerrilla warfare in the enemy's rear and upholding independence and initiative within the united front — 87
3. Support the policy of resistance, unity and progress — 93
4. Consolidating the anti-Japanese base areas and promoting the anti-Japanese democratic movement — 101
5. Strengthening party building, pushing forward the Sinification of Marxism and carrying out the Rectification Movement — 108
6. Seventh Party Congress and the establishment of Mao Zedong Thought as the CPC's guiding ideology, and final victory in the War of Resistance Against Japanese Aggression — 114

CHAPTER 4 - WINNING NATIONWIDE VICTORY FOR THE NEW DEMOCRATIC REVOLUTION

1. Chongqing negotiations and the struggle for peace and democracy — 123
2. Foiling the KMT's military attacks and forming a second front — 129
3. The PLA's shift to strategic offensive — 134
4. Formulation and implementation of national programme for victory while consolidating and expanding the People's Democratic United Front — 138
5. The great strategic decisive battle and collapse of the KMT's reactionary rule — 144
6. The Second Plenary Session of the Seventh Central Committee of the CPC and preparations for the establishment of New China — 153

CHAPTER 5 - THE FOUNDING OF THE PRC AND ESTABLISHMENT OF THE SOCIALIST SYSTEM

1. The founding of the PRC and consolidation of the newly-emerged people's power — 163
2. The War to Resist the US and Aid Korea, land system reform and other democratic reforms — 171
3. National economic recovery and the launch of all types of construction — 180
4. The CPC's general line during the transition period and the beginning of planned large-scale economic construction — 190
5. Basic completion of socialist transformation and the establishment of the socialist system — 195

CHAPTER 6 - EXPLORATION AND TORTUOUS DEVELOPMENT OF SOCIALIST CONSTRUCTION

1. The Eighth National Congress of the CPC and a good start for China's socialist construction — 205
2. Difficulties in exploring the socialist road — 211
3. The tortuous development path of socialist construction — 225

CHAPTER 7 - A MOMENTOUS AND HISTORIC TURNING POINT AND THE ESTABLISHMENT OF SOCIALISM WITH CHINESE CHARACTERISTICS

1. Third Plenary Session of the 11th CPC Central Committee achieves a momentous and historic turnaround — 239
2. Completing the task of setting things right — 248
3. The beginning of rural reform, the establishment of special economic zones (SEZs), and reform and opening up — 254
4. The CPC's 12th National Congress and the comprehensive launch of socialist modernisation — 264
5. The CPC's 13th National Congress and establishment of the party's basic line in the primary stage of socialism — 279
6. Adjustments to National Defence Strategy — 285
7. Formation of the 'One Country, Two Systems' policy — 288
8. Foreign policy adjustments — 292

9. Undergoing the trial of political turmoil, and the completion of governance rectification — 295
10. Deng Xiaoping's southern tour speeches — 305

CHAPTER 8 - PROPELLING SOCIALISM WITH CHINESE CHARACTERISTICS FORWARD INTO THE 21ST CENTURY

1. The 14th CPC National Congress and the establishment of the socialist market economy — 313
2. Strengthening macro-control and economic development to achieve a 'soft landing' — 318
3. The 15th CPC National Congress, the establishment of Deng Xiaoping Theory as the guiding ideology of the party and the thorough advancing of reform and opening up — 321
4. Formulation and implementation of the cross-century development strategy — 330
5. The construction of political civilisation and advanced culture, and the achievement of all-round moderate prosperity in people's lives — 338
6. Active promotion of military reform with Chinese characteristics — 346
7. The return of Hong Kong and Macau to the motherland and the growth of cross-strait exchanges — 349
8. Promoting the construction of a new pattern of comprehensive multi-level foreign relations — 354
9. Promoting construction of the party's new great project — 358

CHAPTER 9 - UPHOLD AND DEVELOP SOCIALISM WITH CHINESE CHARACTERISTICS UNDER NEW CONDITIONS

1. The 16th National Congress of the CPC: the establishment of the important thinking of 'Three Represents' as the party's guiding ideology, and a programme for creating an all-round moderately prosperous society — 369
2. Promoting economic, social and scientific development — 373
3. The 17th National Congress of the CPC and the new arrangements for building an all-round moderately prosperous society — 384
4. Responding to major challenges, and deepening reform and opening up — 388

5. Fulfilling the historic mission of the military on the new stage of the new century	403
6. Promoting the practice of 'One Country, Two Systems' and the great cause of the peaceful reunification of the motherland	406
7. Persisting with peaceful development and cooperation	411
8. Improving the scientific level of party building and establishing the Scientific Outlook on Development as the party's guiding ideology	414

CHAPTER 10 - SOCIALISM WITH CHINESE CHARACTERISTICS

1. The 18th National Congress of the CPC and the Chinese dream of realising the great rejuvenation of the Chinese nation	423
2. Promoting the comprehensive programme of 'five in one'	434
3. Coordinating and advancing the strategic programme of the 'four comprehensives'	456
4. Comprehensively advancing the modernisation of national defence and the military	475
5. Adhering to 'One Country, Two Systems' and advancing the reunification of the motherland	486
6. Comprehensively promoting major-country diplomacy with Chinese characteristics and promoting the building of a community with a shared future for mankind	496
7. The 19th National Congress of the CPC, the decision to take Xi Jinping Thought on Socialism with Chinese Characteristics in the New Era as the party's guiding ideology and securing a decisive victory for building an all-round moderately prosperous society	510
8. Upholding overall party leadership and boosting the quality of party building	521
9. Taking new steps to build state institutions and governance systems	536
10. Pushing ahead various undertakings amid risks and challenges	547
11. Building an all-round moderately prosperous society and embarking on a new journey to fully build a modern socialist state	566
Conclusion	585

One

The Founding of the Communist Party of China and How it Threw Itself into the Powerful Current of the Great Revolution

One night in July 1921, the First National Congress of the Communist Party of China (CPC) was inaugurated secretly in a two-storey private residence in the French Concession in Shanghai. A modern political party of the proletariat which took Marxism-Leninism as its guide to action was born. An epoch-making event, like a blazing torch held aloft, it brought light and hope to the war-ravaged Chinese people who had suffered tremendously in modern times. From then on, they had the backbone for their struggle for national independence and liberation, for the prosperity and strength of the country, and for the happiness of the people; mentally they shifted from passivity to taking the initiative.

1
THE HISTORICAL MISSION OF NATIONAL REJUVENATION AND THE DIFFICULT TASK OF EXPLORING EVERY SOURCE OF POWER

Over the course of several thousand years, the Chinese people created a long-lasting and splendid civilisation, making a marvellous contribution to humanity and becoming one of the great peoples of the world. Following the advent of modern times, however, owing to the aggression of the Western powers and the corruptness of feudal rulers, China was gradually reduced to a semi-colonial, semi-feudal society. The country went to rack and ruin and the people were plunged into misery, causing the Chinese nation to experience suffering of unparalleled proportions.

From 1840 onwards, the Western powers forced China to concede territory and pay indemnities, greedily seizing special privileges through wars of aggression and other means. The main wars included the First Opium War, Britain's invasion of China, 1840-1842; the Second Opium War, the Anglo-French Allied Forces' invasion of China, 1856-1860; the war of French aggression against China, 1884-1885; the Japanese aggression against China, 1894-1895; and the Eight Allied Forces' invasion of China, 1900. Consequently Britain seized Hong Kong, Japan took Taiwan, and Tsarist Russia grabbed the Northeast and Northwest of China. Apart from seizing territory, the Western powers extorted payment of indemnities. For war reparations China paid out more than one billion taels of silver, yet the annual revenue of the Qing Government was no more than 8,000 taels of silver at the time. Through harsher and harsher unequal treaties, the Western powers gained various important privileges. They were able to build ports and concessions, open mines, factories, banks and companies, build railways and churches, and station their armed forces in China; they carved out spheres of influence and enjoyed consular jurisdiction and unilateral most-favoured-nation (MFN) treatment. With regard to politics, the economy, the military and culture, like a giant net penetrating everywhere, hundreds of unequal treaties, regulations and special treaties shackled China, making it unable to move a single step yet blamed for whatever it did, while accordingly the Western powers could do whatever they liked. They controlled China's trading ports, customs, foreign trade and transportation, meanwhile dumping their goods and turning China into a market for their products and a base for extorting raw materials.

The burning down of the Old Summer Palace by Anglo-French forces, the wiping out of the Chinese Northern Fleet in the Sino-Japanese War of 1894-1895, the incursion of the Eight-Power Allied Forces sent by Britain, the United States, France, Germany, Russia, Japan, Italy and Austria that brutally burned, murdered, raped and looted in Beijing… all these events left a painful, indelible memory in the mind of the Chinese people. Representing the interests of the landlord class and the comprador bourgeoisie, the Qing Government had increasingly become the tools of foreign capitalists to rule China, turning itself into a traitorous, decadent and incompetent regime stifling China's vitality. The contradiction between imperialism and the Chinese nation, between feudalism and the popular masses, had become the principal contradiction in Chinese society. The Chinese people lived in suffering and the nation seemed to be on the brink of ruin.

After the Opium War of 1840, the realisation of national rejuvenation has become the greatest dream of the whole nation and a historical mission for the Chinese people fighting for national independence and liberation, for the prosperity and strength of the country and for the happiness of the people. With a tradition of striving unceasingly, they never ceased their struggles to defend national independence and dignity, and safeguard Chinese civilisation. Before the CPC was founded, to change China's lot, many patriotic pioneers, who devoted themselves to the cause of national progress, who would step into the breach as another fell, made unremitting efforts to explore a way to save China. However, no matter whether they were wars of resistance against foreign aggression, the peasant uprising of the Taiping Heavenly Kingdom, the Westernisation Movement of *zhongti xiyong* (keeping Chinese values as the essence, while adopting Western concepts for their practical utility), the Reform Movement of 1898 or the Yihetuan Movement in 1900, also known as the Boxer Rebellion, that started from the grassroots of society and enjoyed broad-based support, owing to their failure to find a scientific theory, a correct path and reliable social forces, one after another they all failed, a result that countless people with lofty ideals regretted to the end of their days.

The Xinhai Revolution of 1911 broke out in October that year. It overthrew the Qing imperial court and established the Republic of China (ROC), ending the autocratic monarchy system that had ruled China for over two thousand years. Although the 1911 Revolution led by Sun Yat-sen failed to change the semi-colonial, semi-feudal nature of the old China, failed to change the tragic lot of the Chinese people, and failed to complete the mission of realising national independence and liberation, yet it developed the modern national democratic revolution in a complete sense. It opened the gate for China to progress and spread the ideology of democracy and a republic, and greatly promoted national ideological emancipation. With its shocking force and influence, it pushed forward China's social transformation, destabilising the reactionary ruling order.

Reality is sometimes cruel. Supported by imperialists and domestic reactionary forces, the Beiyang warlords headed by Yuan Shikai grabbed the fruits of the 1911 Revolution, and the newborn bourgeois republic came to a premature end after an existence of a few months. After Yuan Shikai died, the Beiyang faction of the northern warlords split into the Zhili, Anhui and Fengtian factions. Manipulated by the imperialist powers, China fell into disintegrating, separatist warlord regimes and tangled warfare among warlords. Under the autocratic rule of the feudal warlords, China was sinking deeper and deeper into the abyss of semi-colonial, semi-feudal society.

"Countless money and blood miserably purchased a fake republic." After the 1911 Revolution, China tried restoration of the monarchy, parliamentarianism, a multi-party system, and presidential government. All sorts of political forces and their representatives came on stage, but they all failed to find a correct answer. The social nature of the old China and the miserable situation of the Chinese people remained unchanged. The country was still in a battered state, poor and weak; the Western powers still rode roughshod and seized interests in China while the Chinese people were still living in suffering and humiliation.

History has fully proven that without the guidance of an advanced theory, without the leadership of an advanced political party armed with an advanced theory, going with the tide of historical development, boldly shouldering the historical responsibility and daring to make sacrifices, there was no way the Chinese people could have defeated the reactionaries that weighed on their backs, nor could they have changed their oppressed, enslaved lot.

History was crying out for an entity capable of undertaking to truly lead the Chinese people to accomplish the mission of great rejuvenation, and this task gloriously fell on the shoulders of the representative of the advanced productive forces - the Chinese working class.

2
THE MAY FOURTH MOVEMENT AND THE SPREAD OF MARXISM IN CHINA

THE RISE OF THE NEW CULTURE MOVEMENT AND THE INFLUENCE OF RUSSIA'S OCTOBER REVOLUTION ON CHINA

The founding of the Republic of China failed to bring the Chinese people the anticipated national independence, democracy and social progress; disappointment replaced expectations. The old road was closed, so a new road had to be found. Some progressive Chinese intellectuals began to summarise the lessons of the 1911 Revolution, putting in efforts to sweep away ignorance, to enlighten minds and to free the masses from the trammels of old ideas. The New Culture Movement of ideological enlightenment became the leader of great social change.

In September 1915, Chen Duxiu established *Youth Magazine* in Shanghai, which was later changed to *New Youth*, marking the start of the New Culture Movement. In 1917, he was appointed dean of the School of Letters at Peking University while the editorial department of *New Youth* moved to Beijing. Peking University and *New Youth* became the main front of the New Culture Movement.

Youth Magazine *founded by Chen Duxiu*

The basic slogan of the New Culture Movement was "support democracy and science". Taking evolutionary theories and individuals freeing themselves from old ideas as their main weapons, the movement's initiators vigorously attacked the sages of the past, Confucius being their symbol. They supported new ethics but opposed the old morality. They promoted new literature, including writing in the vernacular language rather than in classical style. Through criticism of Confucius' learning, the movement shook the dominant position of feudal orthodox ideology but opened the floodgates holding back the flow of new ideas. Their action set off a trend that freed minds in Chinese society.

However, the movement still took bourgeois democracy as the national salvation plan. In Europe and America, where the new ideological trends originated, the internal contradictions were acute and, in an extreme fashion, World War One further exposed the inherent, insurmountable contradictions of capitalism. Moreover, the Chinese had suffered repeated failures in their attempts to learn from the West, causing advanced Chinese elements to doubt the feasibility of a bourgeois republic in China. Again, the search for a national salvation programme reached a crossroads.

Just at this moment, in 1917 the salvoes of Russia's October Revolution brought China Marxism-Leninism. From its scientific truth, Chinese advanced elements saw the solution to China's problems. The calls of anti-imperialism sent out by the October Revolution made the Chinese people who had been bullied by the imperialist powers feel "extremely bitter, serious and significant", which gave impetus to progressive Chinese who were inclined to embrace socialism, pushing them into truly understanding the learning guiding the October Revolution. Under such circumstances, a group of intellectuals who were in favour of the road of Russia's October Revolution and in possession of the preliminary ideology of Communism emerged in China.

Li Dazhao was the first to raise the October Revolution banner and the earliest promoter of Marxism-Leninism in China. From July 1918, he published *A Comparison Between the French and Russian Revolutions*, *The Victory of the Common People* and *The Victory of Bolshevism* in praise of the victory of the October Revolution. He pointed out the October Revolution is "the herald of the world revolution in the twentieth century", "the new dawn for all the human beings of the world". He proclaimed that the trend set by the October Revolution would be unstoppable, "We can see that the future of the universe is a world of red flags!" After the May Fourth Movement, he put more energy into promoting Marxism. In *My Views on Marxism*, he systematically introduced Marxist theory to Chinese readers, which greatly influenced ideological circles, causing Marxism to systematically spread in China. In *Further Discussion on Problems and Isms* he refuted the anti-Marxist trend of thought while expounding that Marxism meets China's needs.

Why was the October Revolution that broke out in Russia in 1917 able to bring about such powerful repercussions in China? The fundamental reason lies in the internal changes taking place in Chinese society. When China's ideological circles underwent a drastic change, the Chinese social structure also quietly went through a profound change. During World War One, the major Western imperialist powers were busy fighting in the battlefields in Europe, for the time being they relaxed their economic invasion of China. Therefore, China's national capitalist economy received a relatively fast development and the Chinese working class and national capitalists continued to grow. On the eve of the May Fourth Movement in 1919, the number of industrial workers had reached about two million and they became an increasingly important newly-emerging social force.

The Chinese working class is a great newborn revolutionary class in modern China. Besides the virtues they were associated with the most advanced economic form, highly organised and disciplined, and owning no private means of production, they also had a resolute and thoroughly revolutionary character. In the soil of China's semi-colonial, semi-feudal society, it was inevitable for them to become the most fundamental impetus of the revolution. Meanwhile, students and teachers from all kinds of new educational institutions, and newspaper and magazine journalists quickly increased in number, forming an intellectual circle which was larger in size than the one in the 1911 Revolution period, but equipped with a newer ideology.

The rise of a new people's great revolution became inevitable.

THE MAY FOURTH MOVEMENT MARKED THE GREAT BEGINNING OF THE NEW DEMOCRATIC REVOLUTION

China's diplomatic failure in the Paris Peace Conference was the immediate cause of the May Fourth Movement.

In the first half of 1919, the Entente countries who had won World War One held a 'Peace Conference' in Paris. The Chinese delegation put forward seven proposals including abolishing foreign powers' sphere of influence in China and withdrawing their armed forces from China, a statement demanding the cancellation of the Twenty-One Demands[1] and the exchange of a note. The conference rejected China's reasonable requests but transferred all Germany's rights and holdings in Shandong to Japan. Giving in to the pressure of the imperialist powers, the Beiyang warlord government was preparing to sign the peace treaty. When the news spread back home, the rage of the Chinese people that had accumulated for so long finally erupted like a volcano.

On 4 May, about three thousand students from Beijing staged a protest. They shouted slogans: "Win sovereign rights internationally, eliminate traitors at home"; "Cancel the Twenty-One Demands"; "Return Qingdao to China"; "Put traitors Cao Rulin, Zhang Zongxiang and Lu Zongyu to death"[2]. Breaking out from the blockade of the military and police, from all directions they gathered before Tiananmen. The May Fourth Movement that shocked the country and the whole world had broken out.

In the May Fourth Movement, the Chinese working class began to step onto the political stage as an independent force. From 5 June, the workers in Shanghai spontaneously staged a strike to support the students in Beijing. In a few days' time the workers on strike reached 60,000 or 70,000. Soon afterwards, the workers in Beijing, Tangshan, Hankou, Nanjing and Changsha also went on strike, followed by merchants in many big or medium-sized cities, forming the high tide of the strike which quickly spread to over 20 provinces and a hundred cities.

The May Fourth Movement broke through the narrow circle of intelligentsia, turning it into a nationwide mass movement with participants composed of working class, petty bourgeoisie and capitalist classes. Under pressure, the Beiyang Warlord Government released the arrested students and announced the dismissal of Cao Rulin, Zhang Zongxiang and Lu Zongyu from office. On 28 June, the Chinese delegation did not attend the signing ceremony of the Paris Peace Conference.

Peking University student demonstrators march towards Tiananmen during the May Fourth Movement

The May Fourth Movement has epoch-making significance in modern Chinese revolutionary history, marking the great beginning of the new democratic revolution. By its revolutionary nature of thorough anti-imperialism and anti-feudalism, by its progressive character of seeking national salvation and building up national strength, and by the extensive participation of the masses of all circles and nationalities, it pushed Chinese social progress, promoted the wide spread of Marxism in China, brought about the integration of Marxism and the Chinese workers' movement, and paved the way for the founding of the CPC both ideologically and in terms of officials (cadres). The May Fourth Spirit was imbued with patriotism, progress, democracy and science as the main contents. Patriotism, which was the core, was a milestone in the historical progress of the Chinese people's pursuit of national independence and development.

THE SPREAD OF MARXISM IN CHINA

Round about the time of the May Fourth Movement, from the substantial lessons learned from the Paris Peace Conference, Chinese progressive elements came to realise the true nature of the joint oppression of the Chinese people by the imperialist powers, and this was the direct reason for the further spread of socialist ideology in China. In March or April 1920, *Eastern Miscellany* magazine published the Soviet Government's first declaration on China, which stated that it would give up all the special rights gained by Tsarist Russia at China's expense. This gave a fresh and powerful impetus to the spread of socialist ideology in China. The study and promotion of socialism gradually became the main trend in progressive ideological circles.

It was under such circumstances that many advanced intellectuals of different experience trod on the path of Marxism by various ways after careful and repeated consideration.

Li Dazhao played a primary role in China's early Marxist ideological movement. In 1919, he edited Issue 5, Vol. 6 of *New Youth* featuring a special issue *A Study on Marxism*, while helping a supplement of Beijing's *Morning Review* newspaper to open with a special column entitled *A Study of Marx*.

Chen Duxiu, the ideological leader of the New Culture Movement, also kept to the stand of Marxism. After the May Fourth Movement, he professed, "We should not repeat the wrong path of Europe, America and Japan", yet he clearly proclaimed that China must build a working-class country by revolutionary means.

Mao Zedong, in the *Xiangjiang Review*, of which he was the chief editor, warmly praised the victory of the October Revolution. He believed that this victory would certainly become popularised throughout the world and that we should begin to follow this example. After he went to Beijing for the second time, enthusiastically he sought out and read books about communism, thereby building on his faith in Marxism. Later he recalled, "When it came to the summer of 1920, in theory and some degree of action, I had become a Marxist."

Some veteran members of the Tongmenghui (Revolutionary Alliance) also began to turn to proletarian socialism. Dong Biwu used to recall, "I made revolution with Sun Yat-sen. The revolution made progress, but Sun Yat-sen could not hold onto the reins of government and power was taken away by others. So we began to study the Russian way."

Guided by Marxism, Chinese progressive elements actively threw themselves into the practice of mass struggle. In early 1920, some revolutionary intellectuals in Beijing went to the residential area of the rickshaw pullers to investigate their wretched living conditions. Deng Zhongxia went to Changxindian to propagate revolution to the workers there, beginning to build contacts with industrial workers. The process of integration between the progressive intellectuals and the masses of workers was the process of integration between Marxism and the Chinese labour movement.

---

1. The Twenty-One Demands was a treaty draft proposed by Japan in 1915, aiming to destroy China. It included unreasonable demands such as that Japan control Shandong Province, the three provinces of the Northeast and the eastern part of Inner Mongolia.
2. Cao Rulin, Zhang Zongxiang and Lu Zongyu were three pro-Japan bureaucrats of the Beiyang Warlord Government.

3
THE FOUNDING OF THE COMMUNIST PARTY OF CHINA AND THE FORMULATION OF THE DEMOCRATIC REVOLUTIONARY PROGRAMME

THE BUILDING OF THE EARLY ORGANISATIONS OF THE CPC AND THEIR ACTIVITIES

With the wide spread of Marxism in China and the emergence of a group of progressive intellectuals with a firm belief in Marxism, the ideological conditions were ripe for the establishment of a communist party in China and a contingent of cadres, therefore the task of founding a party of the working class was put on the agenda.

The first ones to come up with the idea were Chen Duxiu and Li Dazhao. They came to realise that if China was to be transformed by Marxism, a proletarian party had to be established to function as the organiser and leader of the revolution. In February 1920, to avoid prosecution by the warlord government, Chen Duxiu secretly left Beijing for Shanghai, accompanied by Li Dazhao. During the journey Li Dazhao and Chen Duxiu discussed the founding of a communist party in China.

In March 1920, Li Dazhao organised a Marxist study society in Peking University. This was the earliest organisation for the study and research of Marxism and an important prerequisite for the founding of the CPC. In April Grigori Voytinsky, the representative of the Russian Communist Party (Bolshevik) and the others arrived in China. They met Li Dazhao in Beijing and Chen Duxiu in Shanghai to discuss the founding of a communist party in China, and these discussions played a certain driving role for the founding of the CPC.

The early organisation of the CPC was established in Shanghai, the centre of the Chinese working class. In May 1920, Chen Duxiu initiated and organised the Marxism Research Association to explore socialist studies and social transformation in China. In August, the CPC's early organisation was established in the editorial department of *New Youth* in Shanghai, with Chen Duxiu as the secretary. In November, the *CPC Manifesto* was drafted, in which it was stated, "The aim of the communists is to create a new society in accordance with communist ideals". This organisation in Shanghai was, in fact, the sponsor organisation of the CPC and the liaison centre for communists all over the country to carry out party-building activities.

In October 1920, Li Dazhao founded an early CPC organisation in Beijing called the 'CPC Small Group'. At the end of that year the group members decided to establish the Beijing branch and Li Dazhao was the secretary.

Contacted and pushed by the organisations in Shanghai and Beijing, one after another, early party organisations were established throughout China. From the autumn of 1920 to the spring of 1921, Dong Biwu, Chen Tanqiu and Bao Huiseng in Wuhan, Mao Zedong and He Shuheng in Changsha, Wang Jinmei and Deng Enming in Jinan, and Tan Pingshan and Tan Zhitang in Guangzhou founded the early party organisations in their own cities, while in Japan and France Chinese students and the progressive elements of the overseas Chinese also founded theirs.

After these organisations were established, a lot of work was carried out, such as: the study and propagation of Marxism and study of China's actual problems; engagement in debate with anti-Marxism trends and help for a group of progressive elements to clarify the distinction between socialism and capitalism, and between scientific socialism and other socialist trends, thereby enabling them to walk along the Marxist road; engagement in publicity and organisational work among the workers, enabling them to begin to accept Marxist education, thereby raising their class consciousness; establishment of socialist youth organisations, organising the members to study Marxism and take part in real struggles, which trained and built up the party's reserve forces.

The *Communist Manifesto* played an extremely important role in the ideological and theoretical preparations for the founding of the CPC. In February 1920, in order to translate the book, Chen Wangdao secretly returned home to Zhejiang. When he was concentrating intently on doing the translation, he was unaware that he had eaten the *zongzi* which he had dipped in ink rather than in sugar, yet saying: "Sweet, very sweet!" "The taste of truth is very sweet." And this sentence demonstrated the thirst of the Chinese communists for the Marxist truth of national salvation, as well as their strong beliefs in communist ideals. In August 1920, the complete Chinese version of the *Communist Manifesto* was published, which was a great event for the spread of Marxism in China.

As the Chinese people and the Chinese nation were undergoing a great awakening and Marxism-Leninism was becoming closely integrated with the Chinese workers' movement, the Communist Party of China (CPC) was born.

THE FIRST NATIONAL CONGRESS OF THE CPC

In July 1921, the First National Congress of the CPC was inaugurated at 106 Wangzhi Road (today's 76 Xingye Road) in the French Concession, Shanghai.[1]

The delegates were: Li Da and Li Hanjun from Shanghai, Zhang Guotao and Liu Renjing from Beijing, Mao Zedong and He Shuheng from Changsha, Dong Biwu and Chen Tanqiu from Wuhan, Wang Jinmei and Deng Enming from Jinan, Chen Gongbo from Guangzhou, Zhou Fohai[2] from Japan and Bao Huiseng who was sent by Chen Duxiu. They represented some 50 party members from all over the country. Maring and Nikolski, the agents from the Communist International (Comintern), also attended. Busy with other work, Chen Duxiu and Li Dazhao did not attend the congress.

The site of the First National Congress of the CPC

Because the site had drawn the attention of secret detectives and was searched by the French Concession police, the delegates moved the last day's meeting to a pleasure-boat in South Lake, Jiaxing in Zhejiang.

The congress decided on the name of the party as the Communist Party of China (CPC). It adopted the first party programme which determined that "the revolutionary army must work together with the proletariat to overthrow the capitalist regime", "the declaration of the dictatorship of the proletariat until the end of class struggle", "the abolition of ownership by capitalists", and the alliance with the Third International. Once founded, with a clear-cut stand the CPC stipulated socialism and communism as the objectives of the struggle and adhered to realising these objectives by revolutionary means.

The congress decided to set up the Central Bureau as the provisional leading organisation of the Central Committee and elected the bureau members with Chen Duxiu as secretary.

The congress declared the official founding of the CPC, an inevitable result of the development of modern Chinese history, of the tenacious search for the Chinese people's national salvation and survival, and of the campaign to realise the great rejuvenation of the Chinese nation. As a party of the most advanced class - the working class, the CPC not only represents the interests of workers, but also of all the Chinese people throughout the nation. Right from the beginning it upheld Marxism as the guide to action, while regarding seeking happiness for the Chinese people and national rejuvenation as its original intention and mission.

The founding of the communist party in China was an epoch-making event, which profoundly changed the direction and course of the development of the Chinese nation in modern times, transformed the future of the Chinese people and nation, and altered the landscape of world development.

The First Congress site in Shanghai and the red boat in the South Lake of Jiaxing were the 'cradle' of the CPC where the party's dream set sail. The pioneers of communism in China established the CPC and developed the great founding spirit of the party, which comprises the following principles: upholding truth and ideals, staying true to our original aspiration and founding mission, fighting bravely without fear of sacrifice, and remaining loyal to the party and faithful to the people. This spirit is the party's source of strength.

THE SECOND NATIONAL CONGRESS OF THE CPC AND FORMULATION OF THE DEMOCRATIC REVOLUTIONARY PROGRAMME

For the newly founded CPC, its most important task was to observe and analyse the actual problems facing China through learning and employing scientific theories. At the time, the most distinctive trouble for China was the internecine warfare among warlords. Manipulated by the imperialist powers, it had become more and more tense. The party realised profoundly that under such turbulent circumstances, if the warlords, big or small, who had brought calamity to the country and the people, could not be overthrown, there could be no talk about realising all their beautiful ideals.

In July 1922 the Second Congress of the CPC was held in Shanghai, attended by 12 people representing 195 party members countrywide.

Through the analysis of China's economic and political situation, the congress announced that Chinese society was characterised by semi-colonialism and semi-feudalism. It pointed out that the party's maximum programme was the realisation of socialism and communism; however, during the initial stage, the minimum programme was to overthrow the warlords and the oppression of the international imperialists, and to unify China as a genuine democratic republic. It pointed out: for the realisation of the revolutionary objective of anti-imperialism and anti-warlordism, the party must unite all the revolutionary parties and bourgeois democrats to form a 'democratic alliance'.

The party had only been founded for one year. However, right away it put forward a clear anti-imperialist, anti-feudal democratic revolutionary programme and rapidly spread it. "Overthrow the great powers and eliminate the warlords" became the common cry of the broad masses of the people. This illustrated that only the CPC armed with Marxism could indicate the direction of the Chinese revolution.

The Second Congress passed the first party constitution, making specific stipulations regarding membership conditions, organisations at all levels and party discipline. It embodied the principles of democratic centralism, which was significant in strengthening the party's self-construction. It also passed a resolution to confirm that the CPC was a branch of the Comintern.

The congress passed a resolution, expounding that the CPC was a political party composed of the most revolutionary elements of the proletariat, "a political party fighting for the proletarian masses". It stressed that all party movements had to penetrate deep into the broad masses and must not depart from them. This was significant for the party's early development of the worker-peasant movement.

The congress elected the Central Executive Committee which elected Chen Duxiu as secretary-general.

THE FIRST HIGH TIDE OF THE WORKERS' MOVEMENT AND THE EARLY DEVELOPMENT OF THE PEASANT MOVEMENT

After the CPC was founded, it devoted itself to organising and leading the workers' movement. In August 1921, the secretariat of the China Labour Association, the general organ for the party to openly engage with the labour movement, was set up. It published the *Labour Weekly* magazine, ran workers' schools, organised industrial labour unions and carried out strikes. This increasingly extended the party's political influence on workers and the whole of society.

Under the party's leadership, starting from the seamen's strike in Hong Kong in January 1922 to the strike of the Beijing-Hankou railway workers in February 1923, a series of strikes set off the first high tide of the Chinese labour movement. In 13 months, a hundred large or small strikes took place throughout the country involving over 300,000 participants. Among the strikes, those staged by the railway workers and miners of Anyuan and the miners of Kailuan were the most representative examples. They fully showed the force of the working class once it was organised.

Members of the preparatory committee of the Anyuan Railway Workers and Miners Club

There were 17,000 workers and miners working for the railroad and mines in Anyuan. In the winter of 1921 Mao Zedong, the party secretary of the Hunan branch, went to Anyuan to make a social investigation, followed by Li Lisan who was sent by the Hunan party organisation to carry out work over there. On Labour Day in 1922, the Anyuan Railway Workers' and Miners' Club was established. Early in September that year, Mao Zedong arrived in Anyuan to plan a strike, followed by Liu Shaoqi. On 14 September the strike started. The workers and miners raised demands for their political rights to be assured and their treatment improved. The courageous struggle of the workers and miners, and the support from all circles of society forced the authorities of the railway and mines to acknowledge part of the conditions raised by the workers and miners, rendering the strike a success.

A general strike by workers on the Beijing-Hankou railway broke out on 4 February 1923 with the aim of establishing the General Labour Union of the Beijing-Hankou Railway. On the 7th, supported by the imperialists, warlord Wu Peifu mobilised the military and police to carry out a bloody suppression of the strikers. They tied Lin Xiangqian, a CPC member and chairman of the Jiang'an branch of the General Labour Union of the Beijing-Hankou Railway to a wire pole, forcing him to order all the workers to go back to work. Lin Xiangqian would rather die than submit and he died heroically. When CPC member Shi Yang, the legal advisor of the Beijing-Hankou Railway Labour Union, was executed, he shouted "long live labourers" when he was shot three times. In the February Seventh Massacre, 52 strikers were killed, 300 were wounded, about 40 were arrested and put in prison, and more than a thousand were sent into exile after being sacked. Thereafter, the labour movement went into a low ebb.

In the process of leading the labour movement, the party's self-construction began to be strengthened. Its organisations at the basic level began to be built in industrial and mining enterprises. With the development of the workers' struggle, a group of outstanding figures emerged, such as Su Zhaozheng, Shi Wenbin, Xiang Ying, Deng Pei and Wang Hebo. One after another, they all joined the party ranks.

While gathering strength to lead the labour movement, the party went to the countryside and undertook a mobilisation of the peasants. In September 1921 a peasant meeting was held in Yuqian Village, Xiaoshan County, Zhejiang Province, proclaiming the founding of the first new-type peasant organisation in China. In July 1922 Peng Pai set up the first secret peasant association in Haifeng County, Guangdong Province. By May 1923, many places in Haifeng, Lufeng and Huiyang counties had set up peasant associations with about 200,000 members. In September, inspired by the labour movement in Shuikoushan and under the leadership of the party, the peasants in Baiguo District of Hengshan County, Hunan Province founded the Yuebei Peasant-Worker Association. They carried out a series of struggles, raising the first banner of the peasant movement in Hunan. Moreover, the party also organised the youth and women's movements.

The worker-peasant movement, particularly the workers' movement, initiated, organised and led by the party, demonstrated the firm revolutionary nature and the combat effectiveness of the Chinese working class. They extended the CPC's national political influence, preparing certain conditions for its cooperation with other revolutionary forces to launch a great national-scale revolution.

---

1. According to later textual research, the precise date for the First National Congress of the CPC was on 23 July 1921. In June 1941, the *Instructions on the Commemoration of the 20th Anniversary of the Founding of the CPC and the 4th Year of the War of Resistance Against Japanese Aggression* established 1 July as the day of commemoration; thereafter 1 July of each year became the commemorative day of the founding of the CPC.
2. In 1938 Zhang Guotao threw in his lot with the KMT and he was expelled from the CPC; Zhou Fohai and Chen Gongbo were expelled from the CPC due to serious violations of party discipline soon after the First National Congress and they turned into traitors during the War of Resistance Against Japanese Aggression.

4
THE FIRST KMT-CPC COOPERATION AND THE RISE OF THE HIGH TIDE OF THE GREAT REVOLUTION

THE THIRD NATIONAL CONGRESS OF THE CPC AND THE ESTABLISHMENT OF KMT-CPC COOPERATION

From the failure of the strike of the Beijing-Hankou railway workers, the Chinese communists realised that the revolutionary force was far below the power of the imperialist and feudal forces. The party realised the importance of forming a broad united front and therefore decided to take the active step of allying itself with the Kuomintang (KMT) led by Sun Yat-sen.

Sun Yat-sen, right now, was dejected by his reliance on warlords fighting warlords and the repeated setbacks in his campaign to overthrow the warlord government. He witnessed the influence demonstrated by the CPC-led labour movement, realising that the CPC was a new revolutionary force full of vigour, so he was willing to cooperate with it. In January 1923, the Executive Committee of the Comintern promulgated *The Resolution on the Relationship Between the CPC and the KMT*, which played a role in promoting the issue.

In June 1923 the Third National Congress of the CPC was held in Guangzhou, attended by about 30 delegates, representing 420 party members nationwide.

The congress correctly evaluated Sun Yat-sen's revolutionary stand and the feasibility of reorganising the KMT. It decided that CPC members could enter the KMT as individuals to realise the KMT-CPC cooperation. It clearly stipulated that when the CPC members joined the KMT, the CPC had to maintain its political, ideological and organisational independence.

The congress made the first revision of the party constitution. Amendments were made, and for the first time it stipulated that there had to be a waiting period for a new member to become an official member, and a member was able to "quit the party of their own free will".

The congress elected the Central Executive Committee and formed the Central Bureau with Chen Duxiu as secretary-general.

After the congress, the KMT-CPC cooperation greatly quickened its pace. The CPC organisations at all levels mobilised their members and the revolutionary youth to join the KMT and actively pushed forward the national revolutionary movement nationwide. In early October 1923, at the invitation of Sun Yat-sen, the Soviet representative Borodin arrived in Guangzhou to be the instructor of the KMT organisations, and later the political advisor. The reorganisation of the KMT quickly entered the practical stage.

In January 1924 the First National Congress of the KMT was held in Guangzhou. Among 165 delegates who attended the opening ceremony, about 20 were CPC members. Li Dazhao was appointed a member of the presidium by Sun Yat-sen.

The *Manifesto of the First National Congress of the Chinese KMT* examined and passed by the First KMT Congress, made a new interpretation of the Three People's Principles, namely, the "New Three People's Principles". In nationalism, it highlighted anti-imperialism; in democracy, it stressed that democratic rights "must be shared by all ordinary people"; in people's livelihood, "an equal share of land ownership" and "capital restraint" were taken as two major principles. In addition to these new interpretations, soon after the congress, Sun Yat-sen put forward the slogan of "land to the tiller". The political programme of the First Congress of the KMT was consistent with many of the basic principles of the CPC's political programme in the democratic revolution stage, and this became the political foundation for the first cooperation of the two parties.

This congress confirmed the principle that CPC members could join the KMT as individuals. It elected the Central Executive Committee of the KMT and 10 CPC members, such as Li Dazhao, Tan Pingshan and Mao Zedong, were elected members or alternate members of the committee, which accounted for approximately a quarter of the total committee numbers. After the congress, the CPC members who took key positions in the Central Party Headquarters of the KMT were: Tan Pingshan, Minister of the Organisation Department; Lin Boqu, Minister of the Peasants

Department; and Mao Zedong, Acting Minister of the Publicity Department.

The First Congress of the KMT, in fact, established the three revolutionary policies: unite with Russia, unite with the communists, and aid farmers and workers, marking the formal establishment of the KMT-CPC cooperation.

THE FORMATION OF THE NEW SITUATION OF THE REVOLUTION AND THE FOURTH NATIONAL CONGRESS OF THE CPC

After the KMT-CPC cooperation centred in Guangzhou where all the national revolutionary forces gathered, a new anti-imperialist, anti-feudal warlord situation quickly developed.

The KMT-CPC cooperation pushed the recovery and development of the labour movement. In July 1924, thousands of workers took part in a strike in the Shamian Concession in Guangzhou to protest against the 'New Police Rule' imposed by the British and French restricting the free entry of Chinese residents. The Chinese police also joined the strikers. The protest lasted for a month and was eventually victorious. In May 1925, the All-China Federation of Trade Unions was founded at the Second National Labour Conference held in Guangzhou.

The peasant movement was also gradually developing. The peasants in all of Guangdong's counties set up peasant associations and organised self-defence corps, launching a struggle against local tyrants, evil gentry and corrupt officials. Starting from July 1924, six sessions of the Peasant Movement Institute were held in Guangzhou presided over by Peng Pai, Mao Zedong and others in which they trained a group of key movement members while the students' and women's movement also started to develop.

To build the backbone for armed revolution recommended by the communists, the First Congress of the KMT decided to establish a military academy for ground forces, the Whampoa (Huangpu) Military Academy. Countrywide, the communists selected large numbers of party members, Youth League members and other revolutionary youths, and sent them to the academy to study. Among the first-term cadets, 56 were party and Youth League members, accounting for 10% of the total number of cadets.

With the joint efforts of the two parties, from south to north, and on an unprecedented scale, the national revolutionary ideology spread extensively throughout the country. In October 1924 Feng Yuxiang, a general of the Zhili clique, staged a coup, overthrowing the Beijing government controlled by the Zhili clique warlord leaders Cao Kun and Wu Peifu, taking control of Beijing and Tianjin, and reorganising his troops as the Nationalist army. He sent Sun Yat-sen a telegram, inviting Sun to go to Beijing to "discuss national affairs". In November, Sun Yat-sen left Guangzhou for Beijing. On his journey, he propagated his views on the convening of a national conference and the abolition of the unequal treaties. Public organisations around the country sent telegrams of support to him, thereby leading to the development of a political publicity movement.

To strengthen leadership of the rising revolutionary movement, in January 1925 the Fourth National Congress of the CPC was held in Shanghai, attended by 20 delegates representing 994 party members countrywide.

The historical contribution of the Fourth CPC Congress lies in that it put forward the issue of leadership of the proletariat in the democratic revolution, the worker-peasant alliance, and the more complete stipulation of the contents of the democratic revolution. It pointed out that when we "oppose the international imperialists", we must also "oppose the feudal warlord politics" and "oppose the feudal economic relationship". This marked significant progress in understanding the Chinese revolution after summarising the experience after the founding of the party, particularly the practical experience in the year's KMT-CPC cooperation.

The congress also decided to strengthen the party's organisation construction throughout the country, to expand the membership, to consolidate party discipline, and clearly stipulated that the party branches were the party's basic organisations.

The congress revised the party constitution, putting forward specific requirements for the construction of party branches, and stipulating that three party members could set up a branch.

The congress elected the Central Executive Committee which elected the Central Bureau with Chen Duxiu serving as secretary-general.

On 12 March 1925 Sun Yat-sen died of illness in Beijing. After the death of Sun Yat-sen, the KMT right-wingers who were originally anti-communist became active again. The KMT left-wingers and right-wingers became more divided, further complicating the situation regarding the united front built on the basis of KMT-CPC cooperation. For the Chinese communists, this was a rigorous test.

THE MAY 30TH MOVEMENT AND THE UNIFICATION OF THE REVOLUTIONARY BASE IN GUANGDONG

The arrival of the great nationwide revolutionary high tide began with the workers' strike in Shanghai against the foreign capitalists in May 1925.

On 15 May, the Japanese owner of the No. 7 Neiwai Cotton Mill in Shanghai shot dead Gu Zhenghong, a mill worker and a CPC member. On 30 May, initiated and led by the CPC, the workers and students in Shanghai took to the streets to protest. The police in the International Settlement suddenly opened fire and shot dead 13 students and workers with countless wounded. This was the May 30th Massacre that shocked the whole of China. In the following days, incidents when the British and Japanese police shot dead Chinese civilians continued to happen in Shanghai and elsewhere.

The May 30th Massacre aroused great indignation among the Chinese people. The rage buried deep in their hearts for years erupted all of a sudden and developed into strikes of workers, students and merchants. The CPC Central Committee decided to set up the Shanghai General Labour Union and the Shanghai Joint Association of Workers, Traders and Students to strengthen its leadership of the movement. Across the country, about 17 million people directly took part in this movement. From business metropolises to remote townships and villages, everywhere sounded the roar of "Down with imperialists" and "Abrogate the unequal treaties". Sparked by the May 30th Massacre as the immediate cause, the unstoppable and powerful tide of the national anti-imperialist movement quickly swept the whole country; this was the May 30th Movement.

The Great Guangzhou-Hongkong Strike numbering 250,000 strikers was an important part of the May 30th Movement. The strikers set up a committee, with party member Su Zhaozhen serving as chairman. The strikers sealed off Hong Kong and the strike lasted for 16 months. About 100,000 organised strikers concentrated in Guangzhou became powerful backers of the Guangzhou Revolutionary Government.

The CPC made great progress in its leadership of the movement. Party membership increased from less than a thousand in early 1925 to 10,000, and party organisations were now established in many places where they had not existed before. To adapt to the new situation, the Central Committee put forward without delay that in a very short time the party would be transferred "from a small group into a centralised political party of the masses". It stressed the importance of educating and training party members, so in Beijing an advanced party school was set up to train cadres.

Under the thriving and advantageous circumstances, the CPC and KMT jointly carried out a campaign to unify the revolutionary base in Guangdong Province. In 1925, after the Eastern and Southern Expeditions, warlords Chen Jiongming and Deng Benyin were wiped out, and the insurgency in Guangzhou staged by warlords Yang Ximin and Liu Zhenhuan was put down. The Guangdong revolutionary base was unified, which prepared a reliable rear base for the Northern Expedition.

The party also attempted to build a revolutionary armed force under its direct command. Supported by Sun Yat-sen, taking some party and Youth League members as the backbone, Zhou Enlai and the CPC Guangdong Branch reorganised the armoured car platoon of the Supreme Headquarters of the Generalissimo into a force commanded by the CPC. Early in 1926, the Independent Regiment of the Fourth Army, the National Revolutionary Army, was built up and its commander was CPC member Ye Ting.

Under the hard work of Li Dazhao, the revolutionary movement in the northern region expanded quickly. From early 1924, the workers' movement in the north gradually turned around its despondent state, staging a recovery and development. A series of strikes were organised in Beijing, Qingdao and Tangshan. In October 1925, an enlarged meeting of the Central Executive Committee of the CPC stressed the importance of the work in the north. The CPC Executive Committee in the North Region was set up with Li Dazhao as secretary. In July 1926, a dozen prefectural committees and several dozen special branches and independent branches were set up in Beijing, Tianjin, Tangshan, Taiyuan and North Manchuria with 2,000 party members. Besides, Li Dazhao and the party's northern organisations worked to win over Feng Yuxiang and his Nationalist army, as well as the campaign to win tariff autonomy rights for the local people. These efforts and struggles demonstrated the awakening of the revolutionary consciousness of the northern public and struck a blow against the reactionary Beijing government controlled by Duan Qirui.

5
THE NORTHERN EXPEDITION AND THE WORKER-PEASANT MOVEMENT

THE SUCCESSFUL ADVANCE OF THE NORTHERN EXPEDITION

In July 1926, the National Revolutionary Army held an oath-taking rally and launched the Northern Expedition. The direct target of the campaign was the imperialist-supported Beiyang warlords. Wu Peifu, Sun Chuanfang and Zhang Zuolin directly controlled 700,000 troops, while the National Revolutionary Army under the control of the Nationalist Government had only about 100,000 soldiers.

Bravely confronting the great disparity in strength between the two forces, guided by Soviet advisors, the National Revolutionary Army formulated a strategy of concentrating a superior force to destroy the enemy forces one by one. Supported by civilians, the Northern Expeditionary Army smashed the enemy resistance along its advancing front. In September they seized Hanyang and Hankou. On 10 October they captured Wuchang, wiping out Wu Peifu's main force. On the battlefield in Jiangxi, the National Revolutionary Army destroyed Sun Chuanfang's main force and captured Jiujiang and Nanchang in early November. In December, they reached the Fujian provincial capital of Fuzhou without a fight. Soon they planned to seize Zhejiang, Shanghai and then join the forces in Nanjing. In February 1927, they entered Hangzhou and suppressed the enemy resistance in the whole of Zhejiang Province. In March, they captured Anqing and Nanjing, and entered Shanghai. Up to that point, the Northern Expeditionary Army had completely captured the region south of the Yangtze River.

Group photo of part of the CPC members engaged in political work in the Northern Expeditionary Army, Nanchang

Meanwhile, assisted by the Soviet Union and the CPC, in September the Nationalist army under the command of Feng Yuxiang held an oath-taking rally in Wuyuan, Suiyuan before sweeping south. In November they controlled Shaanxi and Gansu provinces, and were ready to march east out of the Tongguan pass to meet the National Revolutionary Army.

The Northern Expedition was carried out under the slogans of anti-imperialism and anti-warlordism put forward by the CPC. In the campaign, the party and the Youth League members risked their lives and played a vanguard and exemplary role. The Independent Regiment was the first to attack and enter Wuchang, becoming brave and skilful battle-hardened troops and thereby winning the title of 'Iron Army'. The communists made a tremendous contribution to the National Revolutionary Army's political work and the work of mobilising workers and peasants. The CPC Provincial Committee in Guangdong led the Guangzhou-Hongkong Strike Committee to organise a 3,000-strong contingent of transport, publicity and medical corps manpower to follow the troops north. When the National Revolutionary Army marched toward Changsha, the CPC Provincial Committee in Hunan mobilised workers and peasants to act as guides, to deliver letters, to transport supplies and to carry stretchers. Such a warm scene was seldom seen in the previous wars in China.

The Northern Expedition achieved great success in a short time as a result of the KMT-CPC cooperation.

THE UPSURGE OF THE WORKER-PEASANT MOVEMENT IN HUNAN, HUBEI AND JIANGXI

Following the victory of the Northern Expedition, the worker-peasant movement rose at an unprecedented scale, particularly in Hunan, Hubei and Jiangxi.

The peasant movement rose first in these provinces. In November 1926, Mao Zedong took the position of Secretary of the Peasant Commission of the Central Committee, focusing on the peasant movement in Hunan, Hubei, Jiangxi and Henan. From the summer of 1926 to January 1927, membership of the Hunan Peasant Association increased sharply from 400,000 to 2 million. Once organised, the peasants began to act and started an unprecedented countryside revolution. Mao Zedong pointed out, "The national revolution needs large-scale change in the countryside. The 1911 Revolution didn't have it, so it failed. Now we have it, it's the key factor for achieving the revolution."

The Wuhan Peasant Movement Institute of the KMT Central Committee during the Great Revolution, of which Mao Zedong was the actual director

The thriving development of the peasant movement scared the landlords, gentry and KMT right-wingers to death. They began to attack it, defaming it as a "ruffians' movement" and "very bad". In early 1927 Mao Zedong carried out a 32-day investigation of the Hunan peasant movement. In his *A Report on the Investigation of the Hunan Peasant Movement*, he sharply refuted all the fallacies denigrating the peasant movement inside and outside the party but explained the great significance of the revolution in the countryside. He pointed out that all the revolutionary comrades should march at the head of the peasants and lead them, not follow in the rear, gesticulating at them and criticising them, still less should they face them as opponents. He stressed that the party must rely on the poor peasants to be the "revolutionary vanguard", unite with the middle peasants and other forces that can be won over to establish the peasant associations and armed forces, and take control of all the forces in the countryside, then carry out campaigns to reduce rents for land and interest on loans, and distribute land to the peasants.

In cities, there was also an upsurge in workers' movements. One after another, the General Labour Unions in Hunan and Hubei were set up in September and October 1926. By January 1927, union membership had reached 700,000. Soon the General Labour Union in Jiangxi was also set up. Following the example of the Guangzhou-Hongkong Strike, they organised armed workers' pickets. The workers in Changsha, Wuhan and Jiujiang went on a series of large-scale strikes in succession, and most of them were victorious. The thriving mass anti-imperialist campaigns drove the Nationalist Government to regain the concessions in Hankou and Jiujiang from the British in February 1927.

Driven by the victorious advance of the Northern Expedition and the rise of the worker-peasant movement, starting from October 1926, the Party Central Committee and the Shanghai District Committee organised workers in Shanghai to carry out armed uprisings. The first and second uprisings failed. Then the Central Committee and the Shanghai District Committee jointly formed the highest commanding organ of the uprising - the Special Commission. The Commission members were Chen Duxiu, Luo Yinong, Zhao Shiyan and Zhou Enlai, who was the commander-in-chief of the uprising. Under their direct leadership, the workers in Shanghai successfully launched the third armed uprising on 21 March 1927. On the 22nd, the Shanghai Special Provisional Government was founded, which was the earliest revolutionary power established by the masses in a metropolis.

The third armed uprising of workers in Shanghai was a heroic undertaking of the Chinese labour movement during the Great Revolution period, the pinnacle of the development of the labour movement during the Northern Expedition.

6

THE BREAKDOWN OF KMT-CPC COOPERATION AND THE FAILURE OF THE GREAT REVOLUTION

THE EMERGENCE OF A DANGEROUS SITUATION FOR THE GREAT REVOLUTION AND THE FIFTH NATIONAL CONGRESS OF THE CPC

When the mighty Great Revolution was developing like a raging fire, a submerged current, or a crisis hidden amid victory, was also under way.

Inspired and supported by the imperialist powers, Chiang Kai-shek, who had gradually matured militarily and politically, constantly created anti-communist incidents. In March 1927, he instigated the KMT Army to arrest CPC member Chen Zanxian, who was secretary of the Ganzhou General Labour Union and deputy secretary of the Jiangxi General Labour Union. Despite being forced to sign documents to disband the unions and to end the worker-peasant movement, resolutely and decisively, Chen Zanxian said, "You can kill me, or slay me, but I will never sign the document to disband the Labour Unions!" He called out, "Long live the CPC!" and died heroically.

With the victorious advance of the Northern Expedition, Chiang Kai-shek's anti-communist activities became more and more overt. At this critical moment, the main leader of the party committed the error of compromising and making concessions.

On 24 March 1927, the Northern Expeditionary Army captured Nanjing. That afternoon, with the excuse of protecting their nationals residing in China, British and American warships cruising on the Yangtze River fired shells at Nanjing, inflicting serious casualties on Chinese soldiers and civilians. The Nanjing Incident quickened Chiang Kai-shek's pace of collusion with the imperialist powers. On the 26th, Chiang arrived in Shanghai. He held a series of secret meetings with the imperialist powers, tycoons, financial magnates from Jiangsu and Zhejiang, and underworld gang leaders. In early April, he held a secret meeting in Shanghai, making the decision to "purge the party" by means of violence and to launch a sudden attack on the communists.

On 12 April, Chiang Kai-shek staged an anti-revolutionary coup in Shanghai. Before dawn, large groups of armed hoodlums from the Green Gang, disguised as workers, charged out of the concessions, making a sudden attack on the workers' pickets stationed in the office of the Shanghai General Labour Union. Using the excuse that they had come to mediate, the 26th Army disarmed the pickets. On 13 April, 100,000 Shanghai workers and citizens held a rally, then a demonstration to demand the release of arrested fellow workers and the return of any confiscated firearms. When the procession reached Baoshan Road, the 26th Army suddenly dashed out of buildings and opened fire on the packed demonstrators, killing a hundred at the scene with countless wounded. On the 15th, about 300 workers were killed, 500 were arrested and 5,000 went missing; this was the April 12th Counter-Revolutionary Coup that shocked the country and the whole world.

After the coup in Shanghai, one after another, in Jiangsu, Zhejiang, Anhui, Fujian, Guangdong and Guangxi, KMT reactionaries began to arrest and kill communists and the revolutionary masses on a large scale with the excuse of "purging the party". In Guangdong the number killed reached 2,000, including the noted Communists Xiao Chunü and Xiong Xiong. In the north, the Fengtian warlord Zhang Zuolin also arrested large numbers of communists and revolutionary masses.

On 6 April Li Dazhao, one of the main founders of the CPC, was sadly arrested. In prison he fearlessly fought with the enemy. He strictly kept the party's secrets, and tried to shield and save the comrades who were arrested at the same time as him. In his *Account of My Time in Prison*, he expressed his absolute devotion to the revolutionary cause, "After I received my education in my early teens, I pledged to devote my life to the cause of national liberation, to practice what I believe and strictly enforce what I know. Is it an accomplishment, or a crime? I have no time to care about it." In the face of the enemy gallows, he met his death like a hero, showing his tenacious adherence to the original intention and mission of the communists, his unparalleled loyalty to the cause of the party, and setting an example to be firm in one's ideals and beliefs.

Chiang Kai-shek ordered the closing and disbandment of revolutionary and progressive organisations and the wanton capture and killing of communists and revolutionaries

After Chen Yannian, party secretary of the Jiangsu Provincial Committee, was arrested, he was savagely tortured. With his iron will, he would rather die than submit. On the execution ground, the executioner commanded him to kneel down. He responded loudly, "Revolutionaries are upright and honourable, they face death unflinchingly. They can only stand to die and will never kneel down!" Chin up and chest out, Chen Yannian died a martyr's death.

Faced with the grave situation of the White Terror, Zhao Shiyan, the acting party secretary of the Jiangsu Provincial Committee, voiced his determination, "The CPC is a fighting party. One day it exists, we must fight one day. If unwilling to take part in the struggle, how can one be called a party member?" After he was arrested, he said in an impassioned speech, "People of ideals and integrity do not shrink from sacrificing their lives. The CPC will surely win victory!" He died heroically on the execution ground, sacrificing his youth and blood to the great undertaking of national rejuvenation.

When Xiao Chunü worked in the Peasant Movement Institute and the Whampoa Military Academy, he once said to his students, "A man should be like a candle, giving as much light as the heat can produce in his limited life, to give people light and warmth." He died a hero's death in the White Terror, like a candle that is never extinguished, burning himself but lighting the way forward for the revolution.

The April 12th Counter-Revolutionary Coup was the turning point for the Great Revolution to go from high tide to failure.

On 18 April, Chiang Kai-shek set up another 'Nationalist Government' in Nanjing to represent the interests of the landlord and bourgeois capitalist classes. From then on, China had three opposing governments: the Beijing Government led by Zhang Zuolin, the Nanjing Nationalist Government headed by Chiang Kai-shek and the Wuhan Nationalist Government which continued to maintain the KMT-CPC cooperation.

At this critical moment, from April to May 1927, the Fifth Congress of the CPC was held in Wuhan, attended by 82 delegates, representing 57,967 party members countrywide.

The congress elected the Central Committee. The first plenary session elected the Central Political Bureau (Politburo) and the Standing Committee, Chen Duxiu being secretary-general. It also elected the Central Supervisory Commission, the first central supervision organisation for inspecting discipline in the CPC's history, a significant event in the construction of the party.

After the congress, in accordance with requirements, the Central Politburo passed the resolution to revise the Party Constitution, formally putting forward the organisational principle of carrying out democratic centralism within the party. For the first time, democratic centralism, and the relationship between the party and the Youth League, were written into the Party Constitution, and for the first time it was made clear that the age for joining the party must be above 18 years old.

The Fifth Congress put forward some correct principles, such as to win leadership of the proletarian revolution, to build a revolutionary democratic regime and to carry out agrarian revolution. However, on the issues of how to win the leadership, how to lead the peasants, and particularly how to build a revolutionary armed force led by the party, it failed to put forward any effective and specific measures, so it was hard to undertake the task of saving the revolution.

THE FAILURE OF THE GREAT REVOLUTION AND LESSONS LEARNED

After the Fifth Congress, the crisis in the areas governed by the Wuhan Nationalist Government deteriorated. Hubei, Hunan and Jiangxi provinces all experienced incidents in which the revolutionary organisations were searched and closed down and the worker-peasant leaders were arrested. On 21 May 1927, Xu Kexiang, a KMT military officer, took over the guns of the workers' pickets in Changsha, and captured and executed about 100 CPC members and revolutionary masses. This was the May 21st Incident. After the incident, Changsha was shrouded in White Terror.

On 15 July, Wang Jingwei held an enlarged meeting of the KMT Central Standing Committee. In the name of "separating the CPC from the KMT", he officially broke with the CPC and carried out a large-scale arrest and massacre of communists and revolutionary masses. The KMT-CPC cooperation broke down completely and the Great Revolution initiated by the cooperation of the two parties was declared a failure. Large numbers of China's sons and daughters fell in the reactionary reign of terror. According to incomplete figures, from March 1927 until the first half of 1928, the number of communists and revolutionary masses executed reached about 310,000.

In the White Terror, revolutionaries shed blood like water, but they were not scared. Before he was arrested, Xia Minghan was a member of the Standing Committee of the Hubei Provincial Committee. After he was put in prison, he remained faithful and unyielding. In a letter to his wife, he wrote the proud words, "Keep up the revolution, carry out my will and pledge yourself to spread the truth to the world". His words "beheading is nothing to me, as long as one is true to one's doctrine" vividly expressed that the light of communist ideals and faith would never die out.

The Great Revolution was the people's revolutionary movement participated in by workers and peasants as the main force, while the bourgeois capitalists and the upper petty bourgeoisie were also participants. By its fundamental difference in scale, as well as in form, to the 1911 Revolution, it set off an earth-shaking hurricane, giving a heavy punch to the influence of the imperialists in China. It basically overthrew the reactionary rule of the Beiyang warlords, led to an unprecedented spread of the democratic revolutionary ideology to the whole country, accelerated the awakening of the broad masses of the Chinese people, and pushed forward Chinese social progress. It educated and trained all the revolutionary classes and laid the mass foundation for the future Agrarian Revolutionary War led by the party. In the Great Revolution, the party's organisations developed rapidly and the party's own construction was strengthened. In the six short years from the founding of the party to the failure of the Great Revolution, except for Xinjiang, Qinghai, Guizhou, Tibet and Taiwan, all the other parts of the country had established party organisations or party activities. From about 50 members, the CPC was developed into a political party of 58,000 members, leading about 2.8 million workers and 9.7 million peasants, giving the party a considerable mass foundation.

In the early and middle stages of the Great Revolution, the party's line was correct on the whole. The enthusiasm of the party members, cadres and masses was very high and therefore we won a tremendous victory. The failure of the Great Revolution, speaking objectively, was due to the reasons that the counter-revolutionary forces were strong, the bourgeoisie wavered in their support, and the Chiang Kai-shek clique and the Wang

Jingwei clique betrayed the revolution one after another. Speaking in subjective terms, the party was in its infancy, lacking experience to deal with complicated situations and not good at integrating the fundamental tenets of Marxism with the concrete practice of the Chinese revolution.

The experience and lessons from the rise to the failure of the Great Revolution showed that the party not only must establish a united front, but also always maintain its own independence in order to win leadership of the proletarian revolution by implementing a policy of "both unity and struggle". Meanwhile, according to the national conditions at the time, if victory was to be won, the armed struggle had to be maintained, and an armed force commanded directly by the party had to be organised and built. Besides, the land issue of the peasantry had to be resolved so the masses could be fully mobilised to join the revolution and the revolutionary force could be expanded. Moreover, the party had to strengthen its own construction and democratic centralism. It had to develop the party organisation and focus on the number of members, but what it had to do most was to consolidate them and attach importance to the quality of the membership. Only with a correct understanding and solving these problems could the party lead the Chinese revolutionary cause to success.

Despite the Great Revolution failing, its historical significance would never be obliterated. In fact, it was a great exercise for future victories. It was during this period of time that the communists carried out dynamic work, setting off an anti-imperialist, anti-feudal struggle throughout the country, and writing a heroic and moving page in Chinese revolutionary history. No matter whether the revolution was in high tide or in White Terror, the communists displayed a dauntless and utterly fearless spirit of self-sacrifice and the revolutionary will to die rather than submit. For the supreme interest of the people and the nation, they would not hesitate to go through fire and water, thereby winning the trust of the people.

After the Great Revolution, for both positive and negative reasons, the party accumulated profound experience, and began to explore ways to localise Marxism in China and put forward the basic idea of the new democratic revolution under the leadership of the proletariat, and to understand the importance of an agrarian revolution and the control of a revolutionary armed force. Furthermore, the Chinese people's political consciousness had evidently heightened. All these elements constituted the necessary prerequisites for a new stage of the Chinese revolution - the Agrarian Revolutionary War.

Two

Setting off a Storm of Agrarian Revolution

After the failure of the Great Revolution, China was in a state of White Terror. The young Communist Party encountered a rigorous test never experienced since its founding. Confronted by the bloody massacre of the reactionaries, the CPC and the Chinese people were neither cowed nor conquered nor exterminated. They picked themselves up, wiped off the blood, buried their fallen comrades and went into battle again.

1
RESISTING KMT REACTIONARY RULE BY ARMED STRUGGLE

THE AUGUST SEVENTH CONFERENCE AND THE NANCHANG, AUTUMN HARVEST AND GUANGZHOU UPRISINGS

After Chiang Kai-shek and Wang Jingwei betrayed the revolution, the domestic political situation suddenly reversed. China was shrouded in a bloodbath and the Chinese revolution was at a critical juncture.

In grim struggles and from bloody lessons, the CPC realised profoundly that without a revolutionary armed force, there was no way they could defeat the armed reactionaries, or shoulder the responsibility of leading the Chinese revolution, or win victory, or change the lot of the Chinese people and the nation. Without armed struggle, it was as good as sitting still waiting for death while leaving the whole of China covered in darkness.

On 1 August 1927, under the leadership of the Front Commission of the Central Committee with Zhou Enlai as secretary, He Long, Ye Ting, Zhu De and Liu Bocheng led about 20,000 troops controlled or influenced by the CPC, and in Nanchang they fired the opening shot in an armed struggle against the KMT reactionaries. After a fierce four-hour battle, the troops involved in the uprising captured the city. Soon afterwards, following the plan of the Central Committee, the troops withdrew from Nanchang and marched south to Guangdong Province. In early October they were defeated in Chaozhou and Shantou. Part of the surviving troops moved to the Haifeng and Lufeng areas of Guangdong where they joined forces with the local peasant army, while the main part, led by Zhu De and Chen Yi, moved to southern Hunan where they carried out guerrilla warfare.

The gunshots in Nanchang City were like a flash of lightning streaking across the night sky. The Nanchang Uprising marked the beginning of the CPC's independent leadership of the revolutionary war, the construction of a people's army and aim to seize state power by armed force, opening a new era of the Chinese revolution. Ever since then, the People's Army under the leadership of the CPC bravely plunged into the mighty historical torrent to seek liberation and happiness for the people, and independence and rejuvenation of the nation, closely linking it with the lot of the Chinese people and the nation.

On 7 August, in Hankou, Hubei, the CPC Central Committee secretly held an emergency conference (the August Seventh Conference), which defined the guiding principles of land revolution and armed struggle against the KMT reactionaries. It was a correct guiding principle and a correct conclusion exchanged after the party had paid a bloody price. Mao Zedong, who attended the conference, stressed in his speech, "In future we must pay great attention to the military. We must know that political power grows out of the barrel of a gun."

August Seventh Conference site

This conference was a turning point. It pointed to a new way out for the CPC, which was then an ideologically confused and demoralised organisation, so this made a great contribution to saving the party and the revolution. It was a historical transformation from the defeat of the Great Revolution to the upsurge of the Agrarian Revolutionary War.

After the conference, the party sent many cadres to various places to recover and consolidate the party organisations and launch armed uprisings.

In the capacity of commissioner of the Central Committee, Mao Zedong went to Hunan to convey the spirit of the conference, to reorganise the Hunan Provincial Committee and to lead the Autumn Harvest Uprising. The Front Commission with Mao Zedong as secretary unified 5,000 soldiers of every type into the First Division of the Workers' and Peasants' Revolutionary Army and on 9 September 1927, they launched the Autumn Harvest Uprising in the Hunan-Jiangxi border area. After they were defeated in an attack on the key city of Changsha, Mao Zedong resolutely changed the plan. He led the remaining troops to retreat to Wenjiashi, Liuyang to gather where he held a meeting of the Front Commission. It decided that the troops would go and find a place to stay in the mountainous countryside where enemy rule was weak. From attacking big cities to advancing to the countryside, this was a decisive new starting point in the development history of the Chinese people's revolution.

On 29 September Mao Zedong led the troops involved in the uprising to carry out the famous Sanwan Reorganisation in Sanwan Village, Yongxin County, Jiangxi Province, to build party branches in company-level army units, to set up soldiers' commissions at all levels, and to exercise a democratic system of political equality between officers and men. From then on, the bad practices and harmful styles of the old army among the troops involved in the uprising began to change and organisationally the leadership of the party over the army was established, which was an important start to building a new type of people's army under the leadership of the proletariat.

On 11 December Zhang Tailei, the party secretary of the Guangdong Provincial Committee, Ye Ting and Ye Jianying, led the Guangzhou Uprising. The troops at once occupied most of Guangzhou where they established a soviet government. But they were outnumbered, and the uprising was defeated on the third day. Zhang Tailei and many revolutionaries died heroically. The revolutionary couple Zhou Wenyong and Chen Tiejun were sadly arrested. In February 1928 they held their solemn wedding in the execution ground in Honghuagang, Guangzhou, going to their death unflinchingly.

The Guangzhou Uprising was another brave counterblow against the massacre policy of the KMT reactionaries. The practice proved once again that when the new KMT warlords had powerful armed forces in key cities, it was impossible for the communists to win a victory for the revolution by armed city uprisings, or by attacking and capturing cities.

By early 1928 the party was leading other uprisings. The fairly important ones were the uprisings in Haifeng-Lufeng, Hainan Island, Huang'an, Macheng, Donggu, Yiyang, Hengfeng, Wan'an, South Hunan, Sangzhi, West Fujian, Queshan, Weinan and Huaxian. Although most of them failed due to the fact that the troops involved in the uprising were outnumbered, or the leaders implemented erroneous policies, or the objective conditions were not ripe for an uprising, they made it clear that the spark of revolution could never be stamped out by any counter-revolutionary armed suppression because their cause was just and in accordance with the demands of the people. Some of the troops involved in the uprising kept up their resistance by guerrilla warfare in the remote border areas between provinces, which laid a preliminary foundation for the later further development of the Red Army and its base areas.

THE SIXTH NATIONAL CONGRESS OF THE CPC

The party launched a series of armed uprisings; however, the revolutionary situation was still at a low ebb. Because the party had only been founded for a few years, it was politically immature. Regarding the major issues, such as what was the nature of Chinese society and what were the nature, motivation and prospects for the Chinese revolution, there was a divergence of views and controversy in the party. Therefore, there was an urgent need to convene a national congress. But the situation of White Terror in China was extremely grave. After obtaining the Comintern's permission, the party decided to convene the Sixth National Congress in the Soviet Union.

From June to July 1928 the Sixth Congress of the CPC was held in the suburbs of Moscow with 142 attendees. It passed resolutions on a series of issues regarding politics, the military, organisation and the soviet regime, as well as passing the revised *Constitution of the CPC* and electing a new Central Committee.

The congress scientifically analysed the nature of Chinese society. It clearly pointed out that China was still a semi-colonial, semi-feudal state and the nature of the present Chinese revolution was a bourgeois democratic revolution; China's political situation at the time was between two revolutionary high tides when the first tide had gone but the new one had not yet arrived; and the party's general line was to win over the masses. It shifted the focus of work from trying every means to organise armed insurrections to engaging in long-term arduous mass work. It set out to win over the masses as the paramount task of the party and opposing 'leftist' deviation as the principal danger. This was an important change in the party's work policy.

The party constitution passed by the congress meticulously stipulated the contents of democratic centralism, while formulating new regulations for the system of managing party members and organisations

The line of the Sixth Congress was generally correct. It unified the thinking of the party under the circumstances whereby it was in a state of ideological confusion. After the congress, the whole party implemented this line to restore and rebuild the party organisations, and to take the lead in carrying out work among the masses, which put the Chinese revolution on the right track toward recovery and development.

2
MAO ZEDONG AND THE OPENING UP OF A NEW PATH FOR THE CHINESE REVOLUTION

THE FOUNDING OF THE JINGGANGSHAN REVOLUTIONARY BASE AND THE MARCH INTO SOUTHERN JIANGXI AND WESTERN FUJIAN

After the defeat of the Great Revolution, what could collectively embody the correct direction of the Chinese revolution was the struggle in the Jinggangshan revolutionary base led by Mao Zedong and Zhu De.

After the Sanwan reorganisation, Mao Zedong led the troops involved in the uprising to Jinggangshan, a mountainous area in the middle section of the Luoxiao mountain range bordering Hunan and Jiangxi provinces. The reasons Mao Zedong chose this place to build up a base were: the mass foundation was fairly good because all the border counties of the two provinces had once built party organisations and peasant associations during the Great Revolution period; some of the old-style local peasant armed forces were willing to ally with the Workers' and Peasants' Revolutionary Army; the terrain here was strategically situated and difficult to access, easy to defend but difficult to attack; the surrounding counties had a self-sustaining agricultural economy, making it convenient for the troops to raise funds and obtain grain; it was in the Hunan-Jiangxi border area, far away from the centre ruled by the KMT while conflict existed between warlords of the two provinces, so control over the area was comparatively weak.

Taking advantage of the opportunity when the ruling class had a new internal split, Mao Zedong spared no effort to carry out party-military-political regime building in the border area. In November 1927 he founded the first red political regime - the Workers', Peasants' and Soldiers' Government of Chaling County in the Hunan-Jiangxi border area. In mid-February 1928 he commanded his troops to smash the KMT offensive in Jinggangshan. At that point, the Jinggangshan base was preliminarily established and the border-area party organisation was also gradually being built up.

To the Workers' and Peasants' Revolutionary Army, Mao Zedong demanded that changes be made to the old tradition of caring only about fighting battles but that they should also shoulder three tasks of either fighting battles to wipe out the enemy, or expropriating local tyrants to raise money, or undertaking mass work to mobilise people. In April 1928 he summed up the experiences of the troops engaging in mass work and stipulated that the troops must implement the 'Three Main Disciplines[1] and Six Points for Attention' which were later developed into the 'Eight Points for Attention[2]'. These stipulations embodied the nature of the People's Army and all played a significant role in correctly handling the internal relations within the army and the relations between the military and the people, as well as in annihilating the enemy army.

In late April 1928, Zhu De and Chen Yi led a force of about 10,000 of the troops remaining from the Nanchang Uprising and the Hunan Peasant Uprising Army to move to the Jinggangshan area. They joined forces with Mao Zedong and founded the Fourth Army of the Workers' and Peasants' Revolutionary Army (it was later changed to the Fourth Army of the Workers' and Peasants' Red Army), commanded by Zhu De while Mao Zedong was party representative and secretary of the military commission. Ever since then, the troops led by them were called the 'Zhu-Mao Red Army'. In May the First CPC Congress of the Hunan-Jiangxi Border Area elected a Special Committee with Mao Zedong as secretary.

From successive victories over the Hunan-Jiangxi KMT army's offensive, Mao Zedong and Zhu De summarised the basic principles of guerrilla warfare, namely, that "if the enemy advance, we retreat; if the enemy camps, we harass; if the enemy tires, we attack; if the enemy retreats, we pursue". They led less than four regiments into battle against the KMT's eight or nine, or even 18 regiments, fearing neither formidable enemies nor difficulties but expanding their base day by day.

The struggle in Jinggangshan was inseparable with the Agrarian Revolution. When the base was first founded, land redistribution was only tried in some individual places. Following the gradual consolidation of the base, from May to July 1928 all the counties along the border area set off a surge of land redistribution, meanwhile the *Land Law* was promulgated at the end of the year. From the fact that they had had land redistributed to them, the poor peasants realised that the Red Army was fighting for their interests, therefore, they gave all-out support to every aspect of development of the Red Army and the base, which was the social foundation for the existence and development of the base.

The founding of the Jinggangshan base lit the spark for building armed independent regimes of workers and peasants, and explored the correct path for the revolution to encircle the cities from the rural areas and then seize state power by armed force, a path no one had explored before. The most valuable property left during the Jinggangshan struggle was the Jinggangshan Spirit. Its most important aspects were to have firm belief, to work hard and resolutely, to seek truth from facts, to dare to tread a new path, to rely on the masses and to have the courage to win victory.

In December 1928 the KMT army in Hunan and Jiangxi provinces despatched 30,000 troops and from five directions they launched an attack on Jinggangshan. In January 1929 Mao Zedong, Zhu De and Chen Yi led the Fourth Army's main force to launch an attack on southern Jiangxi and then they joined forces with the Fifth Army that had broken out of Jinggangshan and together they marched to western Fujian. In spring 1930 the southern Jiangxi base and the western Fujian base were formed, and successively the southwestern Jiangxi soviet and the western Fujian soviet were founded, which laid the foundation for the establishment of the central revolutionary base, and also played an inspirational and exemplary role for the development of the Red Army's guerrilla warfare and the construction of bases in all regions.

THE GUTIAN CONFERENCE AND ESTABLISHING THE PRINCIPLES OF PARTY AND ARMY BUILDING

The Gutian Conference was convened at a critical, life-and-death moment for the Chinese Red Army. At the time the Fourth Army was fighting in southern Jiangxi and western Fujian. A divergence of opinion on the issue of army building emerged among the leaders; the purely military viewpoint, the ideology of roving rebel bands and the remnants of warlordism had developed to some extent in the army. After the Eighth Party Congress of the Fourth Army, an attack on Dongjiang was launched but failed, thereby confusing the troops ideologically and lowering their morale. The whole Fourth Army faced a rigorous test.

In December 1929 the Ninth Party Congress of the Fourth Army was held in Gutian, Shanghang County, Fujian Province. A new Front Committee was elected with Mao Zedong being secretary. In accordance with the spirit of the September letter of the Central Committee, the congress passed the *Gutian Conference Resolution* drawn up by Mao Zedong. The most important part of the resolution was on correcting mistaken ideas in the party, which established the principle of building the CPC in terms of ideology and building the army in terms of politics.

Gutian Conference site

With respect to party building, the resolution epitomised a unique way which stressed building the party ideologically. The resolution profoundly expounded the extreme importance of strengthening the ideological construction of the party. It pointed out the manifestations of various non-proletarian ideas, their roots, and the methods for correcting them. Besides, it put forward the tasks of strengthening the party's organisational construction and demanded 'striving to ensure democratic life under centralised guidance', and paying attention to quality when recruiting new party members.

In respect of army building, the resolution stipulated that the Red Army was an armed body for carrying out the political tasks of the revolution, therefore it must absolutely obey the leadership of the CPC and strive wholeheartedly to implement the party's programme, line and policy. It criticised the purely military viewpoint that regarded military affairs and politics as being opposed to each other, while again proposing that the Red Army must shoulder the tasks of fighting battles, raising funds and undertaking mass mobilisation of people, and emphasising that the Red Army's political work must be strengthened, especially its political education work.

The *Gutian Conference Resolution* was a programmatic document for the building of the CPC and the Chinese Red Army. It was an important milestone in the history of building the party and the people's armed forces. The Gutian Conference established the principles of building the party and the army with Marxist ideology, and established the policy, principles and system of the army's political work. It put forward principles as well as directions for solving the fundamental problems of army-building, thereby turning an army mainly comprised of peasants into a new people's armed force of a proletarian nature, thereby realising its rebirth. The foundation of the army political work laid in the Gutian Conference played a decisive role in the Chinese armed forces' survival and development.

The absolute leadership of the party over the army is the soul of the People's Army and it will never change. This fundamental principle and system began in the Nanchang Uprising, was established in the Sanwan Reorganisation and finalised at the Gutian Conference. It is the political character and fundamental strength of the People's Army which makes it completely different to all old-style armies. Thousands upon thousands of revolutionary officers and men were loyal to the CPC, obeyed its orders and followed it. When faced with setbacks, they braced themselves more and more; when faced with hardship, they marched forward courageously, thereby constructing an ever-victorious armoured fist.

After the establishment of the party and army-building principles, the Red Army had an excellent opportunity for great development. In June 1930, the Red Army troops in southwestern Jiangxi and western Fujian were reorganised into the First Army Group of the Red Army, totalling about 20,000 soldiers. In August, the First Army Group and the Third Army Group commanded by Peng Dehuai and Teng Daiyuan were reorganised into the First Front Army of the Red Army, totalling about 30,000 soldiers. Zhu De was the commander-in-chief and Mao Zedong was concurrently the secretary-general of the Front Committee and general political commissar. Consequently, the First Front Army became a Red Army force with the highest combat effectiveness in the whole country.

After Mao Zedong led the Autumn Harvest Uprising troops to Jinggangshan, regarding the question from the party "How long can we keep the Red Flag flying?", in accordance with the actual conditions of the Chinese revolution, he scientifically expounded that in the Chinese revolution where the economic mainstay was agriculture, armed insurrection would be a characteristic. He profoundly demonstrated the objective conditions for the long-term existence and development of red political power, putting forward the idea of an armed independent regime of workers and peasants. In *A Single Spark Can Start a Prairie Fire*, he pointed out that the establishment and development of the Red Army, the guerrilla forces and the Red areas were the key factors in bringing about the high tide of the national revolution. Therefore, the idea of encircling the cities from the rural areas and then seizing state power by armed force took shape. This was the summarisation of the experience of the struggle of the Red Army and the base areas led by the CPC after the defeat of the Great Revolution in 1927, and the creative application and development of Marxism in China.

After the failure of the Great Revolution, the Chinese Communists walked along a unique path to guide the Chinese revolution to recover and to win victory gradually. This path was to encircle the cities from the rural areas and seize state power by armed force.

In semi-colonial, semi-feudal China, under the circumstances that the Great Revolution had suffered a defeat and there was a great disparity in strength between the enemy and us, it was impossible for the Chinese Communists to be like the Russian October Revolution and win victory by firstly occupying key cities and then winning victory nationwide. First they had to build revolutionary bases in the countryside to accumulate revolutionary strength, then seize the cities when conditions were ripe and finally strive for nationwide victory of the revolution.

This correct revolutionary road suited to the Chinese reality was opened up in the collective struggle of the CPC in its leadership over the people, and Mao Zedong made the most outstanding contribution during the process. In practice he not only established a foothold for the armed struggle in the countryside, leading to the creation of the Jinggangshan base and creatively solving a series of fundamental problems that had to be solved so the bases could be maintained and developed in the rural areas, but also in theory, and step by step, he clearly explained the problem of which road the Chinese revolution should follow.

---

1. The 'Three Main Disciplines' were: obey all military orders; don't take anything from workers and peasants; all goods seized must be returned to the public.
2. The 'Eight Points for Attention' were: speak amicably; trade fairly; pay back what is borrowed; pay for any damage; don't hit or scold others; don't damage crops; don't molest women; don't abuse prisoners.

3
THE RED ARMY'S VICTORY IN ITS STRUGGLE AGAINST 'ENCIRCLEMENT AND SUPPRESSION' AND BUILDING REVOLUTIONARY BASES IN RURAL AREAS

RECOVERY AND IMPROVEMENT OF THE REVOLUTIONARY SITUATION

In the two years after the Sixth Congress, because the party implemented resolute changes in how it worked, party organisations achieved substantial recovery and development. By September 1930, according to the statistics of the enlarged Third Plenum, the number of party members nationwide had increased to 122,300. By the end of that year, the party had recovered 17 provincial party committees (provincial work committees) as well as many special, municipal and county party committees. In its arduous struggle in the KMT-controlled areas, the party gained a rich store of underground work experience. The Special Branch of the Central Committee was set up in November 1927. Under the direct leadership of Zhou Enlai, it played an important role in the work to secure the safety of the Central Committee, to rescue arrested comrades, to punish traitors, to gather intelligence, to link up wireless communications among all the soviet areas and to coordinate combat operations with the Red Army in the base areas.

The Central Committee also strengthened its leadership over all Red Armies as well as undertaking work in rural bases and achieved tremendous development in its work. In March 1930 the Red Army forces across China had 13 army units with about 62,000 troops. Apart from the bases in southwestern Jiangxi and western Fujian under the leadership of Mao Zedong, there were also important bases in the border areas of western

Hunan-Hubei, Hubei-Henan-Anhui, Hunan-Jiangxi, Hunan-Hubei-Jiangxi, Fujian-Zhejiang-Jiangxi, and in Zuoyoujiang in Guangxi, Dongjiang in Guangdong and Hainan Island. The building, as well as the development, of the bases were the key factors enabling the revolution to take a favourable turn in this period.

In the western Hunan-Hubei area, in early 1928 He Long arrived at Honghu Lake in Hubei while Zhou Yiqun arrived in Sangzhi in western Hunan. They organised several peasant guerrilla forces, established a new revolutionary force and reorganised them as the Fourth Army of the Workers' and Peasants' Revolutionary Army. In July 1930, in Gong'an, Hubei, they joined forces with the Sixth Army built by enlarging the general units of the western Hubei guerrilla forces, thereby expanding their forces to about 10,000. They established the Second Army Group of the Red Army, with He Long as commander and Zhou Yiqun as political commissar. Before long, they founded the western Hunan-Hubei soviet.

In the Hubei-Henan-Anhui border area, the Red Army guerrilla forces also developed quickly. In the beginning, this base consisted of three parts: the Hubei-Henan border area, southeastern Henan and western Anhui. The Central Military Commission (CMC) sent Xu Xiangqian to the Hubei-Henan border area to take charge of military and command work. In early 1930, the Central Committee decided to establish a special committee there, so they sent Guo Shushen to take on the job as party secretary and to bring the three bases under unified leadership, and founded the First Army of the Red Army. This was the predecessor of the future Hubei-Henan-Anhui Central Bureau and the Fourth Front Army.

In the Hunan-Hubei-Jiangxi border area, after Peng Dehuai and Teng Daiyuan led the Fifth Army's return to the area, they joined forces with the local guerrillas and expanded the force into the Third Army Group of the Red Army, with Peng Dehuai as commander-in-chief and secretary of the front committee, and Teng Daiyuan as political commissar. They founded the Hunan-Hubei-Jiangxi revolutionary base.

In western Guangxi, representatives of the Central Committee, Deng Xiaoping, Zhang Yunyi and Wei Baqun, led part of the forces of the Guangxi Army and the local peasant armies who were under the influence of the CPC to launch the Baise Uprising and the Longzhou Uprising respectively in December 1929 and February 1930. They established the Seventh Army and the Eighth Army of the Red Army, with Li Mingrui as commander-in-chief and Deng Xiaoping as political commissar for both armies, founding the Zuoyoujiang revolutionary base.

THE RED ARMY'S COUNTER-ENCIRCLEMENT STRUGGLE

The tenacious existence and rapid development of the Red Army shocked the ruling circle of the KMT. Chiang Kai-shek gathered forces and launched several large-scale 'encirclement and suppression' campaigns against the Red Army bases and the Red Army.

Their major targets were the Central Revolutionary Base and the First Front Army commanded by Mao Zedong and Zhu De. From October 1930, Chiang Kai-shek mobilised 100,000 troops and launched the first 'encirclement and suppression' campaign against the central soviet area. The First Front Army had about 40,000 troops. Adopting the combat policy of luring the enemy in deep, they wiped out 13,000 of the enemy, successfully crushing the KMT's first 'encirclement' campaign.

Before long, Chiang Kai-shek commanded 200,000 troops and launched the second 'encirclement' campaign against the central soviet area. The First Front Army carried on with the policy of luring the enemy in deep and from 16 to 31 May 1931, they won five victories in a row, sweeping 700 *li* (around 350km) in distance, from the Ganjiang River straight to Jianning in Fujian, wiping out 30,000 of the enemy. They crushed the KMT's second 'encirclement' campaign and further expanded the central soviet area. "In fifteen days we marched seven hundred *li*, crossing the misty waters of the Gan River and green Fujian hills, rolling back the enemy as we would a mat." Full of power and grandeur, Mao Zedong's verses vividly recorded and narrated this inspiring victory.

In June, making himself Commander-in-chief, Chiang Kai-shek gathered 300,000 troops and launched the third campaign against the Red Army. In three months, the Red Army wiped out about 30,000 of the enemy, crushing the KMT army's third 'encirclement' campaign. Afterwards, the two bases in southern Jiangxi and western Fujian linked together, expanding to cover a broad area across more than 20 counties.

Affected by the Red Army's victory, about 17,000 troops of the KMT's 26th Route Army revolted in Ningdu, Jiangxi on 14 December 1931. They were reorganised into the Fifth Army Group of the Red Army, which shocked the KMT troops.

Meanwhile, victory was also won in the other base areas.

In the Hubei-Henan-Anhui border area, from the winter of 1930 to the summer of 1931 the Red Army crushed two KMT 'encirclement' campaigns. In November 1931, following the decision of the Central Committee, the Fourth Army and the 25th Army in this base area reorganised into the Fourth Front Army of the Red Army with about 30,000 troops. Xu Xiangqian was commander-in-chief and Chen Changhao was political commissar.

Victories were also won in the western Hunan-Hubei border area, northeastern Jiangxi, the border areas of Hunan-Jiangxi and Hunan-Hubei-Jiangxi, and in Hainan Island. Meanwhile, after arduous struggles, the founders of the Red Army in the Northwest, Liu Zhidan, Xie Zichang and Xi Zhongxun, also established the Shaanxi-Gansu border base and the northern Shaanxi base (later developed into the Shaanxi-Gansu base which was also called the 'northwestern base'). The distribution of the Chinese revolutionary bases made a change. Not only were there bases in the south, but also in the north of the country, which had a significant influence on the later development of the Chinese revolution.

From the struggle against the 'encirclement' campaigns, the Red Army developed its thinking on military strategy and tactics, which included: wipe out the enemy's effective forces; concentrate a superior force to destroy enemy forces one by one; 'fight when we can win, withdraw when we cannot'; discover the enemy's weakness in mobile warfare; and fight a quick battle to force a quick decision. All these ideas were built on the foundation of peoples' war, solving the problem of how the Red Army defeats a more powerful enemy with inferior strength and backward equipment, thereby adding distinguished contributions to Marxist military theory.

AGRARIAN REVOLUTION AND EVERY ASPECT OF CONSTRUCTION IN THE BASE AREAS

The Agrarian Revolution was one of the basic contents of China's New Democratic Revolution, as well as the manifestation of the practice of the CPC's original intention and mission. The party leading the peasants to 'expropriate local tyrants and redistribute land' was to liberate the broad masses of the peasantry and struggle for the basic interests of the people. Following the establishment and development of the Red Army and the rural revolutionary bases, Agrarian Revolution was carried out extensively.

From the bases in southern Jiangxi and western Fujian, Mao Zedong put forward a series of policies and principles for a thoroughgoing Agrarian Revolution. In April 1929, he presided over the draft *Land Law* in Xingguo County and changed the article 'confiscate all land' stipulated in the *Land Law* on Jinggangshan to 'confiscate all public land and the land of the landlord class'. In July, under his guidance, the resolution passed in the First Party Congress in western Fujian made the stipulation in principle that 'the land of owner-peasants must not be confiscated' and 'take from the haves and give to the have-nots', ensuring that land redistribution was carried out over an area of 300 *li* in western Fujian where more than 600,000 poor peasants obtained land. In February 1930, guided by the principle of equal distribution of land according to population, the whole of Xingguo County and another five counties, as well as parts of Yongfeng County, carried out full-scale land redistribution. In February 1931, Mao Zedong revised the regulations in the *Land Law* on Jinggangshan so that peasants had only land-use rights and were prohibited from selling or buying land but reaffirmed the peasants' ownership of land.

At the same time, the Agrarian Revolution was also carried out rigorously in the revolutionary bases in northeastern Jiangxi, the border areas of western Hunan-Hubei and Hubei-Henan-Anhui, and in Zuoyoujiang, Guangxi and Hainan Island.

In practice over three years, a set of fairly feasible Agrarian Revolution lines, policies and methods were basically taking shape. They were mainly: reliance on poor peasants and farmhands, alliance with middle peasants, restriction toward rich peasants, elimination of the landlord class and turning feudal land ownership into land ownership by the peasants; taking the village as a unit to redistribute land to the population, taking from the haves and giving to the have-nots based on the original farming land.

The political and economic turnaround enabled vast numbers of peasants to quickly distinguish between the superiority of the CPC regime and inferiority of the KMT regime, thereby greatly enhancing their enthusiasm for revolution. They supported the Agrarian Revolution and the CPC. One after another they joined the Red Army and took part in the counter-encirclement struggle. They assisted with front-line work and brought gifts to the Red Army troops, forming a relationship between the party and the masses, between the military and civilians, making them as inseparable as fish and water, and as close as flesh and blood.

Under the circumstances the bases and the Red Army forces continued to develop, in November 1931 the First Congress of the Chinese Soviet Republic was convened in Ruijin, Jiangxi Province. It elected the Central Executive Committee and announced the founding of the Provisional Central Government of the Chinese Soviet Republic. Mao Zedong was elected Chairman of the Central Executive Committee as well as the Peoples' Commission of the Central Executive Committee.

The Chinese Soviet Republic was the first national workers' and peasants' democratic political power in Chinese history, an important attempt of the CPC in power in some areas of China. The establishment of the provisional government of the Chinese soviet, to some extent strengthened its function as the leading centre for all the bases where they were in a state of independence, and politically it also exerted a great influence, giving an impetus to the development of political power, the economy, culture and education in all the bases, as well as self-construction of the party.

The Chinese Soviet Republic practiced a representative congress system of workers, peasants and soldiers, with elected administrators at every level, and with representatives of workers and peasants drawn extensively to participate in managing the regime, and exercising their rights as masters of their own affairs. From November 1931 to January 1934, the Central Revolutionary Base carried out three democratic elections and promulgated the details of Election Law. In many places more than 80% of the total electorate took part in elections. One after another, the other bases also convened their own congresses and elected their own soviet administrators at every level.

The Soviet Government attached great importance to building a righteous and honest government and judicial system. In December 1933, the Central Executive Committee issued a decree to punish acts of corruption and waste, and to seriously investigate and deal with corruption cases. In 1934 it built up an audit supervision system, which played an important role in aspects such as standardising financial revenue and expenditure, investigating and prosecuting corruption and waste, and promoting the building of an honest and clean government. The Provisional Central Government issued 120 laws and decrees, having initially established a legal system with a distinctive class nature and characteristics of the times.

The Soviet Government led the army and the people to actively carry out economic work and to struggle to break through the enemy economic blockade, so that agriculture, industry, commerce, transportation, posts and telecommunications, finance and other economic work had a certain development. Under extremely arduous circumstances, they worked hard to develop culture and education, and all kinds of schools were extensively built to train cadres and people with professional skills.

The party's self-building was also strengthened. Party membership expanded continuously and the party's organisation at every level was improved. The fine style of hard struggle, honesty and self-discipline and maintaining close ties with the masses was nurtured, thereby forging the Soviet Area Spirit with the following as the main contents: being firm in faith, seeking the truth and doing practical work, devoting oneself wholeheartedly to the people, being honest and upright, working diligently in defiance of difficulties, and striving for first-class and selfless dedication.

"The cadres in soviets have a fine style. They bring their own food when they go to handle official business. They wear straw sandals to make revolution in the day and at night they walk along the mountain paths to visit the poor peasants." This folk song was widely sung in the soviet areas and has been handed down to this day, a true portrayal of the Soviet Area Spirit.

Ruijin in Jiangxi Province, the site of the Central Workers' and Peasants' Democratic Government during the Agrarian Revolutionary War period

The thriving scene in the rural revolutionary bases under the leadership of the CPC formed a sharp contrast to the miserable scenes in the KMT-controlled areas where the masses lived in dire poverty, which made the Chinese people living in the abyss of suffering see the light and hope.

4
THE SITUATION AFTER THE MUKDEN INCIDENT AND THE START OF THE CENTRAL RED ARMY'S LONG MARCH

THE OUTBREAK OF THE MUKDEN INCIDENT AND THE RISE OF THE ANTI-JAPANESE NATIONAL SALVATION MOVEMENT

Late in the evening of 18 September 1931, the Japanese Kwantung Army stationed in China's Northeast (Manchuria) by unequal treaties launched an attack on the camp of the Chinese troops and the city of Mukden (now Shenyang). This was the Mukden Incident. The next day the Japanese troops occupied Shenyang. By February 1932 the three provinces of Liaoning, Jilin and Heilongjiang had become Japanese-occupied territory. In March the Japanese puppet state, the Manchukuo, with Puyi at the helm, was established in Changchun, Jilin.

The Mukden Incident was the inevitable result of Japanese militarists' long-term policy of aggression and expansion towards China, and a serious step in turning China into a colony monopolised by Japan.

The unprecedented national calamity aroused an unprecedented national awakening. After the incident, the national contradiction between China and Japan gradually became the main contradiction, a great change took place in China's domestic class relations and the Anti-Japanese National Salvation Movement sprang up rapidly across the country. In Shanghai 35,000 dock workers held an anti-Japanese strike, and in succession, the workers and other labouring masses in Nanjing, Tianjin, Beiping and Hankou presented their petitions to the local governments, making donations and banning the sale of Japanese goods. Young students, the urban petty bourgeoisie and the upper circle of the intelligentsia all voiced their demand to resist Japanese aggression and to practice democracy.

The Communist Party took the lead to hold high the banner of armed resistance against Japan. In September 1931, the CPC Central Committee issued the *Manifesto of the CPC on the Occasion of the Japanese Imperialists' Brutal Occupation of the Three Northeastern Provinces*, unequivocally putting forward, "Oppose the Japanese imperialists' brutal occupation of the Three Northeastern Provinces!" The CPC Provincial Committee in Manchuria gave directions to the party organisations at all levels to carry out an anti-Japanese struggle. The Central Committee despatched Zhou Baozhong and Zhao Yiman to the Northeast to strengthen the party's organisational force. Up until early 1933, one after another, anti-Japanese guerrilla forces, directly under the leadership of the CPC, were established in Bayan, South Manchuria, Haidong, East Manchuria, Ning'an, Tangyuan and Hailun, and they gradually became the main armed forces to resist Japanese aggression in the Northeast.

Japanese Army on top of the Xiaoximen (Small Western Gate) of Shenyang's inner-city wall firing on the city, 19 September 1931

The uprising of the Chinese people in the Northeast became the starting point of the War of Resistance Against Japanese Aggression, meanwhile it uncovered the prelude to the anti-Fascist world war.

The Chinese Nationalist Government repeatedly compromised against Japan's invasion of the Northeast, and in July 1931 Chiang Kai-shek put forward the policy of "resisting foreign aggression after stabilising the country". When the Mukden Incident occurred, the Nationalist Government informed the Northeast Army, "In order to avoid the expansion of the incident, (you) must follow the policy of nonresistance." All of this prompted Japan to attack China with force on a larger scale.

At this moment of national crisis, the KMT camp split up. Ma Zhanshan and Li Du, two generals of the KMT Northeast Army, fought the Japanese in the Northeast. On 28 January 1932, when Japanese troops attacked Shanghai, the Nationalist 19th Route Army commanded by Jiang Guangnai and Cai Tingkai rose to resist. However, under the basic policy of suing for peace, the Nanjing Government signed the Shanghai Ceasefire Agreement and the Tanggu Agreement with the Japanese invaders, which damaged China's sovereignty. In Zhangjiakou, Feng Yuxiang organised the Chahar Peoples' Anti-Japanese Allied Force, but the KMT Government sabotaged it and forced it to be disbanded.

THE CPC'S WORK IN KMT-CONTROLLED AREAS AND THE LEFT-WING MOVEMENT IN LITERATURE AND ART

After the Mukden Incident the national crisis became more and more serious. Under extremely difficult circumstances, CPC members carried on struggles in the KMT-controlled areas, using various positions to carry out their work.

In March 1930 the League of Leftist Writers was founded in Shanghai, followed by many other leftist cultural organisations, such as the Social Scientists Association, the Dramatists Association, the Artists Association, the Educationists Association, the Film Group and the Music Group. Under the leadership of the CPC, this new army of leftist culture actively engaged in activities of publicising Marxism, and revolutionary literature and artistic creation, thereby developing into the powerful Leftist Culture Movement.

With regard to publicising Marxism, leftist social scientists translated and published Volume One of *Das Kapital*, *Anti-Duhring*, *Critique of Political Economy*, *Materialism and Empiriocriticism*. These were the earliest complete Chinese translations of Karl Marx's classics.

Some CPC members maintained close ties with patriotic and progressive personages, such as Soong Ch'ing-ling (Mme Sun Yat-sen) and Lu Xun, to push forward the Anti-Japanese National Salvation Movement and to oppose the authoritarian rule of Chiang Kai-shek. Through massive strongly militant prose, Lu Xun ruthlessly exposed the landlord and comprador cliques' fawning on foreign powers and dictatorship, the shameless pacifism and the cruel cultural 'encirclement and suppression'. As Mao Zedong pointed out, "The road Lu Xun took was the very road of China's new national culture."

Leftist cultural workers also worked hard to cooperate with middle-of-the-roaders to take action together. Some articles written by Lu Xun, Qu Qiubai, Mao Dun and Zhou Yang were published in *Free Talk*, a supplement of the *Shen Bao* newspaper and monthly journal *Literature*. Mao Dun's famous novel *Midnight* was published in January 1933 and reprinted four times in three months. CPC members Xia Yan, Yang Hansheng and Tian Han produced many progressive films which had a large audience in the KMT-controlled areas. With regard to the development of leftist culture, even the KMT media cried out in alarm, "They are like mercury poured onto the ground, so pervasive as to gain entry by every opening."

Influenced by the intense atmosphere of the Anti-Japanese and National Salvation campaign, the *March of the Volunteers*, with music by Nie Er and words by Tian Han, spread rapidly throughout China after its publication, becoming the most powerful voice of the times and playing a tremendous role in mobilising the Chinese people to rise up to resist Japanese aggression and to save the nation. 'The people of China are at their most critical time, everybody must roar in defiance.' Soul-stirring, the song made an indelible impression on people once they heard it. It expressed the grief and indignation of the Chinese people, kindled their strong patriotic feelings, and sang out the heroic spirit of fighting to the death in defending China, thereby becoming an immortal masterpiece of great patriotism.

The leftist culture movement in the KMT-controlled areas in this period trained a group of strong revolutionary culture teams, which played an important role in pushing forward the anti-Japanese and national salvation campaign.

DEFEAT IN THE FIFTH COUNTER-ENCIRCLEMENT CAMPAIGN

In January 1931, under the direct interference of Pavel Mif, secretary of the Far Eastern Bureau, Executive Committee of the Comintern, the enlarged Fourth Plenum of the Sixth Congress of the CPC was held in Shanghai. Wang Ming, who lacked practical struggle experience, was not only by-elected as a member of the Central Committee, but also became a member of the Central Politburo. 'Leftist' dogmatism errors, represented by Wang Ming, began their four-year rule in the CPC's leading organ.

After the plenum, there were a series of unusual situations in the party's work in the KMT-controlled areas, where CPC organisations sustained severe damage. In Shanghai, both members of the Central Committee and the Politburo were less than half. Responding to the proposal of the Far Eastern Bureau of the Comintern, in the second half of September 1931 the CPC Provisional Central Politburo (Provisional Central Committee) was set up with Bo Gu (Qin Bangxian) assuming overall responsibility.

At the end of 1932, Chiang Kai-shek assembled a force of about 30 divisions and launched the fourth 'encirclement' campaign against the Central Revolutionary Base. Meanwhile, under the erroneous domination of dogmatism, Mao Zedong's correct stand was censured, and he was wrongly removed as leader of the Red Army. Zhou Enlai and Zhu De, by applying and developing experiences that had previously proved successful, commanded the Red Army and defeated the KMT's fourth 'encirclement' campaign, while creating a precedent of how to ambush large troop formations in the Red Army's war history.

In the second half of 1933, Chiang Kai-shek launched his fifth 'encirclement' campaign on the revolutionary bases. He assembled one million troops and attacked the Red Army everywhere. Among the one million troops, half of them began the attack on the Central Revolutionary Base from late September.

At this moment, Bo Gu handed the military command to Li De (Otto Braun) who was sent by the Comintern. This leadership had no idea about the actual conditions in China, but mechanically copied their experience in regular positional warfare, holding that the Red Army should 'resist the enemy outside the gates'. After suffering setbacks, they adopted a passive defence strategy and the tactic of 'making short swift thrusts', commanding the Red Army to engage in positional warfare and fortified-position warfare, and battle with the well-equipped enemy, thereby increasingly landing the Red Army in a passive position.

In mid to late April 1934, the KMT army concentrated its forces to attack Guangchang, the northern gateway of the Central Soviet Area. Owing to tactical errors, after 18 days of bloody fighting, the Red Army suffered heavy casualties and Guangchang fell into enemy hands.

In order to move and contain the enemy, and to relieve the pressure on the Central Soviet Area, in early July the Seventh Army Corps of the Red Army was reorganised into the Northbound Anti-Japanese Vanguard. They marched to the Fujian-Zhejiang-Anhui-Jiangxi border area. After joining forces with the 10th Army led by Fang Zhimin, in November the two Red Army forces formed the 10th Army Group. Under the blockade and pursuit of the massive enemy forces, at the end of January 1935 the 10th Army Group suffered heavy losses. After Fang Zhimin was captured, he died heroically in August. In prison he wrote down the immortal writings of *Lovely China* and *Be Poor*, in which he solemnly expressed that "the enemy can only cut off our heads but never shake our faith" and described his expectations for the future, "China certainly has a glorious future". "The mother who has given birth to us will also be decorated most beautifully and join hands equally with all mothers in the world".

START OF THE CENTRAL RED ARMY'S LONG MARCH

In early September 1934, the KMT army stepped up their offensive on the hinterland of the Central Revolutionary Base, making it impossible for the Red Army to turn the tables in the original place. In October, the Central Committee and the Central Revolutionary Military Commission led about 86,000 Red Army main forces and set out on a long journey marking a strategic shift and beginning an unprecedented feat in world history.

This time the central leaders, who had originally practiced the 'leftist' erroneous policy, committed 'escapism' in retreat when commanding a campaign of breakout and strategic shift. Moreover, they turned the strategic shift of position into a house-removal operation, bringing along with the troops the heavy printing machines and the machinery of a war industry. Marching jam-packed along narrow mountain paths the 80,000 troops could often only pass one hill each night.

The KMT's 'pursuit and suppression' army reached 16 divisions, 77 regiments, who laid out four blockade lines. When breaking through the Xiang River, the fourth blockade line, under a pincer-movement attack by the KMT Hunan Army and Guangxi Army, the Red Army paid a heavy price in terms of lives lost. The 34th Division which was assigned to provide cover for the main body of troops became tightly encircled and isolated. It was impossible for them to cross the river. Facing an enemy more than 10 times stronger than them, the division commander Chen Shuxiang was courageous and fearless. He led his men to resist the enemy furiously, building a 'city wall' with their flesh and blood. They fought hard for four days and five nights, winning precious time for the other Red Army forces to cross the Xiang River. He was badly injured and captured. When the enemy carried him on a stretcher to go and take credit for their capture of a Red Army commander, he woke up. He snapped his intestines and died a hero's death. The 34th Division, the 18th Regiment of the Third Army Group, were blocked on the east bank of the Xiang River. They were running out of ammunition and provisions, and in the end most of the troops died heroically. The martyrs' blood dyed the Xiang River red, so a saying spread among the local folk, "Don't drink the water from the Xiang River for three years; don't eat fish from the Xiang River for 10 years."

After crossing the Xiang River, the 86,000-strong Red Army forces were sharply reduced to 30,000.

After the Xiang River campaign, a heated debate was going on in the party regarding the direction of advance. In December 1934 the Politburo held a meeting in Liping, Guizhou Province. According to a proposal put forward by Mao Zedong, the meeting passed a resolution, deciding to give up the plan to join forces with the Second and Sixth Army Groups in northwestern Hunan, but advance instead to northern Guizhou. On 7 January 1935 the Red Army captured Zunyi, a key city in northern Guizhou. A turning point which would decide the fate of the CPC and the Red Army was coming.

5
THE ZUNYI CONFERENCE AND SUCCESS OF THE RED ARMY'S LONG MARCH

THE ZUNYI CONFERENCE REALISED A GREAT HISTORICAL TURNING POINT

In January 1935 the CPC Central Committee held an enlarged Politburo conference to concentrate on resolving the military and organisation problems which had a decisive significance at the time. It elected Mao Zedong as an additional member of the Standing Committee of the Politburo, and entrusted Zhang Wentian to draft the *Resolution of the Central Committee on Summarising the Fifth Counter-Encirclement Campaign* and abolished the 'triumvirate'[1]. Soon after the conference, when marching to the Zhaxi area of Yunnan, the Standing Committee made the decision that Zhang Wentian would replace Bo Gu to take overall charge of the Red Army and Mao Zedong would assist Zhou Enlai on military command matters. Afterwards, a new triumvirate consisting of Mao Zedong, Zhou Enlai and Wang Jiaxiang was set up to be responsible for the military actions of the whole Red Army.

The Zunyi Conference was a life-and-death turning point in the CPC's history. It was held at a time when the Red Army had suffered defeat in its fifth counter-encirclement campaign and setbacks in the early stages of the Long March. It, in fact, established Mao Zedong's leadership over the CPC Central Committee and the Red Army, began to establish the leadership of the correct line of Marxism with Mao Zedong being the principal representative in the Central Committee, and began to form the first generation of CPC central leadership of the Central Committee with Mao Zedong at the core, thereby opening up a new stage of the party independently solving the practical problems of the Chinese revolution and, at the critical moment, saving the party, the Red Army and the Chinese revolution. The distinctive characteristics of the conference were that it held firmly to the truth, amended errors, established the correct leadership of the Central Committee, and creatively formulated and practiced the strategy and tactics suited to the characteristics of the Chinese revolution.

The site of the Zunyi Conference

After the conference, under the command of Mao Zedong and others, according to the changes in the actual circumstances, the Central Red Army flexibly altered its combat direction, outflanking or thrusting deep among the heavily armed enemy troops. From the end of January to late March 1935, the Red Army crossed the Cishui River four times. They then crossed the Wujiang River to the south, feigning an attack on Guiyang. Chiang Kai-shek, who was in Guiyang to supervise operations, urgently moved the Yunnan Army to reinforce Guiyang. As soon as the Yunnan Army was out of Yunnan, in one big stride the Red Army troops immediately made a long-range raid on Yunnan and headed for Kunming. The Yunnan authorities hurriedly moved forces to defend Kunming, thereby weakening their defence of the Jinsha River. The Red Army suddenly turned north and in early May they crossed the Jinsha River.

Up to now, the Central Red Army had shaken off the encirclement, pursuit, obstruction and interception of tens of thousands of KMT troops, crushing Chiang Kai-shek's plan of surrounding and annihilating the Red Army in the Sichuan-Guizhou-Yunnan border area, and winning a victory of decisive significance in its strategic shift of position. This victory was won after a change in the central military leadership, and it fully demonstrated Mao Zedong's superb skills as a military commander.

THE RED ARMY MARCHES NORTH TO JOIN FORCES WITH THREE ARMIES

After the Red Army crossed the Jinsha River, they continued marching north. When they entered the area inhabited by the Yi ethnic group, Liu Bocheng, the Red Army's chief of general staff, formed an alliance with Xiaoyedan, the chieftain of the Guoji Tribe. The Red Army passed through the area untroubled and reached the ferry crossing in Anshunchang on the south bank of the Dadu River. The water in the Anshunchang section ran rapidly and the mountains were steep. It was where Shi Dakai of the Taiping Heavenly Kingdom attempted to take his troops across to the north bank, but eventually they were wiped out. Seventeen Red Army warriors took the lead and part of the Red Army troops successfully fought their way across the river. However, it was impossible for the main body of the Red Army to swiftly cross the river. Taking the opportunity when the enemy was not quick enough to destroy the Luding Bridge on the upper reaches of the Dadu River, a large unit of the Red Army made a forced march covering 340 *li* in two days and reached the bridge. Under intensive enemy fire, a shock brigade consisting of 22 soldiers climbed the iron cable and crossed the Luding Bridge. The Central Red Army successfully crossed the natural barrier of the Dadu River.

After crossing the river, the Red Army scaled Jiajinshan, the first untraversed snow-capped mountain during the Long March. It is situated south of Maogong (today's Xiaojin), 4,000 metres above sea level, 70 *li* up and down. Lack of oxygen caused many deaths among the Red Army soldiers.

After the Central Red Army joined forces with the Fourth Front Army in the Maogong area, to decide the direction for the next action, in June the Politburo held a meeting in Lianghekou. A decision was made that the Red Army should concentrate its main force to attack northward so as to create a Sichuan-Shaanxi-Gansu revolutionary base. Before long, Zhang Guotao proposed that the Red Army move south to Sichuan and Xikang, and his decision cast a shadow over the prospects of the two armies after they joined forces.

In early August, the First Front Army and the Fourth Front Army reorganised into the Left Route Army and the Right Route Army and they were to march north. Mao Zedong, Zhang Wentian and Zhou Enlai led the Central Committee organs and the front-line headquarters to follow the action of the Right Route Army. Zhu De, Liu Bocheng and Zhang Guotao led the Red Army general headquarters to follow the Left Route Army. On 21 August, the Right Route Army set off from Mao'ergai. They crossed over the desolate marshland, waiting for the Left Route Army to join them.

At this moment, Zhang Guotao was self-assured that he had more guns and men, so he brazenly scrambled to gain more power from the party. He raised a host of excuses for not going north but insisted the Right Route Army go south. On 9 September, by telegraph, he ordered Chen Changhao, the political commissar of the Right Route Army, to take the troops south, "to thoroughly carry out inner-party struggles". After Mao Zedong heard about the circumstances, he had an urgent discussion with Zhou Enlai, Zhang Wentian, Bo Gu and Wang Jiaxiang. They then decided to lead the First and Third Armies[2] and the Military Commission Column to march north that very night. The Central Committee sent Zhang Guotao several telegrams demanding that he take the troops north, but he ignored the demands. On 12 September the Politburo held an enlarged meeting in Ejie (today's Gaoji Village) in Diebu County, Gansu Province, passed a resolution regarding Zhang Guotao's error, and renamed the northbound Red Army troops as the 'Shaanxi-Gansu Detachment'.

On 17 September the vanguard of the detachment broke through Lazikou, the natural barrier bordering Sichuan and Gansu provinces. The next day they captured Hadapu where Mao Zedong found out from the newspapers that there was a Communist base of Red Army activities in northern Shaanxi.

Right at this moment, the 25th Army of the Red Army, that had started their Long March from their base in the Hubei-Henan-Anhui border area in November 1934, arrived in the Shaanxi-Gansu base and joined forces with the local 26th and 27th armies of the Red Army, and were reorganised into the 15th Army Group. They crushed the enemy's massive 'encirclement and suppression' campaign, which created the conditions for the Party Central Committee to establish its revolutionary base camp in the northwest. On 27 September the Standing Committee members held a meeting at the Bangluo Township and officially decided that the Red Army would go to northern Shaanxi. Before long, the detachment scaled the main peak of Liupanshan untroubled. 'Today we hold the long cord in our hands, when shall we bind fast the grey dragon?' Mao Zedong's poetry of *Liu Pan Shan - to the Tune of Qing Ping Yue* expressed the invincible revolutionary spirit of the Red Army.

On 19 October the detachment arrived in Wuqizheng in northern Shaanxi. At this point, the Long March, in which the main force of the Central Red Army had trekked 25,000 *li* across 11 provinces, ended in triumph. Mao Zedong wrote his poetry of *The Long March - to the tune of Qi Lü* to artistically and vividly express the heroic and indomitable spirit as well as the revolutionary optimism of the Red Army officers and men, *'The Red Army fears not the trails of the March, making light of ten thousand crags and torrents.' 'Minshan's thousand li of snow joyously crossed, the three armies march on, with smiling faces.'*

The Shaanxi-Gansu base was one of the few revolutionary bases still remaining and in complete shape in the later stage of the Agrarian Revolutionary War. It provided a foothold for the Central Committee and all routes of the Red Army after the Long March, as well as a starting point for the Eighth Route Army that was reorganised from the Red Army to march to the anti-Japanese front line after the breakout of the national War To Resist Japanese Aggression. After the detachment arrived in northern Shaanxi, it restored its former designation of the First Front Army while incorporating the 15th Army Group. From February to July 1936, it carried out the Eastern and Western Expeditions, expanding the Shaanxi-Gansu base into the Shaanxi-Gansu-Ningxia base.

In October 1935 Zhang Guotao, who opposed going north but insisted on going south, set up a separate 'Central Committee' and appointed himself 'Chairman'. The Central Committee sent him telegrams and ordered him to disband this 'Central Committee' and terminate all antiparty activities. Zhang Guotao's attempts to split the party were unpopular among the Fourth Front Army, moreover, the troops going south were decimated by 50% in combat actions; in June 1936 Zhang Guotao was forced to abolish his separatist 'Central Committee'.

From November 1935 the Second and Sixth Army Groups led by Ren Bishi and He Long in the Hunan-Hubei-Sichuan-Guizhou border base area began their Long March from Sangzhi. After going through much hardship and difficulty, they joined forces with the Fourth Front Army in Ganzi, Sichuan in July 1936. The Party Central Committee assigned them to the reorganised 32nd Army which was amalgamated with the Second Front Army with He Long the commander-in-chief and Ren Bishi the political commissar.

After strenuous efforts by Zhu De, Liu Bocheng, Ren Bishi and He

Long and with the support of Xu Xiangqian and the Fourth Front Army cadres and soldiers, the Fourth Front Army and the Second Front Army finally marched north together. On 9 October, the headquarters of the Fourth Front Army arrived in Huining, Gansu Province and joined forces with the First Front Army. On the 22nd, the headquarters of the Second Front Army arrived in Jiangtaipu in Longde, Gansu (now belonging to the Ningxia Hui Autonomous Region). At that point, the three main forces of the Red Army successfully joined forces.

The Long March of the Chinese Workers' and Peasants' Red Army was a great expedition of ideals and beliefs, a great expedition to test truth, a great expedition to arouse the masses and a great expedition to usher in a new phase of the revolution. Its victory adequately demonstrated that the CPC, as well as the Red Army under its leadership, was an invincible force.

In the 25,000-*li* trek of the First Front Army, on average, for every 300 metres there was one soldier who laid down his life. 'Their revolutionary ideals rising above all else'. Hardships, twists and turns, and deaths, the experience of the Long March tested the ideals and beliefs of the Chinese Communists. They proved to the world that their convictions were indestructible. The heroic Red Army officers and men engaged their enemies over 600 times, crossed nearly 100 rivers, scaled more than 40 high mountains and perilous peaks, including over 20 snow-capped mountains with elevations in excess of 4,000 metres, and traversed vast marshlands known as 'death traps'. When they scaled a snow-capped mountain, a comrade froze to death in his thin old clothes. The commander called out for the section chief of military supplies, wanting to know why he did not issue cotton-padded clothing to the dead soldier. But he was told that the deceased was the chief of military supplies. The man who was in charge of garments would rather be frozen to death himself than bundle himself up. It was only with such a lofty ideological level that the Red Army was able to overcome the unparalleled difficulties and conquered the limits of human survival with their indomitable wills, and created a human miracle of monumental proportions.

The victory of the Long March made the CPC immensely politically and ideologically mature. Therefore, it further realised that only by integrating the basic tenets of Marxism with the specific practice of the Chinese revolution and by solving the major problems independently could it lead the revolutionary cause to triumph. This was the truth learned from the bloody lessons as well as through the test of struggles. Tempered by the Long March, the CPC was more and more ideologically mature, and was thereby able to realise the unprecedented unity of the party and the Red Army based on seeking and upholding truth.

The Long March ended with our victory and the defeat of the enemy. In all respects it demonstrated the force of the CPC's nature and objective. It publicised the party's stand and sowed the seeds of revolution, thereby expanding the influence of the CPC and the Red Army. On the march, the Red Army troops received warm support from the masses. While in Shazhou Village in Rucheng County, Hunan Province, three female soldiers stayed overnight with Ms Xu Xiexiu's family. When they departed, they cut their only quilt and left half of it for Ms Xu who said afterwards, "What are Communists? They are those who would give half of their only quilt to the common people." The story of 'half a quilt' enabled the masses to know about the CPC and take it as their own.

The victory of the Long March was a crucial moment for the Chinese revolution to be out of danger. Mao Zedong once vividly pointed out, "The Long March is the first of its kind in the annals of history, it is a manifesto, a propaganda force, a seeding machine." It declared the total defeat of the KMT reactionaries' attempt to annihilate the CPC and the Red Army. It declared the successful strategic shift of the CPC and Red Army, who were shouldering the hopes of the nation, to go north to resist the Japanese. It realised a great turning point for the CPC and the Chinese revolution to march from setbacks to victory. It began a new great advance of the CPC for the realisation of national independence and people's liberation. Although the number of Red Army soldiers that survived was small, they were the valuable essence of the party. They constituted the future backbone to lead the national War of Resistance Against Japanese Aggression as well as the People's Liberation War.

The Long March created the great Long March Spirit, which includes: the interests of the whole people and the Chinese nation are above everything else; the firm revolutionary ideals and convictions embodying the spirit which firmly believes that a just cause is bound to win; the spirit of not being afraid of any difficulties and sacrifice at all costs to save the nation and the people; the spirit of adhering to independence, seeking truth from facts and proceeding from reality in all work; the spirit of taking the interests of the whole into account, strictly observing discipline and closely uniting; the spirit of relying firmly on the masses of people, sticking together with the masses through life and death, going through thick and thin together, and working hard and perseveringly. The Long March Spirit provides a strong spiritual power for the Chinese revolution to go from victory to victory.

In late October 1936, in order to realise the aim of opening up a route for Soviet aid, following the orders of the CMC, part of the Fourth Front Army troops crossed the Yellow River to the west to get ready for the Ningxia Campaign. On 11 November, by the Central Committee's decision, the troops who had crossed the river were addressed as the Western Route Army. Under extremely difficult conditions, the officers and men who had fought deep into the Hexi Corridor fought courageously for four months, wiping out 20,000 of the enemy. However, they were badly outnumbered and ultimately suffered defeat in March 1937. The Western Route Army's heroism and their spirit of dedication to the party and the people descended in one continuous line from the Long March Spirit and became an important part of the CPC's tradition as well as a precious cultural wealth of the Chinese nation.

THE RED ARMY'S GUERRILLA WARFARE IN SOUTHERN CHINA AND THE STRUGGLE OF THE NORTHEAST ANTI-JAPANESE UNITED ARMY

When the main force of the Central Red Army withdrew from its base, the Party Central Committee decided to set up a branch of the Central Committee as well as the Central Military Command of the soviet area, with Xiang Ying as secretary, commander and political commissar concurrently, while the office of the Central Government of the Chinese Soviet Republic was also set up, with Chen Yi as director.

About 16,000 Red Army and guerrilla forces stayed behind at the base. Led by Xiang Ying and Chen Yi, after they gave their support and cover for the main force to make the strategic shift of position, they dispersed and broke out of the enemy encirclement and began to engage in guerrilla warfare. Owing to a great disparity in strength between them and the enemy, they suffered heavy losses. The soviet Branch Bureau carried on leading the forces to carry out guerrilla warfare in the Fujian-Jiangxi border area as well as in western Fujian. At the end of March 1935, Xiang Ying and Chen Yi led about 300 soldiers to the Jiangxi-Guangdong border area. Centred on the Youshan Mountains, they carried out arduous guerrilla warfare. During this period, Chen Yi wrote the verses, 'Since I joined the revolution, I've taken it as my home; the reactionary reign of terror will be ended. Today I die to preserve my virtue intact, the free flowers will be planted all over the world.' This poetry expressed the indomitable and never-give-up revolutionary will and spirit of the Communists when they faced the most difficult situations in their struggle.

Meanwhile, in northern, eastern and central Fujian, as well as in the border areas of Fujian-Guangdong and Anhui-Zhejiang-Jiangxi, and in southern Zhejiang and southern Hunan, and in the border areas of Hunan-Hubei-Jiangxi, Hunan-Jiangxi, Hubei-Henan-Anhui and Anhui-Henan, and on Hainan Island, the party organisations and guerrilla forces also closely relied on the masses and carried out courageous and tenacious guerrilla struggles.

In the Red Army's three-year guerrilla warfare in the south, He Shuheng, He Chang, Mao Zetan, Wan Yongcheng, Gu Bo and Ran Xiaoxian, as well as many other cadres and soldiers who stayed behind to carry on struggles in the soviet base, died heroically. After Qu Qiubai was captured, he remained faithful and unyielding. Before he was escorted to the execution ground, with deep feelings he wrote his last words, 'When the smoke and clouds under my eyes entirely pass me, I shall be carefree.' When reaching a grassy area on the Luohan Ridge, he looked around, then crossing his legs he sat down and said to the executioner, 'This is a good spot, you can open fire now!' Qu Qiubai, who was only 36 years old, died fearlessly a martyr, showing the dauntless spirit of the Communists who treat death as 'going home'.

After the Mukden Incident in 1931, the CPC actively organised and led armed anti-Japanese struggles in the three northeastern provinces of China. From September 1933, the CPC Provincial Committee of Manchuria reorganised all the guerrilla forces led by the CPC into the People's Revolutionary Army of the Northeast. In February 1936, this force and all the guerrilla forces led or influenced by the CPC were reorganised into the Northeast Anti-Japanese United Army.

The United Army created three guerrilla regions in southeastern and northern Manchuria, and eastern Jilin. Until around the time of the breakout of the national War of Resistance Against Japanese Aggression, they were developed into 11 armies, totalling about 30,000 troops. From the Changbai Mountains in the south to Xiaoxinganling in the north, from the Ussuri River in the west to the vast area of the eastern bank of the Liaohe River, they engaged in guerrilla warfare and fought several thousand battles with the Japanese and their puppet troops. They crushed the enemy's 'suppressions' one after another. Their heroic struggles hit the colonial rule of the Japanese in Northeast China hard and pinned down large numbers of Japanese forces. Their actions supported and inspired the nationwide movement of resistance against Japanese aggression and striving for national salvation.

Many heroic and moving figures and deeds emerged from the United Army. In August 1936, before 31-year-old Zhao Yiman met her death, in a letter to her son she said, 'My dearest child! Mum does not educate you in words but in deeds. After you grow up, I hope you will not forget that your mother died for the country!' Zhao Yiman's lofty values of 'being determined to work for the people but not for her own family' vividly annotated the great spirit of the Northeast Anti-Japanese United Army.

---

1. To prepare for the strategic shift of the Central Red Army's main force, in the summer of 1934, a 'triumvirate' consisting of Bo Gu, Li De and Zhou Enlai was set up before the Long March.
2. The First, Third, Fifth and Ninth Army Corps of the First Front Army were changed into the First, Third, Fifth and 32nd armies respectively.

6

STRIVE FOR THE ESTABLISHMENT OF A NATIONAL ANTI-JAPANESE UNITED FRONT

THE DECEMBER NINTH MOVEMENT AND A NEW UPSURGE OF THE ANTI-JAPANESE SALVATION MOVEMENT

After occupying Manchuria, the Japanese invaders stepped up their scramble for North China. In the middle of June 1935, coerced by Japan, the KMT 'Central Army' withdrew from Tianjin and Hebei Province, so the whole of northern China was on the verge of Japanese occupation. In grief and indignation, the students in Beiping called out: "The vast northern China cannot accommodate a peaceful desk!"

Under the leadership of the CPC underground organisations, on 9 December 1935 the students in Beiping held a mammoth anti-Japanese demonstration but were suppressed by the KMT military and police. From then on, the December Ninth Movement rapidly spread to the whole country. In many big or medium-sized cities, students and workers joined in the anti-Japanese salvation movement. In Shanghai and other cities, patriotic personages and organisations set up national salvation associations of all circles, demanding that the KMT Government cease civil war and send troops to resist the Japanese. The anti-Japanese salvation struggle developed into a mass movement of national scale.

In late December, under the leadership of the CPC, the Beiping Students Association organised the Beiping-Tianjin enlarged publicity group and went to the countryside in Hebei to conduct anti-Japanese propaganda, thereby walking along the path of integrating with the workers and peasants. Based on the group, they founded the Chinese

National Liberation Vanguard in early February 1936, which quickly expanded to about 20,000 members, playing an important role in uniting the young people and promoting the anti-Japanese and national salvation movement.

The December Ninth Movement exposed the Japanese plot to annex North China and further monopolise China. It hit the KMT's policy of compromise and concession, meanwhile it greatly promoted a national awakening, marking the arrival of a new upsurge of the Chinese people's anti-Japanese and national salvation movement.

FORMULATION OF TACTICS FOR THE ANTI-JAPANESE NATIONAL UNITED FRONT AND PEACEFUL SETTLEMENT OF THE XI'AN INCIDENT

The new upsurge of the national anti-Japanese salvation movement showed that China was on the eve of a big change in politics. To gather all anti-Japanese forces and form a united front to resist foreign enemies, and this mission historically landed on the shoulders of the CPC.

On 1 August 1935, the CPC delegation to the Comintern drafted the *Letter to All Chinese Compatriots from the Chinese Soviet Government and the CPC Central Committee to Resist Japanese Aggression and Save the Nation (The August First Manifesto)* and soon openly published it. It appealed for an end to the civil war and for the organisation of a national defence government as well as an anti-Japanese coalition force to fight a war against Japan.

In December, the Central Politburo held an enlarged conference in Wayaobu, northern Shaanxi and passed the *Resolution of the CPC Central Committee on the Current Political Situation and the Party's Tasks*. Two days later, at a conference of party activists Mao Zedong gave a report *On Tactics Against Japanese Imperialism*. Both the resolution and Mao Zedong's report clarified the party's basic tactics and task of building a broad anti-Japanese national united front. They criticised the incorrect trends of 'left' adventurism and closed-doorism that had existed in the party for a long time.

After the Wayaobu conference, the party took practical measures to give impetus to the rising anti-Japanese and national salvation movement. At the end of 1935, the Central Committee sent Liu Shaoqi to northern China to recover, reorganise and rebuild the party organisations. He quickly made progress and opened up a new situation in the region.

In the first half of 1936, the Central Committee and the party's representatives to the Comintern sent Feng Xuefeng and Pan Hannian to Shanghai, where they re-established contacts with the party organisations and actively carried out united front work. In May, patriots Soong Ch'ing-ling (Mme Sun Yat-sen), Shen Junru, Zou Taofen, Tao Xingzhi and Zhang Naiqi initiated the establishment of a national salvation association of all circles and advocated 'cessation of civil war and unity against Japan'.

Meanwhile, a breakthrough was made in the united front work of the party with the Northeast Army headed by Zhang Xueliang and the Northwest Army headed by Yang Hucheng who were stationed in the northwestern region of China. By the first half of 1936, hostilities between the Red Army and the KMT's Northeast Army and 17th Route Army had actually stopped.

However, Chiang Kai-shek made no fundamental changes to his policy of 'resisting foreign aggression after stabilising the country'. On 4 December 1936 he went to Xi'an in person to force Zhang Xueliang and Yang Hucheng to 'suppress the Communists'. After Zhang's and Yang's request to resist Japan was rejected, the two generals remonstrated with Chiang Kai-shek backed up with a show of force and detained him. They then published an open telegram to the nation, putting forward eight propositions, which included cessation of civil war and uniting to resist Japan. This was the Xi'an Incident that shocked China and the world.

After detaining Chiang Kai-shek, Zhang Xueliang sent a telegram to the CPC Central Committee that same night. Zhou Enlai, who was despatched by the CPC Central Committee, arrived in Xi'an on 17 December. After the Central Committee gained a clear idea of the situation, while focused on the overall situation of national unity against Japan, it independently decided on the policy of a peaceful settlement of the Xi'an Incident. In accordance with this policy, Zhou Enlai, Zhang Xueliang and Yang Hucheng worked together and, after negotiations, Chiang Kai-shek was forced to promise that he would 'stop suppressing the Communists and unite with the Reds to resist Japan'.

The peaceful settlement of the Xi'an Incident became the pivot for a change in the situation. It played an important role in the establishment of an anti-Japanese national united front based on KMT-CPC cooperation. That basically brought the 10-year civil war to an end and peace at home began to be realised. On the premise of resisting Japan, the second KMT-CPC cooperation became an irresistible trend.

SUMMING UP HISTORICAL EXPERIENCE AND STRENGTHENING SELF-CONSTRUCTION

At the turning point when the Chinese revolutionary process and KMT-CPC relations were about to undergo a great change, the CPC Central

Committee energetically and rigorously strengthened the party's self-construction, particularly the ideological theory construction.

After the Red Army arrived in northern Shaanxi, Mao Zedong and the Central Committee spent a lot of energy on theoretical construction work. In December 1935, in his report *On Tactics Against Japanese Imperialism*, Mao Zedong expounded the party's new policy of an anti-Japanese national united front and systematically explained many problems with the party's political tactics. In December 1936, in his *Problems of Strategy in China's Revolutionary War*, he summed up the controversy within the party on military questions during the Agrarian Revolutionary War and explained the problems of strategy in China's revolutionary war in a systematic way. In summer 1937, in *On Practice* and *On Contradiction*, the two important philosophical works which embodied the theoretical achievement of the localisation of Marxism in China, from the height of Marxist epistemology and dialectics, Mao Zedong emphatically criticised the error of subjectivism, and particularly the error of dogmatism that had long existed in the party. He formulated the Marxist ideological guideline of the party and established the Marxist philosophical thinking with distinctive Chinese characteristics, thereby ideologically and theoretically arming the Chinese Communists. The substantial success of these theoretical constructions greatly pushed forward the localisation of Marxism in China, having undertaken good political and ideological preparations for the coming of the great national resistance against Japanese aggression.

The party also paid attention to strengthening itself organisationally. In accordance with the gist of the Wayaobu conference, the CPC overcame the error of closed-doorism but paid attention to the expansion of party membership, and established and strengthened the party organisations at every level, which made the party organisations and membership ranks develop and grow in strength.

In May 1937, the Central Committee held a congress in the soviet area as well as in the KMT-controlled area, further summing up the party's historical experience and clarifying the party's tasks during the time of resisting Japanese aggression. The party's construction in all aspects was set on a track of healthy development, which laid a solid ideological, political and organisational foundation to meet the coming national War of Resistance Against Japanese Aggression.

The 10 years from the defeat of the Great Revolution until the eve of the national War of Resistance Against Japanese Aggression was an important time when the CPC continued to struggle under extremely difficult circumstances and reached political maturity. It had experienced two rigid tests: the defeat of the Great Revolution and the defeat in its fifth counter-encirclement campaign. The two defeats badly weakened the party's strength, causing it to be on the verge of extinction. However, all along the outstanding elements of the CPC demonstrated their revolutionary optimism full of confidence in the future as well as an indomitable willpower. They calmly responded to the setbacks and quietly immersed themselves in hard work. They miraculously pulled through the darkest times and opened up a new prospect.

The 10-year historical experience proved: the strength of the Chinese Communists came from the principle of practical integration of the universal truth of Marxism with the concrete practice of the Chinese revolution, of closely standing with the overwhelming majority of people in the country, of adhering to the principle of seeking truth from facts, the mass line and acting independently. During those 10 years, with regard to guiding ideology, although the party occasionally made mistakes of rushing things, resulting in serious setbacks to the revolutionary cause, by relying on its own strength it ultimately overcame such errors. It was because of this that, under the complicated situation of domestic class contradictions, the party was able to adopt the correct policies to maintain the main revolutionary achievements in the Agrarian Revolutionary War and strode toward the new historical period of all-out nationwide war against Japan.

Three

The Mainstay of the National War of Resistance Against Japanese Aggression

In the evening of 7 July 1937, the Japanese invading forces brazenly launched the Lugouqiao Incident (also known as the July Seventh Incident). The Chinese troops garrisoned locally put up a fight, which prompted the outbreak of the national War of Resistance Against Japanese Aggression. The day after the incident the CPC Central Committee issued an open telegram to the whole nation, "Beiping and Tianjin are in peril! North China is in peril! The Chinese nation is in peril! A war of resistance by the whole nation is the only way out!" So began the life-and-death struggle which would determine the fate of the Chinese nation.

1
THE PARTY'S LINE OF ALL-OUT RESISTANCE AND FORMULATION OF PROTRACTED WAR POLICY

THE OUTBREAK OF THE ALL-OUT WAR OF RESISTANCE AGAINST JAPANESE AGGRESSION AND THE OFFICIAL FORMATION OF THE SECOND KMT-CPC COOPERATION

The war on China launched by the Japanese militarists was an imperialist war of aggression and an attempt to conquer the whole of China thereby turning it into a colony monopolised by Japan. At the end of July, the Japanese army occupied Beiping and Tianjin, followed by an expanded offensive in northern China along the Beiping-Suiyuan, Beiping-Hankou and Tianjin-Pukou railways, with an attempt to 'subjugate China' within three months.

At this critical juncture of life and death for the nation, a national united resistance was the only way out for China's survival and development. The CPC held high the great standard of resistance and on the day after the Lugouqiao Incident it issued an open telegram to the whole nation, stating, "Let all the people of the whole country, the government and the armed forces unite and build up a national united front as our solid Great Wall of resistance to Japanese aggression!" "Let the KMT and the CPC closely cooperate and resist the new attacks by the Japanese aggressors!" On the same day, the Red Army leaders Mao Zedong, Zhu De and Peng Dehuai sent a telegram to Chiang Kai-shek to express the Red Army officers' and men's willingness "to lay down their lives for the country, to fight the enemy with the aim of protecting our territory and defending our country." To push the realisation of the KMT-CPC cooperation to resist Japanese aggression, the CPC Central Committee sent Zhou Enlai and the others to go and present Chiang Kai-shek with a manifesto, *The Central Committee of the CPC Announces the Manifesto of Cooperation Between the KMT and the CPC*. On 22 September, the KMT's Central News Agency published this manifesto, and on the 23rd, Chiang Kai-shek made a statement in which he, in point of fact, recognised the legitimacy of the CPC. The publication of the CPC manifesto and the statement of Chiang Kai-shek declared the second KMT-CPC cooperation and the formation of the anti-Japanese national united front.

In August, the Revolutionary Military Commission of the CPC Central Committee issued orders, announcing that the Red Army was to be reorganised as the Eighth Route Army of the National Revolutionary Army (Eighth Route Army for short), with three divisions totalling about 46,000 men, and the Front Commission of the Red Army was to be changed into the General Headquarters of the Eighth Route Army, with Zhu De as the commander-in-chief and Peng Dehuai as the deputy commander-in-chief. In September, the Shaanxi-Gansu-Ningxia Base Area was changed into the Shaanxi-Gansu-Ningxia Border Region which would still be the seat of the CPC Central Committee. Soon afterwards, the Red Army guerrilla forces in eight provinces in southern China (except for Hainan Island) were reorganised as the New Organised Fourth Army of the National Revolutionary Army (New Fourth Army, for short), commanded by Ye Ting, with Xiang Ying as deputy commander, and with four detachments totalling 10,300 men.

Unity is strength and only unity can bring victory. It was this standard of anti-Japanese national united front that summoned the whole of China's political parties and groups, people from all walks of life and all the armed forces, summoned all of China's workers, peasants, soldiers, students and merchants, and summoned the Chinese at home and overseas. They united and shared a bitter hatred of the enemy, thereby building a Steel Great Wall of the Chinese nation to resist the Japanese aggressors. In her statement the great patriot Soong Ch'ing-ling (Mme Sun Yat-sen) pointed out, "The CPC is a political party representing the interests of the working and peasant classes. Dr Sun Yat-sen knew that without the warm support and cooperation of these labouring classes, it would be impossible to smoothly realise the mission of the national revolution. In the face of a national calamity, all old grudges should be forgotten and forgiven. The whole of China must unite to resist Japan and strive for final victory." In the KMT, the Chinese Revolutionary League led by Li Jishen and others changed their stand from opposing Chiang Kai-shek and resisting Japanese aggression to supporting Chiang Kai-shek and resisting Japanese aggression. The

National Socialist Party, the Chinese Youth Party, the China Vocational Education Association and the Village Construction School unanimously expressed their support for the government and the KMT-CPC cooperation to resist Japanese aggression. The workers, peasants and intellectuals actively joined in the mighty torrent of the resistance campaign. The national industrialists and merchants made donations to the front line, while some of them even made light of difficulties and dangers, and moved their factories and plants to the interior of the country. Along with the Han people, all the ethnic minorities took an active part in the War of Resistance Against Japanese Aggression. Many Taiwanese compatriots returned to the Mainland and organised all sorts of anti-Japanese organisations and armed forces. In different ways, the compatriots in Macau and Hong Kong, as well as the Chinese overseas also took part in anti-Japanese activities. These new scenes, that had not been seen for a hundred years, marked the unprecedented awakening of an ancient nation. It made the Japanese aggressors suddenly discover that they were facing an unexpected anti-Japanese national united front formed by the whole Chinese nation.

THE PARTY'S LINE OF ALL-OUT RESISTANCE AND THE GENERAL STRATEGIC POLICY OF PROTRACTED WAR

Right from the beginning, the KMT and the CPC had different opinions on the question of how to resist Japan. The Chiang Kai-shek clique pursued the policy of partial resistance, namely, by the efforts of government and army alone, but was unwilling to implement democracy, to improve people's livelihood, not daring to arouse the masses and rely on them to resist Japanese aggression. On the contrary, the CPC insisted that the War of Resistance Against Japanese Aggression must be a total resistance by the whole nation, the KMT one-party dictatorship must be abolished, the people must be given full democratic rights to fight the Japanese, the livelihood of the workers and peasants must be improved, the masses of people must be mobilised, organised and armed to fight the Japanese and turn the War of Resistance Against Japanese Aggression into a genuine people's war.

In August 1937, the CPC Central Committee held an enlarged Politburo conference, known as the Luochuan Conference, in the suburbs of Luochuan in northern Shaanxi and passed the *Ten-Point National Salvation Programme of the CPC* as well as the *Mobilisation of All the Nation's Forces for Victory in the War of Resistance Against Japanese Aggression*, an outline for conducting publicity and agitation drafted by Mao Zedong. The conference stressed that the party must adhere to the leadership of the proletariat in the united front, go all out to launch independent mountain guerrilla warfare in the enemy's rear, and let go of the anti-Japanese mass movement in the KMT-controlled areas. The Luochuan Conference was an important meeting held at a historic turning point when the national War of Resistance Against Japanese Aggression had just broken out. The ten-point programme and the decision passed in the conference marked the official formation of the party's policy of total resistance.

In order to mobilise and organise the masses of the people to carry out total resistance, a clear guiding principle of military strategy had to be put forward. At the time, both the erroneous theories of 'national subjugation' and 'quick victory' found quite some support in society. How would the Sino-Japanese war develop? Could China win? How to win? All these questions needed an urgent and clear-cut solution.

In order to make a preliminary summary of the national resistance experience and to refute all sorts of mistaken viewpoints, yet allow prevalent viewpoints, as well as to systematically explain the party's policy of protracted war, in May and June 1938, Mao Zedong delivered a long series of lectures on his work *On Protracted War*. In the lectures he clearly pointed out, "Will China be subjugated? The answer is no, it will not be subjugated but will win final victory. Can China win quickly? The answer is no, it cannot win quickly and the war must be a protracted one." He gave an analysis of the four fundamental characteristics of the existing contradictions between the two warring parties, namely, that Japan is a powerful imperialist country, China is a weak semi-colonial and semi-feudal country; Japan's war is retrogressive and barbarous, China's war is progressive and just; Japan is a small country which cannot withstand a long war, China is a big country and is capable of sustaining a long war; Japan's unjust war receives meagre support, China's just cause receives abundant support. He further pointed out: the first characteristic determines that Japan can ride roughshod over China for a certain time, so China cannot win a quick victory, but the last three characteristics determine that China will never be subjugated, and after a protracted resistance it is sure to win final victory.

On Protracted War scientifically foretells that the War of Resistance Against Japanese Aggression will experience three stages: strategic defence, stalemate and counteroffensive. It clearly points out that after the three stages, with regard to comparing the strength of the two warring sides, China will surely reach a balance from being inferior, to being superior. Among the three, the stalemate stage may cover a period of considerable length in which China will encounter the worst of hardships, however, it is the hub of the transformation of the whole war. In this stage China's main combat form is guerrilla warfare, supplemented by mobile warfare; war can be cruel, but guerrilla war is capable of winning. Whether China becomes an independent country or is to be reduced to a colony does not lie in whether or not the big cities are lost in the first stage of strategic defence, but will be decided by the degree of effort made by the whole country in the second stage of stalemate. China will gradually grow in strength, provided it perseveres in the War of Resistance Against Japanese Aggression, in the united front and in protracted warfare.

Mao Zedong pens On Protracted War *in a cave dwelling, Yan'an*

On Protracted War stresses that "The army and the people are the foundation of victory" and that "the richest source of power to wage war lies in the masses of the people". It points out that the only correct way for China to strive for victory is to mobilise the masses with full strength and rely on them to carry out a people's war. Therefore, in the whole War of Resistance Against Japanese Aggression the CPC persevered in mobilising and relying on the people, thereby pushing forward the formation of the historical mighty torrent of resistance by the whole nation, and consequently engulfing the Japanese aggressors in the boundless ocean of the people's war.

By making a systematic explanation of the party's general strategic line of a protracted war of resistance, *On Protracted War* is the programmatic document of the CPC leading the way in the War of Resistance Against Japanese Aggression. It not only points out the prospect that final victory can be won only by a protracted war of resistance, but also puts forward a full set of feasible methods of how to mobilise the masses of the people, and in the circumstances of a protracted war, how to constantly weaken the enemy's advantages while growing our own strength to win final victory, thereby greatly enhancing the people's determination and confidence in adhering to a war of resistance. It is rare in history for a speech to be so persuasive and soul-stirring, besides, in every respect the later practice of the war proved that the foresight in *On Protracted War* was perfectly correct and in line with the actual situation.

Meanwhile, Mao Zedong also wrote *Problems of Strategy in Guerrilla War Against Japan*, in which he particularly stressed the great strategic role of guerrilla warfare in the war of resistance.

2

WAGING ANTI-JAPANESE GUERRILLA WARFARE IN THE ENEMY'S REAR AND UPHOLDING INDEPENDENCE AND INITIATIVE WITHIN THE UNITED FRONT

THE EIGHTH ROUTE ARMY MARCHES TO THE ANTI-JAPANESE FRONT

After the Red Army was reorganised into the National Revolutionary Army, they swiftly marched to the anti-Japanese front. At the time, the War of Resistance Against Japanese Aggression was in the stage of strategic defence, which presented two characteristics: firstly, the Japanese army marched deep into the vast territory of China via different routes and their offensive on the front-line battlefields had reached its peak; secondly, the people's army led by the CPC carried out guerrilla warfare in the enemy's rear and it rapidly grew in strength.

At the time, the KMT showed a certain amount of anti-Japanese zeal. Its army had once carried out the Beiping-Tianjin, Wusong-Shanghai, Xingkou, Xuzhou and Wuhan campaigns to defend these cities and, furthermore, they had won victory in Tai'erzhuang, thereby crushing the plans of the Japanese imperialists to 'subjugate China in three months'. However, fundamentally, these campaigns failed to reverse the war situation.

On 13 December 1937, after the Japanese army occupied Nanjing, they carried out a horrifying, six-week long massacre. The number of Chinese civilians as well as the disarmed soldiers who were shot dead, burnt, buried alive or brutally murdered by other means, reached over 300,000. Countless women were raped and children died a violent death. One third of the city's buildings were damaged and large numbers of properties were looted. The once prosperous ancient capital was turned into a hell on earth. The savage massacre, single-handedly created by the Japanese invading army, was an appalling crime against humanity and a very dark page in human history. Facing the extremely barbaric and brutal Japanese aggressors, the Chinese people, who were in possession of great patriotic spirit, did not submit; on the contrary, they developed an unprecedented will to fight the invaders to the last drop of their blood and strengthened their belief in victory by resisting Japan and saving the nation.

After the Eighth Route Army arrived at the anti-Japanese front in Shanxi Province, they won an important victory at the battle of Pingxing Pass. On 25 September 1937, the 115th Division, the main force of the Eighth Route Army, laid an ambush in the Pingxing Pass where they won their first battle. They wiped out a thousand Japanese troops, destroyed 300 Japanese trucks and captured large numbers of army supplies and equipment as well as arms. Soon, the three divisions of the Eighth Route Army were coordinated with the KMT army and carried out the Xinkou Campaign, and in succession, they won a victory in an ambush at Yanmen Pass and in a night raid on the Japanese army's airfield in Yangmingbu. The Xinkou Campaign was the largest and most intensive on the north China battlefield. Moreover, it was a campaign in which the KMT and the CPC cooperated fairly well in fighting the Japanese.

The victory at Pingxing Pass was the first major victory won by the Chinese army after taking the initiative to fight the Japanese after the outbreak of the national War of Resistance Against Japanese Aggression. It shattered the myth that the Japanese army was 'invincible' and greatly boosted the confidence of the whole Chinese army and the people to resist Japanese aggression. It elevated the reputation of the CPC and the Eighth Route Army, leading many people to believe that the CPC was not only determined to resist, but also had the capacity to defeat the enemy. In a letter to his family, Zhu De wrote, this battle "has boosted the morale of the whole front-line army. If all the armies can be like us, it is not a difficult thing to beat back and wipe out the enemy".

After penetrating far behind enemy lines, how should the Eighth Route Army conduct their operations and how should it strike blows at the enemy? The party defined the operational policy that it is basically guerrilla warfare. However, the troops must not slacken their efforts at mobile warfare when conditions are favourable. The people's army under the leadership of the CPC made a major shift in its military strategy, which was the change from mobile warfare in the late stage of the Agrarian Revolutionary War to guerrilla warfare in the War of Resistance Against Japanese Aggression.

Eighth Route Army troops en route to the anti-Japanese front line

OPENING UP BATTLEFIELDS IN THE ENEMY'S REAR AND ESTABLISHING ANTI-JAPANESE BASE AREAS BEHIND ENEMY LINES

After the fall of Taiyuan in November 1937, the guerrilla warfare mainly fought by the communist forces rose to the main position in northern China. Following the Luochuan Conference decision, the armies under the leadership of the CPC focused on the implementation of the strategy behind the enemy lines and they launched independent guerrilla warfare. When the Japanese army relied on their superior force and made fierce advances, and the KMT troops kept on retreating, with simple and crude equipment the Eighth Route Army spread out and boldly drove into the areas behind the enemy lines, where they integrated themselves with the local party organisations to organise work teams, to establish field mobilisation committees or anti-Japanese national salvation associations and semi-political organisations.

On 10 January 1938, the Shanxi-Chahar-Hebei Border Region Provisional Administrative Commission[1] was founded. It was the first united front anti-Japanese democratic regime led and set up by the CPC. The establishment of the anti-Japanese regime behind enemy lines restored the social order which had been descending into chaos after the KMT authorities fled the region helter-skelter, making the broad masses of people see the light toward a brighter future, thereby quickly winning their support.

In April 1938, the Party Central Committee decided that the three Eighth Route Army main forces, originally operating in the mountain areas in Shanxi, should press onward to the flatlands in Hebei and Shandong provinces where they could open up some new anti-Japanese base areas. It was a new challenge for the Eighth Route Army who were used to conducting operations in mountainous areas. Moreover, the New Fourth Army also made use of the mountains and the varied topography of rivers, lakes and tributary streams to carry out guerrilla warfare, thereby opening up a new aspect of guerrilla war behind enemy lines.

The opening up of battlefields in the enemy's rear caused the Chinese War of Resistance Against Japanese Aggression to develop into two strategically, mutually coordinated battlefields, one being the front-line battlefield shouldered by the KMT army, the other being the battlefield in the enemy's rear waged by the communist army. The swift development of the battlefield in the enemy's rear pinned down large numbers of Japanese troops, and this was an important prerequisite for the War of Resistance Against Japanese Aggression to turn from one of strategic defence to one of strategic stalemate.

New Fourth Army troops deploy north and south of the Yangtze River

The guerrilla war carried out by the communist troops in the enemy's rear was an arduous war rarely seen in world history. Confronting the enemy's successive 'mopping-up' operations, the Eighth Route Army officers and men had only very simple and crude weaponry to beat back the enemy. They had no firearms or ammunition support from the rear. Surrounded by the enemy, they established base areas and the majority of them were in remote and backward areas where the material conditions were extremely poor. In November 1937, when the 115th Division of the

Eighth Route Army marched to the Shanxi-Chahar-Hebei border area, it began to snow on Mount Wutai, yet the troops were still in single-layer clothing and straw sandals, and they had to spend the nights in desolate temples. However, after many arduous struggles, they finally held their ground in the enemy's rear and made a breakthrough, and the key to it was that they had gained the support of the people. This was the secret for the people's army to achieve constant progress under difficult circumstances behind enemy lines.

UPHOLDING INDEPENDENCE AND INITIATIVE WITHIN THE UNITED FRONT

In the national War of Resistance Against Japanese Aggression, due to the complicated international and domestic situation, as well as the two different anti-Japanese lines between the CPC and the KMT, the question of how to deal with the relationship between unity and independence, and between unity and struggle, in the united front became a decisive issue for the success or failure of the War of Resistance Against Japanese Aggression. When the nationwide resistance began, the party pointed out that the communists must uphold the principle of independence and initiative within the united front.

At the end of November 1937, Wang Ming, the CPC representative in the Comintern and a member of the Executive Committee of the Comintern, returned to Yan'an from the Soviet Union. He held that "everything passes through the united front" and "everything is subordinate to the resistance against Japan". He restricted the movement of the CPC and the people's army within the limit permitted by the KMT. Moreover, he criticised many correct viewpoints and policies of the party on the question of the united front since the Luochuan Conference. Such erroneous viewpoints of his were resolutely boycotted by Mao Zedong and the other central leaders. In July 1938, the leader of the Comintern also expressed that Mao Zedong's leadership position should be supported in the CPC Central Committee and that Wang Ming lacked practical work experience, so he should not contend for leadership.

From September to November 1938, the enlarged Sixth Plenary Session of the Sixth Central Committee of the CPC was held in Yan'an. For the first time the conference raised the question of localising Marxism in China. Mao Zedong clearly pointed out, "To apply Marxism concretely in China so that its every manifestation has an indubitably Chinese character, that is, to apply Marxism in the light of China's specific characteristics, has become an urgent problem for the whole party to understand and solve."

The plenary session stressed that "our policy is one of independence and initiative within the united front, a policy both of unity and of independence", as well as defining that the general strategic plan for the War of Resistance Against Japanese Aggression in the enemy's rear is to "consolidate northern China and develop central China".

The plenary session reaffirmed the discipline of the party, namely, that: the individual is subordinate to the organisation; the minority is subordinate to the majority; the lower level is subordinate to the higher level; and the entire membership is subordinate to the Central Committee. It also stressed the need for party members to strengthen their study of Marxist theory, "Our party's fighting capacity will be much greater if there are one or two hundred comrades with a grasp of Marxism-Leninism which is systematic and not fragmentary, genuine and not hollow".

During the Hundred Regiments Campaign, the Eighth Route Army sabotages Japanese military transportation lines

The party's enlarged Sixth Plenary Session of the Sixth Central Committee was a conference of great historical significance. Afterwards, at the Seventh National CPC Congress, Mao Zedong said, "The Sixth Plenary Session was to decide China's destiny." This plenary session correctly analysed the situation of the War of Resistance Against Japanese Aggression, stipulated the party's tasks in the new stage of resistance and made an overall strategic plan for the party to realise its leadership in the War of Resistance Against Japanese Aggression. It basically rectified Wang Ming's 'rightist' errors, further consolidating Mao Zedong's leadership of the whole party and made the party reach unanimity of thought and action, thereby promoting the rapid development of all work.

---

1. Initially called the Provisional Administrative Commission. In late January 1938, the word 'Provisional' was omitted after receiving official permission from Yan Xishan, the Military Commission as well as the Executive Council of the Nationalist Government.

3
SUPPORT THE POLICY OF RESISTANCE, UNITY AND PROGRESS

THE SITUATION AND THE PARTY'S POLICY AFTER THE ARRIVAL OF THE STRATEGIC STALEMATE STAGE

After the Japanese army occupied Guangzhou (Canton) and Wuhan in October 1938, they lacked the strength to launch any more large-scale strategic offensives. The Chinese national War of Resistance Against Japanese Aggression entered the stage of strategic stalemate from strategic defence.

Under the general policy of subjugating China, the Japanese invaders readjusted their tactics and gradually deployed their main forces to attack the Eighth Route Army and New Fourth Army in their rear. To the Chinese Nationalist Government, they changed their tactics from mainly military attack, supplemented by political inducement to mainly political inducement, supplemented by military attack. In the Japanese occupied areas, the Japanese stepped up their efforts to prop up the puppet regime and set up and developed treacherous organisations.

Under such circumstances, activities of capitulation, separation and retrogression in the KMT ruling clique became more and more serious. In December 1938, the KMT pro-Japan clique represented by Wang Jingwei openly capitulated and began to put together a puppet central regime. Although the pro-Britain and pro-US KMT clique represented by Chiang Kai-shek continued to resist, their attitude was more and more negative, while their anti-communist trend distinctively increased. Successive anti-communist friction occurred in all places where communist-led anti-

Japanese military personnel and civilians were attacked or killed. There was a serious crisis in solidarity against Japan.

The CPC correctly analysed the complicated international and domestic situation after the War of Resistance Against Japanese Aggression reached the stalemate stage. On 7 July 1939, the Central Committee issued the *Manifesto on the Current Political Situation on the Second Anniversary of the War of Resistance Against Japanese Aggression*, and put forward a clear-cut stand, "Stick to the War of Resistance Against Japanese Aggression to the end and oppose compromise halfway! Consolidate domestic unity and oppose internal division! Strive for national progress and oppose retrogression!" At the critical moment in the national War of Resistance Against Japanese Aggression, the party raised the bright standard of united resistance to the end.

THE DEVELOPMENT OF GUERRILLA WARFARE IN THE ENEMY'S REAR AND THE HUNDRED REGIMENTS OFFENSIVE

During the strategic stalemate period the CPC shouldered the main task of resisting the Japanese aggressors, and guerrilla warfare led by the party behind enemy lines became the principal method of fighting the Japanese.

The key target of the Japanese army's 'mopping-up' campaigns against the anti-Japanese base areas was in the North China region. In spring 1939, the Japanese army in North China drafted the 'public order rectification plan' and carried out a 'total force battle' which integrated the military, the economy, culture and secret services. In the two years from 1939 to 1940, in North China alone, the Japanese army made 109 large-scale 'mopping-up' raids with a force of more than a thousand men, and the total force used in the campaign was over half a million.

Following the strategic policy of 'consolidating northern China', relying on the broad masses of the people the Eighth Route Army pursued guerrilla warfare in mountainous areas while developing guerrilla warfare on the plains. In early November 1939, in coordination with the 120th Division of the Eighth Route Army, the Shanxi-Chahar-Hebei troops carried out the Huangtuling ambush, killing the so-called 'gem of generals' Lieutenant General Norihide Abe, Commander of the 2nd Independent Mixed Brigade of the Imperial Japanese Army. The *New China Newspaper* issued a short commentary about it, saying, "Since the War of Resistance Against Japanese Aggression, this is the first time we've killed an enemy commanding officer at lieutenant general level in battle. It is truly something for us to get excited about!"

In order to implement the strategic policy of 'developing central China', in February 1939, Zhou Enlai was entrusted by the Central Committee to go to southern Anhui where he and the New Fourth Army leaders discussed and decided that the strategic task of the New Fourth Army was to consolidate their position toward the south, to conduct operations toward the east and to develop in a northerly direction. In May 1940, the Central Committee despatched 12,000 Eighth Route Army troops to go south and develop anti-Japanese base areas in Central China along with the New Fourth Army.

In South China, after Guangzhou fell into enemy hands, the CPC organisations in Guangdong Province actively carried out guerrilla warfare and created the Dongjiang Anti-Japanese Base Area and Dongjiang Column. The Red Army guerrilla units which had long fought in Qiongya (Hainan Island) carried out anti-Japanese guerrilla warfare on the island and were later developed into the Qiongya Column.

In the Northeast, the Anti-Japanese United Army led by the CPC kept up a long resistance which imparted a heavy blow to the Japanese army and their puppet troops, becoming a significant force in the nation's War of Resistance Against Japanese Aggression. During this period, the Japanese aggressors carried out successive brutal military 'suppressions' of the United Army. Under extremely difficult circumstances, the United Army kept up an indomitable struggle. In October 1938, when Leng Yun and another seven female soldiers were surrounded by the enemy, they threw themselves into the icy Wusihun River and died heroically for their country. In February 1940, Yang Jingyu, commander-in-chief and concurrently political commissar of the First Route Army of the United Army was caught in a tight encirclement of the Japanese 'suppression' troops in the territory of Mengjiang County (today's Jingyu County); braving bitter cold of minus 40C, he led his troops to fight a bloody battle with the enemy which far outnumbered his force. In the end, all by himself, he held on fighting until he died a hero's death. The brutal enemy opened his abdomen and found that there was not a single grain in his stomach but dry grass, tree bark and cotton fibre.

In over two years from the winter of 1938 to 1940, forces in the enemy's rear led by the CPC pinned down and beat back large numbers of Japanese invaders, while the people's anti-Japanese forces expanded during the fighting with the enemy. Towards the end of 1940, the armed forces led by the CPC had developed to 500,000 in number (excluding the Northeast Anti-Japanese United Army). Furthermore, there were large numbers of local armed forces and guerrilla forces. In northern, central and southern China, 16 anti-Japanese democratic base areas were created, and they played an increasingly important role in the national War of Resistance Against Japanese Aggression.

Many foreign friends travelled thousands of miles to China and participated in the arduous resistance in the enemy's rear. Among them there were a member of the Communist Party of Canada Norman Bethune, German doctor Hans Miller (Doctor of Medicine), American doctor George Hatem (Doctor of Medicine) and Indian doctor Kwarkanath S. Kotnis. In November 1939, in the counter 'mopping-up' operation in the Shanxi-Chahar-Hebei border area, Dr Bethune sadly infected himself when operating on a wounded Eighth Route Army soldier and gave his life to the Chinese people's liberation cause. In December, Mao Zedong cited *In Memory of Norman Bethune* to call on people to learn from Dr Bethune's spirit of absolute selflessness and to be "a noble-minded and pure man, a man of integrity and above vulgar interests, a man who is of value to the people".

On the battlefields in the enemy's rear, following the rapid development of the people's armed forces and the anti-Japanese base areas, as well as the emergence in China at that time of the unprecedented danger of capitulation and difficulty in the War of Resistance Against Japanese Aggression, from August 1940 to January 1941, the Eighth Route Army Headquarters launched a large-scale offensive on the Japanese army in northern China. On the night of 20 August, the troops, guerrilla forces and militias launched a simultaneous attack. With the development of the campaign, the successive troops taking part reached 105 regiments, about 200,000 men. This was the Hundred Regiments Offensive, the largest and longest strategic offensive launched by the Eighth Route Army in northern China since the beginning of the national War of Resistance Against Japanese Aggression. Until early December 1942, the communist army as well as the civilians in the enemy's rear carried out 1,842 combat operations, killing and wounding 25,000 Japanese and puppet troops, capturing 281 Japanese and 18,000 puppet soldiers. They destroyed 470km of railway lines and 1,500km of roads and a large number of the enemy blockhouses and fortified points, as well as capturing a great quantity of guns, artillery and military supplies. The campaign dealt a heavy blow to the Japanese army's 'prisoner's cage policy', elevating the reputation of the CPC and the Eighth Route Army, and inspiring the confidence of the whole nation when the anti-Japanese situation was relatively low.

RESISTANCE IN THE JAPANESE-OCCUPIED AREAS

After large Chinese areas were reduced to occupied areas, the Japanese army practiced barbarous colonial rule and committed unparalleled serious and savage crimes in these areas.

The Japanese army set up secret bases for several germ warfare units in the occupied areas to develop cholera, typhoid and plague viruses, and they carried out barbarous 'vivisection' on the Chinese army and civilians. They also manufactured and provided considerable quantities of chemical weapons and outrageously launched bacteria and poison gas warfare. From the second half of 1940, Unit 731 of the Imperial Japanese Army began to airdrop the viruses onto many places in China, causing large numbers of deaths of Chinese civilians. Moreover, the Japanese army plundered and maimed Chinese labourers, and forced Chinese women to be 'comfort women'.

Moreover, the Japanese army unrestrainedly plundered China's resources and wealth, and by following the policy of 'ideological warfare' they vigorously carried out enslavement education, trying to achieve the aim of killing the national consciousness and rebellious spirit of the Chinese people.

The barbarous acts of the Japanese militarists evoked strong opposition among Chinese people in the occupied areas. Under extremely difficult conditions, the CPC organisations in the occupied areas conducted extensive and in-depth anti-Japanese publicity. They used multiple methods to enlighten the people's national consciousness, to inspire the anti-Japanese enthusiasm of the masses, and to actively mobilise and organise the masses to wage a tit-for-tat struggle against the Japanese invaders. They staged armed insurrections to hit the invaders directly. They established a hidden battle front to carry out effective intelligence work. In 1941, in Datong, the miners staged a strike and an insurrection, and some of the striking miners joined the Eighth Route Army. The Shanxi-Chahar-Hebei Branch of the CPC Central Department of Social Affairs sent people to Beiping, Tianjin and other large and medium-sized cities to organise and liaise with local secret party members, progressive youth and patriotic personages, as well as to infiltrate the enemy where they obtained a large amount of intelligence.

Party organisations in the occupied areas arranged to transfer many cadres and progressive personages through secret liaison lines, and they constantly provided human, material and financial assistance to the Eighth Route Army and New Fourth Army and the base areas. Before the Pacific War broke out in 1941, the Defend China League led by Soong Ch'ing-ling used Hong Kong as its base. With the support of compatriots in Hong Kong and Macau, it liaised with the overseas Chinese and collected large sums in donations to aid the motherland's resistance against Japan. After the Pacific War broke out, the Japanese occupied Hong Kong. The CPC Central Committee and Zhou Enlai, who took charge of the work in the South Bureau, urgently instructed the Eighth Route Army's office in Hong Kong and the leading cadres of the Dongjiang anti-Japanese guerrilla force to rescue the patriotic democratic personages and the personages of cultural circles who were living in Hong Kong. This operation lasted for six months and they rescued 800 people, including He Xiangning, Liu Yazi and Zou Taofeng. After Hong Kong was occupied by Japan, the No. 9 Independent Hong Kong Column of the Guangdong People's Anti-Japanese Guerrilla Force which was established under the leadership of the CPC drove into the enemy's rear where they kept up seaborne as well as urban guerrilla warfare. They often launched attacks on the Japanese and the puppet forces, giving forceful cooperation and support to the guerrilla war in the Guangdong area.

REPELLING AND CURBING THE KMT DIE-HARDS' ANTI-COMMUNIST ONSLAUGHT

During the War of Resistance Against Japanese Aggression, two contradictions about the destiny of the Chinese nation existed. One was the national contradiction, which concerned the life and death of China; the other one was the class contradiction, which concerned whether the whole nation could keep up the resistance to the end and build a new China after the war. The CPC carefully and skilfully handled these two contradictions, either by waging a rational, beneficial and disciplined struggle against the KMT die-hards, or by upholding and safeguarding the anti-Japanese national united front to ensure that the War of Resistance Against Japanese Aggression could develop in the right direction.

From the winter of 1939 to the spring of 1940, the KMT die-hards unleashed their first anti-communist onslaught. The CPC resolutely hit back. On the basis of summing-up the experience of the anti-friction struggle, in order to safeguard, consolidate and expand the anti-Japanese national united front, the CPC formulated the strategic tactics of 'develop progressive forces, win over the middle forces, isolate the die-hard forces', and the self-defence stand of 'if a man does not offend me, I will not offend him; if a man offends me, I will offend him'; as well as the principle of being 'rational, taking advantage and exercising restraint[1]'.

In January 1941, the KMT die-hards created the South Anhui Incident that shocked China and the world. In southern Anhui the New Fourth Army Headquarters and the troops under its command, totalling about 9,000 men, followed the order of the KMT military authorities and moved north. On the journey, they were ambushed and came under fire from all directions by 80,000 KMT troops. Except for 2,000 who managed to break away, one part was broken up and the majority of the 9,000 officers and men were killed or captured. Commander Ye Ting was detained when he went to negotiate with the KMT army, while the deputy commander Xiang Ying was killed in the break-out action. After the incident, Chiang Kai-shek slandered the New Fourth Army for 'turning renegade' and announced the cancellation of its designation.

Facing a grave situation, the CPC still put the overall situation of the War of Resistance Against Japanese Aggression above everything else. Militarily it strictly upheld self-defence, while politically it resolutely hit back. On 20 January 1941, the CMC issued the order to rebuild the New Fourth Army Headquarters with Chen Yi as commander and Liu Shaoqi as political commissar. Meanwhile, the CPC Central Committee published a host of facts to expose the KMT's plot to sabotage the War of Resistance Against Japanese Aggression and put forward 12 solutions to settle the South Anhui Incident, including punishing the chief culprit, releasing Ye Ting and abolishing the KMT one-party dictatorship. The *Xinhua Daily* broke the KMT news embargo and published Zhou Enlai's two handwritten scripts: *Mourn the Deaths South of the Yangtze River*, and *Eternal Rare Injustice, a Leaf in the South of the Yangtze River; Brothers Engaging in Internal Strife, What's the Urgency of Fighting with Each Other?* Zhou Enlai's scripts had strong repercussions in Chongqing as well as throughout the KMT-controlled areas. The CPC's clear-cut stand of putting national righteousness above everything else received the sympathy and support of the people, the middle forces, just personages in the KMT as well as international opinion. In Hong Kong, Soong Ch'ing-ling and He Xiangning waged a protest campaign; the overseas Chinese leader Chen Jiagen sent a telegram to the National Political Council, calling for unity and opposition to Chiang Kai-shek going against the trend of the times. In March 1941, under pressure, Chiang Kai-shek openly assured that there would be no more military operations to 'suppress communists'. By then, the second anti-communist onslaught of the KMT die-hards was defeated.

In spring 1943, Chiang Kai-shek published his *China's Destiny*, an anti-people and anti-communist book, hinting that he would eliminate the CPC and all the revolutionary forces in two years. Then the KMT die-hards took the disbandment of the Comintern in May that year as a pretext to demand the 'disbandment of the CPC' and the 'abolition of the Shaanxi-Gansu-

Ningxia Border Region', while secretly they ordered Hu Zongnan who was stationed in northwestern China with large numbers of troops to get ready to attack the border region. Faced with this threat, the Party Central Committee made the necessary military preparations, meanwhile it took a series of strong measures to hit back politically, thereby halting the KMT's third anti-communist onslaught before it developed into a large-scale armed offensive.

The CPC's policy of upholding resistance, unity and progress successively beat back or prevented three anti-communist onslaughts from the KMT die-hards, which showed that the party had a mature leadership team capable of coping with complicated situations. In the presence of sudden incidents, they were neither panicked into making compromises and concessions, nor did they take risky actions that would give excuses to the forces who were undermining unity and resistance, from which many middle-of-the-roaders saw clearly that the CPC was truly putting the national interest above everything else, not just caring for the interests of one party or one clique. Consequently, the party's political status in the whole country was unprecedentedly improved, providing further evidence that the CPC was the pillar uniting the whole nation in the War of Resistance Against Japanese Aggression.

---

1. 'Rational' refers to the principle of self-defence; 'taking advantage' means only fight where there is a prospect of victory, don't engage in unsure battles where the situation is disadvantageous or unfavourable; 'exercising restraint' refers to the principle of fighting with restraint in terms of not continuing to fight endlessly regardless of the prospects of victory and being willing to negotiate a truce if necessary.

4
CONSOLIDATING THE ANTI-JAPANESE BASE AREAS AND PROMOTING THE ANTI-JAPANESE DEMOCRATIC MOVEMENT

THE ARDUOUS STRUGGLE OF THE ARMY AND THE PEOPLE IN THE ENEMY'S REAR TO REPEL THE ENEMY'S 'MOPPING-UP' AND 'CLEARING-UP' CAMPAIGNS

After the War of Resistance Against Japanese Aggression entered a stage of stalemate, the struggle in the enemy's rear became increasingly serious. The time from 1941 to 1942 was the most difficult period for the Chinese resistance behind enemy lines.

At this time, the aggression of the Japanese and German fascist forces reached its peak. In June 1941, Germany launched a large-scale offensive on the Soviet Union after invading and occupying many European countries. In December, the Japanese army made a surprise attack on the US naval base at Pearl Harbour, starting the war in the Pacific. On 1 January 1942, 26 countries, including China, the US, Britain and the Soviet Union, signed the UN Declaration, officially forming the international anti-fascist united front, creating favourable international conditions for the Chinese people to strive for victory in the War of Resistance Against Japanese Aggression.

The Japanese aggressors were attempting to turn China into a rear base for its Pacific War and were therefore determined to step up their war against China. At the end of 1941, Japan's total military strength expanded to 2.4 million men, among which 1.3 million were in China. Therefore, the Chinese battlefield had become the main battlefield of the world's anti-fascist war in the East and it undertook the task of fighting against the main land forces of the Imperial Japanese Army.

The Japanese army successively carried out the 'public order enhancement campaign' in northern China and exercised brutal colonial rule and economic plunder as well as education aimed at fostering a slave mentality among people in the occupied areas. They launched unprecedentedly brutal and devastating 'mopping-up' and 'clearing-up' campaigns in all of the anti-Japanese base areas. They implemented the barbarous policy of 'burn all, kill all and loot all' and created a no-man's land by using poisonous gas and germ weapons. They attempted to destroy the living conditions of the anti-Japanese army and the people behind enemy lines and to destroy the CPC and its armed forces of resistance in the enemy's rear.

In late January 1941, when 1,500 Japanese troops carried out a 'mopping-up' operation in Panjiayu, Fengrun, eastern Hebei Province, they drove the whole village, including men and women, old and young, into a large courtyard and machine-gunned them, killing about 1,300 villagers and burning down over a thousand houses, creating the unparalleled savagery of the 'Panjiayu Massacre'.

All the resistance base areas led by the CPC in the enemy's rear faced a very difficult and complicated situation. They could either deal with the Japanese and the puppet troops' 'mopping-up' and 'clearing-up' campaigns, or struggle against the military encirclement and economic blockade of the KMT die-hard forces. Under the circumstances, by 1942, the numbers of the Eighth Route Army and New Fourth Army forces were reduced from 500,000 to 400,000, and the total population in the base areas shrank from 100 million to below 50 million. Finance and the economy in the Shaanxi-Gansu-Ningxia Border Region were extremely difficult. In some places the army and the people had almost no clothes to wear, no vegetables to eat or oil to cook with. The soldiers had no socks and the staff had no quilts in winter. Even eating grain was problematic. In order to pull through this difficult time, the party made a timely adjustment to all policies with regard to construction of the base areas. It led the army and the people to carry out heroic struggles against the 'mopping-up' and 'clearing-up' campaigns of the Japanese and puppet troops.

In their struggles, the army and the people in the enemy's rear created many very effective ways to annihilate the enemy, such as sparrow warfare[1], tunnel warfare, mine warfare, sabotage operations and waterborne guerrilla operations. They also created armed work groups and developed the strategic tactics of a people's war. From 1941 to 1942, the Eighth Route Army and New Fourth Army, the guerrilla units and the militias engaged in 42,000 combat operations, killing, wounding and capturing about 331,000 Japanese and puppet troops. Beating back the enemy's 'mopping-up' campaigns in the enemy's rear pinned down and annihilated large numbers of Japanese forces, which became the most important factor in China's ability to sustain a protracted war of resistance, which was also a huge support to the world in its anti-fascist war.

Many heroic and moving deeds emerged among the army and the people during the arduous resistance in the enemy's rear. In September 1941, in the Langya area of western Hebei Province, to cover the move of the party organs, the government and the masses, the Eighth Route Army soldiers Ma Baoyu, Hu Delin, Hu Fucai, Song Xueyi and Ge Zhenglin voluntarily drew the enemy on themselves, and step by step they moved to the edge of a cliff where they fought the enemy by a narrow pass. When they had fired their last bullet, they smashed their guns and then jumped off the cliff. People called them the 'Five heroic men of Langya Mountain'. In March 1943, the New Fourth Army's 'Liu Lao Zhuang Company' all died heroically in a battle fighting the enemy. The deputy commander-in-chief Zhao Shangzhi of the Second Route Army of the Northeast Anti-Japanese United Army, the deputy chief of staff Zuo Quan of the Eighth Route Army and the commander of the Fourth Division of the New Fourth Army Peng Xuefeng, charged at the head of their men and gave their lives to the country in combat. The revolutionary heroism of the army and the people, under the leadership of the CPC in the enemy's rear, who united as one to defy brutal suppression and resist aggression, was the source of strength for us to win victory in beating back the enemy's 'mopping-up' and 'clearing-up' campaigns.

THE GREAT PRODUCTION CAMPAIGN AND CONSTRUCTION OF THE ANTI-JAPANESE BASE AREAS

The great production campaign was an important link for overcoming the difficulties in the anti-Japanese base areas and its general policy was to 'develop the economy and ensure supplies'. In February 1939, when difficulties first appeared, Mao Zedong issued the call to 'use our own hands' to tackle the problem. In 1941, the Party Central Committee once again stressed that we must walk along the road of providing for and helping ourselves by engaging in production. In the spring of that same year, the 359th Brigade of the Eighth Route Army set out and was stationed in Nanniwan to open up the wasteland and grow food grain. Keeping up the spirit of relying on their own efforts and working with stamina and diligence, they turned the barren Nanniwan into the 'good Jiangnan in northern Shaanxi'.

The central leaders set an example and played a leading role in the production campaign. Mao Zedong opened up a patch of wasteland and planted vegetables. Zhu De organised a production team and they reclaimed three *mu* (a fifth of a hectare) of wasteland and grew vegetables. In 1943, when the organs directly under the Central Committee held a competition for spinning cotton into thread, Ren Bishi won the first prize and Zhou Enlai was voted an expert at spinning cotton.

Cadres spinning cotton

In September 1944, Zhang Side, a soldier in the Guards Regiment of the Central Committee was killed by the sudden collapse of the kiln in which he was working to make charcoal. At a memorial meeting for him, Mao Zedong delivered a speech entitled *Serve the People*. He pointed out, "These battalions of ours are wholeheartedly dedicated to the liberation of the people and work entirely in the people's interests." "If we die for the people it is a worthy death."

After the Shaanxi-Gansu-Ningxia Border Region and the anti-Japanese base areas in the enemy's rear in northern China carried out the great production movement, the burden on the people was greatly lightened, the life of the army and the people evidently improved, and the flesh-and-blood relationship between the party and the masses was strengthened. Up to 1945, if the peasants in the border region worked for three years then, except for consumption, there would be grain left for one year, however the ration of grain in the total yield for peasants to deliver to the public came down year by year. From 1943 the organs in the base areas could generally provide themselves with the grain and vegetables for two to three, even six months. The burden on the people only took up 14% of their total income. By the living standard at the time, the base areas realised the requirement of 'working with our own hands' and 'living in abundance'.

With regard to cadre training, and cultural and educational development, the base areas also achieved remarkable success. After the start of the national War of Resistance Against Japanese Aggression, Yan'an, the seat of the Party Central Committee, became the 'sacred place' that revolutionaries yearned to go. Many ardent youths felt they 'must go to the city of Yan'an even by crawling, so long as I'm still breathing'. Poet He Qifang recorded what he saw and heard when he first arrived in Yan'an, "The city gate of Yan'an opens every day. From all directions, with luggage on their backs, burning with hope, young people enter the gate."

The Party Central Committee made the timely decision to take in large numbers of intellectuals and put the development of the anti-Japanese revolutionary cultural movement on the agenda. One after another, cadre schools and specialist schools were set up, such as the Chinese People's Anti-Japanese Military and Political College, the Northern Shaanxi Public School, the Youth Cadre Training Class, the Lu Xun Arts College, the Marxism-Leninism College, the Party School, the Workers and Staff School, the Chinese Women's College, the Minzu College and the Medical School. The party organisation at all levels generally established the system for cadres to undergo on-the-job training, which played an important role in raising the cadres' political and cultural quality. Meanwhile, the party also strengthened construction on the press front of the party's newspapers, journals, the Xinhua News Agency and the Xinhua broadcasting station, and devoted major efforts to developing literary creations and theatrical performances. The Yan'an Natural Science Institute set up in September 1940 was the first special organ of the party to carry out teaching and research in the natural sciences. The base areas also attached great importance to elementary education and made do with whatever was available to set up middle and primary schools.

All the base areas successively implemented 10 major policies, including better troops and simpler administration, unified leadership, the army's obligation to support the government and cherish the people, the 'Three-Thirds-System[2]', and the reduction of rent for land and of interest on loans, which played an important role in overcoming and pulling through difficulties, as well as consolidating the base areas.

Through the accumulation of experience in leading the people to fight the enemy and in their construction of the base areas, the communists in all areas, in the Shaanxi-Gansu-Ningxia Border Region in particular, formed some systematic concepts and styles, and the Yan'an Spirit was their concentrated manifestation. The main content of these concepts and styles was: a firm and correct political orientation, the ideological line of emancipating the mind and seeking truth from facts, the cardinal purpose of serving the people wholeheartedly, the enterprising spirit of self-reliance, and plain living and hard struggle. The Yan'an Spirit cultivated generations of Chinese Communists and is consequently a valuable spiritual wealth of our party.

THE ANTI-JAPANESE DEMOCRATIC MOVEMENT IN THE KMT-CONTROLLED AREAS

At the same time as the CPC focused its strength on launching guerrilla warfare, building anti-Japanese democratic base areas behind enemy lines and leading people in the Japanese-occupied areas to carry out various forms of anti-Japanese actions, it also carried out a lot of effective work in the KMT-controlled areas (customarily called the 'Great Rear').

Under the leadership of the party, the southern provinces gradually recovered and developed the severely damaged party organisations. Attaching great importance to winning over and uniting the middle-element forces, the party made broad contacts with democratic parties and groups, personages with no party or group affiliation, KMT democrats, strong local public figures, personages in national industry and commerce as well as intellectuals, making them understand the CPC's stand, slowly winning their trust, and thereby consolidating the anti-Japanese national united front and pushing forward the development of the anti-Japanese democratic movement in the KMT-controlled areas.

The party strengthened its work in the KMT-controlled areas in northwestern China through various ways. A hundred party members, including Chen Yun, Deng Fa, Chen Tanqiu and Mao Zemin, were sent to Xinjiang to work, to unite and to help all the nationalities in the region to carry out the anti-Japanese struggle.

After the War of Resistance Against Japanese Aggression led by the CPC in the enemy's rear pulled through its most difficult time, it entered the redevelopment period. From 1943, the people's army under the leadership of the party began its offensive against the Japanese and the puppet troops in some areas while, in the same period, in the front-line battlefield there were large-scale retreats in Henan, Hunan and Guangxi provinces. During the eight months from spring to winter 1944, 146 cities and towns were lost, totalling 200,000sq km of national territory, and 60 million compatriots were under the cruel oppression of the Japanese aggressors. From this fact the people drew their conclusion: the KMT ruling clique was incapable of shouldering the task of striving for victory over Japan, was incapable of maintaining China's independence and pushing forward economic development but was becoming an obstacle to China's progress. Abolishing the KMT one-party dictatorship to practice democratic politics so as to strengthen the force of the united resistance had become an increasingly strong demand from the people (including many middle public figures).

On 15 September 1944, following the Central Committee's instructions, in the National Council Lin Boqu formally put forward the CPC's stand of ending KMT one-party rule and suggested that a multi-party coalition government be established. This stand of the CPC evoked strong repercussions both at home and abroad. On 10 October, the Chinese Democratic League published the *Political Proposition for the Last Stage of the War of Resistance Against Japanese Aggression*, demanding immediate termination of the one-party dictatorship and the establishment of a multi-party coalition regime to practice democratic politics. Under the influence of the CPC, the patriotic democratic movement in the Great Rear was developing toward the clear political goal of building a coalition government.

---

1. A type of guerrilla warfare imitating the sparrow's foraging techniques, splitting up into small dispersed independent groups, only gathering into large groups when there is a prospect of victory, otherwise operating in small, dispersed, flexible groups that rapidly break up and disappear if confronted by overwhelming force.
2. The 'Three-Thirds-System' was an important principle practiced by the CPC in all the anti-Japanese base areas in regime construction whereby the CPC member, non-party personages and middle elements each accounted for one-third of the numbers in the anti-Japanese democratic regimes.

5
STRENGTHENING PARTY BUILDING, PUSHING FORWARD THE SINIFICATION OF MARXISM AND CARRYING OUT THE RECTIFICATION MOVEMENT

PUTTING FORWARD THE 'GREAT PROJECT' OF STRENGTHENING PARTY BUILDING

Under the impetus of the national War of Resistance Against Japanese Aggression, the CPC swiftly developed and grew in strength. By the end of 1938, the number of party members increased from 40,000 to 500,000 since the start of the War of Resistance Against Japanese Aggression, thereby putting forward new requirements for the party's self-construction.

In August 1939, the Central Politburo made the *Decision on Party Consolidation*. In October, Mao Zedong published *Introducing 'The Communist'*, in which he put forward the general target and task of party building, namely, "to build a bolshevised CPC which is national in scale, has a broad mass character, and is fully consolidated ideologically, politically and organisationally." He called the party building a 'great project', pointing out that party building must be centred on the party's political line. He also pointed out that the united front, armed struggle and party building were the three fundamental questions for our party in the Chinese revolution. Having a correct grasp of these three questions and their interrelations was tantamount to giving correct leadership to the whole Chinese revolution.

The heart of party rectification was to strengthen the training of party members so as to raise their quality. For this, Chen Yun wrote *How to Be a Communist*, Liu Shaoqi gave a speech on *How to Be a Good Communist* and Zhang Wentian published a series of six articles on *The Rights and Obliga-*

tions of a Communist. These treatises provided important teaching materials for the education of party members and played an important role in party-building work.

Promoting party building as a great project was a great pioneering work of the party. It showed that the CPC had a more conscious and profound understanding of the importance of its self-construction. Meanwhile the implementation of this great undertaking provided a strong political guarantee for the party to play a key role in the War of Resistance Against Japanese Aggression.

SYSTEMATICALLY EXPOUNDING THE NEW DEMOCRACY THEORY

Since the outbreak of the national War of Resistance Against Japanese Aggression, the question of where China is going failed to disappear, on the contrary, following the painstaking propaganda of the KMT die-hards advocating 'one doctrine' and 'one political party', the question was acutely placed before every Chinese person.

As 1939 turned to 1940, in order to systematise the rich experience of the Chinese revolution, explain the party's theory and programme, and answer the question of where China is going, so as to better guide the War of Resistance Against Japanese Aggression and the Chinese revolution, after *Introducing 'The Communist'*, Mao Zedong successively published the important theoretical work *Chinese Revolution and the CPC* and *On New Democracy*.

In these works, Mao Zedong revealed the nature and the main features of the semi-colonial and semi-feudal Chinese society, the main contradictions in Chinese society in modern times and the cause of the occurrence and development of the Chinese revolution. On this foundation, he pointed out that the whole of the Chinese revolutionary movement led by the CPC was the total revolutionary movement consisting of two stages, the democratic revolution and the socialist revolution. However, the Chinese democratic revolution after the May Fourth Movement had already been an anti-imperialist, anti-feudal, new-democratic revolution of the broad masses of the people under the leadership of the proletariat.

Mao Zedong elucidated the fundamental programme of the CPC in the new-democratic revolution stage, namely, in politics, to build "a democratic republic under the joint dictatorship of all anti-imperialist and anti-feudal people led by the proletariat, that is, a new-democratic republic." In the economy, he advocated nationalising the big banks, and big industrial and commercial enterprises which were monopolistic in character and dominated the livelihood of the people and putting them under state operation and administration; confiscating land from landlords and redistributing it to the peasants, and guiding them to develop a cooperative economy; allowing the development of a national capitalist economy and the existence of a rich peasant economy. In culture, he advocated abolition of the comprador-feudal culture in order to develop a national, scientific and mass culture.

Mao Zedong pointed out that the prospect of developing the new-democratic revolution was certainly socialism. The new-democratic revolution and the socialist revolution are two different stages of revolution, we cannot "accomplish the whole task at one stroke", but the two must be, and are bound to be, consecutive without allowing any intervening stage of bourgeois dictatorship.

Mao Zedong summed up the historical experience of the CPC since its founding, pointing out that the united front, armed struggle and party building were the three principal magic weapons for the CPC to defeat the enemy in the Chinese revolution.

The formulation of the new-democracy theory enabled the whole party to have a clear and complete understanding of the nature, content, leadership and development prospects of the revolution at the present stage. This theory became the banner guiding the Chinese people to conscientiously make unceasing progress in complicated circumstances and played a great guiding role in the successful development of the Chinese revolution.

The new-democracy theory was the product of integrating Marxism with the concrete practice of the Chinese revolution. In the past, within the party, people often confused the task of the democratic revolution with that of the socialist revolution. The formulation of this theory scientifically expounded the strict difference and the policy boundaries between the democratic revolution and the socialist revolution, and creatively solved the problem of the connection between the two revolutions.

The formulation and systematic explanation of the new-democracy theory was an important theoretical achievement of the localisation of Marxism in China, underscoring the fact that Mao Zedong Thought had matured into a development theory covering multiple aspects. It armed the Chinese Communists ideologically and greatly enhanced the whole party's consciousness of participating in and leading the War of Resistance Against Japanese Aggression and the new-democratic revolution.

THE RECTIFICATION MOVEMENT AND THE RESOLUTION OF CERTAIN HISTORICAL ISSUES

After the Zunyi Conference, the party's line walked along the correct track of Marxism, however, there was not enough time to serious clear up the ideological subjectivism and dogmatism which had seriously damaged the party's cause. Therefore, it was necessary to carry out a general Marxist ideological education movement to sum up, and to draw on historical experience and lessons to raise the ideological level of the vast numbers of party members, particularly the senior cadres, so as to strengthen the party's cohesion and combat effectiveness.

In May 1941, in a meeting for senior cadres in Yan'an, Mao Zedong delivered the *Reform Our Study* report. From September to October, the Politburo held an enlarged conference (September Conference) and the senior cadres began to study and undertake research work on the party's history. They summed up the party's historical experience and strived to distinguish right from wrong regarding the political line, so as to reach basic unanimity in understanding, which allowed them to prepare for the general rectification of the whole party.

In February 1942, Mao Zedong gave a succession of lectures on *Rectifying the Party's Work Style* and *Opposing Stereotyped Party Writing*, aimed at carrying out a widespread party rectification movement. The main content of the movement was to oppose subjectivism, sectarianism and stereotyped party writing, and to establish a Marxist work style. Combating subjectivism to rectify the style of study was the paramount task of the movement. To overcome subjectivism, party members had to treat Marxism with a scientific attitude. They had to carry forward the Marxist style of study of integrating theory with practice, be realistic and seek truth from facts. Among all of these, investigation and research are the indispensable intermediate link to integrating theory with practice. Moreover, opposing sectarianism to rectify the party's style of work and opposing stereotyped party writing to rectify the style of writing were also important tasks of the rectification movement.

The method of rectification was to conscientiously read documents about the movement. After that they had to associate their individual thoughts, work, history and the work in their local departments to make an examination and carry out criticism and self-criticism. They had to clarify the environment in which mistakes were made, the nature of the mistakes and why they made such mistakes, thereby gradually achieving ideological consensus and putting forward the direction for effort. When they carried out criticism and self-criticism, stress had to be laid on self-criticism. Mao Zedong emphasised that a cautious attitude must be taken when dealing with people, neither vague, perfunctory, nor harming comrades, and this is one of the signs of vigour and prosperity of our party.

During the Rectification Movement, the Central Committee held the Yan'an Forum on Literature and Art in May 1942. In his speech Mao Zedong stressed, "The question of 'for whom?' is fundamental; it is a question of principle." "Our literature and art are for the broad masses of the people, firstly for the workers, peasants and soldiers." Under the guidance of the spirit of Mao Zedong's *Talks at the Yan'an Forum on Literature and Art*, one after another, vast numbers of literature and art workers marched to the anti-Japanese front, and went down to the countryside, to the troops and factories. They contacted the masses, observed and learned from real life, thereby creating large numbers of excellent literary and artistic works, such as *The White-Haired Girl, Brother and Sister Reclaim Wasteland, Driven to Join the Liangshan Rebels* and *Wang Guigui and Li Xiangxiang*, which reflected real life and were therefore loved by the labouring people. Among them, *The White-Haired Girl* was China's first new-style opera collectively created by the artists of the Yan'an Lu Xun Art College. Through a real and legendary story, the opera revealed the vivid theme of the times that 'the old society forces a human into being a 'ghost', while the new society turns the 'ghost' into a human being'.

From September 1943, the rectification of the central leadership came to the stage of discussing the party's historical issues. In order to unify the thinking of the senior cadres, the Politburo convened an enlarged conference to discuss the historical question of the party's line.

On the basis of a thorough summary of historical experience, the enlarged Seventh Plenary Session of the Sixth National Congress of the CPC was convened from May 1944 to April 1945. In principle it passed the *Resolution of Certain Historical Issues*. The *Resolution* summed up the history and the basic experience and lessons since the founding of the party, particularly from the Fourth Plenary Session of the Sixth CPC Congress to the time before the Zunyi Conference. It highlighted the manifestation of the 'leftist' errors in politics, the military, organisation, ideology and the serious harm inflicted. It highly appraised the outstanding contribution of Mao Zedong by applying the basic principles of Marxism to solve the question of the Chinese revolution and affirmed the significance of the establishment of Mao Zedong's leadership of the whole party, thereby enabling the understanding of the whole party, and in particular the senior cadres, to reach a consensus on the basis of Marxism-Leninism concerning the basic question of the Chinese democratic revolution. At that moment the Rectification Movement ended in triumph.

The Rectification Movement was a profound Marxist ideological education movement, which achieved remarkable success. It upheld the correct orientation of combining Marxism with China's reality, making the practical and realistic Marxist ideological line take root in the hearts of the whole party. During the movement, a grand debate was carried out revolving around how to treat Marxist principles from a practical point of view, how to combine the basic principles of Marxism with the reality of the Chinese revolution, and how to deal with some important issues in the history of the party. Through the debate, Marxist ideology was consolidated both within and outside the party, which greatly improved the ideological level of the cadres. Through the Rectification Movement, the party realised a new solidarity and unity under the leadership of the Central Committee, with Comrade Mao Zedong at the core, and laid an important ideological and political foundation for the victory of the War of Resistance Against Japanese Aggression as well as the victory of the new-democratic revolution throughout the country.

The experience accumulated in the Yan'an Rectification Movement had a profound significance on the construction of the CPC.

6

SEVENTH PARTY CONGRESS AND THE ESTABLISHMENT OF MAO ZEDONG THOUGHT AS THE CPC'S GUIDING IDEOLOGY, AND FINAL VICTORY IN THE WAR OF RESISTANCE AGAINST JAPANESE AGGRESSION

THE SEVENTH NATIONAL CONGRESS OF THE CPC

On the eve of the fall of German Fascism and imminent victory in the War of Resistance Against Japanese Aggression, from April to June 1945, on the foundation of the rectification of the whole party, the Seventh National Congress of the CPC was convened in the central auditorium in Yangjialing, Yan'an, attended by 547 official and 208 alternate delegates representing 1.21 million party members nationwide. This Congress shouldered the task of summing up the previous revolutionary experience and greeting victory in the War of Resistance Against Japanese Aggression and guiding China to a bright future.

Mao Zedong submitted the political report *On Coalition Government* and delivered a speech at the conference, while Zhu De made a military report *On the Battlefield of Liberated Areas*, Liu Shaoqi gave *A Report on the Revision of the Party Constitution*, and Zhou Enlai *On the United Front*.

The political line proposed in the congress was: 'Go all out to mobilise the masses to strengthen the people's forces, and under the leadership of our party to defeat the Japanese aggressors, to liberate the people of the whole country and to build a new-democratic China.' For the building of a new-democratic country, the congress once again put forward the slogan of 'Abolish the KMT one-party dictatorship, establish a democratic coalition government', and proposed two specific steps to terminate the KMT one-party dictatorship. First, at the present stage, to establish a provisional coalition government through common agreement among representatives of all parties, and among people with no party affiliation. Second, in the next stage, to convene a national assembly after free and unrestricted elections and form a regular coalition government.

The congress drew up the programme concerning politics, the economy and culture for the new-democratic state. It put forward the grand task of the realisation of China's industrialisation, and in a document it clearly proposed for the first time, 'In the final analysis, the impact, good or bad, great or small, of the policy and practice of any Chinese political party upon the people depends on whether or not, and how much, it helps to develop their productive forces, and on whether it hinders or liberates these forces.'

The meeting hall of the Seventh National Congress of the CPC

The congress generalised the party's fine style of work formed in the long-term struggle as the 'Three Major Styles', namely, integrating theory with practice, forging close links with the masses and practicing criticism and self-criticism. This was a hallmark distinguishing the CPC from all other political parties. In the preparatory meeting for the congress, Mao Zedong stressed the sense of keeping in alignment. He said, "We must keep in alignment with the benchmark of the Central Committee and the congress. Keeping in alignment is the principle, being out of step is real life. But when we are out of step, we shout out keep in alignment."

The congress elected the new Central Committee. On 19 June, the First Plenary Session elected 13 members of the Politburo, with Mao Zedong, Zhu De, Liu Shaoqi, Zhou Enlai and Ren Bishi as secretaries of the Secretariat, and Mao Zedong as Chairman of the Central Committee, Politburo and Secretariat. In August, the Politburo conference made the decision that Mao Zedong serve as chairman of the CMC and Zhu De as vice chairman. This enabled the whole party to achieve unprecedented organisational unity.

The Seventh Congress of the CPC was a very important national congress convened during the new-democratic revolution period. It summed up the historical experience of the tortuous development of the new-democratic revolution in China spanning more than 20 years, formulated a correct line, programme and strategy, and overcame the erroneous ideas within the party. It enabled the whole party, especially the senior cadres, to have a fairly clear understanding of the law of development of China's Democratic Revolution, thereby achieving unprecedented unity on the basis of Marxism-Leninism and Mao Zedong Thought. This congress went down in the party's history and was appraised as being 'a congress of unity and victory'.

ESTABLISHING MAO ZEDONG THOUGHT AS THE CPC'S GUIDING IDEOLOGY

The establishment of Mao Zedong Thought as the guiding ideology of the party and writing it into the party constitution were the historical contributions of the Seventh Congress.

In the *Report on the Revision of the Party Constitution* Liu Shaoqi pointed out, "Mao Zedong Thought is the thought of the unity of Marxist theory and the practice of the Chinese revolution, it is China's communism, China's Marxism." The report generalised the main contents of Mao Zedong Thought, which included: an analysis of the modern world and China's national conditions, the theories and policies of New Democracy, the emancipation of the peasants, the revolutionary united front, the revolutionary war, the revolutionary base areas, and the building of a new-democratic republic and culture.

The Seventh Congress establishing Mao Zedong Thought as the guiding ideology of the CPC was the inevitable choice of modern Chinese history and the development of the people's revolutionary struggle. Mao

Zedong Thought was gradually formed in practice on the basis of the party leading the people to work hard, and through summing up both positive and negative experiences. It was a crystallisation of the collective wisdom of the CPC. It enriched and developed Marxism with original theory, thereby realising the first historical leap in the localisation of Marxism in China, and Mao Zedong was the great pioneer in the process.

After the Seventh Congress, under the guidance of Mao Zedong Thought the comrades of the whole party united as one and fought bravely for final victory in the War of Resistance Against Japanese Aggression and the nationwide victory of the new-democratic revolution.

ALL-OUT COUNTER-OFFENSIVE AND THE GREAT VICTORY IN THE WAR OF RESISTANCE AGAINST JAPANESE AGGRESSION

In the first half of 1945, the world anti-Fascist war entered its final victory stage. In April, the UN Constitutional Convention was held in San Francisco in the US. The Chinese delegation, which included Dong Biwu from the Chinese Liberated Region, attended the convention. China became one of the five founding members of the UN and one of the five members of the Security Council.

On 9 August that same year, the Soviet Red Army marched to the Chinese Northeast battlefield and fought alongside the Chinese army and people against the Japanese, which quickened the process of the complete defeat of the Japanese invaders. On the same day, Mao Zedong published a statement on *The Last Round with the Japanese Invaders*. Soon afterwards, Zhu De, commander-in-chief of the Yan'an Headquarters, issued seven counter-offensive orders. Under the very favourable international situation, the Chinese War of Resistance Against Japanese Aggression entered the stage of an all-out counter-offensive.

Meanwhile, the KMT army was mainly concentrated in southwestern and northwestern China. The majority of the cities and towns and the vital communication lines in northern, central and southern China which were occupied by the Japanese were surrounded by the army and people behind enemy lines under the leadership of the CPC. Following the instructions and orders of the Yan'an Headquarters, the army and people in all the anti-Japanese base areas launched an all-out and fierce attack on the Japanese and puppet troops, and quickly liberated a large swathe of territory.

On 15 August, the emperor of Japan, Hirohito, issued the surrender edict via radio broadcast. Japan surrendered unconditionally. On 2

September, the representative of Japan formally signed the instrument of surrender. The following day, 3 September, became the day of commemoration of the victory of the Chinese People's War of Resistance Against Japanese Aggression.

On 25 October, the Chinese Government held the surrender ceremony in Taiwan. Taiwan and the Penghu Islands, which were occupied by Japan for 50 years, returned to Chinese sovereignty, becoming an important symbol of total victory in the War of Resistance Against Japanese Aggression.

The War of Resistance Against Japanese Aggression was the longest and largest national liberation struggle against foreign aggression in modern China and involved the most sacrifice. Furthermore, it was the first national liberation struggle to achieve complete victory. According to incomplete figures, throughout the war, Chinese casualties for both army and people numbered about 35 million. According to 1937 exchange rates, the direct economic loss for China was US$100 billion and the indirect loss was US$500 billion. The victory of the Chinese People's War of Resistance Against Japanese Aggression became a historical turning point for the rejuvenation of the Chinese nation. Moreover, it was of great and far-reaching significance for the progress of world civilisation. It resulted in the complete defeat of the Japanese invaders, effectively defending China's national sovereignty and territorial integrity, and consequently thoroughly washing away the national humiliation of suffering successive defeats in its struggle against foreign aggression in modern times; it promoted the awakening of the Chinese nation, causing the Chinese people's spiritual and organisational progress to reach unprecedented heights, which laid an important foundation for the CPC to lead the Chinese people to achieve complete national independence and people's liberation; it promoted the great unity of the Chinese nation, carrying forward the great spirit of the Chinese nation with patriotism as the core; it had a great influence on the people of all countries worldwide in winning the anti-fascist war and the great undertaking of safeguarding world peace, thereby remarkably raising China's international status and influence, and causing the Chinese people to win the respect of all the world's peace-loving people and establishing a high-level national reputation for the Chinese nation.

The CPC played a key role in the national War of Resistance Against Japanese Aggression, which was the decisive factor in the war of resistance's achievement of complete victory. Since its founding, the CPC has taken the realisation of national rejuvenation as its historical mission, and is therefore resolutely determined to defend national independence, to safeguard the national interest and to courageously resist foreign aggression. Moreover, it made the supreme self-sacrifice. In the War of Resistance Against Japanese Aggression, at the historical juncture when the nation's existence was in peril, the CPC guided the war of resistance forward with its outstanding political leadership, and correct strategy and tactics. It unswervingly pushed the whole nation to keep up resistance, stick to unity and progress, and oppose compromise, division and retrogression. The CPC held high the banner of the Anti-Japanese National United Front, and resolutely safeguarded, consolidated and developed it, while upholding independence and initiative as well as being united in its resistance against Japan, thereby safeguarding the overall interests of the united resistance of the whole country. The communists courageously fought on the front line of the War of Resistance Against Japanese Aggression, and keeping alive the hope of national salvation, thereby becoming the backbone of the national War of Resistance Against Japanese Aggression. The practice of the war proved that the CPC was the strong core leading the Chinese people to strive for national independence and people's liberation.

In the mighty process of the war, the Chinese people bred the Great Spirit of the War of Resistance Against Japanese Aggression, showing the world the patriotic feeling that everyone is responsible for their country, the national integrity of facing death unflinchingly and that they would rather die than submit, the heroic spirit of defying brute force, fighting to the last drop of blood and having an unyielding faith that they cannot be defeated. The Great Spirit of the War of Resistance Against Japanese Aggression is a valuable spiritual wealth for the Chinese people and it will forever inspire them in overcoming all difficulties and obstacles, and in striving for the realisation of the great rejuvenation of the Chinese nation.

The CPC insisted on mobilising the people and relying on the people. In pushing forward the development of the people's War of Resistance Against Japanese Aggression, its own strength also achieved an unprecedented development and growth. The Eighth Route Army, New Fourth Army and the other people's anti-Japanese forces engaged in 125,000 combat operations against the enemy. They pinned down and annihilated vast numbers of Japanese forces and wiped out the majority of the puppet forces. The battlefields behind enemy lines gradually became the main battlefields of the Chinese People's War of Resistance Against Japanese Aggression. When it came to the end of the war, the number of people in the people's army had grown to around 1.32 million, while the guerrilla forces numbered about 2.6 million. There were 19 anti-Japanese democratic base areas, or liberated areas, under the leadership of the CPC, covering a land area of about a million sq km, with a population of nearly 100 million. Compared to before the War of Resistance Against Japanese Aggression, the proportion of the CPC in the national social and political life increased substantially. This created unprecedentedly favourable conditions for the final victory of the new-democratic revolution on the foundation of the great victory of the Chinese People's War of Resistance Against Japanese Aggression.

Four

Winning Nationwide Victory for the New Democratic Revolution

After winning victory in the War of Resistance Against Japanese Aggression, the Chinese people eagerly hoped for peace and democracy to build a new China. However, on 26 June 1946, the KMT heavily besieged the Central Plains Liberated Area centred on Xuanhuadian Town in the border area between Hubei and Henan provinces, provoking a full-scale civil war. In August, in the face of the difficult situation where the enemy was stronger, Mao Zedong met with American journalist Anna Louise Strong and confidently put forward the famous thesis that "all reactionaries are paper tigers". He said very firmly that the reactionaries would fail, and we would win one day. The reason for this was none other than the fact that the reactionaries represented reaction and we represented progress.

1
CHONGQING NEGOTIATIONS AND THE STRUGGLE FOR PEACE AND DEMOCRACY

THE INTERNATIONAL AND DOMESTIC POLITICAL SITUATION AND THE PARTY'S POLICY AFTER THE VICTORY OF THE WAR OF RESISTANCE AGAINST JAPANESE AGGRESSION

The post-war political environment was conducive to developing China's political situation in the direction of peace and democracy. Internationally, socialist countries and national liberation movements had made new developments, and imperialist powers had been so weakened that they could hardly concentrate forces to interfere in the Chinese revolution. At home, the level of awareness, unity and organisation of the Chinese people had been unprecedentedly improved. They generally yearned for peace after suffering from long-term wars and chaos. The various political forces in the country had undergone profound changes. As a result, the CPC had developed into a major party with national influence and maintained close ties with the democratic forces composed of the democratic parties and democrats in the KMT-ruled areas.

The KMT ruling clique severely hindered the CPC and the Chinese people's active efforts to maintain domestic peace and democracy. The KMT was paying more and more attention to eliminating the CPC and other democratic forces to sustain the KMT's one-party dictatorship and "establish a semi-colonial and semi-feudal country under the dictatorship of the big landlords and the big bourgeoisie."

What's more serious was that the KMT's anti-communist policy got US support. After the end of the Second World War, the US actively expanded outward to establish its dominance in the world based on its strong economic and military power. Controlling China was an essential part of the US global strategy. As stated in a later report by the US National Security Council, the US pursued a long-term and a short-term goal in China at the time. The former was to promote the establishment of a stable and unified pro-American government and the latter was to "prevent the CPC from completely controlling China in the first place." The US took two measures: on the one hand, it required the KMT government to implement a certain degree of reform, including a little formal democracy, to gain sympathy and support from the centrists and induce or coerce the CPC to surrender its army, thereby achieving China's 'unification' under the KMT's leadership. On the other hand, the US gave tremendous economic, political and military assistance to the KMT government and helped transport its troops to seize strategic points.

Chiang Kai-shek's purpose was to fight, but it took time to get ready for it. Therefore, while actively preparing for war, Chiang Kai-shek had to express his willingness to negotiate with the CPC. In mid-to-late August 1945, he invited Mao Zedong to Chongqing three times in a row to 'make grand plans together'. Chiang Kai-shek's wishful thinking was that if the negotiation failed, he would launch civil war and shift the war's responsibility to the CPC.

Based on a sincere desire for peace and a clear understanding of the situation, the CPC Central Committee believed that peace negotiations with the KMT were necessary. Even if they led to a temporary peace, they felt they should strive to grasp the chance. On 23 August, the Politburo of the CPC Central Committee held an enlarged meeting to formulate future policy on dealing with the KMT, namely, "We'll fight if Chiang Kai-shek does; we'll stop fighting if Chiang Kai-shek does". The policy aimed to achieve unity through struggle, thus forcing the KMT to accept, to a certain extent, the people's demands for promoting the achievement of the goal of domestic peace. On 25 August, the CPC Central Committee issued the *Declaration on the Current Situation*, which put forward the slogans of peace, democracy and unity. That night, the Politburo of the Central Committee decided that Mao Zedong and others would go to Chongqing for peace talks with Chiang Kai-shek.

CHONGQING NEGOTIATIONS

On 28 August 1945, Mao Zedong and his party flew from Yan'an to Chongqing. This action fully demonstrated the sincere desire of the CPC to seek the chance for peace. The poet Liu Yazi wrote a poem to praise Mao Zedong's move as 'highly courageous'.

During the Chongqing negotiations, the KMT attempted to abolish the liberated areas and the People's Army in the name of 'unifying the government and military chains of command'. To strive for peace and democracy and debunk rumours that the CPC didn't want peace and unity, the CPC Central Committee made necessary concessions during the negotiations on limiting the jurisdiction of the liberated areas and downsizing the troops of the People's Army. During this period, the Jin-Ji-Lu-Yu[1] Military Region troops, under Liu Bocheng and Deng Xiaoping's command, annihilated 35,000 invading KMT troops led by Yan Xishan in the Shangdang area of Shanxi. The victory deterred KMT military offensives in the liberated areas and strengthened the CPC's position in the negotiations.

After signing the Double Tenth Agreement Mao Zedong returned to Yan'an

The KMT and the CPC formally signed the *Summary of Conversations Between the Government and the Representatives of the CPC* on 10 October which is why the summary is also known as the *Double Tenth[2] Agreement*.

The KMT authorities verbally acknowledged the 'basic policy of peaceful nation-building'. The KMT and the CPC agreed to hold a political consultation meeting attended by various parties' representatives and prominent social figures to discuss the peaceful nation-building plan. The CPC made the significant concessions of agreeing to withdraw its troops from the eight liberated areas in South China and drastically downsizing the People's Army. However, the two sides failed to reach an agreement on the two fundamental issues: the People's Army and the liberated areas' political powers. Mao Zedong flew back to Yan'an on 11 October 1945.

The outcome of the Chongqing Negotiations was a victory for the people's power. Through the negotiations, the KMT recognised the basic policy of peaceful nation-building. Although this recognition was only verbal, it created a situation where the KMT would be in the wrong in front of the whole country and the world by launching a civil war and thus in an unfavourable political position. The talks and the agreement reached also strongly promoted the democratic movements in the KMT-ruled areas.

POLITICAL CONSULTATIVE CONFERENCE

As soon as the *Double Tenth Agreement* was signed, Chiang Kai-shek issued a secret order to attack the liberated areas.

The KMT's strategic intent was to occupy the area south of the Yangtze River completely, focus on seizing strategically essential areas and communication lines in North China to divide and compress the liberated areas, and open access to Northeast China to occupy it entirely.

The CPC was under no unrealistic illusions about the KMT authorities because of its efforts to fight for peace and democracy. The party firmly believed that it could 'never expect the KMT to show kindness because it would not'. It also firmly believed that 'only by relying on our strength, our correct guidance to action, our party's fraternal unity and our good relationship with the people could we establish ourselves in an impregnable position and lay a solid foundation for the realisation of peace, democracy and the building of a new China'.

To defend the fruits of the Chinese people's victory in the War Against Japanese Aggression and strengthen the people's revolutionary forces, the CPC Central Committee successively transferred 110,000 troops and 20,000 cadres from various liberated areas to Northeast China. It established the Northeast Bureau of the CPC Central Committee to exercise centralised leadership in Northeast China with Peng Zhen, and later Lin Biao, as secretary and Chen Yun as a member.

In mid-to-late October, the CPC forces in the liberated areas launched three consecutive campaigns, namely, Pingsui (Beiping-Suiyuan), Jinpu (Tianjin-Pukou), and Pinghan (Beiping-Hankou). They annihilated 110,000 intruding KMT troops, thereby delaying their in-depth march into Northeast China. The military offensive failures did not change the KMT regime's civil war policy at all. It had increased its troops to over 1.9 million to attack the liberated areas by the beginning of December 1945. This act inevitably greatly angered the people who longed for peace and democracy.

In late November 1945, some Kunming students held an anti-civil war current affairs party. Its oppression and sabotage by the KMT enraged the students at large so that more than 30,000 of them staged a general strike. On 1 December, many KMT armed mobs suppressed the students, causing heavy loss of life on the part of the students. Strikes or demonstrations supporting the Kunming students broke out in Chongqing, Shanghai and other parts of China. The December First Movement, with the basic slogan 'Oppose Civil War and Strive for Democracy', put the KMT authorities on the back foot politically.

At this time, Chiang Kai-shek was not yet fully prepared to launch a civil war and he did not dare to tear up the *Double Tenth Agreement* rashly. On 5 January 1946, the KMT and the CPC reached an agreement to cease internal military conflicts. On 10 January, the two sides issued an armistice. On the same day, a Political Consultative Conference opened in Chongqing. A total of 38 representatives from the KMT, CPC, the Democratic League, the Youth Party and people without party affiliation attended the meeting. The meeting lasted for 22 days and concluded on 31 January after passing five agreements, including the *Government Organisation Bill*, the *National Assembly Bill*, the *Peaceful Nation-Building Programme*, the *Military Issue Bill*, and the *Draft Constitution Bill*.

The CPC was ready to implement these agreements earnestly. The day after the Political Consultative Conference's conclusion, the CPC Central Committee issued instructions within the party demanding that the whole party be prepared to fight for the resolute realisation of the Political Consultative Conference's agreement.

However, the KMT-Chiang Kai-shek clique had never intended to implement the Political Consultative Conference's agreement. Soon after the Political Consultative Conference's conclusion, Chiang Kai-shek said at a KMT Central Standing Committee meeting, "I am not satisfied with the draft constitution. Now that it has become a fact and we cannot overturn the bill, we have to pass it temporarily and see what will happen in the future." At the Second Plenary Session of the Sixth KMT Central

Committee Conference held in March, he openly stated that he would 'make a proper remedy for the principal items'.

---

1. Jin-Ji-Lu-Yu refers to the Shanxi-Hebei-Shandong-Henan border region based on the single-character pinyin romanisations for each of these four provinces: Shanxi (Jin), Hebei (Ji), Shandong (Lu) and Henan (Yu).
2. The 10th day of the 10th month of the year.

2

FOILING THE KMT'S MILITARY ATTACKS AND FORMING A SECOND FRONT

FULL-SCALE CIVIL WAR BREAKS OUT

After completing preparations for civil war, a KMT army of 220,000 aggressively attacked the liberated area of the central plains on the border between Hubei and Henan on 26 June 1946. Afterwards, the KMT army launched a large-scale attack on other liberated areas. Full-scale civil war had broken out.

For the people's revolutionary forces, the situation at the beginning of the war was quite tricky. Militarily, the KMT had 4.3 million troops, of which about 2 million were regulars. The total strength of the People's Army in the liberated areas was only about 1.27 million, of which 610,000 were field army troops. The KMT forces outnumbered the People's Army by 3.4 to 1. The KMT army had well-equipped land, navy and air forces, whereas the People's Army in the liberated areas had neither navy nor air force. It was equipped with basic infantry weaponry, including a small number of artillery pieces commandeered from the Japanese and puppet-regime troops.

Economically, the KMT-ruled areas boasted 339 million people and occupied about 76% of the country. The KMT government controlled almost all major cities and most of the country's railways. It also owned most of the country's modern industrial enterprises, and human and material resources. On the contrary, the liberated areas had only 136 million people and a total area accounting for only 24% of the country's land. With few modern industries, they primarily relied on a traditional agricultural economy.

The KMT overestimated its strength. Chiang Kai-shek claimed that the KMT's superiority would surely enable it to 'fight a quick battle to win a quick victory'. Chen Cheng, chief of staff of the KMT army, even threatened to 'wipe out the CPC army in perhaps three to five months at most'.

An important reason for the KMT's audacity to launch a full-scale civil war was the US's backing. Mao Zedong pointed out, "Chiang Kai-shek may have American aid but he is going against the people's will, his troops' morale is low, and his economy is difficult. Although we don't have foreign aid, the people's hearts are with us, our troops' morale is high and we also know how to develop the economy. Therefore, we can defeat Chiang Kai-shek." To foil the KMT's military offensives, the party formulated various guidelines and policies. Politically, it upheld the party's leadership, mobilised the masses, united all the forces that could be united, and established the broadest people's democratic united front. Militarily, it applied the principle of using superior troop concentrations to destroy the enemy one by one and adopted an active defence policy. Its main objective was to eradicate the enemy's viable forces rather than keep or seize cities and other places.

CRUSHING THE KMT'S ALL-OUT ATTACKS AND ASSAULTS AGAINST KEY LOCATIONS

From June 1946 to June 1947, the People's Army was in the strategic defence stage, and the war was mainly conducted in the liberated areas. The first eight months saw the People's Army crush the KMT's full-scale offensive, and the last four months saw the People's Army fighting hard to foil the KMT's attacks against key liberated areas.

From mid-July to late August 1946, under challenging conditions, Su Yu and other Central China Field Army commanders carried out seven consecutive military operations in central Jiangsu (the Central Jiangsu Campaign), annihilating more than 50,000 KMT troops. Reports of victory also came from the Huaibei battlefield, the Jin-Ji-Lu-Yu Dingtao Campaign, the Jin-Cha-Ji[1] North Shanxi Campaign, and the 'Three-Time Swooping Down to Jiangnan and Four-Time Defence of Linjiang' Campaign in Northeast China. These victories boosted the morale of the People's Army, slowed the KMT's offensive momentum, and gained initial experience mainly in destroying the enemy in liberated areas. In the first eight months of the war, the People's Army liberated 135 cities and wiped out 708,000 enemy troops. The victories crippled the KMT's plan to destroy the

People's Revolutionary Forces with the strategy of fighting a quick battle to win quick victory.

In March 1947, the KMT army changed tactics to focus attacks against the liberated areas in northern Shaanxi and Shandong after its setbacks in the full-scale offensives. The People's Army continued to implement the combat policy of active defence. Under the command of Chen Yi, Su Yu and other commanders, the East China Field Army in Shandong first wiped out more than 56,000 troops led by Li Xianzhou, deputy commander-in-chief of the KMT Second Appeasement District, in Laiwu in late February and then annihilated the KMT army's elite main force - the 74th Reorganised Division - with over 32,000 troops in the Menglianggu Campaign in mid-May. These campaigns crushed the KMT army's focused attack on the Shandong Liberated Area.

In northern Shaanxi, 250,000 KMT troops commanded by Hu Zongnan and others launched a surprise attack on Yan'an. The CPC Central Organisation took the initiative to withdraw on 18 March and began fighting from one place to another in northern Shaanxi. Soon, the Central Organisation was divided into three sections: Liu Shaoqi, Zhu De and others formed the Central Work Committee to carry out the tasks entrusted by the CPC Central Committee in North China; Mao Zedong, Zhou Enlai and Ren Bishi led the CPC Central Committee and the PLA Headquarters, as well as a cohort of downsized, better-trained office staffers to remain in northern Shaanxi while commanding the fighting on various battlefields across the country; the Central Rear Committee chaired by Ye Jianying and Yang Shangkun moved to Northwest Shanxi to coordinate the work in the rear.

Northern Shaanxi boasted a solid mass basis, rough terrain and ample room for manoeuvre. Following the CPC Central Committee's instructions, Peng Dehuai and Xi Zhongxun commanded the Northwest Field Corps to deploy 'mushroom' tactics to wear down, exhaust and eliminate the enemy by capitalising on favourable factors such as familiarity with local terrain and mass popular support. Within 45 days of evacuating Yan'an, they fought the Qinghuabian, Yangmahe and Panlong Town battles and won each of them, wiping out more than 14,000 enemy troops. The Northwest Field Corps eliminated Hu Zongnan's 36th Reorganised Division and two brigades in the Shajiadian Campaign later. By August, the People's Army had also crushed the KMT army's focused attack on northern Shaanxi.

While crushing the KMT army's key offensives, the military and civilians in other liberated areas carried out strategic counteroffensives against the KMT troops whose forces had been depleted and had changed to a defensive strategy. The Jin-Ji-Lu-Yu Field Army carried out offensives in northern Henan and southern Shanxi, liberating large parts of those areas. The Jin-Cha-Ji Field Army mounted the Zhengtai (Zhengding-Taiyuan), Qingcang (Qingxian-Cangxian) and Baobei (Northern Baoding) campaigns, linking the Jin-Cha-Ji and Jin-Ji-Lu-Yu liberated areas together. The Northeastern Democratic United Army launched a summer offensive, communicating to link up the East, South, West and North Manchurian bases and changed the People's Army's situation of being divided into two combat groups in North and South Manchuria.

The People's Army wiped out 1.12 million KMT troops in a year's operations in the liberated areas from July 1946 to June 1947 and increased its total strength to over 1.9 million.

After the end of the strategic defence phase, the People's Army entered the second year of the People's Liberation War with a new posture.

THE POLITICAL AND ECONOMIC CRISIS IN THE KMT-RULED AREAS AND WIDESPREAD DEVELOPMENT OF THE PEOPLE'S MOVEMENT

After the outbreak of full-scale civil war, the KMT government levied heavy taxes on the people and issued unlimited banknotes to raise funds for the war. Inflation reached appalling levels like a galloping wild horse. The fiat currency issuance in August 1948 increased by more than 470,000 times compared with the eve of the War of Resistance Against Japanese Aggression in 1937, and commodity prices soared by more than 7.25 million times over the same period. This hyperinflation was equivalent to the blatant pillaging of the people in the KMT-controlled areas. Bureaucratic capital expanded incredibly while industrial and agricultural production shrank drastically. Many national industries and commerce were on the verge of bankruptcy. The number of unemployed people in cities rose sharply as peasants died of starvation everywhere in rural areas. The KMT-ruled areas fell into a severe economic crisis. People from all walks of life across the country were struggling in the jaws of death. They had to unite and fight the KMT government in a life-and-death struggle.

To extricate themselves from the economic crisis, the KMT government further threw in its lot with the imperialist US and betrayed considerable national interests. US products had a monopoly in the Chinese market and dealt a devastating blow to China's national capital. The US troops stationed in China lorded it over people, arousing impetuous indignation among the Chinese people.

In mid-May 1947, the students' anti-hunger and anti-civil war movement rapidly surged across the country. On 20 May, more than 5,000 students from Nanjing, Shanghai, Jiangsu and Hangzhou took to the streets of Nanjing to hold a 'Joint Parade to Save the Educational Crisis', chanting 'oppose hunger', 'oppose civil war' and other slogans. The KMT reactionary authorities suppressed the demonstration. On the same day, more than 7,000 students in Beiping also held an 'anti-hunger' and 'anti-civil war' rally. These student movements were known collectively as the May 20th Movement.

The upsurge of the student movement promoted the proliferation of the entire people's movement. In 1947, more than 3 million workers went on strike in more than 20 large and medium-sized cities across the country. In the countryside, most peasants resisted press-gang conscription, grain levies and tax collection. The struggle between the student-led patriotic democratic movement and the KMT government gradually developed into a second front that worked in tandem with the People's Liberation War. The CPC timely proposed establishing a broad front against national betrayal, civil war and dictatorship based on the struggle for survival of the people in the KMT-ruled areas. The CPC proposal expanded and deepened the struggle on the second front. The KMT government suffered defeat on both the military and political fronts, thereby finding itself besieged by the entire Chinese people.

---

1. Jin-Cha-Ji refers to the border area of Shanxi (Jin), Chahar (Cha) and Hebei (Ji) provinces, based on the single-character pinyin romanisation for each of the three provinces.

3
THE PLA'S SHIFT TO STRATEGIC OFFENSIVE

ADVANCING INTO THE CENTRAL PLAINS AND FULL DEPLOYMENT OF A STRATEGIC OFFENSIVE

After a year of fighting, the war situation had undergone significant changes. In July 1947, the KMT's total force had dropped from 4.3 million to 3.73 million, and the number of its regular troops decreased from 2 million to 1.5 million. The PLA's total strength had increased from 1.27 million to 1.95 million, of which nearly one million were regular troops. Its weaponry had also greatly improved. The CPC Central Committee made a decisive decision to shift to a national counteroffensive immediately without waiting to crush the KMT's strategic offensive completely. This shift involved using the PLA's main force to fight the KMT in its controlled areas. The CPC Central Committee chose the Dabie Mountains in the Central Plains as the main direction of the assault and decided that the Jin-Ji-Lu-Yu Field Army would adopt a leap-forward offensive style in a strategic move to penetrate deep into enemy territory without holding back anything in reserve.

On the night of 30 June 1947, Liu Bocheng and Deng Xiaoping led the 120,000-strong main force of the Jin-Ji-Lu-Yu Field Army to break through the dangerous natural barrier of the Yellow River in one fell swoop, opening the prelude to a strategic offensive. Liu and Deng's army lept a thousand *li* (500 kilometres) and entered the Dabie Mountains at the end of August. They closely depended on the people and fought hard to crush the KMT army's focused attacks. By November, they had wiped out more than

30,000 KMT troops and established democratic regimes in 33 counties. The fundamental reason that Liu and Deng's field army could leap a thousand *li* into the Dabie Mountains and take root there was that the CPC and the PLA were united as one with the people. As Liu Bocheng put it, "We rely on the people, whereas Chiang Kai-shek depends on bunkers."

Chen Geng and Xie Fuzhi led a Jin-Ji-Lu-Yu Field Army unit across the Yellow River and marched into western Henan in late August. Chen Yi and Su Yu led the East China Field Army's main force across the Longhai Railway and entered the Henan-Anhui-Jiangsu Plain in September. By November, the two armies had completed their strategic deployment in the Henan-Shaanxi border area and the Henan-Anhui-Jiangsu border area.

At this point, the three armies had all entered the KMT-controlled areas in a 'triangular' deployment. They fought across the vast areas south of the Yellow River, north of the Yangtze River, and between the Hanshui River in the west and the sea in the east. Supporting one another like an iron triangle, they pressed on the KMT army's Yangtze River defence and posed a direct threat to Nanjing and Wuhan.

Simultaneously, the PLA troops still fighting in the liberated areas also stepped up their attacks and gradually shifted to a strategic offensive and counteroffensive. Lin Biao and Luo Ronghuan led the Northeastern Democratic United Army in a succession of autumn and winter offensives, pinning the KMT troops down and isolating them in Shenyang, Changchun and Jinzhou. The three cities occupied only 3% of the total area of Northeast China. This operation fundamentally changed the war situation in Northeast China.

On 21 April 1948, the Northwest Field Army recaptured Yan'an. On 23 March, Mao Zedong led some personnel from the Central Organisation and the PLA Headquarters across the Yellow River to its east bank and moved to Xibaipo Village (now under the jurisdiction of Pingshan County), Jianping County, Hebei Province. The shift of the PLA into a strategic offensive was of great historical significance.

Mao Zedong pointed out, "This is a turning point in history, where Chiang Kai-shek's 20-year counter-revolutionary rule was going from development to elimination and the century-long imperialist rule in China was going from development to elimination. It is a great event."

"Once this event occurs, it will inevitably lead to national victory."

DEVELOPMENT OF THE LAND SYSTEM REFORM MOVEMENT AND PARTY CONSOLIDATION

The new situation in which the PLA had shifted to a strategic offensive required more widespread and in-depth land system reform in the liberated areas. As Mao Zedong pointed out, "If we can solve the land problem universally and thoroughly, we will have the most basic conditions sufficient to defeat all enemies."

From 4 May 1946, the CPC Central Committee issued the *Instructions on Land Issues*, known as the *4 May Instructions*. By the second half of 1947, two-thirds of the liberated areas had achieved the goal of 'farmers owning their land'. But land system reform had not been carried out in a third of the liberated areas. The reform in some places was not as thorough as expected. Liu Shaoqi presided over the National Land Conference in Xibaipo to formulate the *Outline of China's Land Law* from July to September 1947. The CPC Central Committee approved and promulgated it in October the same year.

Peasants in the liberated areas inserting boundary markers on the land distributed to them

The *Outline of China's Land Law* was a thoroughly anti-feudal agrarian revolutionary programme. It stipulated, "The feudal and semi-feudal land system of exploitation will be abolished. A land system where farmers own their land will be implemented." After the announcement of the outline, the leading agencies at all levels in the liberated areas despatched many land-reform teams to the countryside. They went to the grassroots to mobilise and organise poor peasants to denounce despotic landlords' atrocities, punish them and distribute their land to the poor peasants. They soon started a new surge in land system reform.

Land system reform was a tremendous social change aimed at fundamentally destroying the foundation of China's feudal system. The Chinese people brought it about under the CPC's leadership. It made the peasants, accounting for most of the Chinese population, realise that the CPC was the undisputed champion of their interests. As a result, they consciously rallied around the party. It helped form the solid mass basis for defeating Chiang Kai-shek and establishing a new China. While carrying out land system reform, the effort to consolidate the party organisations was also going on in the liberated areas to address impure ideology, style and members' class status found in some local party organisations, especially rural grassroots party organisations. The party consolidation movement's primary content was to solve major problems existing in grassroots party organisations by looking into party members' and cadres' class status, ideology and style, and rectifying those problems. Party consolidation enabled rural grassroots party organisations to make significant ideological, political and organisational progress, and enabled the party to enjoy closer ties with the masses, thereby providing an essential guarantee for land reform and victory in the war.

4

FORMULATION AND IMPLEMENTATION OF NATIONAL PROGRAMME FOR VICTORY WHILE CONSOLIDATING AND EXPANDING THE PEOPLE'S DEMOCRATIC UNITED FRONT

FORMULATION OF THE NATIONAL VICTORY PROGRAMME, AND RELATED POLICIES AND STRATEGIES

As the PLA shifted to strategic offensive, the CPC issued a call in September 1947 for 'a national counteroffensive to defeat Chiang Kai-shek!' In October, the Chinese PLA Headquarters issued a manifesto that resoundingly put forward the slogan "Down with Chiang Kai-shek! Liberate the whole of China!"

In December 1947, the CPC Central Committee held an enlarged meeting, referred to as the 'December Meeting', in Yangjiagou, Mizhi County, North Shaanxi. At the meeting, Mao Zedong submitted a written report entitled *The Current Situation and Our Tasks*.

The report clarified the party's most fundamental political programme, "Form a united national front to defeat the Chiang Kai-shek dictatorship and establish a democratic coalition government by joining forces with the workers, peasants, soldiers, academics, and businessmen of the oppressed classes, as well as with people's organisations, democratic parties, ethnic minorities, overseas Chinese and other patriotic elements." The report pointed out, "The monopoly capital headed by Chiang Kai-shek, Song Ziwen, Kong Xiangxi and Chen Lifu will be confiscated and returned to the ownership of the new democratic country to protect national industry and commerce. These are the three major economic programmes of the new democratic revolution." The report also summarised the combat experience of the People's Army and put forward the 10 military principles, the core of which is "concentrating superior forces and destroying the enemy individually." According to the report, these strategies and tactics could not be used or dealt with by any anti-people armies because they were based on the people's war. It showed the party's confidence in future victory. This report by Mao Zedong was "a political, military and economic document guiding the entire period of overthrowing Chiang Kai-shek's reactionary ruling clique and establishing a new democratic China."

For some time after the 'December Meeting', the CPC Central Committee concentrated on studying and solving various specific policy and strategic issues of the party in the new situation. That was because, with the successful development of the war of liberation, the liberated areas expanded rapidly, and many cities returned to the hands of the people. The party still lacked experience in adapting to the new and previously unfamiliar situation, and in doing a good job in new districts and cities. In actual work, deviations emerged that infringed on the interests of middle peasants, and national industrial and commercial sectors. There was even the sweeping slogan 'The masses can do whatever they want to', which proved to be wrong.

In response to the above situation, Mao Zedong solemnly warned the entire party, "The enemy is now completely isolated but the enemy's isolation does not mean our victory. If we make a policy mistake, we still cannot win." He emphasised, "Policies and strategies are the life of the party, and leading comrades at all levels must pay full attention to them and must not be careless."

In exploring to gain the experience of taking over the management of cities, the CPC Central Committee approved the *Central Work Committee's Urban Work Experience on Recovering Shijiazhuang* in February 1948. It wrote comments and transmitted *The Northeast Bureau's Instructions on the Protection of Newly Recovered Cities* in June and Chen Yun's *Experience in Taking over Shenyang* in December. As the party adopted a series of correct policies, the newly liberated cities' social order quickly stabilised. Meanwhile, their industrial production was quickly restored and expanded. The moves substantially supported the People's Liberation War.

To ensure the strict implementation of the party's line and various principles and policies, Mao Zedong repeatedly warned the entire party that it was necessary to maintain the party's central unified leadership; strengthen organisation consciousness and party discipline. He urged the party to quickly overcome lack of discipline, 'localism' and the guerrilla mentality—tendencies reinforced by years of guerrilla warfare when we were isolated from each other by the enemy. The CPC Central Committee required all localities to strictly abide by the various policies it had formulated and to establish a system for regularly requesting instructions from, and reporting to, the Central Committee. Simultaneously, it promptly criticised the lack of democratic life within the party and demanded that the party's democratic life be strengthened and the party committees' system be improved.

This was a historical turning point in the winning of the New Democratic Revolution. The party's history proves that it must study foreseeable new situations and problems. It must swiftly formulate correct countermeasures and take effective measures when a major historical turning point arrives. The CPC developed various realistic policies at this historical moment and did a lot to strengthen party members' consciousness of its policies. In this way, the whole party maintained a high degree of unity based on the correct line and policy, and worked in an orderly manner, thereby creating the most important conditions for the coming nationwide victory of the revolution.

THE NEW DEVELOPMENT OF THE PATRIOTIC DEMOCRATIC MOVEMENT LED BY THE CPC AND THE DEMOCRATIC PARTIES' HISTORIC CHOICE

As the War of Liberation advanced victoriously, the people's movement in the KMT-ruled areas witnessed new developments. Most students increasingly placed China's hopes on the victory of the People's War of Liberation. Therefore, they no longer struggled under the banner of 'oppose civil war' but of 'oppose persecution'. In October 1947, Yu Zisan, Chairman of the Student Self-Government Association of Zhejiang University, was unlawfully arrested and died tragically in prison. More than 100,000 students in 12 cities, including Hangzhou, Nanjing, Shanghai and Beiping, launched an anti-persecution struggle against 'illegal arrests, surveillance and killing of youths'. In April 1948, the North China students' protest against the authorities' banning of the North China Student Union, coupled with the Beiping-Tianjin faculty and staff's demand for salary and wage adjustment, kicked up a powerful 'April storm'. Between May and June, another nationwide patriotic movement against US government support of Japanese militarism broke out, thereby completely isolating the reactionary rule of the KMT. The democratic parties and the broad masses of non-party democrats were increasingly inclined to support the People's

Revolution. Some of them had once advocated implementing the 'middle line' of bourgeois democracy in China, known as the so-called 'third path'. However, with the War of Liberation's successful development, the KMT authorities' intensified persecution of patriotic democratic forces, and the CPC's success in publicity and education, the 'middle-line' political ideas, once influential among some democrats and middle-of-the-roaders, quickly went bankrupt. Facing the decisive battle between China's two roads, two futures and two destinies, the original middle-of-the-roaders split. Most of the democratic parties and non-party democrats, such as the Democratic League, stood firmly with the CPC in the struggle against the pseudo-National Congress[1] and the pseudo-constitution. These democrats and non-party democrats played a positive role in the fight against the KMT's dictatorship and civil war policies. Fighting against the KMT in a concerted effort with the CPC, they made continuous progress in their struggle. Cooperation was a highlight of the democratic parties during this period and made the democratic parties an essential part of the CPC-led revolutionary united front.

The major democratic parties of the time included the Revolutionary Committee of the Chinese Kuomintang (RCCK), China Democratic League (CDL), China National Democratic Construction Association (CNDCA), China Association for Promoting Democracy (CAPD), Chinese Peasants' and Workers' Democratic Party (CPWDP), China Zhi Gong Party (CZGP), Jiusan Society (JS), and Taiwan Democratic Self-Government League (TDSGL). They all advocated patriotism and democracy, and opposed national betrayal and dictatorship. In these respects, they were basically consistent with the CPC's new democratic revolutionary platform.

The CPC's policy of vigorously winning over and uniting the democratic parties achieved excellent results. The situation helped the left-wing democrats strengthen their political position.

The democratic parties and democrats actively moved closer to the CPC, which caused the KMT authorities to panic. After murdering Li Gongpu and Wen Yiduo, it assassinated the famous democrat Du Bincheng in Xi'an. It also arrested and kidnapped many members of the CDL's local organisations and attacked or destroyed several newspapers run by left-wing democrats.

In May 1947, the KMT blatantly accused the CDL and the CAPD of 'receiving orders from the CPC and becoming the CPC's ready new tools of riots'. The KMT authorities declared the CDL an 'illegal organisation' in October and forced its headquarters to announce the league's dissolution in Shanghai on 6 November.

In January 1948, Shen Junru and others convened the First Plenary Session of the CDL Central Committee in Hong Kong to restore its headquarters, proclaiming that it would work closely with the CPC in future. Simultaneously, the RCCK also publicly acknowledged CPC leadership. Other democratic parties also clearly stated their stand of participating in the new democratic revolution.

FORMATION OF CPC-LED MULTI-PARTY COOPERATION

On 30 April 1948, the CPC Central Committee issued a call in the slogan to commemorate the May First International Labour Day. It read, "All democratic parties, people's organisations and eminent social leaders, let's quickly convene a political consultation meeting to discuss and hold a People's Congress, and to establish a democratic coalition government!" This call received enthusiastic responses from all democratic parties, people without party affiliation, and people from all walks of life. It marked the open and conscious acceptance of the CPC's leadership by all the democratic parties and people without party affiliation. It was the prelude to the country's establishment through consultations between the CPC and various parties, organisations, and people from all ethnic groups, laying the foundation for the multi-party cooperation and political consultation system led by the CPC.

In January 1949, 55 democratic party leaders and well-known non-party democrats like Li Jishen and Shen Junru, jointly issued the *Opinions on the Current Situation*. They unanimously affirmed that the CPC's proposal on convening a political consultative conference and establishing a coalition government was "consistent with the demands of the people of the whole country." They sincerely expressed that "under the CPC's leadership, we are willing to try our best to work with you on strategies for the rapid success of the Chinese People's Democratic Revolution and the early realisation of an independent, free, peaceful and happy new China." This political statement showed that China's democratic parties and non-party democrats voluntarily accepted the CPC's leadership and were determined to follow the road of the people's revolution and support the establishment of a people's democratic new China.

In the spring of the same year, Mao Zedong proposed that the democratic parties "actively participate in the political process and jointly build a new China." The proposal marked a fundamental change in the status of the democratic parties. They were no longer the opposition parties under the KMT regime. Instead, they would jointly assume the historical responsibility of managing and building a new China under the CPC's leadership. It became the basis for forming the political structure of multi-party cooperation and political consultation under the CPC's leadership.

---

1. The pseudo-National Congress refers to the 'National Assembly' organised by the KMT in November 1946. The 'National Assembly' passed the so-called *Constitution of the Republic of China* to safeguard Chiang Kai-shek's dictatorship.

5

THE GREAT STRATEGIC DECISIVE BATTLE AND COLLAPSE OF THE KMT'S REACTIONARY RULE

THE THREE DECISIVE CAMPAIGNS OF LIAOSHEN, HUAIHAI AND PINGJIN

In the autumn of 1948, the People's Liberation War entered a decisive stage of national victory. By this time, the PLA had grown from 1.27 million at the beginning of the war to 2.8 million, of which 1.49 million were field army troops. With relatively powerful artillery and engineering troops available, the PLA had enhanced its ability to assault fortified positions and gained experience in waging positional warfare.

On the contrary, the KMT army had dropped from 4.3 million at the beginning of the war to 3.65 million, with only 1.74 million troops available for the front line, and their low morale undermined their combat effectiveness. They had to abandon their 'comprehensive defence' strategy and changed to 'key defence'. The PLA had isolated the KMT troops on five battlefields: Northwest China, China's Central Plains, East China, North China and Northeast China. They had difficulty cooperating with each other and could not fight on the same front. The CPC Central Committee and Mao Zedong acted decisively and organised three successive campaigns: Liaoshen (Liaoning-Shenyang), Huaihai and Pingjin (Beiping-Tianjin).

According to Mao Zedong and the CMC's strategic plan, Northeast China became the first choice to start the decisive strategic campaigns. On 12 September 1948, Lin Biao and Luo Ronghuan commanded 1.03 million Northeast Field Army and local armed forces to launch the Liaoshen

Campaign and attacked 550,000 KMT troops isolated in Jinzhou, Changchun and Shenyang. The campaign began with the assault on Jinzhou, cutting off the KMT army in Northeast China. On 14 October, the Northeast Field Army launched a general offensive against Jinzhou. After 31 hours of fierce fighting, it wiped out nearly 90,000 of the KMT defending force.

Jinzhou's liberation prompted some of the KMT troops defending Changchun to revolt and the rest to surrender. It also cut off the KMT troops' retreat route into the area outside the northeast. After the PLA's Northeast Field Army captured Jinzhou, it immediately encircled and wiped out the KMT Army Corps under the command of Liao Yaoxiang despatched from Shenyang to reinforce Jinzhou. The PLA's Northeast Field Army followed up its victory with the hot pursuit of the KMT troops, and liberated Shenyang and Yingkou on 2 November, thereby liberating the whole of Northeast China.

Soon after the Liaoshen Campaign, the East China Field Army, the Central Plains Field Army and some local armed forces totalling over 600,000 troops launched the Huaihai Campaign on an unprecedented scale. The campaign's battlefield centred around Xuzhou and extended from Haizhou in the east, Shangqiu in the west and Lincheng (present-day Xuecheng) in the north, to the Huai River in the south. On 16 November 1948, the CPC Central Committee decided that Liu Bocheng, Chen Yi, Deng Xiaoping, Su Yu, and Tan Zhenlin would form the General Front Committee. It made Deng Xiaoping the committee secretary to assume central command over the East China Field Army and the Central Plains Field Army. Since the KMT troops assembling in this area had superior strength and weaponry, the PLA adopted the tactics of dividing the enemy's heavy forces several times and concentrating its own superior forces to crush them one by one.

From 6 to 22 November 1948, the PLA encircled and wiped out about 100,000 troops of the Huang Baitao Army Corps east of Xuzhou, completing a breakthrough in the middle. The PLA wiped out the Huang Wei Army Corps numbering around 120,000 soldiers that had come a long distance from southern Henan to reinforce the encircled KMT troops and stood out as vulnerable. Meanwhile, the PLA surrounded Du Yuming's three army corps of about 300,000-strong under the command of Qiu Qingquan, Li Mi and Sun Yuanliang. The PLA soon destroyed the attacking army under Sun Yuanliang's command. From 16 December 1948 to 10 January 1949, it destroyed the two army corps with 10 divisions commanded respectively by Qiu Qingquan and Li Mi. With the capture of

Du Yuming alive in the last battles, the Huaihai Campaign came to an end with the PLA's triumph.

During the Liaoshen Campaign, the PLA launches an assault on the Jinzhou Wall

During the Huaihai Campaign, the PLA marches triumphantly while many KMT POWs are escorted off the battlefield

This campaign led to the destruction of the KMT army's main force on the south front and the liberation of the vast area along the middle and lower reaches of the Yangtze River. This area was now connected with the liberated areas in North China. With Nanjing, the KMT government's capital, exposed to the PLA, the KMT's reactionary rule disintegrated.

In between the end of the Liaoshen Campaign and the successful development of the Huaihai Campaign, about a million troops from the Northeast Field Army, the Second and Third Corps of the North China Military Region, and the local armed forces in northern and northeastern China jointly launched the Pingjin Campaign.

According to the CPC Central Committee's strategic plan, the Northeast Field Army's main force entered North China secretly, beginning from November 1948. Together with the Second and Third Corps of the North China Military Region, it completed a manoeuvre to cut off the connection between the KMT troops in Beiping, Tianjin and Zhangjiakou, with the tactics of 'encircling without attacking' and 'separating without encircling'. The PLA subsequently launched its assault in the order of 'striking at the two ends before taking the middle' and captured Xinbao'an and Zhangjiakou in late December. On 10 January 1949, the CPC Central Committee decided to establish the Pingjin Front Line General Committee composed of Lin Biao, Luo Ronghuan and Nie Rongzhen, with Lin Biao as the secretary. After Tianjin's KMT garrison troops refused to accept the PLA's peaceful reorganisation, the PLA launched a general offensive with a strong force on 14 January. After 29 hours of fierce fighting, the PLA conquered Tianjin and wiped out 130,000 KMT garrison troops. The more than 200,000 garrison troops in Beiping were in a desperate situation under the PLA's siege. On 31 January, the troops, led by Fu Zuoyi, accepted the PLA's peaceful reorganisation, resulting in the peaceful liberation of Beiping.

Both the scale and result of the Liaoshen, Huaihai and Pingjin campaigns were unprecedented in China's war history and rare in the world's war history. These three major campaigns annihilated more than 1.54 million KMT troops. They destroyed the main military force that the KMT relied on to maintain its reactionary rule, laying the foundation for the Chinese revolution's victory throughout the country.

The victory of the three significant campaigns was a great victory for Mao Zedong's military thinking. In the three major battles, Mao Zedong and the CMC formulated different combat policies based on the three battlefields' diverse characteristics in Northeast, East and North China. By applying the '10 military principles', they closely integrated the destruction of the enemy's vital forces with the seizure of cities and places, closely integrated the concentration of superior forces with the destruction of powerful enemy army corps, closely integrated large-scale mobile warfare with attacks against fortified positions, and closely integrated military strikes with political struggle. What they did was an important development of Mao Zedong's military thinking in practice.

The three campaigns' victory was also a victory of the People's War. Civilians in the liberated areas provided unprecedented support to the PLA on the front line with tremendous enthusiasm, and inexhaustible human and material resources. They transported all the ammunition to the immense number of PLA troops by carrying it on their shoulders and in wheelbarrows. According to statistics, in the Huaihai Campaign alone, the total number of peasant labourers reached 5.43 million, who transported to the front over 73,000 tonnes of ammunition, and 480,000 tonnes of grain and other military supplies. Chen Yi once said affectionately and vividly that the people and their wheelbarrows brought about the Huaihai Campaign's victory.

After the peaceful liberation of Beiping, the PLA hold a grand entrance ceremony

A small convoy of migrant workers in action in the liberated areas of Shandong during the War of Liberation

CARRY ON THE REVOLUTION TO THE END

Faced with military defeat on the battlefield, the Chiang Kai-shek clique started 'stalling tactics' to gain some breathing space. Chiang Kai-shek's effort to ask for increased aid from the US failed, and 'mediation' efforts by the US, Britain, France and the Soviet Union also fell through. Under pressure from various quarters, he had to issue a 'peace-seeking' statement on New Year's Day, 1949. On 21 January, Chiang Kai-shek announced his "withdrawal from public life." The 'Vice President' Li Zongren became acting 'president'. Although the Li Zongren government verbally expressed its willingness to conduct peaceful negotiations based on the CPC's conditions, it wanted to buy some breathing time to deploy the Yangtze River defence line to "maintain KMT rule south of the river."

The CPC was faced with the question of carrying on the revolution to the end or giving up halfway. On 30 December 1948, Mao Zedong issued a great call to "carry the revolution through to the end" in Xinhua News Agency's New Year's congratulatory message. He stated emphatically that the Chinese people must use revolutionary methods to completely and resolutely eliminate all reactionary forces; they must unswervingly persist in overthrowing imperialism, feudalism and bureaucratic capitalism; and they must topple reactionary KMT rule throughout the country and establish a proletarian-led republic of the people's democratic dictatorship with the alliance of workers and peasants as the main body in the whole country. They must, therefore, move towards a socialist society. On this issue, all those willing to participate in the current revolutionary cause must unite and cooperate instead of establishing an 'opposition' or taking a 'middle-line'.

Mao Zedong issued a statement on the current situation on 14 January 1949. In the statement, he solemnly pointed out that to end the war quickly, achieve true peace and reduce the suffering of the people, the CPC was willing to conduct peace negotiations with the Nanjing KMT government, KMT local governments and KMT military groups on the condition that war criminals would be punished, the pseudo-constitution and pseudo-legal system would be abolished, and all reactionary troops would be reorganised.

Although the CPC had no illusions about Chiang Kai-shek's fake 'peace talks', it made a last serious effort to achieve domestic peace. On 1 April, the CPC delegation headed by Zhou Enlai and the KMT government delegation led by Zhang Zhizhong negotiated in Beiping. After repeated consultations, the CPC delegation proposed the *Domestic Peace Agreement (Final Amendment)* on 15 April and demanded a KMT government response before 20 April. As the KMT government refused to sign the agreement, the negotiations broke down. Chairman Mao Zedong and Commander-in-Chief Zhu De issued an order to march across the country on 21 April.

From the night of 20 to 21 April, under the unified command of the Yangtze River Crossing Campaign General Front Committee with Deng Xiaoping as the secretary, the Second and Third Field Armies launched the Yangtze River Crossing Campaign with the cooperation of the Fourth Field Army Advance Corps and the Central Plains Military Region troops. On the thousand-*li* front line from Hukou in the west to Jiangyin in the east, the mighty million-strong PLA army crossed the Yangtze River via three routes. The KMT's Yangtze River Defence Line that they had spent three-and-a-half months building disintegrated in no time.

The PLA won the Yangtze River Crossing Campaign victory with the help of the people's sampans. The wooden sailboats and fishing boats were the means of production and lifeblood for the people along the Yangtze River. But they supported the Yangtze River Crossing Campaign. By the time the Yangtze River Crossing Campaign began, the PLA had collected more than 20,000 boats of various kinds. Some boatmen used logs to create rafts that measured four metres wide by 10 metres in length. Then they turned them into 'gunboats' by fixing motors on them and cushioning them with cotton wadding.

On 23 April, the PLA occupied Nanjing, the centre of KMT rule, declaring the 22-year KMT reactionary rule's collapse. After Mao Zedong read this good news in the Xiangshan Shuangqing Villa in Beiping, he wrote *Qilü - The PLA's Occupation of Nanjing*.

In the lines of the following *Qilü-style* poem, Mao Zedong expressed his determination to carry on the revolution to the end:

> 'The fleeing bandits, we should press our pursuit.
> Unlike Xiang Yu, our desire for fame should be subdued.'

He used the following lines to reveal the objective laws of human social progress:

> 'Had Heaven any sentiments, they'd also be pretty old;
> Change is the Way: great seas have turned into fields and
> rocky folds.'

The PLA captured Shanghai on 27 May. Its troops moved the newly liberated city because they all slept on the streets instead of disturbing the residents by staying in their private houses. Around that time, the PLA continued to march victoriously in the central, southern, northwestern and southwestern parts of the country, quickly eliminating the remaining KMT troops' resistance by military or peaceful means, thereby liberating a vast swathe of territory. The KMT Chiang Kai-shek clique fled from the mainland to Taiwan.

On the eve of Chongqing's liberation, the KMT reactionaries murdered many communists detained in Baigongguan and Zhazidong. The communist Jiang Zhuyun suffered all kinds of torture by the KMT Juntong (National Bureau of Investigation and Statistics) agents. Steadfast and unyielding, she would rather die than divulge any party secrets. People affectionately referred to her as 'Sister Jiang'.

After the KMT Juntong agents tortured her by driving bamboo skewers into her fingers, she unyieldingly said, "Bamboo skewers are made of bamboo, but communists' will is made of steel." When new China was established and Chongqing was about to be liberated, Sister Jiang died heroically at the age of 29. Many revolutionary martyrs represented by Sister Jiang endured all kinds of torture but they were dauntless and preferred death to surrender. They gave their precious lives to the cause of the Chinese people's liberation, and their spirit is known as the 'Red Crag Spirit'.[1]

---

1. Red Crag is a translation of Hong Yan, the name of the place near Baigongguan and Zhazidong where the KMT murdered Sister Jiang and other communists on the eve of Chongqing's liberation. It is famed for an eponymous novel depicting the heroism of Sister Jiang and other martyrs. Moreover, the colour 'red' stands for revolution and 'crag' symbolises the will of these communists; hence the 'Red Crag Spirit'.

6
THE SECOND PLENARY SESSION OF THE SEVENTH CENTRAL COMMITTEE OF THE CPC AND PREPARATIONS FOR THE ESTABLISHMENT OF NEW CHINA

A BLUEPRINT FOR NEW CHINA

With the CPC-led people's revolution winning countrywide victory being a foregone conclusion, the task of establishing a new China was put on the agenda.

The Second Plenary Session of the Seventh Central Committee of the party in session

In September 1948, the Politburo of the CPC Central Committee held an enlarged meeting. At the meeting, Mao Zedong discussed the state system and government system of the upcoming new China: the class nature and form of composition of state power. The meeting also put forward the basic guidelines for the construction of a new-democratic economy.

The Second Plenary Session of the Seventh Central Committee of the CPC held in Xibaipo in March 1949 stipulated the basic policies that the party should adopt in politics, the economy and diplomacy after the country's victory. It pointed out how China would change from an agricultural to an industrial nation, and from a new democratic society to a socialist society.

The plenary session discussed how to shift the focus of the CPC's mission from the countryside to the cities. It pointed out that the period of encircling cities from the rural areas[1] had ended, and from now on, the period of reversing the trend and having the cities lead the rural areas had begun.

To win countrywide victory was only the first step in a long march. The Chinese revolution was great, but the road after the revolution was longer, and the work was greater and more demanding. To this end, Mao Zedong put forward the concept of 'two musts': "we must have our comrades continue to maintain a humble and cautious work style free from arrogance and rashness, and we must have them continue to keep to the style of hard work and plain living." The concept was an important lesson drawn from China's thousands of years of history of chaos and order; it was an apt summary of the CPC's arduous struggle; it showed deep concern for how to maintain the CPC's vanguard character and purity after its victory, and how to bring about the long-term stability of the newly established people's state power; and it demonstrated a profound understanding of the fundamental purpose of the CPC to serve the people wholeheartedly. The 'two musts' thinking has inspired the whole party to always maintain the glorious tradition of hard work and plain living, always maintain flesh-and-blood ties with the people, and always maintain the party's advanced nature and purity. Mao Zedong also pointed out that we must be alert to the 'sugar-coated bullet' attacks of the bourgeoisie in the face of victory.

On the morning of 23 March 1949, Mao Zedong led the CPC Central Committee body out of Xibaipo, the last rural command post of the Chinese revolution, and set off for Beiping. Before leaving, Mao Zedong said to Zhou Enlai, "Today is the day we enter the capital; entering the capital will be our nationwide 'examination.'"[2]

Zhou Enlai responded, "We must all pass the examination so that we will not be sent back."

Mao Zedong said, "If that happens, it means we will have failed. We must not become Li Zicheng.³ I hope we'll do a good job of taking the exam." On 25 March, Mao Zedong and other CPC Central Committee leaders, the central organs and the PLA Headquarters moved to Beiping. The arrival of the CPC Central Committee and Mao Zedong in Xiangshan, Beiping, marked the shift of the Chinese revolution's focus from the countryside to the cities. It became the General Headquarters that led the War of Liberation to nationwide victory and led the country to the new-democratic revolution's great triumph.

To openly clarify the CPC's proposition on establishing the new China to the people of the whole country, Mao Zedong published an article *On the People's Democratic Dictatorship* on 30 June, stating that the people's democratic dictatorship needed the leadership of the working class. The foundation of the people's democratic dictatorship was the alliance of the working class, the peasantry and the urban petty bourgeoisie, but mainly the alliance of workers and peasants. To carry out China's people's revolution and develop China's economy, it was necessary to unite with the national bourgeoisie. Still, the bourgeoisie could not serve as the leader of the revolution, nor should it have a significant position of state power.

The resolutions of the Second Plenary Session of the Seventh Central Committee of the CPC and Mao Zedong's *On the People's Democratic Dictatorship* laid the theoretical and policy foundation for the establishment of new China. In preparing for new China's establishment, the CPC Central Committee also carefully considered and decided on new China's state structure and ethnic relations. It held that a unitary state structure was more in line with China's national conditions. It also believed that implementing regional ethnic autonomy in a unified country is more conducive to realising the principle of ethnic equality.

CONVENING THE CHINESE PEOPLE'S POLITICAL CONSULTATIVE CONFERENCE AND FORMULATING A COMMON PROGRAMME

The preparations for establishing the new China were carried out through the New Political Consultative Conference (Chinese People's Political Consultative Conference or CPPCC).

In June 1949, the First Plenary Session of the Preparatory Committee for the New Political Consultative Conference was convened in Beiping. It established the Standing Committee of the Preparatory Committee for the New Political Consultative Conference with Mao Zedong as its director. It was responsible for drafting a common programme and government plans, and starting comprehensive preparations for new China's founding.

In September 1949, the First Plenary Session of the CPPCC was convened in Beiping. It marked the great historic victory of the Chinese people's struggle for national independence and the People's Liberation Movement over the past hundred years. It also marked the complete formation of the patriotic united front and national unity as an institutional entity, and the establishment of the CPC-led multi-party cooperation and political consultation system. In his opening speech, Mao Zedong proudly declared to the world, "We have a common feeling that our work will be written in the history of mankind. It will show that the Chinese, who account for a quarter of mankind, have stood up as of now." He also predicted, "An upsurge in economic construction is bound to be followed by an upsurge of construction in the cultural sphere. The era in which the Chinese people were regarded as uncivilised is now at an end. We will emerge in the world as a nation with an advanced culture."

At the First Plenary Session of the CPPCC, delegates vote on a bill by a show of hands

The People's Political Consultative Conference was an organisational form of the people's democratic united front based on the alliance of workers and peasants led by the CPC. Participants in the CPPCC were representatives of the CPC, all democratic parties, persons without party affiliation, people's organisations, the PLA, all regions, ethnic groups and overseas Chinese. The meeting passed the *Organisation Law of the CPPCC* and elected the first National Committee of the CPPCC. On 9 October, Mao Zedong was elected chairman of the National Committee of the CPPCC.

The meeting passed the *Common Programme of the CPPCC*. This *Common*

Programme became the *Magna Carta* of the Chinese people and played the role of the new China's provisional constitution for some time.

The meeting passed the *Organisational Law of the Central People's Government (CPG)*, unanimously elected Mao Zedong as chairman of the CPG, Zhu De, Liu Shaoqi, Soong Ch'ing-ling, Li Jishen, Zhang Lan and Gao Gang as vice-chairmen; and 56 people, including Chen Yi, as members of the CPG Committee.

The meeting approved Beiping as the PRC's capital and renamed Beiping as Beijing. The meeting decided to adopt the Common Era as the year notations, *The March of Volunteers* as the provisional national anthem, and the five-star red flag as the national flag symbolising the nation's unity under the CPC's leadership.

THE REASONS AND FUNDAMENTAL EXPERIENCE FOR THE VICTORY OF CHINA'S NEW DEMOCRATIC REVOLUTION

With the collapse of the KMT's reactionary rule and the PRC's founding, China's new democratic revolution achieved a primary victory.

The occurrence and victory of the Chinese revolution were not accidental. It had profound social roots and a solid mass basis. The brutal oppression and exploitation of the Chinese people by imperialist and feudal forces prompted the Chinese people to embark on the historical path of the great revolutionary struggle against imperialism and feudalism. The KMT ruling clique headed by Chiang Kai-shek relied on the support of foreign imperialists, and the feudal landlord class and the bureaucratic comprador bourgeoisie as its social pillars at home, thereby placing itself in opposition to the Chinese people. After the War of Resistance Against Japanese Aggression, the Chiang Kai-shek clique adhered to his dictatorship and civil war policies, pushing people from all walks of life across the country to starvation and death, thereby forcing them to unite and save themselves.

The Chinese people's resistance struggle was heroic but only under the CPC's leadership were they able to eliminate the doom of failure and move from victory to new victory. Since its birth, the CPC has taken the Chinese people's happiness and the Chinese nation's rejuvenation as its original intention and mission. This initial aspiration and mission are the fundamental driving force that inspires the Chinese communists to keep advancing. The CPC has pointed out the goal of the struggle for the Chinese people, found the way to revolutionary victory in its long-term practice of fighting, and united the Chinese people, who were regarded as 'a pile of scattered sand', into an invincible force with one heart. "Without the CPC, there would be no new China" is a scientific conclusion drawn by the Chinese people based on the modern Chinese revolution's historical experience and a great truth confirmed by them based on their personal experience.

To realise its original aspirations and mission, and realise the ideals and propositions that it has always adhered to, the Chinese communists have advanced wave upon wave as they have been fighting unremittingly. In the meantime, they have made tremendous self-sacrifice. During the 28 years from the CPC's establishment in 1921 to the PRC's founding in 1949, countless outstanding fighters dedicated themselves to the Chinese people's liberation. Many great CPC leaders have given up their lives in the magnificent ongoing fights, such as Li Dazhao, Qu Qiubai, Cai Hesen, Xiang Jingyu, Deng Zhongxia, Su Zhaozheng, Peng Pai, Chen Yannian, Yun Daiying, Zhao Shiyan and Zhang Tailei. Sacrificing their lives heroically in the struggles were also many outstanding generals, such as Fang Zhimin, Liu Zhidan, Huang Gonglue, Xu Jishen, Wei Baqun, Zhao Bosheng, Dong Zhentang, Duan Dechang, Yang Jingyu, Zuo Quan and Ye Ting. The victory of China's new democratic revolution resulted from the long-term sacrifice and efforts made by thousands of martyrs, comrades of the whole party and people of all ethnic groups throughout the country.

The long-term social development and people's practice in history inevitably concluded that socialism is the road for the Chinese to take. For a long time, China faced three options for nation-building. The Beiyang warlords and then the KMT ruling clique represented the first option. They embraced the landlord and comprador classes' dictatorship to keep Chinese society on the track of semi-colonialism and semi-feudalism. Certain middle-of-the-roaders or independents represented the second option. They advocated establishing a bourgeois republic, hoping that it might pursue the independent development of capitalism. The CPC represented the third option. It advocated establishing a people's republic based on the alliance of workers and peasants under the working class's leadership, leading to socialism through new democracy. The Chinese people repeatedly and practically tested these three plans and found that only the third option finally won the support of the broadest masses of the Chinese people, including the national bourgeoisie and its political representatives. It shows the historical inevitability of the truth, 'only socialism can save China'.

In leading the people's revolution, the CPC has accumulated rich experience and forged effective weapons for defeating the enemy. Mao Zedong pointed out, "The united front, armed struggle and party building are the three magic, and the most important, weapons for the CPC to defeat the enemy in the Chinese revolution."

The fact that the CPC has led the revolution to victory teaches us that combining Marxism's basic principles with China's specific reality must be unswerving; that Marxism with Chinese characteristics must be ongoing. The formation and development of Mao Zedong Thought have enabled Marxism to take deep root in China. Once accepted by the Chinese people, this Marxism with Chinese characteristics will become a great material force behind Chinese society's revolutionary transformation. The history of the Chinese revolution has conclusively proved that it is entirely correct for history and the Chinese people to choose Marxism and for the CPC to write Marxism on its banner. It has also confirmed that it is equally valid to integrate Marxist tenets with China's specific reality, to constantly promote Marxism's Sinicization, and to make Marxism keep pace with the times.

The victory of the Chinese People's Revolution completely changed the Chinese people's heavy fate of a century's poverty, weakness and humiliation. The Chinese nation has embarked on a magnificent path to its great rejuvenation.

The victory of the Chinese people's revolution fundamentally changed Chinese society's course of development. It cleared major obstacles and created the political prerequisite for bringing about the transition from new democracy to socialism, establishing a socialist system, and carrying out socialist modernisation. It blazed a broad trail for realising China's prosperity, its people's happiness and national rejuvenation. The Chinese people, oppressed and enslaved for thousands of years, have since become the masters of a new country and a new society.

---

1. The theory and practice of encircling the cities from the rural areas to seize political power by armed force is considered a contribution by Mao Zedong and the CPC to combining Marxist universal truth with Chinese revolutionary practice and is also regarded as an integral part of Mao Zedong Thought.
2. A reference to the Chinese imperial examination system used by the civil service to select candidates for the state bureaucracy that can be traced back to the Sui Dynasty (581-618).
3. Li Zicheng was a Chinese rebel leader who overthrew the Ming Dynasty in 1644 and ruled over northern China briefly as the emperor of the short-lived Shun Dynasty before his death a year later. A theory attributes his failure to his indulgence in a life of pleasure resulting in him losing the drive to succeed after entering Beijing.

Five

The Founding of the PRC and Establishment of the Socialist System

On the afternoon of 1 October 1949, 300,000 soldiers and civilians in the capital Beijing held a grand ceremony for the nation's founding in Tiananmen Square. Mao Zedong solemnly declared, "The Central People's Government of the People's Republic of China has been established today." Fifty-four guns fired 28 salutes, symbolising the 28 years of the party leading the people's struggle. The founding of the PRC opened a new chapter in Chinese history. The CPC, which led and organised the victory of the People's Revolution, became the party in power nationwide and embarked on a new journey leading the people to create a happy and beautiful life. The party's history also opened a new chapter.

1 October has since become the National Day of the PRC.

1
THE FOUNDING OF THE PRC AND CONSOLIDATION OF THE NEWLY-EMERGED PEOPLE'S POWER

THE INITIAL TEST OF THE RULING PARTY

Before the founding ceremony, Mao Zedong presided over the CPG Committee's first meeting. The meeting unanimously resolved to accept the *Common Programme of the CPPCC* as its policy programme, appointing Zhou Enlai as Prime Minister and Minister of Foreign Affairs of the CPG, Mao Zedong as Chairman of the People's Revolutionary Military Committee and Zhu De as Commander-in-Chief of the PLA. Those appointed as heads of the CPG and the State Council included excellent representatives of the CPC, various democratic parties, overseas Chinese, and other patriotic democrats. They also encompassed famous people and experts. The appointments fully embodied the principle of multi-party cooperation and unity to build the country under the CPC's leadership and epitomised the characteristics of the people's democratic regime.

The founding of the PRC ultimately ended old China's history of a semi-colonial and semi-feudal society, ultimately ended old China's state of disunity, completely abolished the unequal treaties imposed on China by the great powers and all the imperialists' privileges in China, realised China's great leap from thousands of years of feudal autocracy to people's democracy, and achieved a high degree of unification in China and unprecedented unity of all ethnic groups. The Chinese have since stood up! Since then, the Chinese people have firmly controlled their destiny and become the masters of their country, society and their own destiny! The development and progress of the Chinese nation have since ushered in a new era!

At 3 pm on 1 October 1949, the founding ceremony was held in Tiananmen Square. Mao Zedong solemnly declared, "The CPG of the PRC has been established today"

The founding of the PRC was a victory of world significance. It broke through the eastern front of imperialism, significantly changed the world's political structure, strengthened the world's peaceful and democratic power, and exerted a profound influence on the process of world history.

The founding of the PRC was the victory of Marxism-Leninism in China and the victory of Mao Zedong Thought, which combined the universal principles of Marxism-Leninism with the concrete practice of the Chinese revolution. This victory enabled Marxism-Leninism and Mao Zedong Thought to gain high prestige among the Chinese people and to be accepted as the guiding ideology by institutions from all walks of life in the PRC, and also expanded its influence worldwide.

After the founding of the long-awaited new China, the revolutionary enthusiasm of people of all nationalities was soaring, and everything took on a new look throughout China. Simultaneously, the CPC and the Chinese people still faced many difficulties that needed to be urgently solved, and many severe tests were still in store.

Militarily, the People's War of Liberation had not entirely ended. The KMT still had more than a million troops fighting stubbornly in Southwest and South China and its coastal islands. In the newly liberated areas, the large number of KMT remnants left behind when it fled colluded with despotic forces and hardened bandits, thereby seriously endangering the establishment and stability of a new social order.

New China inherited a badly damaged economy. Production was shrinking, and people were still living a hard life. The prolonged hyperinflation under KMT rule caused prices to soar and speculation to run rampant. Whether the CPC and the CPG could stop hyperinflation, stabilise the economic situation and gain a financial and then a political foothold, was a new and severe test at the time. It was more demanding than marching into unliberated areas and suppressing bandits.

Internationally, the US, which vainly sought world hegemony, still refused to abandon its position of being an enemy of the Chinese people after the failure of its policy to 'support Chiang Kai-Shek and oppose the CPC' and refused to recognise new China. Simultaneously, it tried its best to prevent other countries from recognising China and to prevent the PRC from restoring its lawful seat in the United Nations (UN). Simultaneously, it politically isolated, economically blocked and militarily encircled new China. Whether the CPC and the Chinese people could win the contest against US imperialism was another severe test.

National governance posed a new test for the CPC. Faced with an arduous construction task, the CPC had to quickly learn new economic construction and national governance skills. More importantly, under the peaceful condition of governing and building the country, the CPC had to continue to maintain its fine traditions and style, and withstand the 'sugar-coated bullet' attacks by the bourgeoisie.

In short, a considerable proportion of the Chinese people still doubted whether the new people's government could establish its foothold and whether the CPC could manage the country well after the founding of new China. The question had to be answered in practice. International friends and enemies were also watching and waiting for the answer.

In the face of the complex situation and various tests, the CPC adopted a series of active and sure-footed policies and measures to lead the people of all nationalities to meet the challenges with confidence and start the great effort to build the new China.

THE ESTABLISHMENT OF LOCAL PEOPLE'S POWER AT EVERY LEVEL

Amid the gun salutes at the PRC's founding ceremony, the PLA continued to march to southern and southwestern China, sweeping away the enemy remnants with invincible might. By the end of 1949, it had liberated southern Fujian and most of Guangdong, Guangxi, Guizhou and Sichuan successively. Yunnan and the Xikang[1] region were peacefully liberated. After Xinjiang declared its peaceful liberation in the northwest, PLA troops entered Xinjiang, thus completing the feat of advancing thousands of miles to the border. In May 1950, the PLA liberated Hainan Island.

By October the same year, after a year of fighting, the PLA had eradicated more than 1.28 million KMT regular troops.

Tibet was the last region to be liberated on the mainland. Since modern times, Western imperialists have coveted Tibet, supporting separatist forces there. After the founding of the PRC, a small number of separatists in the upper class of the Tibetan local government attempted to separate Tibet from the mainland at the instigation of imperialist forces. For this reason, the CPC Central Committee laid down the firm principle of never allowing any foreign troops to divide Tibet and waged a closely coordinated military and political struggle with the upper-level separatist forces in Tibet. In May 1951, the CPG and Tibet's local government signed the *Agreement on Measures for the Peaceful Liberation of Tibet (The Seventeen-Article Agreement)*. In October, the PLA moved into Lhasa. The peaceful liberation of Tibet smashed the attempts of the imperialists and a small number of Tibetan separatists to seek the 'independence of Tibet' and reunified China's mainland.

In the newly liberated areas, the PLA launched a large-scale operation to suppress bandits. By the first half of 1951, it had eliminated more than a million bandits in various places, largely putting down the mainland's banditry, effectively protecting people's lives and work, and stabilising social order.

With the victorious march of the PLA, local people's power at every level was quickly established. By 1951, 29 provinces, one ethnic autonomous region (Inner Mongolia), eight provincial administrative offices, 13 municipal governments, 140 municipal and provincial governments, and 2,283 county governments were established countrywide. What became people's democratic governments had never existed before in Chinese history, are truly supported by the people, and effectively exercise power throughout the country, laying a solid political and organisational foundation for the party to govern the country.

THE FORMULATION AND IMPLEMENTATION OF NEW CHINA'S DIPLOMATIC POLICY

After the Second World War, the world gradually formed a bipolar pattern characterised by the confrontation between the two superpowers: the US and the Soviet Union. The appearance of the two camps between peaceful and democratic forces and imperialism, reflecting the contradictions between the US and the Soviet Union, gave rise to a situation in which two social systems - capitalism and socialism - confronted and interacted with each other. Based on this situation, in the first half of 1949, Mao Zedong successively proposed the three basic diplomatic policies of "making a fresh start," "cleaning the house to invite guests," and "leaning to one side." That is, the PRC would not recognise the old diplomatic relations established by the KMT government with other countries and revoked the privileges enjoyed by imperialist powers in China; aimed to clean up the remnants of imperialist influence in China before considering establishing diplomatic relations with foreign nations; and declared that the PRC would side with socialism and the forces of world peace and democracy.

According to the above policy, the PRC immediately established diplomatic relations with the Soviet Union and successively with 10 other people's democratic countries, including Bulgaria, Romania, Hungary, North Korea, Czechoslovakia, Poland, Mongolia, the German Democratic Republic, Albania and Vietnam. From April 1950 to May 1951, it established diplomatic relations with the four independent Asian nations of India, Indonesia, Burma and Pakistan, and the four European capitalist countries of Sweden, Denmark, Switzerland and Finland. The PRC thereby took a critical step to defeat US attempts to contain and isolate China. In December 1949, Mao Zedong visited the Soviet Union. On 14 February of the following year, China and the Soviet Union signed the *Sino-Soviet Treaty of Friendship, Alliance and Mutual Assistance* and related agreements in Moscow. The treaty and agreements allowed the PRC to go all-out to start its domestic construction and helped China and the Soviet Union to jointly face possible imperialist aggression and to strive for and maintain world peace.

Simultaneously, the PRC abolished the unequal treaties signed between the old China and foreign countries, revoked imperialist powers' privileges, and eliminated their influence in China. The customs management, garrison rights and inland navigation rights that the imperialists had in old China had caused the most damage to China's sovereignty and symbolised China's degeneration into a semi-colony. After its establishment, the PRC first abolished these three rights. October 1949 saw the establishment of the General Administration of Customs of China. From January to September 1950, military management committees in Beijing, Tianjin and Shanghai successively announced their recovery and requisition of foreign barracks. In July 1950, the Finance and Economic Committee of the State Council issued instructions on unified shipping management. The abolition of all the military and economic privileges of foreign countries in mainland China ultimately ended the century-old history of humiliation by foreign countries trampling on China's sovereignty and foreigners swaggering around on China's territory rampant since the Opium Wars.

CONFISCATING BUREAUCRATIC CAPITAL, STABILISING PRICES AND UNIFYING THE NATION'S FINANCES

As the KMT reactionary regime's economic foundation, bureaucratic capital monopolised China's economic lifeline, plundered people's wealth and seriously hindered the development of social productive forces. The confiscation of bureaucratic capital as the property of the people's state was one of the economic programmes of the New Democratic Revolution. By the beginning of 1950, the state had commandeered the bureaucratic capital from more than 2,800 industrial and mining enterprises, and over 2,400 financial companies countrywide. On this basis, a socialist state-owned economy was quickly established. Once established, it became the leading force of the entire social economy and the primary material basis for developing production and economic prosperity in new China. It made essential material preparations for the subsequent socialist transformation.

At the beginning of the CPG's establishment, the fiscal and economic situation was difficult. The abnormal development of speculative capital left over from the old society continued to make waves in the newly liberated cities and exacerbated price increases. Some people even threatened to prevent the Rmb from entering Shanghai even though the PLA could enter it.

Faced with harsh financial and economic conditions, the CPC carefully led a significant struggle to stabilise prices and unify finances.

To stop the market chaos aggravated by capital manipulation, the CPC and CPG adopted necessary administrative measures and drastic economic measures to organise the 'Silver Dollar War' and 'Rice-Cotton War' to fight against speculative capital. In June 1949, the Shanghai Military Control Commission closed the securities building, the financial speculation headquarters. After the liberation of Wuhan, Guangzhou and other cities, underground banks were also seized, severely cracking down on speculators' illegal activities and ensuring the Rmb's legal status. In response to speculative capitalists' move to hoard large amounts of grain, cotton yarn, cotton cloth and coal, which once again set off price turmoil, the Central Finance Committee triggered centralised deployment of related goods and materials. The rapid decline in prices and the tightening of the money supply caused speculators to go bankrupt due to the failure in capital turnover. After these two major 'battles', illegal speculative capital was never able to recover, and the state-owned economy gained the initiative in stabilising the market.

In order to fundamentally stabilise prices, the state found it necessary to balance the nation's fiscal revenue and expenditure, and to balance the supply and demand of market materials. To this end, it felt it was essential to implement unified management and leadership of national fiscal and economic work. In March 1950, the State Council issued the *Decision on Unifying the State's Financial and Economic Work*, deciding to unify the nation's fiscal revenue, goods and material delivery, and cash management. The vigorous implementation of the decision countrywide quickly achieved noticeable results. That year, the nation's fiscal revenue and expenditure were close to equilibrium. Simultaneously, with the implementation of tax rectification measures and the promotion of public debt, national prices were further reduced and stabilised.

Price stabilisation and finance unification constituted a significant victory on the financial and economic fronts after new China's founding, thereby ending the hyperinflation and soaring prices that had caused the people to suffer from the KMT rule since the War of Resistance Against Japanese Aggression. It created favourable conditions for stabilising people's lives, and restoring and developing industrial and agricultural production. This victory caused those people at home and abroad who doubted whether the CPC could do an excellent job of managing the economy to be beside themselves with admiration and to call it a 'miracle'. Facts have proved that the CPC is not only invincible militarily and strong politically but also resourceful economically.

In June 1950, the CPC convened the Third Plenary Session of the Seventh Central Committee to arrange various tasks to restore the national economy. The meeting pointed out that it would take three years to create three conditions to achieve fundamental improvement in the financial and economic situation; the completion of land reform, the rationalisation of existing industry and commerce, and substantial reduction in national institutional expenditure. At the meeting, Mao Zedong gave a speech entitled *Don't Attack on All Sides*, pointing out: Our current general policy is to eliminate KMT remnants, spies and bandits; overthrow the landlord class; liberate Taiwan and Tibet; and fight imperialism to the end. In the face of such a complicated struggle, we must adequately handle relations with the national bourgeoisie, democratic parties, intellectuals and ethnic minorities, and refrain from attacking from all sides to create too many enemies and cause tension throughout the country. Mao Zedong criticised the erroneous thinking of 'being able to eliminate capitalism and implement socialism early' and emphasised that the policy on the national bourgeoisie was still unity and struggle, with unity as the mainstay. It was to control capital instead of squeezing and destroying capital. The Third Plenary Session of the Seventh Central Committee was an important meeting convened by the Party Central Committee in the early days of the founding of new China. The guidelines decided by the plenary session drew up a straightforward plan of action for the CPC's work during the period of national economic recovery.

---

1. The historic province of Tibet spanning the Kham region and western Sichuan which was a province during the Republic of China regime (1928 to 1949) with its capital in Ya'an.

2

THE WAR TO RESIST THE US AND AID KOREA, LAND SYSTEM REFORM AND OTHER DEMOCRATIC REFORMS

RESIST THE US AND AID KOREA, DEFEND THE MOTHERLAND AND PROTECT THE NATION

Just as the Chinese people concentrated their efforts to improve financial and economic conditions, new China was facing the threat of external aggression. On 25 June 1950, the Korean Civil War broke out. The US government immediately decided to intervene in the Korean Civil War and despatched the Seventh Fleet to invade the Taiwan Strait, openly interfering in China's internal affairs and obstructing China's great reunification cause. In early October, the US military ignored the Chinese Government's repeated warnings and flagrantly crossed the 38th parallel, fanning the flames of war on the border between China and North Korea, and directly threatening new China's national security. At the critical juncture, the Workers' Party of Korea and the government asked China to send supporting troops.

Whether it dared, or was even capable of, taking on the US imperialists, the world's biggest, richest economy and strongest military power, was a considerable challenge for the PRC, which had only been established for a year and was in dire need of full-scale reconstruction. Given the extreme disparity between the enemy and itself, could China win if it sent troops to fight? Would it 'draw fire against itself' or 'invite disaster onto its own doorstep', making it difficult to carry out economic construction? The Politburo of the Central Committee held many meetings to comprehensively assess the situation at home and abroad. It not only clearly realised the difficulties it was facing but also made an in-depth analysis of the necessity and feasibility of sending troops to war. Eventually, it made the historic decision to despatch the Chinese People's Volunteer Army to fight in Korea, both to resist the US and aid Korea, and to defend China itself.

On 8 October 1950, Mao Zedong issued an order to form the Chinese People's Volunteer Army with Peng Dehuai as the Commander and Political Commissar. On the 19th, the volunteers crossed the Yalu River with great vigour, a righteous act by an army dedicated to a just cause. The Chinese People's Volunteer Army collaborated closely with North Korean soldiers and civilians in the battles of Onjong, Unsan, Chongchon River and Chosin Reservoir. After that, they built an impregnable defence like a bastion of iron, launched many offensive attacks, smashed the 'strangulation battles', withstood 'germ warfare', and fought the bloody Shanggan-ling Campaign (Battle of Triangle Hill), thereby creating a mighty and majestic annal of war. After arduous battles, the Chinese and North Korean troops defeated their opponents who were armed to the teeth, shattered the myth of the US military's invincibility, and forced the overbearing invaders to sign the *Armistice Agreement* on 27 July 1953. The victory of the War to Resist the US and Aid Korea was a declaration to the world, "The era when Western aggressors have for the past hundreds of years been able to occupy a country by setting up a few cannons on a coast in the East is gone!"

The Chinese People's Volunteer Army crossing the Yalu River to fight in North Korea

In the magnificent War to Resist the US and Aid Korea, the heroic Chinese People's Volunteer Army forged the great spirit of resisting the US and aiding Korea by always giving full play to the spirit of putting the motherland and people's interests above all else, the patriotic spirit of dashing ahead regardless of one's own safety for the sake of the motherland and people's dignity, the heroic revolutionary spirit of gallantly fighting while risking one's own life, the optimistic revolutionary spirit of fearing no hardships and constantly keeping high morale, the loyal revolutionary spirit of generously giving up everything for the fulfilment of the mission entrusted by the motherland and people, and the internationalist spirit of striving for the cause of peace and justice for humanity. Mao Zedong's eldest son, Mao Anying, was the first to join the war in North Korea and died heroically on the Korean battlefield. Faced with powerful and fierce opponents in a harsh and cruel battle environment, the Chinese Volunteer Army soldiers shed their blood and laid down their lives as they fought with 'steely determination' against the enemy. They said, "Behind us is the motherland, so we cannot take a step back for the peace of our compatriots!" They bravely charged forward under heavy enemy gunfire; held their positions under the enemy's wanton and indiscriminate bombardment; built ladders with their bodies; plunged themselves into the enemy troops holding bags of explosives or hand-held pipe bombs; never flinched despite hunger and cold, and dared to fight 'hand-to-hand' in the air. Their death-defying fighting spirit terrified the enemy and shook the earth! More than 300,000 troops and 6,000 groups of individuals rendered outstanding service. Examples include Yang Gensi, who unhesitatingly blew up the enemy troops and himself with a bag of explosives; Huang Jiguang, who blocked an enemy embrasure in a fortified position with his chest to clear the way for his comrades to charge; Qiu Shaoyun, who remained still until his heroic death in a fire caused by incendiary bombs; and Luo Shengjiao, who jumped into the icy water and saved North Korean teenagers' lives at the cost of his own... They composed an epic of heroism that shocked the world and brought spiritual beings to tears. Therefore, the Chinese people refer to them as 'The Most Beloved People'.

The great spirit of the War to Resist the US and Aid Korea spans time and space and will last forever. It must be passed on forever and carried forward from generation to generation.

During the War to Resist the US and Aid Korea, the CPC Central Committee took control of the overall situation, carried out effective war mobilisation, and gave correct guidance on the war. Adopting the guiding principle of fighting while maintaining stability and building the country, the CPC launched a magnificent movement to resist the US and aid Korea, a great struggle concerning the country's future and destiny, with united support from the Chinese people of all ethnic groups. The great victory of the War to Resist the US and Aid Korea was a manifesto that the Chinese people were firm on their feet in the East after they had stood up, an important milestone for the great rejuvenation of the Chinese nation, and of far-reaching significance for China and the world. The war's victory smashed the enemy's conspiracy of massing troops along China's border to strangle new China in the cradle. The victory was 'a punch that can prevent a hundred punches'. That is, imperialist powers dared not invade China because China had gained a firm foothold. After this war, the Chinese people had entirely overcome the centuries-old humiliation of being slaughtered and subjugated in modern times, and discarded the label of 'the sick man of East Asia'. As a result, the Chinese people have emerged from a humble situation into an honourable position. After the battle, the Chinese people defeated the invaders, shook the world, established the important role of new China in Asian and international affairs, and demonstrated new China's status as a major power. Since that war, the PLA has learned about warfare in war practice and greatly promoted the modernisation of national defence and the army: it has become increasingly courageous and combat-effective, gained necessary military experience, and transformed from a single-service army to a force of multiple arms. The war's victory significantly shaped post-war Asia and the world's strategic pattern, greatly encouraged the just cause of the world's oppressed nations and peoples to strive for national independence and people's liberation, and vigorously promoted the progressive cause of world peace and mankind. The war's victory made China safer as a peaceful land, displayed the Chinese people's spirit, shocked the world with the Chinese army's fighting capability, and caused the world to look at China with admiration. It fully demonstrates the Chinese people's steel-like willpower that enables them not to fear ferocious adversaries, their indomitable and awe-inspiring character of courage that makes them dare to fight and win, and their firm determination to maintain world peace. The war's victory proves once again that justice is bound to triumph over power politics, and peaceful development is an unstoppable historical trend.

ABOLITION OF THE FEUDAL LAND SYSTEM AND SUPPRESSION OF THE COUNTER-REVOLUTIONARY MOVEMENT

When the PRC was founded, land reform had not yet been completed in the newly liberated areas, accounting for more than half the country's total population. That severely hindered the development of social productivity. While carrying out the War to Resist the US and Aid Korea, the CPC led the reform in the newly liberated areas to abolish the feudal land system from the winter of 1950 until the end of 1952. On 30 June 1950, the CPG promulgated and implemented the *Land Reform Law of the PRC*. It summed up the CPC's experience and lessons in leading land reform and defined the policy to adapt to the new situation after the PRC's establishment, proposing to preserve the rich peasant economy, keep the middle peasants' land intact, and limit the scope of confiscation of landlords' property. The policy was meant to protect middle peasants and split up the landlord class to reduce resistance to land reform and promote the recovery and development of production. Therefore, it became the fundamental legal basis for guiding land reform in the newly liberated areas. By the end of 1952, except for some ethnic minority areas, land reform on the mainland had basically been completed. Including the old liberated areas, about 300 million landless peasants across the country obtained about 700 million mu^1 of land free of charge, exempting the peasants from paying land rent worth over 30 million tonnes of grain to landlords each year.

The land reform's completion marked the eradication of the landlord class's land ownership, the foundation of the feudal system that had lasted for thousands of years in China. It was also the beginning of the peasants becoming masters of the land, a great historic victory. The success in land reform fundamentally liberated rural productivity, stimulated most farmers to be more politically enthusiastic and more productive, promoted the rapid recovery and development of agriculture, and the development of rural culture and education, and opened the way for industrialising new China.

While carrying out land reform, a campaign began to suppress counter-revolutionaries on a grand scale throughout China. After the Korean War broke out, the counter-revolutionary remnants left behind by the KMT on the mainland became more aggressive. They spread rumours, carried out various sabotage and disruptive activities, harmed and murdered revolutionary cadres and the masses, and attempted to cooperate with outside enemies to subvert the people's power.

In 1950, counter-revolutionaries murdered nearly 40,000 cadres and masses in various places, including 7,000 in Guangxi alone. In October 1950, the Central Committee of the CPC issued the *Instructions on the Suppression of Counter-Revolutionary Activities* and decided to resolutely suppress the heinous counter-revolutionaries steeped in evil doings with no intent of repenting. Starting from December, the movement to suppress counter-revolutionaries began throughout the country. By the end of

October 1951, the counter-revolutionary movement's suppression on a national scale was over.

The movement to suppress counter-revolutionaries wiped out the remaining counter-revolutionary forces left by the KMT on the mainland and eliminated the spies, underground armies, secret societies, and other reactionary organisations. Its success led to unprecedented social stability. The movement effectively helped land reform and the War to Resist the US and Aid Korea.

DEMOCRATIC REFORMS IN EVERY ASPECT OF SOCIETY AND THE 'THREE-ANTI' AND 'FIVE-ANTI' CAMPAIGNS

Centred around land system reform, the CPC also led various democratic reforms, including social transformation.

Democratic reforms were carried out in state-owned industrial, mining and transportation enterprises. Most of these were initially bureaucratic capitalist enterprises. After their takeover, they needed further democratic reforms to further reflect the new socialist production relations. Under the CPC committees' leadership, the enterprises in various places rid themselves of hidden remaining counter-revolutionary forces and abolished the old society's bureaucratic management institutions, such as the feudal gang-master system and the body-search system. They mobilised and organised employees to participate in business management through trade union committees and employee representative meetings, thereby creating a democratic management system to meet production needs. The system aroused the workers' enthusiasm to become masters of the country and boost production. As a result, they made remarkable achievements in the recovery of industrial production.

Reforming the feudal marriage system was another essential aspect of the CPC's promotion of democratic reform and social transformation. On 1 May 1950, the CPG promulgated the *Marriage Law of the PRC*, which was the first law enacted by new China. It stipulated, "The feudal marriage system of marriage by arbitrary decision of any third party or by coercion shall be abolished. Male domination, female subordination and negligence of children's interests shall be prohibited. A new democratic marriage system based on free choice of partners for men and women, monogamy, equal rights for men and women, and the protection of the legitimate interests of women and children shall be applied."

The *Marriage Law* was the most significant change in Chinese society's family life in thousands of years. After the movement to implement the *Marriage Law,* most Chinese began to embrace the idea of freedom of marriage and equality between men and women, which gradually became common practice in society. Most women, who accounted for half of the country's population, were liberated from the shackles of the feudal marriage system, and their social status was greatly improved.

After the implementation of the Marriage Law of the PRC, a couple in the suburbs of Beijing hold a wedding

The struggle to ban vile practices, such as prostitution, drug trafficking, drug abuse and gambling parties left over from the old society, was also an essential part of eradicating social ills and carrying out social transformation. After three years of hard work, prostitution, gambling, drugs and other social diseases that were repeatedly banned in old China and regarded as chronic diseases in Western countries were basically prohibited under the CPC's leadership.

While the War to Resist the US and Aid Korea was the continuation of the anti-imperialist struggle of the Chinese People's Democratic Revolution, land reform and other democratic reforms were the completion of the revolution's anti-feudal struggle. The torrent of revolution washes away the old society's filth, and China's social outlook and social customs underwent tremendous changes. These historical changes consolidated the people's democratic dictatorship and provided the necessary socio-political conditions for restoring and developing the economy.

While the Chinese were trying to increase production and practice strict frugality, corruption, waste and bureaucracy appeared in the CPC and government agencies in various places. The serious situation reported from the Northeast and North China prompted the Central Committee of the CPC to promulgate the *Decision on Streamlining Administration; Increasing Production and Practicing Economy; Opposing Corruption and Waste; and Opposing Bureaucratism* on 1 December 1951. It called for a large-scale mass movement to swiftly and thoroughly expose all large, medium and small corruption incidents, and launched the 'Three-Anti' campaign. In the struggle, the focus was on dealing with typical major cases to heighten the whole party's vigilance and draw the entire society's attention. When Liu Qingshan, Secretary of the Tianjin CPC Prefectural Committee, and Zhang Zishan, Assistant Director of the Tianjin Administrative Office, were sentenced to death for abusing their power to embezzle public funds, engaging in illegal business activities and becoming corrupt and degenerate criminals, it showed the people of the whole country that the CPC would never tolerate the unethical practice of using the ruling party's status for personal gain. Once discovered, corrupt elements were severely punished regardless of their seniority and rank.

The 'Three-Anti' campaign ended in October 1952. This struggle was the CPC's first battle to keep communist members and leading cadres clean and to punish corrupt elements in power. The campaign eliminated the vermin among the cadres, educated most of them, and played a significant role in resisting the old society's vices and the bourgeoisie's bad ideas, fostering a fine party culture and governance style, and helped society adopt a healthy pattern.

During the 'Three-Anti', it was discovered that corruption within the party and government agencies often arose from officials' collusion with illegal businessmen. Many facts showed that a small number of capitalists used various unlawful means to make excess profits and even made first-aid kits from waste or rotten cotton to sell to the Volunteer Army, causing wounded soldiers to become crippled or die. Their malpractice aroused public outrage. In January 1952, the Central Government decided to launch the 'Five-Anti' campaign against bribery, tax evasion, theft of state property, cutting corners, and theft of national economic intelligence in the private business community. During the campaign, the CPC and the government mobilised the masses to wage a struggle of reasoning with business people and exposing their illegal practices. Simultaneously, the Central Government also stated that the positive side of the national bourgeoisie was not to be denied and that its due political and economic status stipulated in the *Common Programme of the CPPCC* was to remain unchanged. In general, attention was to be paid to maintaining the normal progress of economic life.

The 'Five-Anti' campaign ended in October 1952, and it effectively cracked down on the grave 'five poisons' of illegal capitalists. An education campaign on the law-abiding operation of business and commerce was conducted among the national bourgeois industrialists and merchants, promoting a worker supervision system and democratic reform in private enterprises. The education paved the way for the gradual transformation of capitalist industry and commerce in a peaceful manner.

---

1. A unit of land equivalent to an area of around 667 sqm.

3
NATIONAL ECONOMIC RECOVERY AND THE LAUNCH OF ALL TYPES OF CONSTRUCTION

RECOVERY AND INITIAL DEVELOPMENT OF THE NATIONAL ECONOMY

The old Chinese economy was originally highly backward. The Japanese imperialists' war of aggression against China and the KMT reactionaries' war against the people damaged it further. Concentrating efforts to restore the national economy became the CPC and the Chinese people's urgent task. The party and the government made every effort to restore the national economy via the basic policy of 'keeping a balance between the public and private sectors, labour and capital, mutual assistance between urban and rural areas, and domestic and foreign exchanges.'

In agriculture, while inspiring individual farmers' enthusiasm in the economy, the CPC gradually promoted mutual assistance among individual farmers. The state increased its investment in agriculture year by year. It concentrated the country's efforts on the key projects, such as harnessing the Huai River, diverting the Jingjiang flood, and controlling flooding on the lower reaches of the Yellow River. These projects initially changed the situation where river embankments had fallen into disrepair and floods had been frequent in old China. Various localities also vigorously repaired canals and small reservoirs in hilly areas to expand farmland irrigation. These types of infrastructure construction promoted the rapid recovery and development of agricultural production. The country's total grain output increased from 113.2 million tonnes in 1949 to 163.93 million tonnes in 1952, an increase of 44.8%.

Industrially, the focus was on restoring mining, steel, power, machine manufacturing, and other major chemical industries urgently needed by the national economy and people's livelihood. Simultaneously, restoring and increasing textile and other light industrial production also began. In terms of regional distribution, the focus was on restoring the northeast industrial base while developing inland industries and adding several new backbone enterprises in a planned way.

In December 1954, the Kham-Tibet and Qinghai-Tibet highways running through the 'Roof of the World' were opened to traffic

By the end of 1952, the output of major industrial products and light industrial products had exceeded the highest level in history.

In the transportation industry, the state invested a total of Rmb1.77 billion, accounting for 22.6% of the country's total infrastructure investment. The original railway network was basically restored, reconnecting northern and southern China. The Chengdu-Chongqing Railway crossing the Great Southwest's hinterland and the Tianshui-Lanzhou Railway in the northwestern region were also completed. The Chengdu-Chongqing Railway was a section of the Sichuan-Hankou Railway funded for construction in the late Qing Dynasty but not completed for nearly half a century. After the founding of new China, it was completed and opened to traffic in just two years. The country also built and rebuilt some major arterial roads and county-level and township-level highways. The number of roads open to through traffic increased by more than 50% compared with the initial period of the founding of new China. The construction of the Kham-Tibet Highway (now the Sichuan-Tibet Highway) and the Qinghai-Tibet Highway leading to the 'Roof of the World' began in 1950.

The recovery and development of trade was an essential link in promoting the exchange of materials between urban and rural areas, and restoring the entire national economy. After several years of hard work, state-owned and cooperative commerce gradually developed and became the main channel for the circulation of goods. By the end of 1952, a unified state-owned commercial system including various categories had taken shape throughout the country. After stabilising prices and unifying finances, the government took a series of measures to solve the problem of false purchasing power's disappearance triggered by inflation. The steps taken included increasing government placement of orders from private factories for processing materials; purchasing a large amount of agricultural and side-line products to increase rural purchasing power; adjusting the tax burden; appropriately reducing state-owned businesses; educating private-enterprise workers to work hard to complete production tasks; and rationally adjusting the relationships between the public and private sector, between labour and capital, and between production and marketing, to greatly promote private industry and commerce.

After more than three years of hard work by people all over the country, the national economy that had been severely damaged before the founding of the PRC was fully restored and had achieved initial development. At the end of 1952, the total output value of industry and agriculture was Rmb81 billion, an increase of 77% over 1949. The country's fiscal revenue had doubled, and revenue and expenditure were balanced. The income of urban and rural people increased year by year, and their lives generally improved. Compared with 1949, employees' national average wage increased by 70%, and farmers' income generally increased by more than 30%. In the process of economic recovery, the structure of the national economy had also undergone profound changes. The proportion of the state-owned economy increased while the proportion of the private capitalist economy declined year by year. The status of industrial productivity was strengthened while the proportion of modern industry rose, laying the foundation for China's gradual transformation from an agricultural to an industrial nation, and ensuring that the entire country steadily moved towards socialism via new democracy.

OUT WITH THE OLD AND IN WITH THE NEW IN EDUCATION, SCIENCE, CULTURE AND PUBLIC HEALTH

With the upsurge of economic construction, a flurry of cultural construction also began. There were corresponding developments in other aspects of construction.

The cultural construction was to adapt to and promote political change, and to adapt and promote economic construction. To build a national, scientific and popular culture, the CPC led systematic reform of old-school education, and social and cultural undertakings, encouraging all patriotic intellectuals to serve the people.

To control public opinion tools and establish the guiding position of Marxism throughout the country, the CPC and the Central Government placed cultural undertakings such as newspapers, publications, radio stations and news agencies under their unified leadership while taking control of the cities. They were essential tools for publicity and mass communication. The first to the third volumes of the *Selected Works of Mao Zedong* were published from 1951 to 1953, the *Collected Works of Lenin* in 1955, and the *Collected Works of Marx and Engels* in 1956 to help systematically study and promote Marxism-Leninism and Mao Zedong Thought.

In terms of education reform, apart from implementing state leadership over schools, abolishing reactionary political education, and bringing Marxist-Leninist education into schools, there were also two main concerns. First, considering that few working people had access to education in the old society, the CPC and the government formulated an education policy of making 'education serve production and construction, and service workers and peasants, and making schools open to workers and peasants'. The second was to develop and reform higher education. From the end of 1951 to 1953, the Ministry of Education adjusted colleges and universities across the country, significantly increasing enrolment to adapt to the urgent need for professional talent in industrialisation.

In terms of literature and art, the CPC and the government continued to advocate the concept of literature and art serving the people, which included workers, peasants and soldiers. They also put forward the policy of 'letting a hundred flowers blossom, and weeding through the old and bringing forth the new'. The policy pointed out the direction for the prosperity of China's literature and art. Most literary and art workers immersed themselves in social life and created many excellent works of literature and art with revolutionary war and social transformation as their themes. Their works aroused people's political consciousness and the people's enthusiasm for labour.

In terms of scientific work, the CPC and government attached great importance to the critical role of science and technology in construction. The Chinese Academy of Sciences was established at the beginning of new China. The Central Government required that the Chinese Academy of Sciences be used as the national scientific research centre to guide the establishment of local scientific research institutions and simultaneously develop scientific research institutions in universities and industry sectors to gradually form a relatively complete scientific research system. By the end of 1955, China boasted over 400,000 scientific and technical personnel and more than 800 professional scientific research institutes. This contingent played an important role in various areas of development in the country.

In terms of medical and health work, the CPC and the government put forward the guidelines that healthcare should be 'oriented toward workers, peasants and soldiers', focused on 'prevention first', and 'unite Chinese medicine and Western medicine'. Grassroots health organisations and various professional epidemic prevention agencies and teams were established in rural areas, urban neighbourhoods, and in industrial and mining enterprises. At the same time, a large-scale patriotic sanitation campaign was carried out across the country, which greatly improved the backward sanitary conditions in urban and rural areas.

The ideological transformation of intellectuals was an essential condition for China to thoroughly realise all aspects of democratic reform and to gradually realise industrialisation. To give play to their active role in national construction, the CPC attached great importance to unifying, educating and reforming intellectuals. In September 1951, 12 famous Peking University professors responded to the party's call and initiated a political study campaign for Peking University faculty members. Universities in Beijing and Tianjin immediately launched a relatively focused study campaign for ideological transformation. On 29 September of the same year, Zhou Enlai gave a report on *Issues Regarding the Transformation of Intellectuals* to the Beijing and Tianjin University Teachers' Learning Association, encouraging all patriotic intellectuals to try their best to side with the people and the working class. Later, the learning movement gradually expanded to the entire intellectual circle. By studying Mao Zedong's works and carrying out criticism and self-criticism through linking their thoughts to their work practices, most intellectuals criticised the bourgeois and petty-bourgeois ideology by eradicating the influence of feudal comprador ideas. Eventually, they mastered the basic knowledge of Marxism, shifted their standpoint to that of the people, and devoted themselves enthusiastically to new China's construction.

MODERNISATION OF THE ARMY AND NATIONAL DEFENCE

Establishing a solid and modern national defence and building a powerful, regularised and modernised revolutionary army was an important task put forward by the CPC after the founding of new China. Especially after the War to Resist the US and Aid Korea, the CMC systematically summed up the experience of fighting with highly modernised US forces, promoted the PLA's adaptation to the requirements of modern warfare, and gradually implemented a strategic shift from a single service to a combined force of different arms.

A unified command, system, organisation, discipline, and training and close coordination among the services and arms are important conditions indispensable for building a modern national defence. Following the CMC's instructions, the PLA was remarkably streamlined and reorganised. Meanwhile, adjustments were made to the organisation and establishment of the army's leading organs. Based on the original army, the leading agencies and services of the air force, navy, air defence and public security were established. So were the leading agencies and service branches of artillery and armoured force. The PLA developed into an army with a relatively complete range of services.

The CPC's leadership of the army had to be strengthened to build a regular and modern revolutionary army. In April 1954, the Central Committee of the CPC and the CMC promulgated the *PLA Political Work Regulations (Draft)*. It was of great significance to ensure the party's absolute leadership over the army and give play to the PLA as a strong pillar of the consolidation of the people's democratic dictatorship.

In August 1953, the Politburo of the CPC Central Committee approved the first five-year plan's construction arrangements for national defence to strengthen the national defence industry's construction and improve the PLA's weaponry modernisation. In January 1955, the Central Committee of the CPC and Mao Zedong decided to develop atomic energy and atomic bombs. Mao Zedong said, "If we do not want to be bullied by others in today's world, we must have atomic bombs." History has proved that focusing on cutting-edge technology was a far-sighted and courageous strategic decision for China. The development of national defence science and technology and national defence modernisation are of great and far-reaching significance.

The CMC's enlarged meeting convened in March 1956 clarified the strategic policy of active defence for the first time, based on the assessment of the general tendency of the eased international situation while imperialist wars were still possible. The policy pointed out the direction for the

PLA to carry out combat readiness tasks and conduct military training, which led to a new stage of normalising the army and modernising national defence.

STRIVE FOR A PEACEFUL INTERNATIONAL ENVIRONMENT CONDUCIVE TO CONSTRUCTION

To create a favourable peaceful international environment for domestic construction, the CPC required vigorous work and struggle in diplomacy. To develop relations with emerging independent countries, especially those neighbouring China, in December 1953, the Chinese government first proposed the *Five Principles of Peaceful Coexistence* in the negotiations with India on the problems between the two countries, especially the relationship between India and the Chinese region of Tibet. The *Five Principles of Peaceful Coexistence* were later defined as mutual respect for sovereignty and territorial integrity, mutual non-aggression, non-interference in each other's internal affairs, equality and mutual benefit, and peaceful coexistence. It was of great strategic significance and a powerful weapon for new China to carry out activities on the international stage, break through the US's policies of isolation and containment, and expand foreign exchanges. It has not only become the cornerstone of China's foreign policy but also gradually been generally accepted in the international community. It has made historic contributions to promoting a fair and reasonable new type of international relations.

Tensions in Asia eased after the armistice in North Korea. However, the US not only did not want to withdraw its troops from the Korean peninsula and resolve the Korean issue peacefully, but its naval fleet continued to be entrenched in the Taiwan Strait, interfering in China's internal affairs and trying to contain China from the Indochina region. This practice of maintaining international tensions was unpopular. In April 1954, the foreign ministers of China, the US, the Soviet Union, the UK, France and related countries participated in a conference to discuss the North Korean and Indochina issues in Geneva, Switzerland. It was the first time that the PRC had participated in an important meeting to discuss international issues as one of the five major countries. During the meeting, the Chinese delegation led by Zhou Enlai conducted outstanding diplomatic mediation, prompting the conference to reach the accords to restore peace in Indochina, with France withdrawing its troops from Vietnam, Laos and Cambodia, and confirming the three countries' national independence. The Geneva Conference's success further eased the Asian and international situation, and enhanced China's security on its southern border.

In April 1955, Zhou Enlai led a Chinese delegation to attend the Asian-African Conference held in Bandung, Indonesia

In the context of the upsurge of national liberation movements in Asia and Africa, the heads of 29 Asian and African countries' governments held a meeting in Bandung, Indonesia, in April 1955. Zhou Enlai led a Chinese delegation to attend the meeting. He put forward the policy of "seeking common ground while reserving differences," calling on all countries to put aside their differences and strengthen unity and cooperation for the common interests of opposing colonialism. The policy, endorsed by the participating countries, opened the door to extensive exchanges between China and the countries in Asia and Africa. The *Final Communiqué of the Asian-African Conference* adopted at the conference assimilated the Chinese delegation's suggestions and formed the 10 principles for peaceful coexistence and friendly cooperation. The conference was a complete success. During the meeting, Zhou Enlai also issued a statement to the effect that: The Chinese government was willing to sit down and negotiate with the US government to discuss easing tensions in the Far East, especially easing tensions in the Taiwan region. China and the US began talks at ambassadorial level in August 1955.

This fruitful diplomatic work and the associated struggles promoted the easing of international tensions, expanded China's international ties, demonstrated its important role in international affairs, and won a more favourable, peaceful global environment for China's socialist construction.

STRENGTHENING THE PARTY'S SELF-CONSTRUCTION AFTER ITS ACCESSION TO POWER OVER THE WHOLE COUNTRY

After the founding of new China, the CPC attached great importance to the party organisation's construction under the circumstances of its assumption of leadership and governance. Unhealthy trends of arrogance, complacency, bureaucratism and bossiness arose among some CPC members after its victory in the Chinese revolution. In response, the CPC Central Committee issued the *Instructions on Carrying out the Rectification Movement in the Whole Party and the Whole Army*, requiring strict rectification of the party culture, particularly party officials' conduct.

In March and April 1951, the Central Committee of the CPC convened the first national organisation work conference and decided to conduct a general rectification of the CPC's grassroots organisations and start an education campaign among all party members on the eight conditions required of CPC members, especially education on the future of socialism and communism. On this basis, each party member was carefully reviewed and registered. Party members who had made serious mistakes or proved unqualified for party membership were disciplined by the party. Party rectification began in the second half of 1951 and ended in the spring of 1954. After party rectification, 410,000 people were expelled from the party or advised to quit, enhancing the CPC organisation's purity. At the same time, party organisations at all levels actively and cautiously recruited new party members. The number of party members increased from 5.8 million before party rectification to more than 6.369 million. The party ended up by adding a lot of new blood.

In February 1954, the Fourth Plenary Session of the Seventh Central Committee of the CPC passed the *Resolution on Strengthening Party Unity*. The resolution emphasised that party unity is the party's lifeblood and required that the whole party, especially its leading officials, enhance their consciousness of maintaining party unity. In March 1955, the CPC National Congress established the party's central and local supervisory commissions and formed the Central Supervisory Commission through an election.

In general, in the early days of new China's establishment, the whole party's mental outlook was relatively good. It continued to work and fight arduously, and maintained close ties with grassroots Chinese people, as it had done during the revolutionary war period. The complete unity of the CPC Central Committee formed since the Yan'an Rectification Movement and the CPC's Seventh National Congress remained as it had been under the conditions of it being a ruling party throughout the country. A strong and united party acting in unison and striving for the party's correct goals was the most important guarantee for the smooth progress of new China in its early days.

4
THE CPC'S GENERAL LINE DURING THE TRANSITION PERIOD AND THE BEGINNING OF PLANNED LARGE-SCALE ECONOMIC CONSTRUCTION

THE CPC'S INTRODUCTION OF THE GENERAL LINE DURING THE TRANSITIONAL PERIOD

After restoring the national economy, China's development faced a new situation and many new issues. While leading the Chinese people onward, the CPC needed to put forward new tasks and goals.

At the end of 1952, land reform was completed and restoration of the national economy was a success. The two sides in the Korean armistice negotiations had reached agreement on the main issues, and the war was expected to end soon. It meant that China had the conditions to carry out large-scale economic construction in a planned way. The CPC swiftly decided to implement its first five-year plan to develop the national economy beginning from 1953. The programme's main thrust was the country's industrialisation, a long-cherished goal of the Chinese people for hundreds of years and the key to changing China's backwardness and achieving prosperity. Now, the Chinese people were finally able to take a big step forward on the road of industrialisation.

At the same time, some new and accumulated contradictions also appeared in China's social life.

In rural areas, after the land reform, the farmers' scattered and backward individual economies could not meet the growing demand for food and agricultural raw materials in urban and industrial development. The emergence of the gap between the rich and the poor alerted the CPC and the government to polarisation. In the cities, the restriction and anti-restriction struggles between the working class and the bourgeoisie rose and fell from time to time, significantly impacting the country's economic life. This situation prompted the CPC to consider stepping up and expanding the mutual aid and cooperative movement in rural areas and restricting capital in the cities. In this way, a systematic socialist transformation of the national economy began to appear on the agenda.

It was against this background that after nearly a year of deliberation, the Party Central Committee formed and proposed the party's general line for the transition period, which was that, 'it was a transition period from the founding of the PRC to the completion of socialist transformation. During this transitional period, the party's general line and general task was to gradually realise China's socialist industrialisation and realise the country's socialist transformation of agriculture, handicraft industry, and capitalist industry and commerce over a reasonably long period of time.' This general line clearly set the great task of building socialism among the people of the whole country. It was a major strategic step taken by the CPC at a critical moment in history. The realisation of socialism in China is the goal set by the CPC since its founding. But under the historical conditions of a semi-colonial and semi-feudal society, the completion of socialism had to be carried out in two steps: the anti-imperialist and anti-feudal new-democratic revolution had to succeed first before the transition to the socialist revolution could begin. When to transition to the socialist stage depended on specific conditions during the revolutionary practice.

After the founding of new China, with three years of practice under its belt, the CPC Central Committee believed that the time and conditions were ripe for formulating the party's general line during the transition period. It presented to the entire party and the people of the whole country the task of a gradual transition to socialism. The reasons were: first, there was a relatively strong and rapidly developing socialist state-owned economy, which had become an important material basis for the transition to socialism. Second, the CPC and the government had accumulated a lot of experience in the use and restriction of private industry and commerce, and had subjected them to preliminary reformation. Third, the CPC and the government had gained a lot of experience in developing mutual agricultural cooperation and cooperatives in rural areas after the land reform, which had become, in reality, the first step in the socialist transformation of individual agriculture. Fourth, from the international environment's perspective, capitalist countries were in a downturn, and socialist nations were full of vitality for upward development. That was also a factor that led the CPC to believe that it should initiate a gradual transition to socialism.

After the general line of the transition period was put forward, extensive and in-depth study, publicity and education campaigns were carried out throughout the party and the country. The campaigns quickly helped party members reach a consensus and gained the Chinese people's support. The general line became a new programme for uniting and mobilising all the Chinese to build a great socialist country with concerted efforts. The whole party and the people of the entire nation turned their attention to the task of socialist industrialisation. They were highly excited to embrace and throw themselves into the new upsurge of new China's large-scale, planned economic construction.

THE FIRST FIVE-YEAR PLAN AND THE START OF SOCIALIST INDUSTRIALISATION

Formulating a practical and feasible medium-term plan for developing the national economy was an important step in fulfilling the main task of industrialisation stipulated in the general line for the transition period.

The realisation of national industrialisation was the only way for the CPC to lead the Chinese people of all ethnic groups to achieve national independence and prosperity so that China could stand on its own among the world's nations. Mao Zedong said long ago, "Without industry, there would be no solid national defence, no people's welfare and no national prosperity." But in 1952, the starting point of China's industrialisation was still low. Modern industrial output value accounted for only 43.1% of the total output value of industry and agriculture. Heavy industry only accounted for 35.5% of the total industrial output value. The per capita output of many important industrial products was not only far behind the industrialised countries but also lower than newly independent countries like India. In 1954, Mao Zedong described it in a way that left a deep impression on people, "What can we make now? We can make tables, chairs, tea sets, grow grain and grind it into flour. We can also make paper. But we can't make a car, an aeroplane, a tank or a tractor." Especially going through the War to Resist the US and Aid Korea, during which China fought with the world's number-one power, the US, China felt it was more urgent to emerge from industrial backwardness. Considering the above-mentioned practical situation, the CPC Central Committee decided to give priority to the development of heavy industry. It prioritised the basic construction of heavy industry and the defence industry, especially those major projects that were decisive for the country and able to quickly strengthen the country's industrial base and defence capabilities.

As a major country that was economically and culturally backward, China could only take the socialist road to achieve industrialisation under the conditions of the people's democratic dictatorship based on the alliance of workers and peasants led by the working class. Only under the socialist system could China make the best use of the advantage of concentrating its strength to accomplish large undertakings and accelerate the country's industrialisation, and win genuine economic independence.

To prepare for constructing a planned economy, China started to work on the first five-year plan in 1951. During the formulation and implementation of the 'first five-year plan', China did an excellent job of handling several major relationships in the nation's economic construction. Handling the relations included: 1) exerting concerted efforts to develop heavy industry without neglecting agriculture and light industry, and achieving the goal by doing overall planning with due consideration for all concerned and making comprehensive arrangements; 2) scientifically laying out industrial centres by changing the unreasonable situation where most of China's industries were clustered in coastal areas; 3) according to the national strength, actively and steadily determining the average annual growth rate of industrial and agricultural production; 4) appropriately combining production with the improvement of people's lives; 5) aiming at foreign aid while focusing on self-reliance and carrying out construction based on China's domestic strength. These requirements had far-reaching guiding significance for China's subsequent economic development.

Economic construction started in 1953 nationwide in a planned way.

Both urban and rural residents participated in and supported the country's industrialisation quickly and enthusiastically. It was an era of burning passion. The infinite longing for industrialisation stimulated the zeal of workers, farmers and intellectuals for work like never before. "Devote every second to the creation of a socialist society" was a call vividly reflecting the spirit of the times and the enthusiasm for construction inspired by the goal of industrialisation. New China changed almost every day. Good news on the industrial construction front came frequently. In December 1953, Anshan Iron and Steel Company's three major projects: a large steel rolling mill, a seamless steel tube mill, and the No. 7 Ironmaking Furnace all held opening ceremonies to celebrate the start of operations. The construction of large-scale steel companies in Baotou and Wuhan began. On average, one abnormally large project either started or was completed every day. Many primary industrial sectors unavailable in old China were established one by one, and many industrial and mining enterprises were set up in the hinterland. China largely put an end to its traditional backwardness and irrational layout of heavy industries. In the previous five years, the achievements of industrial production far exceeded those of the old China in a hundred years. New China quickly stood up from the ruins, laying the foundation for establishing an independent and complete industrial system, and accumulating valuable experience for socialist construction.

In July 1956, China's first batch of domestically-produced vehicles, 'Jiefang' trucks, were successfully trial-produced at Changchun No. 1 Automobile Manufacturing Plant

5
BASIC COMPLETION OF SOCIALIST TRANSFORMATION AND THE ESTABLISHMENT OF THE SOCIALIST SYSTEM

THE FIRST SESSION OF THE FIRST NATIONAL PEOPLE'S CONGRESS AND THE CONSTITUTION OF THE PRC

With the beginning of the country's large-scale economic construction, strengthening its political and legal superstructure became a significant and urgent task in order to better serve the establishment of the socialist economic foundation. To this end, Mao Zedong presided over and devoted much of his energy to drafting new China's first constitution.

The First Session of the First National People's Congress (NPC) was convened in Beijing in September 1954. A significant contribution to the conference was the adoption of the *Constitution of the PRC* with unanimous approval. Socialist in nature, the constitution embodied the principles of people's democracy and socialism. In the form of a fundamental law, it confirmed the heroic struggle waged by the Chinese people over the past hundred years to oppose domestic and foreign enemies, and to fight for national independence, and people's freedom and happiness. It confirmed the historical changes in which the CPC led the Chinese people in winning the new democratic revolution so that the Chinese people began to hold state power. It established the political system for the Chinese people to exercise their rights as masters. It pointed out the correct path for continuing the struggle to develop a socialist society.

The constitution further established China's political system. It stipulated, "The PRC is a people's democratic country led by the working class and based on the alliance of workers and peasants." "All power in the PRC belongs to the people. The organs through which the people exercise power are the NPC and local people's congresses at all levels." "The NPC, local people's congresses at all levels, and other state organs all practice democratic centralism." The constitution also established the state system's structure: the NPC is the highest organ of state power; the State Council (the CPG) is the highest administrative organ of the state.

Delegates attending the First Session of the NPC walk into the venue

The congress elected Mao Zedong as chairman of the PRC and Zhu De as vice chairman. It elected Liu Shaoqi as chairman of the Standing Committee of the NPC and 13 people, including Soong Ch'ing-ling as vice chairman. It made Zhou Enlai premier of the State Council.

The NPC is China's fundamental political system. Its convening marked the establishment of the people's congress system. The implementation of the people's congress system in China is the Chinese people's marvellous creation in the history of the human political system. It is the conclusion drawn from summarising the painful lessons of Chinese political life since modern times. It is the historical result of more than a hundred years of radical changes and turbulent development in Chinese society. It is the inevitable choice made by the Chinese people to stand up and take control of their destiny. The establishment of a new type of political system in which the people are the masters in a country like China with more than 5,000 years of civilisation and a population of hundreds of millions, is of epoch-making significance in the history of Chinese political development and in the history of world political development.

The system of multi-party cooperation and political consultation under the CPC's leadership is a fundamental political system in China and a new type of party political system grown from Chinese soil. The *Constitution of the PRC* clearly states, 'In the great struggle to establish the PRC, the Chinese people have formed a broad people's democratic united front of all democratic classes, all democratic parties and all people's organisations led by the CPC.' 'The Chinese People's Democratic United Front will continue to play its role' in the future. After the First Session of the First NPC, the CPPCC's task of carrying out the NPC's functions and powers came to an end. In December 1954, the CPPCC held the Second National Committee's first meeting. It passed the *Articles of the CPPCC*, affirming that the people's political cooperation organisation as the people's democratic united front still needed to exist. The meeting clarified the nature, status, role and tasks of the CPPCC after the NPC and the relationship between the CPPCC, the NPC and the government. It further consolidated the people's democratic united front and laid the foundation for China's long-term adherence to the basic political system of multi-party cooperation and political consultation under the CPC's leadership.

An important content of the *Constitution of the PRC* is to establish the relationship of equality, friendship and mutual assistance among all ethnic groups in China as the fundamental law, and to protect the autonomous rights of all ethnic minorities. The constitution stipulates, "The PRC is a unified multi-ethnic country." "Regional autonomy is practised in areas where ethnic minorities live in concentrated communities. All ethnic autonomous regions are inseparable parts of the PRC."

The system of regional ethnic autonomy is a basic political system in our country. It is an essential part of the correct way to solve ethnic problems with Chinese characteristics. It is a significant creation of the CPC to use Marxist ethnic theory to solve Chinese ethnic issues based on the characteristics of Chinese history and reality. In September 1949, the *Common Programme of the CPPCC* determined the implementation of regional ethnic autonomy. In August 1952, the CPG promulgated and enforced the *Implementation Programme for Regional Ethnic Autonomy of the PRC*. The constitution of 1954 standardised ethnic autonomous areas into three levels: autonomous regions, autonomous prefectures and autonomous counties, and ethnic minority areas below the county level set up ethnic townships. The implementation of the system of regional ethnic autonomy is of tremendous and long-term significance for China to maintain the integrity and unity of the country and to promote the unity, mutual assistance and development of all ethnic groups under any complicated international and domestic circumstances.

The fundamental political system of the NPC, the CPC-led multi-party cooperation and political consultation, and the basic political system of regional ethnic autonomy constitute China's socialist political system. It provides a political guarantee for China to establish a socialist economic foundation and relevant economic system.

SOCIALIST TRANSFORMATION OF PRIVATE OWNERSHIP OF THE MEANS OF PRODUCTION AND THE ESTABLISHMENT OF A SOCIALIST ECONOMIC SYSTEM

The socialist transformation of agriculture, handicraft industry, and capitalist industry and commerce also pressed on step by step with the implementation of the first five-year construction plan and the start of socialist industrialisation, and with the proposition and publication of the *CPC's General Line on the Transition Period*.

The socialist transformation of agriculture had started before the general line for the transition period was proposed. In September 1951, the CPC Central Committee formulated the *Resolution on Mutual Aid and Cooperation in Agricultural Production (Draft)*. It emphasised that the mutual aid and cooperative movement had to adopt a policy of steady progress in accordance with the needs and possibilities of production. It had to implement the principles of voluntariness and mutual benefit, adopt model operations to demonstrate new work practices[1], and gradually promote methods and guide farmers to take the road of mutual aid and cooperation. It is necessary to implement the principles of voluntariness and mutual benefit, adopt model operations to demonstrate new work practices and gradual promotion methods, and guide farmers to follow mutual assistance and cooperation. After the promulgation of the general line of the transition period, the CPC Central Committee passed the *Resolution of the CPC Central Committee on the Development of Agricultural Production Cooperatives* in December 1953. The rural mutual aid and cooperative movement pressed on steadily under the guidance of these two resolutions. The initial stage of the agricultural cooperative movement was mainly to develop mutual aid groups for agricultural production. Emphasis shifted to developing agricultural production cooperatives after September 1953. After the large-scale economic construction began that year, the supply of agricultural produce fell short of demand, triggering sharp fluctuation of food prices. After repeatedly weighing up the pros and cons, the CPC Central Committee decided on a state monopoly of grain purchase and marketing in October 1953. A state monopoly over purchasing and marketing of oil crops and edible oil soon followed. The state monopolised the purchasing and marketing of cotton and cotton fabric in 1954. The centralised purchase and marketing of primary agricultural produce and products accelerated the pace of agricultural socialist transformation. The agricultural cooperative movement reached a climax after July 1955.

The agricultural cooperative movement was essentially healthy in the early stage. In 1953, there was some impetuous deviation, which was quickly corrected. The superiority and effectiveness of agricultural cooperation were obvious. Statistics at that time showed that more than 80% of cooperatives increased production and income, and mutual aid groups were generally better than individual farmers. Cooperatives were better than mutual aid groups. Therefore, the mutual aid and cooperative movement were welcomed by the vast number of poor farmers. Participation in cooperatives became a mass action. The establishment of agricultural cooperatives was basically completed by the end of 1956.

On 15 January 1956, at a meeting of more than 200,000 people from all walks of life in Beijing, the capital, to celebrate the victory of socialist transformation, representatives of the industrial and commercial sectors reported success to Mao Zedong

The transformation of capitalist industry and commerce was achieved through state capitalism. The state emphasised developing the primary and intermediate capitalist forms that prioritised processing orders. In 1954, it began to focus on developing public-private partnerships, a high-level form of state capitalism. Due to the rapid development of enterprise production after the formation of public-private joint ventures, most of the private equity dividends exceeded the profits made by the private partners when their enterprises were solely privately owned, prompting more capitalists to request to become partners of public-private joint ventures. At the end of 1954, the State Council decided to adopt the policy of 'unified planning with due consideration for all concerned, arrangement through specialised departments, and transformation by trade' to resolve the contradiction between public and private business entities. The transformation of private industry accelerated after adopting the method of big enterprises helping small ones of the same trade, and advanced enterprises demonstrating better ways of doing things for backward enterprises of the same trade. By the end of 1956, the socialist transformation of capitalist industry and commerce had basically been completed.

The socialist transformation of the individual handicraft industry generally went through three stages of handicraft production cooperative groups, handicraft supply and marketing production cooperatives, and handicraft production cooperatives. Measures were taken in accordance with local conditions and in the forms readily accepted by different handicrafts, from low to high, small to large, and simple to complex. The state adhered to the principle of voluntariness and mutual benefit, and strived to make cooperatives beneficial for producers, the state and consumers. By the end of 1956, the country had completed the process of establishing handicraft cooperatives.

In socialist transformation, the CPC created a series of gradual transition forms from elementary to advanced that were adapted to Chinese characteristics, enabling individual farmers, handicraftsmen and private industrialists to gradually change their old modes of production. Especially for capitalist industry and commerce, China created a unique 'buying out' method. The state did not pay a lump sum of money but allowed capitalists to continue to receive their due dividends from the enterprise for a considerable period. This 'redemption' method not only made it easier for capitalists to accept the transformation but also made private industry and commerce play a positive role in expanding production, stimulating circulation, retaining employment and increasing taxation. The CPC won over most of the national capitalists so that they could play a beneficial role in the socialist transformation, thereby successfully realising the peaceful redemption of the bourgeoisie once envisaged by Marx and Lenin. The CPC's practice provides a creative experience that has enriched and developed the Marxist theory of scientific socialism.

History has proved that the CPC's general line for the transition period was correct. However, in the latter stages of the transformation, there were shortcomings such as requirements for progress proved too rash, work that turned out too rough, changes that proved too fast and too simple, and imposition of uniformity in the form of means of production ownership and economic composition. Nevertheless, as an unprecedented and profound social change, the socialist transformation was completed while ensuring economic development and social stability, winning the Chinese people's support. Its achievements and impact were tremendous and far-reaching.

The socialist transformation was completed in 1956. China's socialist political and economic systems were both established, which meant the establishment of China's socialist system. China, a major country in the East with a quarter of the world's population, entered a socialist society under the CPC's leadership, thereby successfully achieving the most profound and remarkable social change in Chinese history. It was a great historic victory, which laid the fundamental political groundwork and institutional foundation for all the development and progress in contemporary China. From then on, the CPC's primary task was to lead the people of all ethnic groups across the country to vigorously develop social productivity based on the newly established socialist system and to strive for the country's prosperity and the people's happiness.

---

1. This refers to a time-honoured CPC practice of testing out a new work practice or method of operation by setting up model units to demonstrate how to do it and prove that it works before rolling out the practice countrywide. The Chinese have a succinct four-character phrase for this methodology – 典型示范 (*dianxingshifan*) – but there is no similarly elegant way of describing this in English.

Six

Exploration and Tortuous Development of Socialist Construction

On 15-27 September 1956, the Eighth National Congress of the CPC convened in Beijing. It was the first national congress held by the CPC since it came to power. In his opening speech, Mao Zedong stated that the task of the conference was, "to sum up the experience since the Seventh National Conference of the CPC, to unite the whole party and all possible forces that can be united at home and abroad, and to strive to build a great socialist China." He said with confidence, "The power of the liberated Chinese people is endless." "We will definitely be able to build our country into a great socialist industrialised country step by step." People eagerly felt that a new era of comprehensive, large-scale socialist construction had begun in Chinese history.

1
THE EIGHTH NATIONAL CONGRESS OF THE CPC AND A GOOD START FOR CHINA'S SOCIALIST CONSTRUCTION

'TEN MAJOR RELATIONS' AND A SERIES OF NEW POLICIES

The year 1956 was recorded in the annals of the CPC as the basic completion of the socialist transformation of the private ownership of the means of production and the establishment of the socialist system in China. At the same time, it was recorded in the party's annals as the beginning of exploring the Chinese road of building socialism.

How to build socialism in China was a brand-new subject the CPC faced after it came to power. In the beginning, it learned from the Soviet experience. But through practice, the CPC quickly realised the limitations of the Soviet model and recognised some of its shortcomings and mistakes in building socialism. After careful consideration, Mao Zedong proposed to learn from the experience and lessons of the Soviet Union and independently explore the path of socialist construction that suited China's national conditions. The convening of the Eighth National Congress of the CPC marked the party's initial exploration of China's road of socialist construction. The proposal of *On the Ten Major Relations* was the beginning of this exploration.

To prepare for the Eighth National Congress of the CPC and get ready to embrace large-scale economic construction, from the end of 1955 to the spring of 1956, Mao Zedong and other central leaders conducted many thorough and systematic investigations and studies. From February to April of 1956, Mao Zedong listened to reports from 35 ministries and commissions of the State Council on industrial production and economic work, and gradually formed a series of views with guiding significance for China's socialist construction. Mao Zedong clearly stated, "The most important thing is to think independently and integrate the basic principles of Marxism-Leninism with the concrete reality of China's revolution and construction. During the Democratic Revolution, we succeeded in achieving this combination and winning victory in the New Democratic Revolution after suffering a great loss. Now that we are in the period of socialist revolution and construction, we must carry out the second combination to find out how to build socialism in China." At an enlarged meeting of the Politburo of the CPC Central Committee on 25 April, he gave a speech entitled *On the Ten Major Relations* and gave a report to the Supreme State Council on 2 May.

Mao Zedong giving his report On Ten Major Relations *at the Supreme State Council*

The basic policy put forward in *On the Ten Major Relations* was, "We must work hard to mobilise all positive factors, directly and indirectly positive, inside and outside the party, at home and abroad, to build our country into a strong socialist country." It was Mao Zedong's fundamental guiding ideology on how to build socialism. Based on summarising the problems of China's economic construction and the experience of the Soviet Union, the report discussed ten issues, namely the 'ten major relations'.

The first five of the 'Ten Major Relations' mainly discussed economic issues, mobilising various positive factors from all aspects of economic work. The first three 'relations' were between heavy industry, light industry and agriculture; between coastal and inland industries; and between economic construction and national defence. The report emphasised that more attention should be paid to the development of agriculture and light industry in the future. It also suggested that more effort be exerted to utilise and develop coastal industries, reduce the proportion of military and administrative expenses as much as possible, and engage in more economic construction. What was involved here was to open a road to Chinese industrialisation that differed from that of the Soviet Union. The fourth and fifth 'relations' were between the state, the production units and the individual producers, and between central and local governments. The two relations began to involve the reform of the economic system. They proposed arousing the enthusiasm of people from all walks of life and appropriately extending local governments' authority under the premise of consolidating the unified leadership of the central government.

The last five of the 'Ten Major Relations' were between politics, the Han and ethnic minorities, party and non-party, revolutionary and counter-revolutionary, right and wrong, and China and foreign countries. These are all issues concerning the mobilisation of various positive factors in political life, and ideological and cultural life. The report proposed the policy of 'long-term coexistence and mutual supervision' in the relations between the CPC and democratic parties, confirming that the united front and multi-party cooperation under the CPC's leadership must continue to exist and play a role. We must learn advanced science and technology, and enterprise management methods from capitalist countries in the relations between China and foreign countries. But we must also resist and criticise all corrupt systems and ideological bourgeois styles.

On the Ten Major Relations initially put forward several new policies for China's socialist economic and political construction. The report noted that the CPC had gained a new and important understanding of how to build socialism. It was pertinent and provided theoretical guidance for socialist construction at that time and in the future. Mao Zedong said on many occasions, "We mainly borrowed from foreign experience in our economic construction in the past few years. *On the Ten Major Relations* began to propose our own line for construction, and now we have established our own way of doing things."

Before and after that, the CPC also put forward a series of new policies in other areas according to the new situation at home and abroad, and the new national construction tasks. In January 1956, the central government held a meeting on intellectuals. In his report, Zhou Enlai fully affirmed the status and role of intellectuals in socialist construction. He believed that most of them "are already part of the working class" and issued a mobilisation order to "advance to modern science." After the meeting, the State

Council established the Scientific Planning Committee to formulate the *Outline of the 1956-1967 Scientific and Technological Development Vision Plan*.

To promote and develop socialist scientific and cultural undertakings, the CPC Central Committee put forward the 'Double Hundred' policy of "letting a hundred flowers blossom and a hundred schools of thought contend". Around 1956, the CPC also proposed peaceful liberation of Taiwan and advocated that the CPC and KMT should realise a third round of cooperation for the benefit of the nation and the motherland.

The proposal of *On the Ten Major Relations* and a series of new policies vividly showed how the CPC tried to emancipate the mind and explore many ways to find a path of socialist construction adaptable to Chinese conditions. The proposal made necessary ideological and theoretical preparations for the Eighth National Congress of the CPC.

EIGHTH NATIONAL CONGRESS OF THE CPC

From 15 to 27 September 1956, the Eighth National Congress of the CPC convened in Beijing. Mao Zedong made the opening speech, Liu Shaoqi gave a political report, Zhou Enlai reported on the recommendations of the second five-year plan for developing the national economy, and Deng Xiaoping made a report on the revision of the CPC constitution.

The Eighth National Congress of the CPC correctly analysed the changes in the domestic situation and major domestic contradictions, and clearly put forward the main tasks for the CPC and the people of the whole country under the new situation. The congress announced that the contradiction between the proletariat and the bourgeoisie in China had been resolved, the history of the class exploitation system for thousands of years had ended, and the socialist social system had been established in China. The main domestic contradiction has been between the demand to build an advanced industrial country and the reality of being a backward agricultural country, between the people's demand for rapid economic and cultural development and the fact that the current state of the economy and culture cannot meet people's needs. Currently the principal task for the party and the people of the whole country is to concentrate our efforts on solving this contradiction, and to turn our country from a backward agricultural country into an advanced industrial country as soon as possible. The core viewpoint of these expositions is that under socialist conditions, the whole party must work together to develop the productive forces.

The congress adhered to the policy of opposing conservatism and premature development pointed out by the CPC, an economic construction policy of steadily advancing in overall balance. The congress confirmed the concept of 'Three Mainstays and Three Supplements', which means taking state and collective management, planned production and the national market as the mainstays, supplemented with self-employment, free production and the free market. It was a significant attempt to break through the Soviet planned economy model in theory and explore economic system reform. The congress put forward the strategic vision of building a complete industrial system in China within three five-year plans or a little longer, presenting a grand blueprint for developing socialism for the Chinese people.

The Eighth National Congress of the CPC in session

The new party constitution adopted by the Eighth National Congress of the CPC was the first party constitution formulated by the CPC after it came to power. Based on the characteristics of a ruling party, the new party constitution put forward the task of building a socialist society in an all-round way. The new party constitution made many new regulations to implement the party's fundamental principles of democratic centralism. It required that 'the party take effective measures to promote inner-party democracy'. Simultaneously, it emphasised that 'the party's democratic principles cannot deviate from its principle of centralism and that the party is a unified fighting organisation united by discipline that all party members must abide by'. The following was added to party members' obligations, 'maintaining and consolidating party unity' and 'being loyal and honest to the party'.

The First Plenary Session of the Eighth Central Committee of the CPC elected Mao Zedong as chairman of the CPC's Central Committee; Liu Shaoqi, Zhou Enlai, Zhu De and Chen Yun as vice-chairmen; and Deng Xiaoping as general secretary. The above six people constituted the Standing Committee of the Politburo of the CPC Central Committee.

The Eighth National Congress of the CPC announced the completion of the socialist revolution and the establishment of the socialist system. The congress's line was correct, and many new policies and ideas that the congress put forward were creative. This congress's exploration of China's socialist road, at a relatively high historical starting point, achieved preliminary results and had long-term significance for developing the cause of the party and the country.

To solve the remaining problems in the socialist transformation after the Eighth National Congress of the CPC, the central government adjusted economic relations following the principle of 'Three Mainstays and Three Supplements', made initial progress and produced some new ideas for invigorating the economy. At the same time, the CPC adjusted the internal relations of the rural collective economy and launched the gradual reform of streamlining administration and delegating power.

Marked by *On the Ten Major Relations* and the Eighth National Congress of the CPC, the party had made a good start exploring the road to socialist construction in China.

2
DIFFICULTIES IN EXPLORING THE SOCIALIST ROAD

PUTTING FORWARD THE THEORY OF CORRECT HANDLING OF CONTRADICTIONS AMONG THE PEOPLE, THE WHOLE CPC'S RECTIFICATION CAMPAIGN AND THE ANTI-RIGHTIST STRUGGLE

The 20th National Congress of the Communist Party of the Soviet Union convened in February 1956. Khrushchev made a secret report that negated Stalin, causing great shock and ideological confusion in the socialist camp. The international communist movement experienced major setbacks. The situation was a warning that if people could not correctly understand and handle the various contradictions in a socialist society, especially the contradictions among the people, the socialist system would be difficult to consolidate, and socialist construction would be difficult to carry out. In China, there were unstable situations such as a small number of ordinary people causing disturbances in some places due to the rapid completion of socialist transformation in addition to the lingering influence of rash progress in economic construction and the remaining bureaucratism and other problems among officials. The CPC Central Committee and Mao Zedong pondered the contradictions in a socialist society and put forward theories on correctly handling contradictions among the people.

In February 1957, Mao Zedong published *How to Deal with Contradictions Among the People* (later changed to *Problems on Correctly Handling Contradictions Among the People*) at the Supreme State Council. He pointed out that contradictions were universal, and socialist society was also full of contradictions. It is these contradictions that promote the continuous development of socialist society. The basic contradiction in a socialist society is still the contradiction between productivity and production relations, and the contradiction between economic foundation and superstructure. These contradictions could be continuously resolved through self-adjustment and improvement of the socialist system itself. This conclusion scientifically revealed the driving force for the development of socialist society for the first time and laid the theoretical foundation for subsequent socialist reforms.

Mao Zedong also pointed out that in a socialist society, there are two types of contradictions that are fundamentally different in nature: contradictions between ourselves and the enemy, and contradictions among the people. The former needed to be solved by compulsory and dictatorial methods. In contrast, the latter could only be solved by democratic, persuasive, educational methods and the 'unity-criticism-unity' approach. He raised correct handling of the contradictions among the people to the height of national political life. He emphasised that the large-scale turbulent mass class struggle in the revolutionary period had ended and that "our fundamental task has changed from liberating the productive forces to protecting and developing productivity under the new relations of production".

On the Correct Handling of Contradictions Among the People has groundbreaking significance in Marxist development history. Mao Zedong intensely studied socialist society's contradictions and formed a systematic theory about them. It enriched and developed the theory of scientific socialism and had long-term guiding significance for the party and the cause of socialist construction.

According to the spirit of the Eighth National Congress of the CPC and considering the emergence of new situations and problems both inside and outside the party, the CPC Central Committee decided to overcome bureaucratism, sectarianism and subjectivism and correctly handle contradictions among the people by launching the campaign to rectify the party's style. On 27 April 1957, the CPC Central Committee issued the *Instructions on the Rectification Campaign*. Mao Zedong later pointed out that the party hoped to achieve this goal through the rectification campaign, "to create a political atmosphere within the party in which we have both centralism and democracy, both discipline and freedom, and both unity of will and personal ease of mind and vitality." The broad masses of cadres, including many influential people outside the party, actively responded to the call. They put forward a lot of criticism and suggestions on the work of the party and the government, and the ideological style of party and government officials. Most of the opinions were pertinent, sincere and constructive, and greatly benefited the party's rectification and correction of its shortcomings and errors.

However, with the development of the rectification movement, many complicated situations emerged. A small number of people took the opportunity to attack the party and the nascent socialist system. They attacked the CPC leadership in the country's political life as "the party's world," demanded "taking turns to be in charge," and described the system of people's democratic dictatorship as the source of bureaucratism, sectarianism and subjectivism. This abnormal phenomenon caused the party to be on the alert.

In June, the central government demanded the organisation of forces to counter the rightists' offensive. It was necessary and correct to counterattack the offensive by a small number of rightists and to criticise the trend of thought of opposing the party's leadership and the socialist road. However, overestimating the class struggle's seriousness, the CPC treated many contradictions among the people as contradictions between the party and the enemy, and treated many ideological and comprehension issues as political issues, and severely expanded the anti-rightist struggle. This caused a setback for the party's good start in exploring the road of socialist construction in China and became an important lesson in the party's history.

THE 'GREAT LEAP FORWARD', PEOPLE'S COMMUNE MOVEMENT AND EFFORTS TO CORRECT THE 'LEFT'

To change poor and backward China to a better nation as soon as possible, the CPC tried to open new ground in exploring the path of socialist construction. A tendency toward rushing progress in China's economic construction had already become apparent at the beginning of 1956. With the rapid growth of production in some factories and rural areas in 1957, the Chinese people's enthusiasm for building socialism increased remarkably. The CPC believed that it could speed up economic construction. Internationally, the CPC gained a high reputation at the Moscow Congress of Communist and Workers' Parties in November 1957. Meanwhile, the Soviet Union successfully launched the first artificial earth satellite and proposed catching up with and surpassing the US in 15 years. All this greatly encouraged socialists all over the world, including China.

In the winter of 1957, China's agricultural production reached new heights, primarily by building water conservancy projects, raising pigs to stock up manure and improving soil, which was the prelude to the 'Great

Leap Forward'. In May 1958, the Second Session of the Eighth National Congress of the CPC passed the general line of "building socialism with greater, faster, better and more economic results". It might have reflected the general desire of the party and the broad masses of the people to urgently change China's situation of economic and cultural backwardness. But it violated the objective laws that must be followed in economic construction. After the session, the CPC launched an all-round 'Great Leap Forward' campaign across China. It proposed the slogan, "Take grain as the key link and ensure all-round development" and required that the country reach the stipulated food production target in three to five years, or even one or two years, which triggered a severe trend of exaggeration. It also proposed the slogan "Take steel as the key" in industry and required that China reach the goal of producing an otherwise 15-year output of steel a few years in advance to catch up with the UK in steel production, setting off the mass movement of 'backyard furnaces' across the country.

Simultaneously, as the 'Great Leap Forward' developed rapidly, the people's commune movement reached its climax in rural areas. The CPC Central Committee made the *Resolution on the Establishment of People's Communes in Rural Areas* in August 1958. Subsequently, China's rural areas were communised in just over a month. The people's communes established at the beginning of the 'Great Leap Forward' were characterised by 'one big, two public', meaning that the communes were firstly bigger, and secondly, had a higher degree of public ownership, than the cooperatives they superseded. It was, in reality, the so-called 'communist wind' of egalitarianism and appropriation without compensation of the property and labour force of production teams and commune members which seriously harmed the peasants' enthusiasm for production.

It was the urgent desire of the whole party and the people of the entire country to do their utmost to speed up socialist construction so as to gain more initiative. However, the results turned out to be counterproductive because the CPC lacked experience in large-scale socialist construction, deviated from the principle of seeking truth from facts that it had always advocated, and acted based on subjective wishes and will.

During the autumn and winter of 1958, the CPC Central Committee discovered that many things had gone wrong with the 'Great Leap Forward' and the people's commune movement. From the CPC's first Zhengzhou Conference in November 1958 until the early days of the Lushan Conference in July 1959, the CPC Central Committee's leadership rectified malpractices with the people's communes and adjusted the unreasonably high quotas. Through these efforts, the CPC initially contained 'leftist' errors, such as the 'communist wind', the trend of exaggeration, unrealistically high targets, and arbitrary and impracticable directions, which thereby started to improve the situation somewhat. During this period, the CPC Central Committee and Mao Zedong gained some new understanding of the laws of socialist construction. That mainly included: production relations had to be suited to the nature of the production forces; the law of value was a great school and must be used to serve socialism; socialist construction must be carried out in the order of 'agriculture, light industry and heavy industry'; overall balance was vital to managing the entire economy, and the national economy had to develop in a planned and proportionate manner. Understanding these issues was an important reason for the initial results in correcting the 'leftist' trend and the significant results achieved by the CPC in its exploration of China's socialist construction path. However, the correction of 'leftism' was done under the premise of affirming the 'Great Leap Forward" and the people's communes. Therefore, the initial positive results had yet to be consolidated. As the ensuing 'anti-rightist' struggle interrupted the process of correcting 'leftism', coupled with natural disasters and the Soviet Union's perfidious act of tearing up aid contracts, the CPC and the Chinese people were confronted with severe economic difficulties unprecedented since the founding of new China.

NATIONAL ECONOMIC ADJUSTMENT AND THE 'FOUR MODERNISATIONS' STRATEGIC GOALS

Up against severe economic difficulties, the CPC Central Committee and Mao Zedong were determined to conduct serious investigations, correct mistakes, and adjust policies. In November 1960, the CPC Central Committee issued the *Emergency Instruction Letter on Current Policy Issues Among the Rural People's Communes*, requesting that the entire party exert its utmost efforts to resolutely rectify the 'communist wind'. In January 1961, the Ninth Plenary Session of the Eighth Central Committee of the CPC decided to implement the policy of 'adjusting, consolidating, enriching, and improving' the national economy. These two events ended the 'Great Leap Forward' campaign. The national economy began to get on a new track of adjustment.

At the Ninth Plenary Session of the Eighth Central Committee and at the Central Work Conference held in preparation for this plenary session, Mao Zedong called on the whole party to resume the style of seeking truth from facts and investigation. After that, national leaders such as Mao Zedong, Liu Shaoqi, Zhou Enlai, Zhu De, Chen Yun and Deng Xiaoping took the lead in conducting in-depth investigation and research at grassroots level. In March 1961, Mao Zedong presided over drafting the *Draft Regulations Governing Rural People's Communes* (known as the *Sixty Agricultural Items*) to systematically solve the problems existing in the rural people's communes. During the drafting and revision of the regulations, the whole party's understanding continued to deepen and it began to solve the problems with public canteens vehemently opposed by the farmers.

The CPC encouraged the conduct of investigation and research, thereby providing a crucial ideological basis for adjustments in various fields. The CPC centred the industrial sector's adjustments on reducing steel output and other indicators, and rectifying order in enterprises. In September 1961, the central government issued the *Instructions on Current Industrial Issues*, emphasising that China must act decisively to lower industrial production and infrastructure construction indicators to a reliable level, allowing a little wiggle room. Simultaneously, the central government issued trial *Regulations on the Work of State-Owned Industrial Enterprises (Draft)* (also known as the *Seventy Industrial Articles*), which played an active role in restoring and establishing the normal production order of enterprises.

At the Ninth Plenary Session of the Eighth Central Committee of the CPC, Mao Zedong called on the whole party to revitalise the party's style of investigation and research

In conjunction with economic adjustment, adjustments were also made in science, education and culture. The content of the adjustments was threefold: 1) to focus on the relationship between the party and intellectuals, and implement policies on intellectuals; 2) to adhere to the policy of 'letting a hundred flowers blossom and a hundred schools of thought contend'; and 3) to improve the necessary rules and regulations to restore normal order and ensure smooth progress in all aspects of work. To further arouse intellectuals' enthusiasm, Zhou Enlai gave his report *On the Issue of Intellectuals* in March 1962. It affirmed that most Chinese intellectuals were already classified as being working people, and emphasised that the party and government must make the best use of science and scientists in socialist construction.

To further sum up the experience and lessons since the 'Great Leap Forward', reach a common understanding, and strengthen party unity, the CPC held an enlarged Central Committee Work Conference (a 7,000-member conference) in Beijing from 11 January to 7 February 1962. On behalf of the CPC Central Committee, Liu Shaoqi summarised the experience and lessons of economic construction since the 'Great Leap Forward' and analysed the reasons for the shortcomings and errors in his draft written report. On 30 January, Mao Zedong delivered a speech at the conference and made self-criticism, emphasising that "we still have a lot of blindness in our socialist construction activity. We will work hard to conduct investigations and research to figure out the socialist economic laws in the future. It may take China more than a century to catch up with and surpass the world's most advanced capitalist countries."

This reflected the CPC Central Committee's and Mao Zedong's further understanding of the long-term nature of socialist construction. Deng Xiaoping and Zhou Enlai respectively represented the Secretariat of the CPC Central Committee and the State Council in conducting self-criticisms at the conference. They proposed the main methods of restoring the party's fine traditions and overcoming current difficulties.

The 7,000-member congress achieved significant results under the historical conditions of the time. The meeting failed to wipe away the 'Great Leap Forward' and 'anti-rightist' errors from the fundamental guiding ideology. But the more pragmatic attitude towards shortcomings and mistakes, and the spirit of promoting democracy and self-criticism inspired the whole party and strengthened its cohesion. Therefore, the conference played an active role in mobilising the entire party to unite in its struggle to overcome difficulties.

After the 7,000-member conference, the CPC and the central government took the following measures to adjust the national economy: 1) they vigorously reduced the number of employees and urban population; reduced the scale of capital construction, and suspended a large number of capital construction projects; 2) they shortened the industrial front, and took the necessary steps to suspend, merge or transfer industrial enterprises; and 3) they supported agriculture with human and material resources from all areas, and strengthened the leadership of the rural grassroots. As part of the agricultural policy adjustment, some places tried various agricultural production responsibility systems, including contracting production to households. These attempts achieved good results.

Mao Zedong, Liu Shaoqi, Zhou Enlai, Zhu De, Chen Yun, and Deng Xiaoping together at the 7,000-people meeting

After nearly two years of adjustments before and after the 7,000-member conference, various construction undertakings began to develop healthily, starting from the summer of 1963. By the end of 1965, the task of adjusting the national economy was fully completed. As a result, the gross value of industrial and agricultural production exceeded the highest level in history; the ratio between agriculture, light industry and heavy industry improved; the proportional relationship between accumulation and consumption returned to normal; fiscal revenue and expenditure was balanced; the market became stable; and people's living standards improved. The seriously difficult situation brought about by the 'Great Leap Forward' and 'People's Commune' movements, were improved by the arduous efforts of the party and the people.

When outstanding achievements were made in adjusting the national economy, the CPC put forward new goals in due course. At the end of 1964,

Zhou Enlai solemnly proposed the historical task of realising the 'Four Modernisations' at the first meeting of the Third National People's Congress: "in a not-too-long historical period, to build our country into a powerful socialist country with modern agriculture, modern industry, modern national defence, and modern science and technology; and to catch up with and exceed the world's advanced level." The central government also determined the strategic concept of realising the modernisations in two steps starting from the third five-year plan. The first step was to establish an independent and relatively complete industrial and national economic system after three five-year plan periods. The second step was to fully realise the modernisation of agriculture, industry, national defence, and science and technology so that China's economy would be at the forefront of the world. The 'Four Modernisations' have since become the common goal of the CPC and the people of all ethnic groups across the country, and a powerful uniting spiritual force for the Chinese people in their ongoing struggle.

ADHERE TO INDEPENDENCE AND OPPOSE HEGEMONISM

From the mid-1950s to the mid-1960s, the world situation was turbulent. In the Cold War dominated by the two superpowers of the US and the Soviet Union, China faced open and potential threats of aggression, war provocations, and military pressure on many fronts.

Maintaining independence and opposing hegemonism from all sides to safeguard national dignity and national interests was at the centre of the CPC's consideration of international relations.

From the late 1950s to the early 1960s, according to the development of the situation, Mao Zedong raised the issue of the 'middle zone' again, thinking that the middle zone had two parts: one part referred to the many economically backward countries in Asia, Africa and Latin America. The other part consisted of the imperialist countries represented by Europe and the developed capitalist countries. Both these parts opposed US control while the Eastern European countries were against the Soviet Union's dominance. Winning the support of the 'middle zone' and developing relations with Asian, African and Latin American countries became an essential part of China's foreign policy at that time. The establishment of diplomatic relations between China and France in 1964 was a major achievement in opening up the diplomatic situation between China and Western developed countries.

During this period, confrontation between China and the US revolved around US armed intervention in Taiwan, interference in China's internal affairs, and US armed aggression against Vietnam threatening China's security.

In August 1958, the CPC Central Committee and Mao Zedong raised the Taiwan issue by bombarding Kinmen. It dealt a heavy blow to the Chiang Kai-shek clique's arrogant clamouring to 'retake the Chinese Mainland' and the US attempt to engage in 'two Chinas'. It strongly demonstrated the Chinese people's position and determination to oppose US interference in China's internal affairs and safeguard national unity. The struggle against the US by aiding Vietnam that started in 1965 embodied the Chinese people's fearless spirit of opposing the threat of aggression and safeguarding world peace.

Since the late 1950s, the contradictions and conflicts between China and the Soviet Union had intensified daily. The Soviet Union's party regarded itself as the 'boss party' and demanded that the CPC bow to its Soviet-American cooperation strategy to dominate the world militarily and diplomatically. As Deng Xiaoping said, "The real substantive problem is inequality, and the Chinese feel humiliated." The CPC insisted on independence, resolutely withstood the tremendous pressure from the Soviet Union, and safeguarded national sovereignty, national dignity and the CPC's dignity.

THE ACHIEVEMENTS OF 10 YEARS OF SOCIALIST CONSTRUCTION AND THE ENTREPRENEURIAL SPIRIT OF HARD WORK, PLAIN LIVING AND GOING ALL-OUT FOR CHINA'S PROSPERITY

From 1956 to 1966, the decade of building socialism in an all-round way was a decade of the CPC's arduous exploration of China's path to socialist construction. Although it experienced twists and turns, it still achieved undeniably outstanding achievements. The design for the building of industry, scientific research, the development of cutting-edge technologies for national defence, the construction of irrigation and water conservancy projects, and agricultural mechanisation and modernisation all began in that era.

Compared with 1956, the national industrial fixed assets tripled from their original industrial construction prices. In terms of the iron and steel industry, and the further building of China's largest Anshan Iron and Steel Base, Wuhan and Baotou's two major inland iron and steel bases were mainly built in that decade. More than a dozen important sectors in the mechanical industry, including metallurgy, mining, power stations, petrochemical and other industrial equipment manufacturing, aircraft, automobile and engineering machinery manufacturing, were formed. China was able to independently design and manufacture some large-scale modern equipment. In 1964, the self-sufficiency rate of China's main machinery and equipment reached over 90%.

What was particularly prominent was that the petroleum industry had developed into a pillar industry in China's national economy during this period. After completing the construction of the Daqing Oilfield, the Shengli and Dagang oilfields were subsequently developed. By 1965, the country was totally self-sufficient in terms of its domestic petroleum needs, which enabled China to proudly announce that the era when the Chinese lived on 'foreign oil' was over!

The transportation industry developed rapidly. From 1958 to 1965, China added 9,000 kilometres of operational railways countrywide. The Yingtan-Xiamen, Baotou-Lanzhou, Lanzhou-Qinghai, Lanzhou-Xinjiang, Sichuan-Guizhou and Guizhou-Guangxi railways were completed and opened to traffic. Except for Tibet, all provinces, autonomous regions and municipalities directly under the central government were accessible by rail. Trains were available in Fujian, Ningxia, Qinghai and Xinjiang for the first time. Highways, water transportation and aviation also developed significantly.

Irrigation and water conservancy construction made outstanding achievements. The backbone projects of large hubs and various reservoirs played a vital role at that time and would play an essential part for a long time to come. Significant achievements were made in the development of science and technology. On 16 October 1964, China successfully detonated its first atomic bomb, effectively breaking the nuclear monopoly and blackmail by major powers, and enhanced China's international status. China also made breakthroughs in the development of guided missiles and artificial satellites. In terms of basic scientific research, China synthesised bovine insulin crystals in 1965, which was a world first.

China's achievements in education and healthcare were remarkable. From 1957 to 1966, nearly 1.4 million students graduated from higher education institutions, and 2.11 million from secondary and professional schools, respectively 4.9 times and 2.4 times more than from 1950 to 1956. There were great increases in the number of medical and health institutions, and the national urban and rural medical and health network had basically taken shape. Diseases such as smallpox, cholera, schistosomiasis, malaria and plague that seriously endangered people's health had been either exterminated, or effectively controlled. *"We ask the God of Plague, 'Where are you bound?' Flaming paper barges and candle-light illuminate the* sky." Mao Zedong wrote this line to express his admiration for the miracle of eliminating schistosomiasis in China.

Many outstanding literary and artistic works emerged, such as the novels *Song of Youth* and *History of Entrepreneurship*, movies and stage plays such as *The Red Detachment of Women* and *Sentinel Under the Neon Light*, and the opera *Sister Jiang*. The large-scale song-and-dance epic *The East Is Red* was a classic of this period.

The regions inhabited by ethnic minorities saw economic and cultural progress. Many large modern industrial bases were built in many places, ending the history of the absence of modern industries in ethnic minority areas. Several colleges and universities emerged in the regions and turned out a wide variety of specialised talent needed for local construction.

In the past decade, China trained much specialised talent needed to govern the CPC, the country and the army, and to work for the cause of socialist construction. The CPC strengthened its construction and increased its membership. The number of party members nationwide rose from 10.73 million in 1956 to 18.95 million in 1965.

As the *Resolution of Several Historical Questions for the CPC Since the Founding of the PRC* points out, 'the material and technical basis for modernising our

China successfully detonated its first atomic bomb on 16 October 1964

country was primarily established during that period. It was also mainly in the same period that the core personnel for our work in the economic, cultural and other spheres was trained and gained their experience. This was the principal aspect of the party's work in that period'. What makes the CPC and the Chinese people proud is that China also gained spiritually apart from the significant achievements in socialist construction made under the CPC's leadership through arduous exploration.

Chinese of all ethnic groups devoted themselves to the bustling socialist construction with great zeal. Meanwhile, many advanced models and heroes emerged. They changed the world with their poetic deeds and formed the spirit of the times, spanning time and space. The Daqing Oilfield workers represented by Wang Jinxi built China's largest oil base, the Daqing Oilfield, in only three years to eliminate China's 'oil-poor' label as soon as possible. They worked with the spirit of 'We'll work with all our might to build the big oil field even if our lives are shortened 20 years because of this.' They worked with the determination 'to go ahead regardless of whether conditions are favourable or not'. Their heroism forged the patriotic, enterprising, practical and devotional spirit dubbed the 'Daqing Spirit' or 'Iron Man Spirit', as Wang Jinxi enjoyed the nickname 'Iron ManWang '.

Jiao Yulu, secretary of the CPC Committee of Lankao County, Henan Province, led the people in controlling the sand, conserving the water and transforming the sand-covered land into fertile fields to help lift them out of poverty despite his chronic liver disease. With a 'selfless' and serving-the-people attitude, Jiao Yulu interpreted his people-loving, hardworking, truth-seeking, difficulty-braving and self-sacrificing 'Jiao Yulu Spirit' with his deeds. He vividly described it as, "I'll live in the sand, die in the sand and link my life with my county folk."

Under the county CPC committee's leadership, the people of Linxian County, Henan, spent 10 years boring 221 tunnels and building 152 aqueducts across myriad peaks and ridges in the Taihang Mountains to complete the 1,500-kilometre 'Artificial Tianhe' (river in the sky), the Red Flag Canal. Eighty-one people sacrificed their lives for the project. They created a world-changing legend of a generation of Chinese farmers with their heroism epitomised by their slogan, "We vow to transform the rivers and mountains with our lofty aspirations."

Lei Feng, a PLA soldier, was willing to be a screw in the machine of ordinary jobs. He was known for his selfless dedication and readiness to help others, demonstrating his lofty communist sentiment and becoming the most famous name of that era. He died on duty in August 1962 when he was only 22 years old. With Mao Zedong's inscription: 'Learn from Comrade Lei Feng', the 'Lei Feng Spirit' became a symbol of the social customs of new China.

In building new China, the successful development of the 'two bombs and one satellite' was an outstanding achievement of which the Chinese nation feels proud. Many scientists such as Qian Xuesen, Qian Sanqiang and Deng Jiaxian closely linked their ideals with the motherland's fate and the nation's rejuvenation. They are unsung heroes, "making world-shaking accomplishments while remaining anonymous." They sprinkled their blood, sweat and tears on the Gobi Desert and devoted their youth to constructing China's national defence. Their patriotic, selfless, self-reliant, hardworking, team-playing, and high-aiming 'two bombs and one satellite spirit' is forever etched on China's land and has become a valuable, inexhaustible source of aspiration and driving force for the Chinese people.

There were many more such heroes with their inspiring spirits admired by future generations of Chinese. This decade fraught with difficulties was an era of the Chinese people working hard to build the new China, and it was an era of heroes with lofty spirits. In order to create a prosperous and powerful new China, the Chinese people, who had become masters of the country, were racing against time and made a series of achievements like the brand-new and most gorgeous paintings added to the beauty of the motherland's landscape. With their actual deeds, the Chinese fought against difficulties and material temptations with a chivalrous spirit, which is the soul of a nation striving for perpetual survival. Only when a national spirit reaches a certain height can this nation be firm on its feet and move forward courageously in the torrent of history.

3
THE TORTUOUS DEVELOPMENT PATH OF SOCIALIST CONSTRUCTION

BREAKOUT OF THE 'CULTURAL REVOLUTION' AND DIFFICULTIES IN PROGRESS WITH EVERY ASPECT OF WORK

In 1966, just as China overcame serious difficulties in the national economy, completed the task of economic adjustment and began to implement the third five-year plan to develop the national economy, the 'Cultural Revolution' broke out.

Complicated international, domestic, social and historical reasons lay behind the breakout of the 'Cultural Revolution'. After the founding of new China, it had faced a severe external environment for a long time. Hostile imperialists had blockaded China for a long time and pinned their hopes of 'peaceful evolution' on China's third and fourth generations. The Soviet Union put tremendous pressure on China after the deterioration of Sino-Soviet relations. Such an external environment profoundly impacted the CPC's scientific judgment of the domestic political situation and the party's and the country's decisions on China's central tasks and policies. As the CPC quickly entered the historical stage of socialism after protracted and brutal wars, it lacked a scientific understanding of, and a sufficient mental preparedness for, how to build socialism in an economically and culturally backward country. Successful class struggle experience accumulated during past revolutionary wars made it easy for the CPC to follow and copy when observing and dealing with many new contradictions in socialist construction. Therefore, it was apt to treat non-class-struggle issues as class struggles and take class struggles that only existed in a certain scope as the principal contradictions in the entire country, and used a large-scale mass political movement to solve them.

In May 1966, the enlarged meeting of the Politburo of the CPC Central Committee passed the *16 May Notice*. It pointed out, "The representatives of the bourgeoisie who have wormed their way into the party, the government, the army and various cultural circles are a group of counter-revolutionary revisionists. Once the time is right, they will seize power and change from the dictatorship of the proletariat to the dictatorship of the bourgeoisie." In August, the 11th Plenary Session of the Eighth CPC Central Committee passed the *Decision of the CPC Central Committee on the Great Proletarian Cultural Revolution*, which stated that "the focus of this movement is to castigate those in power who are taking the capitalist road." The convening of these two meetings marked the full launch of the 'Cultural Revolution'. From then on, the Red Guard movement surged rapidly. Beginning in January 1967, the 'Cultural Revolution' entered the stage of "going all-out to seize power" and quickly developed into a severe situation of "overthrowing everyone and everything" and even starting a "full-scale civil war." Around February, the older generation of revolutionaries such as Tan Zhenlin, Chen Yi, Ye Jianying, Li Fuchun, Li Xiannian, Xu Xiangqian and Nie Rongzhen strongly criticised the erroneous practices of the 'Cultural Revolution' at various meetings. But their action was framed as the 'February Counter-Current' and was suppressed, with some of the participants personally attacked. By September 1968, revolutionary committees had been established countrywide which, to a certain extent, ended the anarchy in the early stages of the 'Cultural Revolution'. In October, under the circumstances of extremely abnormal intraparty political life, the enlarged 12th Plenary Session of the Eighth CPC National Congress announced that "The CPC has expelled Liu Shaoqi from the party for life and dismissed him from all his posts inside and outside the party." The CPC's Ninth National Congress convened in 1969. It further systematised and legitimised the theory and practice of the 'Cultural Revolution'. Between 1970 and 1971, the Lin Biao counter-revolutionary clique conspired to seize supreme power and instigated a counter-revolutionary armed coup, which objectively declared the failure of the theory and practice of the 'Cultural Revolution'. In 1972, Zhou Enlai proposed to criticise the ultra-left trend, significantly improving every aspect of work.

The 10th CPC National Congress held in August 1973 continued to affirm the political and organisational lines of the Ninth Congress. After the 10th National Congress, Jiang Qing formed the 'Gang of Four' with Wang Hongwen, Zhang Chunqiao and Yao Wenyuan to usurp the supreme power of the party and the country. In January 1975, the first meeting of the Fourth NPC reiterated the goal of realising the four modernisations, appointing Zhou Enlai as prime minister and Deng Xiaoping as first deputy prime minister. The appointments gave CPC officials and ordinary Chinese people hope amid repeated turmoil.

The primary consideration for launching the 'Cultural Revolution' was to prevent capitalism's restoration and seek China's own road to building socialism. As a ruling proletarian political party leader, Mao Zedong constantly observed and pondered the emerging socialist society's practical problems. He paid great attention to the party's consolidation and the people's power created with incredible difficulty. He was highly vigilant against the danger of capitalist restoration to overthrow the party and government. The phenomenon of corruption, privilege and bureaucratism in China must be continuously explored and fought unremittingly.

However, due to the unclear understanding of the law of a socialist society's development and the cumulative development of 'leftist' errors in theory and practice, many correct ideas on socialist construction failed to be implemented, which eventually led to civil unrest.

The 'Cultural Revolution' lasted for 10 years, causing the party, country and people of all ethnic groups to suffer the longest setback and the greatest loss with the most extensive scope since new China's founding. It significantly weakened the CPC organisation and state power, brutally persecuted many officials and ordinary Chinese, and arbitrarily trampled on China's democracy and legal system, plunging China into a serious political and social crisis. In no sense was the 'Cultural Revolution' a revolution nor did it represent social progress. It was civil turmoil wrongly initiated by the CPC leader and taken advantage of by counter-revolutionary cliques. It inflicted severe disasters on the party, the country and people of all ethnic groups, and left an exceedingly painful lesson.

During the 'Cultural Revolution', the party and the people never stopped fighting against 'leftist' errors. It was the resistance and struggle of the whole party and the broad masses of workers, peasants, PLA commanders and fighters, intellectuals and cadres at every level that restricted the destruction of the 'Cultural Revolution' to a certain extent. Socialist construction still made some progress in some critical areas. The 'Cultural Revolution' did not change the nature of the people's power, the people's army and Chinese society.

There is a difference between the 'Cultural Revolution' as a political movement and the 'Cultural Revolution' as a historical period. During this period, China's national economy experienced great ups and downs. But with their joint efforts, the party and the people made encouraging progress in various tasks despite difficulties. After 1969, as the domestic situation became more stable, leaders such as Zhou Enlai, who presided over the government routines, seized the opportunity to resume work in central industrial departments and other comprehensive economic sectors, and strengthened the economy's planning and management. The national economy rebounded in 1969, reversing the continuous decline in the previous two years. The construction in the inland strategic rear areas, where the national defence industry was concentrated, quickly began in an all-out way. Locally the 'five small industrial sectors', namely the small-scale iron and steel, machinery, chemical fertiliser, coal mining and cement industry sectors, also rapidly developed. By the end of the year, China had roughly achieved that year's economic quota and the 'third five-year plan' quota.

In 1971, China began to implement the 'fourth five-year plan'. Because factors such as contradictions in economic work and pursuit of high targets were ignored, the risk of economic construction increased. From 1972 to 1973, in accordance with Zhou Enlai's instructions, the State Council took various measures to adjust the national economy. In the second half of 1973, the economic situation improved significantly. China achieved and even exceeded the planned quota of the national economy. During this period, China included family-planning indicators into its national economic development plan for the first time and formulated the first comprehensive environment-protection document. It also successively imported a batch of technologically advanced complete sets of equipment and stand-alone machines from abroad, which played an essential role in promoting China's technological progress.

During this period, the achievements of the third-front construction were remarkable. In May and June of 1964, Mao Zedong divided the country into the first, second and third fronts, taking account of the strategic layout of economic construction and national defence construction. He raised the issue of building the third front, which soon began. From July 1970 to October 1973, the railway engineering corps' commanders and soldiers successfully built the Chengdu-Kunming, Hunan-Guizhou and Xiangyang-Chongqing railways, overcoming numerous difficulties under the extremely harsh conditions of inaccessible mountainous areas. Their construction changed Southwest China's situation of being beset by a long-term traffic barrier. Large-scale enterprises under construction and completion included such large-scale coal mines as Liupanshui in Guizhou and Baodingshan in Sichuan, and large and medium-sized hydropower stations such as Liujiaxia in Gansu, and Danjiangkou and Gezhouba in Hubei.

By the Jinsha River, the builders ate from 'pots set on tripodal-rock firepits' and slept in 'tents pitched in remote mountains'. They transported thousands of tonnes of large machinery with their manpower. Finally, they built the modern, large-scale Sichuan Panzhihua Steel Base, with workmanship compared to delicate ivory micro-sculpture. Third-front construction largely changed the unbalanced industrial layout of old China. The move of many top-notch military-industrial enterprises, state-owned enterprises (SOEs) and research institutes to West China provided the region with a rare opportunity for development.

China successively built several transport lines and oil pipelines, and completed the Nanjing Yangtze River Bridge in 1968. Designed and built by Chinese engineers, it was the largest road-rail bridge in China at that time. The transformed Baoji-Chengdu Railway became the first electrified railway in China. In 1974, China built the first long-distance oil pipeline from Daqing to Qinhuangdao.

Notable achievements were made in national defence, science and technology, and there were also breakthroughs in civilian science and technology. In October 1966, China successfully conducted a nuclear weapon delivery test for the first time. It also successfully detonated the first hydrogen bomb in June 1967. China successfully launched the Dongfanghong-1 artificial earth satellite in April 1970 and the first recoverable remote-sensing artificial earth satellite in November 1975. In terms of biotechnology, the China Academy of Traditional Chinese Medicine (TCM) successfully extracted a new type of antimalarial drug, artemisinin, in 1972, saving millions of lives globally, especially in developing countries. In 1973, China successfully cultivated the strong dominant *Indica* hybrid rice, another world first.

These significant achievements on the scientific and technological front, especially the achievements in cutting-edge defence technologies, enhanced China's comprehensive national strength, defence strategy and defence capabilities. The achievements also had great political significance. Deng Xiaoping said later, "Without the atomic bombs, hydrogen bombs and satellites we've had since the 1960s, China could not be called a major country with important influence. Neither would it have its current international status." Those were the achievements made by the CPC members, officials and the Chinese people at large in their concerted effort to overcome disturbance and interference.

BREAKING NEW GROUND FOR DIPLOMACY

After the founding of new China, the CPC adhered to a peaceful independent foreign policy.

In the beginning, the 'Cultural Revolution' disrupted Chinese diplomatic operations. In the early 1970s, the international situation had undergone significant changes more than two decades after the Second World War and a new global pattern was beginning to emerge. After many people in multiple areas worked hard for years, China's diplomatic work turned over a new leaf in the 1970s, ushering in a second flurry of activity to establish diplomatic relations after the PRC's founding.

The key to the change of the situation was the easing of relations between China and the US. The US wanted to minimise the impact of its defeat in the Vietnam War as soon as possible and continue to maintain global hegemony. To deal with the Soviet Union's challenge, the US urgently needed to improve its relations with China.

China needed to ease its relationship with the US because it needed to focus on dealing with the immediate and severe threat the Soviet Union posed to its security at that time. It also wanted to resolve the Taiwan issue to achieve the great cause of national reunification, resume and expand international exchanges, and actively participate in international affairs.

After taking office in 1969, President Richard Nixon expressed his intention to improve Sino-US relations. In April 1971, Mao Zedong agreed to invite the American table tennis team to visit China. This 'ping-pong diplomacy', using 'a small ball to turn around the big globe', so to speak, unexpectedly promoted Sino-US relations and brought about changes in the world situation. In July, Henry Kissinger, the US president's assistant for national security affairs, paid a secret visit to China, and the news shocked the world.

In February 1972, US President Nixon visited China. After talks, China and the US issued the *Sino-US Joint Communiqué* in Shanghai on 28 February, marking the beginning of the normalisation of their relations. On 25 October 1971, the 26th UN General Assembly passed *Resolution 2758* by an overwhelming majority, restoring all the PRC's legal rights in the UN, and immediately expelling the Taiwan KMT authorities' representatives from all UN agencies. On 1 November, the five-star red flag of the PRC was raised at the UN for the first time. It was a major victory on the diplomatic front for China.

Since then, as a permanent member of the UN Security Council, China has made unremitting efforts within the UN organisations to accomplish the UN Charter's purposes, maintain world peace, strengthen friendly cooperation among different countries, and promote the cause of human progress.

The relaxation of Sino-US relations directly promoted the improvement of Sino-Japanese relations. Japanese Prime Minister Kakuei Tanaka visited

China on 25 September 1972. China and Japan signed a joint declaration on the establishment of diplomatic relations on 29 September. By the end of 1973, China had completed establishing diplomatic relations with most developed capitalist countries besides the US. It also established formal ties with the European Community (replaced by the European Union in 2009). The cooperation between China and these countries in the economy, trade, science and technology, and culture developed solidly. Relations between China and Eastern European countries were restored, improved and expanded to varying degrees.

Another notable achievement of China's diplomacy during this period was the development of friendly and cooperative relations with many countries in Asia, Africa and Latin America, resulting in another upsurge of establishing diplomatic ties en masse. China established diplomatic relations with more than 40 Asian, African and Latin American countries, and firmly supported these countries in their just struggle to defend their national independence and sovereignty, oppose foreign aggression and interference, and maintain regional and world peace. China supported and promoted unity between these countries. It pledged to strive to break the old international order, in which big countries bullied small ones and rich countries oppressed and exploited poor ones to establish a new international order based on the Five Principles of Peaceful Coexistence.

On 21 February 1972, Mao Zedong met with Richard Nixon in Zhongnanhai

In the early 1970s, Mao Zedong had gradually formed an assessment of the international situation, dividing the world into 'three worlds'. He believed that the Soviet Union and the US, the two superpowers, belonged to the first world; the Western developed countries and Eastern European countries (other than the Soviet Union and the US) belonged to the second world; and the vast developing countries of Asia, Africa and Latin America belonged to the third world. Under the historical conditions at that time, Mao Zedong's assessment helped guide China's diplomacy. It played an essential role in steadfastly opposing the superpowers' hegemonism and war threats, striving to establish and develop friendly and cooperative relations with third-world countries and other types of countries, including the normalisation of relations between China and the US.

The first half of the 1970s was a period of breakthroughs in China's diplomacy. By 1976, China had established diplomatic relations with over 110 countries, which included most countries in the world at that time. China's diplomatic achievements significantly improved the country's security environment and expanded the scope of China's diplomatic activities. It also created a favourable prerequisite, and laid the foundation, for China's reform and opening up, and more active participation in international affairs after the 'Cultural Revolution'.

COMPREHENSIVE REORGANISATION IN 1975

At the beginning of 1975, after the first meeting of the Fourth NPC, Deng Xiaoping, with the support of Mao Zedong and Zhou Enlai, fully presided over the day-to-day affairs of the CPC Central Committee and the State Council. He then carried out drastic rectifications countrywide.

In accordance with Mao Zedong's instructions to ensure stability and unity, and push the national economy forward, Deng Xiaoping clearly and firmly proposed the guiding ideology for rectification. He emphasised that things must be put in order in all fields, including industry, agriculture, commerce, finance and trade, culture, education, science and technology, and the military, with the CPC's rectification at the core and the key being the leading officials. The rectification had to result in a leading group that must be daring and resolute. He wanted the CPC and the country to be stable and united to develop the socialist economy, and the CPC to strengthen its leadership and carry forward its excellent work style. He also put forward the crucial Marxist viewpoint that science and technology are productive forces, requiring that the CPC and the country do a good job in science and technology.

Deng Xiaoping started the rectification operation with the railway sector to turn around the chaotic economy. The CPC Central Committee decided on 5 March 1975 to focus on solving railway transportation problems. Deng Xiaoping despatched a working group to work with relevant local party committees to rectify some severe railway administration issues. The working group replaced a batch of administrators who were persistent factionalists and leading troublemakers. The working group redressed erroneous cases and resolutely adjusted the leadership. It also restored and improved work rules and regulations. The railway rectification led to rectifying all industrial sectors, with the iron and steel sector being next. After several months of rectification, the economic situation improved day by day.

During this period, the CPC Central Committee took some important measures to readjust party organisations and further implemented policies towards officials to reinstate veteran officials brought down in the 'Cultural Revolution' to their original posts as soon as possible. There was remarkable progress in rectifying the army by solving the 'overstaffed, undisciplined, conceited, extravagant and sluggish' problems and readjusting the large units' leadership by implementing policies towards the leaders. In terms of literary and artistic work, the CPC's policy of 'letting a hundred flowers bloom and a hundred schools of thought contend' was re-emphasised, and bans on the publication and performance of some excellent works were lifted.

The *CPC Central Committee's Decision on Speeding up the Development of Industry* and *The Outline Work Report of the Academy of Sciences* were essential documents that systematically put forward the suggestion of rectifying 'leftist' errors and restoring and establishing correct policies. On some issues, it put forward crucial ideas for reforming industry, and scientific and technological work, which mentally prepared the party and the country for subsequent reforms in these two fields.

As a result of the all-round rectification, the situation improved significantly. Social order in most parts of China stabilised and the national economy rebounded rapidly. In 1975, industry and agriculture's total output value and most product output indicators were completed according to the 'fourth five-year plan'. Deng Xiaoping said later, "The move to bring order out of chaos began in 1975." He also said, "When it comes to reforms, in fact, we already experimented with it from 1974 to 1975... We called the reform at that time rectification. We emphasised pushing the economy up, but we restored order first. And we saw results wherever we did that."

END OF THE 'CULTURAL REVOLUTION'

On 8 January 1976, Premier Zhou Enlai, beloved by the people of all ethnic groups across the country, passed away. The 'Gang of Four' issued various prohibitions and tried their best to obstruct and slander mass mourning activities. Their perverse acts enraged the entire Chinese people. From late March onwards, people from all over the country broke through obstructions to hold memorials to commemorate Zhou Enlai. They vented their pent-up anger directly at the 'Gang of Four' as a demonstration of objection to their perversion.

Zhu De, a man of compelling integrity, passed away on 6 July 1976.

Mao Zedong, the top leader of the CPC and the state, passed away on 9 September 1976.

Comrade Mao Zedong was a great Marxist, proletarian revolutionary, strategist and theorist. He was a great pioneer in adapting Marxism to the Chinese context and a great patriot and national hero of China since modern times. He was at the core of the first generation of the CPC Central Committee collective leadership. He was a great man who led the Chinese people to completely change their destiny and that of the country.

In just nine months, three outstanding leaders of the party and the country passed away one after another. The entire CPC and the Chinese people were deeply grieved and worried about the party and the country's future and destiny.

Before and after Mao Zedong's death, the 'Gang of Four' stepped up activities to seize the supreme leadership of the party and the country. Many older generations of revolutionaries were deeply concerned. On the evening of 6 October, Hua Guofeng, Ye Jianying and others represented the Politburo of the CPC Central Committee to implement the party and the people's will to isolate the 'Gang of Four' and take them and their backbone associates in Beijing into custody for investigation. On 14 October, the CPC Central Committee announced the smashing of the 'Gang of Four'. The jubilant Chinese people rushed about spreading the news.

The smashing of the 'Gang of Four' put an end to the 'Cultural Revolution' and restored China's social order. The CPC and the government resumed their work and the country saw its economy put back on the track of healthy development.

The 'Cultural Revolution' was a severe setback in China's exploration of its socialist road. But the CPC eventually corrected this grave mistake by relying on its own strength. History again proved that the Chinese people are great, the CPC can correct its errors, and the CPC and the socialist system have strong vitality. The decade-long 'Cultural Revolution' exposed the severe shortcomings in the CPC and the state's system, policies and governance at that time in an unexpected fashion. As Deng Xiaoping pointed out when summing up the historical experience since 1957, "Twenty years of experience, especially the lessons of the 'Cultural

Revolution', tell us that it won't work without reform. Nor will it work without formulating new political, economic and social policies."

Residents of Beijing, the capital, held rallies and parades in Tiananmen Square to celebrate the decisive victory over the 'Gang of Four'

The time between the founding of new China until the end of the 'Cultural Revolution' was a historical period in which the CPC led the Chinese people in an arduous exploration of the road to socialist revolution and construction. The CPC had developed distinctively creative theories and achieved tremendous successes despite severe setbacks. It led the Chinese people in carrying out socialist construction never seen in the old China which had a history of being 'poor and blank'[1]. China had undergone earth-shaking changes in a short time and established an independent and relatively complete industrial system and a national economic system. With the independently developed 'Two Bombs and One Satellite', China effectively safeguarded its national sovereignty and security, and became a major country with substantial influence in the world. It had accumulated significant experience in socialist construction in a large Eastern country with very low productivity. In exploring the path of socialist construction suited to China's national conditions, the CPC had come to some illuminating revelations. Based on its understanding of the situation, it proposed shifting the party's focus and the country's effort to socialist construction and technological revolution, and taking its own path and exploring a road to socialist construction suited to China's national conditions. It pointed out the basic and major contradictions, and proposed that developing social productivity was the party's fundamental task. It proposed achieving socialist modernisation in two steps and developing China's socialism in two stages. It put forward the theory that there are still commodity production and commodity exchange in a socialist society, so it is necessary to respect the law of value and vigorously develop commodity production. It proposed that the party correctly distinguish and handle contradictions between ourselves and the enemy, and contradictions among the people. Those original theoretical conclusions and achievements made in socialist construction provided invaluable experience and the theoretical and material basis for launching the great initiative of building socialism with Chinese characteristics in the new historical period.

---

1. An excerpt from Mao Zedong's *On Ten Major Relations* where he coined the phrase 'poor and blank' or 'poor and white' (穷二白, *yiqiongerbai*) with regard to China, with 'poor' meaning that there was not much industry and agriculture was not developed while 'white' refers to a blank piece of paper, meaning that the cultural and scientific levels were not high.

Seven

A Momentous and Historic Turning Point and the Establishment of Socialism with Chinese Characteristics

When the Gang of Four was smashed, the whole of China was euphoric. Through this people gained a great expectation that with the rectification of the mistakes of the Cultural Revolution and the complete resolution of the grave situation caused by 10 years of internal disorder, this would enable the party and the country as a whole to rise up once again from the midst of crisis. At that time, the world economy was rapidly developing, and science and technology were advancing with each passing day. General trends of development at home and abroad made it necessary for the CPC to make urgent political decisions and strategic choices on major policies regarding the future and destiny of the party and country. In December 1978, as China arrived at a historical juncture of huge importance, the Third Plenary Session of the 11th CPC Central Committee was held in Beijing. At the conference the historic decision was made to shift the focus of the work of the whole party to the drive for socialist modernisation and implement reform and opening up. This led to the most momentous turnaround in the party's history since the founding of the PRC and initiated a new era of reform, opening up and socialist modernisation.

1
THIRD PLENARY SESSION OF THE 11TH CPC CENTRAL COMMITTEE ACHIEVES A MOMENTOUS AND HISTORIC TURNAROUND

INTERMITTENT ADVANCES AND DISCUSSIONS SURROUNDING THE CRITERION OF TRUTH

After smashing the Gang of Four, the Party Central Committee took resolute and decisive measures to investigate and clean up the factionalist setup of the Gang of Four, resolve miscarriages of justice, adjust and equip the leadership team at all levels of the party, government and military, deploy and launch a campaign to expose and criticise the Gang of Four, and restore normalcy within the party and country. This all led to the development of a stable political situation which the people had long desired.

However, it was not an easy task to eliminate the serious political and ideological turmoil caused by the decade-long Cultural Revolution in a short period of time. This turmoil was mainly incited by the two counter-revolutionary groups of Lin Biao and Jiang Qing, but it was also connected with the long-standing errors of the left within the party. The most prominent obstacle to remedying this serious chaos was the proposal and implementation at that time of the 'Two Whatevers' policy, namely, "we will resolutely uphold *whatever* policy decisions Chairman Mao made and unswervingly follow *whatever* instructions Chairman Mao gave". The 'Two Whatevers' led to a refusal to analyse in any way Mao Zedong's decisions and directives while he was still alive and was, from a theoretical perspective, contrary to the basic principles of Marxism and the party's ideological line of seeking truth from facts. In practice, it also set up obstacles to adhering to the truth and correcting mistakes under the new situation.

Soon after the 'Two Whatevers' had been proposed, on 10 April 1977, Deng Xiaoping, who had not yet returned to leadership, stated in a letter to the Party Central Committee, "We must throughout all generations use accurate and complete Mao Zedong Thought to guide our whole party, the whole army and the whole nation." After this, he repeatedly criticised the 'Two Whatevers' on various occasions. The older generation of revolutionaries, such as Ye Jianying, Chen Yun, Li Xiannian, Nie Rongzhen and Xu Xiangqian, also stressed the need to carry forward the party's fine tradition of seeking truth from facts and resisted the 'Two Whatevers'.

The Third Plenary Session of the 10th CPC Central Committee, held in July 1977, decided to reinstate Deng Xiaoping as a member of the CPC Central Committee, the Politburo of the CPC Central Committee, and the Standing Committee of the Politburo of the CPC Central Committee, and also as vice chairman of the CPC's CMC, vice-premier of the State Council, and chief of staff of the Chinese PLA.

After Deng Xiaoping's return, he took the initiative to take charge of scientific education work and used it as a means to spearhead progress in setting things right. He led the criticism of the 'black-line dictatorship of literature and art' and the 'black-line dictatorship of education' advocated by Lin Biao, Jiang Qing and others, and also overturned the 'Two Estimates'[1] that had been crushingly imposed on the intelligentsia for many years. He also called for respect for knowledge and talent, emphasising that, 'science and technology are the primary productive forces', stating that the intellectual labourers who serve socialism also constitute part of the working people. Since then, the party has reversed its leftist policies towards the intelligentsia, and knowledge and intelligentsia have received renewed recognition from the party and the state, which has significantly boosted morale amongst intelligentsia in various fields, such as science, education, literature and art. Many films and plays which had been prohibited for a long time, such as *Ashima*, *The Peach Blossom Fan*, and *Li Shuangshuang*, were once again screened or staged. Prohibitions on many outstanding Chinese and foreign literary and artistic works were lifted, and mass organisations such as literary and artistic associations and writers' associations resumed their work, and literary and artistic creation gradually became active once more. At the end of 1977, the unified entrance examination system for colleges and universities, which had been interrupted during the Cultural Revolution, was restored. Of the 5.7 million people who took part in the exams, 273,000 were admitted and joyfully stepped onto university campuses. Then, in

March 1978, the National Science Congress was held and a new spring of science arrived.

The 11th CPC National Congress was held from 12 to 18 August 1977. The congress declared that the Cultural Revolution had come to an end and reaffirmed that the fundamental task of the party was to build China into a modernised socialist state before the end of the 20th century. However, limited by historical conditions, the General Assembly still affirmed the theoretical and practical errors of the Cultural Revolution, and failed to fundamentally correct its mistakes. The newly elected Central Committee elected Hua Guofeng as chairman and Ye Jianying, Deng Xiaoping, Li Xiannian and Wang Dongxing as vice-chairmen.

In the two years after the end of the Cultural Revolution, the work of the party and the state advanced, beginning to set things right in some sectors, and economic construction, social undertakings and diplomatic work were restored and developed. Economic construction, various social enterprises and diplomatic efforts were also restored and developed. At that time the people eagerly anticipated that the party and the state would be able to emerge from difficulties swiftly and make great strides forwards. However, due to the long-term impact of the leftist errors during the Cultural Revolution, as well as the restrictions brought about by the imposition of the Two Whatevers, every step forward in the process of setting things right was extremely difficult. As a result, hesitations became apparent in the work of the party and the state. This situation caused many outside the party to wonder, "What kind of stance should we have towards Mao Zedong's directives?" and, "What exactly is it that determines the standards of right and wrong of historical practice?" All this inevitably produced a debate between the two sides of seeking truth from facts and the Two Whatevers.

On 10 May 1978, *Practice Is the Sole Criterion for Testing Truth* was published in *Theory Dynamics*, an internal journal of the Party School of the Central Committee of the CPC. On 11 May, the *Guangming Daily* then published this article on behalf of a commissioned commentator, which *Xinhua* then disseminated nationwide.

The article clearly proposed the perspective that social practice is not only a criterion of truth, but that it is also in fact the *sole criterion* of truth. It also stated with regard to the taboo topics established by the Gang of Four that it was 'necessary to dare to touch on them and ascertain the truth'. It further stated that it would not be right to use ready-made formulas to limit, ride roughshod over and tailor the revolutionary practice of the rapid development of infinite riches, but rather have the courage to study new problems raised by new experiences. This article provoked a strong reaction among the masses of cadres and led to a great debate about the criterion of truth.

Practice Is the Sole Criterion for Testing Truth was actually a well-known tenet of Marxism. However, since it was diametrically opposed to the Two Whatevers and touched upon the ideological rigidity and personality cult which had been prevalent for many years, the debate regarding the criterion of truth was denounced by some from the outset.

However, at the critical juncture, Deng Xiaoping lent his timely and robust support for one specific side. On 2 June 1978, he delivered a speech at the All-Army Political Work Conference, highlighting Mao Zedong's views on seeking truth from facts, and criticising the incorrect attitude of some people towards Mao Zedong and the Two Whatevers of Mao Zedong Thought. He called for "setting things right and casting off our mental shackles so that we can greatly emancipate our minds". With the leadership of Deng Xiaoping and the support of many older revolutionaries, a great discussion on the criterion of truth quickly began to develop throughout the entire party and the whole of society. More than 650 deliberative articles were published in the central and provincial newspapers, forming a great wave of ideological emancipation.

This profound and extensive movement for ideological liberation became the ideological forerunner of the bottom-up reforms, setting things right, and reform and opening up.

Through these debates, thinking within and outside the party about the way forward became increasingly enlivened, with criticism of the far-left *Zeitgeist* that had posed a threat for many years, restoration of the party's Marxist ideological line, and reflections on the twists and turns of the past. From out of this a new situation began to appear and ferment in which China would open up to the outside world and various systems would be reformed.

After smashing the Gang of Four, China's foreign relations rapidly expanded, and party and state leaders went overseas one after another to learn about the outside world. How they could not but painfully sense how much time had been wasted in those years! How great the gap was between China and developed countries in the fields of economics, science and technology, and national management! Hence, a strong sense of crisis and urgency prompted party and state leaders to expedite their study and draw from advanced foreign management experience, and pertinent scientific and technological issues. Through reform and opening up, the overarching approach of accelerating the pace of China's development began to take shape.

In March 1978, Deng Xiaoping pointed out at the National Science

Conference that acting independently does not equate to closing the country to international relations, and self-reliance does not equate to blind xenophobia. He also stated that, "Every people or country should study the strengths of other peoples and countries, and learn from the advanced science and technology of others." At a state retreat held by the State Council from July to September of that year, many department heads proposed reforming the rigid system of economic management and introducing foreign advanced technology and funds. In late September, the National Planning Conference also proposed implementing the following changes to economic work: 1. Focusing attention on the struggle for production and technological revolution. 2. Transforming management systems and methods to align with scientific management methods in accordance with economic laws. 3. Switching from a state of closure or partial closure of the country to international relations to a policy promoting the active introduction of foreign advanced technology and using foreign capital to confidently access international markets.

In September 1978, Deng Xiaoping visited the three provinces of Heilongjiang, Jilin and Liaoning in northeast China. While there, he repeatedly stressed that the world changes every day, that new matters continue to arise and new problems continue to emerge, and that it would not be acceptable for China to close its doors or to fail to exercise its intellectual capabilities and be left behind forever by the rest of the world. He stated that the development of China's productivity must be accelerated in accordance with the favourable conditions of the time in order to improve people's lives. He also proposed that the mass campaign to criticise the Gang of Four should soon be ended, and that there should be a return to normal operations, and also advanced an important proposition whereby the focus of the work of the party and the state should shift to modernisation. This laid the ideological foundation for the subsequent Central Work Conference and the Third Plenary Session of the 11th CPC Central Committee.

THE CONVENING OF THE THIRD PLENARY SESSION OF THE 11TH CPC CENTRAL COMMITTEE

The CPC Central Committee held a work meeting in Beijing from 10 November to 15 December 1978, before the convening of the Third Plenary Session of the 11th CPC Central Committee. The main topic originally identified for the meeting was a discussion of economic work. However, since Deng Xiaoping's proposal to shift the focus before the meeting had been endorsed by the Standing Committee of the Politburo of the CPC

Central Committee, the meeting began with a discussion of the matter of shifting the focus of the work. All present were enthusiastically supportive, and unanimously in favour, of the shift in focus. However, they sensed that if the problem of guiding ideology were not correctly solved, if leftist errors, including the serious errors of the Cultural Revolution, were not corrected, if dogmatism, book worship and ideological rigidity were not overcome, and if the problem of the criterion of truth were not solved, then it would be impossible to truly shift the focus of work.

Deng Xiaoping at the Third Plenary Session of the 11th CPC Central Committee

During the discussions, the Northeast Group proposed that the problems left over from the Cultural Revolution and from before it should be solved systematically, which aroused a strong reaction from the participants. After that, the meeting saw an exchange of ideas on the issue of the criterion of truth, and also heated discussions on economic issues, building the party, and the construction of the country's democratic and legal system, which resulted in a change to the agenda of the meeting. At the meeting there were also even stronger calls to re-establish the party's ideological line of seeking truth from facts. On 25 November, the Politburo made the decision to redress the Tiananmen Incident and the case of the 'Group of 61 traitors led by Bo Yibo', amongst others, and resolved a number of major historical legacies.

On 13 December, Deng Xiaoping delivered an important speech entitled *Emancipating the Mind, Seeking Truth from Facts, Uniting as One and Looking to the Future* at the closing session of the Central Work Conference. In his speech he pointed out that it is necessary to emancipate the mind first, and that only when the mind has been emancipated is it possible to correctly take Marxism-Leninism-Mao Zedong Thought as a guide in order to solve problems left over from the past and solve a range of emerging problems. He said that for a party, a state and a people, if everything starts from books, then ideology becomes rigid and superstition prevails, such that they cannot move forward and their vitality will cease, and the party and state will perish. He stressed that democracy is a crucial condition for emancipating the mind, and that in order to protect the people's democracy, it is necessary to strengthen the rule of law. This is to ensure a legal foundation, compliance with the law, strict law enforcement and investigations of violations. In his speech, Deng Xiaoping proposed the task of reforming the economic system. With heartfelt words he said, "If we do not implement reform now, then modernisation and socialism will be buried."

In his speech he also set out a 'major policy', whereby some regions, companies, and workers and farmers, would be permitted to have a slightly increased income and improved standards of living before others due to their hard work and significant accomplishments. He said this would inevitably result in a demonstration of strength and lead to the economy as a whole continuing to advance in waves, thereby enabling people of all ethnic groups to become wealthy relatively quickly. This speech was a manifesto regarding the emancipation of the mind and establishing a new era and a new path, and in fact became the thematic report of the subsequent Third Plenary Session of the 11th CPC Central Committee.

The Third Plenary Session of the 11th CPC Central Committee was held in Beijing from 18 to 22 December 1978. The plenary session broke the serious shackles of the longstanding errors of the left, thoroughly rejected the erroneous policy of the Two Whatevers, positively appraised the debate on the criterion of truth, and re-established the party's ideological line of seeking truth from facts.

The plenary session also ceased using the slogan 'class struggle as the key link' and promptly and decisively ended the nationwide mass movement to expose Lin Biao and the Gang of Four, and decided to shift the focus of the entirety of the party's work and the attention of the people to the drive for socialist modernisation as of January 1979. It also introduced the task of reform and opening up. The plenary session went on to point out that achieving the four modernisations constituted an extensive and profound revolution, and that it was necessary to adopt a series of new and important economic measures, by implementing serious reforms to the economic management system and management methods, and actively developing mutually beneficial economic cooperation with various countries on the basis of self-reliance.

The plenary session went on to emphasise the need to fully develop democracy and set out the task of democratic institutionalisation and legalisation. It also decided to bolster the democratic centralism of the party, and party rules and regulations, and intensify party discipline. The plenary session also proposed a scientific system for correctly treating Mao Zedong's historical status and Mao Zedong Thought, and specified the path for upholding and developing Mao Zedong Thought.

The plenary session elected additional members of the central leadership organs, and elected the Central Commission for Discipline Inspection, with Chen Yun as its first secretary. Hua Guofeng made a self-criticism with regard to the issue of the Two Whatevers at the Central Work Conference before the plenary session. Although Hua Guofeng still served as chairman of the CPC Central Committee after the plenary session, actually Deng Xiaoping had already become the core of the party's central leadership in terms of embodying the party's correct guiding ideology and the major policies that were to determine reform and opening up, and socialist modernisation.

The successful convening of the Third Plenary Session of the 11th CPC Central Committee marked the end of the period in which the party and the state had only made intermittent progress in work after smashing the Gang of Four. The plenary session re-established the ideological, political and organisational lines of Marxism, and achieved a momentous turnaround of profound significance in the history of the party since the founding of new China, and initiated a new era of reform and opening up, and socialist modernisation in China. The historic decision made by the plenary session to implement reform and opening up was based on a profound grasp of the future and destiny of the party and the country, a profound summary of the implementation of socialist revolution and construction, profound insights into the trends of the time, and a profound understanding of the expectations and needs of the people. Reform and opening up constituted a great awakening of the CPC, and it is this great awakening that engendered the great rebirth of the party from theory to practice. From the beginning of this plenary session, with the great curtain-raising on reform and opening up, and the founding of socialism with Chinese characteristics, Deng Xiaoping Theory gradually formed and developed. The Third Plenary Session of the 11th CPC Central Committee has gone into the glorious history books as a momentous turnaround.

---

1. 'Two estimates' refers to the fact that on the educational front in the 17 years before the 'Cultural Revolution', it was the bourgeoisie that ruled the proletariat, known as the 'black line dictatorship'; mostly the worldview of intellectuals is basically that of the bourgeoisie, they are bourgeois intellectuals.

2
COMPLETING THE TASK OF SETTING THINGS RIGHT

REDRESSING OF UNJUST, FAKE AND FALSE CHARGES ON A LARGE SCALE AND THE ADJUSTING OF SOCIAL RELATIONS

After the Third Plenary Session of the 11th CPC Central Committee, the work of redressing unjust, fake and false charges was comprehensively advanced at the central and local levels, in accordance with the principle of seeking truth from facts and correcting all mistakes.

In the work of redressing unjust, fake and false charges, the most important influence was the *Resolution on the Rehabilitation of Comrade Liu Shaoqi* adopted at the Fifth Plenary Session of the 11th CPC Central Committee in February 1980. The resolution completely overturned the various charges levelled against Liu Shaoqi and restored Liu Shaoqi's reputation as a great Marxist and proletarian revolutionary, and as one of the main leaders of the party and the state. This demonstrates that the CPC is a Marxist political party which seeks truth from facts, corrects all mistakes, as well as being serious, open and candid. The party and the people are also deeply aware of the importance of strengthening democratic centralism and strengthening the construction of democratic and legal systems.

By the end of 1982, the nationwide large-scale work to redress unjust, fake and false charges was largely complete. In total, unjust, fake and false charges against more than 3 million cadres were redressed, and the party membership of more than 470,000 CPC members was restored, enabling them to return to work or take up new leadership positions in a positive frame of mind.

At the same time as dealing with problems left over from the party's history, the party also actively adjusted various aspects of social relations and undertook a significant amount of work. In all parts of the country, reexaminations and corrections were conducted regarding rightist elements who were wrongfully attacked during the expansion of the anti-right struggle in 1957. The CPC Central Committee also announced that those who were formerly industrial and commercial workers had been made workers, that those already workers who were peddlars and craft-workers were being distinguished from the industrial and commercial workers of the former bourgeois class, and that the social status of the vast majority of those who were originally landowners or rich peasants had been converted into that of workers. This series of moves appropriately resolved a large number of contradictions within the party and amongst the people.

The CPC Central Committee attached great importance to the issue of the implementation of policies relating to the intelligentsia. As a result, the state took a series of effective measures, successively enacting regulations on natural science awards and degrees, mustered the initiative of the intelligentsia, and promoted the selection and cultivation of talented individuals. The CPC Central Committee also required that everything possible be done to improve the working and living conditions of middle-aged scientific and technological staff, especially those who were doing practical work on the front line. Respect for knowledge and respect for talented individuals once again prevailed throughout society, and as a result China's educational, scientific and cultural undertakings began to demonstrate great vitality.

Correcting some of the leftist practices of the party in united front work was an important aspect in the adjusting of social relations. In June 1979, speaking at the second meeting of the Fifth Session of the CPPCC National Committee, Deng Xiaoping pointed out that China's united front had already become a broad alliance of socialist workers and socialism-advocating patriots, led by the working class and based on an alliance of workers and farmers. He also stated that all the democratic parties in China had become a political alliance of some socialist workers and some socialism-advocating patriots. From 1978 to 1979, the various democratic parties, the All-China Federation of Industry and Commerce (ACFIC) and the various people's organisations convened separate congresses and elected their respective governing bodies and leaders. In this way, the democratic parties and the ACFIC, which had ceased to be active during the Cultural Revolution, re-established their work.

Redressing unjust, fake and false charges, adjusting social relations, and correctly handling a series of contradictions within the party and amongst the people, served to significantly mobilise the initiative of people of all classes across society. It also played a very important role in promoting social stability, the unity of the people, and the consolidation and development of the patriotic united front, thereby advancing reform and opening up, and socialist modernisation.

The trial of the main perpetrators of the Lin Biao and Jiang Qing counter-revolutionary cliques was a significant matter drawing great attention with regard to the construction of democracy and the rule of law. In September 1980, the 16th Session of the Standing Committee of the Fifth NPC decided to set up the Special Prosecutor's Office of the Supreme People's Procuratorate and the Special Court of the Supreme People's Court to conduct a public trial in the case of the two counter-revolutionary groups of Lin Biao and Jiang Qing. From November 1980 to January 1981, the Special Court of the Supreme People's Court held a public trial of the 10 main perpetrators of the two counter-revolutionary groups, and thereby demonstrated the solemnity of socialist democracy and the rule of law.

RECTIFYING DISORDER IN THE GUIDING IDEOLOGY AND THE *RESOLUTION ON SOME HISTORICAL ISSUES OF THE PARTY SINCE THE FOUNDING OF THE PRC*

After the Third Plenary Session of the 11th CPC Central Committee, in the process of emancipating the mind and bringing order out of chaos, the masses of cadres were freed from the serious shackles of the Cultural Revolution and leftist ideology which preceded it. There also appeared a vibrant situation within and outside the party, whereby people studied new situations and solved new problems, but at the same time there were some noteworthy and alarming phenomena. Some people revealed that they did not understand, and were even resentful towards, the new policy lines in place since the Third Plenary Session of the 11th CPC Central Committee. A few people misinterpreted the 'emancipation of the mind', arbitrarily exaggerated the mistakes made by the party and Mao Zedong, and attempted to reject the party's leadership, the socialist system, and Mao Zedong and Mao Zedong Thought.

In March 1979, in response to these aspects of ideological confusion, Deng Xiaoping delivered a speech on *Uphold the Four Cardinal Principles* at the party's theoretical work retreat. He pointed out that it was necessary to adhere ideologically and politically to the four cardinal principles of keeping to the socialist road, upholding the dictatorship of the proletariat (later expressed as people's democratic dictatorship), upholding the leadership of the Communist Party and upholding Marxism-Leninism and Mao Zedong Thought. These were, he said, the "basic prerequisites for achieving the four modernisations". He also said, "To undermine any of the four cardinal principles is to undermine the whole cause of socialism in China, the whole cause of modernisation". He also proposed an important idea, namely, "Now, in our national construction, we must likewise act in accordance with our own situation and find a Chinese path to modernisation". This speech solemnly declared that the reform and opening up led by the CPC had a clear socialist direction from the outset.

In order to implement reform and opening up, and comprehensively set disorders right, it was crucial to reach conclusions on the major historical issues of the CPC since the founding of new China, so as to unify the ideology of the whole party and the people, and in unity look to the future. In November 1979, under the personal leadership of Deng Xiaoping, the drafting group of the *Resolution on Certain Problems Concerning the History of the Party Since the Founding of the PRC* was established. Over the following two years, Deng Xiaoping convened meetings of the drafting group more than 10 times and presented many important directives on the drafting work. He proposed that the resolution should embody the three general requirements, or the general principles and the general guiding ideology, namely, the most central of the three principles, being: 1. Establishing Comrade Mao Zedong's historical status and adhering to and developing Mao Zedong Thought; and also 2. Conducting an analysis, according to the notion of seeking truth from facts, of the major events of the 30 years since the founding of the PRC, establishing which had been correct and which had been wrong, including making a fair evaluation of the merits of some comrades in positions of authority; and 3. Making a basic summary of the past, one which is rough and not detailed, the purpose being to guide the nation to look to the future in unity. With regard to the evaluation of Mao Zedong's merits and demerits, it was necessary to seek truth from facts and act appropriately. The banner of Mao Zedong Thought was not to be lost, because to lose it would be to negate the party's glorious history. Deng Xiaoping also stressed that Chairman Mao had repeatedly saved the party and the country from crisis, and that without Chairman Mao, Chinese people would, at the very least, have had to continue to grope about in the dark for a long time.

After more than a year of drafting and extensive consultation, the Sixth Plenary Session of the 11th CPC Central Committee adopted the *Resolution* on *Certain Problems Concerning the History of the Party Since the Founding of the PRC* in June 1981. The resolution fundamentally rejected the Cultural Revolution and the errant 'theory of continued revolution under the dictatorship of the proletariat', provided an assessment of some important historical events and important historical figures according to the notion of seeking truth from facts, and scientifically summarised the historical experience of socialist revolution and construction since the founding of new China. The resolution stated that the history of the CPC after the founding of the PRC was, generally speaking, the history of the party leading all the peoples of China to carry out socialist revolution and socialist construction, and to achieve great success, under the guidance of Marxism-Leninism-Mao Zedong Thought. The resolution evaluated Mao Zedong's historical status according to the notion of seeking truth from facts and fully affirmed the great significance of Mao Zedong Thought as the long-standing guiding ideology of the party. The resolution also stated that Mao Zedong was a great Marxist, a great proletarian revolutionary, strategist and theorist. His merits and achievements were primary, his mistakes secondary. The resolution distinguished between Mao Zedong's mistakes in his later years from Mao Zedong Thought, and pointed out that Mao Zedong Thought constitutes the application and development of Marxism-Leninism in China, the summary of the correct theoretical principles and experience of the Chinese revolution that have been proven by practice, and the fruit of the collective wisdom of the CPC. The resolution independently gave a scientific summary of the content and living spirit of Mao Zedong Thought, namely, seeking truth from facts and the Mass Line, and emphasised that Mao Zedong Thought is the precious spiritual wealth of the party, which would guide the party's actions permanently, and that it was necessary to continue to adhere to Mao Zedong Thought in order to enrich and develop the party's theory in line with practical new principles and conclusions. The formation of the resolution shows that the CPC takes a solemn attitude towards its own failures and mistakes, and those of its leading figures, and dares to acknowledge, correctly analyse and resolutely correct them, so that failures and mistakes, along with the successful experience of the party, can together become valuable historical teaching resources.

The resolution also summarised from 10 aspects the main points of the correct road of socialist modernisation that had been gradually established since the Third Plenary Session of the 11th CPC Central Committee, and in essence tentatively proposed the kind of socialism which should be built in China and how to build socialism. The resolution correctly resolved the two important and interrelated historical issues of scientifically evaluating

Mao Zedong's historical status and the scientific system of Mao Zedong Thought, and implementing reform and opening up in accordance with new realities and development requirements, and establishing the correct path of China's socialist modernisation drive, which amply reflects the foresight and political maturity of the CPC Central Committee. The adoption of the resolution marked the completion of the party's victory in setting things right as it related to the guiding ideology. On the recommendation of the Politburo, the Sixth Plenary Session of the 11th CPC Central Committee decided to allow Hua Guofeng to resign as chairman of the Central Committee and chairman of the CMC, electing Hu Yaobang as chairman of the Central Committee and Deng Xiaoping as chairman of the CMC.

3
THE BEGINNING OF RURAL REFORM, THE ESTABLISHMENT OF SPECIAL ECONOMIC ZONES (SEZS), AND REFORM AND OPENING UP

RESTRUCTURING THE NATIONAL ECONOMY

In April 1979, in order to correct the deviation in the guidelines for economic construction present for many years, and to solve the problem of the imbalance of the national economy after the Cultural Revolution, the CPC Central Committee held a work meeting to formally establish the policy of 'restructuring, reform, rectification and improvement' of the national economy, commonly known as the new Eight Character Guidelines. The implementation of the new Eight Character Guidelines was not only an important step in restructuring economic relations, but also in the process for correcting the guidelines for economic construction and exploring the path of socialist modernisation suited to China's national conditions, as well as being the process for promoting reform and opening up.

When discussing the restructuring of the national economy, Deng Xiaoping stressed that there were at least two important features that must be faced in order for China to achieve the four modernisations, one being a weak foundation, and the other having a large population but not much arable land. Chen Yun also pointed out that the main feature of China's social economy was that the rural population accounted for 80% of the total, and that the population was large but there is not much arable land, and that it must be recognised that this was the context within which the Four Modernisations were to be achieved.

In the course of economic restructuring, the CPC Central Committee initially summarised the lessons of economic construction since the founding of new China, and stated that economic construction must start from the realities of national conditions, and follow the laws of economy and nature; that it was necessary to assess capabilities and act accordingly, moving forward step by step based on irrefutable reasoning and pragmatism, so that economic development would be closely integrated with an appropriate improvement in people's lives; and that it was necessary to actively develop foreign economic cooperation and technical exchanges on the basis of independent actions and self-reliance. The restructuring of the national economy and the reform of the economic system were carried out under the guidance of these guidelines.

In December 1981, the Government Work Report adopted by the Fourth Session of the Fifth NPC proposed that it was necessary to start from China's actual situation and walk, at a more appropriate speed, along a new path where the economic benefits would be better and the people would be able to gain more tangible benefits. The report affirmed the results achieved by the restructuring and announced that the 1981 National Economic Plan was expected to be successfully completed and that the goal of stabilising the economy would be basically achieved. The task of national economic restructuring was successfully completed.

RURAL REFORM THE FIRST TO ACHIEVE A BREAKTHROUGH

China is a major agricultural power. As a result, rural development is a decisive factor in determining whether China can develop successfully. Before the Third Plenary Session of the 11th CPC Central Committee, there had been some serious flaws in rural areas, in terms of matters such as egalitarianism, regarding over-centralisation of operational management and distribution, which seriously disincentivised farmers' initiative in production, and as a result agricultural development and the improvement of farmers' lives had been slow. In 1978, there were still 250 million people in the country facing hunger.

In the summer and autumn of 1978, Anhui Province experienced severe drought and the autumn planting was extremely difficult. The provincial party committee decided to lend part of the land to farmers to grow grain and vegetables, with the grain and vegetables produced not being subject to requisitioning or rationing. This measure quickly stimulated the initiative of the masses towards production, and that year the province completed the autumn planting with a surplus. Inspired by 'borrowing land', grassroots cadres and farmers in some parts of Anhui broke through the limitations of the old system and began devolving production responsibility to production units and delegating production responsibility to households. Eighteen farmers in Liyuan Commune in Xiaogang Village, Fengyang County, were brave enough to sign a contract to take on allocated tasks. According to the system of delegating production responsibility to households in Xiaogang Village, they would pledge a part to the country, provide amply for the collective, and then keep the remainder for themselves. This method was simple and effective, and was welcomed by farmers. Some parts of Sichuan, Gansu, Yunnan and Guangdong provinces also relaxed their policies and adopted similar practices. These bold ventures served to lift the curtain on rural economic reform.

For a time, within and outside the party there were different opinions regarding the nature of the system of responsibility for agricultural production, regarding devolving production responsibility to production units, delegating production responsibility to households, and others. Many people feared that these approaches would affect the rural collective economy and deviate from the socialist path of rural development. In May 1980, Deng Xiaoping affirmed the farmers' reform initiative in a speech, saying, "After the relaxation of rural policy, some places suitable for engaging in delegating production responsibility to households have engaged in this practice. The effect has been very good, and changes have been rapid." He stated that worrying about the effect this approach would have on the collective economy was unnecessary because, as long as production in these places developed and there were developments in the social division of labour and the commodity economy in rural areas, then low levels of collectivisation would develop to high levels of collectivisation, and the fragile areas of the collective economy would be reinforced. In September of that year, the CPC Central Committee published an essay entitled *Several Issues Pertaining to Further Strengthening and Improving the Responsibility System for Agricultural Production*, which broke down the age-old practice of equating the concept of delegating production responsibility to households with individual farming and capitalism, and affirmed the implementation of delegating production responsibility to households under the leadership of the production unit. In 1982, the CPC Central Committee issued *Document No. 1*, which clearly stated that all responsibility systems which incorporated the delegating of production responsibility to households and work contracted to households were all aspects of the production responsibility system of the socialist collective economy. With the support of the CPC Central Committee, the household contract responsibility system, mainly in the form of the delegating of production responsibility to households and work contracted to households, was rapidly promoted.

This resulted in fully stimulating farmers' production initiative and promoted the rapid development of agricultural production. In many places, the desired effect was had in only one year, with significant increases in food production, and within a few years the changes were huge.

Farmers who have benefited from a bumper harvest selling their grain to the state

With the implementation of the new management system in the vast rural areas, farming masses had greater autonomy in production and management, and were able to use surplus labour and funds to develop a variety of operations. A large number of township and village industrial enterprises soon emerged in rural areas, as well as a large number of family firms specialising in production and management. This was the beginning of the transformation of rural areas in China towards specialised, commercialised and socialised production.

In the process of advancing rural reform, some places with a relatively solid collective economic foundation continued to implement collective centralised management, reformed their original methods of egalitarian distribution, and gradually advanced towards a high level of collectivisation. Their approach was also in line with the spirit of the CPG's stance of 'if it is appropriate to unify, unify, if it is appropriate to divide, divide'.

Rural reform was the great achievement of Chinese farmers. It is no coincidence that the reform first achieved breakthroughs and success in the countryside. It was determined by China's basic national conditions and the hardships of rural economic development at that time. The Third Plenary Session of the 11th CPC Central Committee provided an important ideological premise for rural reform and created a favourable political environment. As a result, grassroots cadres in vast rural areas and tens of millions of farmers bravely broke through the old system, which had not been conducive to the development of productivity, in order to change the condition of the countryside and their own destinies, thus setting off a great surging tide of reform. Consequently, the great implementation of building socialism with Chinese characteristics began to advance step by step, brought about by the party and the masses.

THE PRELIMINARY STAGES OF THE REFORM OF THE URBAN ECONOMIC SYSTEM

The reform of the urban economic system was far more complicated than that of rural reform. After the Third Plenary Session of the 11th CPC Central Committee, the reform of the urban economic system, with the expansion of enterprise autonomy as the major component, was gradually advanced throughout the country, on the basis of learning from the experience of expanding production and operational autonomy in rural reform. In May 1979, eight major enterprises, including Capital Iron and Steel Company, Tianjin Bicycle Factory and Shanghai Diesel Engine Factory, began piloting reforms. By June 1980, the number of companies participating in the reforms had grown to 6,600. The expansion in the reforms of enterprise autonomy opened a gap in the traditional planned economic system, and initially changed the manner of planned production. In the past this system had only been based on national directives, had not understood the needs of the market, and had not paid attention to product sales or profits and losses, but these reforms now strengthened enterprises' sense of self-management and market awareness.

Urban reform was gradually advanced into the area of economic responsibility on the basis of expanding enterprise autonomy, and the reforms were first piloted in enterprises in Shandong Province in the spring of 1981. In order to implement reforms in the system of economic responsibility, it was necessary to link the economic interests of enterprises and workers with the economic benefits they reap, which would lead the majority of workers to achieve the greatest economic benefit with the least amount of human and material resources with a sense of ownership.

After that, economic accountability was quickly introduced to 36,000 industrial enterprises across the country. Reforms to the commercial distribution system were also being launched at the same time. From 1979, the state re-defined the scope of the state purchasing monopoly and fixed government purchase of agricultural and by-products, relaxed the state monopoly of purchasing and marketing agricultural and by-products, and stipulated that the grassroots organisations of supply and marketing cooperatives could purchase and sell in other counties and provinces, and that collective-owned businesses, individual traders and farmers may also trade over long distances. This created favourable conditions for accelerating the flow of goods between urban and rural areas.

Reform of ownership frameworks also began and, in 1979, a vast swell of educated young people returned to the cities. In order to ease the increasing pressure on employment, the CPC Central Committee and the

State Council decisively adopted a policy of supporting the collective economy and individual economic development of cities and towns, and initiated reforms mainly of the public-sector economy in which various forms of economy coexisted. Under these circumstances, the concept of the 'self-employed' came into being. In Qianmen, Beijing, the Big Bowl of Tea Youth Teahouse set up a stove. In Wuhu, Anhui Province, Nian Guangjiu started the large-scale operation of the 'Idiot Sunflower Seeds' venture. In October 1981, the CPC Central Committee and the State Council stated in their *Decisions on Creating Opportunities, Revitalising the Economy and Solving Employment Problems in Cities and Towns* that, 'Under the fundamental premise of the dominant socialist publicly owned economy, it is a strategic decision of our party to simultaneously implement multiple economic forms and multiple modes of business over a long period of time, and it is by no means an interim measure.' Under the guidance of the new policy, the collective and individual economies developed in new ways, and a new economic form emerged, which was developed jointly by the people, collectives and individual associations.

OPENING UP TO THE OUTSIDE WORLD AND THE ESTABLISHMENT OF SEZS

In the process of advancing reform, opening up to the outside world occurred gradually and major breakthroughs were achieved. Attracting and utilising foreign capital and setting up Sino-foreign equity joint ventures and Sino-foreign cooperative joint ventures (and projects) was an important means and step for opening up to the outside world. In 1979, the China International Trust and Investment Corporation (CITIC) was established to develop international trusts, investment, leasing and other business. In 1980, China regained its representation at the World Bank and the International Monetary Fund (IMF) and joined the International Fund for Agricultural Development. It then went on to begin to acquire loans from these international financial institutions. China also successively signed agreements with Japanese, French, American and other companies to conduct offshore oil exploration and development. With the introduction of the July 1979 *Law of the PRC on Chinese-Foreign Equity Joint Ventures* and later a series of related laws and regulations, Sino-foreign joint equity ventures developed from the ground up. Tourism also swiftly emerged, quickly becoming a prominent aspect of China's opening up to the outside world and developing as a new sector of industry.

The establishment of SEZs constituted a great initiative of the party and the state to promote reform and opening up, and socialist modernisation.

As early as April 1978, after the economic and trade mission despatched to Hong Kong and Macau by the State Planning Commission and the Ministry of Foreign Trade and Economic Cooperation (MOFTEC) conducted its field visit, it proposed that the CPG utilise Bao'an and Zhuhai in Guangdong near Hong Kong and Macau as an export base. In January 1979, Guangdong Province and the Ministry of Transport jointly submitted a report to the State Council proposing the idea of establishing an industrial zone in the Shekou area, which was approved by the CPG. Not long afterwards, the Shekou Industrial Zone was born with charges detonated to blast through the mountains.

Builders of the Shekou Industrial Zone in Shenzhen blasting through mountains

In April 1979, the CPG held a work meeting. Xi Zhongxun, first secretary of the Guangdong Provincial Party Committee, expressed the hope that the CPG would delegate some powers to give Guangdong the necessary autonomy in its external economic activities, specifically allowing export processing zones to be established in Shenzhen, Zhuhai and Shantou, which are adjacent to Hong Kong and Macau. The Fujian Provincial Party Committee also proposed a similar idea, in response to which the CPG expressed its support. Concerning what these areas implementing special policies should be called, Deng Xiaoping said they should be called special zones, and emphasised that the Shaan-Gan-Ning area had been the first to be called a special zone. He said that although the CPG had no money, it could introduce relevant policies so that these locations could establish themselves and blaze a pioneering trail.

In July 1979, the CPC Central Committee and the State Council approved the report of the Guangdong Provincial Committee and the Fujian Provincial Party Committee, confirming that the two provinces were to adopt special policies and flexible measures regarding external economic activities. They were to take the lead and establish their economies as quickly as possible. At the same time, the CPC Central Committee and the State Council also decided to pilot special export zones in Shenzhen and Zhuhai. In May 1980, the CPC Central Committee and the State Council officially decided to name the 'special export zones' as 'Special Economic Zones'. In August of that year, the 15th session of the Standing Committee of the Fifth NPC approved the establishment of SEZs in Shenzhen, Zhuhai, Shantou and Xiamen in the provinces of Guangdong and Fujian. Under the impetus of the strategic decision-making of the CPG, the builders of the special administrative regions, who came from far and near, overcame all obstacles and, through hard work and entrepreneurship, turned Shenzhen and Zhuhai, these once small frontier towns and desolate fishing villages, into vibrant new cities in just a few short years. These people thereby created the audaciously daring, pioneering and hard-working spirit of the special administrative regions. The SEZs became an important showpiece of China's reform and opening up, and revealed to the world the boundless strength of China's new modus operandi.

ON THE REFORM OF THE SYSTEM OF PARTY AND STATE LEADERSHIP

The Third Plenary Session of the 11th CPC Central Committee pointed out that achieving the four modernisations would require a substantial increase in productivity, and would inevitably require multi-faceted changes in socio-economic relations and the superstructure which were not suitable for the development of productivity. Thereafter, the CPC Central Committee earnestly summarised and drew lessons from the past political life of the party and the state in order to reform the system of party and state leadership, and the reforms of the political system were set in motion with democratic institutionalisation and legalisation as the main components. In July 1979, the Second Session of the Fifth NPC deliberated on, and adopted, seven important laws, namely, the *Law for the Organisation of the Local People's Congresses of Various Levels of the PRC*, the *Law for the Election of the NPC and the Local People's Congresses of Various Levels of the PRC*, the *Criminal Law of the PRC*, the *Criminal Procedure Law of the PRC*, the *Law for the Organisation of the People's Court of the PRC*, the *Law for the*

Organisation of the People's Procuratorates of the PRC, and the *Joint Venture Law of the PRC*. In this way, the institutionalisation and legalisation of China's socialist democracy took an important first step forwards.

In the process of promoting the construction of democracy and the legal system, the system of multi-party cooperation and political consultation under the leadership of the CPC was restored and developed. In October 1979, Deng Xiaoping emphasised at a reception held by the CPPCC National Committee and the Central United Front Department that, under the leadership of the CPC, the implementation of multi-party cooperation was determined by China's specific historical and actual conditions and was also a feature and advantage of its political system. Long-term coexistence and mutual supervision, he said, are a long-term and constant approach. That same month, the CPC Central Committee, in a report of the Organisation Department of the CPC Central Committee and the Central United Front Department, pointed out that party committees at all levels must overcome 'monotone' thinking, and earnestly make appropriate arrangements for non-party members, especially those with business and technical expertise, cooperate sincerely with them and work together to serve the interests of the state.

The CPC Central Committee took a series of measures to reform the system of party and state leadership. The Fifth Plenary Session of the 11th CPC Central Committee was convened in February 1980 on the theme of upholding the party's leadership, improving the party's leadership, and improving the party's preparedness to engage in struggle. The plenary session decided to re-establish the Central Secretariat as a regular working body under the leadership of the Politburo and its Standing Committee, and Hu Yaobang was elected general secretary of the Central Committee.

In August 1980, the Politburo held an expanded meeting. Deng Xiaoping gave a speech at the meeting entitled *On the Reform of the System of Party and State Leadership*. He pointed out that problems with the leadership system and organisational system were rather of a fundamental, all-encompassing, consistent and long-term nature. "If these systems are good," he said, "then bad people will not be able to run amuck at will, but if the system is not good then good people will not be able to do ample good, and may even end up doing bad." Deng Xiaoping emphasised that the purpose of reforming the system of party and state leadership was not to weaken the party's leadership or relax the party's discipline, but actually to uphold and strengthen the party's leadership and the party's discipline. This speech clearly defined the basic guiding ideology for the reform of the system of party and state leadership.

Under the premise of upholding the leadership of the party, the party and the government made great efforts to solve problems such as lack of clarity regarding the responsibilities of the party and the government, all the affairs of the party committee, as well as the problems of inefficiency, bloated institutions, over-abundance of personnel, and dilatory work practices. They also increased local authority, expanded democratic rights at the grassroots level, and effectively safeguarded the judicial authority and prosecutorial powers enjoyed by trials and procuratorial organs in accordance with the constitution.

Institutional reform also soon came onto the agenda. In January 1982, Deng Xiaoping pointed out at a meeting of the Politburo that streamlining institutions constituted a revolution, and that the most critical issue was the selection of younger, talented cadres with integrity into the leadership team. As a result of the reform, the bureau-level institutions of the units directly under the CPC Central Committee decreased by 11% and the level of staffing decreased by 17.3%. The number of ministries, central services and offices under the State Council was reduced from 100 to 61, and the level of staffing was also reduced by about one-third. Some 32% of the cadres in the newly formed leadership team were newly selected young and middle-aged cadres, with a drop in the average age from 64 to 58.

In February 1982, the CPC Central Committee made the *Decision on the Establishment of the Retirement System for Old Cadres*, abolishing the system of lifelong tenure for cadres in leadership positions which had existed. A large number of old cadres responded to the call and took the initiative to ask to leave leadership positions, take compulsory or voluntary retirement, or retire from leading posts to assume advisory posts, making way for a group of proven young and middle-aged cadres to take up leadership positions. Through this strategic initiative, the problem of the ageing of the ranks of cadres under special circumstances was solved.

In the just over three years after the Third Plenary Session of the 11th CPC Central Committee, various undertakings flourished, with the process of setting things right getting fully underway and the construction of socialist democracy and the legal system gradually getting on the right track. The reform of the system of party and state leadership was also steadily advanced, whilst reform and opening up, and the adjustment of the national economy achieved positive results. These all served to lay an important foundation for the convening of the Party's 12th National Congress.

4
THE CPC'S 12TH NATIONAL CONGRESS AND THE COMPREHENSIVE LAUNCH OF SOCIALIST MODERNISATION

THE CPC'S 12TH NATIONAL CONGRESS PROPOSES THE IMPORTANT ASSIGNMENT OF 'BUILDING SOCIALISM WITH CHINESE CHARACTERISTICS'

The CPC's 12th National Congress was held from 1 to 11 September 1982 in Beijing. In his opening remarks, Deng Xiaoping emphatically set forth the agenda of, "the integration of the universal truths of Marxism with the concrete reality of China's situation, following the path that is right for China, and building socialism with Chinese characteristics." The major new proposition of "building socialism with Chinese characteristics" answered the important question about which the party and people were most concerned after entering the new period of reform and opening up regarding the path China should take, and it became the great guiding banner of reform and opening up, and socialist modernisation.

Through Hu Yaobang's report entitled *Creating a New Situation in Socialist Modernisation in an All-Round Way*, the General Assembly put forward a guiding principle for the struggle to comprehensively create a new situation. The overall mandate of the party established by the General Assembly in the new historical period was one of uniting the people of all ethnic groups throughout the country, self-reliance, struggling arduously, gradually achieving the four modernisations of industry, agriculture, national defence, and science and technology, and building China into a highly civilised and highly democratic socialist country.

The 12th National Congress of the CPC

The General Assembly proposed that from 1981 until the end of the 20th century, the overall objective of China's economic construction was to strive, under the premise of continuously improving economic benefits, to double the annual output value of the country's industry and agriculture from Rmb710 billion in 1980 to about Rmb2.8 trillion in 2000, so that the people's material and cultural life would reach a moderately prosperous level. The General Assembly also established agriculture, energy and transport, education and science as strategic priorities for economic development. The General Assembly changed the previous target of the end of the 20th century for achieving the four modernisations to achieving moderate prosperity, and resolved the long-standing problem of unnecessary haste, based on strategic guidance. This was a historic decision made by the CPC Central Committee on the basis of lessons learned from history.

Another important contribution of this General Assembly was to put forward the goal of economic construction, while clearly proposing the strategic policy of building a high degree of socialist spiritual civilisation and a high degree of socialist democracy. The General Assembly pointed out that the socialist spiritual civilisation is an important feature of socialism and an important manifestation of the superiority of the socialist system, that the construction of socialist material civilisation and spiritual civilisation should be safeguarded and supported by the continued development of socialist democracy, and that the construction of socialist democracy must be closely integrated with the construction of a socialist legal system. The proposing of these mandates embodied the comprehensive requirements of socialist modernisation, enriched and developed the theory of scientific socialism, and marked the ongoing deepening of the party's understanding of socialism.

The General Assembly also adopted a new *Constitution of the CPC*. The new Party Constitution further expounded on the historical lessons learned from the building of the party and issued a series of new regulations which reflected the new requirements of the realities of the party. The new Party Constitution emphasised that Communist Party members would always be ordinary members of the working people, and stipulated eight obligations of party members, requiring party members to uphold the interests of the party and the people above all else, personal interests to be subservient to the interests of the party and the people, suffering to precede gratification, and that they would serve the public interest wholeheartedly and never abuse public position for their own ends. The party's new constitution also stipulated that joining the party should be done by swearing an oath in front of the party flag, and also stipulated the uniform content of the oath. According to the new Party Constitution, the CPC Central Committee would not have a chairman but rather a general secretary, who was to be responsible for convening meetings of the Politburo of the CPC Central Committee and meetings of the Standing Committee of the Politburo, and presiding over the work of the Secretariat of the CPC Central Committee. Also the CPG and provincial levels were to set up advisory committees as transitional institutions for the replacement of old with new cadres, in order for older comrades, with rich experience but who had retired from the front line, to serve as advisors for the cause of the party. The new Party Constitution stipulated the basic principles of democratic centralism, emphasising that the party should maintain a high degree of ideological and political consistency, and that the party's committees at all levels should implement a system of combining collective leadership with division of individual responsibilities. All people are equal in the face of party discipline and, in addition to party discipline, party members must strictly abide by rules for government discipline and national laws.

The General Assembly elected the Central Committee, the Central Advisory Commission and the Central Commission for Discipline Inspection. The First Plenary Session of the 12th National Congress elected Hu Yaobang, Ye Jianying, Deng Xiaoping, Zhao Ziyang, Li Xiannian and Chen Yun as members of the Standing Committee of the Politburo of the CPC Central Committee, Hu Yaobang as general secretary of the CPC Central Committee, and Deng Xiaoping as chairman of the CMC, and approved Deng Xiaoping as chairman of the Central Advisory Commission and Chen Yun as first secretary of the Central Commission for Discipline Inspection.

The 12th National Congress was the first National Congress held by the party after entering the new era of reform and opening up. Starting from this General Assembly, it was institutionalised that the Party's National Congress would be held every five years, in accordance with the provisions of the Party Constitution.

PROMOTING REFORM OF THE ECONOMIC SYSTEM AND THE FORMATION OF A NEW PATTERN OF OPENING UP TO THE OUTSIDE WORLD

After the 12th National Congress, rural reform was further deepened on a consolidated foundation, and the focus of the reform gradually shifted to cities and comprehensively expanded. From 1982 to 1984, the CPC Central Committee consecutively issued three *Document No. 1s* regarding rural work, and the household contract responsibility system was rapidly spread throughout the country. By 1987, 98% of the country's farmers had implemented the household contract responsibility system, the enthusiasm of hundreds of millions of farmers for production had been greatly improved, and agricultural production had emerged from a state of stagnation. This fundamentally shook up the system of people's communes characterised by 'three-level ownership with the production team as the basis' and the 'integration of government administration with commune management'. In 1982, the new constitution made provisions to change the system of integrated government administration and commune management of rural people's communes, established township governments as the grassroots of political power, and universally set up villagers' committees as mass self-government organisations. By the end of 1984, the country had basically completed the division of government administration and commune management, and the people's commune system, which had been in place for more than 20 years, ceased to exist. This constituted a major reform of the rural economic and political system.

The implementation of the family contract responsibility system created conditions for the development of the rural commodity economy. In 1985, the CPC Central Committee issued *Document No. 1*, deciding to implement a new policy of state-planned procurement contracts for a small number of important agricultural products, such as grain and cotton, in which products other than those procured are freely sold or sold to the state at an agreed price, leaving most of the remaining agricultural by-products to be freely traded on the market, with the state no longer issuing directive plans. This fundamentally changed the policy of fixed-price state purchasing which had been in place for more than 30 years and put the rural economy on track to become a planned commodity economy. Rural reform also brought about the powerful rise of township and village enterprises, with a sizeable rural labour force being liberated from the land, and engaging in industry, commerce and services. Lu Guanqiu of the Wanxiang Tool Factory in Xiaoshan, Zhejiang Province, signed a personal risk contract with the township government to develop the township enterprise from a small workshop into the first Chinese auto parts company to enter the US market. Township enterprises changed the face of China's rural areas with amazing speed and scale. By 1987, the output value of township enterprises reached Rmb476.4 billion, exceeding the value of total agricultural output for the first time. This constituted a historic change in the rural economy.

Rural economic reform was a successful practice, whereby the party started with the realities of the time, reported on the innovations of farmers in a timely manner, and took advantage of the new situation to continuously promote these reforms. China's rural areas, with a population of hundreds of millions, achieved these profound social changes relatively smoothly, and these changes had a profound impact on the development of the rural economy and the entire national economy, as well as on reforms in other areas.

Under the impetus of rural reform, urban reform was also further promoted. In October 1984, the Third Plenary Session of the 12th CPC Central Committee adopted the *Decision of the CPC Central Committee on the Reform of the Economic System*, which raised and expounded on some important theoretical and practical issues regarding the reform of the economic system. The decision broke down the traditional concept of setting the planned economy and the commodity economy in mutual opposition, proposed that China's socialist economy would be a 'planned commodity economy based on public ownership', and also broke down the traditional concept of confusing national ownership with the direct operation of enterprises by state institutions, and stated that 'ownership and management rights can be properly separated'. This was the party's new understanding of the relationship between planning and the market.

After this, urban-focused reforms of the economic system were comprehensively implemented. The central aspect of the reform was enhancing the vitality of enterprises under national ownership, one of the measures of which was implementing contractual management responsibility systems and establishing clear regulations for responsibilities, and rewards and penalties, in order to enhance the sense of responsibility of company operators. By 1987, 80% of the country's SOEs had implemented various systems of contractual management responsibilities. Some enterprises also began to attempt to carry out reforms of the shareholding system. In November 1984, Shanghai Feilo Acoustics Company issued a public offering of shares, becoming the first corporation in Shanghai to pilot joint-stock management after reform and opening up. In November 1986 during a visit to China, the chairman of the New York Stock Exchange (NYSE) was presented by Deng Xiaoping with Rmb50 worth of shares in Shanghai Feilo. This symbolic gesture demonstrated that stocks and shareholdings are not exclusive to capitalism but can also be used by socialist countries.

At the same time as the reform of SOEs, various economic components of different ownership systems were developed. Non-public economic components, such as Sino-foreign equity joint ventures, Sino-foreign cooperation, wholly foreign-owned enterprises and the domestic self-employed workers and private initiatives achieved rapid development with the permission, and under the guidance of, the state. The formation of ownership structures, principally characterised by public ownership and having multiple economic components, created a new set of circumstances for developing the national economy, making people's lives easier and expanding employment.

In accordance with the requirements of developing a socialist planned commodity economy, the state gradually decentralised its planning and management authority over the economy, reduced directive planning and expanded guiding plans. The scope and mode of national macro-control were adjusted and improved, and small commodities and unplanned commodities were regulated by the market. Prices, taxation, finance and other economic levers played an increasingly important role in macro-control and promoted the development of the commodity economy.

Reform of the systems of science and technology, and education were also added to the agenda. In March 1985, the CPC Central Committee made the decision to reform the system of science and technology, stating that economic construction must rely on science and technology, and that work in science and technology must be oriented towards the strategic policy of economic construction. As a result of this, the enthusiasm of the masses of workers in the field of science and technology was greatly stimulated. In March 1986, four scientists proposed to the CPC Central Committee that China should keep in step with advanced levels in the world and develop advanced technologies. Deng Xiaoping was quick to make an announcement in this regard, and in November of that same year, China decided to implement the '863' Plan to develop advanced technologies.

Deng Xiaoping writing his dedicatory inscription for the Shenzhen SEZ

Tens of thousands of scientists in different fields cooperated and tackled key problems together, soon achieving considerable results. In this way, China's research into advanced technologies entered a new stage of development.

In October 1983, Deng Xiaoping proposed that "education should be oriented towards modernisation, the world and the future", thereby indicating the direction for China's educational reform and development. In May 1985, the CPC Central Committee made a decision on the reform of the education system, proposing that the fundamental purpose of the reform of the education system was to improve the level of people's education and produce more numerous and more talented people. The reform of the education system stimulated enthusiasm for education conducted on local and societal levels, and the system of nine years of compulsory education was implemented in a planned and systematic way. Education of all kinds and at all levels was developed, and all kinds of talents continued to emerge in large numbers to meet the needs of modernisation.

After the 12th National Congress, new steps were taken in opening up to the outside world. At the beginning of 1984, Deng Xiaoping visited Shenzhen, Zhuhai, Xiamen and other SEZs and wrote dedicatory inscriptions for them, fully affirming the achievement of constructing the SEZs. At that time, he said, "In our constructing of SEZs and implementing a policy of opening up, there is a guiding principle which must be clear, namely, not to restrain but to release", and also, "The SEZs are windows, being windows for technology, windows for management methods, windows for knowledge, and windows for foreign policy." Deng Xiaoping's trip to southern China and his affirmation of the SEZs ushered in new opportunities for opening up to the outside world. In May 1984, the CPC Central Committee and the State Council decided to open up 14 coastal port cities, namely, Dalian, Qinhuangdao, Tianjin, Yantai, Qingdao, Lianyungang, Nantong, Shanghai, Ningbo, Wenzhou, Fuzhou, Guangzhou, Zhanjiang and Beihai. Then in February 1985, the Central Committee and the State Council issued a notification approving the designation of the Yangtze River Delta, the Pearl River Delta and the region of Xiamen, Zhangzhou and Quanzhou in southern Fujian as coastal economic open zones. As a result, a new multi-level, focused, integrated pattern of opening up was established throughout the country, including SEZs, coastal open cities, and coastal economic open zones. These all constituted a frontier for opening up to the outside world which incorporated two municipalities, 25 provincial cities, 67 counties, and a population of approximately 150 million people. Opening up to the outside world became an important driving force for China's economic and social development.

COMPLETION OF THE SIXTH FIVE-YEAR PLAN AND FORMULATION OF THE SEVENTH FIVE-YEAR PLAN

At the end of 1985, the sixth five-year plan for national economic and social development was successfully completed. During the period of the sixth five-year plan, the output of major industrial and agricultural products increased substantially and national revenue, which had been decreasing each year towards the end of the period of the fifth five-year plan, began instead to increase year on year, resulting in a basic balance of income and expenditure. Significant progress was also made in capital construction and technological transformation, whilst foreign economic trade and technological exchanges opened new horizons. The completion of the sixth five-year plan resulted in more effective solutions to some of the economic problems that had long plagued China in the past. The huge increase in grain and cotton production provided conditions for solving the problem of insufficient food and clothing for the people. The supply of consumer goods became relatively abundant, and many goods which had been rationed and supplied based on coupons in the past, apart from grain and oil, basically no longer needed to be rationed. These achievements and changes were outstanding when compared with the periods of the previous five-year plans since the founding of new China.

Paying attention to economic development while putting social development in a prominent position was a distinctive feature of the sixth five-year plan. Previous five-year plans had been called plans for national economic development, and from the beginning of the sixth five-year plan, the name was changed to plans for national economic and social development. During the period of the sixth five-year plan, the party and the government made arrangements for social development with regard to aspects such as population, labour, employment, the population's income and consumption, urban and rural construction, social welfare, culture, public health, physical education and environmental protection. Family planning was identified as one of China's basic state policies, and the state broadly advocated for each couple to have only one child. Under the historical conditions at that time, the implementation of this policy ensured that population growth was in keeping with the growth of the national economy, which was of great significance for improving people's living standards. During this period, environmental protection was established as a basic state policy. The party and the government made great efforts to solve the prominent problem of environmental pollution, and the environmental conditions of key scenic cities such as Beijing, Hangzhou, Suzhou and Guilin were moderately improved.

On the basis of the smooth implementation of the sixth five-year plan, the CPC Central Committee began to formulate preparations for the seventh five-year plan in 1983. In September 1985, the National Party Congress adopted the *Recommendations of the CPC Central Committee on the Formulation of the Seventh Five-Year Plan for National Economic and Social Development*. On the recommendation of the CPC Central Committee, the State Council formulated a draft plan for the seventh five-year plan. In April 1986, the plan was approved by the Fourth Session of the Sixth NPC.

THE ADVANCE OF SOCIALIST DEMOCRACY AND THE LEGAL SYSTEM

On 4 December 1982, the Fifth NPC adopted the newly amended *Constitution of the PRC*. The constitution, based on the 1954 constitution, corrected the shortcomings of the 1978 constitution and was more complete. The new constitution correctly expounded the historical experience since the founding of new China, specified that the fundamental task of the country in the future was to focus on socialist modernisation, and made clear provisions for China's fundamental and basic political system, basic economic system, the basic rights and obligations of citizens, and the establishment and duties of state institutions, and other major issues, in the form of fundamental laws. The constitution stipulated many new provisions for state institutions, including strengthening the system of people's congresses, re-establishing the positions of national president and vice-president, the establishment by the state of the CMC to lead the national armed forces, and the implementation by the State Council of the system of prime ministerial responsibility, amongst others. These new regulations added new elements and characteristics to the system of socialism with Chinese characteristics.

The implementation of the new constitution accelerated the construction of the legal system. During the Sixth and Seventh NPCs, ninety-six laws were considered and adopted, with emphasis on two aspects; firstly, the formulation of laws to meet the needs of modernisation, economic reforms, and opening up to the outside world, and secondly, the enacting of laws to protect civil rights. In 1986, the campaign of the first five-year plan for popularisation of knowledge of the law was launched throughout the country. After that, a plan for popularising the knowledge of laws was formulated every five years, and legal awareness campaigns were continuously strengthened and deepened.

In developing and perfecting the system of multi-party cooperation and political consultation under the leadership of the CPC, the 12th

National Congress developed the eight character policy of 'long-term coexistence and mutual oversight' into the sixteen-character policy of 'long-term coexistence, mutual supervision, sincere treatment of each other, and sharing weal or woe'. Through this the role of the democratic parties in the political life of the country was further articulated, and the cooperation between the CPC and the democratic parties entered a new stage. In May 1984, in order to improve the system of regional ethnic autonomy, the *Law of the PRC on Regional Ethnic Autonomy* was promulgated, and the system of regional ethnic autonomy was established as a basic political system of the state. In order to promote the construction of grassroots democracy, enterprises and institutions throughout the country generally established workers' congresses, residents' committees in urban areas were further improved, villagers' committees in rural areas were gradually established, and a grassroots mass self-government system of socialism with Chinese Characteristics was gradually formed.

The achievements of the construction of socialist democracy and the legal system, and the reform of the political system represented by the formulation of the 1982 constitution, not only constituted an important strengthening and improvement of China's socialist political system, but also provided an important political guarantee for the deepening of reforms of China's economic system, economic development and social stability.

STRENGTHENING AND IMPROVING PARTY LEADERSHIP

After the Third Plenary Session of the 11th CPC Central Committee, the CPC Central Committee took practical measures to improve party rules and regulations, and rectify the party's style of work, in order to further enhance the party's cohesiveness and preparedness to engage in struggle, and carry forward the party's fine traditions and style of work. In February 1980, the Fifth Plenary Session of the 11th CPC Central Committee adopted the *Several Guidelines on Political Life Within the Party* and announced them to the whole country. The guidelines summarised the lessons learned from the historical political life of the party, concretised the relevant provisions of the party constitution and the principle of democratic centralism, and put forward 12 requirements: adherence to the party's political line and ideological line, adherence to collective leadership and opposition to individual arbitrariness, maintaining the central unity of the party and strictly abiding by the party's discipline, adherence to the party spirit and eradication of factionalism, speaking the truth and ensuring unity of words and deeds, developing intraparty democracy and treating differing opinions correctly, protecting the rights of party members from violation, ensuring that elections fully reflect the will of voters, fighting against wrong tendencies, malefactors and misdeeds, treating comrades who make mistakes correctly, accepting the oversight of the party and the masses, and prohibiting the granting of privileges, and studying hard and being faithful to the party as well as being professional.

After this, the Central Commission for Discipline Inspection held three sessions within the course of one year to promote the implementation of the guidelines. During the symposium held by the Central Commission for Discipline Inspection in November 1980, Chen Yun shrewdly pointed out that, "the work style of the ruling party is a matter of life and death for the party" and called on the party organisations at all levels to raise awareness and strive to strengthen the construction of the party's work style. The publication and implementation of the guidelines played a very important role in restoring and improving intraparty democracy, safeguarding the party's centralisation and unity, ensuring party discipline would be taken seriously, promoting party unity, and ensuring the smooth progress of reform and opening up, and socialist modernisation.

In order to solve prominent problems existing within the party, party-wide consolidation was implemented in stages from October 1983 to May 1987, with the basic task of unifying thought, reorganising work methods, strengthening discipline and purifying organisation, in accordance with the *Decision of the CPC Central Committee on Party Consolidation* of the Second Plenary Session of the 12th CPC Central Committee. The process of party consolidation improved the consciousness of the majority of party members, especially party cadres, in terms of ideology, politics and actions, bringing them into line with the CPC Central Committee, incorporated investigations into serious violations of discipline by a number of party members and cadres, and cleaned up the so-called 'three kinds of people', which included those rebels who followed the counter-revolutionary group of Lin Biao and Jiang Qing during the Cultural Revolution, those with gravely factional ideology, and the 'smash and grab' elements. This consolidation of the party played an important role in solving the problems of intra-party ideology, work style, organisational impurities and poor discipline left over from the Cultural Revolution.

Achieving the four modernisations required a large number of young and vigorous leading cadres at all levels. Under the new situation of reform and opening up, and socialist modernisation, Deng Xiaoping, Chen Yun and other older revolutionaries astutely reminded all party comrades to pay attention to training and selecting qualified successors, and to realise the revolutionisation, rejuvenation, intellectualisation and specialisation of cadres, so that the party's cause would have qualified successors and continue to advance. In accordance with the standards of the four modernisations, the CPC Central Committee accelerated the pace of selecting young and middle-aged cadres. A large number of vigorous, professionally competent and talented young and middle-aged cadres distinguished themselves and shouldered heavy responsibilities. In September 1985, the National Party Congress made large-scale adjustments to the leadership of the CPG, guiding the leadership of the CPG to make great steps in promoting younger staff. This provided a strong impetus to the succession of older cadres by younger ones and improvements in the structure of the cadre ranks, ensuring that the influx into the ranks of new cadres would continue to advance together with the cause of the party.

THE CONSTRUCTION OF SOCIALIST SPIRITUAL CIVILISATION

The objective environment of reform and opening up, and the development of a commodity economy urgently required the strengthening of the construction of socialist spiritual civilisation. In the early 1980s under the attention and leadership of the CPC Central Committee, the 'Five Disciplines, Four Graces and Three Loves' campaign was conducted widely, which focused on civility, politeness, hygiene, order, morality, the beauty of the spirit, language, behaviour and the environment, and love for the motherland, socialism and the CPC. The construction of socialist spiritual civilisation played a positive role in promoting the improvement of the party's work style and the social climate, resulting in the emergence of a number of models for the times.

Jiang Zhuying of the Changchun Institute of Optics, Fine Mechanics and Physics of the Chinese Academy of Sciences, paved the road of chasing light with dedication, worked hard and selflessly, developed China's first optical transfer function test device, and became a model example of intelligentsia. Luo Jianfu of the 771st Research Institute of the Ministry of Aerospace Industry, with indifference towards worldly rewards, courageously tackled problems and made a major contribution to China's aerospace industry, becoming known as the 'Chinese Pavel', reminiscent of the protagonist Pavel Korchagin from the Soviet novel *How the Steel was Tempered*. Zhu Boru, who served with the airforce in Wuhan, served the masses by setting himself alight like a burning coal and gave warmth to others, and became known as the 'new Lei Feng of the 1980s', rejoicing with the masses and sharing their hardships. Gu Wenchang, secretary of the County Party Committee of Dongshan County, Fujian Province, with relentless courage, led the people of Dongshan to fight hard for more than a dozen years to build a protective forest along the coast for the benefit of future generations, thereby erecting an immortal monument in the hearts of the people. The moving achievements of these heroic models provided a powerful spiritual impetus for the entire population to devote themselves to reform and opening up, and modernisation.

In order to build a socialist spiritual civilisation, it is necessary to resolutely resist the mistaken tendency to blindly promote the decadent ideology and culture of the western bourgeoisie, and to firmly oppose the *zeitgeist* of liberalising the bourgeoisie characterised by seeking to deviate from the socialist road and from the leadership of the party. In October 1983, Deng Xiaoping made it clear at the Second Plenary Session of the 12th CPC Central Committee that the ideological front must not engage in spiritual pollution, and that it was necessary to use Marxism to analyse, identify and criticise modern western bourgeois culture. In accordance with the spirit of the plenary session, those engaged in ideology and culture across the country launched a struggle against spiritual pollution and bourgeois liberalisation.

In September 1986, the Sixth Plenary Session of the 12th CPC Central Committee issued The *Resolution of the CPC Central Committee Regarding the Guiding Principles of the Construction of a Socialist Spiritual Civilisation*. The resolution emphasised that the liberalisation of the bourgeoisie, being the denial of the socialist system and the assertion of the capitalist system, is fundamentally contrary to the interests of the people and the tide of history, and is firmly opposed by the people. Based on an overview of the general layout of socialist modernisation, the resolution expounded the strategic position and fundamental tasks of the construction of socialist spiritual civilisation, emphasising the need to cultivate socialist citizens with ideals, morals, culture and discipline, united Chinese people of all ethnic groups with the common ideal of building socialism with Chinese characteristics, and improved the ideological, moral, scientific and cultural quality of the whole Chinese nation. This resolution was the party's first programmatic document on the construction of spiritual civilisation, and it provided the basic guidelines for the healthy development of the construction of a spiritual civilisation in China.

However, because some people, including some senior leading cadres, were not sufficiently knowledgeable about the essence and risks of bourgeois liberalisation and did not do their best to oppose it, the strengthening of the guiding position of Marxism in the construction of spiritual civilisation and the opposing of bourgeois liberalisation emphasised in the resolution of the Sixth Plenary Session of the 12th CPC Central Committee were not diligently implemented. At the end of 1986, there were student protests which affected many cities. In January 1987, the Politburo convened an enlarged meeting at which Hu Yaobang reviewed mistakes on major political principles. The meeting made a serious comradely criticism of Hu Yaobang, and at the same time, honestly affirmed the achievements of his work. The meeting agreed to accept his request to resign as general secretary of the Central Committee and to retain his positions as a member of the Politburo and as a member of the Standing Committee of the Politburo. Zhao Ziyang was elected as acting general secretary. The decision of this enlarged meeting was later confirmed by the Seventh Plenary Session of the 12th CPC Central Committee held in October of the same year.

5
THE CPC'S 13TH NATIONAL CONGRESS AND ESTABLISHMENT OF THE PARTY'S BASIC LINE IN THE PRIMARY STAGE OF SOCIALISM

THE PARTY'S 13TH NATIONAL CONGRESS AND THE 'THREE-STEP' DEVELOPMENT STRATEGY

With the constant deepening of reform and opening up, and the continuous promotion of the cause of socialism with Chinese characteristics, there was a compelling need for the party, on the basis of a profound analysis of the basic national conditions and a summary of practical experience, to provide a clear theoretical and practical answer to the fundamental question surrounding the nature of socialism and how to build it, as well as what basic line should be followed in China's drive for reform and opening up, and socialist modernisation.

The CPC's 13th National Congress was held in Beijing from 25 October to 1 November 1987. There Zhao Ziyang gave a report entitled *Advancing Along the Road of Socialism with Chinese Characteristics*. The General Assembly deliberated and adopted the report and the *Amendments to Some of the Articles of the Constitution of the CPC*.

The prominent contribution of this congress was to systematically expound the theory of the primary stage of socialism and clearly summarise the basic line of the party in the primary stage of socialism. On the eve of the congress, Deng Xiaoping stated that the central task of the whole phase of the history of socialism was to develop productivity. In China's case, he said, the first step was to break free from poverty. Neither poverty nor lethargic development are features of socialism. He also clearly stated that, "Socialism itself is the primary stage of communism, and China is in the primary stage of socialism, which is the stage of underdevelopment. Everything has to start from this reality, and we must formulate plans in accordance with this reality."

The 13th National Congress of the CPC

The CPC's 13th National Congress noted that the primary stage of socialism has two layers of meaning: firstly, Chinese society was already a socialist society, and China must uphold socialism and not depart from it; secondly, Chinese socialist society was still in the primary stage, and it was essential to start from this reality and not move beyond this stage. The congress also noted that the primary stage of socialism does not refer to the initial stage that any country will go through when it enters socialism, but rather to the specific stage that China must go through to build socialism under the conditions of backward productivity and an underdeveloped commodity economy. It would take a minimum of more than one hundred years from the basic completion of socialist transformation pertaining to the private ownership of means of production in the 1950s to the basic realisation of socialist modernisation, and this is all part of the primary stage of socialism. In the primary stage of socialism, the main contradiction is the contradiction between the people's ever-growing material and cultural needs and backward social production. The main task of the party and the state is to develop productivity and advance socialist modernisation. Advancing the theory of the primary stage of socialism became the basic foundation upon which the party formulated the correct line and policies, and provided a powerful theoretical weapon for upholding reform and opening up, as well as for upholding and developing socialism with Chinese characteristics.

Starting from the new understanding of the primary stage of socialism, the congress proposed that the basic line of the party in the primary stage of socialism was to lead and unite the people of all ethnic groups throughout the country and, with a focus on economic construction, adhere to the four basic principles, namely, upholding reform and opening up, self-reliance, and hard work and innovation, and striving to build China into a prosperous and strong, democratic and civilised modern socialist country. In summary, this approach can be described as 'one central task and two basic points', namely the central task of economic construction and upholding the four basic principles, and reform and opening up. Practice has proven that having economic construction as the central task is the key to the prosperity of the country, that the four basic principles are essential to the establishment of the nation, and that reform and opening up is the path to becoming a strong country. This fundamental line is the lifeline of the party and the country, as well as being the source of the people's happiness.

Another major contribution of the CPC's 13th National Congress was the formulation of a 'three-step' strategy for modernisation and development. This was advanced based on Deng Xiaoping's strategic vision of the steps for China's achievement of modernisation. As early as December 1979, Deng Xiaoping stated in his meeting with Japanese Prime Minister Ohira Masayoshi that, "The four modernisations we want to achieve are a distinctly Chinese four modernisations. Our conceptualisation of the four modernisations is not like your conceptualisation of modernisation, but rather of a 'moderately prosperous family'." After that, the CPC's 12th National Congress established the strategic goal of achieving moderate prosperity by the end of the 20th century in two steps. In April 1987, Deng Xiaoping clearly articulated the vision for the 'three-step' modernisation strategy when he met with Alfonso Guerra, then deputy general secretary of the Spanish Socialist Workers' Party and deputy prime minister. This strategic vision was confirmed at the 13th National Congress. This National Congress pointed out that after the Third Plenary Session of the 11th CPC Central Committee the strategic deployment of China's economic construction was divided into three steps: 1. To achieve a doubling of the level of GDP from 1980, and solve the problem of insufficient food and clothing. This task has been largely realised. 2. To further double GDP again by the end of the 20th century and raise people's standard of living to moderate prosperity. 3. To attain the GDP level of moderately developed countries by the middle of the 21st century, with the people being relatively affluent and modernisation having been basically achieved. The 'three-step' development strategy provided a positive and secure plan for the ambitious goal of carrying forward China's courageous diligence, by embodying the ambition of the party and the people to dare to forge ahead, and also reflecting the scientific mindset of starting from actual circumstances and following objective laws. This development strategy constitutes a great achievement of the CPC in exploring the laws of the construction of socialism with Chinese characteristics.

The congress highly appraised the great significance of pioneering the road of building socialism with Chinese characteristics after the Third Plenary Session of the 11th CPC Central Committee in the historical process of the Sinicisation of Marxism, noting that there had been two historic leaps in the process of integrating Marxism with practice in China over the previous 60 years. The first leap took place during the new democratic revolution, when the CPC drew on their experiences of success and failure, found a revolutionary path with Chinese characteristics, and led the revolution to victory. The second leap took place after the Third Plenary Session of the 11th CPC Central Committee, when the CPC began to find a path to building socialism with Chinese characteristics and pioneered a new stage of socialist construction, all on the basis of summing up the experience of both positive and negative aspects of the founding of new China over the previous 30 years and on the basis of studying international experience and the world situation. The congress concluded and summarised a series of scientific theoretical views formed in the practice of reform and opening up, and modernisation from the stages, task, dynamics, conditions and layout of China's socialist construction and the international environment, and from this gave a clearer outline of the theory of building socialism with Chinese characteristics.

The General Assembly elected the Central Committee, the Central Advisory Commission and the Central Commission for Discipline Inspection. The First Plenary Session of the 13th CPC Central Committee elected Zhao Ziyang, Li Peng, Qiao Shi, Hu Qili and Yao Yilin as members of the Standing Committee of the Politburo and Zhao Ziyang as General Secretary of the CPC Central Committee, determined that Deng Xiaoping should be the chairman of the CMC, and approved Chen Yun as chairman of the Central Advisory Commission and Qiao Shi as secretary of the Central Commission for Discipline Inspection. After the 13th CPC National Congress, Deng Xiaoping no longer held the post of member of the Politburo Standing Committee. As the chief architect of China's socialist reform and opening up, and modernisation, he still closely followed the cause of reform and opening up, and modernisation with a strong sense of responsibility and mission, and continued to play an extremely important role in the development of socialism with Chinese characteristics under the leadership of the party.

CONTINUING ADVANCE OF REFORM AND OPENING UP, AND THE BEGINNING OF GOVERNANCE AND RECTIFICATION

In accordance with the deployment of the 13th CPC National Congress, the reform of the economic system in 1988 focused on deepening the reform of the mechanisms of enterprise management. In February of that year, the State Council promulgated the *Interim Regulations on the Contracted Management Responsibility System for Nationally-Owned Industrial Enterprises*. In April, the First Session of the Seventh NPC passed the *Law of the PRC on State-Owned Industrial Enterprises*, making clearer provisions on the principles of reform for the 'separation of two rights' of ownership and management of enterprises, and providing legal guarantees for the reform of the contract management responsibility system for enterprises. The constitutional amendments adopted by the congress gave the provision that, 'The state permits the private economy to exist and develop within the limits prescribed by law. The private economy is a supplement of the socialist public ownership economy', thereby confirming the legal status of the private economy.

The pace of opening up to the outside world increased further. In March 1988, the State Council decided to appropriately expand the coastal economic open zone, newly incorporating 140 cities and counties, including the three provincial capitals of Hangzhou, Nanjing and Shenyang. In April, the First Session of the Seventh NPC formally approved the establishment of Hainan Province and the creation of the Hainan SEZ, reflecting the courage and determination of the CPC Central Committee to accelerate reform and opening up. After this, the beautiful Chinese island of Hainan gained unprecedented opportunities for development and entered a new historical stage of deepening reform and broader opening up.

The development of China's economy accelerated from 1984 to 1988, driven by comprehensive reforms. During these five years, GDP grew at an average annual rate of 12.1%, total industrial output reached more than Rmb6 trillion, and the country's economic strength and national strengths reached a new level. However, in the operation of the economy there also appeared a series of problems related to instability and incongruity, which mainly manifested themselves in rising inflation, imbalances in social production and consumption totals, irrational structure, and so on. The party and the government sought new ways to solve these problems. In early 1985, a 'soft landing' approach was adopted, in which the balance of total social demand and supply was gradually restored in a relatively moderate way, but the desired effect was not achieved. In the summer of 1988, preparations were made to implement a 'price break', by comprehensively promoting price reform and liberalising prices. At a meeting of the Politburo that August, the Politburo adopted the *Preliminary Plan on Price and Wage Reform*, by which it was anticipated to take about five years to resolve the price issue. Although the plan was not formally implemented, the news spread, triggering expectations of high inflation and panic, which sparked a nationwide rush to withdraw savings deposits and the panic buying of goods.

In late September 1988, faced with this grim situation, the Third Plenary Session of the 13th CPC Central Committee advanced a policy for managing the economic environment, rectifying economic order and comprehensively deepening reforms, and decided to shift from accelerating the pace of reform to focusing on the management of the economic environment and rectifying economic order in the following two years, stressing that price reform should not be the only focal point, but that reform must be comprehensive. In accordance with this decision, the State Council took a series of measures to reduce the scale of fixed asset investments and total social demand, to strengthen price control and management, and rectify various types of disorder in the economy, especially in the area of circulation. After approximately one year of governance and rectification, a reasonable degree of control had been attained regarding excessive social demand, but the difficulties of national economic development had not yet been navigated, with some deep-rooted structural and institutional problems still needing further resolution.

6
ADJUSTMENTS TO NATIONAL DEFENCE STRATEGY

After the Third Plenary Session of the 11th CPC Central Committee, national defence and military construction entered a new historical period. Based on a judgment of the changes in the international and domestic situation, the strategic military policy was changed from 'active defence and luring the enemy in deep' to 'active defence'. In September 1981, Deng Xiaoping, speaking at a military exercise and parade in northern China, clearly articulated the overall objective of building a strong modernised and regularised revolutionary army, indicating the direction of military construction in the new era.

In May and June 1985, the CMC held an expanded meeting where a major strategic shift in the guiding ideology of military construction was proposed which aimed to shift the army's work from a state of readiness based on 'fighting an early, large-scale and nuclear war' to a track of peacetime construction. This aimed to make full use of that period of peacetime and, under the precondition of complying with the general situation of the country's economic construction, to implement a policy of increasing the number of elite troops, and to implement basic military construction focused on modernisation in a planned and systematic manner, to reduce the number but improve the quality of troops, and to enhance the combat capability of the army under modern conditions. The commission decided to reduce military posts by one million and approved the *Programme of Military Reform and Streamlining and Consolidation*. From the second half of 1985 to the beginning of 1987, the million-man reduction in military forces, which had received global attention, was largely completed. As a result of the adjustment, the number of PLA military regions was adjusted from 11 to seven, and the General Staff Headquarters, the General Political Department, the General Logistics Department and the various PLA military district organs were reduced in size by nearly half. In 1988, a new system of military ranking was introduced, and a system of civilian cadres was established. The PLA took a significant step forward in increasing the number of elite troops, and in implementing synthesis and efficiency, and a new step was taken in the regularisation of the armed forces. The PLA complied with and served the general situation of the country's economic construction and constantly made new achievements in its participation in socialist construction. A number of military facilities were converted for civilian use, and science and technology for national defence began to be integrated with civil science and technology, training a large number of military and ground personnel, and thereby strongly supporting China's economic construction.

Deng Xiaoping inspecting PLA troops on parade to celebrate the 35th anniversary of the founding of the PRC on 1 October 1984

In the Water Diversion Project from the Luanhe River to Tianjin City and the construction site of the Shengli Oilfield, as well as on site in emergency flood relief, the PLA acted heroically with courage and diligence.

In the late 1970s and 1980s, the PLA performed its duties remarkably in the struggle to defend the sovereignty of China's territory. In February and March 1979, China's border guard units launched self-defence counterattacks on the Vietnamese border. In 1981, an operation was conducted to recapture the Faka and Koulin mountains. The battle to recapture the Laoshan mountains was carried out in 1984 and was followed by years of defensive operations in Laoshan, through which the situation in the border areas was stabilised. In March 1988, a Chinese naval vessel returned fire on a Vietnamese naval vessel that had scuttled in the Chigua Reef area of China's Nansha Islands (known internationally as the Spratly Islands) to engage in provocative actions. These acts of retaliatory self-defence served to defend the integrity of our territorial sovereignty, safeguarded China's national dignity and demonstrated that the PLA is a formidable force.

7
FORMATION OF THE 'ONE COUNTRY, TWO SYSTEMS' POLICY

Achieving the reunification of the motherland has always been the common aspiration of all China's sons and daughters. China must and will be unified. On this issue, the position of the CPC has always been unwavering and clear-cut. After the Third Plenary Session of the 11th CPC Central Committee, the CPC Central Committee and Deng Xiaoping, on the basis of the ideology of Mao Zedong, Zhou Enlai and other older revolutionaries regarding striving for the peaceful liberation of Taiwan, confronted history and reality, and creatively proposed the scientific concept of 'One Country, Two Systems', thereby pioneering a new way to achieve the reunification of the motherland by peaceful means.

In the late 1970s, the Taiwan issue was raised as an important issue on the party and state agenda. On 1 January 1979, the Standing Committee of the NPC issued the *Message to Compatriots in Taiwan*, solemnly proclaiming the major policy of striving for the peaceful reunification of the motherland. After this, the CPC Central Committee further considered the reunification of the motherland from a global perspective. In January 1980, Deng Xiaoping proposed that three things must be done in the 1980s, namely, in international affairs opposing hegemonism and safeguarding world peace, returning Taiwan to the motherland and achieving the reunification of the motherland, and intensifying economic construction. He also expounded many times the strategic vision of achieving peaceful reunification of the motherland on the basis of respecting the reality in Taiwan. In September 1981, Ye Jianying, chairman of the Standing Committee of the NPC, gave a speech in which he comprehensively and systematically expounded the nine principles for Taiwan's return to the motherland and peaceful reunification. Then in January 1982, Deng Xiaoping first proposed the concept of 'One Country, Two Systems'. In June 1983, he further proposed six guidelines for resolving the Taiwan issue, saying that, "After the reunification of the motherland, the Taiwan Special Administrative Region (SAR) may have its own autonomy and may implement a different system from the mainland. Its judiciary will be independent, and the right of final appeal will not be with Beijing. Taiwan can also have its own army, but this may not pose a threat to the mainland. The mainland will not send people to be stationed in Taiwan, and not only will the army not go, but administrative personnel will also not go. Taiwan's parties, administration and military will all be under Taiwan's own control. The CPG will also reserve some positions for Taiwan." These six guidelines further substantiated the concept of 'One Country, Two Systems'.

The concept of 'One Country, Two Systems' was first proposed for the settlement of the Taiwan issue, but it was first actually applied to the issue of the return of Hong Kong and Macau to the motherland and was successful in this. The Hong Kong issue is a historical legacy issue caused by the invasion of China by British colonialists. After the Opium War in 1840, the British Government forced the Qing Government to sign a succession of unequal treaties such as the Treaty of Nanjing, the Convention of Peking, and the Convention for the Extension of Hong Kong Territory, which forcibly occupied Hong Kong Island and Kowloon, and forcibly leased the New Territories. Under the Convention for the Extension of Hong Kong Territory, the period of the lease of the New Territories was 99 years and expired on 30 June 1997. In the late 1970s, the British Government raised the issue of Hong Kong's future status, trying to put pressure on China to gain long-term authority to govern Hong Kong. In December 1981, the CPC Central Committee took the decision to take back Hong Kong on 1 July 1997. The Chinese Government established two principles for dealing with the Hong Kong issue, firstly, that China must take back Hong Kong in 1997 and resume the exercise of sovereignty, and that this must not be delayed, and secondly, that the stability and prosperity of Hong Kong would be maintained under the premise of restoring the exercise of sovereignty.

In September 1982, British Prime Minister Margaret Thatcher visited China to commence the Sino-British negotiations on Hong Kong. Mrs Thatcher argued that Hong Kong's prosperity was reliant on British rule, and that if major changes to British administration were to be implemented or announced at that time, these would have a disastrous effect on Hong Kong and strongly expressed the feeling that the three treaties concerning Hong Kong could not be unilaterally repealed. In this regard, Deng Xiaoping categorically stated that the question of sovereignty was not an issue to be debated, and that in 1997 China would take back Hong Kong, not only the New Territories, but also Hong Kong Island and Kowloon as well. China and Britain conducted negotiations based on this premise. If China were still not to take back Hong Kong in 1997, if 48 years after the founding of the PRC Hong Kong had not been reclaimed, no Chinese leader or government would be able to justify this to the people of China or even to the people of the rest of the world. He went on to say that if announcing that Hong Kong would be taken back would have a 'disastrous effect', as Mrs Thatcher said, then it was necessary for China to face this disaster courageously and decisively.

Deng Xiaoping meeting with British Prime Minister Margaret Thatcher on 24 September 1982

Through this meeting, the Chinese side took the initiative to reclaim Hong Kong, and the fundamental approach for resolving the Hong Kong issue was thus set in accordance with the will of the party and the people.

After more than two years and 22 rounds of difficult negotiations, in December 1984 the Chinese and British governments formally signed a joint declaration on Hong Kong, confirming that the Chinese Government would resume the exercise of sovereignty over Hong Kong on 1 July 1997. After that, Hong Kong entered a transitional period ahead of its return to the motherland.

After this, under the provisions of the 1982 Constitution and on the basis of extensively listening to the views of people from all sectors of Hong Kong society, the *Basic Law of the Hong Kong SAR of the PRC* was deliberated and adopted at the Third Session of the Seventh NPC in April 1990. The Basic Law of Hong Kong established the policy guidelines of the Central Government towards Hong Kong in legal form and laid the legal foundation for the rule of law in Hong Kong.

After initiating the process for Hong Kong's return, the issue of Macau's return was also put on the agenda. Macau, including the Macau Peninsula, Taipa Island and Luhuan Island, had been Chinese territory since ancient times but was gradually forcibly occupied by Portugal from the 16th century onwards. In June 1986, the Chinese and Portuguese governments began negotiations on Macau. The negotiations went relatively smoothly and, in April 1987, the Chinese and Portuguese governments formally signed a joint declaration on Macau, announcing that the Chinese Government would resume the exercise of sovereignty over Macau on 20 December 1999. Macau then entered a transitional period ahead of its return to the motherland, and in March 1993, the *Basic Law of the Macau SAR of the PRC* was deliberated and adopted at a meeting of the Eighth NPC. The preliminary practice implemented to solve the Hong Kong and Macau issues proves that the concept of 'One Country, Two Systems' embodies the principle of achieving the reunification of the motherland and safeguarding national sovereignty, and also takes full account of the history and realities of Hong Kong, Macau and other places, and that it is a creative policy to promote the peaceful reunification of the motherland, which has had a great impact on the international community.

8
FOREIGN POLICY ADJUSTMENTS

On the eve of the Third Plenary Session of the 11th CPC Central Committee, two major initiatives regarding China's foreign affairs were adopted. Firstly, the *Sino-Japanese Treaty of Peace and Friendship* was signed with Japan in August 1978. Secondly, a joint communique on the formal establishment of diplomatic relations with the US was issued in December 1978. After the Third Plenary Session of the 11th CPC Central Committee, with the shift in the party's and state's priorities and the development of reform and opening up, striving for a peaceful international environment conducive to China's modernisation drive increasingly became the consensus of the whole party. Based on the development and changes in the international context, the CPC Central Committee began to make major adjustments to foreign policy, implementing two major changes.

The first change was to alter the view that war was inevitable and imminent, and make new scientific judgments on war and peace. In the 1980s, Deng Xiaoping repeatedly stated that although the danger of war still existed, there had been encouraging developments in the forces constraining war, that the growth of the forces of world peace had surpassed the growth of the forces of war, and that it was possible that there would not be a large-scale world war for a long period of time, and that there was hope for maintaining world peace. In March 1985, Deng Xiaoping clearly advanced the important assertion that "peace and development are the two outstanding issues in the world today", which provided an important foundation for the party and the state to formulate foreign policy in the new era.

The second change was altering the 'one line' strategy. After the establishment of diplomatic relations between China and the US, the US Congress passed the *Taiwan Relations Act*, and continued to interfere in China's internal affairs and undermine China's sovereignty and security. Although China and the US issued a joint communiqué on 17 August 1982, regarding the step-by-step process to be followed until a final and complete settlement of the issue of US arms sales to Taiwan, the US Government has since failed to deliver on its promises. At the same time, the Soviet Union repeatedly expressed its desire to improve its relations with China. Against this background, China changed its past 'one line' strategy of allying with the US and opposing the Soviet Union. In September 1982, the report of the CPC's 12th National Congress solemnly affirmed China's adherence to a foreign policy characterised by acting independently and the development of relations with other countries guided by the Five Principles of Peaceful Coexistence. The report also highlighted the CPC's willingness to 'develop relations with the communist parties and other working-class political parties of other countries in accordance with the principles of independence, full equality, mutual respect and non-interference in each other's internal affairs'. These four principles became the basic principles for the establishment and development of inter-party relations between the CPC and political parties around the world.

In April 1986, the State Council's *Report on the Seventh Five-Year Plan*, approved by the Fourth Session of the Sixth NPC, expounded the main thrust and basic principles of China's independent and peaceful foreign policy from 10 aspects, and summarised the adjustments of China's foreign policy since reform and opening up, and drew conclusions. The report mentioned that China maintains that all countries in the world are equal, irrespective of their size, level of wealth, or relative strength, that the affairs of all countries should be left to the peoples of those nations themselves to attend to, and that the affairs of the world should be resolved through consultations involving all countries, rather than just by one or two superpowers. China will never proclaim itself a hegemony and will resolutely oppose hegemonism, irrespective of origin and form. China will uphold independence at all times and under all circumstances, and determine its own attitude and responses on all international issues according to the various merits and demerits of each issue. China would by no means attach itself to any superpower and would also certainly not form an alliance with any. China would not determine affinities and preferences based on differences and similarities in social system or ideology, and would resolutely oppose any country using similarities or differences in social systems and ideologies as a pretext for occupying the territory, or interfering in the internal affairs, of other countries.

With the adjustments in foreign policy, China's diplomacy was developed in an all-round way, and an external environment conducive to China's reform, opening-up and modernisation drive began to take shape. By 1989, 137 countries had established diplomatic relations with China.

During this period, dealing with Sino-US and Sino-Soviet relations was one of the main aspects of diplomatic work. Although Sino-US relations were severely tested by issues such as arms sales to Taiwan, they maintained steady development in the 1980s. In terms of Sino-Soviet relations, the two countries consulted on the normalisation of relations from 1982 onwards. After the main obstacles affecting Sino-Soviet relations had been basically resolved, Mikhail Gorbachev, chairman of the Presidium of the Supreme Soviet and general secretary of the Communist Party of the Soviet Union, visited China in May 1989, and normalised relations between the two parties and the two nations, which had been ruptured for more than 20 years, providing a good basis for the establishment of a new type of relationship between superpowers that was non-aligned, non-confrontational and did not target third parties.

9
UNDERGOING THE TRIAL OF POLITICAL TURMOIL, AND THE COMPLETION OF GOVERNANCE RECTIFICATION

THE POLITICAL STORM OF 1989

Just when the work of governance and rectification was being further advanced, from late 1988 to early 1989 a very small number of people took advantage of the mistakes in the work of the party and the government, and the anxiety of the people regarding increasing prices, as well as dissatisfaction with corruption among some party members and cadres, and carried out activities to incite opposition to the leadership of the CPC and opposition to the socialist system in several major cities, especially in Beijing.

Hu Yaobang passed away on 15 April 1989. The CPC Central Committee gave due recognition to Hu Yaobang's outstanding contribution to the cause of China's revolution, construction and reform during his 60-year revolutionary career. During the memorial ceremony conducted by the CPG, a very small number of people took the opportunity to spread rumours and enticed the masses to hold demonstrations. In Beijing, a serious incident occurred when a crowd of people stormed the main Xinhuamen entrance of the Zhongnanhai Palace. In other cities, criminal activities such as fighting, smashing, looting and arson were carried out by lawless elements. On 24 April, the Standing Committee of the Politburo analysed developments and concluded that political upheaval of a planned, organised anti-party and anti-socialist nature lay ahead. On 26 April, the *People's Daily* published an editorial entitled *It Is Necessary to Take a Clear-Cut Stand Against Disturbances*, in which it pointed out the nature of the struggle to the party and the people. However, a very small number of people with ulterior motives still incited the masses to occupy Tiananmen Square and continue various illegal activities, which eventually turned into a counter-revolutionary riot.

At a crucial moment for the party and the country, the Politburo, with the resolute and strong support of Deng Xiaoping and other older revolutionaries, relied on the people to stand out against the unrest and took decisive measures on 4 June to quell the counter-revolutionary riots in Beijing. Beijing and other large and medium-sized cities soon returned to normal. The victory of this struggle defended China's socialist administration and upheld public order and the fundamental interests of the people.

The occurrence of this political turmoil was not accidental, but rather the result of the interaction of various domestic and international factors. As Deng Xiaoping pointed out, "This storm would have come sooner or later. This is determined by the international climate and China's own local situation. It was bound to happen and could not be diverted by the will of the people." From an international perspective, after the end of the Second World War the capitalist world passed through a crisis, and under the impetus of the new scientific and technological revolution, productivity developed rapidly. Meanwhile some socialist countries suffered considerable difficulties due to serious mistakes in decision-making, economic construction and social development, and the superiority of the socialist system could not be well developed, affecting the image of socialism in people's minds, thereby creating the misconception that 'socialism is inferior to capitalism'. Political forces in some western countries pursued the 'peaceful evolution' of socialist countries over a long period of time and supported and nurtured various anti-communist and anti-socialist movements. In this sense, this instance of political turmoil was first instigated by international anti-communist and anti-socialist hostile forces and social thinking. From the perspective of the domestic environment, the leaders who presided over the central work for a period of time, while promoting reform and opening up, and developing the economy, failed to diligently implement a policy of opposing bourgeois liberalisation. As a result, the trend towards bourgeois liberalisation was not curbed, but instead became more and more widespread.

This political turmoil prompted the party to think more calmly about the past, present realities and the future. On 9 June 1989, Deng Xiaoping met with cadres having oversight over the forces implementing martial law in the capital to give a clear answer to the fundamental question of the direction of China's development and which route it would take, which was receiving great attention from China and the rest of the world. He pointed out that there was nothing wrong with the line and policy formulated by the Third Plenary Session of the 11th CPC Central Committee, including the 'trilogy' of development strategies, and that the basic line of 'one central task and two basic points' outlined by the 13th CPC National Congress was not wrong. He also underscored that the party would continue to implement unswervingly the basic line and policy that it had formulated. Deng Xiaoping believed that if a mistake had been made, it was that there had not been enough consistency in upholding the four basic principles, and that the basic line and policy had not been used as the fundamental ideology for the education of the people, students, the masses of cadres and also CPC members. If this had not been done adequately, it was because China had not yet been adequately reformed and opened up. Deng Xiaoping's important speech summed up the lessons learned in the previous 10 years of reform and opening up, and pointed out the right direction for China's reform and development after the period of political turmoil.

FOURTH PLENARY SESSION OF THE 13TH CPC CENTRAL COMMITTEE AND THE FORMATION OF A NEW CENTRAL LEADERSHIP

The Fourth Plenary Session of the 13th CPC Central Committee was held in June 1989. In view of Zhao Ziyang's serious mistakes in supporting the unrest and splitting the party at a crucial moment in the struggle for the survival of the party and the nation, the plenary session decided to repeal all of his party leadership roles. The plenary session made adjustments to the members of the central leadership and elected Jiang Zemin as general secretary of the Central Committee.

At the plenary session Jiang Zemin said, "On this occasion the central leadership has made some adjustments to personnel, but the line and basic policies of the Third Plenary Session of the 11th CPC Central Committee have not changed and must continue to be implemented. On this most basic issue, I would like to make two very clear statements [describing the approach we must take]: one is unwavering and unshakable, and the other is complete implementation and consistency."

Before and after the Fourth Plenary Session of the 13th CPC Central Committee, Deng Xiaoping repeatedly stated solemnly that it was now time to truly establish a new third generation of leaders. He said that the third generation of leadership must have a core, that core must be consciously upheld, and that the core was Comrade Jiang Zemin. He stressed that the key to China's problems was for the CPC to have a good

Politburo, especially a good Politburo Standing Committee, and that as long as there were no issues with this aspect, China would be as stable as the age-old mountains. After the plenary session, the new central leadership firmly and comprehensively implemented the party's basic line, taking firm hold of governance and rectification, and deepening reform, and gaining a firm grip of the tasks of building the party, building a spiritual civilisation, and ideological and political work. As a result, the national political situation quickly stabilised, the economic situation gradually improved, and matters on the ideological front took a turn for the better.

Jiang Zemin delivering a speech at the Fourth Plenary Session of the 13th CPC Central Committee

In September 1989, Deng Xiaoping formally signed a request to the Politburo to resign as chairman of the CMC in light of the effective work of the new central leadership. In November, the Fifth Plenary Session of the 13th CPC Central Committee agreed to Deng Xiaoping's request and decided to appoint Jiang Zemin as chairman of the CMC. The plenary session held that Deng Xiaoping, in the fundamental interests of the party and the state, was resigning from his post while he was in good health, fulfilling his long-held wish to step down completely from the leadership post, and demonstrating the broad open-mindedness of a great proletarian revolutionary. Comrades at the meeting praised him highly for his example in abolishing the life-long system of leading cadres.

After the Fourth and Fifth Plenary Sessions of the 13th CPC Central Committee, the central leadership successfully achieved the promotion of a new generation to replace the old, which was of great significance for ensuring the stability and continuity of the party's policies and achieving lasting stability for the party and the country.

STRENGTHENING THE PARTY'S CONSTRUCTION, AND IDEOLOGICAL AND POLITICAL WORK

The party withstood the test amidst political turmoil and also became deeply aware of its own problems. Deng Xiaoping pointed out that the riots had cleared the party's minds and that it was vital that the party establish itself. After the Fourth Plenary Session of the 13th CPC Central Committee, the CPC Central Committee made great efforts to firmly proceed with building the party.

In August 1989, the CPC Central Committee issued a notice on strengthening the party's construction. Then, in accordance with the spirit of the notice, party organisations at all levels carefully investigated and purged key figures and priority issues from the period of political turmoil in the autumn and winter of 1989 and the spring of 1990 in order to ensure the purity of the party's ranks. Subsequently, party-wide education was conducted to ensure all party members were fully qualified and party members were also re-registered. At the same time, standards for party membership were made stricter, and some outstanding elements who had been cultivating and assimilating enterprises or who were from the front line of rural production joined the party.

With regard to strengthening construction of the party's ideology, there was a focus on educating party and government cadres at or above the county level on the basic theories of Marxism-Leninism-Mao Zedong Thought, and regularising and institutionalising this education, in order to help them to distinguish right from wrong in a complex environment and discern the correct direction to follow. According to the regulations of the CPC Central Committee, all members who enter leadership must undergo relevant study at the party school, and other leading members must go to the party school regularly to receive training in rotation.

After reflecting on the period of political turmoil, the CPC Central Committee stressed the need to carry forward the fine traditions of the party, foster close ties between the party and the masses, and the cadres and the masses, advance party construction to fight corruption and advocate probity, and resolutely fight against corruption and corrupt elements. Jiang Zemin stated clearly at the Fourth Plenary Session of the 13th CPC Central Committee that, "the eyes of the people of all ethnic groups throughout the country are watching us closely to see if we can come up with practical actions to punish corruption". In July 1989, the CPC Central Committee and the State Council decided to do seven things of public concern in curbing corruption and setting an example of integrity and hard work, starting with the leading comrades of the CPC Central Committee and the State Council. In March 1990, the Sixth Plenary Session of the 13th CPC Central Committee adopted the *Decision of the CPC Central Committee on Strengthening the Party's Ties with the Masses*. The implementation of these measures yielded good results.

In order to solve the problem of the weakening of the party's leadership, the CPC Central Committee stressed that the leadership of the CPC and the basic socialist political system must be upheld, that China's national character and basic systems must not be destabilised, and that no state governmental organs or social and political organisations would be permitted to deviate from the leadership of the CPC. These requirements would support the fundamental guarantee of social stability and economic development in China. Meanwhile, in terms of leadership structure, the CPC Central Committee further adjusted the relationship between the party and the organs of state power, and other social and political organisations, gradually restored party leadership groups that had been abolished from state organs, economic organisations and cultural organisations, strengthened construction of the party in enterprises, rural areas and universities and colleges, and gave play to the role of grassroots party organisations as the political core and battle fortress.

The party attached great importance to strengthening ideological and political work amongst the people, especially young students. Deng Xiaoping, in analysing the causes of the period of political turmoil, said that the biggest mistake of the previous 10 years had been education, mainly in terms of ideological and political education, the approach to which had fluctuated between being firm and being soft. After the Fourth Plenary Session of the 13th CPC Central Committee, the committee took a series of strong measures to overcome the problem of the softer approach. From 1990 to 1991, the Marxist theory of party building and the history of the CPC were studied by party members and cadres, and socialist ideological education was conducted among the masses. China's modern history and education regarding national conditions also received more and more attention from all sides. Consequently, the system of ideological education and work methods was restored and improved.

The party also strengthened its leadership of the front line of news and public opinion. In November 1989, Jiang Zemin made a speech at a seminar on news work organised by the Publicity Department of the CPC Central Committee, expounding the basic principles of socialist journalism, demanding that newspapers, radio and television be the mouthpieces of the party, the government and people, adhering to the party's principles regarding journalism, and opposing absolute freedom of the press. This session also advanced adherence to the principle of mainly positive publicity and playing the correct guiding role of public opinion. The strengthening of the party's construction and ideological and political work promoted China's political and social stability and created vital ideological and political conditions for governance and rectification and the deepening of reforms.

RESPONDING TO INTERNATIONAL INSTABILITY

After the period of political turmoil in 1989, the US Government and US Congress issued statements slandering and attacking the Chinese Government and announcing a series of 'sanctions'. In July, the G7 summit and the European Community announced the suspension of high-level political contacts with China and the deferral of World Bank loans, amongst other measures. A short while later, the international situation changed dramatically, with the collapse of the Soviet Union and radical changes in Eastern Europe, and the global socialist movement hit a low point.

In the face of a wave of anti-China sentiment set off by some Western countries led by the US and the incessant anti-China rhetoric, Deng Xiaoping repeatedly stressed the need to maintain stability and persevere with reform and opening up, and being sure to do one specific thing well, namely, taking care of China's own affairs. The key was for China to succeed in this aspect. He cautioned that the fundamental purpose of Western pressure on China was to force it to abandon socialism. China must resolutely buck this pressure and resist with a clear-cut stance. He said that although international public opinion may bring pressure on China, it was vital to be calm and collected, maintain the approach of acting independently, refusing to be misled, and not being afraid of anything. As long as China followed the socialist path which it had itself chosen, none would be able to crush it.

In September 1989, at the meeting to celebrate the 40th anniversary of the founding of the PRC, Jiang Zemin firmly stated, "Attempts to exclude and isolate China are unwise and impossible. No economic sanctions will shake our determination to revitalise China and adhere to the socialist road, nor will they shake our belief in friendly relations with the peoples of the world."

The party and the government identified two priorities for diplomacy in the early 1990s in order to turn the tide on the situation and take the initiative, firstly, to develop good-neighbourly diplomacy, stabilise and actively develop relations with neighbouring countries, and strengthen solidarity and cooperation with developing countries, and secondly, to break the 'sanctions' imposed by western countries and restore and stabilise relations with developed Western countries.

Party and state leaders made every effort to actively develop diplomatic activities. Between 1990 and 1992, China and Indonesia restored diplomatic relations, Sino-Vietnamese relations were normalised, Sino-Indian relations were greatly improved, diplomatic relations were established with Saudi Arabia, Singapore, Israel and South Korea, the transition from Sino-Soviet to Sino-Russian relations was successfully achieved, and normal relations were established or developed with newly independent Eastern European countries after the collapse of the Soviet Union. By the end of August 1992, 154 countries had established diplomatic relations with China. China also succeeded in its bid to host the UN's Fourth World Conference on Women in Beijing in 1995. Instead of being isolated by Western 'sanctions', China actually played an active role in international affairs.

China conducted a rational, favourable and justified struggle against the 'sanctions' imposed by some Western countries, which were headed by the US. China's leaders took stock of the situation and adopted a policy of political and economic integration, and official and civil integration, pushing for Japan to take the lead in lifting 'sanctions' against China in 1990. Soon after this a number of other Western countries and international organisations also lifted their 'sanctions' against China. By the end of 1991, China's relations with most Western countries were basically back on track.

The US took the lead in 'sanctioning' China, but also gradually came to realise that isolating China may not be in its own best interests. From July to December 1989, US President George W Bush twice sent the president's assistant for national security affairs, Brent Scowcroft, to China as a special envoy. At the most difficult stage of Sino-US relations, Deng Xiaoping said, "In order to resolve the past, the US should take the initiative, and only the US can take the initiative", and "If they want China to beg, it's not going to happen. Even if it drags on for a hundred years, the Chinese will not beg for the lifting of sanctions." At the same time, China continued to actively communicate with the US side with a vision that maintained a visionary and sagacious view of the overall situation. After the Gulf crisis broke out, the US had to reconsider improving relations with China in order to get China's support on the Gulf issue. In November 1993, at the invitation of US President Bill Clinton, Chinese President Jiang Zemin attended the first Informal APEC Leadership Conference in Seattle, USA. During this conference, the top leaders of the two countries held an official meeting. Through its efforts, China effectively responded to the external challenges of the political turmoil of 1989. The 'sanctions' imposed by Western countries did not succeed in defeating or isolating China, but instead were eventually dismantled. China's reform, opening up and modernisation drive gained a more favourable international environment and its diplomacy firmly advanced in all directions.

THE EFFECTS OF GOVERNANCE AND RECTIFICATION, AND COMPLETION OF THE SEVENTH FIVE-YEAR PLAN

After the political storm, the CPC Central Committee put the work of governance and rectification, which had been delayed, back on the agenda. In November 1989, the Fifth Plenary Session of the 13th CPC Central Committee made the *Decision of the CPC Central Committee on Further Governance and Rectification, and Deepening Reform*, which determined that, on the basis of curbing inflation and stabilising the economic situation, the task of governance and rectification should be basically completed in three years or a little more than three years from 1989. This stage of governance and rectification was implemented in two steps, firstly, focusing on starting the economy and pursuing moderate economic development at the same time as adjusting the economic structure, and secondly, gradually shifting the focus of governance and rectification, and deepening reform to adjusting the industrial structure and improving economic efficiency.

During the period of governance and rectification, the people's 'basket of vegetables' became one of the focal points of attention of all levels of government. In 1988, the state began implementing the 'Vegetable Basket Project' to establish a central and local production base for meat, eggs, milk, aquatic products and vegetables. Through the process of governance and rectification, the overheated economy cooled significantly, the national economy maintained a rate of growth appropriate for the actual situation, and the contradiction between the balance of supply and demand was significantly eased. Inflation, a significant concern of the people, was effectively controlled, the turmoil in the circulation sector initially eased, and market order improved markedly. In March 1992, the Fifth Session of the Seventh NPC announced that the main tasks of governance and rectification had been basically completed and that one particular phase of economic development could be completed on schedule.

During the period of governance and rectification, the targets for national economic and social development set out in the seventh five-year plan were mostly achieved or even exceeded by the end of 1990, and the strategic objectives of the first step were achieved ahead of schedule. The people's living standards were further improved, and in the vast majority of the country the problem of insufficient food and clothing was solved and China began to move towards becoming a moderately prosperous society.

Reform and opening up continued to advance, and major breakthroughs were made in some areas. The establishment of the stock exchange also constituted a landmark step in deepening reforms. In

December 1990, the Shanghai Stock Exchange was officially opened, and was the first stock exchange to open on the mainland since reform and opening up. In July 1991, the Shenzhen Stock Exchange was also officially opened. The operation of these two exchanges made the centralised trading of stocks a reality, thereby creating stock exchanges in Shanghai and Shenzhen of national significance and promoting the development of the shareholding system. In October 1990, Zhengzhou Grain Wholesale Market opened and introduced a futures trading mechanism, which constituted the beginning of futures trading in China. The successful opening of the Shanghai and Shenzhen exchanges and the introduction of futures trading mechanisms sent a strong signal to the world that China's reform and opening up would move forward unflinchingly.

The development and opening up of Pudong, Shanghai, was a major step in the expansion of opening up. Pudong refers to a triangular area east of the Huangpu River, southwest of the mouth of the Yangtze River, and north of the Chuanyang River, adjacent to the Bund, the most bustling part of Shanghai. This land with great potential for development, had not been effectively developed for a long time, and was what some people saw as being aptly called *Lannidu*, or 'muddy crossing', which contrasts sharply with the prosperous Puxi of today. In April 1990, the CPC Central Committee and the State Council approved the development and opening up of Pudong, turning Pudong into an economic and technological development zone and implementing certain policies pertaining to SEZs. This was a major strategic decision made by the CPC Central Committee after having comprehensively studied international and domestic trends and grasped the overall situation of reform and development. As a result of this, a brand new and profound chapter in China's reform and opening up was launched. Hundreds of thousands of builders drove into Pudong, built bridges, roads, factories and buildings, and an export-oriented, multifunctional, modern Pudong New Area in the Yangtze River Delta emerged. This not only promoted the rapid development of Shanghai, but also had a strong ripple effect on the reform and opening up, and economic development of the Yangtze River Delta, the whole Yangtze River Basin and the entire country. With the completion of the task of governance and rectification, and the successful completion of the seventh five-year plan, the undertaking of reform and opening up, and socialist modernisation was about to enter a new phase.

10
DENG XIAOPING'S SOUTHERN TOUR SPEECHES

With the collapse of the Soviet Union and the upheavals in Eastern Europe, the practice of socialism in the world hit a low point. After the end of the Cold War, the world began to move towards multi-polarisation, the process of economic globalisation accelerated, and some of China's neighbouring countries demonstrated strong momentum in their development. However, the development of China's socialist cause faced great difficulties and pressure. After the process of governance and rectification, China's economy turned a corner, but the deep-seated problems existing in the operation of the economy had not yet been fundamentally resolved. The serious twists and turns in the path of socialism throughout the world also had a certain negative impact on China, with some people lacking confidence in the future of socialism, and some people began to doubt reform and opening up, raising the question of whether it was right for China to follow socialism or capitalism. Whether or not the party's basic line could be upheld, and the opportunity could be seized and development accelerated to advance reform and opening up, and modernisation became a major issue that CPC members had to face and resolve. From 18 January to 21 February 1992, Deng Xiaoping, at the advanced age of 88, visited Wuchang, Shenzhen, Zhuhai and Shanghai at a critical juncture in the history of the party and the country. He looked and observed attentively as he travelled and made a series of important statements.

Regarding how to advance reform and opening up, Deng Xiaoping pointed out in his speeches that revolution is the liberation of productivity, and that reform is also the liberation of productivity. He said that in order to carry out reform and opening up more courage was needed to dare to experiment with new approaches. If you get it right, he said, you must try boldly and venture boldly. He also said that an inability to advance reform and opening up, and venture boldly, and nothing but mere talk, implied a fear of many aspects of capitalism and means ending up walking the capitalist road. The key is the question of whether to follow socialism or capitalism. The standard of judgment for decisions should mainly be based on discerning whether the proposed choice is conducive to the development of the productivity of a socialist society, whether it is conducive to strengthening the comprehensive national strength of a socialist country, and whether it is conducive to improving people's living standards. In response to some people's criticism and decrying of reform and opening up, Deng Xiaoping stressed that the right can ruin socialism, and the 'left' also has the capacity to ruin socialism. He said that China should be wary of the right, but mainly focus on guarding against the 'left'. He pointed out that it might take another 30 years before China would be able to develop a more mature and finalised system in all areas. Policies and guidelines under this system would also be more permanent.

On 23 January 1992, Deng Xiaoping pointed out during his visit to Guangdong that the province should take several steps and strive to catch up with the 'Four Little Dragons' of Asia within 20 years

Regarding the relationship between a planned and a market economy, Deng Xiaoping pointed out that a more planned economy or more of a market economy, did not constitute the essential difference between socialism and capitalism. Both planned and market economies are economic tools. He pointed out clearly that the essence of socialism is to liberate and develop productivity, eliminate exploitation and polarisation, and ultimately achieve shared prosperity. He also pointed out that in order to win out in the comparison with capitalism, socialism must boldly absorb and learn from all the achievements of civilisation created by human society, and absorb and learn from all the advanced modes of operation and management that reflect the pattern of modern socialised production in all countries of the world, including developed capitalist countries.

Seizing the opportunity to speed up development is one of the major issues that Deng Xiaoping repeatedly stressed in his speeches. He pointed out that some of China's neighbouring countries and regions were developing faster than China, and that if China did not develop or developed too slowly, the people would have problems as soon as they tried to make comparisons. He said that in seizing the opportunity to develop, the key was to develop the economy. Development was of overriding importance. In the long process of modernisation from that time onwards, several certain stages of relatively fast development and relative efficiency were necessary and conceivable. He stated with great conviction that this was the ambition China must have. Deng Xiaoping believed that the key to solving China's development problems was to adhere to the party's basic line and not waver. He also stressed that the key to adhering to the party's line, principles and policies since the Third Plenary Session of the 11th CPC Central Committee was to adhere to 'one central task and two basic points'. If China were to not uphold socialism, not reform and open up, not develop the economy, and not improve people's lives, then it would be on the road to disaster. The basic lines should be managed for a hundred years without wavering.

In his speeches Deng Xiaoping also expounded some other important thoughts of strategic guiding significance. He stressed that in the whole process of reform and opening up, it was necessary to always pay attention to adhering to the four basic principles. The dual approach must be upheld, with one hand firmly grasping reform and opening up, and one hand firmly combating all kinds of criminal activities. Both hands should be firm and if they are it would be possible to accomplish the construction of socialist spiritual civilisation. It was, he said, vital to oppose corruption throughout the whole process of reform and opening up. He also said that the key to whether China's affairs could be successfully managed, whether socialism and reform and opening up could be upheld, whether the economy could be developed swiftly, and whether the country could experience long-term stability lay, in a sense, with the people. At the end of the day, the key was that the internal workings of the CPC should be in order without any disorder.

Faced with the low point in world socialism, Deng Xiaoping confidently asserted that he firmly believed that the number of people in the world in favour of Marxism would increase because Marxism is a science. There was no need to panic or think Marxism would disappear or be gone or fail. That was utterly inconceivable. In some countries, there had been serious twists and turns, and socialism seemed to have been impaired, but the people in those places had been trained and learned things from it, and would promote socialism in a healthier direction. He stressed that the consolidation and development of the socialist system would require a long period of time and would require the unremitting efforts of several, a dozen, or even dozens of generations of Chinese people. It was important to continue on the path of building socialism with Chinese characteristics. The period of time between then and the mid-21st century would be very important and all-out efforts were necessary.

One of the notable statements of Deng Xiaoping during his tour was that, "The vigour of spring greets the eyes as the east wind comes." Deng Xiaoping's speeches during his southern tour expounded a series of brand-new ideas and dispelled the fog of people's thinking just like a strong east wind. They answered theoretically many important questions which had long troubled and bound people's thinking, and constituted another manifesto for emancipating people's minds and seeking truth from facts to advance reform and opening up, and modernisation to a new stage. This manifesto not only had a very important guiding role for the 14th CPC National Congress, which was about to be convened, but also had great and far-reaching significance for the whole cause of China's socialist modernisation drive.

His speeches during his southern tour brought Deng Xiaoping's glorious achievements in life to a new height. Comrade Deng Xiaoping is recognised by the whole party and the people of all ethnic groups as an outstanding leader with great prestige, a master Marxist, a great proletarian revolutionary, statesman, military expert and diplomat, the chief architect of China's socialist reform and opening up, and modernisation drive, the pioneer of the path of socialism with Chinese characteristics, and the principal founder of Deng Xiaoping Theory. Without Deng Xiaoping, Chinese people would not have the new life they have today, and China would not have the new context of reform and opening up or the bright prospects provided by socialist modernisation. As one of the great men of his generation, Deng Xiaoping's magnificent achievements and scientific theories have changed and will continue to change and influence China and the world.

Eight

Propelling Socialism with Chinese Characteristics Forward into the 21st Century

In the second half of 1992, the CPC held its 14th National Congress. After Deng Xiaoping's southern tour speeches, there was much interest both domestically and internationally in the new steps China's reform and opening up would take. In the process of guiding the drafting of the report of the 14th CPC National Congress, Jiang Zemin went to the Central Party School on 9 June 1992 to give a speech entitled *Deeply Understanding and Fully Implementing the Important Spirit of Comrade Deng Xiaoping's Speeches to Accelerate and Improve Economic Construction, and Reform and Opening Up*. This was, in fact, a 'briefing' to solicit opinions and seek consensus on the report of the 14th National Congress. In his speech, Jiang Zemin cited several references to the goal of economic restructuring, expressing a preference for using the term 'socialist market economy'. After the meeting, Jiang Zemin solicited the views of Deng Xiaoping and other comrades. Deng Xiaoping agreed, and said that, as a result, the 14th National Congress would now have a clear theme. Hence, Jiang Zemin's speech made important ideological and theoretical preparations for the convening of the 14th CPC National Congress.

1
THE 14TH CPC NATIONAL CONGRESS AND THE ESTABLISHMENT OF THE SOCIALIST MARKET ECONOMY

THE 14TH CPC NATIONAL CONGRESS

The 14th CPC National Congress was held in Beijing from 12 to 18 October 1992. There Jiang Zemin gave a report entitled *Accelerating the Pace of Reform and Opening Up, and Modernisation in Order to Win a Greater Victory in the Cause of Socialism with Chinese Characteristics.*

The congress took three profoundly significant decisions. The first was to seize the opportunity to accelerate development and concentrate efforts on economic development. The congress noted that the accelerated development of China's economy was not only a major economic issue, but also a major political one. Now that domestic conditions were right and the international environment was favourable, there were both challenges and more opportunities, and it was a good time to accelerate development. The congress adjusted the planned pace of economic development in China in the 1990s, adjusting the original annual GDP growth rate of 6% to 8-9%, and proposed that, by the end of the 20th century, the overall quality and comprehensive national strength of China's national economy would reach a new level, with GDP exceeding the originally planned level of quadruple that of 1980, and people's lives achieving moderate prosperity with regard to food and clothing.

The second decision was to determine that the goal of the reform of China's economy was to establish a socialist market economy. The congress pointed out that determining the kind of model required for reforms of China's economy was a major issue which related to the entirety of socialist modernisation. At the heart of this problem was a proper understanding and handling of the relationship between planning and the market. The development of practice and the deepening of understanding required that the party clarify that the goal of China's economic reforms was to establish a socialist market economy in order to further liberate and develop productivity. The socialist market economy to be established in China was combined with the basic systems of socialism, the purpose of which was to make the market play a fundamental role in the allocation of resources under the macro-control of a socialist state, so that economic activities would meet the requirements of the law of value and adapt to changes in supply and demand.

The third decision was to lay out the task of arming the whole party with Comrade Deng Xiaoping's theory of building socialism with Chinese characteristics. The congress report summarised the main content of the theory of building socialism with Chinese characteristics from nine aspects, namely the development path, the stages of development, fundamental tasks, the impetus for development, external conditions, political guarantees, strategic steps, leadership and reliance on strength, and the reunification of the motherland. Stating this theory answered for the first time relatively systematically a series of basic questions about how to build socialism, how to consolidate and develop socialism in China, a country with a relatively backward economy and culture, and imbued and developed Marxism with new ideas and viewpoints.

The General Assembly deliberated and adopted the report and the *Constitution (Amended) of the CPC*. The amendments to the CPC Constitution incorporated the theory of building socialism with Chinese characteristics and the party's basic line that China was in the primary stage of socialism. They also stated clearly that the building of the party must be closely knit with the party's basic line, enforce strict governance of the party, and make the building of the party the strong core in the process of leading the people continuously forwards along the road of socialism with Chinese characteristics. The amendments further incorporated a clarification of the importance of discipline, stipulated that party discipline constituted rules of conduct for the party's organisation at all levels and by which all party members must abide, required party organisations and party members to strictly implement and maintain party discipline and consciously accept the constraints of the party's discipline.

The congress elected the 14th Central Committee and the Central Commission for Discipline Inspection, and decided not to re-establish a Central Advisory Committee. From the 12th to the 14th CPC National Congresses, the Central Advisory Committee assisted the CPC Central

Committee in conducting much fruitful work, and made historic achievements for the party, the country and the people in the new historical period, completing their mission in remarkable fashion.

The First Plenary Session of the 14th CPC Central Committee elected Jiang Zemin, Li Peng, Qiao Shi, Li Ruihuan, Zhu Rongji, Liu Huaqing and Hu Jintao as members of the Standing Committee of the Politburo of the CPC Central Committee, and Jiang Zemin as general secretary of the Central Committee. It also decided that Jiang Zemin should be the chairman of the CMC and approved Wei Jianxing as secretary of the Central Commission for Discipline Inspection. Under the impetus of Deng Xiaoping's southern tour speeches and the spirit of the 14th CPC National Congress, China's reform and opening up embarked on a new chapter. Enthusiasm was at a high throughout the country, and the economy developed rapidly. The eyes of the world were also focused on China, and there was a boom in the numbers of those coming to China to invest. Marked by Deng Xiaoping's southern tour speeches and the 14th CPC National Congress, China's reform and opening up, and socialist modernisation drive entered a new stage of development.

FORMULATION AND IMPLEMENTATION OF PROGRAMME TO ESTABLISH SOCIALIST MARKET ECONOMY

The decision to establish a socialist market economy constituted a major decision made by the 14th CPC National Congress. China's practice since the period of reform and opening up began fully proved that the original economic system could no longer meet the requirements of the development of social productivity, and that repairs here and there could not come close to solving the problem. It was vital to implement fundamental reform of the planned economy and establish a socialist market economy which could make the market play a fundamental role in the allocation of resources and which would be full of vitality.

However, people still had different understandings regarding the reasons for putting the word 'socialist' in front of 'market economy'. In this regard, Jiang Zemin clearly pointed out that the word 'socialist' could not be lacking, and that it was not superfluous, or a case of ruining the drawing of a snake by overdoing it through adding legs but, on the contrary, this was a case of bringing the drawing of a dragon to life by dotting the eyes. He said that the 'eyes' in this case referred to the nature of China's market economy, and that China's creativity and characteristics were embodied in this. This demonstrated that China's socialist market economy must be integrated with China's national conditions and could not be exactly the same as western countries, or copy or imitate them. The socialist market economy possessed both the commonality of the common form of market economies as well as China's distinctive characteristics, and it was crucial to deal with the relationship between the role of stimulating the market and strengthening macro-control.

Integrating the basic socialist system with the market economy and establishing the socialist market economy was the result of more than 10 years of arduous exploration of reform and opening up, and constituted a great initiative by the CPC and a great development of Marxism by Chinese Communists, as well as a major breakthrough in the history of socialist development. It played an extremely important role in China's reform and opening up, and economic and social development.

In accordance with the decision of the 14th CPC National Congress, the Central Committee and the State Council made a series of interrelated institutional reforms and policy adjustments, while firmly formulating overall plans and implementing them in a planned and systematic manner.

In November 1993, the Third Plenary Session of the 14th CPC Central Committee deliberated and adopted the *Decision of the CPC Central Committee on Certain Issues Concerning the Establishment of a Socialist Market Economy*, further solidified the objectives and basic principles of economic restructuring put forward by the 14th National Congress, and formulated an overall plan for the establishment of a socialist market economy. The basic framework of this plan was to establish a system of modern enterprise, a unified and open market system, a sound system of macro-control, a reasonable income distribution system and a multi-level social security system on the basis of adhering to public ownership as the main approach and the common development of various economic components. The reform of China's economy began to advance towards the goal of establishing a socialist market economy.

In accordance with the requirements of the CPC Central Committee on the establishment of a socialist market economy, the State Council made a series of arrangements in succession to accelerate the pace of institutional reform in the areas of finance, taxation, banking, foreign trade, foreign exchange, planning, investment, prices and circulation.

The reforms brought about an increase in supply capacity and material enrichment. After 1992, China fully liberalised grain purchase and sale prices and operations. In fact, almost all consumer goods, not only grain, were priced by the markets. Price reforms, which had once suffered setbacks, achieved remarkable success. In 1993, China abolished food coupons and ended the 40-year-old system for the purchase and marketing of grain, and the coupons, once vital for people's lives and used for commodities such as grain and oil, became a relic of history.

The reform of SOEs was the central link in establishing the socialist market economy but was itself also not without difficulties. During this period, the reform of SOEs began to move from the previous stage of decentralisation and policy adjustment to the new stage of mechanism conversion and system innovation. From the end of 1994, the State Economic and Trade Commission, the Commission for Economic Restructuring and relevant departments selected 100 large and medium-sized SOEs to carry out a pilot project to establish a modern enterprise system.

After that, more than 2,700 SOEs were selected in succession across the country to participate in the pilot. The State Council also selected 18 cities to carry out the pilot of the comprehensive 'optimisation of capital structure' reforms and adopted a variety of policies to achieve key breakthroughs in reducing the debt burden of enterprises, separating social service functions, and rerouting surplus personnel. These reforms and adjustments all accelerated the pace of transition from a planned economy to a socialist market economy on the basis of practical steps, and the fundamental role of the market in the allocation of resources was significantly enhanced. All across China reform and opening up was comprehensively advanced and there was a rapid development of economic construction.

2

STRENGTHENING MACRO-CONTROL AND ECONOMIC DEVELOPMENT TO ACHIEVE A 'SOFT LANDING'

ECONOMIC DEVELOPMENT ACHIEVES A 'SOFT LANDING'

In the process of rapid economic development, unilateral pursuit of high-speed advances by some places and departments, coupled with gradual lapses in the original mechanisms of macro-control and with new regulatory mechanisms not yet having been perfected, resulted in excessive increases in investments in fixed assets, an overheated property market and development zones, turmoil in the financial order, rising prices and other new problems. The CPC Central Committee discovered these developments relatively quickly and in the first half of 1992 repeatedly warned that it was vital to prevent overheating, stressing the need to deepen reform efforts in order to avoid only making an issue out of expanding the scale of investment, in order to prevent the occurrence of the duplication of new construction and overstocking of products. In April 1993, the CPC Central Committee held an economic briefing focused on solving problems, such as indiscriminate raising of capital, and borrowing and overheating in the property market and development zones.

In June of that year, the CPC Central Committee and the State Council published their *Opinions on the Current Economic Situation and Strengthening Macro-Control*, and decided to adopt 16 measures focused on rectifying financial order, mainly aiming to strictly control the issuance of money, resolutely resolve violations in capital lending, resolutely stop all kinds of indiscriminate raising of capital, strictly control the total credit volume and stabilise prices on the foreign exchange market. Accordingly, the State

Council successively convened a National Financial Work Conference and National Financial and Taxation Work Conference in order to strengthen the financial, fiscal and taxation aspects of rectification efforts.

This macro-control, apart from taking necessary administrative and organisational measures, mainly focused on the use of economic and legal means from accelerating the transformation of the old and new systems to finding a way forward and taking prominent problems in economic management as the impetus for accelerating the reform and construction of the socialist market economy. Through three years of hard work, macro-control achieved remarkable results, investment overheating was effectively controlled, financial order gradually improved, the total amount of credit was controlled, prices were gradually liberalised and the extent of price rises decreased significantly. This macro-control successfully curbed inflation while maintaining the rapid pace of economic growth. It also achieved a 'soft landing' from overheating and inflation to high growth and low inflation, avoided significant ups and downs in the economy, and laid the foundation for the healthy development of the economy and for later successfully withstanding the impact of the Asian financial crisis.

COMPLETION OF THE 'EIGHTH FIVE-YEAR PLAN'

In the process of strengthening macro-control and deepening reform, the main indicators proposed in the eighth five-year plan were completed or exceeded, and remarkable achievements were made in national economic and social development. During the period of the eighth five-year plan, the national economy continued to grow rapidly, with GDP growing at an average annual rate of 12.3%, reaching Rmb6.113 trillion in 1995, five years ahead of the original target of quadrupling the GDP of 1980 by the year 2000. The lives of urban and rural people continued to improve, with the per capita disposable income of urban residents increasing by 7.9% annually and the per capita net income of rural residents increasing by 4.3% per annually. China's various undertakings developed comprehensively, and social productivity, comprehensive national power and people's living standards reached a new level.

In September 1995, the Fifth Plenary Session of the 14th CPC Central Committee adopted the *Recommendations of the CPC Central Committee on Development of the Ninth Five-Year Plan for National Economic and Social Development and the Vision 2010 Goals*, and made new arrangements to achieve the strategic development objectives of the second step during the ninth five-year plan, namely, in the context of China's population being expected to grow by about 300 million compared with 1980, to achieve a quadrupling of per capita GDP by the year 2000 compared with 1980, basically eradicating poverty, and achieving moderate prosperity in people's lives, accelerating the construction of a modern enterprise system, and achieving the initial establishment of a socialist market economy. The *Recommendations* confirmed the main goals for 2010 as achieving a doubling of GDP compared with 2000, further enhancing the moderate prosperity of people's lives, and the formation of a relatively complete socialist market economy. The *Recommendations* emphasised that the key to achieving the goals was to implement two fundamental changes of comprehensive significance: firstly, the transformation of the economy from a traditional planned economy to a socialist market economy and, secondly, transforming the mode of economic growth from extensive to intensive, and promoting the sustained, rapid, and healthy development of the national economy and all-round social progress.

In his speech at the close of the plenary session, Jiang Zemin expounded the 12 important relationships in the socialist modernisation drive. Among these 12, the most important one pertained to correctly handling the relationship between development and stability. He stressed that reform was the driving force, development was the goal and stability was the prerequisite in order to promote reform and development in an environment of political and social stability, and to achieve long-term political and social stability in the midst of advancing reform and development. This constituted a profound summing up of the historical experience of China's reform and opening up, and socialist modernisation drive.

3
THE 15TH CPC NATIONAL CONGRESS, THE ESTABLISHMENT OF DENG XIAOPING THEORY AS THE GUIDING IDEOLOGY OF THE PARTY AND THE THOROUGH ADVANCING OF REFORM AND OPENING UP

THE 15TH CPC NATIONAL CONGRESS

On 19 February 1997, Deng Xiaoping, the chief architect of China's socialist reform and opening up, and modernisation drive, passed away. At that time the world was watching to see if the CPC could continue along the path of socialism with Chinese characteristics pioneered by Deng Xiaoping.

From 12 to 18 September 1997, the 15th CPC National Congress was held in Beijing. Jiang Zemin delivered a report entitled *Holding High the Great Banner of Deng Xiaoping Theory for All-Round Advancement of the Cause of Building Socialism with Chinese Characteristics into the 21st Century*.

The congress noted that the issue of banners was of paramount concern. Banners indicate direction and embody values. For the first time, the congress employed the concept of 'Deng Xiaoping Theory' as a banner to guide the party forward. The congress stressed that to adhere unswervingly to the party's line since the Third Plenary Session of the 11th Central Committee was to uphold unswervingly the banner of Deng Xiaoping Theory. In the new period of reform and opening up, and socialist modernisation, and in the new phase of the journey into the new century, it was, he said, vital to hold high the great banner of Deng Xiaoping Theory and use Deng Xiaoping Theory to guide the whole cause and each aspect of the work of the party.

The congress put forward the party's basic programme in the primary stage of socialism and expounded the basic economic, political and cultural characteristics and requirements for building socialism with Chinese characteristics. The congress elaborated anew on such important issues as the ownership structure and the form of manifestations of public ownership in the primary stage of socialism in China, the rule of law and the construction of a socialist country under the rule of law, and the construction of the culture of socialism with Chinese characteristics. The congress pointed out that the common development of an economy centred around public ownership, but that having multiple forms of ownership is a basic approach to the economy in the primary stage of socialism in China. The public ownership economic model includes not only the state-owned economy and the collective economy, but also the state-owned and collective components of the mixed-ownership economy. The state-owned economy plays a leading role in economic development and is mainly embodied through the control of the economy. Public ownership can and should be diversified. The non-public economy is an important part of China's socialist market economy. Governing the country according to the rule of law is the basic strategy for the party to lead the people and govern the country, an objective need for the development of the socialist market economy, an important symbol of the progress of social civilisation, and an important safeguard for the long-term stability of the country. To build a culture of socialism with Chinese characteristics is to develop a socialist culture oriented towards modernisation, the world, and the future, ethnic and scientific masses, guided by Marxism and aimed at cultivating citizens with ideals, morals, culture and discipline. These discussions reflect the deepening of a further ideological and theoretical understanding of the party from exploring and answering the question regarding the nature of socialism and how it is to be built.

At the same time that the second step of China's economic development 'three-step' strategy was about to be achieved, the congress put forward further plans on how to achieve the goal of the third step, and put forward a new 'three-step' development strategy. This new strategy aimed to double China's GDP in the first decade of the 21st century compared with the level of GDP in the year 2000, in order to further advance the level of moderate prosperity of people's lives and form a more perfect socialist market economy, to further develop the national economy and further perfect various systems by the time of the 100th anniversary of the founding of the CPC through 10 further years of hard work, and to basically achieve modernisation and complete the building of a prosperous, strong, democratic and civilised socialist country by the middle of the 21st century, a hundred years after the founding of the PRC. The congress made strategic deployments for the sake of China's development into the following century, centred on this development strategy.

The congress stressed that in accordance with the overall objectives of a great new undertaking in the process of the party's construction, the party should strengthen its construction in a comprehensive manner in terms of ideology, organisation and style of work, continuously raise its level of leadership and governance, constantly enhance its ability to fight corruption and forestall moral degradation, and lead the people to complete new historical tasks with new dynamics and a greater capacity for struggle.

The congress deliberated and adopted the report and the *Amendment to the Constitution of the CPC* and elected the 15th Central Committee and the Central Commission for Discipline Inspection. The First Plenary Session of the 15th CPC Central Committee elected Jiang Zemin, Li Peng, Zhu Rongji, Li Ruihuan, Hu Jintao, Wei Jianxing and Li Lanqing as members of the Standing Committee of the Politburo, and Jiang Zemin as general secretary of the Central Committee. It also appointed Jiang Zemin as chairman of the CMC, and approved Wei Jianxing as secretary of the Central Commission for Discipline Inspection.

ESTABLISHING DENG XIAOPING THEORY AS THE PARTY'S GUIDING IDEOLOGY

The 15th CPC National Congress wrote Deng Xiaoping Theory into the Party Constitution along with Marxism-Leninism-Mao Zedong Thought as the guiding ideology of the party. This was a historic decision made by the party after nearly 20 years of successful practice of reform and opening up, and socialist modernisation, displaying the determination and conviction of the whole party to comprehensively advance socialism with Chinese characteristics founded by Deng Xiaoping, and also reflected the consensus and aspirations of the people.

The report of the 15th CPC National Congress stated that Deng Xiaoping Theory was gradually formed and developed under historical conditions characterised by peace and development during the implementation of China's reform, opening up and modernisation drive, and on the basis of summing up the historical experience of China's socialist victories and setbacks, and drawing on the historical experience of the successes and failures of other socialist countries. Deng Xiaoping Theory grasped the fundamental questions surrounding the nature of socialism and how to build it, answered for the first time relatively systematically a series of basic questions regarding building socialism with Chinese characteristics, and guided the party to formulate the basic party line during the primary stage of socialism. Deng Xiaoping Theory is a relatively complete scientific system covering economics, politics, science and technology, education, culture, ethnicity, military affairs, diplomacy, the united front and party construction which links together fields such as philosophy, political economics and scientific socialism, but is also a scientific system which needs to be further enriched from all aspects.

Deng Xiaoping Theory has pioneered a new realm of Marxism, constitutes a new stage in the development of Marxism in China, can be identified as the Marxism of contemporary China, and amounts to the groundbreaking creation of the theoretical system of socialism with Chinese characteristics. The 15th CPC National Congress profoundly expounded the historical status and guiding significance of Deng Xiaoping Theory, and pointed out that Marxism-Leninism and China's reality had merged and achieved two historic leaps and two great theoretical accomplishments. The theoretical achievement from the first leap was the correct theory and summary of experiences regarding Chinese revolution and construction, proven by practice. Its main founder is Mao Zedong, and the party refers to it as Mao Zedong Thought. The theoretical achievement from the second leap was the theory of building socialism with Chinese characteristics, the main founder of which is Deng Xiaoping, and the party refers to it as Deng Xiaoping Theory. These two theoretical achievements constitute the crystallisation of the practical experience and collective wisdom of the party and the people.

THE COMPREHENSIVE PROMOTION OF RURAL REFORM, AND THE REORGANISATION AND TRANSFORMATION OF SOES

After the 15th CPC National Congress, the CPC Central Committee adopted a series of important measures to accelerate and advance reform, and re-emphasised the importance of firmly grasping two specific major aspects, one being to strengthen the basic position of agriculture, and the other to competently handle large and medium-sized SOEs.

On the issue of rural reform and development, during his visit to agricultural and rural areas in Jiangxi in March 1995, Jiang Zemin reiterated and further expounded Deng Xiaoping's ideology regarding the 'two leaps'[1] in agricultural reform and development. He pointed out that maintaining the stability of, and unchanging and constant improvements in, the household contract responsibility system over a long period of time, and gradually embarking on the road of intensification and collectivisation in the long term, constituted the general direction of rural development.

With the acceleration of the pace of establishing the socialist market economy, the awkward contradiction between China's agricultural management system and industrial structure, and the market economy, became increasingly prominent. To this end, the CPC Central Committee proposed a policy for the strategic adjustment of the agricultural structure in a timely manner. In October 1998, the Third Plenary Session of the 15th CPC Central Committee adopted the *Decisions of the CPC Central Committee on a Number of Major Issues Regarding Agricultural and Rural Work*, which proposed the basic establishment, by 2010, of a rural economy suited to the requirements of developing a socialist market economy on the basis of a household contract management system and supported by an agricultural socialised service system, an agricultural product market, and a state support and protection system for agriculture. The plenary session's policy of steadfastly implementing a 30-year extension of the land contract period gave many millions of farmers the peace of mind for production and operation on contracted land and promoted the development of agriculture.

In order to solve the problem of insufficient food and clothing of farmers and increase in income in poor areas, the party and the government implemented many measures to step up efforts to alleviate poverty. Since the 1980s, the party and the government have carried out, organised and planned large-scale poverty alleviation efforts throughout the country. The *Development-Oriented Poverty Reduction Programme* formulated and implemented in 1994, proposed to basically solve the problem of insufficient food and clothing for 80 million rural poor people within approximately seven years. During the implementation of the plan, the central government invested a total of Rmb112.7 billion in poverty alleviation funds. By the end of 2000, the number of poor people living without sufficient food and clothing in rural areas had fallen to 32.09 million, representing a fall to approximately 3.5% of the rural population. Production and living conditions improved significantly in 592 poverty-stricken national-level counties, and most administrative villages achieved electrification, the construction of access roads, and postal and telephone access, thereby alleviating poverty in these areas.

While promoting rural reform, pilot work on establishing reforms in the modern enterprise system by SOEs, which began at the end of 1994 in accordance with the objectives of clear property rights, clear rights and responsibilities, separation of government and enterprises, and scientific management, achieved initial results. However, due to causes including historical baggage and heavy social burdens, coupled with the impact of the 1997 Asian financial crisis, SOEs faced unprecedented difficulties. In order to reform SOEs, it was necessary to seek new ideas to achieve new breakthroughs.

The 15th CPC National Congress advanced the goal of reforming SOEs and getting out of poverty within three years, which meant that it would take approximately three years to enable most large and medium-sized loss-making SOEs to emerge from their difficulties through reform, reorganisation, transformation and strengthening of management, so that most key large and medium-sized SOEs could preliminarily establish a modern enterprise system. After the 15th CPC National Congress, comprehensive reforms of SOEs were implemented with the goal of establishing a modern enterprise system. The State Council implemented an approach to reform involving re-employment projects, in accordance with a series of measures to encourage mergers, regulate bankruptcy, redirect laid-off workers, reduce staff and increase efficiency. It also commenced a comprehensive three-year battle to relieve various industries by taking the textile industry as the sector for initial breakthrough by employing debt-to-equity swaps, special funds for national technical reform, listing SOEs on the stock market, policy-based closures, bankruptcies and other measures.

In 1998, China National Petroleum Corporation, China Petrochemical Corporation, Shanghai Baosteel Group Corporation and a number of other large enterprise groups operating in accordance with market requirements were successively formed, which constituted an important first step towards the establishment of a modern enterprise system. These large SOEs operated in accordance with market requirements, ceased to assume administrative functions, and enhanced their capacity for self-development and international competition. Small SOEs leveraged the advantages of their small size to employ restructuring, joint operations, mergers, leases, contract-based management, joint-stockholding, sales and other forms to speed up the pace of reform. By the end of 2000, the three-year goal of reforming and relieving large and medium-sized SOEs had been basically achieved, while the profits of state-controlled enterprises had substantially increased and most key large and medium-sized SOEs had preliminarily established a modern enterprise system.

In the process of accelerating economic restructuring and deepening the reform of SOEs, in order to solve the problem of mass lay-offs of workers, the CPC Central Committee repeatedly emphasised that the vast number of employees of SOEs had made great contributions to the country over the preceding several decades, and that it was necessary, with enthusiasm and a heightened sense of responsibility, to mobilise the forces of the whole party and the whole of society to successfully provide basic living protection and re-employment opportunities for laid-off workers of SOEs.

In 1996, Shanghai took the lead in creating a re-employment service centre and vigorously promoted re-employment projects. After developing this 'public interest project' throughout the entire country, bridges were built from enterprises to the market to redirect workers of SOEs. In June 1998, the CPC Central Committee and the State Council issued a circular calling for the initial establishment of a social security system and employment mechanism adapted to the requirements of the socialist market economy within approximately five years. In accordance with the arrangements of the central government, all levels of government established three layers of protection for laid-off workers, namely, protection of basic living, unemployment insurance and protection for a minimum standard of living for urban residents, and initiated the reform of the social security system focusing on workers' pension insurance and medical insurance. Many places also strengthened vocational training, led workers to change their concept of options for career change, actively developed tertiary industries, and broadened employment channels. These measures guaranteed the basic living of laid-off workers and, to a large extent, resolved the difficulties and risks of the reform of SOEs.

THE FORMATION OF A COMPREHENSIVE PATTERN OF OPENING UP TO THE OUTSIDE WORLD

Deepening reform domestically and broadening opening up to the outside world are closely linked. In the very complex international environment of the 1990s, the CPC Central Committee astutely observed and firmly grasped the irreversible development trend of economic globalisation, and unswervingly upheld the basic state policy of opening up to the outside world, making great strides in the promotion of opening up to the outside world. The Third Plenary Session of the 14th CPC National Congress and the 14th CPC Central Committee proposed that the regions opened up to the outside world should be expanded to form a multi-level, multi-channel and comprehensive open set-up, make full use of both international and domestic markets and resources from both, and actively promote strategic measures such as quality and market diversification.

With the gradual implementation of some preferential policies and flexible measures in inland areas which had first been implemented in the SEZs, discussions appeared among some cadres in SEZs as to whether SEZs were no longer 'special', whether they should continue to be referred to as 'special' and whether they should continue to be developed. In 1994, the CPC Central Committee made it clear that the central government's determination to develop SEZs remained unchanged, that its basic policy towards them remained unchanged, that their historical status and role in the country's reform and opening up, and modernisation drive remained unchanged, and that they should 'enhance their strengths in innovation and take them to the next level'.

The 15th CPC National Congress further stated that opening up to the outside world was a long-term basic state policy, and that it was necessary to adopt a more proactive approach towards the rest of the world, develop a comprehensive, multi-level and broad pattern of opening up, develop an open economy, and enhance international competitiveness. In February 1998, the Second Plenary Session of the 15th CPC Central Committee profoundly expounded the lessons learnt from the Asian financial crisis and proposed that China should not only be bold in, but also adept at, participating in international economic and technical cooperation and competition under the conditions of economic globalisation. As such, China should not only make full use of the various favourable conditions and available opportunities for its development, but also clearly understand and prevent in a timely manner all kinds of adverse effects and risks that may thereby be brought about, steadily promote opening up to the outside world, seek to avoid harm and exploit beneficial opportunities, as well as take the initiative in various ways. After this, the CPC Central Committee further pointed out that economic globalisation was a 'double-edged sword', carrying with it advantages and disadvantages for China's development. Hence, it was vital not only to unswervingly implement opening up to the outside world, but also to adhere to acting independently, to enhance risk awareness, strengthen preventive work, effectively safeguard China's economic security, and develop and grow in a better manner.

According to these important decisions, China expanded, under the vigorous efforts of the CPC Central Committee and the State Council, the opening up of coastal, inland, border, river and provincial capital cities, and established a number of economic and technological development zones and tariff-free zones, while also clarifying the development strategy for the economic takeoff of the Yangtze River Delta spearheaded by the Pudong New Area of Shanghai, and also determining that Shanghai should be established as an international economic, financial and trading centre by the beginning of the 21st century. By 1997, a new composition of multi-level, multi-channel and comprehensive opening had gradually been formed in coastal, river, border and inland areas.

Joining the WTO constituted a historic event in China's process of reform and opening up, and also an important juncture in the further promotion of comprehensive, multi-level and broad opening up. In July

1986, the Chinese Government applied for the restoration of China's GATT status and began negotiations with the various parties. After the founding of the WTO in January 1995, China began to engage in intensely competitive bilateral negotiations with WTO members one at a time. There were many ups and downs during this process and Sino-US negotiations were particularly complex and difficult. China negotiated for 15 years from the time of the restoration of its GATT status to the time of its accession to the WTO. Throughout this period the CPC Central Committee always attached great importance to the WTO and worked diligently.

On 10 November 2001, the Fourth WTO Ministerial Conference, held in Doha, Qatar, approved the decision to permit China's accession to the WTO. On 11 December 2001, China officially became the 143rd member of the WTO. The integration of the global economy is the general direction of history, and for China's economy to develop China must go down to the ocean of the global market and dare to swim; if it dare not go to sea to brave the wind and rain and face the world, then one day it will inevitably drown in the sea and die. Therefore, China bravely marched into the global market. Experience since then has proven that China's accession to the WTO gave China's economy a favourable position to participate in the process of globalisation, thereby opening up new horizons for opening up to the outside world and gaining a wider space for China's development. This, in turn, had a profound impact on promoting the reform and modernisation of the economy.

---

1. On 3 March 1990, Deng Xiaoping, in a conversation with several comrades in charge of the Central Committee, pointed out that from a long-term perspective the reform and development of China's socialist agriculture should take two leaps. The first leap was the abolition of the people's communes and the implementation of the household contract-based responsibility system. This constituted a huge step forward, which needed to be persisted with over a long period of time. The second leap was to meet the needs of scientific farming and the socialisation of production, to develop moderate-scale management, and to develop the collective economy. This was a further huge step forward, but one that required an extensive process.

4
FORMULATION AND IMPLEMENTATION OF THE CROSS-CENTURY DEVELOPMENT STRATEGY

A STRATEGY FOR INVIGORATING CHINA THROUGH SCIENCE AND EDUCATION

Modern international competition, in the final analysis, is the competition of comprehensive national strength, and the key area is competition in the field of science and technology. The formulation and implementation of the strategy for invigorating the country through science and education was gradually formed on the basis of the increasing attention paid to the promotion of science and technology in China's modernisation drive. In 1993, the *Law of the People's Republic of China on the Progress of Science and Technology* was promulgated and implemented, constituting the first law on science and technology in new China. In May 1995, the CPC Central Committee accurately analysed the development trends of science and technology and the domestic and international situation, made a decision on accelerating scientific and technological progress, and decided to implement the strategy of invigorating the country through science and education.

Invigorating the country through science and education meant fully implementing the idea that science and technology are the primary productive forces, upholding an emphasis on the central importance of education, placing science and technology and education in an important position in economic and social development, and enhancing the country's scientific and technological strength and its ability to make the transformation of productivity a reality. It also meant improving the quality of science and technology and culture of the entire nation, transforming economic construction to be characterised by a reliance on scientific and technological progress and improving the quality of workers, and accelerating the accomplishment of China's prosperity and strengthening. Implementing the strategy of invigorating the country through science and education required constant improvements in China's innovative capabilities. On 26 May 1995, Jiang Zemin emphasised at the National Conference on Science and Technology that innovation is the soul of a nation's progress and the inexhaustible driving force for a country's prosperity and development, and that a nation without innovative capabilities would find it difficult to stand tall in the forest of the world's advanced nations. He said that China must study and introduce foreign advanced technology, while at the same time persevering unremittingly in striving to improve the country's independent research and development capabilities.

Jiang Zemin addressing a National Conference on Science and Technology

After the CPC Central Committee put forward the strategy of invigorating the country through science and education, in 1997 it organised and implemented the *National Basic Research Programme* (the *973 Programme*) to strengthen basic research work guided by national strategic objectives, while continuing to implement the *863 Programme*. The CPC Central Committee was also keenly aware that IT is a scientific and technological innovation with profound transformative significance, and emphasised the need to actively promote the integration of industrialisation and information technology, and achieve a leap forward in development by employing

IT to provide the impetus for industrialisation. During this period, great achievements were made in the development of science and technology in China. In November 1999, the successful launch of China's first unmanned test spacecraft, Shenzhou-1, marked a major breakthrough in China's manned space flight technology. The advent of the Shenwei computer in 1999 broke the blockade of China in high-performance computer technology by western nations.

In order to incentivise the masses of scientists and technologists to achieve lofty goals, the CPC Central Committee, the State Council and the CMC decided to honour 23 scientific and technological experts who had made outstanding contributions to the development of the Two Bombs and One Satellite, on the occasion of the 50th anniversary of the founding of new China. The CPC Central Committee and the State Council decided to establish the Highest Science and Technology Award starting in the year 2000, and on 19 February 2001, the National Science and Technology Awards Conference was held for the first time. Wu Wenjun, a famous mathematician, and Yuan Longping, the 'father of hybrid rice', won the 2000 Highest Science and Technology Award, which reverberated strongly across the country.

In the area of education, the CPC Central Committee and the State Council promulgated the *Outline for Education Reform and Development in China* in February 1993, which clearly stated that it was vital to give education priority and a strategic position in the process of development, and to strive to improve the ideological, moral, scientific and cultural level of the whole nation, stressing that this was the fundamental grand plan for achieving the modernisation of China. In September 1995, the *Education Law of the PRC* came into effect, providing legal guarantees for the development of education. In the same year, the state officially launched *Project 211* which, gearing towards the 21st century, focused on the construction of about a hundred institutions of higher learning and a number of key disciplines. In 1999, the state began to implement *Project 985*[1], which focused on supporting several universities to create world-class universities and a number of top-quality disciplines. The state rationally adjusted the composition and structure of colleges and universities, promoted the reform of higher education and the joint running of schools in various forms, gradually changed the longstanding situation of the fragmentation and duplication in the construction of higher education, and made the allocation of educational resources more rational. In elementary education and vocational and technical education, a new system of government-led schools integrating social participation was gradually formed. The state greatly increased investments in education, strongly supporting the reform of the education system and the development of education.

SUSTAINABLE DEVELOPMENT STRATEGY

In the context of China's rapid and extensive economic growth and increasing economic scale, the issue of sustainable development attracted more and more attention from the CPC Central Committee. After the *UN Conference on Environment and Development* in 1992, the CPC Central Committee and the State Council announced clearly that a sustainable development strategy would be implemented in China. In 1994, China published its *Agenda 21: White Paper on China's Population, Environment and Development in the 21st Century*, setting out an overall strategy, response and action plan for sustainable development. The 15th CPC National Congress and the First Session of the Ninth NPC held in March 1998 made the sustainable development strategy an important task of China's cross-century development, upheld the basic state policy of family planning and environmental protection, and correctly handled the relationship between economic development, population, resources and the environment. Under the active promotion of the party and the government, the implementation of the sustainable development strategy made significant progress in a number of important areas. In 1996, the State Council published its decision on a number of issues related to environmental protection, vigorously promoted the work of setting functional regional standards to control the total amount of emissions from major pollutants, sources of industrial pollution and the environmental quality of key cities accordingly. It also comprehensively pioneered the prevention and control of water pollution in Huaihe, Haihe, Liaohe and Taihu, Dianchi and Chaohu, as well as acid rain pollution control zones and sulphur dioxide pollution control zones. After the 15th CPC National Congress, the State Council promulgated the *National Ecological Environment Construction Plan* and the *Outline of the Plan for the Development of China's Nature Reserves*, and made a series of provisions for the prohibition of straw burning and its comprehensive utilisation, and cracking down on the illegal killing and managing of, wild animals. The State Council also pioneered the comprehensive management of soil erosion, initiating projects such as the protection of natural woodland, reforestation (and returning to grasslands) of some agricultural lands, the Beijing–Tianjin sandstorm source control, and implemented a system of paid use of resources, increasing year by year efforts for ecological and environmental protection.

In 1978, the CPC Central Committee made a strategic decision to build large-scale protective forests in key areas of northwest, north and northeast China impacted by sandstorms and soil erosion, and initiated the establishment of three protective forests under the *Three-North Shelterbelt Programme*. Through unremitting efforts, by 2001 China successfully completed the first phase of establishing these forests, and the forest coverage achieved by the programme, initially set up as the great green wall to prevent southward encroachments by sandstorms, reached 10%. The project became known as the greatest ecological project in the world. In the process of its establishment, a number of advanced models of anti-desertification, afforestation and ecological improvement emerged, such as Saihanba Forest Farm and Youyu County.

THE GREAT WESTERN DEVELOPMENT STRATEGY

China's territory is vast, and there are significant variations in the natural environment and the conditions for development in different regions. For a long time, development was unbalanced and uncoordinated. Through the period of construction after the founding of new China, and especially after the dawn of reform and opening up, the western region of China accumulated a considerable material and technological base. However, compared with eastern China, transportation, communications and other infrastructure was weak, its economic level was lagging behind for a long time, and the development of culture, education, health and other areas lagged significantly behind.

Gradually narrowing the disparity in levels of regional development, achieving the coordinated economic and social development of the entire country, and finally attaining to the common prosperity of all the people is the essential requirement of socialism and is also a major problem related to China's overall development which spans the centuries. As early as September 1988, Deng Xiaoping put forward the strategic concept of the 'two overall situations'[2]. He pointed out that, "the coastal areas should accelerate opening up to the outside world so that this vast area with a population of 200 million can develop more rapidly, in order to provide the impetus for better development in the interior, which is a matter with significant implications for China's overall situation. Inland areas should also give careful consideration to the reality of this overall situation. On the other hand, once development has reached a certain point, coastal areas will be required to do more to facilitate the development of inland areas. This too is a reality of the overall situation. At that time, coastal areas will have to comply with this reality." In his southern tour speeches in 1992, he also stressed that once a level of moderate prosperity had been achieved at the end of the 20th century, it would be necessary to give prominence to solving this problem.

In mid-to-late December 1995, during his inspection visits to Shaanxi and Gansu, Jiang Zemin began to ponder and mull over accelerating the opening up and development of western China. He proposed that efforts should be made to accelerate the pace of development in western China through the strong support of the state and the multi-faceted support of other regions, especially the more developed regions. At that time, the most prominent and urgent problem facing western China was the protection and management of the ecological environment. In August 1997, Jiang Zemin issued instructions in the *Investigative Report on the Management of Soil Erosion and the Construction of Ecological Agriculture in the Northern Shaanxi Region*, proposing the necessity of making concerted efforts to plant trees, green deserts, construct ecological agriculture, and create a beautiful northwest region with beautiful mountains and rivers. Subsequently, the State Council adopted a series of measures in the western region, such as the reforestation and restoration to grasslands of farmlands, and migration and opening up. With nationwide support, the people of western China proactively revised the structure of agricultural production, planted trees on a large scale, and went to war against desertification.

At the turn of the century, China's comprehensive national strength was significantly enhanced, economic restructuring accelerated, economic and social development in eastern China accumulated a certain degree of strength, and the conditions for the state to support the accelerated development of western China were basically in place. The conditions were just right. In September 1999, the Fourth Plenary Session of the 15th CPC Central Committee made the decision to implement the strategy for the development of western China, calling for the accelerated development of central and western China, and areas inhabited by ethnic minorities through measures such as giving priority to the construction of infrastructure and increasing fiscal transfers. In October 2000, the Fifth Plenary Session of the 15th CPC Central Committee made further arrangements, and the implementation of the great western development strategy was fully activated. After this, the State Council made an announcement on the implementation of a number of policies and measures for the great western development strategy, and made it clear that the scope for the application of policies for the development of western China would include 12 provinces, autonomous regions and municipalities, namely, Sichuan, Yunnan, Guizhou, Tibet, Chongqing, Shaanxi, Gansu, Qinghai,

Xinjiang, Ningxia, Inner Mongolia and Guangxi under the direct jurisdiction of the central government.

With the approval of the State Council, the Xiangxi Tujia and Miao Autonomous Prefecture in Hunan Province, and the Enshi Tujia and Miao Autonomous Prefecture in Hubei Province and Yanbian Korean Autonomous Prefecture in Jilin Province were attended to in terms of practical work in accordance with the relevant policy measures developed in western China. In order to support the grand development of western China, the State Council formulated and promulgated specific policies on finance, taxation, banking, foreign capital and foreign trade, means of attracting talented individuals and science and technology education, increased fiscal transfers and expanded the scale of public investment in western China.

In addition, a large number of key projects were successively commenced, such as the Qinghai-Tibet Railway, West-East Gas Pipeline and West-East Electricity Transmission, and the pace of the construction of infrastructure was significantly accelerated, which strongly promoted the economic and social development of western China. The implementation of the great western development strategy constituted a major strategic decision within the overarching vision of the CPC Central Committee, and it was of great and profound significance for promoting the coordinated development of eastern and western China and ultimately achieving common prosperity, safeguarding national unity, social stability and national security, and expanding the space for strategic manoeuvering regarding national development.

THE STRATEGIES OF 'INTRODUCING' AND 'GOING OUT'

Since reform and opening up, China has developed itself by actively introducing foreign capital, advanced technology and management experience, and has made great achievements. The strengthening of China's economic strength and the accelerated development of economic globalisation require China to grasp the opportunity to boldly 'go out' and make full use of both international and domestic resources and markets. Only in this way is it possible to make up for shortages in domestic resources and markets, and come up with technology, equipment, products and services, so that China will be better prepared to introduce new technologies, develop new industries, and gradually form its own transnational corporations and thereby be more able to be competitive in the context of economic globalisation.

In July 1996, Jiang Zemin proposed during his visit to inspect work in

Tangshan, Hebei Province, to intensify research into the huge topic of how SOEs could 'go out' in a focused and organised manner and make good use of international markets and foreign resources. In December 1997, Jiang Zemin, in his meeting with representatives of the National Foreign Investment Work Conference, further explained the fact that 'introducing' and 'going out' are two closely linked, mutually reinforcing and equally vital aspects of China's basic state policy of opening up to the outside world. This constituted a grand strategy, which was not only important for opening up to the outside world, but also for economic development. In October 2000, the Fifth Plenary Session of the Fifteenth CPC Central Committee proposed "implementing the 'going out' strategy and achieving a new breakthrough in striving to utilise domestic and foreign resources and markets".

In accordance with this strategic arrangement, China's opening up developed from the past focus on 'introduction' alone, to an integration of both 'introduction' and 'going out'. A group of capable and strong enterprises went to Africa, Central Asia, the Middle East, Eastern Europe, South America and elsewhere to invest in factories and actively participate in international cooperation, and they maintained steady growth in various forms of foreign economic cooperation. By the end of 2001, China had participated in 195 overseas resource cooperation projects with a total investment of US$4.6 billion and 6,610 foreign enterprises had been established, into which the Chinese side had invested US$8.4 billion. The average investment in overseas projects amounted to US$2.52 million, which was an increase of nearly 30% from the previous year. China National Petroleum Corporation, China Petrochemical Corporation and other key large-scale enterprises played a leading role in the implementation of overseas investment strategy and were the first fledgling examples of multinational companies. The strategies of 'introducing' and 'going out' promoted the development of an open economy in China, accelerated the process of China's economic integration into the global economy, and expanded China's space for economic development. This was yet another visionary strategic decision made by the CPC Central Committee on the development path of China's socialist cause into the new century.

---

1. These projects are named after the year and month in which they were launched with, for example, 985 signifying May 1998.
2. To bear in mind the 'two overall situations' means to have a global vision and strategic thinking, to see the general trend, to have a clear direction, and to take a long-term view, to nurture opportunities in crises and to adapt to change as new situations arise.

5
THE CONSTRUCTION OF POLITICAL CIVILISATION AND ADVANCED CULTURE, AND THE ACHIEVEMENT OF ALL-ROUND MODERATE PROSPERITY IN PEOPLE'S LIVES

SOLID PROGRESS IN ESTABLISHING THE RULE OF LAW AND THE CONSTRUCTION OF POLITICAL CIVILISATION

Developing socialist democratic politics and building a socialist political civilisation is an important goal of socialist modernisation. The 14th CPC National Congress asserted that it was necessary to actively promote reform of the political system in order to bring about significant progress in the construction of socialist democracy and the rule of law. The 15th CPC National Congress ensured that the rule of law became a basic strategy in the context of the party leading the people to govern the country, and proposed that under the leadership of the party and on the basis of the people's ownership, China should be governed according to the rule of law, socialist democratic politics with Chinese characteristics should be developed, and a socialist country ruled by law should be established.

In order to meet the needs of establishing a socialist market economy, after the 14th CPC National Congress, party committees and government organs at all levels implemented drastic reforms to the administrative system, and party and government institutions in accordance with the principles of the separation of government and enterprise, and streamlining, uniformity and efficiency. After the 15th CPC National Congress, the reform of the administrative system and the transformation of government functions was further intensified. The reforms focused on strengthening the departments responsible for macro-economic control, adjusting and reducing the professional economy sector, and strengthening the departments responsible for the supervision of law enforcement. After that, a series of measures which pertained to the transformation of government functions were adopted to deepen administrative reform, such as reforming the administrative examination and approval system, and regulating the bidding system.

After the 14th CPC National Congress, the construction of the country's legal system entered the 'fast lane'. It should be noted that the socialist market economy is also an economy governed by the rule of law. In March 1993, the first session of the Eighth NPC enshrined in the constitution the implementation of a socialist market economy in China. After that, the pace of legislation regarding the socialist market economy accelerated significantly, and the *Company Law of the PRC* was adopted at the fifth session of the Standing Committee of the Eighth NPC in December of that year.

In February 1996, Jiang Zemin gave a speech on the rule of law at a lecture organised by the CPC Central Committee, in which he changed the existing reference to 'ruling the country with law' to 'ruling the country by law', pointing out that ruling the country by law constituted an important policy for the party and the government to manage state and social affairs. In 1997, the 15th CPC National Congress changed its goal of ruling the country by law from 'building a country with a socialist legal system' to 'building a socialist country ruled by law'. The change from 'legal system' to 'rule of law' may seem like a minor one, but it is highly significant. The 'legal system' itself accounts for only one aspect and element of the rule of law, but the 'rule of law' is the method and strategy for governing the country. In this way, the basic strategy of the party leading the people to govern the country by the rule of law was formally established.

In order to implement this basic strategy, the NPC and its Standing Committee made it a top priority to strengthen legislative work and improve the quality of legislation, enacted legislative laws, amended marriage laws, and promulgated and implemented a number of laws on the development of a socialist market economy, such as securities laws and contract laws. In order to meet the needs of broadening opening up to the outside world, in particular regarding joining the WTO, the law on Sino-foreign joint equity ventures, the law on Sino-foreign cooperative ventures, the law on foreign-funded enterprises and a number of laws and regulations related to the protection of intellectual property rights were amended in a timely manner.

In March 1999, the Second Session of the Ninth NPC enshrined in the constitution the principle of 'governing the country according to the rule of law and building a socialist country ruled by law'. This constituted an important achievement in the development of socialist democratic politics and marked a new stage in the construction of a socialist democratic legal system in China.

After the 15th CPC National Congress, the CPC Central Committee gradually established adherence to the organic unity of the party's leadership, the ownership of the people and the rule of law as the basic principle of socialist democratic politics in China. Under the guidance of this basic principle, the system of people's congresses, the system of multi-party cooperation and political consultation under the leadership of the CPC, and the system of regional ethnic autonomy were improved. The patriotic united front was also strengthened, the democratic management systems of autonomy of rural villagers, urban residents, workers' congresses and other forms of enterprise were continuously developed, and the construction of grassroots democracy in urban and rural areas was gradually strengthened.

Strengthening ethnic and religious work is an important part of socialist political construction. During his inspection visit to Xinjiang in August and September 1990, Jiang Zemin proposed that people of all ethnic groups should establish the perspective that the Han are inseparably linked to ethnic minorities, that ethnic minorities are inseparably linked to the Han, and that ethnic minorities are mutually inseparable from each other. The 1992 Central Ethnic Work Conference called for the continued consolidation and development of socialist ethnic relations based on equality, solidarity, mutual assistance, common development and common prosperity. The 1993 National United Front Work Conference proposed that the party's religious policy should be fully and correctly implemented, the management of religious affairs should be strengthened in accordance with the law, and religion should be actively guided to adapt to socialist society. In 1994, the CPC Central Committee and the State Council convened the third symposium on Tibet-related work, formulated a series of policies and measures to accelerate Tibet's development and maintain social stability, made major decisions by various departments of the central government and 15 provinces and cities to assist Tibet, and created a new situation of national support for Tibet. In the context of concern of the leadership of the CPC Central Committee and the support of the whole country, the masses of cadres in Tibet inherited and carried forward the 'spirit of old Tibet' and made remarkable achievements in Tibet's reform, opening up and modernisation drive. During this period, the party and the state strengthened the development of resources and infrastructure in ethnic areas, implemented the central fiscal transfer system, increased investment in ethnic education, implemented a movement to revitalise the borders and make the people there more prosperous, implemented counterpart assistance in coastal provinces and cities, increased efforts to combat poverty in ethnic areas, and vigorously promoted social stability and economic and cultural development in ethnic areas.

THE CONSTRUCTION OF SPIRITUAL CIVILISATION AND THE STEADY DEVELOPMENT OF ADVANCED CULTURE

In the 1990s, the CPC Central Committee upheld the principle of 'doing two jobs at once and attaching equal importance to each', emphasised that spiritual civilisation should be focused on construction, mobilised the strength of the whole party and society to continue to promote the construction of socialist spiritual civilisation, and vigorously developed the culture of socialism with Chinese characteristics, and in so doing made new progress and achievements.

In order to further adhere to the 'two serving' policy of 'serving the people and serving socialism' and carry out the 'double-hundred' policy of 'Let a hundred flowers bloom; let a hundred schools of thought contend', as well as promoting the main theme and prospering socialist culture, the Central Publicity Department, starting from 1991, organised the implementation of selection activities for the 'Five-One Project'[1] Awards for the construction of spiritual civilisation to encourage cultural and artistic workers to deepen their lives and permeate deeply amongst the masses, and to create outstanding works to meet the spiritual and cultural needs of the masses. In March 1996, the Fourth Session of the Eighth NPC included the construction of spiritual civilisation in the overall plan for national economic and social development, and advanced the mutual promotion and coordinated development of the construction of material civilisation and spiritual civilisation.

In October 1996, the Sixth Plenary Session of the 14th CPC Central Committee issued the *Resolution of the CPC Central Committee on Strengthening the Construction of Socialist Spiritual Civilisation,* emphasising the need to arm people with scientific theories, guide people with correct public opinion, shape people with noble spirit, inspire people with excellent works, cultivate socialist citizens with ideals, morals, culture and discipline, and arrange the construction of socialist spiritual civilisation under the new situation. After this plenary session, activities for the creation of mass spiritual civilisation, mainly focused on the creation of civilised cities, villages and towns, and industries, among others, were vigorously implemented throughout the country. Youth volunteer action, such as

'Project Hope' and other activities, also received positive responses from people in all walks of life for promoting throughout the country the Chinese national virtues of taking joy in helping others and helping those in distress. The cultural, technological and health-related activities of the 'three down to the countryside' movement for bringing about rural development in three aspects penetrated deeply into vast rural areas, especially the former revolutionary base areas in remote border regions, bringing the opportunity for the enjoyment of spiritual culture to the rural masses, and also enabling them to obtain abundant information and technology, health-related knowledge and medical services.

Building the culture of socialism with Chinese characteristics constituted a new proposition put forward by the 15th CPC National Congress. The 15th National Congress emphasised that, as far as its main content was concerned, the culture of socialism with Chinese characteristics is consistent with socialist spiritual civilisation, is an important force to unite and inspire the people of all ethnic groups throughout China, and is an important symbol of comprehensive national strength. After the 15th CPC National Congress, the state implemented a 'boutique strategy' for cultural construction, energetically developed non-profit cultural undertakings, and strengthened the construction of cultural infrastructure and major cultural projects. A number of outstanding works reflecting the spirit of the times and close to the reality of people's lives continuously emerged. The cultural life of the masses became increasingly colourful, a healthy and civilised social atmosphere was gradually enhanced, and the ramparts of socialist culture continued to be strengthened.

Strengthening the construction of socialist ideology and morality is an important and central link in the development of advanced culture. During this period, the CPC Central Committee gave priority to the strengthening of ideological and moral construction, advancing the important ideology of 'rule by virtue'. In January 2001, at the National Conference of Publicity Ministers, Jiang Zemin stated clearly that, "In the process of building socialism with Chinese characteristics and developing a socialist market economy, we should unswervingly strengthen the construction of the socialist legal system and rule the country according to law, and at the same time, we should also continue to strengthen the construction of socialist morality and rule the country by virtue. With regard to the governance of a country, the rule of law and moral governance have always been mutually complementary and mutually reinforcing. Both are indispensable and must not be abandoned."

In September 2001, the CPC Central Committee published the *Outline for the Implementation of the Construction of Civic Morality*, proposing to closely integrate the construction of the legal system and morality, and the rule of law and rule by virtue in order to form and develop a system of socialist morality. Through vigorously advocating the basic moral code of 'patriotism and observance of the law, courtesy and honesty, unity and friendship, diligence and self-improvement, dedication and devotion' in society as a whole, socialist moral construction was continuously deepened and expanded, and the moral quality of the masses of cadres and the people was unceasingly enhanced.

COMPLETION OF THE NINTH FIVE-YEAR PLAN AND THE BROAD ACHIEVEMENT OF MODERATE PROSPERITY IN THE LIVES OF THE PEOPLE

In the process of advancing the cause of socialism with Chinese characteristics into the 21st century, the party united and led the people to unswervingly deepen reform and opening up, accelerate modernisation, and successfully met various serious risks and challenges, achieving great results.

In the second half of 1997, a financial crisis broke out in countries in Southeast Asia, leading to the appearance of a downward trend in China's total foreign trade imports and exports, and resulting in serious difficulties for economic construction. Faced with the impact of the financial crisis, the CPC Central Committee clearly advanced the guidelines of firm confidence, situational awareness, proactively preempting risks, remaining calm in the face of adversity, making all-out efforts, and moderating harm and exploiting beneficial opportunities. It also resolutely adopted measures to expand domestic demand, implemented a proactive fiscal policy and prudent monetary policy, increased investment and strengthened the construction of infrastructure. Furthermore, the CPC Central Committee increased the livelihood security of people on low and middle incomes, improved people's lives, adopted measures to increase export tax rebates and combat smuggling, and made every effort to increase exports and boost economic growth in many ways. These responses quickly achieved results. After 1997, China's economy continued to grow, and foreign trade exports began to rebound sharply from the latter half of 1999. Faced with economic recession and sharp currency devaluations in many countries, China fulfilled its promise not to devalue the yuan, played a key role in overcoming the Asian financial crisis, fully demonstrated its role as a responsible power and contributed to alleviating the global financial crisis.

In the summer of 1998, China was hit by a major flood on a scale rarely ever seen. The Yangtze, Nenjiang and Songhua rivers experienced record-breaking severe floods, as did the Xijiang in the Pearl River Delta and the Min River in Fujian, affecting 230 million people. In this time of crisis, the CPC Central Committee attached great importance to the safety and interests of the people in disaster areas, making decisive decisions and carefully implementing them. Party and state leaders came to the front line in the fight against the floods, and more than 300,000 soldiers from the PLA, People's Armed Police and military officers participated in the bitter sweat-and-blood fight against the floods to build strong embankments which could not be broken. The people in disaster areas made selfless sacrifices for the public good and the whole country strongly supported the military and civilians on the front line, achieving a comprehensive victory in the fight against the floods. In the struggle against the floods, the party and the people forged a magnificent flood-beating spirit characterised by strong and unbreakable unity, tenacious struggle and fearlessness, unyielding perseverance and the courage to win.

In the midst of reform and opening up, some erroneous tendencies and undesirable phenomena emerged in China from time to time under the influence of the infiltration and subversive activities of hostile foreign forces. In April 1999, in response to the incident in which a very small number of people used 'Falun Gong' to bewitch the people and destabilise society, the CPC Central Committee led the people to resolutely and decisively carry out a major political struggle against the evil cult of 'Falun Gong', promptly outlawing this evil cult in accordance with the law, mobilised all sectors of society to denounce the heresies of the evil cult of 'Falun Gong', and carried out educational transformation of the people who had been blinded by the threat, thereby maintaining social and political stability.

Its victory in dealing with the Asian financial crisis and a series of major struggles fully demonstrated the ability of the CPC Central Committee to manage the meta-narrative, meet challenges and protect against risks, and thereby demonstrated the superiority of China's socialist system. As a result, the party and the people became more confident as they pressed ahead.

In the process of meeting various difficulties, risks and challenges, new achievements were made in reform, opening up and modernisation. By 2000, the main tasks of the ninth five-year plan had been completed or surpassed, with GDP reaching Rmb9.9776 trillion, with an average annual growth rate of 8.6%. Also, the goal of quadrupling the 1980 value of GDP per capita was achieved in 1997, three years ahead of schedule, and the output of major industrial and agricultural products ranked among the highest in the world, with the shortage of commodities having been basically ended. The income of urban and rural residents greatly increased, and quality of life improved significantly. Overall progress was achieved in various undertakings and national strength was further enhanced. During this period, the world-famous Yangtze River Three Gorges water conservancy project successfully dammed the great river. Significant progress was also made in the construction of a number of cross-century mega-projects, such as the new rail passage for coal transportation from west to east and a multi-million-tonne steel base, amongst others. The construction of a gas pipeline for the west-to-east supply project, and the expansion of the Qinghai-Tibet Railway between Xining and Golmud were also successively launched.

By the year 2000, China had successfully achieved the transformation from a planned economy to a socialist market economy, the basic framework of the socialist market economy had been preliminarily established, and the institutional environment for economic and social development had undergone major changes.

The successful completion of the ninth five-year plan marked the accomplishment of the strategic goal of the second step of socialist modernisation in China, and the overall achievement of moderate prosperity in people's lives laid a good foundation for moving towards the strategic goals of the third step. This constituted a great achievement in China's reform and opening up, and socialist modernisation, and a new milestone in the history of the development of the Chinese nation.

In October 2000, the Fifth Plenary Session of the 15th CPC Central Committee adopted the *Recommendations of the CPC Central Committee on the Formulation of the 10th Five-Year Plan for National Economic and Social Development*, which laid out a new blueprint for economic and social development.

---

1. 'Five' here refers to high-quality books, plays, films, TV dramas (film), and collections of creative and persuasive articles. As of 1995, high-quality songs and radio plays have been included in the list, but the name 'Five-One Project' has remained unchanged.

6
ACTIVE PROMOTION OF MILITARY REFORM WITH CHINESE CHARACTERISTICS

In the 1990s, faced with new military changes in the world, the CPC Central Committee and the CMC advanced the general requirements for military construction in the new era characterised by 'political qualification, military excellence, excellent work ethics, strict discipline and powerful safeguards', with a view to achieving and maintaining consistent levels of quality. They also made a series of strategic plans and arrangements for military construction and preparations for military struggle and promoted military reform with Chinese characteristics.

Jiang Zemin inspecting Chinese PLA troops at the 50th anniversary celebration of the founding of the PRC on 1 October 1999

The Gulf War, which broke out in early 1991, showed the world a new picture of warfare, and high-tech weapons and equipment became an important factor in determining the success or failure of a war. From the point of view of military technology and types of warfare, this was the turning point from mechanised warfare towards the informatisation of warfare and triggered a wave of global military reform. The CMC paid close attention to this, and Jiang Zemin participated in three symposiums on the Gulf War, stating that it was necessary to clearly observe the changes in the international situation and study how to fight the wars of the future, as well as develop national defence technology and possess a 'trump card' in terms of weapons and equipment. In January 1993, an expanded meeting of the CMC formulated the strategic military policy of active defence in the new era, implemented major adjustments in strategic guidance, clarified the objectives and tasks of the preparation for military struggle under the new situation by the whole army, proposed to establish the basis of preparation for military struggle on winning local wars using modern technology, especially high-technology, and gave further depth to the strategic military policy of active defence.

In December 1995, the expanded meeting of the CMC adopted the *Outline of the Plan for Military Construction for the Ninth Five-Year Plan Period*, which clearly put forward the military strategy of building a strong military using science and technology, and the strategic idea of 'Two Fundamental Shifts'. These shifts pertain to, in terms of preparation for military struggle, shifting from preparing for local wars under general conditions to preparing to win local wars using modern technology and especially high-technology and, in terms of military construction, shifting from a quantitative model to a qualitative and performance-based model, and from a manpower-intensive to a technology-intensive model. The expanded meeting of the CMC held in December 2000 proposed that the construction of China's military should complete the dual tasks of mechanisation and informatisation, and the new idea of achieving a leap forward in development.

In order to promote military reform with Chinese characteristics and follow the path of establishing elite soldiers with Chinese characteristics, initial adjustments and streamlining were implemented across the entire military structure from the second half of 1992 to the end of 1994. In September 1997, the 15th CPC National Congress announced that China would reduce the number of military posts by a further half a million within three years, on top of the reduction in military posts by one million in the 1980s. Through this adjustment and streamlining, the Chinese PLA took a step towards synthesis and miniaturisation, downsizing and diversification. In order to meet the needs of military reform with Chinese characteristics, the CPC Central Committee and the CMC also made major adjustments and reforms to the systems of military logistical support, military academies, service of active-duty soldiers, and in particular systems for non-commissioned officers.

After the mid-1990s, the state increased its investment in national defence and military construction on the basis of sustained and rapid economic growth. Various branches of the PLA diligently implemented the policy of establishing a strong and high-quality military by way of science and technology, accelerated the development of national defence technology, and weapons and equipment, made achievements at an advanced level in aviation, aerospace, ships, weapons, military electronics, engineering and physics, and made significant progress in microelectronics, information, sensing and communications technology. In particular, breakthroughs were achieved in the development of a number of cutting-edge weapons, including submarine-launched missiles and mobile strategic missile development, laying a new and important technical foundation for the modernisation of China's military weapons and equipment.

The PLA has always adhered to the fundamental principles and systems of the party's absolute leadership over the armed forces and has given top priority to ideological and political construction in all aspects of construction. During this period, the CPC Central Committee and the CMC revised, formulated and implemented the *Regulations on the Political Work of the Chinese PLA*, the *Decision on Certain Issues of the Ideological and Political Construction of the Army Under the Conditions of Reform and Opening Up, and the Development of a Socialist Market Economy*, and thereby continuously strengthened officers' and soldiers' consciousness of military spirit, always maintained the PLA's strong revolutionary will and vigorous fighting spirit, and provided strong assurances for various tasks focused on enabling China's military to complete preparations for military struggle.

7

THE RETURN OF HONG KONG AND MACAU TO THE MOTHERLAND AND THE GROWTH OF CROSS-STRAIT EXCHANGES

THE VICTORIOUS RETURN OF HONG KONG AND MACAU TO THE MOTHERLAND

After Hong Kong entered the transitional period of reunification with the motherland, early cooperation between the Chinese and British governments in resolving the Hong Kong issue was basically smooth. After 1989, especially after the upheavals in the Soviet Union, the British Government miscalculated the situation, violated relevant provisions of the Sino-British Joint Declaration, put up numerous obstacles to the smooth transition of Hong Kong, and obstructed and opposed the resumption of the exercise of sovereignty over Hong Kong by the Chinese Government. In response to this, the party and government engaged in a reasonable and modest measure-for-measure struggle. In order to ensure a smooth transition and maintain Hong Kong's long-term prosperity and stability, at the end of 1992 the CPC Central Committee proposed a China-centred and fully prepared approach. After that, the Chinese Government, in accordance with the Basic Law of the Hong Kong SAR, stepped up its preparations for the resumption of the exercise of sovereignty over Hong Kong and preparations for the establishment of the Hong Kong SAR. On 11 December 1996, the Selection Committee for the First Government of the Hong Kong SAR elected Mr Tung Chee-hwa as the first chief executive of the Hong Kong SAR by secret ballot. On 16 December, the Central Government appointed Mr Tung Chee Hwa as the first chief executive of the Hong

Kong SAR. At this point, all preparations for Hong Kong's return to the motherland were basically ready.

At midnight on 30 June 1997, the Hong Kong Convention and Exhibition Centre was brightly lit and there the world-famous handover ceremony between the Chinese and British governments in Hong Kong was held. At 23:59 on 30 June, the British and Hong Kong flags were slowly lowered, symbolising the declaration of the end of a century and a half of British colonial rule over Hong Kong. On 1 July, at 00:00, the band played the national anthem of the PRC, and the flags of the PRC and the Hong Kong SAR of the PRC were raised. Jiang Zemin, president of the PRC, solemnly declared that the Chinese Government had resumed the exercise of sovereignty over Hong Kong.

The handover ceremony at the Hong Kong Convention and Exhibition Centre on 1 July 1997

After a hundred years of vicissitudes, Hong Kong's triumphant return to the embrace of the motherland washed away the century-old shame of the Chinese nation and completed the achievement of the important step of the complete reunification of the motherland. This is indeed an utterly historic event in the annals of the history of the Chinese nation. Hong Kong compatriots thereafter became the true masters of this part of the motherland, and Hong Kong embarked on a broad road of common development and eternal unity with the motherland.

At the same time as preparations for Hong Kong's return were under way, the pace of Macau's return was also accelerating. On 15 May 1999, the

Selection Committee of the First Government of the Macau SAR elected Mr Edmund Ho Hau Wah as the first Chief Executive of the Macau SAR by secret ballot. On 20 May the central government appointed Mr Edmund Ho Hau Wah as the first Chief Executive of the Macau SAR.

The handover ceremony at the Macau Cultural Centre on 20 December 1999

From midnight on 19 December to the early hours of 20 December 1999, the Chinese and Portuguese governments held a handover ceremony in Macau. Jiang Zemin, president of the PRC, solemnly declared that the Chinese Government had resumed the exercise of sovereignty over Macau.

The Song of the Seven Sons, written by the famous poet Wen Yiduo in 1925, relates and expresses the strong desire of Macau compatriots to return to the motherland, and at that moment in 1999 it became a reality. Macau's triumphal return is another monument erected by the Chinese people on the road to accomplishing the great cause of reunifying the motherland.

After the reunification with the motherland, as special administrative regions directly under the central government, Hong Kong and Macau were reintegrated into the system of national governance. The central government administers Hong Kong and Macau in accordance with the constitution and the Basic Law of the SARs, and the corresponding systems and institutions of the SARs were also established. Hong Kong and Macau became more and more closely connected with the rest of China. Faced with the severe impact of the Asian financial crisis and the adverse effects of changes in the international economic environment, with the strong support of the central government, the SAR governments responded calmly and people from all walks of life worked together to properly handle a series of economic and social problems, and maintain the stability and prosperity of Hong Kong and Macau. The facts clearly show that 'One Country, Two Systems' is the best solution to the problems of Hong Kong and Macau left over from history, and also the best institutional arrangement for maintaining long-term prosperity and stability after the reunification of Hong Kong and Macau.

GROWTH OF CROSS-STRAIT EXCHANGES

As mainland China developed, after years of efforts by compatriots on both sides of the Taiwan Strait, the KMT authorities in Taiwan opened up in October 1987 to restricted visits to relatives. In November of that year, the first group of Taiwan compatriots to visit their relatives travelled to the mainland via Hong Kong. In this way, 38 years of cross-strait disconnection was broken, and cross-strait people-to-people, economic and cultural exchanges gradually began.

On this basis, the CPC Central Committee steadily promoted the development of cross-strait relations. In March 1992, the Association for Relations Across the Taiwan Straits and the Taiwan Straits Exchange Foundation began transactional talks. In November, the two sides reached a consensus on how to express their adherence to the one-China principle and reached a consensus that 'both sides of the Taiwan Strait belong to one China and will work together to seek national reunification', which later became known as the 1992 Consensus.

In April 1993, Wang Daohan, president of the Association for Relations Across the Taiwan Straits, and Koo Chen-fu, chairman of the Straits Exchange Foundation, held successful talks in Singapore, signed four agreements, including the *Joint Agreement of the Koo-Wang Talks*, and established a cross-strait institutionalised consultation mechanism, marking an important step in cross-strait relations. In March 1994, the Sixth Session of the Standing Committee of the Eighth NPC adopted the *Law of the PRC on the Protection of Investments by Taiwan Compatriots*, which provided legal protection for Taiwanese business investments, further promoting the development of cross-strait economic relations and the growth of exchanges in other areas.

However, after Taiwan's leader Lee Teng-hui came to power, with the support and connivance of the US and other external anti-China forces, Taiwan gradually reneged on the one-China principle, and activities promoting so-called 'Taiwanese independence' became rampant. The CPC Central Committee scientifically analysed the situation in Taiwan and considered that it was necessary to curb the separatist forces promoting 'Taiwanese independence' and combat their threatening manner, as well as to study in depth the application and development of the policy of 'peaceful reunification; One Country, Two Systems' under the new situation. On the occasion of the traditional Spring Festival Chinese holiday on 30 January 1995, Jiang Zemin delivered a speech entitled *Continuing the Struggle for the Completion of the Great Work of the Reunification of the Motherland*, which put forward eight propositions for developing cross-strait relations and promoting the peaceful reunification of the motherland at that point in time. He emphasised that adhering to the one-China principle is the basis and prerequisite for achieving peaceful reunification, and that China would not commit to renouncing the use of force, although this force would not be used against compatriots in Taiwan, but rather against attempts by foreign forces to interfere with China's reunification and the conspiracy to bring about 'Taiwanese independence'. The speech not only reflected the Chinese government's firm determination to accomplish the great cause of reunification of the motherland, but also fully took into account the aspirations of compatriots in Taiwan and the actual situation of Taiwan, thereby drawing significant attention and a positive response both within China and overseas.

However, Lee Teng-hui went further and further down the road of 'Taiwanese independence' and fomenting division. In June 1995, Lee Teng-hui visited the US in a so-called 'private capacity', openly establishing the concept of 'two Chinas' within the international community, and in July 1999 he reprehensibly introduced the so-called 'two-state theory'. When Chen Shui-bian, leader of Taiwan's Democratic Progressive Party, came to power in March 2000, he refused to accept the one-China principle and rejected the *1992 Consensus*.

In response to the incessantly intensifying separatist activities fomenting 'Taiwan independence' by some on the island of Taiwan and by foreign hostile forces, the CPC Central Committee took decisive measures to launch a struggle in the political, military, diplomatic and public opinion arenas. From the second half of 1995 to the first half of 1996, the PLA conducted a series of large-scale military exercises in the Taiwan Strait and the waters around Taiwan which shook the world and demonstrated the strong determination of the Chinese Government and the Chinese people to safeguard national sovereignty and territorial integrity. This effectively combated the threatening manner of the Taiwanese separatist and hostile foreign forces fomenting 'Taiwanese independence'.

8
PROMOTING THE CONSTRUCTION OF A NEW PATTERN OF COMPREHENSIVE MULTI-LEVEL FOREIGN RELATIONS

In the early 1990s, with the collapse of the Soviet Union and the upheavals in Eastern Europe, the international landscape and situation were highly complicated. The CPC Central Committee has always put the sovereignty and security of the country first, actively responded to new changes in international relations, and the impact and challenges of the rapid development of science and technology, held a clear-cut stance on opposing hegemonism and power politics, safeguarded the interests of the large numbers of developing countries, united all forces that can be united, promoted world peace and development, and promoted the establishment of a just and reasonable new international political and economic order.

During this period, China proposed to the international community the development of a new model for relations between major powers, mainly characterised by non-alignment, non-confrontation and non-targeting of third parties. In accordance with this principle, China established a basic framework for the development of bilateral relations with Russia, the US, France, the UK, Japan and the EU, amongst others, suited to the 21st century. Advocating and committing to the development of a new model of relations between major powers is conducive to breaking the monopoly of Western countries, led by the US, on international affairs, and demonstrated China's sincerity, wisdom and strength in encouraging the world towards multipolarity and international relations towards democratisation.

After the collapse of the Soviet Union, China also re-established diplomatic relations with Russia. Through negotiations the two sides resolved issues in most areas on their shared border, which had been left over from history, in an appropriate manner. In April 1996, China and Russia announced the *Partnership for Developing Strategic Coordination Based on Equality and Benefit, and Oriented Towards the 21st Century*.

In the 1990s, China's relationship with the US became extremely complicated. Relations between the two countries experienced several major twists and turns as the US continued to adhere to a policy towards China of so-called engagement plus containment. On 8 May 1999, NATO, led by the US, bombed the Chinese embassy in the Federal Republic of Yugoslavia. On 1 April 2001, a US warplane collided with a Chinese one in Chinese airspace in the South China Sea. Faced with barbaric atrocities committed by the US against China's sovereignty and various incidents instigated in the context of their bilateral relations, China engaged in a measure-for-measure struggle and thereby safeguarded national sovereignty and dignity.

Developing amicable neighbourly relations with neighbouring countries and regions, maintaining peace and stability in surrounding areas, and promoting common development, are among the important objectives of China's diplomacy. During this period, China made important progress in developing amicable neighbourly and cooperative relations. Between 1997 and 2002, the *Joint Declaration of the Summit of the PRC and ASEAN Heads of State* was issued, and China advocated and promoted the establishment of the China-ASEAN Free Trade Area and signed the *Framework Agreement on Comprehensive Economic Cooperation Between China and ASEAN*.

In April 1996, the heads of state of China, Russia, Kazakhstan, Kyrgyzstan and Tajikistan met in Shanghai and formally established the 'Shanghai Five' mechanism. On this basis, in June 2001, China, Russia, Kazakhstan, Kyrgyzstan, Tajikistan and Uzbekistan signed the *Declaration on the Establishment of the Shanghai Cooperation Organisation*. The Shanghai Cooperation Organisation (SCO) was the first regional cooperative organisation to be established by China's participation and advocacy, and named after a Chinese city, and the 'Shanghai Spirit' of 'mutual trust, mutual benefit, equality, consultation, respect for diverse civilisations and the pursuit of common development' which it advocates, has had an important impact on contemporary international relations. Since the establishment of the SCO, member states have strengthened exchanges and cooperation in security, economics and the humanities, played an important role in opposing hegemonism and power politics, and guarding against 'colour revolutions'[1], effectively combated and curbed the forces of violent terrorism, ethnic separatism and religious extremism to maintain the overall stability of the region, and promoted the economic and social development of member states.

Group photo at the 9th Informal APEC Leadership Meeting on 21 October 2001

At the same time as implementing a strategy of stabilising surrounding areas, China strengthened friendly and cooperative relations with developing countries in other regions. In October 2000, the 'Forum on China-Africa Cooperation - Ministerial Conference Beijing 2000' was held in Beijing and adopted the *Beijing Declaration of the Forum on China-Africa Cooperation* and the *Programme for China-Africa Cooperation in Economic and Social Development*. China's relations with Latin American and Caribbean countries also developed rapidly and in depth, and China established diplomatic relations with all countries in South America except Paraguay.

China has also taken an active part in various fields of multilateral diplomacy with a more open attitude. On 7 September 2000, at the initiative of China, the heads of the five permanent members of the Security Council, China, the US, Russia, the UK and France, attended the UN's Millennium Summit. In February 2001, the Bo'ao Forum for Asia was established in Bo'ao, Hainan. This was the first non-official international conference organisation to be permanently located in China, with equality, reciprocity, cooperation and mutual profitability as its main theme, and it has become a link between Asia and people from different sectors who are concerned about Asia to enhance understanding, friendship and cooperation. In October of that year, China also successfully hosted the Ninth Informal APEC Leadership Meeting in Shanghai, which had a positive impact on promoting economic recovery and development in the Asia-Pacific region.

At the turn of the century, China established a new pattern of comprehensive multi-level foreign relations, becoming more and more proactive in the context of fierce international competition and struggle, constantly expanding its strategic international space and significantly increasing its international influence.

---

1. Colour revolutions, also known as 'flower revolutions', refer to non-violent movements for regime change that occurred at the end of the 20th century in countries such as the former soviet republics (CIS countries) and Central Asia, and later in movements such as the Arab Spring. Participants often adopted a colour or flower as their symbol.

9
PROMOTING CONSTRUCTION OF THE PARTY'S NEW GREAT PROJECT

CLARIFYING THE OVERALL GOAL OF THE PARTY'S CONSTRUCTION AND TWO HISTORICAL ISSUES

In the 1990s, the CPC Central Committee scientifically analysed the new situation the party faced regarding its own construction, actively explored the goals, tasks and avenues for strengthening party building under the conditions of developing a socialist market economy, and took a series of important measures to strengthen and improve party building.

In September 1994, the Fourth Plenary Session of the 14th CPC Central Committee made the *Decision of the CPC Central Committee on Several Major Issues Concerning Strengthening Party Building*, which raised party building in the new era to the level of a 'new great project' and clearly set out the overall goal of party building. The 15th CPC National Congress further expressed this overall goal as the need to build the party into a Marxist political party armed with Deng Xiaoping Theory, serving the people wholeheartedly, fully consolidated ideologically and politically, able to withstand all kinds of dangers, always staying ahead of the times, and leading the whole nation to build socialism with Chinese characteristics.

In response to the profound changes evident in the global situation, national conditions and party affairs at the turn of the century, Jiang Zemin stressed at the Fourth Plenary Session of the 15th Central Commission for Discipline Inspection in January 2000 that in order to govern the country, it was first necessary to govern the party, and that the party must be strictly governed. He said that if party governance is strong and robust, then the country will be governed correctly and effectively. He comprehensively put forward the two historical issues of 'improving the level of leadership and governance, and enhancing the ability to fight corruption, forestall moral degeneration and withstand dangers', and called on the whole party to seriously study and solve problems, so that the party would become stronger and more vigorous, and lead the people of all ethnic groups to continue to advance triumphantly.

The proposal of the overall goal of party building and the two historical topics refined the party's understanding of the law of self-construction, enriched the Marxist theory of party building, adapted to the new demands for party building made by developing the socialist market economy, and pointed out the direction for strengthening and improving party building under the new historical conditions.

COMPREHENSIVELY STRENGTHENING PARTY BUILDING AND LAUNCHING 'THREE STRESSES' EDUCATION

In accordance with the requirements of the overall goal of party building, with regard to the two historical issues, the CPC Central Committee closely integrated the promotion of reform and opening up, and the implementation of the development of a socialist market economy on the journey of development into the new century, made solid progress in all aspects of party building, and made significant new headway.

During this period, the CPC Central Committee insisted on arming the whole party and educating cadres and the people with Deng Xiaoping Theory. They took ideological and political work as the lifeline of economic work and all other work, and inherited and carried forward the fine traditions of the party, constantly innovating and making improvements in content, form, methods, means, mechanisms, and so on. In accordance with the principle of gaining a view of the overall picture and coordinating the approaches of all parties, the committee further strengthened and improved the leadership of the party, not only to ensure the central role of the leadership of the party committees, but also to fully utilise the role of the people's congresses, the government departments, the CPPCC committees and people's organisations. In accordance with the principles of 'collective leadership, democratic centralisation, case-specific consultations, and decisions through meetings', the party further improved the deliberative and decision-making mechanisms within the party committees, established and improved the decision-making mechanisms integrating leaders, experts and the masses, and gradually improved the mechanisms for scientific and democratic decision-making. The party also attached great importance to the training and selection of outstanding young cadres, and accelerated the pace of recruiting new personnel to replace retiring personnel at all levels of leadership, as well as formulating regulations and standpoints on the work of grassroots organisations, such as implementing organs, universities, SOEs, rural areas, associations and non-government organisations (NGOs), and guided and promoted the construction of grassroots organisations of the party in various spheres. These measures made the self-construction of the party significantly stronger and ensured the healthy development of the cause of reform and construction.

With the development of the socialist market economy, new social strata, economic organisations and social organisations appeared in China. In order to adapt to the new situation, the CPC Central Committee promptly advanced the need to 'enhance the party's class base and expand the party's mass base', accelerated the formation of party organisations in new economic organisations and new social organisations, and continuously expanded the coverage of the party's work. From August 2001 onwards, the party commenced pilot work on the development of party members in the new social classes.

Strengthening the construction of the leadership team and improving the quality of leading cadres was the key to advancing the new great project of party building. In November 1995, Jiang Zemin, during his tour of work being conducted in Beijing, stated that it was vital for cadres engaged in education, especially those in leadership roles, to be given prominent positions as a key link in the chain, and advanced the requirement for leading cadres at all levels to 'pay more attention to theoretical study, improve their political awareness, and act with integrity'. This is known as the 'three stresses' and all three are closely linked and bound together. The core aspect is improving political awareness, and this requires persistent study and must embody integrity. From November 1998 to the end of 2000, the whole party carried out education regarding the party's spirit and work style among leadership teams and cadres, group by group, with theoretical study, political awareness and integrity as the main content.

The educational approach of the 'three stresses' is a creative and exploratory move to strengthen party building under new historical conditions, especially in building leadership teams and the ideological and political formation of leading cadres, and it constitutes the enrichment and development of the spirit of the Yan'an Rectification Movement in the early

1940s and the party's 'three important styles of work', namely integrating theory with practice, maintaining close ties with the masses and practicing self-criticism, in the new historical period. In the educational approach of the 'three stresses', the masses of cadres earnestly took up the weapons of criticism and self-criticism, widely listened to the opinions of the masses, sought out problems in leadership work and within themselves, launched a proactive and healthy ideological struggle, universally received a profound Marxist education, and experienced rigorous training in political life within the party.

In the new stage of reform and opening up, under the active promotion of party organisations at all levels, the majority of party members and cadres consciously strengthened training in the party's spirit, strove to improve themselves and always stood at the forefront of the times, emerging as a great multitude of outstanding CPC members typified by Kong Fansen. Kong went to Tibet twice to work for a total of 10 years and worked his heart out in a self-sacrificial manner. He struggled arduously and achieved outstanding political accomplishments, but unfortunately died in 1994 in the line of duty. He has become known as 'the role model of leading cadres'. These excellent CPC members amply displayed the work style of party members of the time and became the pioneers of the age of reform and opening up, and modernisation.

PROMOTING THE BUILDING OF A CLEAN AND HONEST PARTY WORK STYLE, AND THE FIGHT AGAINST CORRUPTION

Under the new conditions of reform and opening up, and developing a socialist market economy, the CPC Central Committee persevered in prioritising taking firm hold of building a clean and honest party work style and the fight against corruption, understanding that these are related to the survival of the party and the country. In August 1993, Jiang Zemin proposed at the Second Plenary Session of the 14th Central Commission for Discipline Inspection the importance of competently conducting anti-corruption work in three ways. Firstly, leading party and government cadres at all levels should lead the way in modelling integrity and self-discipline. Secondly, the party should concentrate its efforts on the investigation and handling of a number of major cases. Thirdly, cadres everywhere should take firm hold of the prominent problems in their own department in their own region and put a stop to several unhealthy trends with which the masses were dissatisfied. After this, the CPC Central

Committee and the State Council focused on the supervision and inspection of the integrity and self-discipline of leading cadres at all levels of the party and government, concentrated their efforts on investigating and handling major cases, and put an end to unhealthy trends in the three aspects of work against which the reaction of the masses was very strong, and gradually formed a three-pronged approach in anti-corruption work.

In order to strengthen work in the fight against corruption and the advocacy of probity, the CPC Central Committee and the State Council further improved relevant organs. In January 1993, the Central Commission for Discipline Inspection and the Ministry of Supervision were co-located. In November 1995, the General Administration for Combating Corruption and Bribery of the Supreme People's Procuratorate was established. During this period, the CPC Central Committee formulated the *CPC Disciplinary Regulations (Pilot)* and the *Regulations on the Implementation of the Responsibility System for the Construction of a Clean and Honest Party Work Style*, as well as *Some Guidelines for the Political Integrity of Leading CPC Cadres (Pilot)* and other intra-party regulations. At the same time, it was also stipulated that the income of leading cadres at or above the county level of party and government organs should be declared, gifts received by the staff of party and state organs in the course of domestic official activities should be registered, and the use of hospitality-related expenses for the business of SOEs should be reported to the workers' congress. A code of conduct for clean government for leading cadres was preliminarily established, gradually forming a party leadership system against corruption and a party work mechanism characterised by unified leadership, joint control by the party and government, and organisation and coordination conducted by the Central Commission for Discipline Inspection, with individual responsibility taken by each department, all of which depended on the support and participation of the masses. In order to further promote the establishment of a clean and honest work style within the party, the Sixth Plenary Session of the 15th CPC Central Committee adopted the *Decision of the CPC Central Committee on Strengthening and Improving the Establishment of the Party's Work Style* in September 2001, which made comprehensive arrangements to strengthen the establishment of the party's style of work.

The CPC Central Committee also made resolute decisions that military, armed police forces and political and legal organs should cut their ties with business activities and with party and government organs and their operational enterprises, on the implementation of the separation of revenue and expenditure, bidding for projects, and government procurement systems, and worked hard to prevent and curb corruption at the source. Party committees, and government and discipline inspection and supervision organs at all levels continued to step up their efforts to combat corruption, solemnly investigated and dealt with cases of violations of discipline and law, especially with regard to the investigation and handling of a number of major cases. This all engendered a greater deterrent effect and maintained the serious nature of party discipline and national law. The establishment of a clean and honest party work style and the fight against corruption achieved initial results.

However, some cases of corruption within the party continued despite repeated prohibition, and some cases even grew increasingly serious. One important reason for this is that differing degrees of weakness and lax party governance existed in some party organisations, resulting in over-lenience and inadequate levels of strictness in the implementation of discipline and systems through lax education, management, and supervision of party members and cadres, and particularly of leading cadres. Practice shows that the construction of a clean work style within the party and the fight against corruption are not only a fierce battle, but also a protracted one. The fight against corruption and advocacy of probity must be relentless, and the alarm bells must long ring in the fight against corruption and the forestalling of moral degeneration.

PROPOSAL OF THE IMPORTANT IDEOLOGY OF 'THREE REPRESENTS'

In the process of advancing the great cause of socialism with Chinese characteristics and the new great project of party building, the CPC, with Comrade Jiang Zemin as its main representative, scientifically analysed the situation within China and overseas, and the historical position of the party and the historical mission it shoulders, considered in depth the new situation and new problems it was facing, deepened the party's understanding of the nature of socialism and how to establish it, as well as the kind of party which should be built and how to build it. This led to the gradual advancing of the important ideology of the 'Three Represents'.

During his visit to inspect work in Guangdong from 21 to 25 February 2000, Jiang Zemin clearly advanced the demands of the 'Three Represents'. He said, "Our party has won the support of the people because our party, in times of revolution, construction and reform, has always represented the requirements for the development of cutting-edge productivity in China, the orientation of China's advanced culture, and the fundamental interests of the vast majority of the Chinese people, and has worked tirelessly to achieve the fundamental interests of the country and the people through the formulation of the correct line and policy." On 14 May Jiang Zemin, while in Shanghai presiding over a symposium on party building in Jiangsu, Zhejiang and Shanghai, further expounded that always achieving the 'Three Represents' was the foundation for party building, the cornerstone of its governance and the source of its strength.

On 1 July 2001, Jiang Zemin systematically expounded the important ideology of the 'Three Represents' in a speech at the meeting to celebrate the 80th anniversary of the founding of the CPC. He pointed out that the party should always represent the requirements for the development of cutting-edge productivity in China, namely the party's theory, line, agenda, guidelines, policies and work, and that it was necessary to strive to comply with the laws of the development of productivity, to embody the requirement of continuously promoting the liberation and development of social productivity and, in particular, to embody the requirement of promoting the development of cutting-edge productivity, and through the development of productivity to continuously raise people's living standards. He also pointed out that the party must always represent the orientation of China's advanced culture, namely the party's theory, line, agenda, guidelines, policies and work, and that it was necessary to embody and develop national, scientific, mass and socialist culture requirements which are oriented toward modernisation, the world and the future, in order to promote the continuous improvement of the ideological, moral, scientific and cultural quality of all China's ethnic groups, and constantly provide spiritual impetus and intellectual support for China's economic development and social progress. He further pointed out that the party should always represent the fundamental interests of the vast majority of Chinese people, namely the party's theory, line, agenda, guidelines, policies and work, and that it was necessary to persist in establishing the fundamental interests of the people as the starting point and destination, and fully utilise the enthusiasm, initiative and creativity of the people so that the people may continually obtain tangible economic, political and cultural benefits on the basis of continuous social development and progress.

The important ideology of the 'Three Represents' constitutes the basic summary of the party's historical experience of always maintaining a progressive nature, which not only adheres to the basic principles of Marxism, but also reflects the new requirements of the development and changes in the modern world and China for the work of the party and the state, and inherits, enriches and develops Marxism-Leninism-Mao Zedong Thought and Deng Xiaoping Theory with new ideas, perspectives and inferences. It is also a powerful theoretical weapon to strengthen and improve party building and to promote the self-improvement and development of socialism in China. The propounding of the 'Three Represents' made important ideological and theoretical preparations for the convening of the 16th CPC National Congress and for the entire party to complete its sacred historical mission in the 21st century which abounds with hope and challenges.

Nine

Uphold and develop socialism with Chinese characteristics under new conditions

On 5 to 6 December 2002, Hu Jintao, newly elected general secretary of the Central Committee of the CPC led his comrades of the Central Committee Secretariat to Xibaipo in Pingshan County, Hebei Province for a period of study and investigation revisiting Mao Zedong's important statement on the 'Two Musts'[1]. Hu Jintao called on all comrades in the party, especially leading cadres, to vigorously continue their hard work and always keep in mind their purpose of wholeheartedly serving the people; they should remember that their power should be wielded for the benefit of the people, that their love should be tied to the people, and that everything should be done for the profit of the people, thereby withstanding a new test and providing excellent results in the task of leading the people to achieve the goal of building an all-round moderately prosperous society, and to continue to create a new situation in the cause of socialism with Chinese characteristics. This trip to Xibaipo demonstrated the feelings and goals of CPC members at this new stage of the new century.

---

1. The 'Two Musts' were originally put forward by Mao Zedong on 5 March 1949 at the Second Plenary Session of the Seventh Central Committee of the CPC, demanding that the whole party must keep a clear head before victory, withstand the test of ruling power after seizing power throughout the country, and ensure that party members continue to remain humble. He also pointed out that party members must ensure that they continue to maintain the style of hard work, being cautious not arrogant, and not being irritable.

1

THE 16TH NATIONAL CONGRESS OF THE CPC: THE ESTABLISHMENT OF THE IMPORTANT THINKING OF 'THREE REPRESENTS' AS THE PARTY'S GUIDING IDEOLOGY, AND A PROGRAMME FOR CREATING AN ALL-ROUND MODERATELY PROSPEROUS SOCIETY

THE 16TH NATIONAL CONGRESS OF THE CPC

The 16th National Congress of the CPC was held in Beijing from 8 to 14 November 2002. Jiang Zemin presented a report entitled *Building an All-Round Moderately Prosperous Society and Building a New Position in the Cause of Socialism with Chinese Characteristics*.

The conference systematically summarised the 13 years of struggle and fundamental experience since the Fourth Plenary Session of the Thirteenth Central Committee of the CPC. The report pointed out that these experiences were linked to the historical experience of the party itself since its establishment. In the final analysis, our party must always represent the developmental requirements of China's advanced production forces, the direction of China's progressive culture, and the fundamental interests of the overwhelming majority of Chinese people. The conference put forward requirements for the comprehensive implementation of the important thinking of the 'Three Represents' elaborated above.

The conference put forward the goal of building an all-round moderately prosperous society. The congress stated its belief that, through the joint efforts of the whole party and the people of all ethnic groups in the country, we have successfully achieved the first and second goals of the 'three-step' strategy of modernisation, and the people's lives have generally reached a level of all-round prosperity. However, it must be noted that our country is still in the primary stage of socialism and will remain so for a long time. The current prosperity of our society is still low-level, incomplete, and unevenly distributed. The increasing material and cultural needs of the people are in direct contrast to our retrograde social development. The contradiction between the two is still the main stalling point within our society. To consolidate and improve the current level of prosperity in our society requires sustained hard work. The conference pointed out that the first 20 years of the 21st century constitute a period of important strategic opportunities for our country that must be firmly grasped in order to attain the great benefits they offer. In the first 20 years of this century, our country must concentrate its efforts on building a higher level of prosperity within society that can bring all-round benefits to more than one billion people. In this way, the economy can develop, democracy can be reinforced, science and education will be more advanced, culture will be more flourishing, society will be more harmonious, and people's lives will be improved and become more substantive. This is a developmental process that must be followed in order to achieve the third-step strategic goal of modernisation. It is also a key stage for perfecting a socialist market economic system and expanding our opening up to the outside world. After this stage of development, we must continue for several decades the struggle to achieve basic modernisation by the middle of this century and to build our country into a prosperous, strong, democratic and civilised socialist nation. The conference also proposed the goal of building an all-round moderately prosperous society in terms of economy, politics, culture, society and environmental responsibility. It emphasised that, by optimising structure and improving efficiency, the nation will strive to quadruple the 2000 level of GDP by the year 2020.

The conference reviewed and approved the report and the *Constitution of the CPC (Amendment)*. The amendment to the party constitution clearly stipulated that the CPC was the vanguard of the Chinese working class, and also the vanguard of the Chinese people and the Chinese nation. It was the central core of the cause of socialism with Chinese characteristics. It represented the developmental requirements of China's advanced production forces and also of China's progressive culture. The way forward encompassed the fundamental interests of the overwhelming majority of Chinese people. Expressing the nature of the party in this way was conducive to mobilising the enthusiasm, initiative and creativity of the broad masses of party members, and to uniting the broad masses of the ordinary people on the shared journey to the construction of socialism with Chinese characteristics. The amendment to the party constitution added that the party must follow the principle of taking an overview of the prevailing situation and ensuring the coordination of all parties involved. It also added provisions for the party leadership group to play the core leadership role; it clarified that application for party membership should be extended to leading members of other social strata; it also added details of the establishment of grassroots party organisations to liaise with local areas and local neighbourhood associations. The amendment to the party constitution also added a chapter entitled The Party Emblem and the Party Flag, emphasising the importance of reinforcing the appeal of the party emblem and the party flag and their role in enhancing the party's cohesion and influence.

The General Assembly elected the 16th Central Committee and the Central Commission for Discipline Inspection. The First Plenary Session of the 16th CPC Central Committee elected Hu Jintao, Wu Bangguo, Wen Jiabao, Jia Qinglin, Zeng Qinghong, Huang Ju, Wu Guanzheng, Li Changchun and Luo Gan as members of the Politburo Standing Committee, and Hu Jintao as general secretary of the Central Committee. It appointed Jiang Zemin as chairman of the CMC and approved Wu Guanzheng as secretary of the Central Commission for Discipline Inspection. In September 2004, the Fourth Plenary Session of the 16th CPC Central Committee appointed Hu Jintao as chairman of the CMC.

The 16th National Congress of the CPC was the first to be held in the new century. The conference clearly answered important questions such as what flag the CPC would fly, what path it would take, and what development goals it would achieve at this early stage of the new century. It showed to the world that at that early stage of the new century, the banners held high by the CPC were the banners of Marxism-Leninism, Mao Zedong Thought and Deng Xiaoping Theory, and the banner of the important thinking of the 'Three Represents'. The road that the CPC intended to travel was the road of socialism with Chinese characteristics. The goals that the leadership of the CPC wished to achieve in the first 50 years of the new century were of building an all-round moderately prosperous society and consequently implementing modernisation. Since then, the Chinese people have already embarked on that new journey.

ESTABLISHING THE IMPORTANT THINKING OF 'THREE REPRESENTS' AS THE PARTY'S GUIDING IDEOLOGY

A historic contribution of the 16th National Congress of the CPC was to incorporate the important thinking of the 'Three Represents' into the Party Constitution along with Marxism-Leninism, Mao Zedong Thought and

Deng Xiaoping Theory as a guiding ideology that the party must uphold for a sustained period of time.

The 16th National Congress of the CPC comprehensively explained the scientific connotations and fundamental requirements of the important thinking of the 'Three Represents'. The conference emphasised that the important thought of the 'Three Represents' was advanced on the basis of scientific consideration of the historical position of the party. It represented the inheritance and development of Marxism-Leninism, Mao Zedong Thought and Deng Xiaoping Theory, and reflected the new requirements of the development and changes of the contemporary world and China on the party and the state, and was a powerful theoretical weapon for strengthening and improving the construction of the party and promoting the self-improvement and development of the socialist system. They represented the crystallisation of the collective wisdom of the entire party. The conference pointed out that the key to implementing the important thinking of the 'Three Represents' lay in rigorously keeping pace with modern developments. The core of this lay in maintaining the progressive nature of the party and the essence lay in continuing to govern in the interests of the common people. Consistent achievement of the 'Three Represents' is the foundation of our party, the foundation of its governance, and the source of its strength. For this reason, the whole party had always to maintain the mentality of advancing with the times, and constantly opening up new fields for the development of Marxist theory. Development had to be regarded as the party's top priority in governing and rejuvenating the country, and constantly creating new prospects for modernisation. We had to fully mobilise all positive factors continuously to add new strength to the great rejuvenation of the Chinese nation; we had to promote party building with the spirit of reform and continuously inject new vitality into the body of the party.

After the 16th National Congress of the CPC, the party Central Committee adopted a series of measures to promote the study and implementation of the important thinking of the 'Three Represents'. All regions and departments conscientiously implemented the requirements of the Central Committee, continuously pushed the study and implementation of the important thinking of the 'Three Represents' to new heights, and effectively promoted the development of various undertakings of the party and the country.

2

PROMOTING ECONOMIC, SOCIAL AND SCIENTIFIC DEVELOPMENT

PUTTING FORWARD THE SCIENTIFIC OUTLOOK ON DEVELOPMENT

Just as all regions and departments were striving for the goal of building an all-round moderately prosperous society proposed by the 16th National Congress of the CPC and vigorously pushing forward reform, opening up, and socialist modernisation, our country encountered a sudden epidemic of atypical pneumonia (commonly called SARS).

In mid-to-late February 2003, the SARS epidemic spread through parts of Guangdong and into northern China in early March. Thereafter it spread to 26 provinces, autonomous regions and municipalities across the country in mid-to-late April. The SARS epidemic posed a serious threat to the lives, health and safety of the people, and had a serious impact on economic and social development. The Party Central Committee and the State Council insisted on putting people's lives, health and safety first. With one hand, they promptly undertook the vital tasks of ongoing prevention and treatment, and with the other, they maintained an unshakable hold on the centre of economic development. In this they took the hugely important strategic decision to pursue the double victory of gaining control of the epidemic and advancing economic development. Under the strong leadership of the Party Central Committee and the State Council, the people of all ethnic groups throughout the country vigorously promoted the spirit of unity, mutual aid and courage to overcome difficulties, all coupled with a determination to win. In doing so, the nation effectively controlled the SARS epidemic and maintained rapid economic growth. In June, the World Health Organisation (WHO) announced the lifting of the travel warning against Beijing. In this, our country achieved a significant victory in the fight against SARS.

The victory in the fight against SARS fully demonstrated the tremendous superiority of our socialist system. At the same time, the occurrence and spread of atypical pneumonia also revealed that a period of rapid economic development in our country had brought to the fore new contradictions and new problems, such as insufficient development coordination, lagging public health development and inadequate emergency response mechanisms. This spurred the Party Central Committee to engage in profound consideration of how China's development should adapt to this new situation. The important theoretical and practical question of 'what kind of development to achieve and how to develop' has historically faced the Chinese Communists.

At the late August and early September 2003, during a tour of inspection in Jiangxi, Hu Jintao advanced the 'Scientific Outlook on Development' and stressed that it should be firmly established as a means to achieve development that was coordinated, comprehensive and sustainable. In October, for the first time, the Third Plenary Session of the 16th Central Committee of the CPC proposed the Scientific Outlook on Development in an official party document, emphasising the need to 'adhere to people-oriented thinking, establish a comprehensive, coordinated and sustainable development outlook, and promote an all-round economic, social and human development'.

Hu Jintao investigating the prevention and treatment of SARS in rural areas of Sichuan while on a visit to medical staff at Fushun County People's Hospital in Zigong City on 12 May 2003

On 10 March 2004, Hu Jintao delivered a comprehensive elaboration on the scientific connotations, basic requirements and guiding principles of the Scientific Outlook on Development at the Central Population, Resources and Environmental Work Forum. He pointed out that to adhere to the people-oriented principle is to achieve the goal of all-round human development; and that to seek and promote development from the fundamental interests of the people, to continuously meet the people's growing material and cultural needs, and to effectively protect the people's economic, political and cultural rights is to allow the fruits of development to benefit everyone. Comprehensive development means placing economic growth at the core, thereby comprehensively advancing economic, political and cultural growth, and realising economic development and overall social progress. Coordinated development means coordinating urban and rural development, regional development, and economic and social development while also coordinating the harmonious development of the relationship between man and nature, domestic development and opening to the outside world. It requires the promotion of the complete coordination of productivity and production relations, and of the economic foundation and superstructure; it also requires the promotion of the coordination of every stage of economic, political and cultural growth. Sustainable development requires promotion of the harmonious relationship between man and nature, and the realisation of the coordination of economic growth with population, resources and environmental considerations. We must also persevere in following the paths of productivity growth, raising the standard of living and cultivating a sound ecological culture. In all these ways we can guarantee sustainable growth for generation after generation.

The Scientific Outlook on Development is the Party Central Committee's summary of the experience of more than 20 years of reform and opening up; it was an important inspiration for overcoming the SARS epidemic, and an urgent requirement to promote the building of an all-round moderately prosperous society. Since the Scientific Outlook on Development was first advanced, it has been continuously enriched and improved in practice, and has played an important guiding role in the development of the cause of socialism with Chinese characteristics.

IMPROVING THE SOCIALIST MARKET ECONOMY SYSTEM AND PROMOTING SOUND AND FAST ECONOMIC DEVELOPMENT

After the reform and opening up, especially since the 14th National Congress of the CPC, our country had initially established a socialist market economy system, which greatly promoted the development of our society's productivity. However, there were still many imperfections in the socialist market economic system and further reforms were needed.

In October 2003, the Third Plenary Session of the 16th Central Committee of the CPC approved the *Decision of the Central Committee of the CPC on Several Issues Concerning the Improvement of the Socialist Market Economic System*. This proposed vigorous development of a mixed-ownership economy involving state-owned capital, collective capital and non-public capital; relaxation of market access, allowing non-public capital to enter infrastructure, public utilities and other industries, and fields that are not prohibited by laws and regulations; the establishment of a modern property rights system with clear ownership, clear rights and responsibilities, strict protection and smooth circulation; the establishment of a system that is conducive to the gradual change of the dual economic structure of urban and rural areas, and other major policy measures. This *Decision* showed that our party had further deepened its understanding of the development of the market economy under socialist conditions and had further improved its ability to understand and use the laws of the market economy. By means of this plenary session, our country's reform of the economic system was steadily advanced in key areas and through key links.

Consolidating and developing the publicly owned economy and giving full play to the leading role of the state-owned economy are important aspects of improving the basic economic system. Across the country, central, provincial and municipal levels have successively established state-owned assets supervision and management committees to change the previous practice of government being directly involved in managing enterprises; this was to ensure that the responsibility for maintaining and increasing the value of state-owned assets was properly fulfilled. Following the requirements of the *Decision* that the shareholding system should be the main form of enacting public ownership, the reform of the shareholding system of SOEs was continuously promoted and developed through various channels such as standardised listing, Sino-foreign joint ventures, mutual equity participation, and mergers and acquisitions. After the reform, a number of new SOEs emerged that were able to seize market opportunities and respond to the challenges of the international market. These became the pillars of the national economy, and the vitality, control and influence of the state-owned economy were significantly enhanced by them.

While being unshakeably committed to the consolidation and development of the public sector of the economy, we should be equally unswerving in encouraging, supporting and guiding the development of the non-public sector as well. In February 2005, the State Council issued a number of opinions on encouraging, supporting and guiding the development of the non-public economy. These included promoting individual and private enterprises, proposing to relax market access for the non-public economy and allowing non-public capital to enter the fields of monopoly industries, public utilities, social undertakings and financial services, and encouraging participation in the reorganisation of SOEs. With the continuous improvement of the policy planning environment, non-public enterprises were able to develop rapidly. The output value created during this period exceeded half of GDP, and the proportion of tax paid to the country increased. This all played an increasingly important role in promoting economic growth, expanding employment and activating the market.

By enacting continuous and deepening reforms, the party and the government took timely measures to increase macro-control in response to problems such as excessive growth in fixed asset investment, excessive money supply and credit, and excessive foreign trade surpluses that emerged in the process of industrialisation and urbanisation. After 2003, the central government proposed that the twin gateways of land and credit must be strictly controlled, and policies for natural resources such as land must be used as macro-control measures. Due to such timely measures, the economy was slowly cooled after the second quarter of 2004, and the excessive growth of investment in some industries was curbed to some extent.

While strengthening macro-economic regulation and control, the Party Central Committee also proposed new development policies based on the new conditions of economic and social development. In October 2006, the Sixth Plenary Session of the 16th Central Committee of the CPC put forward the new requirement of 'promoting sound and rapid economic development'. Sound and speedy development emphasises the need to maintain stable and rapid economic growth and prevent major fluctuations. It also demands persistence in seeking quick solutions focused on optimising structure, and continuous strenuous efforts to improve quality and efficiency. The guidance for economic development changed from 'fast and good', which had stood for so many years, to 'good and fast'. Although this was only a change in the order of the words 'good' and 'fast', it actually reflected the essential requirements of scientific development.

Through reforms in key areas and key links, as well as through the effective implementation of macro-control and timely adjustment of guidelines, some outstanding contradictions in economic operations were alleviated, and the national economy maintained rapid growth, improved structure and increased efficiency. It found itself in a good and stable position with no major fluctuations. By 2007, our country's overall economy rose to become the fourth largest in the world, and its total import and export volume rose to third in the world.

ADVANCING THE STRATEGIC GOAL OF BUILDING A HARMONIOUS SOCIALIST SOCIETY

The goal of our party's unremitting struggle is to achieve social harmony and to build a better society. In the new century, in the face of profound changes in the economic system, profound changes in the social structure, profound adjustments in the pattern of priorities and profound changes in ideological concepts, the Party Central Committee, following the overall pattern of the cause of building socialism with Chinese characteristics and the construction of an all-round moderately prosperous society, has taken a firm and targeted grip on the development of our country. In doing so it has proposed major strategic goals for building a harmonious socialist society while taking account of specific phase characteristics and using objective analysis of prominent contradictions and problems affecting social cohesion.

In November 2002, when the 16th National Congress of the CPC stated the goal of building an all-round moderately prosperous society, it identified the requirements for achieving a more harmonious society. In September 2004, the Fourth Plenary Session of the 16th Central Committee of the CPC clearly defined the major strategic task of building a harmonious socialist society and identified improving the ability to build such a society as an important element in strengthening the party's ability to govern.

In October 2006, the Sixth Plenary Session of the 16th Central Committee of the CPC passed the *Decisions of the Central Committee of the CPC on Several Major Issues Concerning the Construction of a Harmonious Socialist Society*. These proposed the principles of democracy and the rule of law as: fairness and justice, honesty and friendship, vitality, stability and order, and harmony between people. The overriding requirement of natural and peaceful coexistence is the construction of a harmonious socialist society. The *Decisions* emphasised that it is necessary to adhere to people-oriented principles and always to take the fundamental interests of the overwhelming majority of the people as the starting point and the goal of all the work of the party and the country. In this way development is for the people, development depends on the people, and the fruits of development are shared by the people, and the overall development of people is promoted. The *Decisions* also proposed policies and measures for building a harmonious socialist society.

The proposal of the major strategic goal of building a harmonious socialist society introduced the important aspect of 'social construction' to the overall blueprint for the cause of socialism with Chinese characteristics. It thereby expands the 'trinity' of economic construction, political construction and cultural construction into a fourfold combination of economic construction, political construction, cultural construction and social construction.

PROMOTING THE COORDINATED REGIONAL DEVELOPMENT OF URBAN AND RURAL AREAS

The imbalance of regional urban and rural development was an outstanding problem that restricted our country's economic and social development. After the Scientific Outlook on Development was advanced, the Party Central Committee earnestly implemented its requirements and undertook a series of major decisions and actions for the overall planning of regional urban and rural development.

After the implementation of the Western Development Strategy at the turn of the century, in accordance with the central government's policy of focusing on first and appropriately phased progress, efforts were made to strengthen infrastructure construction in the western region. These focused on the construction of landmark projects such as the West-to-East Electricity Transmission, West-to-East Gas Transmission and the Qinghai-Tibet Railway. The Qinghai-Tibet Railway is known as the 'Railway Closest to Heaven'. Under harsh natural conditions, the construction teams overcame the three universal major engineering and technical problems of perennially frozen soil, intense cold, lack of oxygen and ecological fragility and, in doing so, built the world's highest-altitude railway. This plateau railway, which is the longest ever built, stands as a miraculous achievement in the history of railway construction. On 1 July 2006, the 1,956km-long Qinghai-Tibet Railway was opened to traffic, so ending Tibet's historic lack of railways. It gave an enormous boost to the rapid development of the snow-covered plateau and the improvement of the lives of people of all ethnic groups and became the 'oxygen line' for the economic and social development of Tibet. The comprehensive implementation of the strategy for the development of the western region has succeeded in bringing continuous new prospects for the economic and social development of the western region.

The Qinghai-Tibet Railway opens to traffic at the head of the Tuotuo River Bridge in Qinghai Province, where local people welcome the 'Qing 1' train departing from Golmud

With the in-depth implementation of the Western Development Strategy, the Party Central Committee focused on achieving coordinated regional development and made a series of major decisions such as revitalising the northeast and other old industrial bases, and promoting the growth of the central region, thereby shaping and enriching the overall regional development strategy. Through the implementation of major industrial restructuring projects in the northeast, a number of key enterprises such as the Daqing Oilfield and China First Automotive Works (FAW) significantly improved their technological levels, and their independent innovation and advanced manufacturing capabilities continued to increase. In addition, a number of resource-based cities such as Fuxin, Liaoning and others achieved appropriately phased results in their trial economic transformation. With the support of the central government, the central region fully implemented its growth. A number of competitive industries and products continued to emerge. The formation of conurbations, urban belts and urban circles accelerated, further highlighting the advantages of connecting the western and eastern regions. The state approved the Shanghai Pudong New Area and the Tianjin Binhai New Area as national pilot areas supporting comprehensive reform, and actively promoted the development and opening up of key areas such as the Yangtze River Delta and the west coast of the Taiwan Strait. The eastern region took full advantage of its location and position in the vanguard of reform to achieve model innovative development. The three major metropolitan areas of the Yangtze River Delta, the Pearl River Delta and the Beijing-Tianjin-Hebei region continue to maintain their status of the 'three engines' of our country's economic development.

The coordination of urban and rural development was another important task in promoting scientific development and social harmony. The Fourth Plenary Session of the 16th Central Committee of the CPC undertook in-depth analysis of the development process of industrialisation in other countries, and clearly defined the important thesis of the 'two trends'. These were that 'it is a universal trend that in the initial stage of industrialisation, agriculture supports industry and provides the necessary accumulation of resources; however, once the process of industrialisation has reached a certain point, it is also a universal trend that industry feeds back into agriculture, and cities support the countryside. This is how to implement the coordinated development of industry and agriculture, and cities and rural areas.' The Central Committee believed that, after decades of development, our country had generally entered that stage of development in which industry promotes agriculture and cities lead the countryside. It was then the necessary work of the whole party to coordinate urban and rural economic and social development, and to solve the problems of agriculture, rural areas and farmers. The most important thing was to adhere to the policy of 'give more, take less and loosen control' and to strive to increase farmers' income. Since 2004, the central government has published the annual *No. 1 Document* on the issue of 'agriculture, the rural areas and farmers'. In October 2005, the Fifth Plenary Session of the 16th Central Committee of the CPC clearly proposed the major strategic task of building a new socialist countryside and made the necessary arrangements for the task.

The party and government adopted a series of major measures to effectively reduce the burden on farmers.

On 29 December 2005, the 19th Meeting of the Standing Committee of the 10th NPC decided that the *Regulations of the PRC on Agricultural Taxes* would be repealed from 1 January 2006. As a result, the state no longer levied separate taxes on agriculture, and an ancient tax that had existed in our country for 2,600 years was ended. A series of local fees attached to agricultural taxes were also cancelled. The abolition of agricultural taxes and various surcharges fundamentally reversed the overburdening of farmers and brought tangible benefits to hundreds of millions of farmers. Wang Sanni, a farmer in Qinglian Village, Lingshou County, Hebei Province, threw her own money into a 'Farewell Tian Fu Ding', a cast bronze tripod inscribed with text commemorating the abolition of the agricultural tax in order to express her joy at the abolition of the tax in a special way, and to ensure that future generations would always remember this historic move.

The state also implemented comprehensive rural reforms and collective forest rights system reforms that included township institutions, rural compulsory education, and county and township financial management system reforms. Rural reform and development opened a new chapter in the great process of building a new socialist countryside.

COMPLETION OF THE 10TH FIVE-YEAR PLAN AND FORMULATION OF THE 11TH FIVE-YEAR PLAN

At the turn of the century, some people in Western countries propounded the so-called 'theory of China's economic collapse'. However, facts have proved that China's economy has not only not collapsed but has become an important force in the development of the global economy.

During the five years of the '10th five-year plan', our country negated the impact of the Asian financial crisis, successfully defeated the SARS epidemic, overcame major natural disasters, calmly responded to the new changes in joining the World Trade Organisation (WTO), and lost no time in promoting reform and opening up, and strengthening and improving macro-control. The economy maintained steady and rapid development, and social productivity and overall national strength reached new levels. In the five years from 2001 to 2005, GDP grew by 57.3%, with an average annual growth rate of 9.5%. People's lives improved significantly, people's housing conditions were greatly improved, cars quickly became part of ordinary households, and popular tourism consumption greatly increased. Not only did domestic consumption during the Golden Week holiday boom, more and more people went abroad and travelled all over the world.

During the '10th five-year plan' period, our country's per capita GDP exceeded US$1,000, and economic and social development entered a critical period. With the completion of the '10th five-year plan', the Party Central Committee thoroughly studied and understood a series of important phased features of our country's development during this period, paying great attention to the existing challenges and risks, and working hard to overcome them by formulating the '11th five-year plan' in response.

In October 2005, the Fifth Plenary Session of the 16th CPC Central

Committee passed the *Proposals of the Central Committee of the CPC on Formulating the 11th Five-Year Plan for National Economic and Social Development*. The principal feature of the *Proposals* was their emphasis on the overriding necessity of using the Scientific Outlook on Development to guide overall economic and social development and of ensuring that the Scientific Outlook on Development was applied across the entire process of reform, opening up and modernisation. The *Proposals* had two outstanding elements: one was to emphasise that, on the basis of optimising structure, improving efficiency and reducing consumption, the per capita GDP in 2010 would be double what it had been in 2000. This per capita indicator of GDP was higher than that previously proposed and the goal of doubling the value was even more ambitious; the other element was to incorporate energy consumption into the target system for the first time, proposing that energy consumption per unit of GDP should be reduced by about 20% from the end of the 10th five-year plan period. In March 2006, the Fourth Session of the 10th NPC reviewed and approved the *Outline of the 11th Five-Year Plan for the National Economic and Social Development of the PRC*.

The goals, tasks and policy measures defined in the 11th five-year programme not only connected with the goal of building an all-round moderately prosperous society, they also reflected the objective requirements and phased characteristics of economic and social development. The 11th five-year programme also changed, for the first time in 50 years, the wording of the name from 'plan' to 'programme'. This simple change represented the practical positioning of medium and long-term planning under the conditions of the socialist market economy and reflected major changes in our country's development philosophy, economic system and government functions.

3

THE 17TH NATIONAL CONGRESS OF THE CPC AND THE NEW ARRANGEMENTS FOR BUILDING AN ALL-ROUND MODERATELY PROSPEROUS SOCIETY

THE 17TH NATIONAL CONGRESS OF THE CPC

From 15 to 21 October 2007, the 17th National Congress of the CPC was held in Beijing. Hu Jintao delivered a report entitled *Hold High the Great Banner of Socialism with Chinese Characteristics and Strive for New Victories in Building an All-Round Moderately Prosperous Society*.

The conference made an incisive summary of the '10 combinations' of invaluable experience of reform and opening up, and expounded on the fundamental connotations of the road to socialism with Chinese characteristics. The conference emphasised that the fundamental reasons for all the achievements and progress we made since the reform and opening up were: the opening up of the road to socialism with Chinese characteristics and the establishment of the theoretical system of socialism with Chinese characteristics. In order to hold high the great banner of socialism with Chinese characteristics, the most fundamental thing is to adhere to the path of socialism with Chinese characteristics and to the theoretical system of socialism with Chinese characteristics.

The conference comprehensively and systematically explained the historical background, scientific connotations, spiritual essence and fundamental requirements of the Scientific Outlook on Development.

The conference undertook in-depth analysis of the development of, and changes in, the international and domestic situation, and the new characteristics of our country's development at this early stage in the new century. It also made comprehensive arrangements for the realisation of the grand goal of building an all-round moderately prosperous society and detailed the new requirements involved in the five aspects of: the economy, politics, culture, society and ecological awareness. Looked at in comparison with the goals set by the 16th National Congress of the CPC, these new requirements not only connected closely with them, thereby maintaining continuity, they also enriched them in line with the new conditions and circumstances. Consequently, the goal of building an all-round moderately prosperous society was also made more comprehensive, richer in content and more specific. In particular, in accordance with the reality of sustained and rapid economic development, the 17th National Congress of the CPC adjusted the goal proposed at the 16th National Congress of the CPC, achieving economic growth by 2020 which would quadruple the GDP of 2000 and proposed instead the more demanding goal of achieving a per capita GDP by 2020 that was quadruple that of 2000. These new goals profoundly reflected the new developments in the party's thinking on governing the country, and vividly embodied the essential requirements and fundamental spirit of the Scientific Outlook on Development.

The conference reviewed and approved the report and the *Constitution of the CPC (Amendment)*. The amendment to the party constitution added the overall pattern of the cause of socialism with Chinese characteristics, and comprehensively promoted the content of economic construction, political construction, cultural construction and social construction, while reflecting our party's understanding of the laws of the CPC's governance, the laws of socialist construction and the laws of human social development. In addition, it was stipulated that the Party Central Committee and provincial, autonomous region and municipal committees implement an inspection system to help strengthen internal party supervision and promote anti-corruption measures; it was further stipulated that party cadres must establish a correct view of political performance and ensure that their actual performance could meet the test of good practice, the people and historical experience; new regulations were also added to promote open party affairs, develop intraparty democracy, and strengthen and improve the management of floating party members.

The congress elected the 17th Central Committee and the Central Commission for Discipline Inspection. The First Plenary Session of the 17th CPC Central Committee elected Hu Jintao, Wu Bangguo, Wen Jiabao, Jia Qinglin, Li Changchun, Xi Jinping, Li Keqiang, He Guoqiang, and Zhou Yongkang[1] as members of the Politburo Standing Committee, and Hu Jintao as general secretary of the Central Committee; Hu Jintao was elected chairman of the CMC and He Guoqiang was approved as secretary of the Central Commission for Discipline Inspection.

A SUMMARY OF THE THEORETICAL SYSTEM OF SOCIALISM WITH CHINESE CHARACTERISTICS

The major contribution to political theory made by the 17th National Congress of the CPC was the creative proposal and profound explanation of the political theory that resulted from the second leap forward of Marxism in China, namely, the theory of the system of socialism with Chinese characteristics.

The theoretical system of socialism with Chinese characteristics was gradually formed through the excellent practice of the party's leadership in reform and opening up, and socialist modernisation. The 17th National Congress of the CPC proposed for the first time that the theoretical system of socialism with Chinese characteristics should be considered a scientific theoretical system that includes Deng Xiaoping Theory and the important thinking of the 'Three Represents', as well as other major strategic thinking such as the Scientific Outlook on Development. This theoretical system upholds and develops Marxism-Leninism and Mao Zedong Thought, and has condensed the wisdom and hard work of generations of Chinese Communists to lead the people in unremitting exploration and practice. It is the latest achievement of the Sinification of Marxism and the most valuable political and spiritual treasure of the party. It is the common ideological basis for the unity and struggle of the people of all ethnic groups across the whole nation. The congress emphasised that the theoretical system of socialism with Chinese characteristics is an open theoretical system that is constantly evolving and must be cherished, persisted with over the long term and continuously developed.

The congress pointed out that the Scientific Outlook on Development is based on the fundamental national conditions of the primary stage of socialism in summarising our country's development practice, learning from foreign development experience, and adapting to new development requirements. The first essential of the Scientific Outlook on Development is development; its core is people-oriented; its basic requirement is comprehensive coordination and sustainability; and its fundamental method is overall planning. To continue to build an all-round moderately prosperous society and to develop socialism with Chinese characteristics at this new stage of development, we had to closely follow Deng Xiaoping Theory and the important thinking of the 'Three Represents' as our guides, and thoroughly implement the Scientific Outlook on Development.

The congress held that the Scientific Outlook on Development is a major innovation in the theoretical system of socialism with Chinese characteristics and decided to include this achievement in the party constitution. The party constitution clearly stipulates that the Scientific Outlook on Development is a scientific theory that is in line with Marxism-Leninism, Mao Zedong Thought, Deng Xiaoping Theory and the important thinking of the 'Three Represents', and is an important guiding principle for our country's economic and social development. It is a major strategic idea that socialism with Chinese characteristics must adhere to and implement.

---

1. In December 2014, in view of Zhou Yongkang's serious violation of discipline, after reviewing his case, the Central Committee of the CPC decided to expel him from the party. In June 2015, Zhou Yongkang was sentenced to life imprisonment by Tianjin No. 1 Intermediate People's Court. and deprived of political rights for life for the crimes of accepting bribes, abusing power and deliberately leaking state secrets.

4
RESPONDING TO MAJOR CHALLENGES, AND DEEPENING REFORM AND OPENING UP

RESPONDING TO THE INTERNATIONAL FINANCIAL CRISIS AND OTHER CHALLENGES

The US subprime mortgage crisis that began in 2007, evolved into a global financial crisis in 2008, and it quickly spread from the financial sector to the real economy, and from the US to the world's other major economies. The fierceness of its onslaught, the speed of its spread and the depth of its influence had not been seen since the world economic crisis in the late 1920s and early 1930s. After the outbreak of the subprime mortgage crisis in the US, the Party Central Committee paid close attention to the development of the crisis, especially the risks and impacts that it might bring to our country's economic development, and they emphasised the need to establish awareness of the crisis and to make preparations for it.

By September, the impact of the international financial crisis on our country was intensifying rapidly. The economic growth rate in the fourth quarter showed a sharp decline, foreign trade exports were difficult, and employment pressures rapidly increased. The Party Central Committee and the State Council made comprehensive analyses and accurate judgments, and initiated a calm response. They shifted the focus of macro-control onto preventing an excessively rapid decline in economic growth; implemented a proactive fiscal policy and a moderately loose monetary policy; strove to expand domestic demand, especially consumer demand; and put together a package plan that included a major increase in government investment, implementation of structural tax cuts, and extensive implementation of an adjustment and revitalisation plan for 10 key industries.

After much hard work, our country took the lead in the world in achieving economic recovery. From the second quarter of 2009 onwards, the economy stopped falling and rebounded, with a full-year growth rate of 9.2%. The facts proved that our country's methods, policies and measures to deal with the impact of the international financial crisis were generally effective. However, some of the economic stimulus policies adopted needed time to take effect and, at the same time, there were also still many outstanding contradictions and problems in our country's economic development. In order to fundamentally solve the problem of stable and healthy economic development, a determined advance and even deeper reforms were needed.

On 12 May 2008, an earthquake measuring 8.0 on the Richter scale struck Wenchuan in Sichuan Province. It killed 87,000 people, affected more than 46.25 million people, and caused a direct economic loss of more than Rmb845.1 billion. Under the leadership of the Party Central Committee, China swiftly organised earthquake relief activities with the fastest rescue speed, the widest mobilisation range and the greatest practical input in history. The Party Central Committee acted with the good of the people at the heart of their intentions, showed respect for science and responded firmly, decisively and calmly. The people across the country shared the burden of adversity and worked together. Men, women, children and soldiers ignored personal danger and forged ahead. Help came from all directions for every area in distress and the advantages of our system of all coming together in the face of great disaster were amply demonstrated. During this magnificent earthquake relief operation, countless people, facing the danger of death themselves, risked their lives for the sake of others at the moment of life and death. Parents carried their children to safety, teachers used their bodies to shelter their students from the threat of death. At the moments of greatest danger, party members and cadres came rushing to the fore to confront the calamity. Moving and heroic songs were written amongst the ruins left by the earthquakes, demonstrating the great spirit of the people in the face of the disaster, coming together in a spirit of unity, defying hardship with perseverance and respect for science.

After winning a major victory in the earthquake relief struggle, the party and the government quickly formulated a post-disaster recovery and reconstruction plan for the disaster area. They decided to complete the task of post-disaster recovery and reconstruction in three years, and mobilised the strength of the nation to provide complementary support. People of all ethnic groups across the country, compatriots from Hong Kong, Macau and Taiwan, and overseas Chinese contributed to the earthquake relief and post-disaster reconstruction in many different ways. By the end of September 2010, the reconstruction task was essentially completed one year ahead of schedule, and the infrastructure, productivity and standard of living of the people in the disaster-stricken areas greatly exceeded their pre-disaster levels. This all constituted a miracle of post-disaster reconstruction.

From 2008 to 2010, the party and government led the people in the fight against severe natural disasters, such as extreme weather in the form of rain, snow and freezing temperatures in the south, the violent earthquake in Yushu, Qinghai, and the massive torrents and mudslides in Zhouqu, Gansu, and together our nation achieved the victory of restoration and reconstruction. Also, under the rule of law, the severe violence in Lhasa and other places on 14 March 2008 was resolutely quelled and properly dealt with.

The crime and serious violence of looting, burning and destruction of property in Urumqi on 5 July 2009 was resolutely handled and the sabotage activities of violent terrorist forces, ethnic separatist forces and religious extremist forces were suppressed, thereby maintaining national unity and social stability.

These successful responses to various difficulties, dangerous situations and challenges fully illustrate our party's ability to withstand a variety of risks and manage complex situations. They demonstrate the strong leadership of the party and the political advantage of our country's socialist system in its ability to concentrate its efforts on major issues. There is no difficulty that cannot be overcome by the heroic Chinese people's fearless spirit.

ACCELERATING TRANSFORMATION OF ECONOMIC DEVELOPMENT METHODS AND DEEPENING REFORM OF IMPORTANT AREAS

Accelerating the transformation of the means of economic development, and deepening the reform of important areas to achieve that acceleration was a profound change in the economics of our country.

In order better to solve the structural contradictions accumulated in the economy over a long period of time and the challenges of the pattern of extensive economic growth, the 17th National Congress of the CPC proposed the strategic task of accelerating the transformation of the pattern of economic development. The change from the frequently used expression 'pattern of transformation of economic growth' to 'pattern of transformation of economic development', only involves one word, but it has very profound connotations. The 'transformation of the pattern of economic development' not only covers all the meaning of the 'transformation of the pattern of economic growth', but it also emphasises the new and higher requirements of the concept, purpose, strategy and approach of economic development. This fully reflects the party's deepening understanding of the laws of economic development.

The impact of the international financial crisis further highlighted the problems of unbalanced domestic and external demand, uncoordinated investment and consumption, irrational industrial structure and unsustainable development patterns. The Fifth Plenary Session of the 17th Central Committee of the CPC held in October 2010 clearly indicated that accelerating the transformation of economic development was the main theme of economic and social development during the 12th five-year plan. The Party Central Committee also made a new summary of the basic requirements for accelerating the transformation of the pattern of economic development, clearly requiring the strategic adjustment of the economic structure as the main direction, with scientific and technological progress and innovation as an important support; taking the protection and improvement of people's livelihood as the fundamental starting point and goal; regarding the construction of a resource-saving and environment-friendly society as an important focus, and reform and opening up as a powerful driving force. In accordance with these requirements, the party and the state successively adopted a series of measures which: adhere to the strategy of expanding domestic demand; adhere to the path of new industrialisation with Chinese characteristics; steadily promote energy conservation, emissions reduction and ecological environmental protection; implement, in depth, the overall regional development strategy, and actively and steadily promote urbanisation. In this, a new step was taken to promote the transformation of the pattern of economic development.

The lag in the transformation of the economic development mode was caused by many factors, but the biggest sticking point was that the institutional mechanism was irrational. To this end, the Party Central Committee emphasised that through continuous deepening of reforms, the market's fundamental role in resource allocation should be more systematically brought into play, and a macro-control system conducive to scientific development should be formed to provide a powerful driving force and institutional guarantee for economic and social development.

In terms of ownership reform, the strategic adjustment of the state-owned economy and the reform of large SOEs were accelerated. Starting from 2006, centralised enterprises increased their merger and reorganisation efforts. The number of centralised enterprises under the supervision of the State-Owned Assets Supervision and Administration Commission (SASAC) decreased from 159 in 2007 to 117 in 2011. More than 80% of the assets were concentrated in petroleum and petrochemical, power, defence and communications industries, and also key areas including transportation, mining and metallurgy. In all of them, the overall quality and competitiveness of SOEs was greatly enhanced. As SOEs became stronger and better, the party and government adhered to the 'two unshakable'[1] policy and actively guided and encouraged the healthy development of the non-public sector of the economy. In May 2010, the State Council issued several opinions on encouraging and guiding the healthy development of private investment, and the institutional environment for the development of the non-public economy was further improved.

In terms of rural reform and development, the central government clearly declared on the 30th anniversary of the reform and opening up, that the existing land contracting relationship should remain stable and unchanged for a significant period. The Third Plenary Session of the 17th Central Committee of the CPC held in October 2008 made the *Decision of the Central Committee of the CPC on Several Major Issues in Promoting Rural Reform and Development*, emphasising that agriculture is a strategic industry that stabilises the world and stabilises people's hearts, and requires that the red line of 1.8 billion *mu* of arable land be firmly maintained in order to promote the integration of urban and rural economic and social development. After that, the central government further increased its financial investment in agriculture and introduced a series of agricultural policies to strengthen benefits and profits for farmers. Centred on the implementation of direct grain subsidies, it implemented subsidies for grain farmers, subsidies for the purchase of agricultural machinery and comprehensive subsidies for agricultural materials. These measures fully mobilised the enthusiasm of grain farmers. From 2004, our country's grain output achieved continuous growth for eight years, reaching 570 million tonnes in 2011. The per capita net income of farmers also increased year on year.

In terms of opening up to the outside world, the level of openness of the economy was comprehensively improved. China fulfilled its commitment to join the WTO and significantly reduced tariffs. By 2010, the overall tariff level was reduced to 9.8%, far below the average level of developing countries. At the same time, large-scale clean-up and revision of laws and regulations was carried out. Beginning in 2001, the central government cleaned up more than 2,300 laws, regulations and departmental rules over a 10-year period, and local government cleaned up more than 190,000 local policies and regulations. After the outbreak of the international financial crisis, China actively responded to the rapid changes in the external environment, promptly introduced policies and measures to stabilise foreign demand, implemented market diversification strategies, and made important progress in foreign trade, use of foreign capital and foreign investment. In the 10 years between 2002 and 2011, when it joined the WTO, China's global ranking for trade in goods rose from sixth to second. China's opening-up policy of equality, mutual benefit, cooperation and win-win results not only benefited 1.3 billion Chinese people, but also benefited people from all over the world, and gave a strong impetus to the development of the world economy.

COMPLETION OF THE 11TH FIVE-YEAR PLAN AND FORMULATION OF THE 12TH FIVE-YEAR PLAN

During the 11th five-year plan period, in the face of complex changes in the domestic and foreign environment and major risks and challenges, the Party Central Committee kept a firm grasp on development, the first priority for governing and rejuvenating the country, gave full play to the political advantages of the socialist system and also to the fundamental role of the market in resource allocation. They accelerated reform, opening up and modernisation, and new historical changes took place in the country's outlook.

The economy developed steadily and rapidly, and the national economy reached new levels. During the period of the '11th five-year programme', GDP grew at an average annual rate of 11.3%. In 2010, it exceeded Rmb40 trillion. The total economic output surpassed that of Germany and Japan successively, and jumped to become the second largest in the world after the US. The per capita disposable income of urban residents and the per capita net income of rural residents increased by 9.7% and 8.9%, respectively. People's living standards improved significantly.

Rapid economic development requires technological innovation to provide impetus, while at the same time creating conditions for technological progress. Following the proposal for building an innovative country in 2005, the central government further proposed the implementation of an innovation-driven development strategy in 2012. In accordance with this strategy, the state increased investment in science and technology, organised the implementation of 16 major science and technology projects and technological innovation projects, and 10 major industry revitalisation plans and strategic emerging industry development plans. They achieved a number of major independent successes at the cutting edge of science and in strategically contested areas, and made important new breakthroughs in fields such as manned spaceflight, lunar exploration and supercomputers. Following the first manned spaceflight of the *Shenzhou V* spacecraft in 2003, five years later, the *Shenzhou VII* spacecraft astronauts successfully carried out the first Chinese spacewalk, achieving a major milestone advance in the development of our country's space technology. In 2007, *Chang'e-1* completed its first lunar exploration. The Chinese nation's dream, for thousands of years, of flying to the heavens had finally become a reality. In August 2008, the Beijing-Tianjin intercity high-speed railway opened for operation, marking China's entry into the era of high-speed rail. In addition, news poured in continuously of successes with the Three Gorges Water Conservancy Project, the Qinghai-Tibet Railway, the South-to-North Water Diversion, the West-East Electricity Transmission, the West-East Gas Transmission and other major construction projects, all of which amply demonstrated our country's brilliant achievements in reform, opening up and modernisation.

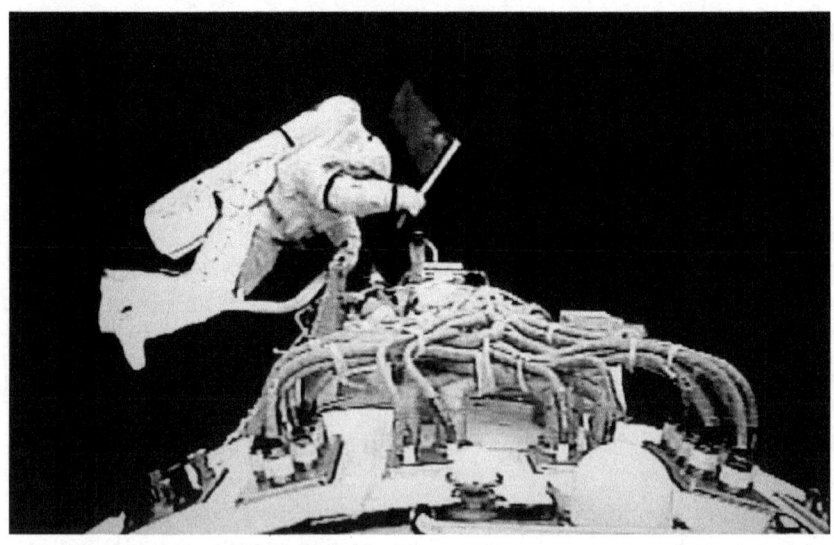

On 27 September 2008, astronaut Zhai Zhigang waves the Chinese flag on a spacewalk outside the Shenzhou VII space craft

During the '11th five-year programme' period, our country also managed many major events. From 8 to 24 August 2008, the 29th Summer Olympic Games were held in Beijing, followed by the 13th Paralympic Games. The Chinese team ranked first in the gold medal list at the

Olympics and ranked first in both the gold medal and the overall medal lists at the Paralympic Games, achieving honour both in sports performance and spiritual culture. The Chinese people successfully hosted a unique and high-quality Olympic Games, fulfilling the century-long expectations of the Chinese nation, fulfilling their solemn promises to the international community, and further enhancing mutual understanding and friendship with people from all over the world. From 1 May to 31 October 2010, the World Expo with the theme of 'Better City, Better Life' was held in Shanghai. This was the first official World Expo to be held in a developing country. In 184 days, 246 countries and international organisations participated in the exhibition, and 73.08 million people visited the exhibition, writing a new chapter in the story of exchange and mutual learning between the Chinese people and the people of other countries in the world.

The arena of the 29th Summer Olympic Games in Beijing, 2008

Entering the second decade of the 21st century, the Party Central Committee comprehensively analysed the international and domestic situations it faced and advanced the important opinion that our country's development during the '12th five-year plan' period was still at a stage of important strategic opportunities from which many achievements could be accomplished. In October 2010, the Fifth Plenary Session of the 17th Central Committee of the CPC passed the *Proposals of the Central Committee of the CPC on Formulating the 12th Five-Year Programme for National Economic and Social Development*.

We will make overall plans for continuing to advance towards the goal of building an all-round moderately prosperous society at a new historical starting point. Distinctively, the *Proposals* clearly advanced the scientific development theme of the 12th five-year plan, the main thrust of which was to change the mode of economic development. In March 2011, the Fourth Plenary Session of the 11th NPC approved the *Outline of the 12th Five-Year Plan for National and Social Development of the PRC*.

ACTIVELY AND STEADILY PROMOTING THE CONSTRUCTION OF DEMOCRACY AND THE RULE OF LAW

Entering the new century, in compliance with the requirements of the times and the expectations of the people, the Party Central Committee insisted on unifying the leadership of the party with the people as masters of the country and in accordance with the rule of law while adhering to the path of the political development of socialism with Chinese characteristics.

The framework of the People's Congress system was further strengthened. In May 2005, the Central Committee of the CPC forwarded *Several Opinions of the Party Group of the NPC Standing Committee on Further Giving Full Play to the Role of NPC Representatives and Strengthening the System Construction of the NPC Standing Committee*. In March 2010, the Third Session of the 11th NPC passed the newly revised NPC and Local People's Congress election laws, which made it clear that, in the circumstances of our country's rapid economic and social development, continuous urbanisation and huge changes in the urban-rural population structure, the urban and rural representatives to the People's Congress would be elected according to proportional representation of the population. From the first half of 2011 to the end of 2012, the nation completed the first elections to the people's assemblies at county and township levels following the revision of the electoral law. This demonstrated that, for the first time in the history of new China, the system of 'same vote same power' in urban and rural areas had been enacted, thereby better embodying the principles of equality of all people, equality of regions and equality of ethnic groups.

The pace of establishment of scientific legislation and democratic legislation was also accelerated. By the end of 2010, a socialist legal system with Chinese characteristics composed of laws, administrative regulations and local regulations with the constitution as the head, and the laws of multiple legal departments such as constitutional law, civil law and commercial law as the backbone, and composed of laws, administrative regulations and local regulations, was formed. This was an important milestone in the history of the construction of our country's socialist democracy and legal system, and an important sign of the ongoing maturing of the socialist system with Chinese characteristics.

The underlying political system was further improved and developed.

The 17th National Congress of the CPC, for the first time, brought the system of community-level self-governance into the grassroots level of the socialist political system with Chinese characteristics, and promoted it as a fundamental project for the development of socialist democratic politics. Both in the cities and in the countryside, community-level democratic elections, democratic decision-making, democratic management and democratic supervision were practiced more and more extensively. Hundreds of millions of people managed their affairs in accordance with the law, enjoyed more and more practical democratic rights, and the overall vitality of community-level democracy was greatly increased. By the end of 2012, more than eight rounds of general elections for village committees had been held in rural areas. More than 98% of village committees across the country had implemented direct elections, and the average participation rate of villagers reached 95%; cities had held more than six rounds of general elections for neighbourhood committees.

PROMOTING THE GREAT DEVELOPMENT AND PROSPERITY OF SOCIALIST CULTURE

The building of a socialist culture to strengthen the nation was a major strategic decision made by the party as it entered the new century. The 17th National Congress of the CPC emphasised the need to promote cultural development and prosperity more consciously and proactively, and to enhance the country's cultural soft power. The Sixth Plenary Session of the 17th Central Committee of the CPC held in October 2011 adopted the *Decisions of the Central Committee of the CPC on Several Major Issues Concerning Deepening Reform of the Cultural System and Promoting the Great Development and Prosperity of Socialist Culture*, which proposed adhering to the development path of socialist culture with Chinese characteristics and striving to carry out the strategic task of building a socialist culture to strengthen the nation. Our country's cultural reconstruction entered a new stage of development.

The building of a socialist core value system was a major innovation in ideological and cultural construction. In March 2006, when Hu Jintao participated in a joint discussion between the Democratic League and the Democratic Progressive Committee at the Fourth Session of the 10th National Committee of the CPPCC, he proposed the establishment of a socialist concept of honour and disgrace. In October, the Sixth Plenary Session of the 16th Central Committee of the party proposed the task of building a socialist core value system. Since then, the construction of this system has been integrated into the whole process of national education, and spiritual and cultural development. The whole of society has extensively engaged in ideological and spiritual education, patriotic education, national environmental education and practical policy education, through which the people have further strengthened their faith and belief in the leadership of the CPC, in the socialist system, in the project of reform and opening up, and in the overall aim of creating an all-round moderately prosperous society.

In order to achieve cultural prosperity and cultural development, it was a priority to establish a cultural system compatible with the socialist market economy. In December 2005, the Central Committee of the CPC and the State Council issued several opinions on deepening reform of the cultural system, clarifying that reform of the cultural system should focus on reforming the market, reshaping market systems, improving macro management, transforming government functions and other such key development areas. As of 2012, the restructuring of state-owned business units such as publishing and distribution, film and television drama production, and television broadcasting and transmission were complete, and the group system reform of state-owned art academies had also essentially been accomplished.

In the process of systemic cultural reform, the state increased investment and reformed mechanisms to propel the construction of a public cultural service system into the fast lane. The establishment of shared cultural resource projects, extending television coverage across all villages, building comprehensive cultural centres in country townships and other such projects that provide cultural enrichment to the people, was essentially the realisation of the project to ensure that 'every county had a library and a culture hall, and every township had an all-purpose cultural centre'. At the same time, it also actively promoted free access to museums, memorial halls, public libraries, art galleries, culture halls (centres) and so on, thereby emphasising the prominence of the role of public culture in benefiting the people's welfare.

The reform of the cultural system greatly stimulated the vitality of ongoing cultural innovation and creativity, and the rise and development of the culture industry became a notable feature of cultural reform and development as our country entered the new century. Through reform, many cultural institutions that used to 'eat the emperor's grain' transformed themselves into commercial entities that operated independently, took responsibility for their own profits and losses, and developed and limited themselves, thereby greatly improving the supply of cultural products in our country. By 2012, the total output value of the national cultural industry exceeded Rmb4 trillion; the variety and total volume of published books ranked first in the world; the output of movies remained above 500 year on year, making it the world's third largest film industry; annual output of television dramas, numbering tens of thousands of episodes, made our country the world's largest producer. Emerging cultural industries such as cultural innovation, digital publishing, mobile multimedia, animation and games also all underwent rapid development.

ACCELERATING SOCIAL DEVELOPMENT WITH THE FOCUS ON IMPROVING PEOPLE'S LIVELIHOODS

The people are the participants in reforms and share in the benefits of the resulting developments. The resolution of issues affecting the daily life of the people is determined not only by social harmony and stability, but also by popular support and the consolidation of the foundations of party rule. During this period, taking economic development as their foundation, the Party Central Committee adhered to the concept of development for the people, development dependent on the people, and development results shared by the people. In doing so, they focused on the people's most immediate, most direct and practical interests, and strove to solve the problem of economic and social development that is known as: 'One leg too long and one leg too short'. It was determined to speed up social construction focused on improving people's lives by striving to ensure that everyone enjoyed their rights to education, employment, medical and old-age care, and housing.

Educational equality is an important foundation of social equality. After the 16th National Congress of the CPC, the state substantially increased education funding, established a new mechanism for guaranteeing rural compulsory education funding, completely exempted rural compulsory education tuition and miscellaneous fees, implemented the 'two exemptions and one subsidy'[2] policy in rural areas in the west, and further improved the national scholarship and scholarship funding system. They ensured that education resources were focused on rural areas, remote areas, ethnic minority areas and poverty-stricken areas, and strove to ensure that all of the people had access to excellent education opportunities. By 2008, all compulsory education in urban and rural areas was exempted from tuition and miscellaneous fees, benefiting 160 million students, reducing the financial burden on hundreds of millions of families, and ensuring that all school-age children in compulsory education were able to 'go to school without spending money'. The enrolment rate reached 99.5%. The degree of uptake of higher education also increased. In 2012, the gross enrolment rate for higher education reached more than

30%, providing the opportunity for many more students to receive higher education.

The party and the government were firm on taking employment as the foundation of people's livelihoods and did everything possible to expand employment. At the same time, laws and regulations such as the *Employment Promotion Law* and the *Labour Contract Law* were promulgated and implemented to provide legal guarantees for solving employment equality issues. After the outbreak of the international financial crisis in 2008, our country's employment situation came under new pressure. For a time, securing employment became the top priority of all levels of government from central to local. All areas implemented more active employment policies to help college graduates find jobs, open up new job opportunities for farmers, to do the same to help urban families in difficulties find jobs, and to encourage entrepreneurship to drive employment. At the end of 2011, the number of employed people in urban and rural areas in our country reached 760 million, maintaining an overall stable level of employment.

Medical and health care are of vital importance to people's livelihoods. From 2003, our country began to implement a new type of rural cooperative medical system in parts of the western region. It was then launched nationwide in 2006 and covered the whole country by the end of 2008, with 814 million rural residents participating. This new type of rural cooperative medical system, in which individuals participate voluntarily, focuses on overall planning for major illnesses but also takes care of minor illnesses. There is a low level of individual financing but mostly it is subsidised at both state and local government levels. It has been warmly welcomed by the majority of farmers.

Establishing and improving the social security system was an important goal for the building of an all-round moderately prosperous society. Following the 16th National Congress of the CPC, the Party Central Committee adhered to the policy of broad coverage and basic insurance. The system was designed to be multi-level and sustainable, focusing on basic pension, basic medical care and securing a minimum standard of living. Consequently, they accelerated the establishment of a social security system that covered urban and rural residents and was compatible with economic development. In rural areas, a series of major systems such as the new rural cooperative medical care, rural minimum living security and rural endowment insurance systems were introduced one after another; in urban areas, the scope continued to expand to include both urban employees and urban residents, but especially non-public enterprise employees, flexible employees, and migrant workers and social security recipients. By 2012, the number of people participating in various types of endowment insurance in our country reached 790 million, and the basic urban and rural pension insurance system was fully established. The number of people participating in various types of medical insurance exceeded 1.3 billion, and universal medical insurance was effectively achieved; the minimum living security system also achieved full coverage. Consequently, the urban and rural social assistance system had essentially been established and a social safety net covering the largest population in the world had effectively been completed.

With reform and development entering a critical period, social contradictions were always likely to occur. The party and government at all levels actively explored new ways and means to improve social management and services in response to new situations and new problems that arose. Initially, the Party Leadership Committee and the government were responsible for the social management structure for social cooperation and public participation. They strove to resolve contradictions at the grassroots level and nip them in the bud. At the same time, they actively explored the establishment and improvement of an emergency management system to further improve their ability to respond to and manage public emergencies, and the level of that response. In this process of profound and rapid economic and social transformation, our country maintained social and political stability through the strengthening of social management and social service measures.

INCREASING ENVIRONMENTAL PROTECTION

Entering the 21st century, our country's development was facing more and more obvious constraints on resources and the environment, and the people's need for solutions to ecological and environmental problems were becoming more and more urgent. In accordance with the requirements for accelerating the construction of a resource-conserving, environmentally-friendly society, central and local governments took measures to take our country's environmental protection work to a new level.

In order to continuously strengthen environmental protection, our country formulated or revised the *Cleaner Production Promotion Law*, the *Circular Economy Promotion Law* and the *Water Pollution Prevention and Control Law* among others, and was the first developing country to formulate and implement a national plan to address climate change. The 11th five-year plan also clearly stipulated that energy consumption per unit of GDP would be reduced by about 20% compared with the end of the 10th five-year plan period; the total discharge of major pollutants would be reduced by 10%; and the forest coverage rate would be increased to 20%.

From the central to the local level, the pursuit of green GDP began to replace the previous practice of pursuing simple GDP.

The party and the government attached great importance to energy conservation and emission reduction, and focused on taking effective measures with steel, nonferrous metals, chemicals, building materials and other industries. In accordance with the law, they also eliminated a large number of small thermal power stations, small coal mines and other retrograde power sources. At the same time, the Huaihe River and Taihu Lake and other sites were identified as key river basins and efforts were made to carry out water pollution control projects so that rivers and lakes that were overwhelmed by pollution could be restored to health. In 2011, among the 189,000km of rivers that were evaluated nationwide, the proportion of rivers with Grade I-III water was 64.2%. The urban sewage treatment rate reached 83.6%.

The Party Central Committee and the State Council took the major decision to steadfastly pursue the project of returning farmland to forests in order to solve the problems of serious soil erosion and frequent river flooding. By 2008, a total of more than 400 million *mu* of farmland was returned to forest across the country, which is equivalent to rebuilding a state-owned forest area covering Northeast China and Inner Mongolia. In addition, our country continued to implement a series of key ecological and environmental protection projects such as the Qinghai Sanjiangyuan Nature Reserve Ecological Protection and Construction Project, the Beijing-Tianjin Sandstorm Source Control Project, and the Rocky Desertification Comprehensive Control Project. By 2013, the national forest coverage rate reached 21.63%, and desertified land achieved a historic change from 'sand advancing, man retreating' to 'man advancing, sand retreating'.

Through unremitting efforts, the trend of increasing environmental pollution and ecological destruction in our country slowed down, and environmental protection was put into effect.

---

1. The 'two unshakable' policy refers to, one, the need to 'unswervingly consolidate and develop the public ownership economy' and, two, to 'unswervingly encourage, support, and guide the development of the non-public economy'. This policy was advocated by General Secretary Xi Jinping as being an important component for the united front work of the private economy in the new era.
2. 'Two exemptions and one subsidy' refers to provision of free textbooks for elementary and junior high school students from poor families and exemption from fees, and subsidies for certain boarders' living expenses.

5
FULFILLING THE HISTORIC MISSION OF THE MILITARY ON THE NEW STAGE OF THE NEW CENTURY

At an expanded meeting of the CMC in December 2004, Hu Jintao proposed new requirements for the historic mission of the military. He indicated that the military should provide an important guarantee for the CPC in the consolidation of its ruling position; should provide a strong security guarantee during this period of strategic opportunity for national development; should provide strong strategic support for the safeguarding of national interests; and play an important role in maintaining world peace and promoting common development.

In April 2005, Hu Jintao clearly stated that we should adhere to the implementation of the Scientific Outlook on Development in national defence and army building; promote the comprehensive, coordinated and sustainable development of national defence and army building, and realise the combination of a prosperous country and a strong army. In December, Hu Jintao provided a systematic elaboration of the implementation of the Scientific Outlook on Development in national defence and army building.

Army building requires giving ideological and political construction pride of place. In October 2006, Hu Jintao proposed building a revolutionary army that obeyed the party's command, served the people and fought bravely. In December 2008, at an expanded meeting of the CMC, Hu Jintao proposed that the core values of contemporary revolutionary soldiers should be: "to be loyal to the party, to love the people, to serve the country, to be dedicated to their mission and to always advocate honour". The whole army whole-heartedly cultivated the core values of contemporary revolutionary soldiers and carried out in-depth education on historical campaigns, ideals and beliefs, fighting spirit and the socialist view of honour and disgrace. Through this, the creativity, cohesion and combat efficiency of party organisations at all levels in the army was continuously enhanced. A number of advanced groups and individuals emerged from across the armed forces, including the heroic manned spaceflight group.

Hu Jintao reviewing PLA troops at the 60th anniversary celebration of the founding of the PRC on 1 October 2009

The whole army concentrated on making preparations for military conflict as the prime impetus for modernisation of the army. With the increasingly prominent role of informatisation in modern warfare, in 2004, the CMC expanded and perfected a military strategy for the new age and proposed that the underlying aim of their preparations should be to win local wars under informatisation conditions. To meet the requirements of China's special military reform, the central government adjusted and reformed the structure of the military. From 2003 to 2005, the PLA reduced its personnel by 200,000 and focused on streamlining its forces. At the same time, it strengthened the strategic management functions of the Military Commission Headquarters, promoted the construction of new combat capabilities and pursued the development of expert, unified, versatile and efficient combat forces. The army also continuously accelerated the pace of implementation of modern logistics and, building on the foundation of the unification of the three services, fail-safe systems, methods, tactics and management models were built that met the requirements of warfare under the new conditions of informatisation.

Focusing on building an informatised army and winning informatised wars, the process of transforming models to generate combat effectiveness was accelerated. The army actively promoted the transition from military training under mechanised conditions to military training under informatised conditions, and successfully organised a series of major joint campaigns and tactical training exercises. Efforts were made to improve independent innovation capabilities for national defence technology, weapons and equipment, in order to rapidly develop up-to-date weapons and equipment supported by military information systems. This effectively saw the construction of a weapon and equipment system with second-generation components forming the main body but with third-generation components as the backbone, thereby laying a solid material foundation for the transformation of combat effectiveness. In September 2012, our country's first aircraft carrier, the *Liaoning* was officially delivered to the navy.

The armed forces and the armed police also successfully completed a series of urgent, difficult, dangerous and burdensome operations. They actively participated in the rescue and relief operations against SARS, the freezing rain and snow emergencies in the south, the Wenchuan and Yushu earthquakes, and the Zhouqu floods and mudslide emergencies. They participated in the evacuation of overseas Chinese from Libya, justifying the name 'soldiers of the people' with their effective actions. The Chinese military also actively participated in joint military exercises with many countries, UN peacekeeping operations and escort duties to the Gulf of Aden and the waters of Somalia, thereby fully demonstrating its excellent military capabilities and presenting an admirable image of our nation as a force in military matters, a force for civilisation and a force for peace.

6
PROMOTING THE PRACTICE OF 'ONE COUNTRY, TWO SYSTEMS' AND THE GREAT CAUSE OF THE PEACEFUL REUNIFICATION OF THE MOTHERLAND

PROMOTING THE PRACTICE OF 'ONE COUNTRY, TWO SYSTEMS'

In the new century, the central government continued unswervingly to implement the principles of 'One Country, Two Systems', 'Hong Kong people ruling Hong Kong' and 'Macau people ruling Macau', allowing a high degree of autonomy, strictly in accordance with the Constitution and the Basic Law of the SAR, and fully supporting the economic and social development of Hong Kong and Macau.

After the handover, the democratic political system of the Hong Kong SAR was enacted in accordance with the law. The Standing Committee of the NPC exercised the powers conferred by the Constitution and the Basic Law of the Hong Kong SAR, and successively interpreted the relevant provisions of the Hong Kong Basic Law and its annexes in 1999, 2004, 2005 and 2011. According to the Basic Law and relevant interpretations of the Standing Committee of the NPC, in December 2007, the 31st meeting of the Standing Committee of the 10th NPC decided that in 2012 appropriate modifications could be made to the post of the fourth chief executive of the Hong Kong SAR and the specific method for forming the Fifth Legislative Council; that the election of the fifth chief executive of the Hong Kong SAR in 2017 should be conducted by universal suffrage; and that after the chief executive was selected, the election of the Legislative Council of the Hong Kong SAR should also be implemented by universal suffrage.

The democratic political system of the Macau SAR also progressed in accordance with the provisions of the Basic Law. In December 2011, the 24th meeting of the Standing Committee of the 11th NPC explained *Article 7 of Annex 1* and *Article 3 of Annex 2 of the Macau Basic Law*, clarifying the procedures for amending the method for the formation of the chief executive of the Macau SAR and the Legislative Council. At the start of the new century, the central government promptly adopted a series of policy measures such as opening up travel to Hong Kong and Macau for some mainland urban residents; expanding Hong Kong's Rmb currency business; and promoting mainland companies' listing in Hong Kong to help Hong Kong and Macau emerge from the Asian financial crisis, get rid of the impact of SARS, and restore economic growth by the administration of a 'cardiac stimulant'. In 2003, the Mainland, Hong Kong and Macau signed the *Closer Economic Partnership Arrangement (CEPA)* and its respective supplementary agreements to eliminate institutional barriers in trade and investment between Hong Kong, Macau and the Mainland, and to continue to promote the relationship between the Mainland, Hong Kong and Macau. The liberalisation of trade in goods and services, and the facilitation of investment in China resulted in a mutually beneficial, win-win situation for all parties. After the outbreak of the international financial crisis, the central government issued a series of policies and measures to provide Hong Kong with strong support for responding to the crisis. The central government also increased its support for Macau's economic development and appropriate diversification; supported Macau's construction of a world tourism and leisure centre; approved the construction of a new campus for the University of Macau on Hengqin Island in Zhuhai; and supported the development of economic and trade relations between the Macau SAR and Portuguese-speaking countries.

With the strong support of the central government, cooperation between the Mainland and Hong Kong and Macau was continuously strengthened, and cooperation mechanisms were established in nine provinces, regions and associated areas including Guangdong and Hong Kong, Guangdong and Macau, Beijing and Hong Kong, Shanghai and Hong Kong, and the Pan-Pearl River Delta, in order to continuously expand the development space for Hong Kong and Macau. The central government also actively promoted the cooperative development of Shenzhen Qianhai, Zhuhai Hengqin, and Guangzhou Nansha as the focuses of Guangdong, Hong Kong and Macau cooperation. The economies of Hong Kong and Macau achieved relatively rapid expansion. In 2011, Hong Kong's GDP increased by 54% compared with 1996 before the return to the motherland; Macau's GDP more than quadrupled from the year 2000, with an average annual growth rate of 12.5%. Hong Kong and Macau maintained social stability and their economies became more prosperous, demonstrating the strength and vitality of the 'One Country, Two Systems' policy.

In July 2012, at the 15th anniversary celebration of Hong Kong's return to the motherland, Hu Jintao emphasised that 'One Country, Two Systems' was the best institutional arrangement for Hong Kong to maintain long-term prosperity and stability after its return. It was essential to adhere to a comprehensive understanding and implementation of the 'One Country, Two Systems' policy; strictly to follow the Basic Law; adhere to the 'One Country' principle and respect the differences between the 'Two Systems'; safeguard central authority and guarantee the high degree of autonomy of the SAR; safeguard the overall interests of the country and protect Hong Kong society. The interests of all walks of life, support for Hong Kong's active development of foreign exchanges and opposition to external forces' interference in Hong Kong affairs are all organically interconnected and none of them should be neglected at any time.

PROMOTING THE PEACEFUL DEVELOPMENT OF CROSS-STRAIT RELATIONS

In resolutely maintaining the stability and prosperity of Hong Kong and Macau, the Party Central Committee unswervingly promoted the great cause of the peaceful reunification of the motherland in accordance with the principle of 'peaceful reunification and One Country, Two Systems'.

In the new century, the separatist activities of an 'independent Taiwan' intensified. The Chen Shuibian authorities in Taiwan attempted to use 'constitutional reform' to separate Taiwan from China through their so-called 'constitution' and 'laws', and this had a serious impact on the peaceful and stable development of cross-strait relations. The Party Central Committee's interactions with Taiwan were characterised by giving more prominence to opposing and containing the notion of an 'independent Taiwan'. On 4 March 2005, Hu Jintao raised four points regarding the development of cross-strait relations, emphasising that our country will never waver in adhering to the one-China principle, never give up efforts for peaceful reunification, never change the implementation of the policy of putting our hope in the people of Taiwan, and always oppose 'Taiwan independence'. These four 'never' propositions have produced significant repercussions on both sides of the strait and on the international community. On 14 March, the Third Session of the 10th NPC passed the 'Anti-Secession Law' with a substantial majority, emphasising the fact that should the 'Taiwan independence' separatist forces cause Taiwan to separate from China under any pretext or by any means, or should any unforeseen event occur that caused Taiwan to separate from China, or should there be a complete breakdown of the possibility of peaceful reunification, the country might adopt non-peaceful methods and other necessary measures to defend its sovereignty and territorial integrity. This amply demonstrated the shared will and firm determination of the entire Chinese people to oppose an 'independent Taiwan' and safeguard national unity and territorial integrity. The Taiwan policy thereby entered a new stage of 'using law to contain independence and using law to promote reunification'.

At the same time, the Central Committee of the CPC actively promoted cross-strait party exchanges. On 29 April 2005, General Secretary of the CPC Central Committee Hu Jintao met with Lien Chan, Chairman of the Chinese KMT, in Beijing and exchanged the first handshake in 60 years between the leader of the CPC and the leader of the KMT. As a result of the meeting, the *Common Vision for Cross-Strait Peaceful Development* was published, and the KMT and the CPC came together over a series of issues. In April 2006, the CPC and the Chinese KMT jointly hosted the first Cross-Strait Economic and Trade Forum, and in October, they jointly hosted the Cross-Strait Agricultural Cooperation Forum. Through the platform of these forums, the mainland has introduced a number of policy measures to promote cross-strait exchanges and cooperation to the benefit of our compatriots in Taiwan, thereby promoting the development of cross-strait relations.

In March 2008, the DPP (Democratic Progressive Party), which stubbornly adhered to the 'independent Taiwan' stance, stepped down and the KMT came back to power, making positive changes to the situation in Taiwan. On 31 December, at a symposium to commemorate the 30th anniversary of the publication of the *Letter to Compatriots in Taiwan*, Hu Jintao comprehensively and systematically explained his important thoughts on the peaceful development of cross-strait relations and put forward six proposals to promote the peaceful development of cross-strait relations. He pointed out that promoting the peaceful development of cross-strait relations was the only way to achieve peaceful reunification and was an important signpost for the further promotion of the development of cross-strait relations.

Both sides of the Taiwan Strait were committed to the improvement and development of cross-strait relations in the spirit of 'building mutual trust, setting aside disputes, seeking common ground while reserving differences, and creating a win-win situation'. In June 2008, the Association for Relationships Across the Taiwan Strait and the Taiwan Strait Foundation resumed formal consultations on the basis of the *1992 Consensus*[1]. In

December, cross-strait direct sea, air and postal services were officially launched, and the cross-strait comprehensive direct reciprocal 'three links'[2] took a historic step forward. In June 2010, the signing of the *Framework Agreement on Cross-Strait Economic Cooperation* promoted the formalisation and institutionalisation of cross-strait economic cooperation. With the gradual normalisation of cross-strait economic and trade relations, cross-strait exchanges in academic, cultural, educational, news, sports and religious fields continued to deepen.

The Strait Forum was held every year from 2009 and in June 2011, personal visits of mainland residents to Taiwan were officially launched. The Chinese Government was also assiduous in handling Taiwan-related diplomatic issues such as Taiwan's participation in the World Health Assembly and the APEC Leaders' Informal Meeting. It effectively safeguarded the legitimate rights and interests of our Taiwan compatriots and attended to their well-being in assisting them in handling foreign-related disputes. This series of measures was not only welcomed and praised by the people on the island of Taiwan, but also consolidated the one-China approach of the international community by adding positive factors to the peaceful development of cross-strait relations.

---

1. The *1992 Consensus* refers to a consensus reached by the PRC and Taiwan after talks held in Hong Kong in October 1992 that 'both sides of the strait adhere to the one-China principle'.
2. The 'three links' refers to three links across the Taiwan Strait, comprising two-way cross-strait direct postal, trade and shipping links.

7
PERSISTING WITH PEACEFUL DEVELOPMENT AND COOPERATION

In the new century, the Party Central Committee conformed to the world trend of seeking peace, development and cooperation, and committed itself unswervingly to follow the path of peaceful development. On 22 April 2005, Hu Jintao proposed the promotion of the construction of a 'harmonious world' at the Asia-Africa Summit in Jakarta. In October 2007, the report of the 17th National Congress of the CPC reiterated that 'people from all countries should work together to promote the building of a harmonious world of lasting peace and common prosperity'. For the first time, the diplomatic goal of building a harmonious world was reflected and confirmed in the documents of the Party Congress. In order to promote the building of a harmonious world, China suggested the fundamental pattern for diplomatic relations should be that 'the major powers are the crux; neighbours are at the forefront; developing nations are the foundation, and multilateralism is centre stage', and that all parties should actively pursue fruitful diplomatic activities.

Overall, relations between the major powers generally saw both stability and development. In January 2011, Hu Jintao was invited to pay a state visit to the US. The two heads of state issued a Sino-US joint statement, reaching an important consensus on building a mutually respectful, mutually beneficial and win-win cooperative partnership. In 2008, China and Russia resolved the historical border issue on the eastern sector of the Sino-Russian border, and the strategic, cooperative partnership continued to deepen. China and the EU established a comprehensive strategic partnership in 2003. After that, economic and trade cooperation between the two sides developed rapidly, and the EU maintained its position as our country's largest trading partner for eight consecutive years. Sino-Japanese relations continued to develop amidst twists and turns. In May 2008, Hu Jintao visited Japan and the leaders of the two countries jointly published the *China-Japan Joint Statement on Comprehensively Promoting Strategic Mutually Beneficial Relations*.

In September 2012, in response to the Japanese government's so-called 'nationalisation' of the Diaoyu Islands, the Chinese government issued the *Statement of the Government of the PRC on the Baseline of the Territorial Seas of the Diaoyu Islands and Their Affiliated Islands* and the white paper on *The Diaoyu Islands Are Inherently Chinese Territory* and passed measures such as regularising legal enforcement patrols, implementing management of the Diaoyu Islands and their adjacent waters, and resolutely defending national sovereignty.

China carried out high-level visits and exchanges with neighbouring countries and promoted the process of regional cooperation. Led by China, in 2007, the member states of the Shanghai Cooperation Organisation signed a long-term good-neighbour friendship and cooperation treaty. China and ASEAN signed the *Declaration on the Conduct of Parties in the South China Sea* in November 2002, laying a political foundation for relevant countries to carry out pragmatic cooperation and joint development in the South China Sea. In January 2010, the 'China-ASEAN Free Trade Area' was officially launched, benefiting nearly one third of the world's population.

On 15 September 2005, Hu Jintao delivered a speech entitled Efforts To Build a Harmonious World of Lasting Peace and Common Prosperity *at the summit meeting on the 60th anniversary of the founding of the UN*

Significant progress was made in the solidarity and cooperation between China and developing nations, and China successively issued policy documents on Africa, Latin America and the Caribbean. In November 2006, the Beijing Summit of the Forum on China-Africa Cooperation was held. The declaration of the summit formally announced the establishment of a new type of China-Africa strategic partnership. China continued to provide assistance to developing countries according to its capacity, and its solidarity and cooperation with developing nations was continuously strengthened.

From its place in the multilateral arena, China promoted the resolution of international and regional hotspots. After the outbreak of the international financial crisis, China promoted the reform of the world economic governance mechanism by attending the G20 Leaders' Summit, the APEC Leaders' Informal Meeting, and hosting the Annual Bo'ao Forum for Asia Meeting. We promoted the establishment of the BRICS (Brazil, Russia, India, China and South Africa) leaders' meeting mechanism. Beginning in 2009, BRICS leaders held regular meetings to enhance the representation and voice of emerging market nations and developing countries in global governance. China also actively participated in international cooperation on global issues such as security and counterterrorism, and amply demonstrated its role as a responsible world power.

During this period, the Chinese government followed the principle of 'diplomacy for the people' and prudently handled major emergencies such as the evacuation of overseas Chinese, hostage rescues and labour disputes, especially during February and March 2011, when tensions rose in Libya. There, China quickly organised, in orderly fashion, the largest evacuation of overseas Chinese citizens (including compatriots from Hong Kong, Macau and Taiwan) since the founding of the PRC. We safely evacuated all 35,860 Chinese citizens in Libya back to China, effectively safeguarding the personal safety and legal rights of Chinese citizens overseas.

8
IMPROVING THE SCIENTIFIC LEVEL OF PARTY BUILDING AND ESTABLISHING THE SCIENTIFIC OUTLOOK ON DEVELOPMENT AS THE PARTY'S GUIDING IDEOLOGY

STRENGTHENING THE BUILDING OF THE PARTY'S GOVERNING CAPACITY AND ITS ADVANCED NATURE

Building an all-round moderately prosperous society in the new century and on a new stage highlighted new and higher requirements for the party's ability to govern. The Party Central Committee adhered to the central tenet of building governance capacity of an advanced nature, closely integrating the practice of governance and administration, and it continued comprehensively to promote the great new project of party building.

The 16th National Congress of the CPC advanced the proposition of 'strengthening the party's governing ability'. In September 2004, the Fourth Plenary Session of the 16th Central Committee of the CPC passed the *Decision of the Central Committee of the CPC on Strengthening the Construction of the Party's Governing Capability*. This served to advance the exposition of the goals of rule by science, rule by the people and rule according to the law and all their ramifications. It also explicitly raised the necessity of continuously improving our capacity to control the socialist marketplace, our ability to develop socialist democratic government and to construct a harmonious, socialist society, and our ability to respond to international situations and to handle foreign affairs. At the plenary meeting, Hu Jintao emphasised that it was necessary to carry out comprehensive, systematic and in-depth research on the major issues of who power is held for, who holds it and how they wield it; it was also necessary to conduct in-depth research into the whole government system and to strive to perfect the party's ruling strategy, to make its system more complete, its methods more scientific and to consolidate its foundations.

In order to implement the requirements of the 16th National Congress of the CPC and the Fourth Plenary Session of the 16th Central Committee, the party led the national legislature in scientific and democratic legislation, revision of the constitution and the *People's Congress Election and Organisation Laws*, and promulgation of the *Supervision Law of the Standing Committee of the People's Congress* at all levels. The fundamental political system was improved and the party's ruling system became more complete, thereby providing a standardised legal framework for strengthening the party's ability to govern. The Party Central Committee also made arrangements to deepen the reform of the administrative management systems and institutions; strengthen the deployment of the work of the CPPCC, the People's Court, and the People's Procuratorate; organically unify the party's leadership and the people's control of the country under the rule of law. This expanded democracy, the scientific rule of the party and rule by the people, as well as continuously improving the capabilities of the rule of law.

In November 2004, the Party Central Committee issued a document to make arrangements for the entire party to carry out education activities centred on the practice of the important thinking of the 'Three Represents' that would maintain the progressive nature of party members. In January 2005, Hu Jintao put forward the important proposition of 'building the progressive nature of the party in the new era' at the special report meeting on that subject, emphasising that this was a fundamental task in building the Marxist party itself. The progressive education activities were carried out in three batches from January 2005, and essentially ended in June 2006. These activities focused on solving outstanding problems of party members and party organisations in terms of ideology, organisation, method and tasks, and achieved fruitful results.

After the 16th National Congress of the CPC, which concentrated on the central tenet of strengthening the party's ability to govern and building its progressive nature, the Party Central Committee also proposed and implemented a series of important measures to strengthen party building. These were: the call for senior cadres to take the lead in implementing education; establishing a collective study system for the Politburo of the Central Committee; establishing a system for the central and local party committee standing committees at all levels to be responsible to the whole committee, report work and accept supervision including responsibility for the party's congressional representative proposal system, proposal processing and response mechanism; reforming the cadre personnel system, implementing open selection and competition for posts; increasing the intensity of party building work through new economic and social organisations, and expanding the coverage of grassroots party organisations. The Party Central Committee also decided to establish the China Pudong Cadre College, the China Jinggangshan Cadre College and the China Yan'an Cadre College; also, to organise large-scale multi-level training, and strive to improve the ability and quality of party members and cadres.

IMPROVING THE LEVEL OF SCIENCE IN PARTY BUILDING

While writing the Scientific Outlook on Development into the Party Constitution, the 17th National Congress of the CPC made arrangements for activities involving the in-depth study and practice of the Scientific Outlook on Development throughout the party. From September 2008 to the end of February 2010, the whole party carried out in-depth study and practice of the Scientific Outlook on Development. These activities focused closely on the general requirements for party members and cadres to raise their level of education and scientific development, and for the people to see the benefits. This essentially achieved the goals of improving ideological understanding, solving outstanding problems, innovating systems and mechanisms, promoting scientific development, and strengthening grassroots organisations.

In these activities, the Party Central Committee deployed new decision-making processes on how to strengthen and improve party building to meet changes in the global, national and party situations. In September 2009, the Fourth Plenary Session of the 17th Central Committee of the CPC adopted the *Decision of the Central Committee of the CPC on Several Major Issues Concerning Strengthening and Improving Party Building Under the New Situation*, which proposed the major task of improving the scientific level of party building. After that, the Party Central Committee repeatedly emphasised its insistence on arming the whole party with a theoretical system of socialism with Chinese characteristics and guiding party building with scientific theories; establishing and improving an institutional system with the party constitution and democratic centralism at its core, and bolstering the structure of the party with scientific systems; finding creative solutions to new problems in party building raised by contemporary developments and social changes, and using scientific methods to advance the process.

Focusing on improving the scientific level of party building, the Party

Central Committee focused on promoting the construction of the party system, revised and promulgated the work regulations of the party and state organs at grassroots level, implemented the interim regulations on the accountability of party and government leading cadres and other measures, thereby effectively solving the problems raised by the whole process. In May 2012, the Central Committee of the CPC issued the *Regulations on the Formulation of Internal Party Laws and Regulations of the CPC* to promote strict scientific, democratic governance, and governance by law, by strictly regulating the formulation, approval, filing and rectification of internal party regulations.

In order to consolidate and expand the results of the party's in-depth study and practice of the Scientific Outlook on Development, the Party Central Committee decided in April 2010 to carry out the process of 'creating advanced grassroots party organisations and striving to be outstanding party members' among the party's grassroots organisations and party members. This was considered an important part of the regular work of party building. All regions, departments and units made their own contribution in promoting scientific development and social harmony, in serving the people, and strengthening grassroots organisations to fully realise the role of the grassroots organisations as battleground fortifications with party members in the vanguard. Yang Shanzhou, former secretary of Baoshan Prefecture Committee of Yunnan Province, fulfilled his vow that, "As long as I am alive, my service to the people will not stop". After his retirement from office, he rolled up his bedding and headed into the mountain regions. He volunteered for a further 22 years and led the local people in turning 56,000 *mu* of barren mountain land into a fertile oasis. Guo Mingyi, an employee of Ansteel Group emulated Lei Feng every day for decades and was known as 'Lei Feng's Heir' for the new era. In their pioneering activities and striving for excellence, Yang Shanzhou and Guo Mingyi aroused an enthusiastic response from party members, cadres and ordinary people alike, and there was an upsurge of emulation of these two men all across the country.

ESTABLISHING A ROBUST SYSTEM FOR THE PREVENTION AND PUNISHMENT OF CORRUPTION

Enhancing the ability to resist corruption, prevent degeneration and guard against the concomitant risks was a historical issue that the ruling party faced for a long time. The Party Central Committee always maintained a clear understanding of the long-term, complex and arduous nature of the building of a party ethos, cleaning up government and fighting corruption.

To do so, they focused on maintaining the party's progressive nature and purity, and prioritised the building of a party ethos, maintaining clean government and fighting corruption. In October 2003, the Third Plenary Session of the 16th Central Committee of the CPC proposed the goal of establishing and improving a system of punishment and prevention of corruption that was compatible with the socialist marketplace economic system and emphasised education, process and supervision.

In the fight against corruption, a pattern was gradually established for leading cadres to be honest and self-disciplined, to investigate cases of violations of discipline and law, and to correct unhealthy practices in their relevant departments and industries. With regard to the leadership system and mechanisms for fighting corruption and upholding integrity, a functioning system of unified leadership of the party committee, joint management of the party and government, organisation and coordination of the Discipline Inspection Commission and other responsible departments was formed, which relied on the support and participation of the masses. In terms of the operation of the levers of power, structures and mechanisms were established and revised to ensure that powers of decision-making, execution and supervision restrained, and were coordinated, with each other.

In respect of the construction of the systems to fight corruption and uphold integrity, the government drew up *Criteria for Honest and Clean Governance by CPC Leaders, Regulations on Disciplinary Measures of the CPC, Regulations on Reporting Personal Matters by Leading Cadres,* and *Interim Regulations Strengthening the Management of the Movement of State Workers and Their Spouses and Children Living and Working Outside China*. In February 2006, our country became a signatory of the UN Convention Against Corruption and international cooperation in fighting corruption was strengthened.

In terms of investigating major and important cases in accordance with the law, while continuing to investigate and punish all key cases, our country focused on investigating and handling cases of collusion between officials and businesses, trading of power and money, and the soliciting and accepting of bribes by leading cadres, any cases that acted as 'shields' for criminal organisations, cases that seriously infringed the interests of the people and corruption cases behind serious incidents involving the populace and accidents with major liability implications. From November 2007 to June 2012, disciplinary inspection and supervision agencies across the country filed more than 643,700 cases, closed more than 639,000 cases, and imposed more than 668,000 party disciplinary and political sanctions. More than 24,000 people were handed over to the judicial authorities for suspected crimes. In particular, after the 16th National Congress of the CPC, a number of major violations of discipline and law, including the case of Chen Liangyu, were resolutely investigated and dealt with, demonstrating the strong determination of the Party Central Committee to fight corruption.

In terms of correcting unhealthy practices that harm the interests of the people, the Party Central Committee carried out special operations to prevent public funds from going abroad (crossing the border) through travel and tourism, gave special attention to problems with official vehicles, did the same for problems in the field of engineering and construction, and investigated and dealt with a large number of violations of discipline and law. While carrying out in-depth special measures, our government also stepped up efforts to rectify ethics by correcting anomalies in the fields of education, medical care, land acquisition and demolition, land and mineral resource management, food and drug safety, environmental protection, safety in manufacturing, construction and management of affordable housing, law enforcement and the judicial system. They addressed all behaviour that harmed the interests of the people, and earnestly safeguarded the joint rights and interests of the people thereby achieving very significant social benefits.

Through unremitting exploration and effort, the scientific level of party building was continuously improved, which played an important role in maintaining the party's purity and progressiveness, and provided the party's leadership with a strong guarantee of reform, opening up and socialist modernisation. However, it was also important to recognise that the soil for breeding corruption still existed, and the fight against corruption was still serious and complex. In some localities and departments, the phenomenon of corruption became more serious, with regional corruption, systemic corruption, co-ordinated family corruption and cumulative corruption all seriously damaging the physical health of the party. Unswervingly to bolster the party's leadership, unremittingly to strengthen party building and resolutely to curb the spread of corruption still required arduous efforts from the entire party.

ESTABLISHING THE SCIENTIFIC OUTLOOK ON DEVELOPMENT AS THE PARTY'S GUIDING IDEOLOGY

After the Scientific Outlook on Development was first proposed, it went through a process of practice, interpretation, re-practice and re-interpretation. The theoretical connotations were continuously enriched and practical results continued to emerge. The Scientific Outlook on Development provided new scientific answers to major issues such as what kind of development to achieve under the new situation and how to achieve it. Overall, it raised the party's understanding of the laws of socialism with Chinese characteristics to a new level.

In 2012, the 18th National Congress of the CPC officially established the Scientific Outlook on Development as the party's guiding ideology. The conference highlighted that, in summarising the course of 10 years of struggle, the most important things were to adhere to the guidance of Marxism-Leninism, Mao Zedong Thought, Deng Xiaoping Theory and the important thinking of the 'Three Represents'; to bravely promote theoretical innovation based on practice; and to focus on persisting with and developing socialism with Chinese characteristics. All these elements advanced a series of closely inter-connected new ideas, viewpoints and theories which served to form and implement the Scientific Outlook on Development. The Scientific Outlook on Development is the product of combining Marxism with contemporary Chinese reality and the particular characteristics of the times. It is a concentrated expression of the Marxist world view and methodology for development and has opened up a whole new realm for the development of contemporary Chinese Marxism. The Scientific Outlook on Development is an important part of the theoretical system of socialism with Chinese characteristics, the crystallisation of the collective wisdom of the CPC and a powerful ideological weapon that guides all the work of the party and the country. The Scientific Outlook on Development, together with Marxism-Leninism, Mao Zedong Thought, Deng Xiaoping Theory and the important thinking of the 'Three Represents', is the guiding ideology that the party must uphold for a long time to come.

Establishing the Scientific Outlook on Development as the party's guiding ideology was an important decision and a historic contribution made by the party's 18th National Congress. The conference pointed out that, in facing the future, the in-depth implementation of the Scientific Outlook on Development was of great practical and far-reaching historical significance for the adherence to and development of socialism with Chinese characteristics. The Scientific Outlook on Development had to be implemented as part of the overall process of our country's modernisation drive and should be reflected in all aspects of party building.

Ten

Socialism with Chinese Characteristics Enters a New Era

In November 2012, the 18th National Congress of the CPC enacted the replacement of the old central leadership with the new. At the First Plenary Session of the 18th CPC Central Committee, the newly elected General Secretary of the Central Committee, Xi Jinping, acknowledged, "The baton of history has been passed to us. We must certainly live up to this trust, be loyal to the party, loyal to the nation, loyal to the people and use our own wisdom, strength and dedication so that we can face history, face the modern era and face the people, taking pride in our achievements." Since then, concentrating on the overall task of realising socialist modernisation and the great rejuvenation of the Chinese nation, a series of theoretical and practical innovations have unfolded one after another, and the curtain of a new era of socialism with Chinese characteristics has been gradually raised.

1
THE 18TH NATIONAL CONGRESS OF THE CPC AND THE CHINESE DREAM OF REALISING THE GREAT REJUVENATION OF THE CHINESE NATION

THE 18TH NATIONAL CONGRESS OF THE CPC

From 8 to 14 November 2012, the 18th National Congress of the CPC was held in Beijing. On behalf of the 17th Central Committee, Hu Jintao presented a report entitled *Unswervingly Marching on the Road of Socialism with Chinese Characteristics and Striving to Build an All-Round Moderately Prosperous Society*.

The 18th National Congress of the CPC was a highly important meeting held as our country entered the decisive stage of building an all-round moderately prosperous society. The themes of the conference were: holding high the great banner of socialism with Chinese characteristics guided by Deng Xiaoping Theory, the important thinking of the 'Three Represents', and the Scientific Outlook on Development; emancipating the mind; reforming and opening up; gathering strength; overcoming difficulties; unswervingly following the path forward on the road to socialism with Chinese characteristics; and striving to build an all-round moderately prosperous society.

The main theme throughout the conference was to uphold and develop socialism with Chinese characteristics. The conference emphasised that the path of socialism with Chinese characteristics, the theoretical system of socialism with Chinese characteristics, and the practical system of socialism with Chinese characteristics are the fundamental achievements of the party and the people over 90 years of struggle, creation and consolidation. They must be cherished, persisted with and continuously developed. The overall foundation for building socialism with Chinese characteristics is the fundamental stage of socialism, and the overall layout for it comprises the 'five in one' of socialist economic construction, political construction, cultural construction, social construction and ecological civilisation construction. The overall task is to enact socialist modernisation and the great rejuvenation of the Chinese nation. The conference proposed to build an all-round moderately prosperous society within a hundred years of the founding of the CPC, and to build a wealthy, democratic, civilised, harmonious and modern socialist country within a hundred years of the founding of the PRC.

On 15 November 2012, Chinese President Hu Jintao cordially shakes hands with the newly elected General Secretary of the Central Committee and Chairman of the CMC, Xi Jinping

Based on the actual situation of our country's economic and social development, the conference determined the goals of building an all-round moderately prosperous society, namely: sustained and healthy economic development; continuous expansion of people's democracy; significant enhancement of cultural soft power; overall improvement of people's living standards; and significant progress in the construction of a resource-saving and environmentally friendly society. The conference emphasised that, in order to build an all-round moderately prosperous society, it is necessary to use greater political courage and wisdom; not to miss the opportunity to deepen reforms in important areas; to resolutely eliminate all ideological concepts and institutional defects that hinder scientific development; to build a systematic, scientifically standardised and effective system; and to make all aspects of the system more mature and more consistent.

In accordance with the overall plan of the 'five in one' ideology and the goal of building an all-round moderately prosperous society, the conference made comprehensive arrangements for promoting the construction of socialism with Chinese characteristics and emphasised the need to accelerate the improvement of the socialist market economy system and the transformation of economic development methods; to adhere to the path of socialism with Chinese characteristics; to carry out political development and advance reform of the political system; to steadfastly promote the building of socialist cultural power; to strengthen social construction in the improvement of the people's lives through innovative management; to vigorously promote the construction of an ecological culture; to accelerate the modernisation of national defence and the military; to enrich the practice of 'One Country, Two Systems' and promote the reunification of the motherland; and to continue to promote the noble cause of world peace and human development.

The conference emphasised the need to comprehensively promote the great new project of party building through the spirit of reform and innovation, and to comprehensively improve the scientific level of party building. It was necessary to firmly grasp the central themes of strengthening the party's ability to govern while emphasising the progressiveness and purity of the process; to persist in liberating thought, revolutionising innovation, and in insisting that the party must manage the party. It was also necessary to strictly regulate the party; to comprehensively strengthen the party's ideological, organisational and work processes, and its anti-corruption processes and systems; to strengthen self-purification, self-improvement, self-led innovation and self-led enhancement of abilities in order to build an educated, service-oriented and innovative Marxist ruling party with a strong leadership core capable of ensuring that the party will always be a strong player in the cause of socialism with Chinese characteristics.

The conference elected the 18th Central Committee and the Central Commission for Discipline Inspection. The First Plenary Session of the 18th CPC Central Committee elected Xi Jinping, Li Keqiang, Zhang Dejiang, Yu Zhengsheng, Liu Yunshan, Wang Qishan and Zhang Gaoli as members of the Politburo Standing Committee, and Xi Jinping as General Secretary of the Central Committee; confirmed Xi Jinping as Chairman of the CMC;

and approved Wang Qishan as the Central Committee Secretary of the Disciplinary Inspection Committee.

On 15 November 2012, at a meeting with Chinese and foreign reporters, Xi Jinping solemnly promised on behalf of the new central leadership group that, "The people's yearning for a better life is our goal." "We must always keep in touch with the people, share joy and sorrow with the people, fight in unity with the people, stay on duty night and day, work diligently and strive to give history and the people satisfactory answers. It takes a good blacksmith to make steel. Our responsibility is to work with all party comrades to uphold the principle that the party should supervise its own conduct and run itself with strict discipline, effectively solve major problems in the party, improve our conduct and maintain close ties with the people. By doing so, we will ensure that our party remains the core of leadership in advancing the cause of socialism with Chinese characteristics."

Xi Jinping was elected as General Secretary of the 18th Central Committee

AMENDMENTS TO THE CPC CONSTITUTION

The 18th National Congress of the CPC deliberated and unanimously passed the *Constitution of the CPC (Amendment)* proposed by the 17th Central Committee.

The main content of the revision of the party constitution was: positioning and elaborating on the Scientific Outlook on Development, and establishing the Scientific Outlook on Development together with Marxism-Leninism, Mao Zedong Thought, Deng Xiaoping Theory, and the important thinking of the 'Three Represents' as our party's guiding ideology; acknowledging that the principal achievements of socialism with Chinese characteristics, namely the establishment of the socialist system with Chinese characteristics, following the road to socialism with Chinese characteristics and the formation of a theoretical system of socialism with Chinese characteristics, are the fundamental reasons for all our achievements and progress since the reform and opening up; they have enriched the results of persisting in reform and opening up, and emphasised that only reform and opening up can develop China, develop socialism and develop Marxism. In addition, the revision improved the content of the overall plan for the cause of socialism with Chinese characteristics, incorporated the construction of ecological culture, enriched the content of economic construction, political construction, cultural construction and social construction, and added paragraphs about the construction of ecological culture. The content of the overall requirements for strengthening party building was enriched, and some new requirements were put forward with regard to party members, grassroots-level party organisations and party cadres.

The 18th National Congress of the CPC revised the party constitution to make the content more scientific and complete so that it could more effectively play the fundamental normative and guiding role of advancing the party's cause and strengthening the party's structure.

ADVANCING THE CHINESE DREAM OF REALISING THE GREAT REJUVENATION OF THE CHINESE NATION

Under the new historical conditions, continuing to write the great essay on upholding and developing socialism with Chinese characteristics requires concentration, spiritual support and guidance. On 29 November 2012, Xi Jinping first proposed and expounded the Chinese dream of realising the great rejuvenation of the Chinese nation when he visited the exhibition *Road to Rejuvenation*. He declared, "Realising the great rejuvenation of the Chinese nation is our greatest dream in modern times. This dream embodies the long-cherished wishes of many generations of Chinese people, reflects the overall interests of the Chinese nation and the Chinese people, and is the common expectation of every Chinese son and daughter." The proposal of the Chinese dream permeates the past, the present and the future of the Chinese nation, and conveys the firm determination and confidence of the new central leadership group in shouldering the task of national rejuvenation.

Later, Xi Jinping further elaborated and enriched the fundamental implications, practical methods and dependable strengths of the Chinese dream on important occasions such as the First Session of the 12th NPC. Xi Jinping observed that the core content of the Chinese dream is the great rejuvenation of the Chinese nation, and its essence is the prosperity of the country, the rejuvenation of the nation and the happiness of the people. To realise the Chinese dream, it is necessary to follow the Chinese road, which is the road of socialism with Chinese characteristics; to promote the Chinese spirit, which is the national spirit with patriotism at its core, and the spirit of the times with reform and innovation at its core. This is where the strength of the great unity of all the peoples of China lies. The Chinese dream is the dream of the country, the nation and the dream of every Chinese son and daughter. In the final analysis, the Chinese dream is the people's dream. It must be realised by the people and must continue to benefit the people. The Chinese dream is a dream of peace, development, cooperation and mutual benefit. It not only benefits the Chinese people but also the people of the whole world.

On 29 November 2012, the 18th Politburo Standing Committee came to the National Museum of China to visit the exhibition Road to Rejuvenation

The Chinese dream integrates the needs of the country, the yearning of the nation and the expectations of the people. It embodies the overall interests of the Chinese nation and the Chinese people, expresses the common vision of every Chinese son and daughter, and becomes a lofty melody that stirs the hearts of the Chinese people. It has become the greatest common denominator and the largest concentric circle for the unity and struggle of the Chinese nation, and a spiritual banner that inspires the Chinese people to unite, forge ahead and open up the future.

UPHOLDING AND DEVELOPING THE STRATEGIC PLAN OF SOCIALISM WITH CHINESE CHARACTERISTICS

Socialism with Chinese characteristics has been the theme of all the party's theory and practice since the reform and opening up. After the 18th National Congress of the CPC, the Party Central Committee with Comrade Xi Jinping at the core has united and led the entire party and the people to continue to uphold and develop socialism with Chinese characteristics with great political courage and unrelenting enterprising spirit. On 5 January 2013, at the opening ceremony of the seminar for new and alternate members of the Central Committee to study and implement the spirit of the 18th National Congress of the CPC, Xi Jinping emphasised that we must unswervingly adhere to and develop socialism with Chinese characteristics. Xi Jinping declared that socialism with Chinese characteristics is the dialectical unity of the theoretical logic of scientific socialism and the historical logic of Chinese social development. It is scientific socialism rooted in the land of China, reflecting the wishes of the Chinese people, and adapting to the development and progress requirements of China in line with the times. It is a comprehensive construct. A prosperous society is the only way to accelerate socialist modernisation and realise the great rejuvenation of the Chinese nation. Socialism with Chinese characteristics is socialism and does not involve any other doctrines. The basic principles of scientific socialism must not be lost. If they are, it will no longer be socialism. The two historical periods before and after the reform and opening up are two interrelated periods with significant differences, but in essence they are both practical explorations of how our party can lead the people in socialist construction. The two are by no means separate from each other, let alone fundamentally opposed. Xi Jinping also pointed out that upholding and developing socialism with Chinese characteristics is like writing a long essay, and the task of our generation of communists is to continue to write that essay. These important statements profoundly explain the fundamental theoretical and practical issues of socialism with Chinese characteristics, and have greatly contributed to the ideological consensus of the whole party and the people of the whole country to adhere to and develop socialism with Chinese characteristics.

In order to uphold and develop socialism with Chinese characteristics at a new historical starting point, we must prepare for a great struggle with many new and unfamiliar characteristics. To lead this great struggle effectively, we must first build the party effectively. On 4 December 2012, Xi Jinping presided over a meeting of the Politburo of the Central Committee and determined to start by establishing the appropriate ethos and further strengthen party building. The meeting reviewed and approved the eight regulations of the Politburo of the Central Committee on improving work ethos and keeping close contact with the ordinary people. The new central leadership tackled the spirit of implementing the eight regulations head on, with complete thoroughness and penetrated deeply into the process of building an appropriate ethos. All this greatly improved the party's image and prestige in the eyes of the people.

After the 18th National Congress of the CPC, reform and opening up reached a new historical juncture and reform, in particular, entered a critical period and a deep-water zone. Whether the banner of reform and opening up could continue to be held high became the new litmus test for the party's opening up of a new field of action in governing the country and building socialism with Chinese characteristics. From 7 to 11 December 2012, Xi Jinping made his first tour of inspection since being elected as general secretary, choosing to visit Guangdong, a place which led our country in reform and opening up. Confronting the problems and deep-seated contradictions inherent in development, he observed that China's reform had entered a critical period and a deep-water zone, so it was essential not to miss the opportunity and to use greater political courage and wisdom to deepen reforms in important areas. It is necessary to adhere to the correct direction of reform and opening up, to dare to gnaw hard bones and to dare to break through the barriers of ideological concepts and entrenched interests, so that reform and opening up can continue unhindered.

Eliminating poverty is the bottom line when building an all-round moderately prosperous society, and it was the first issue that the new central leadership aimed to solve. From 29 to 30 December 2012, shortly after the end of the 18th National Congress of the CPC, Xi Jinping went to Fuping County, Hebei Province, to visit and offer his sympathy to the people in need there. He inspected poverty relief and development work, listened overnight to local labour reports, and held a long conversation with the cadres and the ordinary people. When he had fully understood the situation, Xi Jinping observed, "In building an all-round moderately prosperous society, the most difficult and arduous work lies in rural areas, especially in those which are poverty-stricken. Without a moderately prosperous society in such rural areas, it is impossible to build an all-round moderately prosperous society." With this in mind, Xi Jinping made a strategic declaration of war on poverty and issued a mobilisation order to the entire party and the country to join in the campaign.

In just over a month after the 18th National Congress of the CPC, the new central leadership shouldered their responsibility to the nation, the people, and the party in leading them into the new era and on a new journey with the overall goal of realising the Chinese dream of the great rejuvenation of the Chinese nation. The building of a new work ethos was the entry point to promote the great new project of party building, and the comprehensive deepening of reform and opening up was the fundamental driving force in advancing the great cause of socialism with Chinese characteristics. The party and the country would soon advance into new territory and show a new spirit.

On 13 December 2014, Xi Jinping shook hands and talked with villagers during a tour of inspection in Yongmaowei Natural Village, Shiye Township, Dantu District, Zhenjiang City, Jiangsu Province

With the continuous deepening of reforms and the development of undertakings, reforms and improvements in various fields, the reforms became more comprehensive and systematic, and their relevance and interaction were significantly enhanced; it was difficult to achieve qualitative results by individual breakthroughs, piecemeal adjustments and running repairs. Xi Jinping declared that it was necessary to thoroughly study top-level design and overall planning for comprehensively deepening systemic reform; to strengthen research and judgment on the relevance of the various reforms, and to organically integrate system reforms into economic, political, cultural, social, ecological and theoretical innovations. It is also necessary to ensure that all these types of innovation, and others too, are organically connected. In the five years after the 18th National Congress of the CPC, the Party Central Committee held seven plenary meetings to make decisions and take action on major issues such as government institutional reform and functional transformation, comprehensively deepening reforms and comprehensively advancing the rule of law within the party. The overarching 'five in one' programme consisted of building a socialist economy with Chinese characteristics, political construction, cultural construction, social construction and ecological civilisation construction. The overall strategic plan of the 'four comprehensives' consisted of the comprehensive construction of an all-round moderately prosperous society; the comprehensive deepening of reforms; the comprehensive governing of the country according to law; and the comprehensive running of the party according to the law. These two strategies, the 'five in one' and the 'four comprehensives' coordinated with each other and supported each other, and this had the effect of accelerating the pace of both theoretical and practical innovation.

CLARIFYING THE CORE POSITION OF GENERAL SECRETARY XI JINPING

After the 18th National Congress of the CPC, Xi Jinping took charge of the new central leadership group and, with great political courage and a strong sense of responsibility, put forward a series of strategies embodying new thinking and new concepts; introduced a series of major policies; launched a series of major actions and important tasks; solved a series of long-term problems that had been demanding attention; managed many major matters that had been long neglected; and pushed the party and the nation to make historic achievements and historic changes. In doing all this, he propelled socialism with Chinese characteristics into a new era.

In his new practice of state governance, Xi Jinping, as the supreme leader of the party, the country and the military, has demonstrated firm belief and conviction, a clear stance on behalf of the people, extraordinary political wisdom, tenacious will, strong historical responsibility and superb political skill, all of which have won the support of the entire party, of the whole army and of people of all ethnic groups. He has also been highly acclaimed by the international community. Xi Jinping fully understands the general trend of the times, met the requirements of new practice, and has complied with the new expectations of the people. He has advanced a series of major ideological viewpoints, further enriched and developed the party's scientific theories, and provided outline programmes for achieving new goals at the new historical starting point. In engaging in the new struggle, Xi Jinping became the heart of the Party Central Committee and the heart of the entire party.

Before the 6th Plenary Session of the 18th Central Committee of the CPC, there was a general consensus and a strong voice both inside and outside the party that, in order to maintain the authority of the Party Central Committee and its centralised and unified leadership, Xi Jinping's core position on the Party Central Committee and in the party as a whole must be clarified and sustained. This was the common aspiration of the entire party and of the people of all ethnic groups in the country. It was an urgent requirement to promote comprehensive and strict governance of the party, to increase the party's creativity, cohesion and combat-effectiveness, and a fundamental guarantee for maintaining the correct direction of the party and the nation's course. After full deliberation, in October 2016, the Sixth Plenary Session of the 18th Central Committee of the CPC clarified General Secretary Xi Jinping's core position on the Party Central Committee and in the party as a whole, and formally proposed the 'Party Central Committee with Comrade Xi Jinping as the core'. In October 2017, the 19th National Congress of the CPC included General Secretary Xi Jinping's core position on the Party Central Committee and in the party as a whole into the party constitution. Establishing General Secretary Xi Jinping's core position was the practical choice, the choice of history, and the choice of the whole party and the people. General Secretary Xi Jinping became the core of the Party Central Committee and the core of the whole party, which is a position worthy of great respect. Resolutely safeguarding the core position of General Secretary Xi Jinping and the authority of the Party Central Committee and its centralised and unified leadership were the major political achievements of the party's 18th National Congress. They represented the common will formed by the whole party in the ongoing forging of the revolution. They were acts of great and far-reaching significance that gathered the strength of the party and of the people to advance the great cause of socialism with Chinese characteristics and the great cause of national rejuvenation.

2
PROMOTING THE COMPREHENSIVE PROGRAMME OF 'FIVE IN ONE'

Entering the new era, the Party Central Committee with Comrade Xi Jinping at the core has taken charge of the overall situation, made scientific decisions, and persisted in the overall promotion of the comprehensive 'five in one' programme of building a socialist economy with Chinese characteristics, political construction, cultural construction, social construction and ecological civilisation construction. They are promoting the comprehensive development and progression of socialism with Chinese characteristics. In the five years after the 18th National Congress of the CPC, our country's reform and opening up and its socialist modernisation have made historic achievements and undergone historic changes.

MAJOR ACHIEVEMENTS IN ECONOMIC CONSTRUCTION

Since the 18th National Congress of the CPC, the economic situation at home and abroad has been extremely complicated, involving many situations that have not been encountered since the reform and opening up. In the face of these new situations and challenges, the Party Central Committee has reviewed the current situation, accurately grasped the general trend of our country's economic development and advanced a series of major conclusions with regard to our country's overall economic development, thereby successfully controlling the overall economic situation and making major achievements in building the economy.

Whether the economy and society can maintain sustained and healthy development is fundamentally determined by whether the party's leadership role in economic and social development is well executed. In November 2012, Xi Jinping observed that it was necessary to steadfastly promote the sustained and healthy development of our country's economy in accordance with the general aim of seeking progress while maintaining stability. In December of the same year, the Central Economic Work Conference clearly stated that the party's leadership over economic affairs must be strengthened. Since then, the Party Central Committee has continuously improved the party's systems and mechanisms for guiding economic affairs, established a system for the regular analysis and study of the economic situation and major economic issues, strengthened their analysis and understanding of the overall development situation, formulated major policies and strategies in a timely manner, made major decisions and performed important work to ensure that the party's leadership over economic affairs is properly implemented. It has provided an important guarantee for promoting cooperation between all parties in running the economy.

In August 2013, the State Council formally approved the establishment of the China (Shanghai) Pilot Free Trade Zone. Since then, the pilot free trade zone has gradually expanded, giving rise to a crop of reproducible and extendable policies, expanding the room for reform and opening up, and improving the level of openness in the economy.

In November 2013, the Third Plenary Session of the 18th Central Committee of the party devised a comprehensive plan and deployment strategy for deepening reforms, emphasising that the core issues in reforming the economic system were to properly manage the relationship between the government and the market, so that the market could play a decisive role in the allocation of resources; to better realise the role played by the government; and to achieve major theoretical breakthroughs and major practical innovations, as signposts for the direction needed for deepening reform of the economic system. Reform of the economic system was comprehensively promoted and breakthroughs were made in some fundamental reforms. Through reform, the Central Committee will further improve the overall market mechanism; eliminate monopolies; allow the price mechanism full play; enhance the vitality of the market; maximise use of the government's role in various forms of administrative economic adjustment, market supervision, social management, public services and environmental protection; and strengthen the vitality of the state-owned economy, its control, influence and safeguarding capabilities in order to stimulate the activity and creativity of the private sector and inject a strong impetus into overall economic development.

In December 2013, the Central Urbanisation Work Conference was held, which clarified the guiding ideology, main goals, basic principles and key tasks for advancing a new type of urbanisation. In March 2014, the Central Committee of the CPC and the State Council issued and implemented the *National New Urbanisation Plan (2014-2020)*. At the end of 2014, the *Opinions on Pilot Work of System Reform on Rural Land Requisition, Market Entry of Collectively Operated Construction Land and Rural Residential Land* were reviewed and approved. In December 2015, the Central Urban Development Conference was held, which clarified the overall thinking and key tasks of urban development. In October 2016, the General Office of the Central Committee of the CPC and the General Office of the State Council issued the *Opinions on Improving the Separation of Rural Land Ownership Rights, Contract Rights and Management Rights*. The 'separation of three rights' was another major institutional innovation in rural reform following on from the household contract responsibility system.

Taking into account the particular characteristics and work requirements of our nation's situation in the 'three superimposed stages' of economic development, namely, increasing the speed of change, the painful period of structural readjustment and the period needed to digest previous stimulus policies, in 2013, Xi Jinping came to the momentous conclusion that our nation's economy had entered a new normal stage. Under this new normal, the main characteristics of our nation's economic development are: the growth rate has shifted from high-speed to medium-to-high-speed, the mode of development has shifted from scale and speed to quality and efficiency, and economic restructuring has shifted from incremental capacity growth to adjustment of inventory and optimised growth. At the same time, the driving force for development has shifted from relying mainly on the input of resources and low-cost labour to being innovation driven. These changes are part of an inevitable process for our national economy's evolution to a stage with a more advanced structure, an optimised division of labour and a more logical framework. Achieving such extensive and profound changes is a new and huge challenge. Understanding the new normal, adapting to the new normal and spearheading the new normal are the overriding logical paths for our country's economic development during this period.

In order to adapt to, firmly grasp and spearhead our new normal economic development, it is necessary to further clarify the main direction, the overall thinking and the principal focus of the work involved. In October 2015, the Fifth Plenary Session of the 18th Central Committee of the CPC reviewed and approved the proposal for the '13th five-year plan' which clearly advanced the concept of people-centred development and proposed the concept of development based on innovation, coordination, environmental awareness, openness and sharing. These new concepts of development embody the development thinking, direction and focus of our country in the new era. They serve to manage the overall situation, to manage the fundamentals and to manage the long-term direction. They reflect the party's deepening understanding of the laws of economic and social development.

At the 11th meeting of the Central Financial Leading Group in November 2015, Xi Jinping proposed for the first time the promotion of 'supply-side structural reform'. Adapting to and leading the new normal economy through supply-side structural reform was a major strategic initiative on the part of the Party Central Committee. In a speech at the Central Economic Work Conference that December, Xi Jinping gave a comprehensive explanation of the supply-side structural reforms from theory to practice, emphasising the five major tasks of reducing overcapacity, reducing inventory, deleveraging, reducing costs and making up shortfalls. It clarified that macro-policy had to be stable, industrial policy accurately targeted, micro-policy flexible, reform policy pragmatic and that social policy had to guarantee social needs.

In August 2016, Baotou Iron and Steel Group's ironworks dismantle a blast furnace to eliminate outdated production capacity

With 'three eliminations, one reduction and one supplement' as the starting point, the Party Central Committee vigorously promoted supply-side structural reform. Focusing on iron, steel, coal and other industries to intensify efforts to reduce capacity, the central government allocated Rmb100 billion of special bonus funds to support the initiative by redistributing employees. In adhering to the stance that housing should be used for living and not for speculation, and by following the urban classification policy and guidance, the reduction in surplus commercial housing in third-tier and fourth-tier cities achieved significant results, and the trend of rising house prices in popular cities was controlled; through steady, ongoing deleveraging, controlling the scale of debt and increasing equity financing, the asset-liability ratio of industrial enterprises continued to decline, the increase in the macro-leverage ratio was significantly narrowed and overall stability was promoted. The pilot business tax reform to value-added tax (VAT) was fully launched; by taking multiple measures to reduce costs, reduce government-funded projects by 30%, reduce enterprise-related fees set up by the central government by more than 60% and gradually reduce the proportion of payments for endowment, medical, unemployment, employment injury, maternity insurances and Housing Provident Fund, it was possible to promote the reduction of costs in the fields of energy, logistics and telecommunications; by highlighting the key points and increasing the strengths to make up for shortfalls, it was possible to achieve conspicuous results in the promotion of supply-side structural reform.

After the 18th National Congress of the CPC, in response to issues relating to the overall long-term situation, the Party Central Committee proposed and implemented a series of major development strategies, including: the coordinated development strategy for Beijing-Tianjin-Hebei, focusing on the relief of Beijing's non-capital-related functions; the construction of the Yangtze River Economic Belt guided by environmental protection and the avoidance of large-scale development; the 'Belt and Road' construction and the construction of the Guangdong-Hong Kong-Macau Greater Bay Area with the goal of promoting mutually beneficial cooperation; implementing a new quality-oriented urbanisation strategy with people at the heart of the process; strengthening incentives to implement innovation-driven development strategies and a national food security strategy with basic grain self-sufficiency and absolute security of food supply; and promoting a new strategy for energy security focused on energy consumption, energy supply, energy technology, revolutionary new energy systems and on strengthening international energy cooperation. They also formulated and implemented an action plan to make our country a manufacturing powerhouse; established a national emerging industry venture capital guidance fund; promoted the development of big data and implemented the 'Internet+'[1] action plan; accelerated the technological transformation of traditional industries, the cultivation of emerging industries and the development of modern service industries; and focused on cultivating new development stimuli. They encouraged high-level essential enterprises to participate in overseas infrastructure construction and to share manufacturing capacity, and to promote Chinese equipment on the world stage. These major strategies have had a profound impact on our country's economic development and reform.

Under the accurate guidance of the new development concept, the Party Central Committee adhered to the overarching theme of seeking progress while maintaining stability, focusing on the promotion of supply-side structural reforms, and proactively adapting to, adopting and leading the new normal economic development. By doing so, they achieved significant results in economic development while maintaining medium-to-high-speed economic growth and improving both quality and efficiency. From 2013 to 2017, the average annual GDP growth exceeded 7%; in 2017, the total GDP reached Rmb82.08 trillion, ranking second in the world, accounting for about 15% of the world economy, and becoming the main source of world economic growth and stability. Infrastructure construction made rapid advances, agricultural modernisation progressed steadily, and the level of urbanisation showed solid improvement. The new open economy was maturing, and foreign trade, foreign investment and foreign exchange reserves were all firmly at the forefront of world financial affairs. A number of landmark scientific and technological achievements were made, including manned spaceflight, lunar exploration projects, quantum communications and manned deep-sea diving. The new impetus focused on new industries, and new business types and models, was continuously reinforced and became an important force in promoting the steady growth of our country's economy and the transformation and upgrading of its economic framework. The inclusiveness of growth and the sense of gain of the people continued to increase, and the steadiness of improvement made the upward trend more obvious. Our country's economic growth moved from being mainly driven by the manufacturing industry to being jointly driven by the manufacturing and service industries; from being mainly driven by investment to being driven by both consumption and investment; and from being a major exporting country to being a major exporting and importing country. This represents the attainment of a goal we had long been aiming for. The major structural changes enacted, economic strength, economic framework, economic vitality and resilience, and influence on global economic development all reached a new level.

MAJOR STEPS TAKEN IN THE CONSTRUCTION OF DEMOCRATIC POLITICS

In terms of national politics, the thinking that was used to plan and promote China's socialist democratic political construction had to focus on the fundamental structures, the overall situation and the long-term development path. China is a large developing country and sticking to the correct path of political growth is a major issue that has a fundamental bearing on the nation's overall situation.

On 4 December 2012, at the meeting where people from all walks of life in the capital commemorated the 30th anniversary of the promulgation and implementation of the current constitution, Xi Jinping summarised the core implications of the political development path of socialism with Chinese characteristics, emphasising that the key to adhering to that path was to uphold the party's leadership and to use the organic unity of the rule of law to ensure that the people are the masters of the country. All of this should be undertaken with the goal of enhancing the vitality of the party and the country, and mobilising the enthusiasm of the people, expanding socialist democracy and developing socialist political civilisation.

At the celebration of the 60th anniversary of the founding of the NPC, on 5 September 2014, Xi Jinping further elaborated on the historical, theoretical and practical logic of the political development path of socialism with Chinese characteristics and gave a penetrating summary of that system's primary characteristics and advantages. He also presented a list of important criteria for evaluating whether a country's political system is democratic and effective. This principally depends on: whether the country's leadership can be replaced in an orderly manner; whether the entire people are in a position to manage state and social affairs, and manage economic and cultural undertakings in accordance with the law; whether there are no impediments to the people's free expression of their needs and interests; whether all levels of society can effectively participate in national political life; whether national decision-making is both scientific and democratic; whether all levels of talent can enter the national leadership and management system through fair competition; whether the ruling party complies with the constitution and laws it establishes; whether the ruling party can achieve leadership over state affairs in accordance with the provisions of the constitution and laws; and whether the wielding of power can be effectively restricted and supervised.

After the 18th National Congress of the CPC, the Party Central Committee concentrated on: increasing and expanding the advantages and characteristics of our country's socialist democratic politics as being the key issue; giving full play to the core leadership role of the party in overseeing the overall situation and coordinating all involved parties; upholding the principle that all power in the country belongs to the people; supporting and improving the system of multi-party cooperation and political consultation under the leadership of the CPC; upholding and improving the system of ethnic regional autonomy; upholding and improving the system of mass grassroots autonomy; adhering to and improving the system and principles of democratic centralism; continuing to promote the institutionalisation, standardisation and proceduralisation of socialist democratic politics, and making better use of the socialist political system with Chinese characteristics. The superiority of the party continues to provide a complete system guarantee for the prosperity and long-term stability of the party and the country.

The People's Congress system was subject to constant improvement. By adhering to the comprehensive rule of law and firmly grasping the key policy of improving the quality of legislation, the levels of scientific legislation, democratic legislation and legislation firmly aligned with the law were continuously raised. In March 2015, the Third Session of the 12th NPC made important amendments to the *Legislative Law of the PRC*, granting local legislative powers to cities divided into districts in accordance with the law, clarifying the power and scope of local legislation, and further improving our country's legislative system.

The 12th NPC and its Standing Committee strengthened legislation in key areas. As of September 2017, 22 new laws were enacted, 110 laws were revised, 37 decisions on legal and other major issues were passed down, and nine legal interpretations were handed down. The socialist legal system with Chinese characteristics centred on the constitution was improved. They persisted in correct and effective supervision, and earnestly performed the supervisory duties of the People's Congress in accordance with the law. They implemented the Party Central Committee's system for improving the discussion processes and decision-making of the People's Congress on major issues and the system for reporting to the People's Congress at the appropriate level before major decisions of government at all levels were promulgated. They were conscientious in discussing and deciding major issues at the NPC and ensured greater efficiency in the employment of the functions of the organs of state power. The work of deputies continued to deepen and expand as the proportion of representatives of front-line workers, farmers, professional and technical personnel, and the number of representatives of migrant workers among the deputies to the NPC increased, and those deputies solemnly undertook to perform their duties in accordance with the law. It became increasingly common for deputies to attend Standing Committee meetings, participate in law enforcement inspections and in the activities of special committees and work committees. This further smoothed the channels for public expression and the reflection of social conditions.

Consultative socialist democracy has developed extensively and at many levels. It is a form of democracy unique, exclusive and original to China's socialist democratic politics, and it is an institutional arrangement that effectively guarantees that the people are the masters of the country. At the beginning of 2015, the Central Committee of the CPC issued its *Opinions on Strengthening the Construction of Socialist Consultative Democracy*, which systematically planned the development path of consultative democracy at the highest level. Seven forms of consultation, including political parties, people's congresses, government departments, CPPCC committees, people's organisations, communities, and social organisations, have continuously achieved new results in promoting the development of extensive and multi-layered institutionalisation of consultative democracy, thereby greatly enriching democratic formats, broadening democratic channels and deepening the democratic implications of the system. During the five years from the 18th National Congress to the 19th National Congress of the CPC, there were more than 110 consultation meetings, symposiums and briefings held by the Party Central Committee or commissioned by relevant departments. Among them, Xi Jinping hosted or attended more than 20 times.

The system of multi-party cooperation and political consultation has made further developments under the leadership of the CPC. In May 2015, the CPC Central Committee issued the *Regulations on the Work of the United Front of the CPC (Trial Implementation)*, which for the first time made 'participating in political consultation under the leadership of the CPC' one of the basic functions of democratic parties, and expanded the basic functions of the democratic parties to 'participation in and discussion of politics, and democratic supervision and participation in political consultations led by the CPC'. From November 2012 to November 2017, all the democratic parties pooled their particular strengths, characteristics and advantages, to focus on the vigorous advancement of supply-side structural reforms; the in-depth promotion of new urbanisation and 'Belt and Road' construction; promoting technological development and independent innovation; and vigorously revitalising and upgrading the real economy and other major issues. Experts and scholars were organised to conduct in-depth investigations, and a total of 496 suggestions were submitted to the CPC Central Committee and the State Council. Of these, suggestions for accelerating the construction of the Pingtan Comprehensive Experimental Zone and scientifically setting the GDP growth rate during the '13th five-year plan' period were also translated into major decisions by the party and the state. The CPPCC also insisted on integrating consultative democracy throughout the performance of its functions, persisted in promoting democracy and enhancing unity, mutual coherence, advocacy, governance and consensus building, and constantly improved the system of specialised consultative institutions. The National Committee of the CPPCC implemented the major reform measures of the CPPCC Central Committee on the structure of the CPPCC's democratic consultative process. It improved its framework with the plenary meeting as the overall lead, the special political standing committee meetings and themed consultations as the focus, and the biweekly consultation forums, counterpart consultations and proposal handling committees as the day-to-day mechanisms for discussion and political structuring. These arrangements fully mobilised the positivity, initiative and creativity of CPPCC members' participation in the political process.

The system of regional ethnic autonomy was effectively implemented. After the 18th National Congress of the CPC, the Party Central Committee attached great importance to the economic and social development of ethnic regions, improved differentiated regional policies, optimised transfer payments and counterpart assistance mechanisms, and implemented plans to promote the development of ethnic regions and ethnic groups with small populations, in order to rejuvenate and enrich the people and to ensure that ethnic minorities and ethnic regions worked with the whole country to achieve comprehensive prosperity and modernisation. They wholeheartedly implemented the party's ethnic and religious policies, held high the banner of ethnic unity, carried out comprehensive publicity and education on ethnic unity and progress, prompted all ethnic groups to cherish each other, and guided the people of all ethnic groups to increase their identification with the great motherland and the Chinese nation in recognising Chinese culture, the CPC and the road of socialism with Chinese characteristics, thereby further forging their consciousness of the community of the Chinese nation. Ongoing strengthening of the construction of the provisions and regulations of the ethnic regional autonomy law was implemented, the legal system around ethnic affairs was continuously improved, and the ethnic regional autonomy system continued to prove its vitality and superiority, all of which effectively promoted the modernisation of the overall governance of ethnic affairs.

The grassroots self-government system flourished. The people were extensively and directly involved in the management of social affairs through village committees, residents' committees and employee representative assemblies. Local rules and regulations or local self-government predominated in rural areas across the country, while urban communities generally formulated resident conventions or regulations for resident autonomy. The system of autonomy at the grassroots level with urban and rural (residential) self-government at its core and democratic election, democratic consultation, democratic decision-making, democratic management and democratic supervision as its main body was enacted in principle and continuously improved. This ensured that the people participated in politics in an orderly manner at all levels and in all fields. In daily life, our country's grassroots democracy played a hugely important role on a daily basis.

In March 2015, the villagers of Houhuang Village, Licheng District, Putian City, Fujian Province set up a banner encouraging voting at the villager supervision seminar on the 'circulation' of ancient dwellings; 'circulation' refers to regulations stipulating how the ownership or use rights of ancient houses can be legally transferred

The patriotic united front continued to consolidate and develop. The Party Central Committee successively convened the Central United Front Work Conference, the Central Ethnic Work Conference, the National Religious Work Conference, the Second Central Xinjiang Work Conference, the Sixth Central Tibet Work Conference and the National United Front Work Conference for People from New Social Strata. The party's first internal party regulations on the united front, the *Regulations on the Work of the CPC on the United Front (Trial Implementation)* and a series of normative documents were put into effect. The united front was constantly innovating, developing and consolidating, and played an important role as a magic weapon in the cause of socialism with Chinese characteristics.

GREAT PROGRESS IN IDEOLOGICAL AND CULTURAL CONSTRUCTION

Culture is the soul of a country and a nation. Culture rejuvenates the country and brings prosperity: when culture is strong, a nation is strong. To strengthen confidence in the path, theory, system and culture of socialism with Chinese characteristics, in the final analysis, is to strengthen cultural confidence. On 17 May 2016, Xi Jinping observed at a Philosophy and Social Science Work Symposium that: "Cultural confidence is a more basic, deeper and more lasting force." On 28 June, Xi Jinping attended the 33rd Collective Study Meetings of the 18th Politburo where he firmly advanced the idea of the 'four confidences': confidence in the socialist road with Chinese characteristics, confidence in political theory, confidence in the system and confidence in culture. The last named is clearly included in the 'four confidences'. By calling for the strengthening of cultural confidence, the Party Central Committee meant adhering to the path of socialist cultural development with Chinese characteristics and inspiring the cultural innovation and creativity of the entire nation.

The party's leadership of ideological work has undergone profound changes. As people's ideological activities become more independent, selective and varied, these changes have taken place in the hierarchies of public opinion, media patterns and communication methods, and ideological work has become more complex in both domestic and international environments. In order to strengthen and improve publicity and ideological work, from 2013 to 2016, the Party Central Committee successively convened the National Publicity and Ideological Work Conference, the Literature and Art Work Symposium, the Party's News and Public Opinion Work Symposium, the Network Security and Informatisation Work Symposium, the Philosophy and Social Sciences Work Symposium, the National Party School Work Conference and the National University Ideological and Political Work Conference. Xi Jinping delivered a series of important speeches profoundly addressing the major theoretical and practical issues of publicity, and ideological and cultural work under new historical conditions. The Party Central Committee made a series of major departmental restructurings and, among other documents, issued the *Guiding Opinions on Promoting the Integrated Development of Traditional Media and Emerging Media*, the *Opinions on the Implementation of Network Content-Building Projects* and *Party Committee (Party Group) Means of Implementing the System for Job Responsibilities for Ideological Work*. Through unremitting efforts, they took a firm grip on the field of ideology, showed the courage to wield the knife and take firm control of leadership responsibilities in managing, articulating and unifying the people, thereby establishing an upward trend towards greater unity. The guiding position of Marxism in our country's socialist ideology was further consolidated. Party organisations and government departments at all levels took effective measures to continue their good work in strengthening Marxist publicity and education, and making top priorities of the in-depth study, dissemination and implementation of the spirit of General Secretary Xi Jinping's series of important speeches, new ideas and new strategies on state governance.

This ensured that, in reinforcing the study, dissemination and implementation of socialism with Chinese characteristics and the Chinese dream, our ideological arsenal was more effective, the tenets of our belief were more firmly voiced, our positive energy was stronger, and the ideological unity of the whole party and of society was consolidated.

CULTIVATING AND PRACTICING THE CORE VALUES OF SOCIALISM

In pursuit of the cultivation and practice of the core values of socialism, the 18th National Congress of the CPC proposed to advocate prosperity, democracy, civilisation, harmony, freedom, equality, justice and the rule of law, patriotism, dedication, integrity and friendliness. In December 2013, the General Office of the CPC Central Committee issued their *Opinions on Cultivating and Practicing the Core Values of Socialism*, requesting that the cultivation and practice of the core values of socialism be integrated into the entire process of national education and incorporated into the practice of economic development and social governance. The whole of society in general carried out patriotic education activities and mass initiatives to improve ethical standards. Core socialist values were incorporated into the national education system and promoted in teaching materials, classrooms and in students' thinking. Some major issues of commemoration were raised to the national level. The state adopted legal procedures to establish 3 September as the Anniversary of the Victory of the Chinese People's War of Resistance Against Japanese Aggression, 13 December as the National Memorial Day for the Victims of the Nanjing Massacre, 30 September as Martyrs Memorial Day, and so on. In December 2015, the CPC Central Committee issued the *Opinions on Establishing and Improving the Party and National Meritorious Commendation System*, and the Standing Committee of the NPC reviewed and approved the *Law of the PRC on National Medals and National Honorary Titles*. By affirming the historical merits of models of meritorious service, establishing benchmarks and displaying banners, the formation of a good atmosphere for the whole of society to learn from others, advocate heroes and strive to be pioneers was promoted.

In order to ensure the inheritance and continuation of China's outstanding traditional culture, and to promote its creative transformation and innovative development, more and more traditional classics, opera, calligraphy and other content were brought into the classroom and onto the campus, and integrated into the national education system. Different localities adopted various methods to breathe new life into cultural relics displayed in museums, historical sites and remains, and the texts of ancient books, so that they could play an important role in promoting the excellence of Chinese traditional culture.

Intensive effort was put into cultural undertakings, and cultural industries were vigorously developed in order to continue to provide people with a rich spiritual diet. Great persistence was demonstrated in putting social benefit at the forefront, in unifying social and economic benefits and in fully implementing a new round of systemic cultural reform. The *Law of the PRC on the Guarantee of Public Cultural Services* came into effect in March 2017, realising the legal protection of the people's basic cultural rights and interests, and improving the modern cultural industrial and market systems. In the context of greater downward pressure on the economy, the cultural industry maintained a relatively rapid growth rate. As of the end of 2017, the added value of our country's cultural industry reached Rmb3.47 trillion and its share of GDP rose to 4.2%. Coordinated foreign cultural exchanges, cultural dissemination and cultural commerce, accelerated the promotion of Chinese culture overseas.

CONTINUOUSLY IMPROVING PEOPLE'S LIVES

Entering the new era, with the improvement of the level of economic and social development, the people's yearning for a better life became stronger, the needs of the people's livelihood became increasingly complex and diverse, and the task of protecting and improving people's livelihood proved very onerous. The Party Central Committee was committed to putting the people at the heart of things; taking the improvement of their well-being as the fundamental goal of development by focusing on making up for the shortfalls in people's livelihoods; providing education for young children; ensuring fair income from work; and treating illnesses and caring for the elderly. A series of ground-breaking results were achieved in the provision of support, housing and supplementary aid for the weak and infirm, so that the benefits of reform and development would be shared more and more equitably between everybody.

Employment is the biggest source of livelihood for the people, and is a matter of great importance, so it must be solved with great efforts. In the face of structural employment pressure, the Party Central Committee implemented a priority employment strategy and a more active employment policy, introduced and improved various preferential policies for entrepreneurship, vigorously developed vocational education and vocational training, and increased assistance to enterprises to stabilise jobs. From 2013 to 2017, more than 13 million new jobs were created in urban areas each year, and the registered unemployment rate in urban areas remained at a low level. The employment infrastructure was continuously optimised, and tertiary industry became the sphere that absorbed the most jobs. The proportion of urban employees increased from 48.4% in 2012 to 53.4% in 2016. The number of employed people in urban areas exceeded that in rural areas, and the pattern of urban-rural employment underwent a historic change. The labour force in the central and western regions showed a clear trend towards finding jobs as locally as possible and towards a return to hometowns to start new businesses. Party committees and governments at all levels continued to improve labour relations coordination and dispute mediation mechanisms, resolutely prevented and corrected employment discrimination, established a long-term mechanism for resolving wage arrears of migrant workers, and generally promoted the building of harmonious labour relations across the whole of society.

Income is the source of people's livelihood. The party and the government adhered to the principle of distribution according to work, strove to broaden the channels of residents' labour and property income, and improved the systems and mechanisms for distribution according to need. They were resolute in the synchronisation of residents' income growth and economic growth, labour remuneration and labour productivity, by 'expanding the middle, raising the base, lifting the upper limits and eliminating the illegal', narrowing the income distribution gap and promoting a more reasonable and orderly income distribution. Through reform and improvement of the income distribution system, the income of residents and their economic development increased at the same pace, as did labour remuneration and labour productivity. From 2013 to 2017, the national per capita disposable income of residents increased from Rmb18,311 to Rmb25,974. In 2017, the ratio of per capita disposable income between urban and rural residents was 2.71, a decrease of 0.17 from 2012.

Education is the foundation of our great plan. Education holds the hopes of hundreds of millions of families for a better life and building an educationally powerful country is the fundamental project for the great rejuvenation of the Chinese nation. The Party Central Committee closely followed the implementation of the fundamental task of deepening education reform and striving to build a comprehensive education system that makes all-round development of moral, intellectual, physical, aesthetics and labour education so that the foundations for the main framework of the socialist education system with Chinese characteristics are firmly established. Since 2012, the proportion of GDP accounted for by national fiscal expenditure on education was maintained at more than 4%. Education equality was better guaranteed by the comprehensive improvement of the basic conditions for running compulsory education in rural areas, the nutrition improvement plan for rural compulsory education students, and the in-depth implementation of the student subsidy system for the whole period of compulsory education. Governments at all levels continued to expand the provision of high-quality educational resources and strove to solve the problems of 'school choice fever' and 'difficulty in finding kindergarten places' with which the people had registered strong dissatisfaction. In 2017, the gross enrolment rate for pre-school education reached 79.6%, the net enrolment rate for primary school-age children reached 99.91%, the gross enrolment rate for junior high school reached 103.5%, the consolidation rate of nine-year compulsory education was 93.8%, and the gross enrolment rate for high school education reached 88.3%. More than 90% of disabled children were given the opportunity to receive education, and more than 80% of the children of migrant workers attended public schools in the area they had moved into. The gross enrolment rate for higher education reached 45.7% and was about to move from the popularised phase to the generalised phase. The structure of the teaching contingent was greatly strengthened, and the establishment of a complete system of educational ethics covering universities, middle and primary schools was accelerated.

Social security is the foundation of people's livelihood. It was essential to adhere to the policy of full coverage, basic protection, multi-level sustainability, and to continuously reinforce reform in order to build the world's largest social security system. In order to significantly enhance the fairness and sustainability of the system it was necessary to establish a unified basic pension insurance system for urban and rural residents, promote the reform of the pension insurance system for government agencies and institutions, establish a central adjustment system for the basic pension insurance fund for enterprise employees, and start the investment in and operation of the pension insurance fund. In 2017, the number of people participating in basic pension insurance for urban employees was 401.99 million, and the number of people participating in basic pension insurance for urban and rural residents was 512.55 million. With a total of 1,176,640,000 people in receipt of basic pension insurance, universal participation was essentially achieved. The number of people participating in unemployment insurance, work injury insurance and maternity insurance reached about 200 million, covering most occupational groups. Through hard work, a multi-level social security system covering urban and rural residents was gradually established.

The Healthy China Strategy was comprehensively implemented. In August 2016, at the National Health and Hygiene Conference, Xi Jinping emphasised that people's health should be given strategic priority for development, in order to accelerate the construction of a healthy China and to intensify efforts to ensure people's all-round health throughout their lives. The conference proposed a health and hygiene policy for the workplace with grassroots reform and innovation as the driving force, and prevention as the main focus. It gave equal weight to Chinese and Western medicine, and aimed to integrate health considerations into all policies, and to encourage the people's participation in building and sharing hygiene and health policy and practice. In October, the *Outline of the Healthy China 2030 Plan* issued by the Central Committee of the CPC and the State Council made comprehensive arrangements for the building of a healthy China. In accordance with this policy and its deployment, medical and health system reforms emphasised the linkage of medical care, medical insurance and medicine, and promoted the integration of prevention and treatment, joint prevention and control, and group prevention and group control, while continuously advancing the change in emphasis from treatment of disease to management of health.

Strengthening and creative reform of social governance was undertaken with institutional innovation as the key. The aim was, by faithfully following the path of socialist social governance with Chinese characteristics, to transform the advantages given by the party's leadership and the socialist system into social governance benefits; to continuously improve the socialist social governance system with Chinese characteristics; and to involve the leadership of the party committee, government responsibility, social coordination and public cooperation in a social governance system guaranteed by the rule of law. This represented the first steps in building a pattern of social governance based on joint construction, joint governance and shared responsibility. The focus of social governance was shifted to the grassroots level, and more resources, services and management were decentralised and reallocated in that direction. By strengthening grassroots grid-based service management and making full use of advanced technologies such as big data and artificial intelligence to create a comprehensive, three-dimensional social security prevention and control system, the public security risk prediction, and early-warning and prevention capabilities for the whole of society were greatly improved. Emphasis was placed on reforming the management systems of social organisations, promoting their healthy and orderly development, giving better play to their role in society, and achieving a benign interaction between government rule, social regulation and residents' autonomy. Through thorough and extensive special operations to crack down on violent terrorist activities, the risk of violent terrorist attacks was effectively controlled and prevented.

ECOLOGICAL CIVILISATION CONSTRUCTION ACHIEVES REMARKABLE RESULTS

After the 18th National Congress of the CPC, the Party Central Committee with Comrade Xi Jinping at the helm took on the construction of ecological civilisation as an important part of the overall strategy for promoting the 'five in one' programme and the coordinated promotion of the 'four comprehensives' strategic programme. They put the concept that 'lucid waters and lush mountains are invaluable assets' in the vanguard of the promotion of historic, transformative and comprehensive changes in our country's ecological environmental protection.

A healthy ecological environment is the most inclusive contributory factor to the well-being of the people's livelihood and welfare. After more than 30 years of sustained and rapid development, environmental problems accumulated over the years have entered a stage of high intensity and frequency in some locations. This is not only a major political issue related to the party's mission and purpose, but also a major social issue related to the people's livelihood.

In building an ecological civilisation, the most important thing is to establish rules and regulations, and to protect the ecological environment with the strictest systems and the strictest rule of law. In November 2013, the Third Plenary Session of the 18th Central Committee of the CPC determined to incorporate 'eco-civilisation system reform' into the programme of comprehensive reforms and proposed to reinforce the reform of the ecological civilisation system by closely focusing on building a beautiful China, accelerating the establishment of a suitable ecological civilisation system, and improving all-round land development. The systems and mechanisms of development, resource conservation and utilisation, and ecological environment protection serve to promote the establishment of a new pattern of harmonious development and modernisation between Man and Nature. In 2015, the CPC Central Committee and the State Council successively issued the *Opinions on Accelerating the Construction of Ecological Civilisation* and the *Overall Plan for the Reform of the Ecological Civilisation System*. Implementing a comprehensive system deployment required the establishment of a complete ecological civilisation system by 2020 with clear property rights, diverse participation, and equal emphasis on incentives and restraints. Under the guidance of these top-level plans, the construction of the ecological civilisation system was comprehensively implemented and continuously developed, and a series of major breakthroughs were achieved.

Promoting the construction of ecological civilisation is inseparable from strong supervision of the ecological environment. After the 18th National Congress of the CPC, some instances of serious damage to the ecological environment were rigorously investigated and dealt with. The Party Central Committee made it clear that the party and the government would have the same responsibility for protecting the ecological environment under the principle of dual responsibility, and strictly implemented the responsibility of the cadres for the same task. From 2015 to 2020, two rounds of central ecological and environmental protection inspections were carried out, which played a key role in solving outstanding ecological and environmental problems and promoting high-quality economic development. Called the 'strictest in history', the new environmental protection law has been in force since 2015, and it has made unprecedented efforts to combat environmental violations. From 2015 to 2020, 930,600 instances of ecological environment administrative penalties were imposed nationwide, with fines amounting to Rmb57.864 billion.

From protection to restoration, it was firmly established that the concept of protecting the ecological environment meant protecting productivity, and improving the ecological environment meant developing productivity, and striving to make up for ecological shortcomings. From 2013 to 2017, 460 million *mu* of newly afforested land nationwide were added, 638 million *mu* of forest maintenance was completed, and the national forest coverage rate reached 21.66%. By the end of 2017, 126 million *mu* of desertified land had been treated in our country. Desertification had been curbed on the whole, and the key control areas had been significantly improved. The area of desertified land was reduced by 1,980 square kilometres annually. The historical transformation from 'sand advancing, humans retreating' to 'humans advancing, sand retreating' was achieved. The proportion of Grade I-III bodies of water in nationally controlled sections of surface water in the country increased to 67.9%, and the proportion of water bodies rated lower than Grade V dropped to 8.3%. The water quality of major rivers was steadily improved. Compared with 2013, the average concentration of inhaleable particulate matter in cities at prefecture-level and above decreased by 22.7% in 2017, and the average concentration of PM2.5 in key regions such as Beijing-Tianjin-Hebei, the Yangtze River Delta and the Pearl River Delta decreased by 39.6%, 34.3% and 27.7% respectively.

In realising the comprehensive advancement of ecological civilisation construction, the national land development and protection system and the planning system have been continuously improved. The planning of major function-oriented zones, the promotion of development in strict accordance with the positioning of major function-oriented zones, and further optimisation of the programme for land and space development, were all implemented. In August 2015, the State Council issued the *National Marine Major Function Zone Planning*, and our country's main function-zone strategy realised its full extension to cover both land and sea territories. The Party Central Committee advocated a simple, moderate, green and low-carbon lifestyle. The creation of green homes, green schools, green communities, green shopping malls and green buildings was widely carried out.

Yu Village, Anji County, Zhejiang Province, has embarked on the green road to 'ecological beauty, industrial prosperity and prosperity for the people'

It was emphasised that the country's mountains, rivers, forests, land and lakes form a community of shared life, and the protection of the ecosystem was comprehensively increased. Through a series of important measures such as the complete cessation of commercial logging of natural forests, the implementation of pilot projects for closed and protected areas on desertified land, the intensification of the project of returning farmland to forests and pastures, the complete cessation of new reclamations, and the promotion of large-scale land greening, meant that forests, grasslands, wetlands and other important areas of ecological function were restored. The system of river chiefs and lake chiefs was fully implemented on all rivers and lakes across the country. Full-coverage ecological protection and compensation in key districts and areas, and a level of compensation in line with the economic and social development status, were realised;

exploration of the implementation of cross-regional and cross-basin compensation pilot projects was undertaken; and the operating mechanisms for compensation for ecological damage, guaranteed payment to beneficiaries and reasonable recompense to ecological guardians, all took shape.

Active participation in global environment and climate governance was undertaken. Our country took the lead in issuing the *China National Plan for Implementing the 2030 Agenda for Sustainable Development* and implementing the *National Climate Change Plan (2014-2020)*. In December 2015, China actively encouraged the UN Climate Change Conference in Paris to produce the historic document of the Paris Agreement. During the 2016 G20 Summit in Hangzhou, Xi Jinping, on behalf of the Chinese Government, formally deposited the instrument of ratification of the Paris Agreement with the UN. China actively fulfils its international obligations on biodiversity protection and makes continuous efforts towards global environmental governance. China's concepts and strategies for the construction of ecological civilisation have been widely recognised by the international community.

Ecological and environmental issues are, in the final analysis, issues of development methods and lifestyles. During this period, the formation of our country's green development mode was accelerated. We implemented dual control systems for overall resources and intensity of usage, strictly observing the red line of water resources, and strictly controlling the scale of new land for construction. We promoted the revolution in energy production and consumption, and the adjustment to the energy infrastructure structure accelerated. China became the world's largest user of new and renewable energy. Comprehensive conservation of resources was effectively promoted, and the intensity of energy resource consumption dropped significantly. We significantly raised the standards of ecological and environmental protection, forcing the transformation and upgrading of traditional industries, continued to resolve the problem of severe environmental pollution, resource consumption, indefensibly backward practices and excess production capacity. The development of energy-saving and environmental protection industries and a recycling economy was accelerated. Through the development of green financial products such as green credit, green bonds and green insurance, and pilot projects such as carbon emission rights and emission rights trading, more social capital was directed to invest in green industries, major environmental protection infrastructure construction, ecological protection and restoration projects, and model villages. Construction has become a hot spot for investment.

With the continuous advance of green development methods, a green lifestyle has increasingly become a common concern and common pursuit of the people. The Party Central Committee advocates a simple, moderate, green and low-carbon lifestyle, opposes extravagance, waste and unreasonable consumption, and guides the formation of a civilised and healthy lifestyle. The supply of green products and services continues to increase, and new business formats such as the sharing economy, service leasing, and second-hand transactions are booming. Energy-saving, environmentally friendly and renewable products are favoured by consumers. Initiatives such as the 'Clear Your Plate Campaign' or 'CD (Cook-on-Demand) Campaign' to reduce food waste and promote healthy eating, and low-carbon travel have received positive responses from the whole society. Content in the national education and training system regarding valuing ecology, protecting resources and caring for the environment has been greatly strengthened. The consciousness and initiative of the whole party and the country to implement the concept of green development have been significantly enhanced, and the previous situation in which the ecological environment was ignored, has changed significantly.

---

1. 'Internet+' refers to 'Internet + traditional industries' and the process whereby information and internet platforms are used to integrate the internet with traditional industries and use the advantages and characteristics of the internet to create new development opportunities.

3
COORDINATING AND ADVANCING THE STRATEGIC PROGRAMME OF THE 'FOUR COMPREHENSIVES'

PROPOSAL FOR THE STRATEGIC PROGRAMME OF THE 'FOUR COMPREHENSIVES'

In November 2013, the Third Plenary Session of the 18th Central Committee of the CPC carried out a systematic deployment of comprehensively deepening reforms and made decisions on several major issues concerning those reforms, clarifying the current and future direction, goals and tasks of the reforms. In October 2014, the Fourth Plenary Session of the 18th Central Committee of the CPC conducted a special study on the establishment of the rule of law, adopted decisions on several major issues concerning the comprehensive promotion of the rule of law, and made a strategic plan for the establishment of the rule of law in China, clarifying the nature of the central task. The two decisions made by the Third and Fourth Plenary Sessions of the 18th Central Committee of the CPC formed companion chapters, making reform and the rule of law like the two wings of a bird and the twin axles of a car, effectively promoting the development of an all-round moderately prosperous society. With the development of good practice, the party continuously deepened its understanding of the laws of state governance. In December, shortly after the closing of the Fourth Plenary Session of the 18th Central Committee of the CPC, during a tour of inspection in Jiangsu, Xi Jinping proposed for the first time to coordinate the building of an all-round moderately prosperous society, to deepen comprehensive reforms, to govern the country in every respect, and to administer party discipline.

In February 2015, Xi Jinping made a speech at the opening ceremony of the seminar for leading cadres at provincial and ministerial level to study implementation of the spirit of the Fourth Plenary Session of the 18th Central Committee of the CPC concerning the comprehensive governance of the country according to the letter of the law. In that speech, he clearly positioned the 'four comprehensives' as the overriding strategic programme. Within the 'four comprehensives' programme, each 'comprehensive' has great strategic significance focused on the overall situation. At the same time, the 'four comprehensives' complement each other, promote each other and work with each other, with a tightly connected internal strategy. They are an organic whole that unifies both goals and strategies. The 'four comprehensives' strategic programme captures the main contradictions and their principal aspects, embodies materialist dialectics, and forms the party's overall grasp of governance in the face of new circumstances.

Following the special studies of the Third and Fourth Plenary Sessions of the 18th Central Committee of the CPC on comprehensively deepening reforms and comprehensively advancing the rule of law, the Party Central Committee successively convened the Fifth and Sixth Plenary Sessions of the 18th Central Committee of the party to build an all-round moderately prosperous society and to make the necessary important arrangements through strictly enforcing party discipline and conducting targeted studies. The Fifth Plenary Session of the 18th Central Committee of the CPC held in October 2015 clearly advanced the fresh development concepts of innovation, coordination, greenness, openness and sharing based on a deep understanding and grasp of the new normal economic development. The *Proposals of the CPC Central Committee on Formulating the 13th Five-Year Plan for National Economic and Social Development* as approved by the plenary session, were guided by the new development concept and clarified our country's strategic thinking on development, the direction of that development and its focus during the '13th five-year plan' period. In October 2016, the Sixth Plenary Session of the 18th Central Committee of the CPC conducted a special study on the issue of comprehensive and strict governance of the party and provided fundamental compliance in order to strictly control political life within the party under the new circumstances, to cleanse the internal political ecology and to improve internal supervision. They also provided an important system guarantee for comprehensive and strict party governance.

The 'four comprehensives' strategic programme was a new strategy for governance and administration determined by the party in grasping the new characteristics of our country's development in the new era. The top-level design for promoting reform and opening up, and modernisation embodied the strategic goals and measures for the long-term development of the party and the country. The 'four comprehensives' strategic programme was a new strategy for the party to grasp the new characteristics of our country's development and the fundamental, overall and urgent major issues in the development of the party and the country. It drew up top-level plans to promote reform and opening up, and modernisation concentrating on the strategic goals and measures for the long-term development of the party and the country. The general promotion of the 'five in one' overall plan and the coordinated promotion of the design of the 'four comprehensives' strategic programme indicated that the party's grasp of the law of building socialism with Chinese characteristics had reached unprecedented new heights.

WHOLEHEARTED PROMOTION OF THE PROCESS OF BUILDING AN ALL-ROUND MODERATELY PROSPEROUS SOCIETY

The building of an all-round moderately prosperous society is a principal aspect of the 'four comprehensives' strategic programme. The Party Central Committee led the entire party and the people of all ethnic groups in the country in the move towards the grand goal of building an all-round moderately prosperous society by 2020 as decreed by the 18th National Congress of the party. In achieving this task, the emphasis is not just on the 'moderately prosperous' part; even more important and more difficult to achieve is that it should be 'all-round'. If all the people are not prosperous, then the society cannot be considered 'all-round' or 'comprehensive'.

Whether a society is moderately prosperous or not, depends on the villagers and countryfolk. Rural areas, especially poverty-stricken areas, are the biggest obstacle to an all-round moderately prosperous society. Xi Jinping observed, "Poverty is not socialism. If poverty-stricken areas are impoverished for a long time, their outlook cannot change for a long time, and the people's lives will not significantly improve for a long time. This does not reflect the superiority of our country's socialist system and it is not socialism." Also, "With greater determination, more precise thinking and more powerful measures, we will take extraordinary steps to implement poverty alleviation projects to ensure that the rural poor under our country's current standards will be lifted out of poverty, as will all poor counties, and the overall problem of regional poverty will be resolved."

After the 18th National Congress of the CPC, the Party Central Committee increased investment in poverty alleviation and brought in new methods so that the whole process entered a new phase. The key to poverty alleviation lies in precision, and that is where success or failure lie. Only by accurate, targeted 'prescriptions' for people and places, attacking the causes of poverty, and the different types of poverty, can we get rid of the 'roots of poverty'. During a tour of inspection in Hunan in November 2013, Xi Jinping imaginatively proposed the important concept of 'precise poverty alleviation', emphasising the need "to seek truth from facts, adapt measures to local conditions, to provide calibrated guidance and precise poverty alleviation". This marked a major change in the methods our country used for poverty alleviation.

Xi Jinping has a discussion with villagers in Shibadong Village, Paibi Township, Huayuan County, Xiangxi Tujia and Miao Autonomous Prefecture in Hunan Province during a tour of inspection on 3 November 2013

With the implementation of targeted strategies, our country continued to make new breakthroughs in poverty alleviation. The *Proposals of the CPC Central Committee on Formulating the 13th Five-Year Plan for National Economic and Social Development* approved by the Fifth Plenary Session of the 18th Central Committee of the CPC took poverty alleviation in rural communities as the basic symbol of building an all-round moderately prosperous society. The key was to make up for the 'shortcomings' of economic and social development as soon as possible to ensure that, under our country's current standards, the rural poor would be lifted out of poverty and need by 2020. All regions had to roll up their sleeves and solve the overarching problem of regional poverty. Subsequently, the CPC Central Committee and the State Council issued the *Decision on Winning the Tough Fight Against Poverty*, focused on the steady realisation by 2020 of the poverty alleviation and development goals known as the 'two no worries and three guarantees' (the rural poor to have no worries about food or clothing, and to have safe and secure access to compulsory education, basic medical care and housing). There would also be adherence to the 'six precisions' of targeted support aims, targeted project management, targeted use of funds, targeted household measures, targeted posting of officials in villages (at first secretary level) and targeted poverty alleviation actions. In response to the questions: 'who to support'; 'who will support', 'how to support', 'how to withdraw' and other key issues, they also proposed the implementation of the 'five batches': developing productivity to get rid of poverty, relocating to get rid of poverty, providing eco-compensation to get rid of poverty, developing education to get rid of poverty, and securing basic needs through social security. These and other engineering projects sounded the advance and led the charge against the obdurate problem of poverty alleviation.

During this period, the strengthening of industrial poverty alleviation, the rapid development of specifically advantageous industries in poverty-stricken areas, poverty alleviation through tourism, PV (photovoltaic) projects and e-commerce, all served to strengthen the vitality and motivation of endogenous development in poverty-stricken areas. Through ecological poverty alleviation, poverty alleviation through relocation, the returning of farmland to forest and grassland and so on, the ecological environment of poverty-stricken areas was significantly improved, achieving a win-win situation in the twin battles on one battleground of ecological protection and poverty alleviation. Through the building of infrastructure and public services, the basic conditions in impoverished areas, especially rural areas, were significantly improved and their overall appearance changed for the better. Through the organisation of poverty identification and poverty exit strategies and the implementation of poverty alleviation projects, grassroots governance and management levels in poverty-stricken areas were significantly improved, and the cohesion and combat effectiveness of rural grassroots party organisations were enhanced. Through the selection of first secretaries and work teams stationed in villages, government cadres were trained and rural skills were cultivated. As of the end of 2017, a total of 435,000 first secretaries and 2.78 million cadres had been selected and despatched to poor villages. The population of the rural poor decreased by more than 68 million, and 8.3

million people were relocated for poverty alleviation. The overall incidence of poverty dropped from 10.2% to 3.1%.

In order to ensure the smooth progress of poverty alleviation, the Party Central Committee insisted on giving full play to the government's central input and leading role; on giving full play also to the roles of both the government and society; on deepening the east-west cooperation in poverty alleviation; on enacting poverty alleviation designated by the party and government agencies, poverty alleviation by the army and armed police forces and by participation of social forces. Poverty alleviation involved building a pattern in which special poverty alleviation, industrial poverty alleviation and social poverty alleviation complemented each other; increasing the investment of financing for poverty alleviation; giving full play to the role of capital markets to support the development of poverty-stricken areas; attracting social funds to participate in poverty alleviation; and forming more funds for poverty alleviation channels and diversified investment. As of January 2017, 267 developed counties in the east and 390 poor counties in the west were paired up, thereby promoting poverty alleviation and coordinated regional development in the western region. By the end of 2017, 46,200 private enterprises nationwide had helped 51,200 villages, invested Rmb52.7 billion to implement industrial poverty alleviation projects, and donated Rmb10.9 billion to carry out public welfare assistance, all of which has motivated and benefited more than 6.2 million registered poor people.

The expansion of middle-income groups has a bearing on the realisation of the goal of building an all-round moderately prosperous society. While the 16th National Congress of the CPC put forward the goal of building such a society, it also articulated, for the first time, the goal of 'increasing the proportion of middle-income earners'. The 17th National Congress of the CPC proposed that 'middle-income earners should make up the majority', and the 18th National Congress of the CPC proposed the task of 'continuous expansion of the middle-income group'. The Third Plenary Session of the 18th Central Committee of the CPC re-emphasised this task when studying the comprehensive deepening of reforms and the Fifth Plenary Session of the 18th Central Committee did the same when studying the 13th five-year plan. Focusing on the stable expansion of the middle-income group, the party and the government put forward a series of key directions for theoretical and practical innovation, and successively introduced a series of new policies, which strongly promoted the expansion of the middle-income group. Through unremitting efforts, our country has formed the world's largest middle-income group, with more than 400 million people.

COMPREHENSIVELY DEEPENING REFORM AND MAKING MAJOR BREAKTHROUGHS

Comprehensively deepening reform is a key breakthrough link in the 'four comprehensives' strategic programme. Entering the new era, the Party Central Committee has promoted comprehensive and deepening reforms, and those reforms have shown a trend of forceful, multiple breakthroughs and rapid but steady, in-depth progress.

In November 2013, the *Decisions of the Central Committee of the CPC on Several Major Issues Concerning Comprehensive Deepening of Reform* were approved by the Third Plenary Session of the 18th Central Committee of the CPC and stood at the strategic height of the overall development of the cause of socialism with Chinese characteristics. They constituted a top-level design and overall plan for comprehensively deepening reform: they clarified the guiding ideology, objectives, tasks and major principles of comprehensively deepening reform, and laid out the scientific plan, the strategic focus, the priorities, main directions, working mechanisms, promotion channels and timetables, all of which constituted the road map for comprehensively instituting deeper reforms. The plenary session made it clear that the overall goal of comprehensively deepening reforms was to improve and develop the socialist system with Chinese characteristics, and to promote the modernisation of the national governance system and governance capabilities. It was required that by 2020, decisive results should be achieved in reforms in important areas and key links, and a complete system aligned with scientifically-determined norms should be formed, in order to operate an effective institutional system and make all aspects of that system more mature and more consistent. The plenary session made a series of new breakthroughs on major theoretical and policy issues, and put forward new viewpoints and conclusions such as 'making the market play a decisive role in the allocation of resources and giving fuller play to the role of government' and 'promoting the development of extensive and multi-layered institutionalisation of consultative democracy'. It also promulgated 336 major reform initiatives in the fields of economics, politics, culture, society, ecological civilisation and party building. The significance of the Third Plenary Session of the 18th Central Committee of the party was epoch-making. It opened a new era of comprehensively deepening reforms and promoting reforms through the overall design of the system and created a new situation in our country's reform and opening up.

Comprehensively deepening reforms is a complex system project that requires the establishment of a higher-level leadership mechanism. In

December 2013, the central government established a central leading group for comprehensive reform headed by Xi Jinping, which was responsible for the overall design, coordination, promotion and supervision of implementation. This fully reflects the great importance the Party Central Committee places on reform and demonstrates the Party Central Committee's determination to carry out reform. It is conducive to giving play to the party's role as the core leadership in coordinating all parties, and also to ensuring the systematic, integrated and synergistic nature of the reform. It helps to ensure that all tasks and links of comprehensively deepening reform are implemented. In the five years after the 18th National Congress of the CPC, 38 meetings of the Central Leading Group for Comprehensively Deepening Reforms were held, which reviewed and approved 365 important reform documents, determined 357 key reform tasks, and introduced more than 1,500 reform measures in important areas and key links. Breakthroughs were made and the main framework for reforms in major areas was fundamentally established.

In the practice of reform, the Party Central Committee emphasised that reform of the economic system should be the crux. When this is brought into play, the market should play a decisive role in the allocation of resources and the government should be more effective. It proposed and promoted supply-side structural reforms, in rural areas the 'separation of three rights' relating to land rights, deepening the reform of state-owned assets and SOEs, developing a mixed-ownership economy, co-constructing the 'Belt and Road', establishing free trade pilot zones and other such new ideas and initiatives. It promoted continuous breakthroughs in reforms in the fields of SOEs, taxation and finance, technological innovation, land systems, opening up to the outside world, culture and education, judicial affairs, environmental protection, retirement, employment, medicine and health, party building and discipline inspection. All this served markedly to change the situation in which the shortcomings of various systems and mechanisms hindered the creativity and development vitality of the whole of society.

In the development process of advancing comprehensive and deepening reforms, the Party Central Committee focused on basic, long-term and systematic system design. It implemented comprehensive standards, openness and transparency for improving the state-owned assets management system, focusing on capital management and strengthening state-owned assets supervision. It steadily promoted the reform of the taxation and financial systems, improved the integration of urban and rural development systems and mechanisms, built a new open economic system, promoted the development of a wide-ranging and multi-layered system of consultative democracy, and ensured that judicial organs independently exercised judicial and procuratorial powers in accordance with the law. Institutional arrangements were made for an anti-corruption leadership system and working mechanism, the establishment of the National Security Committee, the improvement of the natural resource asset property rights system, and the deepening of national defence and military reforms. The system of national governance and governance capabilities was also improved as part of the continuous improvement of the overall system.

TAKING FIRM STEPS TO COMPREHENSIVELY PROMOTE THE RULE OF LAW

Comprehensively advancing the rule of law is a fundamental requirement for solving a series of major problems in the development of the liberation and enhancement of social vitality, the promotion of social fairness and justice, the maintenance of social harmony and stability, and ensuring the long-term stability of the country. At the Central Political and Legal Work Conference in January 2014, Xi Jinping emphasised that the maintenance of overall social stability should be the basic task, the promotion of social fairness and justice the core value target, and the protection of people's work and livelihood the fundamental goal, with the focus on making the people feel that fairness and justice are enacted in every judicial case. He also emphasised that it was necessary to ensure the independent and fair exercise of judicial and prosecutorial power in accordance with the law, to improve the mechanisms for wielding judicial power, improve the judicial guarantee system for human rights, and strive to break through institutional, procedural and security barriers so as to continuously improve judicial credibility.

In October 2014, the Fourth Plenary Session of the 18th Central Committee of the CPC passed the *Decision of the CPC Central Committee on Several Major Issues Concerning Comprehensive Promotion of the Rule of Law*, clarifying that the overall goal of comprehensively promoting the rule of law is to build a socialist legal system with Chinese characteristics and a country governed by the rule of socialist law. This general goal not only clarified the nature and direction of comprehensively advancing the rule of law, but also highlighted the focus of the work and its scope, and had the overall purpose of guiding the plan as a whole. Focusing on this general goal, the plenary session proposed more than 180 major reform measures, covering all aspects of the rule of law. In April 2015, the 11th meeting of the Central Leading Group for Comprehensively Deepening Reforms reviewed and approved the *Implementation Plan for Important Measures of the Fourth Plenary Session of the 18th Central Committee of the CPC (2015-2020)*. In this way, a construction blueprint and general ledger were provided for the subsequent promotion of the comprehensive rule of law.

In the implementation of comprehensively governing the country according to the law, the Party Central Committee attached great importance to the role of the constitution, and it was clear that the first stage of adhering to the rule of law must be the governing of the country in accordance with the constitution. In November 2014, the Standing Committee of the 12th NPC established 4 December, in law, as National Constitution Day. In July 2015, it was clearly stipulated that state employees should publicly take the constitutional oath when taking office, and solemnly pledge to be loyal to the constitution, to the motherland and to the people.

Establishing a complete system of laws and regulations, and guaranteeing good governance with good laws are the prerequisites and foundations for comprehensively governing the country according to law. The legislature made a point of starting from the national conditions and accelerating the advancement of national security legislation, promulgating a series of laws related to national security such as the *National Security Law, National Intelligence Law, Anti-Espionage Law, Anti-Terrorism Law, Cyber Security Law, Foreign NGO Activities Management Law, National Defence Traffic Law* and *Nuclear Safety Law* to provide a solid legal guarantee for safeguarding national security, core national interests and other important interests. At the same time, legislative work in key areas such as the economy, society, people's livelihood, culture and the ecological environment continued to advance. As of September 2017, our country had 260 such laws in force. The socialist legal system with Chinese characteristics centred on the constitution was continuously being improved.

The establishment of a government under the rule of law is a key task in the promotion of the comprehensive rule of law, and it has a leading, exemplary role in the building of a country and a society subject to the rule of law. Starting from the basic requirements for the performance of all their functions in accordance with the law, all localities comprehensively sorted through, adjusted, reviewed and confirmed the powers of government departments and announced them to the public. In December 2015, the CPC Central Committee and the State Council issued the *Implementation Outline for the Construction of a Government Under the Rule of Law (2015-2020)*, proposing that by 2020, the overall goals and action plans for government under the rule of law, comprising 'functional science, statutory rights and responsibilities, strict law enforcement, openness and justice, honesty and high efficiency, and law-abiding honesty' would essentially be completed. In January 2016, the State Council launched a pilot programme for compiling lists of powers and responsibilities in seven departments including the National Development and Reform Commission. The 'lists of powers' and 'lists of responsibilities' were used to clarify the boundaries of government powers and promote the implementation of the reform of 'delegation of power, streamlining of administration and optimisation of government services'. As of the end of 2017, the number of items for administrative examination and approval by the departments of the State Council had been reduced by 44%, and the approval of non-administrative licensing had been completely terminated.

The reform of the judicial system focusing on the judicial accountability system was promoted. Following the planning of the central government, starting from 2014, the following trial reform initiatives were all launched across the country by 2016: the nationwide categorisation of judicial personnel; the improvement of the judicial responsibility system; the improvement of the professional security of judicial personnel; and the pilot reform of unified management of personnel, property and procuratorates of local courts, and procuratorates at and below the provincial level. An operating mechanism for judicial power with unified powers and responsibilities was established through the full implementation of the reforms of the judicial responsibility system, of a quota system for judges and prosecutors, and the introduction of the mechanisms which 'let the trial judge be responsible for the judgement' and 'the arbiter be responsible for his decision'. This gave judges and prosecutors lifelong responsibility for the quality of their cases in accordance with the law and continued to improve the clarification of their powers and responsibilities. There was a focus on improving judicial credibility, advancing reform of the trial-centred litigation system and ensuring that the facts of the investigation, review and prosecution could withstand legal tests. The reform of the leniency system for punishment following confession of guilt was deepened, the operating mechanism of expedited procedures was implemented, including the promotion of the classification of cases on grounds of complexity, severity and speed. This was all part of the drive to build a multi-level litigation system. The six circuit courts of the Supreme People's Court covered six regions, and a downward shift in the centre of gravity of that highest judicial organ was achieved. The system of people's jurors and people's supervisors was also improved. In order to gradually resolve the difficulties in litigation reported by the masses, a comprehensive reform of the registration system was implemented, and the case-filing review system was changed to a case-filing registration system. In this way it could be ensured that cases were firmly established, litigation was properly conducted, supervision was strengthened, false litigation was punished in accordance with the law and the court system was kept running in good order. By deepening the comprehensive supporting reforms of the judicial accountability system, the systems and mechanisms of investigative power, prosecutorial power, adjudicatory power and executive power that complement and restrict each other, were further improved. In this way, the establishment of a complete, standardised and efficient law enforcement, and judicial control and supervision system was accelerated. After this new round of judicial reform, a new judicial management system and an operating mechanism for judicial power were gradually established, and fairness and justice became the bright background of the new era.

The building of a law-abiding society was continuously strengthened to serve as the foundation for the comprehensive rule of law. In 2016, the Central Organisation Department and four other departments jointly issued the *Opinions on Improving the System of Studying and Using Laws for National Staff*, aiming directly at the 'key minority' of leading cadres, and urging national staff to take the lead in respecting the study of the law and adherence to it. In March, the Central Committee of the CPC and the State Council put forward the *Seventh Five-Year Plan of the Central Publicity Department and the Ministry of Justice on Publicity and Education of the Rule of Law Among Citizens (2016-2020)*. Work began on its dissemination and popularisation. The *Opinions on the Implementation of the Law Popularisation Responsibility System of 'Whoever Enforces the Law' of State Organs* issued in May 2017, for the first time clearly identified the state organs as the main bodies responsible for publicity and education regarding the rule of law. Implementing the requirement of 'whoever enforces the law will popularise the law' and adopting a 'taking the bull by the horns' approach to the system of responsibility for popularising the law, a pattern of 'big law popularisation' featuring unified leadership by the party committee, division of labour and responsibility, with everyone performing their allotted duties, and co-management of the overall project, gradually took shape.

OUTSTANDING RESULTS ACHIEVED BY STRICT AND COMPREHENSIVE PARTY GOVERNANCE

Strict and comprehensive administration of the party is the fundamental guarantee for coordinating and promoting the 'four comprehensives' strategic programme, and it has been the shining theme of the Party Central Committee's efforts in party building since the party's 18th National Congress. Xi Jinping observed that under the new historical conditions, if we want to better carry out the great struggle with many new historical characteristics and advance the great cause of socialism with Chinese characteristics, we must push forward with redoubled efforts in the great new project of party building and be unswerving in its pursuit. We must promote comprehensive and strict party governance, and earnestly build and manage it. Strict and comprehensive party governance is a constant process, and there can be no thought of stopping to take a breath or a rest. We must always maintain a calm and clear mind, strengthen our courage and perseverance, reinforce our political consciousness of its necessity, and continue to promote the comprehensive and in-depth development of strict party governance.

At the Central Economic Work Conference in December 2013, Xi Jinping observed that socialism with Chinese characteristics has many different traits and characteristics, but the most essential one is adherence to the leadership of the CPC. In July 2016, Xi Jinping emphasised at the celebration of the 95th anniversary of the founding of the CPC that the most essential feature of socialism with Chinese characteristics is the leadership of the CPC, and the greatest advantage of the socialist system with Chinese characteristics is also the leadership of the CPC.

To uphold the leadership of the party, the first priority is to uphold the authority of the Party Central Committee and the centralised and unified leadership. In January 2014, Xi Jinping pointed out at the Third Plenary Session of the 18th Central Commission for Discipline Inspection, "The Central Committee, the Politburo of the Central Committee, and the Standing Committee of the Politburo of the Central Committee are the core of the party's leadership and decision-making." To reflect this requirement, on 16 January 2015, the Politburo Standing Committee meeting listened specifically to the reports on the work of the Standing Committee of the NPC, the State Council, the National Committee of the CPPCC, the Supreme People's Court and the Supreme People's Procuratorate. On 23 January the Politburo meeting of the Central Committee listened to the related comprehensive report.

In October 2016, the Sixth Plenary Session of the 18th Central Committee of the CPC reviewed and approved the *Several Guidelines on Political Life Within the Party Under the New Situation* and the *Regulations on Inner-Party Supervision of the CPC*. The *Guidelines* emphasised that "resolutely safeguarding the authority of the Party Central Committee and ensuring that the entire party's orders and prohibitions are where the future and destiny of the party and the country lie and are where the fundamental interests of the people of all ethnic groups in the country also lie." This plenary session clarified the core position of General Secretary Xi Jinping in the Party Central Committee and the party as a whole, which also reflected the common aspirations of the entire party, the entire army and the people of all ethnic groups. It is where the fundamental interests of the party and the country lie and is the fundamental guarantee for upholding and strengthening the party's leadership. The plenary session also called on all party comrades to unite around the Party Central Committee with Comrade Xi Jinping at its core, to firmly establish the necessity for political awareness, overall situation awareness, core awareness and alignment awareness, and to unswervingly maintain the authority of the Party Central Committee and the centralised and unified leadership.

In order to strengthen the party's overall leadership, the Central Committee further strengthened and improved the relevant systems and mechanisms. In January 2015, the Central Committee of the CPC issued the *Opinions on Strengthening and Improving the Party's Group Work*, emphasising that the party's leadership is the fundamental guarantee for success in our collaborative labours. In June, the Central Committee of the CPC issued the *Regulations on the Work of the Party Group of the CPC (Trial)*. This was the CPC's first special internal party regulation of the party's group work. In December, the Central Committee of the CPC issued the *Regulations on the Work of Local Committees of the CPC*, which further improved the institutional basis for local party committees to play the role of core leadership and improved the operating mechanisms of local party committees. In October 2016, the central government held a national SOE party-building work conference to make systematic arrangements for solving the problems of party leadership in SOEs, particularly the weakening, diminishing, failing and marginalisation of party building. The meeting emphasised the need to uphold the party's leadership of SOEs and determined singlemindedly to bring about a new era of party building in SOEs. In December, the Central Committee of the CPC and the State Council issued the *Opinions on Strengthening and Improving the Ideological and Political Work in Colleges and Universities Under the New Situation*, which required that party building be implemented throughout and that the party's leadership of colleges and universities should be re-emphasised.

The strict and comprehensive administration of the party starts with the question of approach. In the new era, the strict governance of the party begins with the establishment of rules by the Politburo of the Central Committee and the implementation of the spirit of the eight central regulations. The eight regulations are the first important internal party regulations formulated after the 18th National Congress of the CPC, and they are also a decisive entry point for improving the overall approach. Xi Jinping emphasised that communist party members will always be ordinary members of the working people. Except for personal interests and work powers within the scope of laws and policies, no communist party member should seek any personal interests or privileges and must oppose both the idea and the manifestation of privilege. Our party is firm in its opposition to the "four winds of decadence" (formalism, bureaucratism, hedonism and extravagance), to corruption and to privilege in thought and deed, and has introduced a series of rectification measures regarding the office space, official cars, secretarial equipment and official consumption of leading cadres, strictly regulating their privileges. The benefits enjoyed by some cadres, in both their work and their personal lives, have been effectively curbed. Discipline inspection and supervision processes at all levels started with the management of public funds, food and drink, travel, gift giving and other unhealthy practices, and breakthroughs in specific issues led to an overall change in the atmosphere of both the party and society as a whole. This served to consolidate the hearts and minds of the party and the people for the in-depth promotion of strict party governance.

Discipline was placed centre stage with firm insistence on strict political discipline and observance of the rules. At the first meeting of the 18th Politburo of the Central Committee on 16 November 2012, Xi Jinping emphasised that "everyone must take the lead in observing the party's organisational principles and the rules of political life within the party, understanding the rules and observing discipline". At the Second Plenary Session of the 18th Central Commission for Discipline Inspection in January 2013, Xi Jinping further observed that the most important thing for strict party discipline is strict political discipline. Political discipline is the most important, fundamental and critical discipline. The meeting also proposed that the party's discipline inspection agencies at all levels should put the maintenance of the party's political discipline first, strengthen supervision and inspection of the implementation of political discipline, eradicate interest groups formed by the interweaving of political corruption and economic corruption, and eliminate major hidden political dangers. Disciplinary commissions at all levels strove to resolve the issue of ignoring political discipline and political rules, and seriously investigated and punished public statements that violated the spirit of the Central Committee. In the five years after the 18th National Congress of the CPC, a total of 15,000 cases of violations of political discipline were filed for review and 15,000 were punished, including 112 central management cadres. This served effectively to maintain the centralised and unified leadership of the party. In October 2015, the revised *Code of Integrity and Self-Discipline of the CPC* and *Regulations on Disciplinary Actions of the CPC* were issued.

The *Regulations* insisted on positive advocacy, with the focus on morality and reaffirming the party's ideals, beliefs and purpose. Their adherence to well-established and respected standards set a high moral tone that was obvious to all. They laid out a 'list of negatives' and focused on establishing rules and integrating the disciplinary requirements of the Party Constitution into 'six disciplines'. In order to strengthen the enforcement of discipline, the Party Central Committee adhered to the policy of criticising former mistakes severely to prevent them happening again and criticising people in order to help them; they proposed the constructive use of the 'four forms'[1] of supervision and discipline, strengthened daily supervision and management and, by being more constructive in the application of the primary form of discipline, the benefits of having a disciplinary framework were made more and more apparent.

Corruption is the biggest threat facing the party and seriously erodes the foundations of party rule. In the face of a period of relatively serious corruption in the party, the Party Central Committee, led by Comrade Xi Jinping, was determined to "punish hundreds of people so as not to lose hundreds of millions of others" and insisted on taking the war against corruption to all areas without exception and with zero tolerance. Simultaneously and unswervingly 'fighting tigers' and 'swatting flies', deepening cooperation in international anti-corruption law enforcement, tightening the international surveillance of 'Skynet'[2], the committee met corruption with the force of a thunderclap and continued to present a strong deterrent. In the five years after the 18th National Congress of the CPC, 440 party members and cadres at or above the provincial military level and other central management cadres were approved for investigation by the Party Central Committee. Among them were 43 members and alternate members of the 18th Central Committee, and nine members of the Central Commission for Discipline Inspection. Discipline inspection and supervision agencies across the country handled 2.674 million pieces of information, filed 1.545 million cases and sanctioned 1.537 million people. Among that number were more than 8,900 cadres at the department and bureau level and 63,000 cadres at the county and division level; 58,000 cases of suspected criminal activity were transferred to the judicial authorities for handling. In particular, Zhou Yongkang, Bo Xilai, Guo Boxiong, Xu Caihou, Sun Zhengcai, Ling Jihua and others were resolutely investigated and dealt with for serious violations of discipline and law. The strict and comprehensive governance of the party, with anti-corruption as the key, achieved major strategic results. The goal of deterrence from corruption was realised for a start. The net of incorruptibility was drawn tighter and tighter, the dams against corruption grew stronger and stronger, and the overwhelming momentum of the struggle against corruption was established and consolidated.

Management of the party must start with the political life within the party; strict management of the party must start with imposing strictness on political life within the party. In October 2016, the Sixth Plenary Session of the 18th Central Committee of the CPC conducted an in-depth analysis of the new situation and new problems facing party building and put forward clear measures for handling the weak links in party political life and party supervision. They set a comprehensive standard for internal political life and purified the political ecology within the party, emphasising that the whole party must firmly establish political awareness, overall awareness, core awareness and consistency awareness, and consciously maintain a high level of consistency within the Party Central Committee, led by Comrade Xi Jinping, in ideological and political action.

The Party Central Committee adhered to the close integration of ideological party building and system governance, focusing on solving ideological problems, reinforcing the 'master switch', and continuing to consolidate the ideological foundation for comprehensive and strict party governance. Following the instructions of the 18th National Congress of the CPC, from June 2013 to September 2014, the whole party carried out mass party-line education and implementation activities centred on serving the people in an honest and down-to-earth way. In 2015, the 'three stricts and three realities'[3] special education was implemented among leading cadres at county level and above. In 2016, the 'two learning and one doing'[4] learning and education programme was carried out among all party members. In 2017, the general delivery of the 'two studies and one action' learning and education programme was carried out. Institutional arrangements and implementation continued to promote comprehensive and strict party governance across the range from 'key minorities' to the broad body of party members, in both centralised and regular education. The ideals and beliefs of the whole party became firmer and party spirit became stronger.

By tightening the net of the system across the board, the party governance system can be constantly improved in accordance with regulations. In November 2013, the Central Committee of the CPC issued the *Outline of the Five-Year Plan for the Formulation of Central Party Regulations (2013-2017)*, proposing that "after five years of hard work, we will have established the main areas of party building and party work, and adapted to the management system. We will have built the framework of the party's internal laws and regulations that is required to make the life of the party more standardised and procedural". Also, "by the 100th anniversary of the founding of the party, a comprehensive system of internal party laws and regulations with scientific content, strict procedures, complete supporting facilities and effective operation, will be established." The Central Committee of the CPC issued the *Opinions on Strengthening the Construction of the Party's Laws and Regulations,* proposing to improve the party's laws and regulations in accordance with the principle of "regulating the main body, standardising behaviour, and standardising supervision." The Party Central Committee continuously improved the party and state supervision system. In the five years after the 18th National Congress of the CPC, the Party Central Committee revised the *Regulations on Inspections of the CPC* twice, formulated a five-year plan for inspections by the Central Committee, organised 12 rounds of inspections, and inspected 277 party organisations. This was the first time in the party's history that full coverage of inspections during one term of office was achieved. They revised the regulations on supervision within the party, strengthened supervision and inspection of the state of the party's political life and the implementation of party-line principles and policies, and resolutely maintained the authority of the Party Central Committee's centralised and unified leadership. Through the implementation of the combination of individual and team postings, the central-level party and state organs have been fully staffed in terms of discipline inspection units with consistent titles and management systems. They have deepened reform of the national supervision system, built an authoritative and efficient national anti-corruption agency under the party's unified leadership, achieved full inspection coverage of all public officials, and continuously improved the supervision system of the party and the state.

The key to the strict administration of the party is the strict administration of officials and the careful selection and training of the standard of cadres that the party and the people need. The main issue in the work of cadres is being sure of the specific qualifications and character of the people selected. At the National Organisation Work Conference in June 2013, Xi Jinping proposed, for the first time, the standards for good cadres as being, "firm conviction, service to the people, diligence and pragmatism, courage to assume responsibility, honesty and purity". In order to implement the standards for good cadres in the new era, the Central Committee of the CPC revised and issued the *Regulations on the Selection and Appointment of Party and Government Leading Cadres* and other regulations and documents to strengthen the leadership and gatekeeping role of the party organisation and effectively solved the outstanding problem of biased selection of people based only on vote, status, earning potential or age. The Party Central Committee continuously intensified reform of the cadre and personnel system in response to such 'old problems' in the work of cadres. In July 2015, the General Office of the Central Committee of the CPC issued the *Provisions on the Promotion and Demotion of Leading Cadres (Trial Implementation)*, which clarified the indications for demotion, standardised the methods of demotion and cleared the paths for demotion. This played an important role in supporting the building of an employment-oriented and political environment in which the capable were promoted, the superior rewarded, the mediocre demoted and the inferior dismissed. In August 2016, the General Office of the Central Committee of the CPC issued the *Opinions on Preventing 'the Promotion of Sickness' among Cadres*, which clearly set out the requirements of the 'four musts for all mentions'[5] to ensure that candidates are loyal, pure and responsible. In order to strengthen the management and supervision of cadres, in February 2017, the Central Committee of the CPC revised the *Provisions on Leading Cadres Reporting Matters Related to Individuals* and formulated the *Measures for the Handling of the Results of the Verification of Personal Reports on Relevant Matters by Leading Cadres* to improve and strictly implement the characteristically Chinese system for the reports of leading cadres on personal matters.

1. The 'four forms' of supervision and discipline enforcement refer to frequent criticism and self-criticism, and both oral and written enquiries, conducted so that "red face and sweating" when under examination becomes the norm. Party violations that are lightly punished with minor organisational adjustments should become the majority of disciplinary cases; those with heavy punishments and major demotions should be in a minority; the most serious violations of discipline and suspected violations of the law that merit full investigation should be very few in number.
2. 'Skynet' is a CCTV documentary programme on the rule of law focused on promoting justice and righteousness. It uses real cases to construct suspense stories with the aim of deterring crime.
3. The 'three stricts' refers to: strict self-cultivation, strict use of power and strict self-discipline; 'three realities' refers to: seeking to be practical, starting an undertaking and facing up to reality as an adult.
4. 'Two learning' refers to learning the party constitution and party rules by reviewing a series of speeches; 'one doing' refers to becoming a qualified party member.
5. 'Four musts for all mentions' refers to the need to properly vet the files of cadres before recommending them for promotion; the 'four musts' relate to the fact that: their personnel files 'must' be reviewed; reports regarding personal matters 'must' be reviewed; the opinions of the discipline inspection and supervision organs 'must' be heard, and letters and visits with specific clues 'must' be investigated to prevent so-called 'promotion with illness', in other words, to prevent promotion of someone who is not fit for the job.

4
COMPREHENSIVELY ADVANCING THE MODERNISATION OF NATIONAL DEFENCE AND THE MILITARY

ESTABLISHING THE PARTY'S GOAL OF STRENGTHENING THE ARMY IN THE NEW ERA

The world today is undergoing major changes of a kind not seen in a century. The international strategic landscape has changed profoundly and international military competition has become increasingly fierce. China is at a critical stage in its development from a large country to a strong one. A strong country must have a strong army, as a strong army can ensure national security. In November 2012, the First Plenary Session of the 18th CPC Central Committee elected Xi Jinping chairman of the CMC. At the beginning of his tenure, with the strategic overview of realising the Chinese dream of the great rejuvenation of the Chinese nation, Xi Jinping keenly seized on the world's new military revolution and made overall plans for a series of major projects in the modernisation of national defence and the military in the new age. In December, when meeting with leading cadres above division level of the troops stationed in Guangzhou, Xi Jinping presented the "dream of a strong military" for the first time, pointing out that, where the military is concerned, the dream of a strong country is also the dream of a strong military. To achieve the great rejuvenation of the Chinese nation, it is necessary to persist in the combination of a prosperous country and a strong army, and to build and consolidate national defence and the military.

To realise the dream of a strong army, it is necessary to have a clear idea of what kind of a strong People's Army is needed and of how to build it in the new era. At an enlarged meeting of the CMC at the end of 2012, Xi Jinping proposed striving to build a People's Army that obeys the party's command, can win battles, and has a good work ethic. In March 2013, when attending the Plenary Session of the PLA Delegation to the First Session of the 12th National People's Congress, Xi Jinping made it clear that, under the new circumstances, building a People's Army that obeys the party's command, can win battles, and has a good work ethic was the party's target for a strong military. In February 2016, at an enlarged meeting of the CMC, Xi Jinping further proposed the requirements for achieving the goal of strengthening the military and building a world-class army.

In reaching the goal of strengthening the army, obeying the party's command was the soul of the process, as it determined the political direction of the process; being able to win battles was the core, reflecting the fundamental capabilities of the army and the fundamental orientation of its construction; a good ethic was the guarantee that linked the nature, purpose and qualities of the army. The goal of strengthening the army clarified the focus of the process and reflected the high degree of unity with the party's army-building principles, the fundamental functions of the army and its unique political advantages. It represented the Party Central Committee's strategic plan and top-level design for national defence and army building, and the party's overall strategy for building and administering the military.

In strengthening the country and the army, strategy comes first. In accordance with the national security and development strategy, and adapting to the requirements of the situation and tasks in the new historical period, the Party Central Committee and the CMC continuously enriched and perfected the content of their active defence strategy thinking, and advanced with the times to strengthen strategic military guidance. In November 2013, the Third Plenary Session of the 18th Central Committee of the CMC proposed to innovate and develop military thinking and strengthen military strategic guidance. In 2014, the CMC formulated military strategic guidelines to meet the new circumstances. The policy continued to follow the practice of proactive defence, holistically planning both combat and the cessation of hostilities, maintaining legal rights and social stability, deterrence and actual combat, conducting military exercises in times of both peace and war, recognising that the preparation for military conflict is based on winning informatised local wars, and regarding conflict at sea as the strategic focus. All this served to strengthen the enthusiasm and initiative of the strategic guidance. In May 2015, the first white paper on China's Military Strategy was officially published. The white paper focused on the military strategy of active defence to meet the new circumstances, clearly adjusted the basis of conflict preparation, innovated basic combat thinking, optimised the military strategic layout, and resolutely safeguarded national sovereignty, security and development interests. It was a concentrated expression of the development and practical achievements of the People's Army's military strategy.

CARRYING OUT A STRATEGY OF BUILDING THE ARMY POLITICALLY IN THE NEW ERA

To implement the party's goal of strengthening the army in the new era, the most important thing was to obey the party's command. From 30 October to 2 November 2014, the First Military Political Work Conference of the new century was held in Gutian Town, Shanghang County, Fujian Province. Xi Jinping delivered an important speech at the meeting, emphasising that revolutionary political work was the lifeblood of the revolutionary army, and clearly proposed the theme of political work in the army for the new era, which was to closely focus on the realisation of the Chinese dream of the great rejuvenation of the Chinese nation, and to provide a strong political guarantee for the realisation of the party's goal of strengthening the army under the new circumstances.

Xi Jinping emphasised that the military's political work could only be strengthened and not weakened. The four fundamentals of ideals and beliefs, party spirit and principles, standards of combat effectiveness, and trust in political work must be upheld, and every effort should be made to firmly sustain the soul of the army and manage senior and middle-level cadres. Ethos building, the fight against corruption, cultivation of fighting spirit, and innovation and development of political work were the other five key tasks.

Xi Jinping observed that the political work of the army was essentially the work of the party leading and controlling the army. As an armed force that carried out the party's political tasks, the People's Army had to uphold the party's absolute leadership, unswervingly listen to and follow the party, and fight wherever the party directed. His speech systematically summarised a set of fine traditions formed by the long-term practice of military political work and emphasised that these fine traditions were the fundamental principles and content of military political work and must be passed on from generation to generation.

The All-Army Political Work Conference was an extremely important meeting held at a crucial point in the development of the party, the country and the army, and it embarked on a new journey of ideological party building and political army building. From the perspective of the developments of the time and the overall strategic situation, Xi Jinping's important speech profoundly clarified a series of major issues in the party's ideological and political building of the army, and established a new era in political army building strategy. It was an expertly structured document that spearheaded the building of the People's Army in the new era and created a whole new appreciation of the situation.

In December 2014, the Central Committee of the CPC handed down the *Decision on Several Issues Concerning the Political Work of the Army Under the New Situation*. Since the end of 2014, the whole army had been carrying out the 'four rectifications' of thinking, personnel, organisation and discipline, as well as special clean-up and rectification of cadre work and cadres' work style, inspection and rectification of finances, and promotion of political rectification in the correct spirit of the reinvigoration of political discipline. In February 2015, the CMC formulated the *Overall Deployment Plan for Implementing the Spirit of Armywide Political Work* and issued to the entire army the general plan and mission statement for the implementation of the political army building strategy. The People's Army focused on absolute loyalty, turning the blade inward and scraping the poison out of the bones, particularly in addressing the serious violations of laws and regulations by Guo Boxiong, Xu Caihou and others, and thoroughly eliminating their poisonous influence, and purifying the political ecology. The People's Army focused on cultivating the army's soul and strove to cultivate a new generation of revolutionary soldiers with soul, ability, loyalty and morality, and to forge strong troops with iron beliefs, iron convictions, iron discipline and an iron sense of duty.

The CMC Chairman Responsibility System is a fundamental system for upholding the party's absolute leadership over the People's Army. In order to make the implementation of the CMC Chairman Responsibility System stricter and more practical, in November 2012, the CMC revised the CMC's Work Rules explicitly including the CMC Chairman Responsibility System. In April 2014, the CMC issued the *Opinions on Implementing the CMC Chairman Responsibility System and Establishing and Improving the Relevant Work Mechanisms*, establishing the 'three mechanisms' of requesting instructions, supervision and inspection, and provision of information to service the various requirements of the operating mechanisms of the CMC Chairman Responsibility System. By reforming and reshaping the military leadership and command system, and optimising the scale, structure and composition, a brand new system structure that was more conducive to the implementation of the CMC Chairman Responsibility System could be formed.

Taking the Political Work Conference of the Whole Army as an important jumping-off point, the People's Army of the new era underwent an ideological baptism, repacked its bags and set off again. It thoroughly implemented the Political Army Building Strategy, restored and carried forward the glorious military tradition and work ethic, and effectively channelled political ecology into laying a solid political foundation for army building and reform.

DEEPENING NATIONAL DEFENCE AND MILITARY REFORM

In the face of long-term institutional obstacles, structural contradictions and policy issues that restricted national defence and army building, the Party Central Committee and the CMC took reform as the key to attacking the stubborn diseases that had accumulated for many years, and resolutely eliminated the shortcomings of various systems and mechanisms. By doing so they aimed to reshape the People's Army as a whole and form a powerful position from which to advance reforms and strengthen the army. They deepened the reform of national defence and the armed forces, made great breakthroughs decisively and on a grand scale, proceeding steadily but rapidly, pushing forward with great intensity, and thoroughly reached into every sphere of interest, encompassing an unprecedented field of influence.

In November 2013, the Third Plenary Session of the 18th Central Committee of the party included the deepening of national defence and military reform as a separate section in the decisions of the session, included it in the overall plan for comprehensively deepening reforms, and elevated it to the status of a matter concerning the will of the party and the conduct of the state. In March 2014, the CMC's Leading Group for Deepening Reform of the Army and National Defence, headed by Xi Jinping, held its first plenary meeting. Following that, the relevant work institutions were established to conduct research, provide evidence and draft the reform plan. In July 2015, Xi Jinping chaired and convened the Standing Committee of the CMC and the Standing Committee of the Politburo of the Central Committee to review and approve the *Overall Plan for Deepening National Defence and Army Reform*, and a complete set of solutions to deep-seated contradictions, major innovation breakthroughs, and the distinctive plan for reform of the People's Army emerged fully formed from their cocoon.

In November 2015, the CMC's Reform Work Conference was held to make overall arrangements for deepening the reform of national defence and the military. After the meeting, the CMC issued the *Opinions on Deepening the Reform of National Defence and the Army*, which clarified the guiding ideology, basic principles and overall goals of the reform, drew a road map and timetable for the reform, and laid out a leadership management system and a joint operations command system. It detailed the main tasks of reform, such as the size and structure of the army, the organisation of the army, the training of new-type military personnel, policy systems, the development of military-civilian integration and the command and management systems of the armed police force and their structure. It stated that the rule of military law required efforts to build a system that could be victorious in information warfare and that a modern military force system with Chinese characteristics was necessary to undertake the tasks and missions to further improve the military system in its expression of socialism with Chinese characteristics.

Starting from the end of 2015, the reform of the leadership and command system was carried out first, focusing on breaking down institutional obstacles. In accordance with the general principle of 'the CMC exercising overall leadership, the theatre commands responsible for military operations and the services focusing on developing capabilities' the 15 functional departments of the CMC were all adjusted and reorganised, and the leadership of the ground force, the rocket force, the strategic support force, and the joint logistics support force were all re-established within the management system of the 'CMC-Services-Troops'. They improved the CMC's joint operations command structure, established a joint theatre operations command structure, adjusted the seven military regions to five major theatre commands, implemented joint logistics support system reforms, and built a 'CMC-theatre commands-troops' operational command system. This round of reforms at the top level broke down the long-established systems of general departments, military area commands and the force composition with a dominating ground force, and achieved a historic change in the organisational structure of the military.

Starting from the end of 2016, the scale, structure and strength of the military were reorganised in progressive reforms focused on solving structural contradictions. In accordance with the requirements of adjusting and optimising the structure, developing new types of forces, straightening out overall proportions and reducing the size of the forces, the size of the army was optimised, the total number of active military personnel was reduced from 2.3 million to 2 million, and personnel in administrative and non-combat units were streamlined. They adjusted the overall format of the army, focusing on reducing the size of the ground force, optimising the internal structure of the various services and units, and greatly increasing the proportion of new combat effectiveness; they adjusted the composition of combat forces, implemented the 'group army-brigade-battalion' system for the main combat forces and optimised institutional strength. This round of reforms established a powerful modern military system with Chinese characteristics and promoted the transformation of the military from a quantity-focused organisation to one focused on quality and efficiency, and from a personnel-driven model to a technology-driven model.

Before the 19th National Congress of the CPC, a historic breakthrough was made in the reform of national defence and the army, and a new pattern of 'the CMC exercising overall leadership, the theatre commands responsible for military operations and the services focusing on developing capability' was formed, through which the People's Army organisational framework and power hierarchy were revolutionised.

Technology is the core combat capability of modern warfare. The Party Central Committee and the CMC made strategic plans for innovation in national defence technology. In January 2016, the CMC's Science and Technology Committee was established. In July 2017, at the establishment meeting of the newly adjusted Academy of Military Sciences, the National Defence University, the National University of Defence Technology and a symposium for the main leaders of military academies, scientific research institutions, and training institutions, Xi Jinping proposed to fully implement the strategy of revitalising the army through science and technology, and of relying on technological progress and innovation to shift the models for military construction and generation of combat effectiveness onto the track of innovation-driven development. In August, at a meeting celebrating the 90th anniversary of the founding of the Chinese PLA, Xi Jinping observed that the comprehensive implementation of the strategy of revitalising the army through science and technology would serve to continuously speed up the contribution of technological innovation to the building of the People's Army and the development of combat effectiveness.

In aiming at the world frontiers of military science and technology, the People's Army persisted in striving for technological innovation, relying on the strategic basis of independent innovation, and making a series of strategic deployments around the development of new combat forces; they also accelerated the development of high-tech weapons and equipment, increased the pace of major engineering projects, and accelerated the development of cutting-edge strategic disruptive technologies. By these means, a whole series of remarkable successes were achieved.

Strictly governing the army in accordance with the law is the basis for strengthening the army and an important part of the People's Army's drive to deepen reform and promote modernisation. In October 2014, the Fourth Plenary Session of the 18th Central Committee of the CPC incorporated the rule of law as applied to the army into the overall scheme of the comprehensive rule of law. In December, Xi Jinping emphasised at an enlarged meeting of the CMC that strictly administering the army according to the law was the basic strategy of the party's army building and military administration, the more modern and information-based the army is, the more it needs to be rooted in the law. It was necessary to change the way the military was governed in accordance with the requirements of the rule of law, and to strive to achieve the 'three fundamental changes', namely, changing from relying solely on administrative orders to a fundamental change in administration according to law; changing from relying solely on habit and experience for development to relying on regulations and systems; and changing from a commando-style, activity-based approach to a fundamental shift toward handling affairs according to regulations. In February 2015, the CMC issued the *Decision on Further Promoting the Rule of Law and Strictly Governing the Army Under the New Situation*, making comprehensive arrangements for strengthening the military's rule of law, requiring the establishment and improvement of a system with Chinese characteristics for the rule of law in the military, and the formation of a comprehensive, rigorous and efficient overall military system. The legal system, the military rule of law enforcement system, the military rule of law supervision system, and the military rule of law guarantee system all served to improve the standard of the rule of law in national defence and army building.

In accordance with the requirements of the Party Central Committee and the CMC, the People's Army reformed and made innovations to the two-level military legislative system of the 'CMC - theatre commands, services and arms, and armed police forces', and standardised its legislative powers. In May 2017, the *Regulations on Military Legislation Work* came into effect, providing a legal basis for, and basic compliance with, military legislation in the new era. They promulgated military laws such as the *Law on National Defence Transportation*, revised common regulations such as the *Outline of Army Grassroots Construction* and established regulatory systems and codes of conduct for military construction and development in the new era.

Strict administration of the army started from the implementation of the eight central regulations. In December 2012, the *Ten Regulations of the CMC to Strengthen Its Work Style* were promulgated, and the agencies and leaders of the CMC took the lead. After the 18th National Congress of the

CPC, the CMC decided to establish an inspection system, set up inspection agencies and carry out inspections across the army. As of February 2017, the first round of inspections and return visits to military commission agencies and larger units had been completed. They went on to establish and improve the supervision system of the rule of law, set up a new Commission for Disciplinary Inspection of the CMC and a Political and Law Commission of the CMC, regulated the establishment of the Audit Office of the CMC, implemented station audits and established a system of contact points for supervision of local behaviour. In order to maintain the nature and true qualities of the People's Army, in November 2015, the CMC Reform Work Conference made the decision to completely suspend the military's external paid services. In February 2016, the CMC issued the *Notice on the Complete Cessation of Paid Service Activities of the Army and the Armed Police Forces*, clarifying the intention to systematically stop all paid service activities of the army and military police forces within about three years.

FOCUSING ON THE ABILITY TO WIN BATTLES, AND STRENGTHENING MILITARY TRAINING AND PREPARATION

In the modernisation of national defence and the armed forces in the new era, the Party Central Committee and the CMC focused on preparing for war and taking responsibility for core activities. They took the 'essential criterion of a strong army' as being able to fight and win wars as the core necessity to achieve the party's goal of strengthening the army in the new era. All minds should be focused on combat and all tasks should be combat-oriented in order to comprehensively improve the ability to prepare for war in the new era, and to ensure that the troops can come when they are called on, fight when they arrive, and win when they fight.

At the end of 2012, at an enlarged meeting of the CMC, Xi Jinping clearly proposed that, in order to be prepared for war in the new era, the only fundamental standard was the firm establishment of combat effectiveness, requiring combat effectiveness standards to be integrated throughout every aspect of the entire process of army building. In March 2014, a 'discussion on combat effectiveness standards' was launched throughout the army, with level-by-level inspections and everyone participating in the process. This achieved a high degree of consensus on the training of elite soldiers and the route to victory.

Working from the requirements of actual combat, the People's Army paid great attention to real military combat training, and insisted on using combat to lead training, using training to advance combat techniques and maintaining consistency in combat training. In March 2014, the CMC issued its *Opinions on Improving the Level of Actual Combat Training in the Military* and made a systematic deployment of its recommendations. In the same month, an armywide lead military training supervision group was established to conduct and supervise the army's military training. At the end of 2015, the Military Commission and the theatre commands, the services, and the armed police forces set up training and supervision departments as part of the establishment of a military training supervision system. In November 2016, the CMC issued the *Interim Provisions on Strengthening Actual Military Combat Training*, which put forward firm measures and regulations for the implementation of actual military combat training. The holding to account of units and individuals whose military training was lax and inappropriate caused an improvement in the level of actual combat training of the troops.

To meet the requirements of joint operations, the People's Army further advanced joint operations training to accelerate the improvement of integrated joint operations capabilities. In January 2015, a series of regulations and documents including the *Interim Regulations on Joint Campaign Training of the Chinese PLA* were issued systematically to regulate the organisation and implementation of joint training in various fields and at various levels. In 2016, the establishment of a two-tier joint command organisation of the Military Commission and the theatre commands opened up a new field of joint warfare and joint training with coordination as the key element, which served continuously to improve joint combat capabilities and all domain operations capabilities based on network information systems.

To implement the decisions and deployments of the Party Central Committee and the CMC, the entire army carried out extensive targeted training and military exercises based on missions in various different strategic directions. Each theatre command organised a series of real-time joint military exercises in the 'Eastern', 'Southern', 'Western', 'Northern' and 'Central' theatres; the army conducted extensive military training exercises; the navy expanded long-voyage training; the air force strengthened systematic and real-time, case-based training across its territory; the rocket force organised confrontational test training; there was real-time training at brigade and regiment level; strategic support forces and joint logistics support forces actively integrated into the joint combat system; the armed police forces implemented a series of exercises such as 'Guardians'; the joint training exercises between Chinese and foreign forces were strengthened, as was international military cooperation. All these and other measures helped the People's Army make significant progress in preparations for military conflict. During this period, the

People's Army efficiently carried out major tasks such as maritime rights protection, anti-terrorism and stability maintenance operations, emergency rescue and disaster relief, international peacekeeping, Gulf of Aden escort duties and humanitarian rescue operations. These served to safeguard national sovereignty, security and development interests, and boosted the prestige of the country and our military in the eyes of the world.

5
ADHERING TO 'ONE COUNTRY, TWO SYSTEMS' AND ADVANCING THE REUNIFICATION OF THE MOTHERLAND

MAINTAINING THE LONG-TERM PROSPERITY AND STABILITY OF HONG KONG AND MACAU

'One Country, Two Systems' is a great initiative of the CPC. Entering the new era, the Party Central Committee will study new circumstances and new situations; will properly deal with complex situations; will eliminate all kinds of interference; will fully and accurately implement the 'One Country, Two Systems' policy; will keep a firm grip on the central government's comprehensive governance power over Hong Kong and Macau as granted by the constitution and the basic law; and will deepen exchange and cooperation between the Mainland and the Hong Kong and Macau regions. These actions will carry the practice of 'One Country, Two Systems' on to achieve great and ambitious new successes.

In December 2012, when Xi Jinping listened to a report by the chief executive of the Hong Kong SAR, he solemnly reiterated that the central government's policy of implementing 'One Country, Two Systems' and strictly following the basic law would remain unchanged; the determination to support the chief executive and the government of the SAR in governing and performing their duties in accordance with the law would not change; and the policies to support the development of the economy, to improve people's livelihoods, to promote democracy and to promote harmony in the two SARs of Hong Kong and Macau would also not change. At the same time, he emphasised that the key was to fully and accurately understand and implement the 'One Country, Two Systems' policy, and earnestly respect and maintain the authority of the basic law.

With the full support of the central government, the government of the Hong Kong SAR promoted the reform of the electoral system in accordance with the decision of the 31st meeting of the Standing Committee of the 10th NPC. In June 2014, in response to some people's vague and one-sided understanding of the principles and policies of 'One Country, Two Systems' and the basic law in Hong Kong, the State Council Information Office published a white paper entitled *The Practice of 'One Country, Two Systems' in the Hong Kong SAR*, which systematically explained the central government's basic policy for Hong Kong. The policy highlighted the important viewpoints of the central government's comprehensive governance over Hong Kong and played a role in clarifying the root meaning of the policy. Following the relevant report submitted by the chief executive of the Hong Kong SAR, on 31 August, the 10th meeting of the Standing Committee of the 12th NPC passed the *Decision on the General Election of the Chief Executive of the Hong Kong SAR and the Method for the Formation of the Legislative Council* in 2016, confirming the core elements and institutional framework of the universal suffrage system for the chief executive of the Hong Kong SAR. At the end of September, the illegal 'occupy Central' activity planned by some people in Hong Kong broke out. In the face of the complex and severe situation in Hong Kong, the central government was consistent in fully and accurately implementing the 'One Country, Two Systems' policy, upholding the principle of an uncompromising bottom line, coordinating all parties involved, and fully supporting the Hong Kong SAR government in lawfully quelling the 79-day illegal 'occupy Central' activity and the subsequent 'Mong Kok riot'. In this way, the overall stability of Hong Kong was maintained.

In December 2014, Xi Jinping attended the celebration of the 15th anniversary of Macau's return to the motherland and the inauguration ceremony of the fourth government of the Macau SAR. He observed that to continue to promote the cause of 'One Country, Two Systems', it was necessary to firmly grasp the fundamental purpose of 'One Country, Two Systems', and jointly safeguard national sovereignty, security, development benefits, and the long-term prosperity and stability of Hong Kong and Macau; it was also necessary to adhere to the rule of law in Hong Kong; to guarantee the practice of 'One Country, Two Systems' in accordance with the law; to adhere to the principle of 'One Country' and respect the differences between the 'Two Systems'; to safeguard the central authority and guarantee the high degree of autonomy of the SAR, and give play to the strong supporting role of the motherland. This should be organically combined with enhancing the competitiveness of Hong Kong and Macau, and it should not be neglected at any time. In December 2015, when Xi Jinping listened to the report of the chief executive of the Hong Kong SAR, he further emphasised that the central government must adhere to two points in implementing the 'One Country, Two Systems' policy: first, to be unswerving, unchanging and unshakeable; second, to be precise and comprehensive in guaranteeing that Hong Kong's practice of 'One Country, Two Systems' should not be twisted out of shape or deformed, and should always move in the right direction.

In advancing the practice of 'One Country, Two Systems', the central government attached great importance to the rule of law in Hong Kong and Macau, contained and cracked down on 'independent Hong Kong' forces in accordance with the law, and resolutely safeguarded the core national and fundamental interests of the Hong Kong and Macau SARs. In November 2016, in response to the very few elected members of the sixth legislative council of the Hong Kong SAR who proclaimed 'Hong Kong independence' and engaged in other speeches and actions, the Standing Committee of the NPC took the initiative to interpret Article 104 of the Hong Kong Basic Law and clarified the meaning and obligations of their oath to uphold the law. These were to support the relevant agencies and judicial organs of the Hong Kong SAR Government in prosecuting and passing judgment on certain members, disqualifying them from office, and safeguarding the authority of the rule of law under the Basic Law in Hong Kong. In accordance with the spirit of the NPC Standing Committee's interpretation of the law, the Macau SAR took the initiative to add a 'prevention of independence' clause to the legislative council election law to nip potential trouble in the bud. The central government also took corresponding measures to improve the chief executive's reporting system, exercised its substantive power to appoint the chief executive and principal officials in accordance with the law, and strengthened publicity and education about the national constitution and basic law.

In administering Hong Kong and Macau in accordance with the law, the party and the state focused on overall development strategy, starting from the requirements of maintaining the long-term prosperity and stability of Hong Kong and Macau, actively planning and fully supporting the economic and social development of Hong Kong and Macau, and the improvement of people's livelihoods, and promoting the advantages of Hong Kong, Macau and the Mainland complementarity, mutually beneficial cooperation and common development. In March 2016, the outline of the national '13th five-year plan' clearly proposed to enhance the status and functions of Hong Kong and Macau in the process of national economic development and opening up to the outside world; to support Hong Kong and Macau in participating in the country's two-way opening up and the 'Belt and Road' project; and to promote and upgrade closer economic and trade relations and deepen financial cooperation between the Mainland and Hong Kong. During this period, the central government supported Hong Kong in hosting the 'Belt and Road' Summit Forum and joining the Asian Infrastructure Investment Bank, and supported Macau in hosting the 8th APEC Tourism Ministers' Meeting and the 4th and 5th Ministerial Forums for Economic and Trade Cooperation between China and Portuguese-speaking countries. The central government also issued a series of policies and measures to support the Mainland, Hong Kong and Macau in strengthening exchanges, cooperation and common development. The Mainland and Hong Kong implemented mutual recognition arrangements for funds, and successively implemented financial interconnection policies such as 'Shanghai-Hong Kong Stock Connect', 'Shenzhen-Hong Kong Stock Connect' and 'Bond Connect'. This not only served to steadily promote the opening up of our country's financial market, but also consolidated and enhanced Hong Kong's competitiveness as an international financial centre. Under the comprehensive economic partnership agreement (CEPA) framework, the Mainland signed service trade agreements with Hong Kong and Macau respectively, fundamentally liberalising the trade in financial services. The Mainland and Hong Kong signed investment agreements, and economic and technological cooperation agreements to promote the construction of cross-border infrastructure and the facilitation of customs clearance of people and goods between the Mainland and Hong Kong and Macau.

From 29 June to 1 July 2017, Xi Jinping attended the celebration of the 20th anniversary of Hong Kong's return to the motherland and the inauguration ceremony of the Fifth Government of the Hong Kong SAR; he also undertook an inspection of the Hong Kong SAR. During his stay in Hong Kong, Xi Jinping advanced important concepts, ideas and proposals such as 'three beliefs'[1] 'four leads'[2] and 'four always'[3]. He observed that in the 20 years since Hong Kong returned to the motherland, the practice of 'One Country, Two Systems' had achieved universally recognised success. He emphasised that 'One Country' was the root, and only with deep roots could the plant flourish; 'One Country' was the foundation, and the foundation had to be solid for the project to prosper. It was essential to firmly establish awareness of the concept of 'One Country', to adhere to the 'One Country' principle, and to correctly handle the relationship between the SAR and the central government. Any activity that endangered national sovereignty and security, challenged the central authority and the authority of the basic law of the Hong Kong SAR, or used Hong Kong to infiltrate and sabotage the Mainland, would cross a red line and should never be allowed. Development is a constant theme, the foundation of Hong Kong, and the golden key to solving various of its problems. Backed by the motherland and facing the world, Hong Kong has many favourable development conditions and unique competitive advantages. It was essential to build a socialist system in the Mainland and a capitalist system in Hong Kong, adhering to the foundation of 'One Country' and making good use of the benefits of the 'Two Systems'. These important statements had an important guiding role for the steady and far-reaching practice of 'One Country, Two Systems' in Hong Kong, and for the Hong Kong SAR to improve its governance and planning for long-term development.

From 2012 to 2016, Hong Kong's GDP grew at an average annual rate of 2.6% in real terms, which was higher than the average growth rate of advanced economies over the same period. Hong Kong's status as an international financial, shipping and trade centre was continuously consolidated, and its status as a global offshore Rmb business hub and its function as an international asset management centre were continuously strengthened. Macau's per capita GDP ranked among the highest in the world, and its social projects reached a new level. The successful practice of 'One Country, Two Systems' proved once again that 'One Country, Two Systems' is not only the best solution to the historic problems of Hong Kong and Macau, but also the best institutional arrangement for maintaining long-term prosperity and stability after the return of Hong Kong and Macau. It is feasible, achievable and popular.

PROMOTING THE PEACEFUL DEVELOPMENT OF CROSS-STRAIT RELATIONS

Promoting the peaceful development of cross-strait relations and the reunification of the motherland is an inevitable requirement for realising the great rejuvenation of the Chinese nation. Faced with the difficulties and challenges of the peaceful development of cross-strait relations as they enter the deep-water zone, the complex changes in the situation in Taiwan and the surrounding circumstances, the Party Central Committee maintained a high degree of strategic confidence and strategic determination, holding firm to the correct direction of cross-strait relations, and unswervingly adhering to the government policy concerning Taiwan and the Mainland, firmly grasping the leadership and initiative in cross-strait relations, and promoting major progress in those relations.

In February 2013, when Xi Jinping met with Lien Chan, Honorary

Chairman of the Chinese KMT and people from all walks of life in Taiwan, he emphasised that it was the responsibility of the new CPC Central Committee to continue to promote the peaceful development of cross-strait relations and to promote the peaceful reunification of the two sides. Xi Jinping pointed out that compatriots on both sides of the strait belong to the Chinese nation, and this natural blood bond cannot be broken by any force; the basic fact that both sides of the strait belong to one China cannot be changed by any force; the exchanges and cooperation between the two sides of the strait are unique, and the imperatives of this mutually beneficial interest cannot be suppressed by any force; all Chinese people are determined to stand on their own among the nations of the world through their unremitting labours and this kind of common aspiration of the whole nation cannot be blocked by any force. In June, the Fifth Straits Forum with the theme of *Focusing on Family Love and Sharing Dreams* was held in Fujian. On the Taiwan side, there were 22 counties and cities, 37 sponsors, more than 30 representatives from different sectors and nearly 10,000 people from the grassroots participating in the forum. In October, when Xi Jinping met with the honorary chairman of the Taiwan Cross-Strait Common Market Foundation, Siew Wan-chang emphasised that increasing cross-strait political mutual trust and consolidating a common political foundation were the keys to ensuring the peaceful development of cross-strait relations. The longstanding political differences between the two sides of the strait will eventually, gradually be resolved. The heads of the relevant departments on both sides could also meet to exchange opinions on all matters that concerned cross-strait relations.

In February 2014, after consultations between the two sides of the Taiwan Strait, the Taiwan Affairs Office of the State Council and the Mainland Affairs Commission of Taiwan established a normalised communication mechanism based on the common political basis of the *1992 Consensus*. It has played a positive role in the peaceful development of relations and the promotion of cross-strait exchanges and cooperation in various fields. The signing of the *Agreement on Cross-Strait Services Trade* and other agreements played an important role in promoting the peaceful development of cross-strait relations and enhancing the interests and well-being of compatriots on both sides of the strait. The KMT and the CPC made good use of the platform for regular communications, strove to expand cross-strait economic and cultural exchanges and cooperation, continued to hold cross-strait economic, trade and cultural forums, and formed a number of common recommendations such as 'actively advancing the negotiation and implementation of follow-up agreements on the cross-strait economic cooperation framework agreement'. Most of these initiatives were transformed into the common or separate specific policies and measures on both sides of the strait that have brought tangible benefits to compatriots on both sides. The Mainland adhered to the concept of 'two sides of the strait, one family' and a community with a shared future on both sides of the strait, and continued successfully to host the Cross-Strait Forum, the Annual Meeting of Cross-Strait Entrepreneurs Summit, the Cross-Strait Youth Festival, the 'Shanghai-Taipei City Forum', the Zhongshan Forum and other opportunities for extensive interactive cooperation and platforms for gathering public opinion, and allowing grassroots people to communicate more enthusiastically.

When Xi Jinping and Taiwan leader Ma Ying-jeou met in Singapore on 7 November 2015, they exchanged views on further promoting the peaceful development of cross-strait relations. Xi Jinping emphasised that Chinese people on both sides of the strait are fully capable and wise enough to solve their own problems and jointly make greater contributions to world and regional peace, stability, development and prosperity. Standing at a new starting point for the development of cross-strait relations, both sides of the strait should bear the overall interests of the nation in mind, keep up with the progress of the times, join hands to consolidate the peaceful development of cross-strait relations, and jointly realise the great rejuvenation of the Chinese nation. Xi Jinping put forward four points, emphasising that the common political foundation for both sides of the strait is unshakeable, namely: consolidating and deepening the peaceful development of cross-strait relations, doing more to support the well-being of compatriots on both sides of the strait, and working together to achieve the great rejuvenation of the Chinese nation. This was the first meeting between leaders of the two sides of the strait since 1949. It set a precedent for direct dialogue and communication between leaders of the two sides and opened up new space for the future development of cross-strait relations. Following the consensus reached by the leaders of the two sides of the strait, the Taiwan Affairs Office of the State Council and the Mainland Affairs Council of Taiwan established and launched a 'cross-strait hotline'.

After the Democratic Progressive Party (DPP) came to power in 2016 and the political situation on the island of Taiwan underwent major changes, the momentum of peaceful development of cross-strait relations was severely impacted. In March, when Xi Jinping participated in the deliberations of the Shanghai delegation at the Fourth Session of the 12th NPC, he emphasised that our country's policy on the Mainland-Taiwan issue was clear and consistent, and would not alter because of changes in Taiwan's political situation. In November, Xi Jinping met with Hung Hsiuchu, the then chairman of the Chinese KMT, and emphasised that as long as it was conducive to the promotion of the friendship and well-being of compatriots on both sides of the strait, as long as it was conducive to promoting the peaceful development of cross-strait relations, and as long as it was conducive to safeguarding the overall interests of the Chinese nation, both the KMT and the CPC should do their utmost to ensure matters continue to be handled as well as possible. In appropriately responding to changes in the situation in Taiwan, the Party Central Committee continued to strengthen exchanges and interactions with political parties, organisations, counties, cities and individuals that agree with the *1992 Consensus* on the island; to support the peaceful development of cross-strait relations; to promote cross-strait exchanges and cooperation in various fields and economic organisations; and to integrate development and firmly safeguard the overall situation of peaceful development of cross-strait relations. In June 2015, the State Council revised the *Administrative Measures for Chinese Citizens Travelling to and from the Taiwan Region*, exempting Taiwanese residents from visa procedures for travelling to and from the Mainland and implementing the card-type Taiwan Compatriot Entry Permit. During this period, relevant departments issued more than 20 policies and measures to provide more convenience and create better conditions for Taiwan compatriots to study, work and live on the mainland. In order to provide convenient conditions for Taiwanese youths coming to the mainland for internship, employment and entrepreneurship, the Taiwan Affairs Office of the State Council and relevant provinces and cities established 53 cross-strait youth employment and entrepreneurship bases and model sites, which attracted more than 1,000 Taiwan-funded enterprises and teams. New progress was made in cross-strait education exchanges and cooperation, and cultural exchanges and cooperation became more numerous. Cross-strait trade unions, youth, women, sports, health, religion, clan and folk beliefs, and other fields and sectors continued to exchange views, enhancing the Chinese culture of compatriots on both sides of the strait, and these emotional links further consolidated the foundations of public opinion in favour of cross-strait cooperation.

RESOLUTELY OPPOSING AND CONTAINING 'TAIWAN INDEPENDENCE' SEPARATIST FORCES

The biggest realistic threat to the peaceful development of cross-strait relations are the 'Taiwan independence' forces and their separatist activities. After the 18th National Congress of the CPC, the Central Committee of the party was deeply aware of major changes in the situation in Taiwan, and always focused on the overall and long-term interests of the Chinese nation, firmly safeguarded national sovereignty and territorial integrity, resolutely opposed and curbed any form of 'independent Taiwan' separatist acts, and ensured general stability was maintained in the situation in the Taiwan Strait.

In March 2014, the 'anti-Cross-Strait Service Trade Agreement incident' occurred on the island of Taiwan, which was essentially an 'anti-China' incident instigated and supported by 'Taiwan independence' and other external forces behind the scenes. The process and pace of the peaceful development of cross-strait relations were considerably affected. After the DPP authorities advocating 'Taiwan independence' came to power in May 2016, they refused to recognise the *1992 Consensus* that embodies the one-China principle, unilaterally undermined the political foundation for the peaceful development of cross-strait relations, and condoned support for various forms of 'departure'. The separatist activities of 'de-Sinicisation' and 'gradual Taiwan independence' incited the opposition of public opinion on both sides of the strait, obstructed and undermined cross-strait exchanges and cooperation in various fields, and attempted to rely on foreign opinion to support their ideas, thus posing a severe challenge to the peaceful development of cross-strait relations.

The Party Central Committee remained highly vigilant against all kinds of 'Taiwan independence' activities, resolutely opposed *'de jure* Taiwan independence' separatist activities, resolutely curbed 'gradual Taiwan independence' from eroding the foundations of peaceful reunification and was determined never to leave any room for any form of 'Taiwan independence' separatist activities. Before and after the situation in Taiwan changed, Xi Jinping made many speeches, emphasising that 'Taiwan independence' incites enmity and confrontation among compatriots on both sides of the strait, undermines national sovereignty and territorial integrity, undermines peace and stability across the Taiwan Strait, and obstructs the development of cross-strait relations, which can only bring serious harm to compatriots on both sides of the strait. Compatriots on both sides of the strait must unite in determined opposition to resolutely curb any form of 'Taiwan independence' separatist acts, safeguard national sovereignty and territorial integrity, and never allow the historical tragedy of national division to repeat itself. In this way, the Party Central Committee has drawn a clear red line for the Taiwan authorities and the 'Taiwan independence' forces and formed a powerful deterrent. The Taiwan issue is China's internal affair. The Chinese Government firmly opposes external forces playing the 'Taiwan card' and making waves in the

Taiwan Strait, and resolutely struggles with the negative Taiwan-related trends of certain countries, in order that more and more countries and people come to understand and support the just cause of China's efforts to maintain national unity.

---

1. 'Three beliefs' refers to Hong Kong compatriots believing in themselves, in Hong Kong and in the country.
2. 'Four leads' means that representatives from all walks of life in Hong Kong are expected to take the lead in supporting the chief executive and the new SAR government in governing in accordance with the law; to take the lead in achieving unity; to take the lead in caring for youth; and to take the lead in promoting exchanges and cooperation between Hong Kong and the mainland.
3. 'Four always' refers to: always accurately grasping the relationship between 'One Country' and 'Two Systems'; always acting in accordance with the constitution and the basic law; always focusing on the top priority of development; and always maintaining a harmonious and stable social environment.

6

COMPREHENSIVELY PROMOTING MAJOR-COUNTRY DIPLOMACY WITH CHINESE CHARACTERISTICS AND PROMOTING THE BUILDING OF A COMMUNITY WITH A SHARED FUTURE FOR MANKIND

PROPOSING MAJOR-COUNTRY DIPLOMACY WITH CHINESE CHARACTERISTICS

Entering the second decade of the 21st century, the world's multi-polarisation, economic globalisation, social informatisation and cultural diversification have developed in depth. Emerging market countries and developing countries have risen rapidly, the international balance of power has become more even, and the system of global governance has become even more important. The international structure is evolving rapidly and the world is undergoing major changes and adjustments. The relationship between China and the rest of the world has undergone profound changes. Our country has approached the centre of the world stage as never before, and its interconnection and interaction with the world have become unprecedentedly close. The great rejuvenation of the Chinese nation has entered a critical period. The development and changes of the world and China are both intertwined and turbulent, and China's diplomacy is standing at a new historical taking-off point.

In the face of major changes in the world unseen in a century, the Party Central Committee has meticulously planned our country's diplomatic efforts and proposed that it is necessary to coordinate the domestic and international situations, improve the overall diplomatic structure, comprehensively promote multilateral diplomacy with major countries, neighbouring countries and developing countries, and make diplomatic efforts in a variety of fields. The work to be done is the strategic task of striving for a suitable international environment for building an all-round moderately prosperous society.

In November 2014, Xi Jinping clearly proposed the strategic thinking of advancing major-country diplomacy with Chinese characteristics at the Central Foreign Affairs Work Conference. He pointed out that China must have its own major-country characteristics in such diplomacy. In the interests of consolidating practical experience, it is necessary to enrich and develop the concept of diplomatic work so that our country's diplomatic work has a distinctive Chinese character, Chinese style and Chinese ethos. We must hold high the banner of peace, development, cooperation and mutual benefit; coordinate domestic and international interests; coordinate the two major issues of development and security; firmly grasp the main aim of adhering to peaceful development and promoting national rejuvenation; and safeguard national sovereignty, security and development interests. We must do all this in order to create a more favourable international environment for peaceful development, maintain and extend the important strategic opportunity period for China's development, and provide a strong guarantee for the realisation of the 'two centenary[1]' goals and the realisation of the Chinese dream of the great rejuvenation of the Chinese nation.

The Party Central Committee comprehensively promoted major-country diplomacy with Chinese characteristics and proposed a comprehensive diplomatic framework. In doing so, it advocated the construction of a community with a shared future for mankind; implemented the 'Belt and Road' initiative; initiated the establishment of the Asian Infrastructure Investment Bank; set up the Silk Road Fund; and hosted the first International 'Belt and Road' Initiative High-level Conference and many other multilateral conferences such as the International Cooperation Summit Forum which have promoted reform of the global governance system. Our country's international influence, charisma and creativity have further improved, shaping the unique style of China's diplomacy, embarking on a new path of major-power diplomacy with Chinese characteristics, creating a suitable external environment for realising the Chinese dream of the great rejuvenation of the Chinese nation, and making a major new contribution to world peace and development.

ADVOCATING AND PROMOTING CONSTRUCTION OF A COMMUNITY WITH A SHARED FUTURE FOR MANKIND

In light of the unprecedented changes in the world over the last century, mankind faces many common risks and challenges. Hegemonism, power politics and neo-interventionism have arisen; protectionism and unilateralism have continued to rise; wars, terrorist attacks, famines and epidemics have emerged one after another; traditional and non-traditional security issues have become complex and intertwined; and the world is full of uncertainty. People are worried about the future of mankind and hope that new wisdom will provide new solutions.

In March 2013, Xi Jinping delivered a speech at the Moscow Institute of International Relations, advocating the construction of a community with a shared future for mankind. After that, at a series of other major international occasions, Xi Jinping delivered in-depth elaboration of the concept of building a community with a shared future for mankind, which had an extensive influence on international opinion. In September 2015, Xi Jinping attended the General Debate of the 70th UN General Assembly at the UN headquarters in New York and delivered an important speech. He closely linked the building of a new type of international relations centred on mutually beneficial cooperation with the building of a community with a shared future for mankind, and further enriched and developed the idea of such a community.

On 17 January 2017, Xi Jinping delivered a keynote speech at the annual meeting of the World Economic Forum in Davos. He pointed out that economic globalisation is an objective requirement for the development of socially productive forces and an inevitable result of technological progress. It is not the creation of a few individuals or a few countries. Facing the opportunities and challenges brought by economic globalisation, the correct choice is to make full use of all opportunities, to cooperate to meet all challenges, to guide the trend of economic globalisation, to create a dynamic growth model, a model of open mutually beneficial cooperation, a model of fair and reasonable governance and a model of balanced and inclusive development. As long as we firmly establish a sense of community with a shared future for mankind, work hand in hand, share responsibility and help each other to overcome difficulties together, we will surely make the world a better place and make people happier. On 18 January 2017, Xi Jinping delivered a keynote speech at the UN headquarters in Geneva. Faced with the question of 'what's going on in the world, what do we do?', Xi Jinping put forward the Chinese plan of "building a community with a shared future for mankind, achieving mutually beneficial sharing", systematically explained the theoretical connotations and path to the goal of building a community with a shared future for mankind, and advocated the construction of a clean and beautiful world of lasting peace, universal security, common prosperity, openness and tolerance. This major concept, with a broad international vision and a high degree of responsibility, clarified misunderstandings, demonstrated the path for development, and guided the way forward for the world as it found itself at a crossroads.

Xi Jinping delivers a speech at the Moscow Institute of International Relations

Building a community with a shared future for mankind involves facing major changes in the world unseen in a century and contributing Chinese wisdom and Chinese solutions to various complex problems facing mankind. This has been widely recognised by the international community. In March 2017, *Building a Community with a Shared Future for Mankind* was written into Resolution 2344 of the UN Security Council.

This concept is an embodiment of excellent traditional Chinese cultural wisdom. It embodies the common aspirations and pursuits of all mankind, reflects the inevitable trend of people all over the world yearning for peace, development and prosperity, and has become a vivid banner leading the trend of the times and the progress of human civilisation.

ACTIVELY PROMOTING 'BELT AND ROAD' INTERNATIONAL COOPERATION

The 'Belt and Road' initiative is a great practice of major-power diplomacy with Chinese characteristics. In the autumn of 2013, Xi Jinping proposed the initiative of jointly building the Silk Road Economic Belt and the 21st Century Maritime Silk Road. In November, 'promoting the construction of the Silk Road Economic Belt and the Maritime Silk Road and forming a new pattern of all-round opening up' was included in the *Firm Decisions on Major Issues of Deepening Reform Made by the CPC Central Committee at the Third Plenary Session of the 18th Central Committee*. In June 2014, at the Sixth Ministerial Conference of the China-Arab Cooperation Forum, Xi Jinping officially used the term 'Belt and Road' for the first time, and systematically explained the spirit of the Silk Road and the principles that should be adhered to in the construction of the 'Belt and Road'. The construction of the 'Belt and Road' was formally proposed as a brand-new model of cooperation and a plan for common prosperity and development.

With the introduction of the 'Belt and Road' initiative, the 'Belt and Road' construction plan was launched. In November 2014, the 'Strengthening Connectivity Partnership' host partner dialogue was held in Beijing. Xi Jinping proposed to focus on Asian countries, rely on economic corridors, use transportation infrastructure as the breakthrough mechanism, build financing platforms as the starting point and use suggestions for cooperation with people-to-people exchange as the linking medium. He pointed out that interconnection means to build a comprehensive, three-dimensional, broad interconnected network. It is an open system full of vitality and teamwork, clearly indicating the direction and path of the 'Belt and Road' construction. In December, the Central Committee and the State Council issued the *Strategic Plan for the Construction of the Silk Road*

Economic Belt and the 21st Century Maritime Silk Road. In March 2015, the National Development and Reform Commission, the Ministry of Foreign Affairs and the Ministry of Commerce jointly issued the *Vision and Actions for Promoting the Joint Construction of the Silk Road Economic Belt and the 21st Century Maritime Silk Road*, covering the timeline and background of the 'Belt and Road' construction. The principles of co-construction, frameworked thinking, focus on cooperation, and cooperation mechanisms adhered to the principles of mutual consultation, co-construction and sharing, and strove to achieve policy communication, facility connectivity, unimpeded trade, financing and people-to-people connections. Consequently, a clearer outline of the 'Belt and Road' international cooperation platform was presented to the world.

Construction of the 'Belt and Road' is a major strategic measure of our country's opening up and a top-level design for economic diplomacy. It is also a new platform for exploring new models of global governance and promoting the construction of a community with a shared future for mankind. It has attracted widespread attention and response from the world. In May 2017, the first 'Belt and Road' International Cooperation Summit Forum was held in Beijing. Xi Jinping attended the opening ceremony and delivered a keynote speech, emphasising that the 'Belt and Road' should be built as a road of peace, prosperity, openness, innovation and civilisation. The heads of state and government of 29 countries attended the forum, and more than 1,600 representatives from more than 140 countries and more than 80 international organisations participated in the forum. The leaders' round table summit issued a joint communiqué which reached broad consensus on promoting cooperation among all parties to build the 'Belt and Road'.

As of the end of September 2017, 74 countries and international organisations had signed cooperation documents with China to jointly build the 'Belt and Road'. The countries of the 'Belt and Road Initiative' on joint-building came from Asia, Europe, Africa, Latin America, the South Pacific and other regions.

Under the guidance of clear vision and planning, and with the joint efforts of the people of all the countries along the 'Belt and Road', the construction of the 'Belt and Road' has gradually developed from concept to action and into actual international cooperation. From 2014 to 2016, the total trade volume between China and countries along the 'Belt and Road' exceeded US$3 trillion. China has invested more than US$50 billion in countries along the 'Belt and Road'. As of October 2017, China had signed more than 130 bilateral and regional transport agreements with countries along the 'Belt and Road' and opened 356 international road passenger and freight transport routes with relevant countries; China and 43 countries along the route had direct air flights numbering about 4,200 flights per week; more than 50 China-Europe express rail routes opened, with a total of more than 5,000 trains. The 'steel camel caravan' departing from China reached more than 30 cities in 12 European countries.

FORGING A GLOBAL PARTNERSHIP

To achieve the great rejuvenation of the Chinese nation and promote the building of a community with a shared future for mankind, it is necessary to actively develop global partnerships and expand the convergence of interests with other countries. Based on the various forms of partnerships that have been established with many countries in the world, the Party Central Committee plans to comprehensively promote diplomacy and multilateral cooperation among major countries, neighbouring countries and developing countries, and to forge more inclusive and constructive global partnerships. By building a global partnership network, China's 'truth, affinity and sincerity' will continue to grow bigger and bigger.

Relations between major powers are related to global strategic stability. It is essential to promote the establishment of an overall stable and balanced framework for relations between major powers. As a ballast stone for maintaining world peace and stability, Sino-Russian relations have always been one of the key directions of China's diplomacy. In March 2013, Xi Jinping went to Russia to meet Vladimir Putin on his first visit after assuming the presidency. Since then, China and Russia have maintained frequent high-level exchanges, and the two heads of state have met more than 20 times on different occasions. In July 2017, the two heads of state signed the *Joint Statement of the PRC and the Russian Federation on Further Deepening the Comprehensive Strategic Partnership of Cooperation*, making a comprehensive plan for the development of China-Russia relations, and the Sino-Russian comprehensive strategic partnership of coordination continued to move to a higher level. In terms of Sino-US relations, China has always maintained that, as the largest developing country and the largest developed country in the world, they should accept their responsibilities to mankind, history and the people, and treat their bilateral relations with the utmost seriousness. In June 2013, Xi Jinping visited the US. He met with Barack Obama and they agreed to work together to build a new type of major-power relationship between China and the US. In April 2017, Xi Jinping visited the US again and met with Donald Trump. The two sides established four high-level dialogue mechanisms within China-US relations, covering diplomatic security, comprehensive economics, law enforcement and cyber security, and social affairs and the humanities. China-EU relations have continued to deepen and expand. In November 2013, China and the EU jointly formulated and released the China-EU Cooperation 2020 Strategic Plan. Both parties agreed to work further to promote the development of the China-EU comprehensive strategic partnership. In March 2014, Xi Jinping visited Europe and the EU headquarters. The level of development of China-EU relations has been enriched, and exchanges and cooperation have become deeper, more comprehensive and balanced. The relations between China and European countries are showing an excellent momentum of competitive development and mutual promotion.

China and its neighbouring countries are close to each other, share a common destiny and a respect for each other's virtues, all of which are the foundations for shared development and prosperity. In October 2013, the Party Central Committee held the first symposium since the founding of new China on neighbouring country diplomacy, emphasising the basic policy of such diplomacy, which is to adhere to the principle of being good companions and to maintaining good, peaceful and prosperous relations in order to advance the neighbourly diplomatic ideas of 'friendship, sincerity, mutual benefit and tolerance'. At the Central Foreign Affairs Work Conference in November 2014, Xi Jinping emphasised the need to earnestly pursue success in neighbouring diplomacy and to build a community with a shared future for neighbouring countries. After the 18th National Congress of the CPC, Xi Jinping travelled throughout Northeast Asia, South Asia, Southeast Asia, Eurasia and other regions, essentially attaining a complete set of high-level exchanges with neighbouring countries and playing a leading strategic role in deepening mutual trust and promoting cooperation. We will continue to simultaneously deepen mutually beneficial cooperation and interconnection with neighbouring countries and promote construction of the 'Belt and Road'. Through this construction, neighbouring countries will be better served, and the pattern of interdependence and integration of interests between our country and neighbouring countries will be more stable. The Lancang-Mekong[2] cooperation mechanism was officially launched in 2016. It has become a link to promote friendly exchanges between the people of the six Lancang-Mekong countries and made important contributions to the economic and social development of the countries in the basin.

The huge number of developing countries are our natural allies in international affairs. During his visit to Africa in March 2013, Xi Jinping advanced the concept of 'truth, affinity and sincerity' for Africa for the first time. In October, at the Neighbouring Diplomacy Work Symposium, Xi

Jinping emphasised adherence to the correct view of justice and benefit, and provided as much more assistance to developing countries as was within his capacity. By adhering to the correct concept of justice and benefit, and the concept of true friendship and sincerity, our country has continuously strengthened its unity and cooperation with developing countries. The collective dialogue mechanism with developing countries has been deployed to its fullest extent and cooperation in all directions has reached maximum coverage. In terms of China-Africa relations, at the Johannesburg Summit of the Forum on China-Africa Cooperation in 2015, China proposed and implemented the *Ten Major Cooperation Plans* between China and Africa, ushering in a new era of mutually beneficial cooperation and common development between China and Africa. In terms of China-Arab relations, we have carried forward the spirit of the Silk Road, strengthened the alignment of strategies and actions, and profoundly advanced construction of the 'Belt and Road', driving all-round China-Arab cooperation to a new level. The forward-looking China-Arab strategic partnership of comprehensive cooperation and common development continues to deepen, and the driving mechanism of cooperation is becoming more mature. In terms of China-Latin America relations, we have promoted the co-founding of the China-Latin America and the Caribbean Community Forum and proposed to draw up a new blueprint for China-Latin America cooperation in jointly building the 'Belt and Road'. We are forging a path of cooperation across the Pacific through the ongoing deepening of a comprehensive cooperative partnership of equality, mutual benefit and common development between China and Latin America that will usher in a new era of China-Latin America relations. In September 2015, our country and the UN jointly held a South-South Cooperation Roundtable to promote the development of South-South cooperation to a higher and deeper level and to promote the growth of developing countries.

Party diplomacy, economic diplomacy, humanities diplomacy, civil diplomacy and so on, are the social foundation for the development of relations between states. After the 18th National Congress of the CPC, under the centralised and unified leadership of the Party Central Committee, the political parties, the government, the military, local governments and NGOs coordinated and cooperated with each other to build an environment of great coordination in our country's foreign affairs.

LEADING RECONSTRUCTION AND REFORM OF THE GLOBAL GOVERNANCE SYSTEM

As the balance of international change and global challenges increase, it is an inevitable trend to strengthen global governance and promote reconstruction and reform of the global governance system.

China is a participant, defender and reformer of the contemporary international order, striving to contribute Chinese wisdom and strength to global governance. In March 2014, Xi Jinping attended the Third Nuclear Security Summit held in The Hague, in the Netherlands, and for the first time put forward a 'rational, coordinated and progressive' concept of nuclear security. In November, the 22nd APEC Leaders' Informal Meeting held in Beijing agreed the establishment of a future-oriented Asia-Pacific partnership, launched the Asia-Pacific Free Trade Area process, and approved the *APEC Connectivity Blueprint (2015-2025)*. A total of more than 100 cooperation projects were successfully agreed in nearly 30 fields. At the G20 Hangzhou Summit in September 2016, China led all parties in formulating a series of guiding principles and indicator systems on important issues such as innovative growth, structural reform, multilateral investment, climate change and sustainable development. The *G-20 Leaders Hangzhou Summit Communiqué* was published, and 28 core outcome documents were approved, all of which strongly promoted transformation of the G20 from a crisis response mechanism to one for long-term governance. Our country also successfully hosted diplomatic events such as the CICA[3] Shanghai Summit and the BRICS Summit in Xiamen. Xi Jinping proposed building an innovative, dynamic, interconnected and inclusive world economy, and provided Chinese solutions for solving the various global challenges faced by society.

Our country actively participated in the formulation of governance rules in a number of emerging fields and promoted the reform of unfair and unreasonable arrangements in the global governance system. In October 2013, during his visit to Indonesia, Xi Jinping proposed to establish the Asian Infrastructure Investment Bank. In January 2016, the Asian Infrastructure Investment Bank opened and became the first multilateral financial institution initiated by China. In December 2014, China set up a special Silk Road Fund and began operations focusing on construction of the 'Belt and Road' and promoting infrastructure, resource development, production capacity cooperation and financial cooperation with relevant countries and regions. In July 2015, China promoted the establishment of the New Development Bank, headquartered in Shanghai, to support the infrastructure construction and sustainable development of member countries. With the rise of China's international status, the number of Chinese people holding major positions in specialised agencies of the UN and other important international organisations has continued to increase. In 2016, China's share in the IMF jumped from sixth to third largest. In the same year, the Renminbi was included in the IMF's special drawing rights currency basket. China's power and influence in international discourse have been significantly enhanced.

Group photo of G20 Hangzhou Summit leaders

Our country has constructively participated in solving international and regional hotspot issues, adhered to its position as a developing country, striven to safeguard the common interests of developing countries, and initiated a series of international organisations and cooperation mechanisms with developing countries at their heart. It has achieved full network coverage of multilateral mechanisms in developing countries. Our country earnestly fulfils its responsibilities, abides by international rules, meets international obligations, and takes coordinated actions with the international community to jointly respond to global challenges such as climate change, international counter-terrorism, nuclear safety and international non-proliferation. In addition, our country strongly supports the economic and social development of the Middle East and Africa, contributes to solving the refugee problem, actively participates in the formulation of rules in emerging areas such as the internet, the polar regions, the deep sea, outer space and biosecurity as part of a democratic and transparent global internet governance system. As of September 2017, China has successively carried out in-depth cooperation with more than 70 countries and regions in combating cybercrime, proposed an international anti-drug cooperation programme featuring shared responsibility and social governance, and united countries in carrying out international law enforcement actions such as returning fleeing criminals, recovering stolen goods and combating telecommunications fraud. We fully participated in law enforcement security cooperation within the framework of international and regional organisations such as the UN, Interpol, the Shanghai Cooperation Organisation, China-ASEAN, and so on. We established the Mekong River Basin law enforcement security cooperation mechanism, and the New Asia-Europe Land Bridge Security Corridor International Law Enforcement Cooperation Forum. China firmly supports and actively participates in UN peacekeeping operations and is the country with the largest number of peacekeepers among the five permanent members of the UN Security Council.

RESOLUTELY SAFEGUARDING NATIONAL SOVEREIGNTY, SECURITY AND DEVELOPMENT INTERESTS

On 1 July 2016, Xi Jinping observed in his speech at the celebration of the 95th anniversary of the founding of the CPC, "China does not covet the rights and interests of other countries, nor is it jealous of the development of other countries, but we will never give up our legitimate rights. We do not cause trouble nor are we afraid of anything. No foreign country should expect us to compromise our core interests, nor expect that we will swallow any bitter fruit that harms our sovereignty, security and development interests. The Party Central Committee continues to enrich and develop methods and means to safeguard national interests; to resolutely defend national sovereignty, security and territorial integrity; to firmly curb and crack down on all forms of separatism; to actively protect economic and financial security; to effectively safeguard overseas interests; and to prevent and resolve various risks as they arise. All this provides the strong support necessary for reform, development and national rejuvenation.

China has carried out diplomacy related to Xinjiang and Tibet in a down-to-earth manner, responded to groundless accusations and won the understanding and support of most countries on the UN platform and internationally. We have resolutely defended territorial sovereignty and maritime rights and interests, and effectively curbed all kinds of schemes and actions that violated our country's homeland security. In respect of the

South China Sea issue, we have persisted in a rational, beneficial and disciplined struggle for rights protection. While resolutely responding to interference and intervention by foreign forces, we should also strengthen communication with relevant countries in the region, increase mutual trust, properly handle differences and focus on cooperation. The Chinese government has successively issued a number of official declarations such as the *Statement of the Government of the PRC on Territorial Sovereignty and Maritime Rights and Interests in the South China Sea* and we have reiterated China's position on the South China Sea issue on many international occasions, effectively safeguarding China's territorial sovereignty and maritime rights and interests in the South China Sea. At the same time, we have insisted on resolving specific disputes through dialogue and negotiation, and steadily advanced the consultation process of the *South China Sea Code of Conduct* to stabilise the maritime situation. China has eliminated interference and completed the expansion project of some of the garrisoned islands and reefs in the Nansha Islands (Spratly Islands) as scheduled, and historic progress has been made in safeguarding rights in the South China Sea. The Yongxing (Township) Working Committee and Management Committee of Sansha City, established in July 2014, marked the birth of China's first grassroots government city in the Xisha Islands (Paracel Islands) and reefs, and further established our country's sovereignty in the form of government agencies. Since 2015, the Huayang, Chigua, Zhubi, Yongshu and Meiji Lighthouses have successively been built and put into use, thereby safeguarding our country's sovereignty and maritime rights in the South China Sea. With regard to the Diaoyu Islands (Senkaku Islands) issue, China adheres to principles and conducts reasonable actions on the basis of established history and international law. It has published statements and articles stating that 'the Diaoyu Islands belong to China' on multiple diplomatic occasions and in respected media in several countries, established East China Sea Air Defence Identification Zone of the PRC and carried out enforcement of navigation law in the waters of the Diaoyu Islands. This exercise of national sovereignty in accordance with the law has fully demonstrated the firm determination and will of the CPC, the Chinese Government and the Chinese people to defend the country's territorial sovereignty.

We have actively maintained peace and stability in our surrounding areas and insisted on solving problems through dialogue and consultation. While adhering to principles and continuously improving our management and control capabilities, China insists on negotiating and communicating through diplomatic and military channels to maintain peace and stability in the Sino-Indian border area. Our country actively practices the solution of hot issues with Chinese characteristics, persists in brokering peace and promoting talks, and advances the process of political settlement of the Korean Peninsula issue. China is also actively mediating on the issue of peace and reconciliation in Afghanistan, calling for dialogue between India and Pakistan, and mediating between Myanmar and Bangladesh. These actions have made important contributions to the stability of the regional situation.

We effectively safeguard the security of our overseas interests, protect the security and legitimate rights and interests of overseas Chinese citizens, organisations and institutions, and strive to build a strong security system for overseas interests. In September 2014, the Global Consular Protection and Service Emergency Call Centre of the Ministry of Foreign Affairs was launched, which can provide care and assistance to Chinese citizens who encounter difficulties overseas at any time. In the five years since the 18th National Congress of the CPC, China has also successfully repatriated stranded compatriots from countries with sudden wars or major natural disasters, and successfully organised nine evacuation operations for overseas citizens. As of September 2017, it had handled more than 100 cases of kidnapping or assault of Chinese citizens abroad, and 300,000 other cases of various types requiring consular assistance. Under the overall framework of the construction of our national security system, a unified and efficient security protection system for overseas enterprises and foreign investment has been established. China has also reached a number of agreements or arrangements to facilitate personnel exchanges with other countries. As of September 2017, there were 64 countries and regions that have conditional visa exemption or visa-on-arrival arrangements for ordinary Chinese passports, and 41 countries have concluded agreements with China to simplify visa procedures. It is safer and more convenient for Chinese citizens to travel than ever before and their interests were effectively safeguarded.

---

1. The 'two centenaries' are to commemorate the founding of the CPC in 1921 and of the PRC in 1949.
2. China, Cambodia, Laos, Myanmar, Thailand and Vietnam comprise the six Lancang-Mekong countries. The name Lancang-Mekong is derived from the great Mekong River which flows along their borders whose upper reaches in China (Yunnan and Qinghai provinces) are called the Lancang River.
3. The Conference on Interaction and Confidence-Building Measures in Asia (CICA).

7
THE 19TH NATIONAL CONGRESS OF THE CPC, THE DECISION TO TAKE XI JINPING THOUGHT ON SOCIALISM WITH CHINESE CHARACTERISTICS IN THE NEW ERA AS THE PARTY'S GUIDING IDEOLOGY AND SECURING A DECISIVE VICTORY FOR BUILDING AN ALL-ROUND MODERATELY PROSPEROUS SOCIETY

THE 19TH NATIONAL CONGRESS OF THE CPC

The days from 18 to 24 October 2017 witnessed the 19th National Congress of the CPC in Beijing, with the participation of 2,280 official representatives and 74 specially invited representatives of more than 89 million CPC members across the country.

Xi Jinping made a report entitled *Secure a Decisive Victory in Building an All-Round Moderately Prosperous Society and Strive for the Great Success of Socialism with Chinese Characteristics for a New Era* on behalf of the 18th Central Committee. The theme of the congress was: do not forget the original aspirations, bear the mission firmly in mind, uphold the great banner of socialism with Chinese characteristics, secure a decisive victory in building an all-round moderately prosperous society, strive for the great success of socialism with Chinese characteristics and untiringly struggle to realise the Chinese dream of the great rejuvenation of the Chinese nation.

The congress highly praised the historic achievements and shifts made by the CPC and the state since the 18th National Congress of the CPC. During the last five years, the CPC, with its political courage and strong sense of responsibility, put forward a series of new concepts, new ideas and new strategies, issued a series of important policies and guidelines, implemented a deluge of major moves, promoted a battery of important work, solved multitudes of protracted, unsettled problems, fulfilled the tasks long since unfinished and stimulated historic shifts of the party and the country. The CPC Central Committee with Comrade Xi Jinping at the core bravely faced up to the major risks and tests posed to the party and the prominent problems existing within the party. With tenacious will and quality, the central committee rectified incorrect styles of work, battled against corruption, punished evil-doings and nipped serious hidden dangers within the party and the country in the bud. The political life of the party took on a new look; the party's political ecology took a remarkable turn for the better; its creativity, cohesive force and fighting capacity was notably enhanced; its unity and solidarity became further consolidated; the relations between the party and the masses significantly improved; the party became stronger and more reinvigorated during transformations, providing a solid political guarantee for the development of the party and the country. The last five years smiled at the all-round, groundbreaking accomplishments and profound, fundamental changes.

Xi Jinping reports to the congress on behalf of the 18th Central Committee

The report of the 19th National Congress of the CPC clearly pointed out that the original aspiration and mission of CPC members was to strive for the happiness of the Chinese people and the great rejuvenation of the Chinese nation, which is the fundamental drive for CPC members to forge ahead. Focused on realising the greatest Chinese dream of the great rejuvenation of the Chinese nation in modern times, the report reviewed the course of hard struggles in the century since the founding of the CPC and stressed that we are closer to that goal and have more confidence and capability to realise that goal than ever before. As the saying goes, 'The last leg of a journey marks the halfway point.' The great rejuvenation of the Chinese nation can't be realised hands down. All the party members must be ready to make more arduous, tougher efforts. We must go through great struggles to develop the great party, carry forward the great cause and achieve the great goal. The 'four greats' are tightly interrelated, mutually complementary and interactive, with developing the great party playing a decisive role.

Correctly understanding the historical position and development stage of the party and the people's cause is the fundamental basis to pinpoint the central phased task of the party and formulate its policies and guidelines. The vital political judgment of socialism with Chinese characteristics in the new era was made at the congress. Socialism with Chinese characteristics has entered a new era. It means that the Chinese nation has realised the significant leap from backwardness to prosperity and strength, and has seen the bright prospects of the great rejuvenation of the Chinese nation after experiencing all sorts of hardships since modern times. It means that scientific socialism will be invigorated in China in the 21st century and the great banner of socialism with Chinese characteristics has been held high in the world. It means that the path, theories, systems and culture of socialism with Chinese characteristics have been in continuous development. It has expanded the path for developing countries to strive for modernisation. It offers new choices for countries and nations in the world hoping to accelerate development while keeping their own independence. It has delivered China's wisdom and schemes to solve the common problems of mankind.

The congress put forth that the major problem of Chinese society has become the conflict between people's rising demand for a better life and unbalanced, inadequate development. It is a historic change concerning the overall situation and poses many new requirements for the work of the party and the country. The contradictions between people's rising material and cultural demands and the backward social production, and those between people's rising demands for a better life and unbalanced, inadequate development are the inevitable results of economic and social development.

We should embark on the new journey with high ambitions for new development. The congress, aiming to accomplish the 'two centenary goals', made strategic deployment and arrangements for the new journey to secure a decisive victory of building an all-round moderately prosperous society and building a country of socialist modernisation in a comprehensive way. The report pointed out that the period from the 19th to the 20th National Congress of the CPC was the intersection phase to fulfill the 'two centenary goals'. We should build an all-round moderately prosperous society, realise the first centenary goal and rise on the momentum to set out on the new journey of fully building a modern socialist country and march towards the second centenary goal. Given the international and domestic situations and China's development situation, arrangements can be made in two stages from 2020 to the middle of the century. In the first stage, from 2020 to 2035, socialist modernisation should be basically realised after 15 years of efforts on the basis of building an all-round moderately prosperous society. In the second stage, that is, another 15 years from 2035 to the middle of the century, we should strive to build China into a great modern socialist country that is prosperous, strong, democratic, culturally advanced, harmonious and beautiful.

In accordance with the overall layout of the 'five in one' programme, that is, to promote coordinated economic, political, cultural, social and ecological advancement, the congress made all-round arrangements for economic, political, cultural, social and ecological development. The report pointed out that we should implement a new concept of development and build a modernised economic system; complete the systems whereby the people are the masters of their own affairs and further develop socialist democracy; heighten cultural confidence and promote prosperity and thriving socialist culture; improve people's livelihood and strengthen social governance; step up structural reform of ecological civilisation and build a more beautiful China. The congress also made important arrangements for the construction of national defence and the armed forces, and the work concerning Hong Kong, Macau and Taiwan, as well as foreign affairs. The report stressed persistently seeking the path of building a strong army with Chinese characteristics and promoting the modernisation of national defence and the army; adhering to the 'One Country, Two Systems' policy and advancing national reunification; firmly adopting the path of peaceful development and building a community with a shared future for mankind.

The congress explicitly brought forth the general requirements of party building in the new era, namely:

to uphold the full leadership of the party, adhere to the principle that the party should supervise its own conduct, see to it that self-governance is exercised fully and with rigour, take the construction of the party's long-term ruling ability, advancement and incorruptible nature as the principal line, take the party's political development as the command, stand firm in support of its ideals and principles, mobilise all party members' enthusiasm, initiative and creativity, comprehensively promote the party's political construction, ideological construction, organisational construction, party conduct construction, discipline construction and institutional construction, carry forward anti-corruption efforts, constantly boost the quality of party building and build the party into a vigorous Marxist ruling party always advancing in the forefront of the times, winning people's heartfelt support, bravely exercising self-targeted revolution and withstanding all kinds of tests.

Meeting of the newly-elected members of the Standing Committee of the Politburo with Chinese and foreign journalists covering news of the 19th National Congress of the CPC

The congress approved the passage of the report, the *Constitution of the CPC (Amendment)* and the report on the work of the Central Commission for Discipline Inspection and selected the 19th Central Committee and the Central Commission for Discipline Inspection. The First Plenary Session of the 19th Central Committee of the CPC elected Xi Jinping, Li Keqiang, Li Zhanshu, Wang Yang, Wang Huning, Zhao Leji and Han Zheng as members of the Standing Committee of the Politburo, and appointed Xi

Jinping as general secretary of the Central Committee and chairman of the CMC, and Zhao Leji as secretary of the Central Commission for Discipline Inspection.

ESTABLISHING XI JINPING THOUGHT ON SOCIALISM WITH CHINESE CHARACTERISTICS IN THE NEW ERA AS THE PARTY'S GUIDING IDEOLOGY

Aimed at the long-term development of the socialist undertaking with Chinese characteristics, the 19th National Congress of the CPC prudently brought forward Xi Jinping Thought on Socialism with Chinese Characteristics in the New Era, determined it to be the party's long-term guiding ideology, and included it in the party constitution to ensure the party's guiding ideology keeps pace with the times.

Since the 18th National Congress of the CPC, the Central Committee with Comrade Xi Jinping at the core has systematically answered the major questions as to what kind of socialism with Chinese characteristics should be adhered to and developed, and how to achieve that end, and such questions as the overall objectives, overall tasks, overall layout, strategic layout, orientation, method, motive force, strategic steps, external conditions and political guarantees for development. Besides, based on new practice, it also made theoretical analysis and gave policy guidance in terms of China's economy, politics, the rule of law, science and technology, culture, education, people's livelihood, ethnic minorities, religion, society, ecological civilisation, national security, national defence and army, the 'One Country, Two Systems' policy and national reunification, the united front, diplomacy and party building, and developed Xi Jinping Thought on Socialism with Chinese Characteristics in the New Era.

The report of the congress comprehensively set forth the scientific connotations and practical requirements of Xi Jinping Thought on Socialism with Chinese Characteristics in the New Era via 'Eight Clarifications' and 'Fourteen Perseverances'.

'Eight Clarifications' refers to: clarify that the general assignment to adhere to and develop socialism with Chinese characteristics is to realise socialist modernisation and the great rejuvenation of the Chinese nation, and build China into a prosperous, strong, democratic, civilised, harmonious, beautiful and powerful state featuring socialist modernisation in two steps by the mid 21st century; clarify that the present contradiction in Chinese society is that between the rising demands of the people for a better life and unbalanced, inadequate development, the thought of people-centred development must be followed to incessantly promote people's development in all respects and shared prosperity; clarify that the 'five in one' programme is the overall design of the cause of socialism with Chinese characteristics and the strategic layout is the 'four comprehensives', stressing to strengthen confidence in the path, theory, system and culture; clarify that the general objective of comprehensively deepening reforms is to improve and develop socialism with Chinese characteristics and promote the modernisation and capability of the national governance system; clarify that the general goal of comprehensively advancing the rule of law is to set up the system of rule of law under socialism with Chinese characteristics and build China into a socialist country governed by the rule of law; clarify that the goal of building a strong army in the new era is to build a people's army following the command of the party, competent in winning battles, with a fine style of work and ranking among the world's first-class armies; clarify that diplomacy with Chinese characteristics should promote the construction of a new type of international relations and a community with a shared future for mankind; clarify that the most essential feature of socialism with Chinese characteristics is the leadership of the CPC and the greatest advantage of the socialist system with Chinese characteristics is the leadership of the CPC and the fact that the party is the supreme political leader. The general requirement of party building in the new era was put forward, highlighting the central status of political construction in party building.

'Fourteen Perseverances' refers to: persevere with party leadership over all work, persevere with the principle of taking people as the centre, persevere with deepening all-round reforms, persevere with upholding a new concept of development, persevere with making people the masters of their own lives, persevere with law-based governance of the country, persevere with the socialist core value system, persevere with safeguarding and improving people's livelihood in development, persevere with harmonious coexistence of man and nature, persevere with a holistic approach to national security, persevere with the party's absolute leadership of the people's army, persevere with 'One Country, Two Systems' and national reunification, persevere with building a community with a shared future for mankind and persevere with strict and comprehensive party governance. The 'Fourteen Perseverances' form the basic strategy for persevering with and developing socialism with Chinese characteristics in the new era.

The sound integration and unity of the 'Eight Clarifications' and 'Fourteen Perseverances' reflect the fact that the Central Committee with Comrade Xi Jinping at the core has deepened the recognition of the laws of socialism with Chinese characteristics and reflects the distinctive features of combining theory with reality, and unifying epistemology with methodology. In the new era, we should perfectly implement the party's basic theories, basic guidelines and basic strategies to constantly advance the cause of socialism with Chinese characteristics.

The congress pointed out that Xi Jinping Thought on Socialism with Chinese Characteristics in the New Era is the inheritance and development of Marxism-Leninism, Mao Zedong Thought, Deng Xiaoping Theory, the theory of 'Three Represents' and the Scientific Outlook on Development, the latest outcome of the localisation of Marxism in China, the crystallisation of the practical experience and collective wisdom of the party and the people, the important part of the theory of socialism with Chinese characteristics and the guide to action to realise the great rejuvenation of the Chinese nation by party members and the Chinese people, which should be upheld for the long term and developed continuously. After the guiding role of Xi Jinping Thought on Socialism with Chinese Characteristics in the New Era was determined at the 19th National Congress of the CPC, the constitutional amendment passed at the First Session of the 13th NPC of the PRC in March 2018 incorporated Xi Jinping Thought on Socialism with Chinese Characteristics in the New Era into the constitution, making the state's guiding ideology keep pace with the times and reflecting the common will of the Chinese people of all ethnic groups and the common wish of the whole society.

General Secretary Xi Jinping is the main founder of Xi Jinping Thought on Socialism with Chinese Characteristics in the New Era. With his extraordinary courage, excellent political wisdom and strong sense of mission as a Marxist statesman, ideologist and strategist, Xi Jinping proposed a series of groundbreaking concepts, ideologies and strategies, and played a decisive role and made a decisive contribution to the creation of this ideology.

Xi Jinping Thought on Socialism with Chinese Characteristics in the New Era upholds the Marxist position, views and methods, adheres to the fundamental principles of sound socialism, summarises the experiences and lessons of the worldwide socialist movement, enriches and develops Marxism with brand-new ideology and forms a systematic, sound theoretical system. This thought featuring a serious and complete system, strict logic, with abundant connotations and great profundity shines with the brilliance of Marxist truth. This thought connects Marxist philosophy, political economy and scientific socialism, is connected with history, reality and the future, penetrates into the fields of reform, development and stability, domestic affairs, diplomacy, national defence and party governance, the nation and the armed forces, stands firm in support of ideals and principles, reflects people's sincere feelings and high consciousness and self-confidence, clearly displays the orientation of problem-solving, is brimming with intrepidity and brings the party's recognition of the law concerning the communist party's governance, the law concerning socialist construction and the law of social development of humanity to a new height.

Xi Jinping Thought on Socialism with Chinese Characteristics in the New Era has made original contributions to developing Marxism. It is an open, continuously developing and scientific theory keeping abreast with the times on the basis of combining theory with practice, and is to be continuously developed, enriched and improved with the deepening of the great practice of socialism with Chinese characteristics in the historical process of guiding the great social revolution and self-revolution. Xi Jinping Thought on Socialism with Chinese Characteristics in the New Era comprises his thoughts on building up strong armed forces, the economy, diplomacy, ecological civilisation and rule of law. Practice knows no bounds, and neither does theoretical innovation. Xi Jinping Thought on Socialism with Chinese Characteristics in the New Era, as Marxism in modern China in the 21st century, is sure to realise its innovative development with the changing times and the deepening of practice.

Theoretical arming should closely follow theoretical innovation. To further arm the mind, guide practice and promote work with Xi Jinping Thought on Socialism with Chinese Characteristics in the New Era, the central committee has took implementing this thought as the primary political task after the 19th National Congress of the CPC, took a raft of monumental moves to deepen and fully implement this thought, practically integrated the learning and application of it and unified knowledge, conviction and actions.

AMENDMENT TO THE CONSTITUTION OF THE CPC

Amending the *Constitution of the CPC* was geared to the objective requirement of keeping the party's guiding ideology abreast of the times, the inevitable need to push ahead the undertaking of the party and the country, the strategic move of advancing the new great project of party building and the practical need to implement the spirit of the 19th National Congress of the CPC. Determining Xi Jinping Thought on Socialism with Chinese Characteristics in the New Era as the party's guiding ideology and including it in the constitution were the greatest highlights of the amendment and the most prominent historical contributions. A consensus was reached at the congress that Xi Jinping Thought on Socialism with Chinese

Characteristics in the New Era was determined to be the party's guide to action in the *Constitution of the CPC* together with Marxism-Leninism, Mao Zedong Thought, Deng Xiaoping Theory, the theory of 'Three Represents' and the Scientific Outlook on Development.

The amendment to the party's constitution fully reflected the party's achievements in theoretical, practical and institutional innovations after the 18th National Congress of the CPC and sufficiently manifested the major theoretical viewpoints and strategic thinking determined in the party's report at the 19th National Congress of the CPC. For instance, socialist culture with Chinese characteristics, together with the socialist path, theoretical systems and institutions with Chinese characteristics, was included in the party's constitution; the party's constitution clarified the ambitious goal of realising the 'two centenary goals' and the Chinese dream of the great rejuvenation of the Chinese nation; the party's constitution was amended according to the new major problems prevailing in China summarised at the 19th National Congress of the CPC; plenty of new contents were also included in the party's constitution, for instance, giving full play to the decisive role of the market and the government in resource allocation, pushing ahead supply-side structural reforms, building the socialist legal system with Chinese characteristics, promoting wide-ranging, multilevel and institutional development of consultative democracy, cultivating and practicing socialist core values, stimulating creative transformation and development of fine traditional Chinese culture, tightly controlling leadership over ideology, enhancing and bringing forth new ideas of social governance, pursuing a holistic approach to national security, realising that lucid waters and lush mountains are invaluable assets and, acting on this understanding, continuing to bolster the political loyalty of the armed forces, strengthening them through reform and technology, and running them in accordance with law, building the people's forces into world-class forces that obey the party's command, can fight and win, and maintain excellent conduct, creating a strong sense of community for the Chinese nation, upholding justice while pursuing shared interests, working to build a community with a shared future for mankind and promoting construction of the 'Belt and Road Initiative'. The amendment played a significant role for party members to more consciously and firmly implement the basic theories, guidelines and strategies of the party and better pursue and develop socialism with Chinese characteristics.

The amendments kept the party's guiding ideology abreast of the times, vigorously pushed ahead the development of the party and the country in the new era, and tremendously promoted the new construction of the great party; the amended party's constitution fully reflected the latest outcome of the localisation of Marxism in China, a set of major strategic ideologies put forth by the Central Committee since the 18th National Congress of the CPC and the new experience in the work and construction of the party.

8
UPHOLDING OVERALL PARTY LEADERSHIP AND BOOSTING THE QUALITY OF PARTY BUILDING

The general requirements of party building in the new era proposed in the report of the 19th National Congress of the CPC strengthened top-level design and overall deployment for the new project of party building, clarified the purposes, policies, principal lines, entire layout and objectives of party building for the new era, further answered the historic subject of 'what kind of party-building and how to build such a party', pointed out the direction and basis of ensuring party leadership over all work and improving the quality of party building.

ENSURING PARTY LEADERSHIP OVER ALL WORK

History has provided ample evidence that without the CPC, there would have been no new China and no national rejuvenation. The party exercises overall leadership over all areas of endeavour in every part of the country and is the highest political force. Xi Jinping clearly expounded the core leadership of the party. He stressed: "It is an effort vividly described that 'a myriad of stars surround the moon'. The 'moon' is the CPC." The party's leadership is the fundamental guarantee for doing well in all the work of the party and the country, and is the 'magic cudgel' for the party to overcome all difficulties and risks. The 19th National Congress of the CPC determined "the defining feature of socialism with Chinese characteristics is the leadership of the CPC; the greatest strength of the system of socialism with Chinese characteristics is the leadership of the CPC; the party is the highest force for political leadership" as an important part of Xi Jinping Thought on Socialism with Chinese Characteristics in the New Era. Meanwhile, it included this monumental political principle into the party constitution and prioritised "upholding party leadership over all work" as the basic strategy of upholding and developing socialism with Chinese characteristics in the new era. It is the most fundamental summary of the experience of the CPC and the Chinese people in upholding and developing socialism with Chinese characteristics, and the concentrated embodiment of confidence in the path, theory, system and culture.

Vote by ballot for the Amendment (Draft) to the Constitution of the PRC at the First Session of the 13th NPC of the PRC

The Amendment to the Constitution of the PRC was passed at the First Session of the 13th NPC of the PRC in March 2018. On the basis of determining the party's leadership in the preamble to the constitution, it clearly stipulates in the general principles that the leadership of the CPC is the most essential feature of socialism with Chinese characteristics and strengthens the party's leadership over the whole situation and coordination of all quarters concerned. As the fundamental law, the constitution determines party leadership, reflects the true national conditions of China, enhances the people's awareness of party leadership, effectively implements party leadership in the whole process and in every aspect of the state's work, and ensures the advancement of the undertakings of the party and the country in the right direction.

Overall party leadership is concrete rather than abstract, and must be reflected in every aspect of governance and administration of state affairs, and the design, arrangement and operation of the organisations, systems and institutions of state power to ensure its full coverage and to further strengthen it. In practice, efforts should be made to unceasingly improve the system of upholding overall party leadership and strengthen the leading position of party organisations among its counterparts. The party committees (groups) set up in state organs, public institutions, mass organisations, social organisations, corporations and other organisations should abide by the unified leadership of the party committees that approved their establishment, regularly report back on their work and ensure the implementation of the party's guidelines, policies, decisions and deployment. Accelerated efforts should be made to set up and complete party organisations in new types of economic and social organisations to ensure full coverage of party organisations for party work.

The Fourth Plenary Session of the 19th Central Committee of the CPC held in October 2019 prioritised upholding and improving the institutional system of party leadership, highlighted its dominant position and focused on oversight over the crucial points of national governance. The decision of the plenary session stressed, 'the party should exercise overall leadership, coordinate work in all areas and exercise its leadership in all areas, respects and links of state governance'. It provides a vigorous institutional guarantee for enhancing overall party leadership in the new era.

In October 2020, the Fifth Plenary Session of the 19th Central Committee of the CPC took upholding the party's overall leadership as the primary principle to be followed for the economic and social development in the 14th 'five-year plan' period, clarified that we must adhere to and improve the institutions and mechanisms of the party leading economic and social development, and the system with Chinese characteristics, continuously improve the ability and level of implementing new development philosophy and building a new development pattern, thereby providing a fundamental guarantee for high-quality development.

UPHOLDING THE AUTHORITY OF THE CENTRAL COMMITTEE AND ITS CENTRALISED, UNIFIED LEADERSHIP

Local affairs should be handled under centralised party leadership. The Central Committee is the 'commander-in-chief' in the big picture of the state governance system and the pillar of socialism with Chinese characteristics. Upholding the overall leadership of the party is to uphold the centralised, unified leadership of the Central Committee. It is the overarching principle of party leadership and the most fundamental political rule which should not be neglected or shaken at any time. We should grasp the major issues and let go of the minor ones. As Xi Jinping stressed, we must strengthen our consciousness of the need to maintain political integrity, think in big-picture terms, follow the leadership core, and keep in alignment (the 'Four Consciousnesses'). Our entire party must strengthen our confidence in the path, theory, system, and culture of socialism with Chinese characteristics (the 'Four Confidences'), guarantee the unity, solidarity and action in concert of the entire party, and ensure that the party exercises overall leadership and coordinates work in all areas. After the 19th National Congress of the CPC, the Central Committee lodged a series of specific requirements for upholding the core position of General Secretary Xi Jinping on the Central Committee and in the party as a whole, and upholding the Central Committee's authority and its centralised, unified leadership (the 'Two Upholds').

In October 2017, the meeting of the Politburo of the Central Committee of the CPC reviewed *Several Provisions of the Politburo of the Central Committee of the CPC on Strengthening and Upholding the Centralised and Unified Leadership of the Central Committee* and pointed out that the Politburo should take the lead in establishing the 'Four Consciousnesses', strictly abide by the party constitution and the party's political criteria, fully implement all the requirements of the 19th National Congress of the CPC to enhance and maintain the centralised, unified leadership of the Central Committee, consciously fulfil the responsibilities, carry out work under the centralised, unified leadership of the Central Committee with Comrade Xi Jinping at the core and firmly uphold the core position of General Secretary Xi Jinping on the Central Committee and in the party as a whole. According to the *Provisions*, all the members of the Politburo should give a written annual report on their work to the Central Committee and General Secretary Xi Jinping, which has been an important institutional arrangement to strengthen and uphold the centralised, unified leadership of the Central Committee.

In August 2018, the *Regulations of the CPC on Disciplinary Measures* amended and issued by the Central Committee added the contents of 'Two Upholds' and 'Four Consciousnesses', made specific regulations about doing away with such actions as being inconsistent with the Central Committee on major principles, keeping hold of a mountain-stronghold mentality, insufficiently implementing the decisions and arrangement of the Central Committee, bending the rules and behaving in a double-dealing and duplicitous manner, and provided powerful disciplinary guarantees for the party organisations, members and contingents of officials at all levels to maintain a high degree of consistency with the Central Committee in terms of political stance, orientation, principle and path, and for the party members to strictly enforce orders and prohibitions.

In January 2019, the Central Committee issued the *Opinions on Strengthening the Political Construction of the CPC* which was a vital policy decision made by the Central Committee to strengthen the party's political construction in the new era. The *Opinions* further took 'Two Upholds' as the primary task of strengthening the party's political construction and stressed that, to uphold and strengthen the overall party leadership, the most important thing is to firmly maintain the authority and centralised, unified leadership of the Central Committee and the most crucial thing is to resolutely maintain the core position of General Secretary Xi Jinping on the Central Committee and in the party as a whole. Concurrently, the Central Committee issued the *Regulations of the CPC on Requesting Instructions and Reporting on Major Matters* stressing that reports must be made to the Central Committee on the major policies and guidelines relating to the overall work of the party and the country, the major principles and problems in the construction of the economy, politics, culture, society, ecological civilisation and the party, the issues under the centralised, unified management of the Central Committee over national security, the compatriots of Hong Kong, Macau and Taiwan, foreign affairs, national defence, and the army and other major issues that can only be led and decided by the Central Committee. The *Regulations* boast great significance for firmly implementing the 'Two Upholds', ensuring the solidarity, unity and action in concert with the entire party and fully promoting the institutionalisation and normalisation of reporting in comprehensive and sound ways.

The Fourth Plenary Session of the 19th Central Committee of the CPC explicitly set forth 'fully improving the systems of firmly maintaining the authority and the centralised, unified leadership of the Central Committee' and stressed pushing the entire party to boost the 'Four Consciousnesses', strengthening the 'Four Confidences', fulfilling the 'Two Upholds', consciously keeping a high degree of consistency with the Central Committee with Comrade Xi Jinping at the core in thinking, politics and acting in concert, and practically implementing the maintenance of General Secretary Xi Jinping's core position on the Central Committee and in the party as a whole. Efforts should be made to improve the leadership system of the Central Committee leading major work, strengthen the role of the Central Committee in decision-making and consulting, improve the mechanism of implementing the major decisions of the Central Committee and strictly implement the system of reporting to the Central Committee for strict enforcement of orders and prohibitions. Efforts should be made to safeguard the party's centralised and unified organisational system, form a rigorous system featuring thorough connection of the organisations of the Central Committee and the local areas, and at the grassroots level, and its powerful enforcement. The system provides vigorous guarantees for strengthening the authority and centralised, unified leadership of the Central Committee.

In September 2020, the Central Committee issued the *Regulations on the Work of the Central Committee of the CPC* which stipulated that upholding party leadership over all work and ensuring centralised, unified leadership of the Central Committee should be taken as its primary principle to carry out its work. It also stressed that the Central Committee, the Politburo and the Standing Committee of the Politburo are the central pivots of the party's organisational system and should chart our course, craft overall plans, design policy, and promote reform in carrying forward the socialist undertaking with Chinese characteristics. Only the Central Committee has the right to decide and explain the issues relating to the entire party and the whole country. The *Regulations* prioritised cementing the work of the Central Committee and the status, organisation, authority and methods of its leadership as well as its decision-making, deployment and self-construction so as to provide the fundamental basis to secure the centralised, unified leadership of the Central Committee over the work of the party and the country.

Upholding the core position of General Secretary Xi Jinping on the Central Committee and in the party as a whole, as well as the authority and the centralised, unified leadership of the Central Committee is the major political achievement and invaluable experience of seeing governance over the party exercised fully and rigorously. All departments and all regions should carefully implement the requirements of the Central Committee, formulate and issue specific regulations and methods relating to the 'Two Upholds' according to the realities. Guidance should be given to party members and cadres for their learning to boost the 'Four Consciousnesses', strengthen the 'Four Confidences' and fulfil the 'Two Upholds'. Through their continuous efforts, their political stance, consciousness and competence have seen remarkable improvement, the party's solidarity and unity have been consolidated and the decision-making authority of the Central Committee has been secured.

GIVING TOP PRIORITY TO PARTY POLITICAL CONSTRUCTION

The party's political construction decides the direction and effects of party building and is the 'soul' and 'foundation' of party building. In October 2017, the 19th National Congress of the CPC proposed the main topic of the party's political building, included it into the overall layout of party building, gave top priority to it, clarified its strategic position in the new era and grasped the fundamental problem of seeing governance over the party exercised fully and rigorously. It stressed: the party's political building is the fundamental construction of the party and decides the orientation and effects of party building. It is the primary task of the party's political building to ensure that the entire party obeys the Central Committee and upholds its authority and centralised, unified leadership. All party members must closely follow the party's political line, strictly observe its political discipline and rules, and closely align themselves with the Central Committee in terms of political stance, direction, principles and path. We must foster values like loyalty, honesty, impartiality, adherence to fact, and integrity; guard against and oppose self-centred behaviour, decentralism, behaviour in disregard of the rules, a silo mentality, nice-guyism, sectarianism, factionalism and patronage. We must resolutely oppose double-dealing and duplicity.

The *Opinions of the CPC Central Committee on Strengthening the Party's Political Construction* clearly pointed out that strengthening the party's political building is aimed at cementing political belief, strengthening political leadership, boosting political competence, purifying political ecology and realising solidarity, unity and action in concert with the entire party. The *Opinions* implemented and reflected the fundamental requirements of the 'Two Upholds', gave full play to the commanding role of the party's political building in every aspect of party building, and applied political standards and requirements in this process. The *Opinions* stressed fulfilling the 'Two Upholds' with correct understanding and actions and resolutely preventing and rectifying the erroneous words and deeds deviating from the 'Two Upholds'.

The National Conference on Inspection Work, that is, the Third Round of the Inspection Work Mobilisation and Deployment Conference of the 19th Central Committee, was held in March 2019. It stressed carefully carrying out political supervision over the inspection work in the new era, urging fulfilment of the fundamental task of the 'Two Upholds', tightening political discipline and rules, removing formalism and bureaucratism, stimulating materialisation and normalisation of political supervision, and driving implementation of the Central Committee's fundamental policies.

At the meeting of democratic life of the Politburo held in December 2020, Xi Jinping further stressed enhancing political consciousness, handling problems from a political perspective, grasping the overall political situation and constantly improving political judgment, perception and power of execution.

To fulfil these requirements, the Central Committee focused on the party's political attributes, mission, objectives and political pursuits, guided the entire party to boost the 'Four Consciousnesses', strengthen the 'Four Confidences', fulfil the 'Two Upholds' and bear in mind the country's most fundamental interests, integrated the party's political building in the whole process of making and fulfilling the major decisions and deployments of the party and the country, continuously implemented the supervision, examination and accountability mechanisms on the major decisions and deployments of the Central Committee and the important instructions of General Secretary Xi Jinping, strictly looked into issues in violation of the party's political line and that destroyed the party's centralism and unity, and saw governance over the party exercised fully and rigorously, and developing in depth and breadth with political measures.

INTENSIFYING AND ADVANCING THE PARTY'S SELF-REVOLUTION

The CPC can lead the Chinese people to carry out great social revolution and self-revolution. Bravely conducting self-revolution is the most distinctive characteristic of the CPC and the political gene in the blood of CPC members. The fundamental reason for the CPC to become the backbone of the Chinese people and the Chinese nation is that it has always kept the spirit of self-revolution, redressed its own disadvantages and solved its own problems.

Efforts should be made to advance the self-revolution of the party. The report of the 19th National Congress of the CPC clarified the general layout of party building, "We should fully promote the political, ideological, organisational construction, party conduct and discipline development of the party, implement institutional improvement and combat corruption." Xi Jinping pointed out: "We must uphold the party constitution as our fundamental rules, give top priority to party political work, combine efforts on ideological work and institution building, and strengthen every aspect of party competence. We will continue to strengthen the party's ability to purify, improve, and reform itself. We must demonstrate greater political awareness of the fact that full and rigorous self-governance is a never-ending journey, we must continue advancing the great project of party building in the new era and must ensure that the party preserves its essence, colour and character."

The ideological construction is the basic construction of the party. An important reason why the CPC can grow through difficulties and hardships is that our party has always attach importance to ideological and theoretical party building. The 19th National Congress of the CPC stressed giving top priority to standing firm in support of the ideals and principles in ideological party building, arming the entire party with Xi Jinping Thought on Socialism with Chinese Characteristics in the New Era, giving education and guidance for the entire party to firmly bear in mind the party's tenets and solving the fundamental issues. In only a week after the closing of the 19th National Congress of the CPC, Xi Jinping led the Standing Committee of the Politburo to visit the former site of the First National Congress of the CPC in Shanghai and the Red Boat in the Southern Lake, Jiaxing prefecture-level city, Zhejiang Province to review the history of party building and the oath to be a party member, declaring the firm political convictions of the new leading group. Xi Jinping pointed out: only when we do not forget our original aspirations, firmly bear in mind our mission and strive forever can we make the party always young and vigorous. The campaign on the theme of 'staying true to our founding mission' was launched from the top down among the entire party in two batches in late May 2019. It is the practice of the party to reform itself and ensure strict self-governance in all respects.

The Liuzhou Steel Group in the Guangxi Zhuang Autonomous Region organises party members to review their oath to join the party

To consolidate the achievements of thematic education, the Fourth Plenary Session of the 19th Central Committee of the CPC brought forth the view of establishing the system of not forgetting our original aspirations and staying true to our founding mission so as to regularise and institutionalise the requirements for all party members. In September 2020, the

General Office of the CPC Central Committee (hereinafter referred to as the General Office) issued the *Opinions on Consolidating and Deepening Educational Achievements on the Theme of 'Remain True to Our Original Aspiration and Keep Our Mission Firmly in Mind'* to promote the implementation of various results of thematic education.

While doing a good job of centralised intraparty education, the Central Committee persistently organised learning and education among party members, promoted party organisations at all levels to cement ideological building, armed the entire party with Xi Jinping Thought on Socialism with Chinese Characteristics in the New Era, and organised party members and cadres to study *Xi Jinping: The Governance of China* and excerpts from a series of key statements and important reading materials such as the *Outline for Studying Xi Jinping Thought on Socialism with Chinese Characteristics in the New Era*. Party members and cadres read original works, studied original texts, achieved enlightenment, constantly cemented the foundations of their belief, strengthened spiritual building and steered their ideology in the correct direction.

The party's organisational line for the new era was implemented. The party's power came from organisations. Stronger organisation redoubled the party's power. At the National Conference on Organisational Work in July 2018, Xi Jinping proposed and set forth the party's organisational line in the new era and pinpointed the direction of advancement of party building and organisational work in the new era. The organisational line of the party in the new era is to fully implement Xi Jinping Thought on Socialism with Chinese Characteristics in the New Era, focus on organisational system construction, put forth efforts to cultivate loyal, pure and responsible cadres of high calibre, exert ourselves to attract outstanding, dedicated, patriotic talent with both political integrity and professional competence, adopt a morality-oriented talent policy and appoint people on their merits to provide solid organisational guarantees to uphold and strengthen party leadership in all respects, and to uphold and develop socialism with Chinese characteristics. The proposal of the organisational line of the party in the new era provided a sound basis for enhancing the party's organisation building and an important guarantee for boosting the party's creativity, coherence and fighting capacity. Led by the party's organisational line in the new era, the party's organisation building has been continuously reinforced thanks to persistent rectification of weak and slack primary party organisation, overall progress and perfect mastery of grassroots party organisations. A group of excellent party members has emerged, namely, Zhang Guimei, Zhong Nanshan, Huang Wenxiu, Zhang Fuqing, Zheng Derong and Zhang Liming; the 'Hard-Boned Sixth Company', the party committee of Beijing Ditan Hospital Affiliated to Capital Medical University and the general party branch of Qingheju Community, Gongren Village, Qingshan District, Wuhan. Nationwide advanced grassroots party organisations have played a positive role as the stronghold of fighting. As of 5 June 2021, the total CPC membership reached 95.148 million, there were 4.864 million grassroots party organisations, among which 273,000 were grassroots party committees, 314,000 were party general branches and 427,700 were party branches. The party's political leadership, ideological guidance, mass organising capacity and social appeal have been unceasingly beefed up.

The party's style of work is the image of the party and the barometer of the relations between the party and the people, and the feelings of the people. The first meeting of the Politburo after the 19th National Congress of the CPC listed party conduct construction on its work agenda, reviewed the *Detailed Rules of the CPC Politburo to Implement the Eight-Point Decision on Improving Party and Government Conduct*, further standardised, detailed and improved related contents according to the new circumstances and new problems during the implementation of the eight-point decision of the Central Committee in the past years, became more geared to practical work, provided more guidance and enabled more operability. It solved the prominent problems of formalism and bureaucratism, prioritising grassroots burden alleviation as the key point of party conduct construction. In March 2019, the General Office of the CPC Central Committee issued the *Notice to Solve the Prominent Problem of Formalism for Grassroots Burden Alleviation* which clearly defined the year of 2019 as the 'Year of Grassroots Burden Alleviation'. In April 2020, the General Office issued the *Notice to Persistently Remove Formalism Troubling the Grassroots and Provide a Strong Party Conduct Guarantee for Decisive Victory in Building an All-Round Moderately Prosperous Society*. In October 2020, the Fifth Plenary Session of the 19th Central Committee of the CPC set forth 'continuously rectifying formalism and bureaucratism, and practically alleviating the burden of the grassroots'. Party conduct construction started from details, focused on constant and long-term efforts, delivered practical work and let the entire party and the people see the changes and hopes from the actual effects of party conduct improvement, establishing the party's credibility and winning popular support for seeing governance over the party exercised fully and rigorously. An opinion survey by the National Bureau of Statistics (NBS) shows that 95.7% of people thought the eight-point decision was effectively implemented and the practices of formality for formality's sake, bureaucratism, hedonism and extravagance were successfully rectified in 2020, 14.4% up over 2013; 95.8% of people thought that the effort of seeing governance over the party exercised fully and rigorously was quite effective in 2020, 16.5% up over 2012.

Discipline should become the high-tension line. Discipline enforcement is the fundamental solution to seeing governance over the party. The party should exercise effective self-supervision and practice strict self-governance in every respect according to strict discipline and rules, pushing party members to draw red lines in ideology and define boundaries for behaviour. All departments and all regions launched discipline education campaigns, incorporated intraparty disciplinary punishment rules into the contents of learning from the Theoretical Studies Centre of the Party Committee (Group) and the courses of party schools, profoundly analysed typical cases of cadres committing severe disciplinary violations, gave scope to its warning, frightening and educational effects, cultivated and guided party members and cadres, especially leading cadres, to strictly discipline themselves according to the party constitution so as to raise their consciousness of discipline, the party constitution and party rules, to know the boundaries and baseline, turn heteronomy into inherent pursuit and develop a good habit of abiding by the party constitution and party discipline. The Politburo stressed in a meeting in July 2018 that efforts should be made to consolidate and develop normalised achievement in strict discipline enforcement and strict punishment for severe discipline violation, establish institutions, establish rules, give priority to implementation and enforcement, fully implement rules and discipline, give full scope to the role of disciplinary construction as a weapon for addressing both symptoms and root causes, genuinely turn iron discipline into consciously-followed daily practice of party members and cadres, and further promote governance over the party in depth and breadth.

The system is fundamental and long-term. In February 2018, the Central Committee issued the *Formulation of Intraparty Rules of the CPC in the Second Five-Year Plan (2018-2022)* to meet the requirements of upholding and strengthening overall party leadership and promoting party building in all respects led by political party building, and made top-level planning for intraparty institutional improvement in the next five years. The Central Committee paid more attention to boosting intraparty regulation enforcement, clarified the rigid standards of the institutions and prevented the institutions from becoming 'scarecrows'. In September 2019, the Central Committee issued the *Regulations on the Responsibility for Regulation Enforcement Within the CPC (Trial)*. The *Regulations* clarified the responsibilities of party organisations, members and cadres of all levels and kinds for execution, raised requirements for supervision, examination and responsibility investigation, and was an important move to fundamentally address the problem of 'hard execution' of intraparty regulations and to promote full, deepened implementation of intraparty regulations. The *Regulations*, together with the concurrently issued *Rules on Making Laws and Regulations Within the CPC* and *Rules on Recording and Reviewing Laws and Normative Documents Within the CPC*, further conducted a whole chain of institutional norms for work relating to intraparty regulations and became the 'rules' of making and implementing party regulations. In order to continue to tweak the responsibility system, which is the 'oxe's nose[1]' of strict party governance, the General Office issued the *Regulations on the Entire Responsibility of the Party Committee (Group) to Oversee Party Governance* in March 2020. As of May 2021, there were 210 laws and regulations within the CPC Central Committee, 162 inner-party laws and regulations of ministries and commissions, and 3,210 local party regulations, forming a system of inner-party laws and regulations with the party constitution as the foundation, the standards and regulations as the backbone, and covering all aspects of party leadership and party building.

The construction of party conduct, and honest and clean government, and the struggle against corruption are always ongoing. After the 19th National Congress of the CPC, Xi Jinping stressed that corruption, the top risk of the party in power, still existed and was open to increase; the situation was still severe and complex; the construction of the party and of an honest and clean government, and the struggle against corruption should be pushed ahead without any letup. The Central Committee persistently struggled against corruption, adopted a tough stance against corruption, continued to see that there were no no-go zones, that no ground was left unturned, and no tolerance was shown for corruption. We imposed tight constraints, maintained a tough stance and a long-term deterrence, punished both those who took bribes and those who offered them. We looked into and resolutely punished daredevils who didn't stop their wrongdoing after the 18th National Congress of the CPC and especially after the 19th National Congress of the CPC. We continuously redressed the issues of corruption and bad party conduct, and thoroughly investigated the 'protective umbrella' for the corruption in poverty alleviation, people's livelihood and gang-related criminality. In order to stamp out official corruption, we strengthened deterrence so they didn't dare to be corrupt, strengthened the cage of institutions so they were unable to be corrupt, and strengthened vigilance over them so they had no desire to be corrupt, while concurrently rectifying incorrect styles of work, combating corruption, deepening reform, improving institutions, stimulating interconnected governance, integrating those who exercised public power into the scope of unified supervision and realising full coverage and not turning a blind eye to combating corruption. More efforts should be made to deepen reform through cases, take cases as a mirror, enhance education on party spirit and clean government, and the awareness so that they have no desire to commit acts of corruption. With the unswerving efforts of the entire party, a sweeping victory in the fight against corruption has been secured and comprehensively consolidated. The outstanding contradictions and problems within the party were purified.

The supervision system of the party and the country is an important institutional guarantee for the party to realise self-purification, self-improvement, self-innovation and self-development under the conditions of holding long-term power. After the 19th National Congress of the CPC, integrated efforts were made to promote reform of the party's discipline inspection system, the state's supervision system and the discipline inspection and supervision authorities, and to increasingly improve methods of power supervision fully covering discipline inspection and supervision, monitoring, stationed supervision and inspection tours; to give full play to the role of intraparty supervision as the political leader and integrate supervision into regional governance, departmental governance, trade association governance, grassroots governance and company governance; to promote integrated implementation of the entity responsibilities of the party committees (groups), the responsibilities of the party secretaries as the people primarily responsible and the responsibilities of the discipline inspection commissions; to persist in the dominance of intraparty supervision, continuously improve the power supervision system and promote organically connected and coordinated supervision by people's congresses, democratic supervision, administrative supervision, judicial supervision, auditing supervision, accounting supervision, supervision by statistical means, public supervision, and supervision through public opinion to form a resulting force of normal, long-term effects. In October 2019, the Fourth Plenary Session of the 19th Central Committee of the CPC made significant institutional arrangements for 'upholding and improving the supervision system by the party and the state, and strengthening the restrictions and supervision of power operation', clearly proposed to establish the supervision system featuring unified party leadership, full coverage, authority and high efficiency, enhanced the seriousness, cooperation and effectiveness of supervision, formed a power operation mechanism featuring sound decision-making, resolute execution and forceful supervision, and set up an integrated mechanism so that power executors dared not, could not and had no desire to commit acts of corruption, and ensured that the power endowed by the party and the people was always used to seek happiness for the people. In March 2021, the Central Committee issued *Opinions on Strengthening the Supervision of the 'Top Leaders' and the Leading Groups*, proposing to improve the system of party and state supervision, to promote active supervision and conscious acceptance of supervision, and to form a pattern of paying attention to each level and implementing supervision at all levels.

---

1. 'Oxe's nose' means the crux of a matter, or the key to resolving a problem.

9

TAKING NEW STEPS TO BUILD STATE INSTITUTIONS AND GOVERNANCE SYSTEMS

SYSTEMATIC AND HOLISTIC RESTRUCTURING OF THE PARTY AND STATE ORGANISATIONAL STRUCTURE AND MANAGEMENT SYSTEM

The Central Committee listed deepening the institutional restructuring of the party and the state on its agenda to uphold and strengthen party leadership, to adhere to and improve the socialist system with Chinese characteristics, and to promote the modernisation of the state governance system and capacity by fulfilling the functions of the party and state institutions. In February 2018, the Third Plenary Session of the 19th Central Committee of the CPC passed the *Decision of the CPC Central Committee on Institutional Reform of the Party and the State*, and the *Scheme to Deepen Institutional Reform of the Party and the State*, and made overall arrangements in five respects such as improving the institution of overall party leadership, optimising the government and functional setup, reorganising institutions across the party, government and armed forces, and society as a whole in an integrated manner, making a reasonable layout of local agencies and promoting legalisation of the size of government bodies. On 17 March, the First Session of the 13th NPC approved the institutional reform of the State Council. The overall goal of comprehensively deepening reform is to establish the institutional restructuring system of the party and the state featuring a complete system and sound, standard and efficient operation, to form a party leadership system providing overall leadership and coordinating the efforts of all involved, a government governance system featuring clearly defined responsibility and law-based administration of government, world-class armed forces with Chinese characteristics, the mass work system of wide connection with the people and serving the people, to promote the NPC, the government, the CPPCC, the supervisory organs, the judicial organs, the procuratorial organs, people's organisations, enterprises and public institutions as well as social organisations to take concerted actions, to enhance synergy under unified party leadership and comprehensively boost the governance capacity and level of the state. The goal attaches importance to solving the issues of long-term mechanism and creates advantageous conditions for improving the socialist system with Chinese characteristics.

Deepening institutional reform of the party and the state is the first formidable task to implement the decision and arrangements of the party after the 19th National Congress of the CPC and a systematic and integral restructuring of the organisational structure and the management system of the party and the state. After the Third Plenary Session of the 19th Central Committee of the CPC, all reforms and deployments were rapidly implemented in unity from the Central Committee to the local governments and made solid progress. In March 2018, the newly-established State Supervisory Committee of the PRC was inaugurated and launched into operation, and the institutional reform of the party and the state was in full swing. In November, all the institutional restructuring schemes for 31 provinces (regions and municipalities) were released. The Central Committee strengthened the degree of overall planning, clarified the art of reform, handled the work relating to people, executed strict discipline, promoted a tiered roadmap in the sequencing of the Central Committee, the provinces and the organisations below the provincial level, and completed the overall reform in more than one year. Twenty-five agencies at the ministerial level were newly built and reorganised, 31 leadership management organisations at the ministerial level were readjusted and optimised, and notices were issued concerning the 'Three Determinations[1]' stipulations for 39 departments and the adjustment of the responsibilities of 25 departments. The size of government bodies was generally streamlined. The institutional reform optimised the institutional framework and management systems of all kinds and at all levels of the Central Committee and the local governments. The reconstruction completed the systems of party leadership, government management, the armed forces and mass work, systematically enhanced party leadership, government executive ability and the fighting capacity of the armed forces, improved the organisational structure of the NPC and the CPPCC, and made great strides in maturing and finalising the structure of party and state institutions, and modernising the national governance system and capacity.

The strengthening of overall party leadership was effectively achieved and the structure of party and state institutions under centralised, unified party leadership was completed. It was the signature accomplishment of the institutional reform to implement party leadership in all fields, respects and links in terms of institutional functions. The institutional reform strengthened party leadership in such major work as deepening reform, law-based governance of the country, the economy, national security, network information, diplomacy, size of government bodies, military and civilian integration, auditing, education, agriculture and rural areas, enriched departmental responsibilities for party organisation, publicity, the united front, politics and law, party building in institutions, education and training, and reinforced the major functions in centralising and coordinating the system. Through the reform, the party boosted its capacities in steering the orientation, planning the overall situation, making policies and stepping up reform. The party's position of providing overall leadership and coordinating all aspects was consolidated.

The important content of the institutional reform was to deepen reform of the national supervision system and unified party leadership in the struggle against corruption. The 19th National Congress of the CPC required deepening reform of the state supervision system, conducting pilot work throughout the country and setting up supervisory commissions in provinces, municipalities and counties countrywide. As of February 2018, supervisory commissions at the provincial, municipal and county levels nationwide had been all set up. The Third Plenary Session of the 19th Central Committee of the CPC took setting up the State Supervisory Committee as the primary task of deepening institutional reform of the Central Committee. The First Session of the 13th NPC approved the amendment to the constitution and the *Law of the PRC on Administrative Supervision* and determined the constitutional position of the State Supervisory Committee as a state institution. The reform of the state supervision system was a major reform of China's political system with a close bearing on the overall situation and was the top-level design of the national supervisory system. Supervisory commissions at the national, provincial, prefectural and county levels were set up and the unified party leadership in the struggle against corruption was strengthened. It ensured that supervision covers everyone working in the public sector who exercises public power. An authoritative, efficient oversight system with complete coverage under the party's unified command was established.

The institutional reform of the party and the state made dedicated arrangements for the reform of mass organisations, further improved the system of unified leadership of the party committees over mass work, made the mass organisations more political, advanced and popular with the people, and vigorously reorganised institutions across the party, the government, the armed forces and society. The mass organisations played a better role as bridges linking the party with the people.

In July 2019, Xi Jinping delivered an important speech at the meeting summarising the institutional reform of the party and the state, and fully affirmed its effectiveness and invaluable experiences, including upholding overall party leadership over institutional reform, following the principle of construction before destruction, optimising the coordination and efficiency of institutional functions, synchronising the work of the Central Committee and the local governments, unifying and coordinating reform and rule of law, and implementing ideological and political work in the whole process of reform. Practice proves that the strategies and decisions of the party and the state for institutional reform fully manifested the political advantages of the centralised, unified party leadership and China's socialist system.

COMPREHENSIVELY INTENSIFYING THE DEPTH AND BREADTH OF REFORM

After the 19th National Congress of the CPC, the party pushed ahead the comprehensive deepening of the depth and breadth of reform, systematically integrated the theoretical, institutional and practical achievements of the reform after the Third Plenary Session of the 18th Central Committee of the CPC, drew up a clearer top-level design for comprehensively deepening reform in the new era, focused on making preparations in the early stage and accumulations in the middle stage, and finally attached priority to enhancing system integration and synergy.

In November 2017, the First Session of the Comprehensive Deepening Reform Leading Group of the 19th Central Committee pointed out that the party's centralised, unified leadership over reform should stay unchanged, the general objectives for improving and developing the socialist system with Chinese characteristics and improving the modernisation of the national governance system and capacity should stay unchanged, and the value orientation of people-centred reform should stay unchanged whatever the circumstances. In May 2018, the Leading Group for Comprehensively Deepening Reform of the 19th Central Committee established after the Third Plenary Session of the 19th Central Committee of the CPC reviewed and passed the *Implementation Plan of the Important Reform*

Measures in the Report of the 19th National Congress of the CPC (2018-2022), sorted the 158 reform measures determined at the 19th National Congress of the CPC, listed such elements as the initiating units, the start and end date, the destination path and the forms of achievements of the reform, drew up the 'general work plan' of the comprehensive deepening of reform for the next five years, and made a pledge to 'ensure to comprehensively fulfil the objectives and tasks put forth at the 19th National Congress of the CPC by 2022'.

With the decisive achievements of reform in important areas and key links in 2020 as the benchmark, comprehensively deepening reform will keep fighting hard and gnaw hard bones. A set of major reform measures were successively issued, including deepening institutional reforms of the party and state, and setting up the State Supervisory Committee; setting up and improving the urban-rural integration development system, mechanism and policy system, and accelerating the establishment of the macro control system compatible with the requirement of high-quality development; promoting reform and innovation in pilot free trade zones, supporting Hainan to deepen its reform and opening up in all areas, supporting the Xiong'an new district of Hebei to take the initiative to break through and supporting the building of Shenzhen into a pilot demonstration area of socialism with Chinese characteristics; promoting state-owned capital to invest in and operate the companies for pilot corporate reform, strengthening oversight over non-financial enterprises investing in financial institutions, setting up a science and technology innovation board and implementing a pilot area registration system for the Shanghai Stock Exchange, stimulating integration and sharing of public resource trading platforms and giving more liberty to institutions of higher learning and scientific research institutions for scientific research; implementing national vocational education reform, setting up pilot schemes for national industry-university construction and improving the educational supervision mechanism; reforming the comprehensive supervisory system over the medical industry, reforming and improving the vaccine management system and carrying out pilot areas for regional medical centres.

The year 2018 marked the 40th anniversary of China's reform and opening-up initiative. In December, the Central Committee held a grand celebration for the 40th anniversary of the initiative. At the ceremony, Xi Jinping reviewed the brilliant history of China's reform and opening up over the past 40 years, summarised the great achievements and invaluable experiences of the reform and opening up, and showed the confidence and determination of the Chinese people to persevere to the end in the new era. He stressed, "We are in the middle of a torrential wave and halfway along a steep mountain road. We will either forge ahead or drift downstream in the face of more difficulties. Reform and opening up has undergone numerous hardships and dangers but still has to make an arduous journey. All members of the party and the Chinese people of all ethnic groups are exposed to more glorious missions, tougher tasks, more severe challenges and greater work." Efforts should be made to mobilise the whole party and the Chinese people of all ethnic groups to push the reform and opening up ahead in the new era and untiringly struggle to realise the 'two centenary goals' and the Chinese dream for the great rejuvenation of the Chinese nation.

By the end of 2020, the fundamental frameworks in all areas had been established and historic shifts, system remodelling and integration had been realised in many areas, laying a solid foundation for developing a set of institutions that are well conceived, fully built, procedure-based, and efficiently functioning and mature systems in all respects. In December 2020, the 17th Session of the Comprehensive Deepening Reform Leading Group of the 19th Central Committee scrutinised the appraisal report on summarising the comprehensive deepening of reform since the Third Plenary Session of the 18th Central Committee of the CPC, reviewed the monumental process of reform in recent years and pointed out that it was a profound reform of thought, theory and methods of reform pertaining to organisations, state institutions and governance systems with the wide participation of the people. The session stressed that we had overcome numerous difficulties but would still face more. We should continuously combine pushing ahead reform with serving the overall situation of the work of the party and the state, deepening reform with system integration, promoting reform with precautions against fatal risks and reinvigorating innovation with gathering power to move ahead so as to open up a new situation of reform in the new stage of development.

UPHOLDING AND IMPROVING THE SOCIALIST SYSTEM WITH CHINESE CHARACTERISTICS, AND PROMOTING THE MODERNISATION OF THE STATE GOVERNANCE SYSTEM AND GOVERNANCE CAPACITY

China's domestic and foreign circumstances have gone through profound changes, which have raised new requirements for institutional construction. Institutional construction is more about solving in-depth problems related to systems and mechanisms, and places higher requirements on the nature of systems, integration and synergy of the reforms. Accordingly, the task of establishing rules and systems is heavier. It requires more effort to uphold and improve the socialist system with Chinese characteristics and promote the modernisation of the state governance system and governance capacity. In October 2019, the Fourth Plenary Session of the 19th Central Committee of the CPC reviewed and passed the *Decision of the CPC Central Committee on Upholding and Improving the Socialist System with Chinese Characteristics and Promoting the Modernisation of the State Governance System and Governance Capacity*, systematically summarised China's monumental achievements and the remarkable advantages of its state institutions and national governance system, thoroughly answered the major political question 'what to uphold and consolidate, and what to improve and develop', profoundly expounded the fundamental, basic and important systems supporting the socialist system with Chinese characteristics and made top-level design and overall deployment for stimulating the modernisation of the national governance system and governance capacity. The plenary session systematically sorted, integrated and sublimated the institutions of the party and the state, depicted the magnificent blueprint of upholding and improving the socialist system with Chinese characteristics and provided a powerful institutional guarantee for realising the great rejuvenation of the Chinese nation.

The plenary session clearly proposed the general objective of upholding and improving the socialist system with Chinese characteristics and stimulating the modernisation of the national governance system and governance capacity. By the centenary of the founding of the CPC, the institutions in all areas will have matured and seen significant effects; by 2035, the institutions in all areas will basically realise the modernisation of the national governance system and governance capacity; by the centenary of the founding of the PRC, the modernisation of the national governance system and governance capacity will be comprehensively realised, the socialist system with Chinese characteristics will be more consolidated and its superiority will be fully displayed. To realise the general objective, the *Decisions* made new institutional arrangements for upholding and improving the institutional system of party leadership, the institutional system with the people as the masters of the country, the socialist legal system, the socialist administrative system, the basic economic system, the advanced socialist cultural system, the people's livelihood security system, the social governance system and the ecological civilisation system with Chinese characteristics, the system of the party's absolute leadership over the people's army and the supervision system of the party and the state. The plenary session stressed: it is imperative to uphold and improve the fundamental, basic and important systems supporting the socialist system with Chinese characteristics, to consolidate the foundation, to carry forward the advantages, to supplement the shortages, to overcome the weaknesses, to develop a set of institutions that are well conceived, fully built, procedure-based and that function efficiently, to boost systematic governance, law-based governance, comprehensive governance and source governance, to convert China's institutional advantages into national governance efficiency and to fully manifest the strengths of China's institutional advantages and the strong vitality of 'China's governance'.

The socialist system with Chinese characteristics, like a towering tree, is a well-conceived, complete, scientific system. Socialism with Chinese characteristics is its fundamental, basic and important system, and establishes the overall framework of the national institutional and governance system. The plenary session summarised the practical experiences and made new summaries on the basis of the fundamental, basic and important systems clarified by the CPC, for instance, determining the basic socialist economic system as taking public ownership as the main form, allowing diverse forms of ownership to develop side by side, applying distribution on the basis of labour, allowing coexistence of diverse modes of distribution and implementing the socialist market economy system; clearly putting forth 'the fundamental system of upholding Marxism as the guiding ideology'; further expounding the socialist rule of law with Chinese characteristics, the socialist administrative system with Chinese characteristics, the system prospering and developing advanced socialist culture and making overall arrangements for guaranteeing the urban and rural people's livelihood, the system of jointly-built social governance, governed and enjoyed, the system of ecological civilisation, the system of absolute party leadership over the People's Army, the 'One Country, Two Systems' policy and the supervision system of the party and the state. These systems made institutional arrangements for domestic affairs, diplomacy, national defence, governance of the party, the nation and the armed forces, as well as various undertakings of the party and the state. They were the general principles and basis of the socialist system with Chinese characteristics.

Confirming and consolidating the fundamental, basic and important systems of the country through the constitution and laws, and applying the coercive force of the state to guarantee their implementation are the important guarantee for the systematic nature, normalisation, coordination and stability of the national governance system. With the development of the times and the advancement of the reform, the modernisation of national governance has more urgent requirements for a scientific and complete system of legal norms. In May 2020, the Third Plenary Session of the 13th NPC passed the *Civil Code of the PRC*, which was the first codified law in the history of new China and a signature achievement of the construction of socialist systems and rule of law with Chinese characteristics in the new era. The *Civil Code* made systematic integration of the prevailing civil law and made modifications and improvements according to the new circumstances and problems, reflecting equal protection for the rights for life, health, property security, trading convenience, welfare, dignity and esteem. In November, the Central Committee held a meeting on law-based governance of the country and stressed unswervingly upholding the socialist rule of law with Chinese characteristics and promoting modernisation of the national governance system and governance capacity on the path of the rule of law. In December, the Central Committee issued the *Implementation Outline of Building a Law-Based Society (2020-2025)* which pointed out that building a law-based society is an important part of modernising the national governance system and governance capacity, and made arrangements to accelerate the building of a law-based society. In the same month, the Central Committee issued the *Construction Plan of the Rule of Law in China (2020-2025)* and made specific arrangements for setting up systems for complete legal norms, efficient implementation, rigorous supervision and powerful guarantees, and a system governing intraparty regulations.

Practice is the most convincing benchmark to judge whether a system is feasible, efficient and useful. The CPC led the Chinese people in creating 'two miracles' in the long struggles. The first miracle was China's rocketing economic growth. China made large strides in catching up with the times, completed its industrialisation in mere decades, a feat which took developed countries centuries to achieve, and leaped to be the world's second largest economy, with its comprehensive national strength, scientific and technological capabilities, national defence capabilities, tremendously elevated cultural influence and international influence, and notably improved people's livelihood leading to the Chinese nation standing in the east of the world in a brand new posture. The other miracle was long-term social stability. As China boasts long-term social harmony and stability, and the Chinese people live and work in peace and contentment, China has become one of the countries with the most sense of safety recognised by the international community. The emergence of the 'two miracles' was the inevitable result of the long, untiring struggles of the Chinese people led by the CPC and the remarkable advantages of China's state institutions and governance system.

GRAND CELEBRATION OF THE 70TH ANNIVERSARY OF THE FOUNDING OF THE PRC

The year 2019 marked the 70th anniversary of the founding of the PRC. The party and the central government held solemn, magnificent celebrations in a fervent atmosphere.

On 29 September, the Central Committee held the National Medal and National Honorary Title Granting Ceremony of the PRC in the Great Hall of the People. Xi Jinping granted medals to the medal and title winners, and gave an important speech, stressing that only by upholding heroes can one breed heroes, and that striving to be heroes can give birth to a multitude of heroes; greatness comes from the ordinary and the ordinary breeds greatness; as long as we have firm ideals and faith, and the spirit of persistent struggle, and come down to earth to do ordinary things well, any ordinary person can enjoy an extraordinary life and any ordinary work can create extraordinary achievements.

In the evening of 29 September, a variety show entitled *The Struggle of China's Sons and Daughters*, a large-scale music and dance epic, was held in the Great Hall of the People to celebrate the 70th anniversary of the founding of the PRC.

Square-shaped parade to celebrate the 70th anniversary of the founding of the PRC

During the Commemoration of the Martyrs Day on 30 September, a ceremony was held to offer baskets of flowers to the people's heroes in front of the Monument to the People's Heroes in Tiananmen Square, with the participation of party and state leaders headed by Xi Jinping and people from all walks of life in Beijing.

On the morning of 1 October, the ceremony to celebrate the 70th anniversary of the founding of the PRC was held with great pomp and ceremony in Tiananmen Square. Xi Jinping delivered an important speech on the Tiananmen Gate Tower, stressing that socialist China is now standing majestically in the east of the world and no power can shake China's great status or stop the advancing steps of the Chinese people and the Chinese nation. Afterwards, a grand military parade was held and 59 echelons comprising up to 15,000 officers and soldiers were reviewed. About 100,000 people held a parade with the theme of 'Building the Chinese Dream with One Heart'. That night, festivities were held in Tiananmen Square to celebrate National Day with the joyful participation of party and state leaders, and more than 60,000 people from all walks of life in Beijing.

A large-scale achievement exhibition entitled 'Great Historical Journey and Brilliant Achievements' was held from September in the Beijing Exhibition Hall to celebrate the 70th anniversary of the founding of the PRC. Up to 3.15 million visitors attended the exhibition and the page views of the online exhibition gallery exceeded 140 million in more than three months.

The local departments in different areas also organised and launched diverse festivities, publicity and education activities.

The celebration for the 70th anniversary of the founding of the PRC was a grand occasion for China. Its magnificence, generosity, elegance, orderliness and harmonious rites and music fully demonstrated the glorious accomplishments of the PRC during 70 years, vigorously manifested the prestige of China and the Chinese army, tremendously bolstered the national spirit and extensively gathered the strength of all sides. It showed the cohesion of the entire party, the whole army and the Chinese people of all ethnic groups being of one mind marching towards the goal of building an all-round moderately prosperous society when the first centenary goal was to be achieved; it declared the ideals shared by all the Chinese people to realise the Chinese dream for the rejuvenation of the great Chinese nation; it was the grand occasion for the PRC to strike a pose on the stage of the modern world undergoing unprecedented changes while China still stands proudly erect in the east of the world and becomes stronger.

---

1. 'Three Determinations' determine the organisation (the nature of the unit, such as administration, business, etc.), determine the functions (what are the powers and responsibilities of the unit), and determine the structure and number of people within the organisation.

10

PUSHING AHEAD VARIOUS UNDERTAKINGS AMID RISKS AND CHALLENGES

MAKING OVERALL PLANS FOR DOMESTIC AND INTERNATIONAL SITUATIONS AND PRIORITISING DEVELOPMENT AND SECURITY

The complicated and ever-changing domestic and foreign environment requires us to treat and tackle various conflicts and challenges from a comprehensive, dialectical and long-term perspective, and adapt to new situations and new requirements. The key is to take a correct view of history, the big picture and the outlook on development, and make overall plans for the domestic and international situations. The most important and crucial is to make a better plan for the strategic, great rejuvenation of the Chinese nation and the turbulent situation of the world not seen for a century. Xi Jinping pointed out, "Leaders and cadres should bear in mind two overall situations, first, the strategic overall situation of the great rejuvenation of the Chinese nation and, second, the turbulent situation of the world not seen for a century. It is the basic starting point for us to plan our work."

Making overall plans for development and security, being keenly aware of potential dangers and thinking of potential problems in times of peace comprise another important principle of the party to administer the country. After the 18th National Congress of the CPC, the Central Committee with Xi Jinping at the core decided to set up the National Security Commission of the CPC, proposed and implemented a holistic view of national security, initially set up the main framework of the national security system, developed the theoretical system of national security, improved the national security strategy system, established the national security work coordination mechanism and strengthened every aspect of national security work. Facing the complex situation of increasing risks and challenges at home and abroad after the 19th National Congress of the CPC, the Central Committee persistently took both the domestic and international situations into consideration, made overall arrangements for development and security, and united and led the Chinese people of all ethnic groups to overcome difficulties and progress towards the grand goals set at the 19th National Congress of the CPC.

On 5 January 2018, at the opening ceremony of the seminar on learning and implementing Xi Jinping Thought on Socialism with Chinese Characteristics in the New Era and the spirit of the 19th National Congress, Xi Jinping proposed to the new and alternate members of the Central Committee and the leaders and cadres at ministerial and provincial levels that 'Three Consistents' should be adhered to, that is, consistently upholding and developing socialism with Chinese characteristics, consistently promoting the new great construction of the CPC and consistently being keenly aware of potential dangers, and taking precautions against risks and challenges. He reviewed the interrupted process of the rejuvenation of the Chinese nation in modern times and reminded the entire party that the path ahead might not be plain sailing and more prudence should be taken even when achievements were made and strategic, subversive faults should be strictly avoided; he stressed that we should prevent and control all kinds of risks and attach priority to preventing the overall risks prone to delaying or interrupting the great rejuvenation of the Chinese nation.

On 21 January 2019, at the opening ceremony of the seminar for the main leaders and cadres at ministerial and provincial levels on sticking to the bottom-line thinking and exerting efforts to prevent and dispel major risks, Xi Jinping profoundly analysed the prevention and dissolution of risks in politics, ideology, the economy, science and technology, society, the external environment and party building, and explicitly raised the relevant requirements. Xi Jinping stressed, "In the face of sudden and perplexing changes in the international situation, the complex and sensitive surroundings and the arduous, onerous tasks of reform, development and stability, we should always keep alert to risks such as 'black swan' events, unforeseen and unlikely occurrences that typically have extreme consequences, and 'grey rhino' events, highly obvious yet ignored threats; take the initiative to prevent risks and have the ingenuity to tackle and dispel risks and challenges; prepare to prevent and withstand risks and take the strategic initiative to launch battles to head off dangers and turn adversities into opportunities." At the opening ceremony of the seminar for middle-aged and young cadres of the Party School of the Central Committee of the CPC (the National Academy of Governance) for the autumn term in 2019 held on 3 September, Xi Jinping further stressed that we are faced with golden historic opportunities but concurrently a set of major risks and tests. We should carry forward the fighting spirit and boost our fighting capabilities to achieve the objectives and tasks determined by the party.

Giving priority to development and safety concerns the grand goal of realising the Chinese dream of the great rejuvenation of the Chinese nation. At a Politburo meeting on 30 July 2020, the objective of the high-quality development stage was upgraded from 'four mores' originally to 'five mores', adding 'more safety' to 'more quality, more efficiency, more equality and more sustainability'. The Fifth Plenary Session of the 19th Central Committee of the CPC held in October stressed taking both the domestic and international situations into consideration, giving priority to development and security, paying more attention to preventing and dispelling major risks and challenges, and realising the unity of the quality, structure, scale, speed, efficiency and safety of development. The Fifth Plenary Session of the 19th Central Committee of the CPC integrated taking both the domestic and international situations into consideration in the guiding ideology of China's economic and social growth during the '14th five-year plan' period, and specially made strategic arrangements for, and highlighted the important status of, national security in the overall work of the party and the state.

APPROPRIATELY TACKLING ALL KINDS OF RISKS AND CHALLENGES

Sticking to the bottom-line thinking, being keenly aware of potential dangers and exerting efforts to prevent and dispel major risks comprise the important content of Xi Jinping Thought on Socialism with Chinese Characteristics in the New Era. Xi Jinping has repeatedly stressed the necessity of being keenly aware of potential dangers, and preventing risks and challenges. The Central Committee made in-depth analysis, research and judgment of the major risks and challenges relating to the development of national security, society and overall stability, and put forth countermeasures against them. The main risks include those relating to political security, ideological security, economic growth, scientific and technological security, social stability, ecological security, biological security, the external environment, party building and major public-health risks. Besides, he also stressed preventing and dispelling the risks for food security, energy security, nuclear security and military security.

After 2018, China's external situation went through profound and complicated changes. In particular, the US was unilaterally bent on provoking economic and trade frictions between China and the US, imposed all-round suppression of China and brought about a negative impact on China's economic operations. The Central Committee kept a close eye on it and handled it appropriately. After March, China adopted powerful countermeasures and persistently safeguarded its own legitimate interests; meanwhile, China stuck to its basic stance of dispelling disputes through dialogue and consultation, and strove to stabilise bilateral economic and trade relations. China declared to the world its principle and stance that China was not willing, nor afraid, to fight but had to fight in the trade war; China adopted countermeasures to safeguard the legitimate interests of the country, free trade and multilateral mechanisms as well as the common interests of the people of all countries. The stance won the wide support of the Chinese people and the universal recognition of the international community. During the COVID-19 pandemic, some politicians in Western countries headed by the US made the utmost efforts to stigmatise China, shook off their responsibilities for their ineffective fight against the pandemic, and took China as the scapegoat. We took a clear-cut stance in the struggle of public opinion, reasonably refuted wrong opinions, exposed their lies and revealed their base conduct and ugly deals to the rest of the world.

In July 2018, a meeting of the Politburo proposed the requirements of 'Six Stabilises', that is, to stabilise employment, stabilise finance, stabilise foreign trade, stabilise foreign investment, stabilise investment and stabilise anticipated work to stabilise the macro-economy and boost confidence in tackling the complicated situation and various challenges. In December 2018, the Central Economic Work Conference further proposed the guideline of 'consolidation, enhancement, promotion and unblocking of development' and pointed out the direction of further promoting unshakeable, high-quality development with supply-side reform as the principal line. In June 2019, the 'Amendment Incident' broke out in Hong Kong and the 'One Country, Two Systems' policy encountered unprecedented challenges. The Central Committee with Xi Jinping at the core sized up the situation, made decisions and firmly supported the chief executive of the Hong Kong SAR, the Hong Kong government and police force to take a series of moves to suppress and punish violent and criminal activities, stem violence and chaos, and restore order. The incident fully exposed the institutional loophole in maintaining national security in Hong Kong.

In May 2020, the Third Plenary Session of the 13th NPC passed the *Decision of the NPC on Establishing and Improving the Laws and Execution Mechanism for Safeguarding National Security in the Hong Kong SAR* and authorised the Standing Committee of the NPC to formulate related laws to practically prevent, stem and punish any behaviour and activities severely jeopardising national security like splitting the country, subverting the state's political power, and organising and implementing terrorist activities as well as the interference of foreign and overseas forces in the affairs of the Hong Kong SAR. In June, the 20th Session of the Standing Committee of the 13th NPC passed the *Law of the PRC on Safeguarding National Security in the Hong Kong SAR* and incorporated it into *Annex III of the Basic Law of the Hong Kong SAR*. Clearly released and implemented locally by the Hong Kong SAR, it made specific legalised, normalised and clarified institutional arrangements to safeguard national security. In July, the Committee for Safeguarding National Security of the Hong Kong SAR and the Office for Safeguarding National Security of the CPG in the Hong Kong SAR were successively set up. The implementation of the *Law of the PRC on Safeguarding National Security in the Hong Kong SAR* was the most important move by the Central Committee to handle Hong Kong affairs, cement the institutional shield to safeguard national security in Hong Kong and to exert formidable force to prevent, stem and punish crimes jeopardising national security.

In August 2020, the 21st Session of the Standing Committee of the 13th NPC decided that the Sixth Legislative Council of the Hong Kong SAR should continue to fulfil its obligations after 30 September 2020 for no less than one year until the beginning of the tenure of the Seventh Legislative Council. As requested by the chief executive of the Hong Kong SAR, in November, the 23rd Session of the Standing Committee of the 13th NPC decided on the qualifications for members of the Legislative Council and established the general rule that any member of the Legislative Council affirmed according to law to be non-compliant with the basic law, and the statutory requirements and conditions for allegiance to the Hong Kong SAR should be disqualified. Meanwhile, it clarified that members of the Sixth Legislative Council whose nomination was judged to be invalid during the election of the Seventh Legislative Council should be disqualified. This further demonstrated the political rule that 'Hong Kong should be governed by people who are Chinese patriots as well as Hong Kong patriots while rioters should be eliminated'. According to the decision of the Standing Committee of the NPC, the Hong Kong SAR Government later declared the disqualification of related members of the Legislative Council according to law, fully manifesting the dignity of the constitution and the basic law. On 11 March 2021, the Fourth Session of the 13th NPC deliberated and adopted the *Decision of the NPC on Improving the Electoral System of the Hong Kong SAR*, authorising, in accordance with the *Decision*, the Standing Committee of the NPC to improve the electoral system of the Hong Kong SAR and amend Annex I: *Method for the Selection of the Chief Executive of the Hong Kong SAR* and Annex II: *Method for the Formation of the Legislative Council of the Hong Kong SAR and Its Voting Procedures* to the *Basic Law of the Hong Kong SAR of the PRC*. On 30 March, the two amendments were voted through by the 27th Meeting of the 13th NPC Standing Committee. The NPC and its Standing Committee amended and improved the electoral system of Hong Kong according to law, providing the institutional guarantee for the comprehensive implementation of the principle of 'patriots administering Hong Kong', and ensuring the steady practice of 'One Country, Two Systems' in Hong Kong in the long run.

To reinforce centralised, unified leadership over the work in Hong Kong and Macau, in February 2020, the Central Committee decided to establish the CPC Leading Group over Hong Kong and Macau Affairs to replace the former Central Coordination Group for Hong Kong and Macau Affairs and set up the Leading Group Office which was incorporated into the Hong Kong and Macau Affairs Office of the State Council. It was an important strategic decision of the Central Committee to face up to changes in the world not seen in a century and new changes in the internal and external environment of Hong Kong and Macau, and was a significant adjustment of the leadership structure of Hong Kong and Macau affairs. It further enhanced the centralised, unified leadership of the Central Committee over Hong Kong and Macau affairs in terms of institutional setup and political institutions, not merely playing a vital role in bringing the chaos in Hong Kong back to orderliness, and exerting far-reaching influence on the further long-term practice of the 'One Country, Two Systems' policy.

Firmly unite with Taiwan compatriots to jointly fight against 'Taiwan independence' and encourage reunification. The white paper entitled *China's National Defence in the New Era* released in July 2019 pointed out that the PLA will resolutely defeat anyone attempting to separate Taiwan from China and will safeguard national unity at all costs. It showed once again the stern stance of the CPC and the Chinese Government to resolutely fight against Taiwan separatism and forces of foreign interference, and explicitly marked out the red line that should not be passed. After the election in Taiwan in 2020 with the DPP continuing to be in power, the Taiwan separatists made an erroneous judgment of the situation and launched repeated provocations in an attempt at promoting progressive

Taiwan independence and seeking Taiwan independence in legal principle, confusing the Taiwan situation and posing numerous risks and challenges to Taiwan affairs. A symposium on the 15th anniversary of the implementation of the *Anti-Secession Law* was held in Beijing in May 2020. The symposium stressed tightly crushing the separatist scheme of 'Taiwan independence' and resolutely safeguarding national sovereignty and territorial integrity. In August, as for the negative tendency of some big powers toward the Taiwan issue and erroneous signals to the Taiwan separatists, all military services of the PLA in the Eastern Theatre Command sent out troops in different directions, successively organised combat exercises with live ammunition and resolutely counterattacked the provocative acts aiming to fabricate Taiwan independence and to separate Taiwan from China.

Meanwhile, China carried out diplomacy involving Xinjiang and Tibet, refuted groundless accusations and won the understanding of most countries in the UN and in other international platforms; persistently safeguarded its territory, sovereignty and maritime rights and interests, dared to fight, was good at fighting, maintained dignity and interests, displayed its responsibilities for newly-rising affairs, toughly carried out diplomatic warfare, legal principle warfare and public opinion warfare, effectively curbed various plots and actions infringing on China's territorial security, firmly safeguarded China's sovereignty, security and development interests, and comprehensively boosted China's international status and influence.

PURSUING THE PATH OF A STRONG ARMY WITH CHINESE CHARACTERISTICS

In October 2017, the 19th National Congress of the CPC clarified that the party aims to build a people's army that obeys the party's command, can fight and win, and maintain excellent conduct, made new strategic arrangements and stressed basically realising mechanisation, making large strides in IT-based construction, boosting strategic capabilities by 2020, striving to basically realise modernisation of national defence and the army by 2035, and building the people's army into a world-class force by the middle of the century.

The Fifth Plenary Session of the 19th Central Committee of the CPC in October 2020 put forth stepping up modernisation of national defence and the army, and realising the combination of a prosperous country and a strong army; implementing Xi Jinping Thought on building a strong army and the military strategies and guidelines for the new era; upholding the party's absolute leadership over the People's Army, continuing to bolster the political loyalty of the armed forces, strengthen them through reform and technology, and run them in accordance with law, accelerating mechanisation, the application of IT and intelligence, integrated development, comprehensively strengthening military training and war preparedness, boosting the strategic capability of safeguarding national sovereignty, security and development interests, and ensuring realisation of building a strong army by the time the PLA marks its centenary in 2027.

The 19th National Congress of the CPC incorporated adhering to the party's absolute leadership over the people's army into the basic strategies of upholding and developing socialism with Chinese characteristics in the new era, included 'the CMC implementing the chairman responsibility system' into the party constitution and established the leadership system as the fundamental law of the party; solemnly wrote Xi Jinping Thought on building a strong army into the party constitution and established its guiding role in the construction of national defence and the army. The meeting on party construction of the CMC was held in August 2018. Afterwards, the *Decision on Strengthening Party Building in the Army for the New Era* was issued, making strategic deployment for cementing party leadership and party building of the army for the new era, and further enhancing the political loyalty of the armed forces. The CMC issued the *Opinions on Comprehensively Strengthening Army Management* in January 2019. The Fourth Plenary Session of the 19th Central Committee of the CPC in October made new deployment for the military commission chairman responsibility system and further improved its institutions, standards and procedures. Concurrently, the plenary session set forth building the socialist military policy-making system with Chinese characteristics, seeing that the modernisation of our national defence and our forces is comprehensively promoted, and ensuring realisation of the party's goal of building a strong army in the new era.

In November, the CMC held a grassroots construction conference, issued the *Decision on Strengthening Grassroots Army Building in the New Era* and consolidated the 'Three Excellent[1]' grassroots to set up new standards of grassroots construction, and vigorously ensure that the party's absolute leadership over the army goes directly to the grassroots level and to the officers and soldiers. In November 2020, the Politburo reviewed the *Regulations on Military Political Work* and demanded comprehensive implementation of the CMC chairman responsibility system to secure absolute loyalty, purity and reliability.

Xi Jinping reviews PLA troops on parade at a ceremony to celebrate the 70th anniversary of the founding of the PRC on 1 October 2019

Talent is the key to building and developing a strong army. In October 2020, the CMC issued the *Decision on Promoting the Establishment of the Three-in-One New Military Talent Training System*. The whole army actively adapted to the new situation, tasks and requirements, and built up the talent teams such as commanders for joint operations and talent for new types of operation, high-level scientific and technological innovation, and high level strategic managers. The situation that tapped the initiatives of a variety of talent for innovation initially took shape.

Building a strong army boils down to essentially boosting the army's fighting capacity, focusing on fighting, coupling all work with fighting, and ensuring the army is at the call of the party and bound to win. As a pivotal move of military training and war preparedness, since January 2018 when the CMC organised the mobilisation meeting of the entire party, Xi Jinping issued a mobilisation order to the entire party on the occasion of the new year for four consecutive years to set up the distinctive orientation of military training. In November 2020, the *PLA Joint Operation Field Manual (Trial)* was enacted in and became the top-level regulation on fighting in the new era. In the same month, the CMC training meeting proposed to accelerate the setting up of a new military training system, the transformation and upgrading of military training, and overall enhancement of the training level and fighting capacity.

At the new historical starting point and facing up to profound changes in the national security environment, the requirements of the times were to promote the country's prosperity, build a strong army and strengthen national defence and the army focused on realising the Chinese dream, and to build strong armed forces through political loyalty, reform, science and technology, talent and rule of law. The task of building strong armed forces registered historical achievements with the reshaping of the political ecology, form of organisation, power system, and style and image. By November 2020, mechanisation of the army had been basically completed, IT application had come a long way and the people's armed forces had taken solid strides on the path of building a powerful military with Chinese characteristics.

EXPLORING NEW PROGRESS IN MAJOR-COUNTRY DIPLOMACY WITH CHINESE CHARACTERISTICS

Since the 19th National Congress of the CPC, world multipolarisation has geared up development, the polarisation and composition of international relations has become more complicated, the international situation has faced profound adjustment and the balance of power has developed in a more balanced direction.

In the face of rising protectionism and unilateral bullying, China is in favour of globalisation, holds fast to the free trade mechanism and sticks up for multilateralism. From domestic diplomacy to international conferences and from policy publicity to practical moves, China has been incessantly giving clear signals of expanding opening up and standing fast to the correct side of the advance of history.

The report of the 19th National Congress of the CPC took promoting the construction of a community with a shared future for mankind as one of the basic strategies of upholding and developing socialism with Chinese characteristics in the new era and wrote it into the amended *Constitution of the CPC*. November 2017 saw the CPC host the World Political Parties High-level Dialogue Meeting in Beijing themed 'Working Together Towards a Community with a Shared Future for Mankind and a Better World: Responsibilities of Political Parties'. In March 2018, the First Session of the 13th NPC approved the *Amendment to the Constitution of the PRC*, incorporating the content of building a community with a shared future for mankind in the preamble and officially nominating the thought of building a community with a shared future for mankind as a national resolution. In 2018, 'a community with a shared future for mankind' was successively incorporated into the documents on the achievements of the ministerial conferences, and numerous bilateral and multilateral high-level contacts of the Forum on China-Africa Cooperation Beijing Summit, Shanghai Cooperation Organisation Qingdao Summit and China-Arab States Cooperation Forum, gathering the prestige of all parties to jointly build a community with a shared future for mankind.

At the Bo'ao Forum for Asia Annual Conference 2018, Xi Jinping solemnly declared that "China will never shut the door to opening up but will open it wider". The First China International Import Expo was held in Shanghai in November 2018. It was the first global state-level expo themed on imports and a pioneering work in the development history of international trade.

The 'Belt and Road' initiative has up till now become the most popular worldwide public product and largest cooperation platform. In August 2018, Xi Jinping proposed carrying out overall planning for the construction of the 'Belt and Road' with more care, seeking high-quality development, benefiting the countries and people along the line, and building a community with a shared future for mankind. In 2019, China successfully held the Second Belt and Road Forum for International Cooperation. In 2020, amid the COVID-19 pandemic, the High-level Video Conference on Belt and Road International Cooperation reached the consensus of building a 'Health Silk Road' and developed the favourable tendency of building a high-quality 'Belt and Road'.

China-Europe Railway Express operated 12,400 frequencies and transported 1.135 million TEUs in 2020, up 50% and 56% respectively year-on-year, breaking through the 10,000-trip-per-year barrier for the first time, running stably more than 1,000 times per month and becoming the 'steel camel caravan' helping countries along the line to withstand the pandemic.

China conforms to the times, promotes the global governance system to develop in a fairer and more reasonable direction, and has become the mainstay amid the world's chaos. At the G20 Summit, the Sino-French Forum on Global Governance, the St Petersburg International Economic Forum, the BRICS Summit, the Conference on Dialogue of Asian Civilisations, the Leaders' Summit on Climate and the Global Health Summit, Xi Jinping comprehensively explained the essence and connotations of multilateralism in modern times, advocated the outlook on global governance featuring broad consultation, common development and shared growth, building a community of life together for mankind and nature, and a global community of health for all, and voiced the just call to practice multilateralism, resist unilateralism and oppose hegemonism. China vigorously advocates mutual respect for different civilisations, equal treatment, cultural harmony, openness, inclusiveness, mutual learning, advancing with the times and innovative development, leading the international trend forward with China's concept of civilisation and arousing strong resonance among all sides.

In September 2020, China proposed the *Global Initiative on Data Security* and advocated that global digital governance should uphold multilateralism, give consideration to security and development, and uphold fairness and justice.

In September 2020, Xi Jinping declared at the UN Assembly that China's carbon dioxide emissions would peak by 2030 and China would realise carbon neutrality by 2060. This commitment showed China's function and responsibility as a responsible power in environmental protection and addressing climate change.

In January 2021, speaking at the 'Davos Agenda' of the World Economic Forum, Xi Jinping called for: "Let the light of multilateralism light up the road of mankind ahead and continuously march towards building a community with a shared future for mankind!"

China is a driver of the stabilisation of, and collaboration between, big powers. In 2019, Xi Jinping paid a historic visit to Russia. The heads of the two states jointly declared the establishment of the China-Russia Comprehensive Strategic Coordination Partnership and signed a communique to cement the stabilisation of the modern global strategy, further stabilising the China-Russia Comprehensive Strategic Coordination Partnership. In 2020, the China-Russia bilateral trade in goods reached US$107.7 billion, breaking through the threshold of US$100 billion for three years consecutively. China's proportion in Russia's foreign trade volume was further advanced and China was Russia's number-one partner for 11 years in succession. In June 2021, the Chinese and Russian presidents issued a joint declaration, formerly declaring the extension of the *Sino-Russia Treaty of Good-Neighbourliness and Friendly Cooperation*. The close cooperation between China and Russia set an example for a new type of international relations.

The China-US relationship has caught the world's attention and is related to the interests of all countries. However, it is undergoing the severest test since the establishment of diplomatic relations more than four decades ago. In the face of the bullying and provocations by anti-China forces, China has launched rational, favourable and temperate counterattacks to safeguard its national sovereignty, security, development and interests, upheld the norms of international relations and international fairness and justice, and maintained the legitimate rights and interests of all countries, especially the developing countries. Meanwhile, China has maintained stability and continuity of its US policy, adopted a firm and calm attitude, constructively handled and controlled discrepancies, and has worked hard to strategically stabilise the international system.

China and European countries have tightened their bond of common interests, strengthened coordination and cooperation, enhanced mutual trust, firmly safeguarded multilateralism and jointly addressed global challenges. In 2020, both parties completed the EU-China Comprehensive Agreement on Investment, enriching the EU-China comprehensive strategic partnership with the new content of the times. In February 2021, the cooperation between China and Central and Eastern European countries registered up to 90 dossiers for practical cooperation worth a total of up to US$13 billion, a record high. In July, Xi Jinping held a virtual summit with the French and German leaders, expressing the hope that China and the EU will expand consensus and cooperation, adhere to the construction of overall stability and balanced development of major-country relations, and play an important role in properly addressing global challenges.

Under the correct guidance of Xi Jinping's diplomatic thinking, China has not only kept a generally stable relationship with the big powers but also comprehensively improved and developed relations with surrounding countries.

China is a builder of regional integration and development. China-ASEAN relations have stepped into a new stage of all-round development. In July 2020, 'China+Five Central Asian Countries' held the first foreign ministerial video conference. The *Joint Communique of the Foreign Ministerial Video Conference of 'China+Five Central Asian Countries'* was approved and issued at the conference, and all sides reached a nine-point consensus on promoting cooperation between China and Central Asian countries, and stimulating peaceful regional development. In November, China officially signed the *Regional Comprehensive Economic Partnership (RCEP)* with 10 ASEAN countries, Japan, South Korea, Australia and New Zealand, signalling the official launch of the free trade zone with the largest population, the greatest economic and trade scale, and the most development potential in the world at present.

South-South Cooperation has stepped into a new stage. The year 2018 was the 'Year of South-South Cooperation' for China's diplomacy, in which China realised dialogues with developing countries at the China-CELAC[2] Forum, the China-Arab States Cooperation Forum and the Forum on China-Africa Cooperation (FOCAC). The Beijing Summit of FOCAC was successfully held in September 2018. Xi Jinping brought forth "not interfering with African countries' exploration of the development path suitable for their national conditions, not interfering with African countries' internal affairs, not imposing China's ideas on others, not adding any political conditions to African aid and not seeking political interests in investment and financing in Africa", establishing China's self-discipline standards in its cooperation with Africa and manifesting China's moral code in international development cooperation.

The Second Ministerial Meeting of the China-CELAC Forum in January 2018 issued a special statement on supporting and joining in the 'Belt and Road' initiative, and worked out an action plan for China and the CELAC countries to cooperate in priority fields. The Ninth Ministerial Meeting of the China-Arab States Cooperation Forum was held in 2020, displaying the collective strength of China and Arab States to jointly fight against the pandemic and jointly respond to challenges, and their political will to help each other and share weal and woe with each other, and planning the path of advancement in their practical cooperation and joint development.

Party diplomacy is an important part of the state's overall diplomacy, and an important embodiment of major-country diplomacy with Chinese characteristics. From the end of November to the beginning of December 2017, a high-level dialogue meeting between the CPC and the world's political parties was held in Beijing. In July 2021 the CPC and World Political Parties Summit was convened. Xi Jinping delivered a keynote speech, stressing that as an important force behind human progress, political parties need to set the right course forward and shoulder their historical responsibility to ensure people's well-being and pursue human progress.

Under the correct guidance of Xi Jinping's diplomatic thinking, China has calmly addressed complicated, profound changes in the international situation, appropriately tackled new difficulties and challenges arising therefrom, persistently safeguarded national interests, deeply expanded friendly cooperation, positively exhibited its responsibility as a big power and has made great efforts to explore the new situation of major-country diplomacy with Chinese characteristics for the new era.

FIGHTING AGAINST THE COVID-19 PANDEMIC AND THE GREAT SPIRIT OF RESISTANCE TO THE DISEASE

At the outset of 2020, unexpectedly COVID-19 hit China, which was a major public health emergency featuring the fastest spread, the widest infection, making it the most difficult to prevent and control since the founding of the PRC and the severest pandemic worldwide this century.

After the outbreak of COVID-19, the Central Committee gave top priority to epidemic prevention and control. Xi Jinping personally gave directions, made arrangements, prioritised safeguarding people's lives and physical health, and proposed the general requirements for proceeding with confidence, pulling together in times of trouble, carrying out scientific prevention and control, and implementing targeted countermeasures. From Lunar New Year's Day, Xi Jinping successively chaired 14 meetings of the Standing Committee of the Politburo, four meetings of the Politburo and many important party meetings, made resolute decisions with keen insight, gave sound guidance, tackled matters calmly and soberly, prudently made arrangements to win the battle against coronavirus and protect Hubei Province, including Wuhan City, sized up the situation to work out important strategies and led the entire party, the whole army and the whole nation to fight and win the battle against the pandemic by mobilising all resources and blocking the spread of the virus as soon as possible.

A medical staffer taking good care of a COVID-19 patient in Hubei

Under the strong leadership of the Central Committee, the Chinese people met challenges together, worked as one, gave support to those in difficulty and set up a line of defence for epidemic prevention and control. White-clad medical staff were brave rescuers who went into the teeth of danger. More than 540,000 medical staff in Hubei, including Wuhan, fought against the virus and more than 40,000 medical staff from 346 national medical teams resolutely rushed to the frontline of the epidemic prevention and control. People from all walks of life shouldered their duties, SOEs and public hospitals bravely took on heavy responsibilities, more than 4.6 million grassroots party organisations charged forward, more than four million community workers guarded day and night, all sorts of private enterprises, civilian-run hospitals, charity organisations, nursing homes and welfare homes exerted all their efforts. Party members and cadres took the lead in the struggle, PLA officers and men, armed police forces and police officers mustered their courage and fought in the vanguard, scientific researchers tackled critical problems, millions of deliverymen busied themselves delivering goods despite the virus, more than 1.8 million health workers worked from dawn till dusk, journalists worked at the front and tens of millions of volunteers and ordinary people made quiet contributions.

After arduous efforts, China initially curbed the spread of the epidemic in just over a month, controlled new local cases each day to be no more than 10 within about two months, registered decisive victory against the epidemic in Hubei, including Wuhan, in about three months, annihilated epidemic clusters and scored monumental strategic accomplishments in epidemic prevention and control.

The Party Central Committee adjusted the general prevention and control strategy to 'prevent imported cases and a rebound in indigenous cases' without any delay and promoted the work of epidemic prevention and control to change from unconventional, emergency prevention and control to normalised prevention and control. As requested by the Hong Kong SAR and under the centralised deployment and command of the Central Committee, the National Health Commission organised the Mainland Nucleic Acid Testing Support Team to assist in fighting the virus in Hong Kong; after the epidemic was controlled in Macau, Guangdong and the Macau SAR established a health code and a mutual recognition mechanism for nucleic acid test results, enabling normal contacts between Macau and Mainland China to be gradually resumed. China researched and developed detection kits, took the lead worldwide in vaccine research and development, and allowed all Chinese people to be vaccinated for free.

Despite huge pressure in the fight against the epidemic, China always upheld the concept of building a community with a shared future for mankind, positively launched international and regional cooperation in fighting against the epidemic, and advocated building a community of health for mankind. As of May 2021, China had provided US$2 billion in assistance to developing countries affected by the pandemic to fight the pandemic and restore economic and social development, provided anti-pandemic material assistance to more than 150 countries and 13 international organisations, supplied the world with more than 280 billion masks, 3.4 billion protective suits, 4 billion test kits, provided vaccine assistance to more than 80 developing countries in urgent need, and exported vaccines to 43 countries, giving strong support to other countries for epidemic prevention and control.

Against the impact of the epidemic, the Central Committee made overall plans for epidemic prevention and control, and economic and social growth, and strengthened its countermeasures by implementing macro policies. At the meeting on deployment for epidemic prevention and control, and economic and social growth on 23 February 2020, Xi Jinping pointed out that we should treat China's growth from a holistic, dialectical and long-term perspective, boost confidence and proceed with confidence; we should turn pressure into impetus, transform risks into opportunities, strengthen policy regulation and unleash the maximum potential and greatest functions. At a meeting on resolving poverty alleviation on 6 March, Xi Jinping stressed giving consideration to epidemic prevention and control, and poverty alleviation, alleviating poverty with more resolve, supporting resumption of production for industries enjoying poverty relief, prioritising support for poor labour forces to return to work and helping the epidemic-afflicted poor population shake off poverty. A 17 April meeting of the Politburo proposed comprehensively implementing the 'Six Guarantees' while strengthening the 'Six Stabilises', that is to say, guarantee people's employment, guarantee basic livelihood, guarantee the main market players, guarantee food and energy security, guarantee stable industrial and supply chains, and guarantee grassroots operation. Efforts were made to carry out the 'Six Stabilises' and 'Six Guarantees', which stabilised basic economic operations, won the time and conditions to pull through and provided pivotal guarantees for tackling all kinds of risks and challenges. The Central Committee and the State Council issued a set of bailout policies for the afflicted enterprises, took various measures to increase employment, stimulate investment and consumption, and stabilise the industrial and supply chains, stimulated the development of new commercial activities, promoted orderly recovery of all industries like transportation, restaurants, shopping malls, supermarkets and cultural tourism, implemented a package of policies to support Hubei's development and resumed classes in batches. With the effects of these policies, China's economy achieved a positive growth rate in the second quarter which continued into the third quarter with more robust rejuvenation. With positive growth in the first three quarters, China took a worldwide lead in rejuvenation and became the world's only major economy to experience positive growth in 2020.

A grand awards ceremony for COVID-19 fighters was held on 8 September 2020. Xi Jinping conferred medals on Zhong Nanshan, winner of the PRC Medal, and to Zhang Boli, Zhang Dingyu and Chen Wei, winners of the national honorary title 'People's Hero'. At the awards ceremony, honours were given to advanced individuals and collectives, outstanding CPC members and advanced grassroots party organisations for COVID-19 fighters.

Xi Jinping profoundly expounded the great anti-epidemic spirit of putting life first, all the people being of one mind, disregarding one's own safety, respecting science and sharing weal and woe. 'Life first' collectively reflects the profound tradition of kindheartedness of the Chinese people and the people-centred value pursuit of CPC members. 'All the people being of one mind' indicates the unity and mighty force of the Chinese people being united as one and sharing weal and woe. 'Disregarding one's own safety' mirrors the indomitable, all-conquering will of the Chinese people to overcome difficulties. 'Respecting science' collectively demonstrates the practical character of the Chinese people to be realistic, pragmatic, pioneering and innovative. 'Sharing weal and woe' displays the moral principle and sense of responsibility of the Chinese people to be united, work in concert and love peace. Xi Jinping pointed out, "In the same vein of the characteristics, natural endowment and cultural genes of the Chinese nation formed over a long period of time, the great spirit to fight the pandemic is the inheritance and development of patriotism, collectivism and socialism, and the vivid interpretation of the Chinese spirit, and enriches the contents of the national spirit and the characteristic mood of the age."

On 8 September 2020, a National Commendation Conference on Combating the Novel Coronavirus Pandemic was held in the Great Hall of the People

The COVID-19 epidemic accelerated the evolution of the global landscape and evidently increased the instabilities and uncertainties of the world in the face of new conflicts and challenges in the complicated international environment and facing up to the new characteristics and requirements resulting from the principal contradictions in Chinese society. The Central Committee took into consideration the overall strategy for the great rejuvenation of the Chinese nation and the unprecedented, turbulent situation, led the entire party and the whole nation to overcome difficulties and start afresh with tenacious will, and worked hard to seize the initiative amid crisis, open up a new situation in the turbulent conditions and move towards the goal of the great rejuvenation of the Chinese nation.

---

1. The 'Three Excellent' grassroots refers to strengthening and improving the army at grassroots or basic level. The first 'excellent' is to be aware of one's responsibilities; the second is to see things through from start to finish; the third is to focus on effectiveness and accountability.
2. CELAC refers to the Community of Latin American and Caribbean states.

11
BUILDING AN ALL-ROUND MODERATELY PROSPEROUS SOCIETY AND EMBARKING ON A NEW JOURNEY TO FULLY BUILD A MODERN SOCIALIST STATE

COMPLETE VICTORY IN POVERTY ALLEVIATION

Alleviating poverty, improving people's livelihood and gradually realising common prosperity are the essential requirements of socialism with Chinese characteristics and the significant historical mission of the CPC. Xi Jinping stressed, "In building an all-round moderately prosperous society and realising the first centenary goal, it is a landmark indicator for all the rural poor to be lifted out of poverty." "History has fully proven that the regime is supported by the people and the people are the pillars of the regime. People's support decides the survival of the party." The Central Committee with Xi Jinping as the core leader upheld people-centred development thinking, gave high priority to poverty alleviation for the governance and administration of state affairs, to building an all-round moderately prosperous society and to realising the first centenary goal, gave full scope to the party leadership and the political advantages of China's socialist system, adopted a range of original, unique and monumental moves, and organised the tough battle of poverty alleviation featuring the largest scale and the highest intensity in human history. The 19th National Congress of the CPC issued a mobilisation order to the entire party and all the Chinese people to win the battle of poverty alleviation in October 2017. The Party Central Committee and the State Council worked out *Instructions to Win the Three-Year Poverty Alleviation Campaign* in June 2018. Xi Jinping called on the whole nation at the two sessions in March 2019 to "go out to fight, rise to the challenge, take real action and adopt measures tailored to specific local conditions", blowing the battle horn of the poverty alleviation campaign. The Fourth Plenary Session of the 19th Central Committee of the CPC proposed in October "resolutely winning the battle of poverty alleviation, consolidating the accomplishments of poverty alleviation and setting up a long-term mechanism to wipe out relative poverty."

Xi Jinping paid close attention to poverty alleviation. He once came to 14 destitute areas and successively held seven meetings on poverty alleviation in Shaanxi, Guizhou, Ningxia, Shanxi and Sichuan. At the critical moment of fighting the COVID-19 epidemic in March 2020, Xi Jinping resolutely attended a meeting on poverty alleviation, delivered an important speech and mobilised the entire party and the social forces of the whole country to secure final victory in poverty alleviation. A working mechanism was set up, with the Central Committee making overall plans, the provincial government taking overall responsibility and the municipal, county and township governments taking responsibility for implementing practical work. The system of job responsibilities of top leaders of the party and government administration was strengthened. The party secretaries of five levels took charge of the work of poverty alleviation and the official positions of the leaders of the party and government administration of the poor counties were maintained. Cumulatively more than three million cadres of the institutions, SOEs and public utilities above the county level were assigned to personally offer assistance in the villages, forming the poverty-alleviation pattern featuring 'poverty alleviation via special projects, trade and society'. With the positive participation of the whole society under the tough leadership of the Central Committee, all party members played the role of the vanguards in targeted poverty alleviation for the real poor and helping them out of destitution. Emphasis was placed on poverty alleviation coupled with spiritual encouragement, knowledge, technology and thinking, implementing east-west collaboration in poverty alleviation and fulfilling the task of poverty alleviation in destitute areas. Decisive victory in the poverty alleviation campaign was secured in 2020 with the all-out efforts of the entire party and the whole country. The day, 23 November 2020, marked an extraordinary day that deserves to be recorded in history, on which China's last nine destitute counties shook off poverty. After eight consecutive years of efforts, 832 counties nationwide were lifted out of poverty, all of the 128,000 destitute villages got rid of poverty and a destitute population of up to 100 million threw off poverty, and absolute poverty and overall regional destitution were eliminated. At a summary and commendation meeting for poverty alleviation held in the Great Hall of the People on 25 February 2021, Xi Jinping solemnly declared

China had secured overall victory in poverty alleviation. It was a glorious moment for the Chinese people, the CPC and the Chinese nation!

The solution of absolute poverty, a headache of the Chinese nation for thousands of years, was of historical significance, and was a signature achievement of China in building an all-round moderately prosperous society. The achievement absorbed the wisdom and painstaking efforts of all members of the party and the Chinese people of all ethnic groups. It was obtained by a multitude of cadres and ordinary people in a down-to-earth manner, manifesting the political superiority of the CPC leadership and the Chinese socialist system. Shaking off poverty was not the end but the starting point of new life and new struggles. The Central Committee made it clear that the destitute counties, villages and households lifted out of poverty should still uphold related policies for some time and continue with the responsibility, policy, assistance and supervision concerned to effectively prevent the return of new poverty. The Party Central Committee and the State Council issued special opinions on the establishment of a five-year transition period to gradually realise the smooth transition from concentrating resources to support poverty alleviation to comprehensively promoting rural vitalisation. In April 2021, the 28th Session of the 13th NPC Standing Committee adopted the *Law on the Promotion of Rural Vitalisation of the PRC*. After poverty has been shaken off, all departments and regions should successively issue follow-up policies and promote a stable working system for transformation of poverty-alleviation achievements with rural rejuvenation strategies.

Victory in the battle against poverty laid a solid foundation for achieving the first centenary goal, strengthened the foundation of the party's governance and consolidated the socialist system with Chinese characteristics. Such problems as starvation and miserable lives that had once troubled the Chinese people have been generally eradicated, which has tremendously enhanced people's sense of attainment, happiness and security.

Winning the battle of poverty alleviation delivered historic contributions to the human undertaking of poverty alleviation provided by Chinese wisdom and planning. China spent just decades wiping out poverty which was not thoroughly eliminated in Western developed countries for centuries, a decade ahead of the objective of poverty alleviation in the 2030 Agenda for Sustainable Development and took the lead in the global undertaking of poverty alleviation. The magnificent feat will be recorded in the history of social development of the human race, powerfully showing to the world the superiority of the party's leadership and of the socialist system with Chinese characteristics.

THE GOAL OF BUILDING AN ALL-ROUND MODERATELY PROSPEROUS SOCIETY HAS BEEN ACHIEVED ON SCHEDULE

Since the strategy of building a moderately prosperous society was raised at the outset of China's reform and opening-up initiative, the CPC has always cherished the goal of fulfilling people's yearning for a better life and generations of Chinese people have ceaselessly worked hard for it. Since the 18th National Congress of the CPC, especially during the 13th five-year plan period and in the face of the complicated international situation and onerous tasks of domestic reform, development and stability, and in particular the severe impact of COVID-19, the Central Committee with Xi Jinping as the core leader remained true to our original aspirations and kept our mission firmly in mind, united and led the entire party and all the people of different ethnic groups to forge ahead in an innovative and enterprising spirit, enthusiastically pressed on with all undertakings of the party and the country, lifted China's economic strength, scientific and technological strength, comprehensive national strength and people's living standard to a new stage, and registered the historical victory of building an all-round moderately prosperous society.

China's economic strength rose dramatically and its economic structure was continuously optimised. GDP reached Rmb101.6 trillion, accounting for about 17% of the world's economy and ranked second worldwide in 2020. Per capita GNI (gross national income) broke through the US$10,000 barrier, reaching the standard of medium and high-income countries, according to World Bank criteria. Grain output was steady above 650 million tonnes for six consecutive years from 2015 to 2020, the value added of the manufacturing industry ranked first worldwide for years and the output of more than 220 kinds of industrial products ranked first worldwide. From 2013 to 2019, China's annual average rate of contribution to the growth of the world's economy approached 30% and became the locomotive of world economic growth. Total retail sales of consumer goods was close to Rmb40 trillion and consumption further increased its rate of contribution to economic growth. Investment in key areas such as the high-tech industry, agriculture and society grew continuously and rapidly. The equipment manufacturing industry and high-tech industry gathered speed, the digital economy and the platform economy surged forward, and tertiary industry became the 'new engine' of economic growth.

Major strategies were implemented to accelerate the interactive development of the 'four tectonic plates' comprising Eastern, Central, Western and Northeastern China, coordinated development of the Beijing-Tianjin-Hebei region, development of the Yangtze River Economic Belt, construction of the Guangdong, Hong Kong and Macau Bay Area, integrated development of the Yangtze River Delta and ecological protection and high-quality development of the Yellow River basin. A new type of urbanisation was steadily promoted. By the end of 2019, the urbanisation rate of the permanent-resident population hit 60.6%; infrastructure was increasingly improved, with the scale of high-speed railways, expressways, installed power generating capacity and internet infrastructure all ranking first worldwide. Meanwhile, China was also the largest goods-trading country and the country with the largest foreign exchange reserves.

The Hong Kong-Zhuhai-Macau Bridge

In 2020, the role of scientific and technological innovation was highlighted and R&D input was enlarged. China's appropriation expenditure on R&D was Rmb2.4426 trillion, increasing by Rmb1.0256 trillion over 2015 and ranking second worldwide; the amount of funds invested in R&D reached 2.24% of turnover, up 0.18% over 2015, reaching the level of a moderately developed country; the rate of contribution of science and technology hit 60.2%; the overall strength of basic research has been significantly strengthened, the overall level of chemistry, materials, physics, engineering and other disciplines has been significantly improved, a number of major original achievements have been made in quantum information, stem cells, brain science and other cutting-edge directions. China has successfully organised a number of major basic research tasks, such as Chang'e-5 returning samples of extra-terrestrial objects and Tianwen-I Mars' exploration, rendezvous and docking of manned spacecraft with the Tianhe core module. China notched up a large group of marked achievements in some primary and frontier domains, and leapt from being a 'back marker' to 'parallel running' to being the 'front runner'. China's IP output ranked top globally, with its volume of patent applications via the *Patent Cooperation Treaty* ranking first worldwide in 2019. In 2020, China's innovation index ranking was 14th worldwide and its educational level became better than the worldwide average. The average schooling years of the working-age population increased from 7.18 in 2000 to 10.75 in 2020, primary education was strengthened and developed, and higher education became popularised.

China's ecological environment made marked improvements. The environmental problem is a key to measuring whether building an all-round moderately prosperous society is accepted by the people. The 19th National Congress of the CPC determined environmental control as one of the three major efforts to secure a decisive victory in building an all-round moderately prosperous society. In May 2018, the National Ecological Environment Protection Convention was convened to prevent and control pollution. In June 2018, the Central Committee and the State Council issued the *Opinions on Comprehensively Enhancing Ecological Environment Protection and Winning Victory in Pollution Prevention and Control*, unveiling the campaign to safeguard a blue sky, blue water and clean earth. In 2020, the proportion of days with good air quality in Chinese cities above the prefecture level was 87.0%, up 5.8% over 2015; the mean concentration of PM2.5 was 33 mcg/cum, down 28.3% over 2015. In 2020, the proportion of nationwide fine surface water quality (I-III) was 83.4%, up 17.4% over 2015; the water quality of the whole length of the stem stream of the Yangtze River reached Class II; the energy consumption structure was continuously optimised. In 2020, the consumption of clean energy like natural gas, hydropower, wind power and nuclear power accounted for 24.3% of the total energy consumption, up more than 6% over 2015; the consumption of non-fossil fuel energy accounted for more than 15% of the total energy consumption and the energy consumption per unit of GDP dropped more than 13% compared with 2015. China has become the first worldwide in utilisation of new and renewable energy resources.

The reform and opening-up initiative was constantly deepened, comprehensive, in-depth reform saw vital breakthroughs and some domains realised historical reform, system reshaping and overall restructuring. Improvements were accelerated in the property rights protection law system, and key elements of market-oriented allocation reform continued to be intensified. The system of reform of state-financed enterprises and SOEs was basically formed and the economy with different types of ownership such as private enterprises developed soundly. Reforms to streamline administration, delegate power, and improve regulation and services scored brilliant results. During the '13th five-year plan' period, newly-increased tax cuts amounted to about Rmb7.6 trillion. The global ranking of the business environment jumped from 78th in 2017 to 31st in 2019. Reform and opening up was continuously expanded, the 'bringing in' and 'going out[1]' advanced as a whole, the management system for the pre-establishment national treatment of foreign investment coupled with negative list[2] was comprehensively implemented, negative lists were drastically curtailed, China's overall tariff level was lowered to 7.5% and joint construction of the 'Belt and Road' registered abundant achievements. As of late January 2021, China had signed 205 documents with 140 countries and 31 international organisations on cooperation in 'Belt and Road' construction. China's inventory of foreign investment increased from US$500 billion in 2012 to US$2.3 trillion in 2020, ranking third worldwide.

The living standard of the Chinese people was noticeably boosted. In 2020, the per capita disposable income of Chinese citizens hit Rmb32,189, a real growth rate of 31.3% over 2015. The annual average growth rose by 5.6% from 2016 to 2020, much faster than the growth rate of per capita GDP in the same period. The quality of life of residents was markedly improved, consumption increased rapidly, they had more than enough food and clothing, home appliances were universally used and multitudes of ordinary families bought cars for daily use. The Engel's coefficient[3] of Chinese nationals was 30.2% in 2020, down 12% over 2000. The average life expectancy of citizens increased from 35 years old in 1949 to 77.3 years old in 2019. The world's largest social security system was established. By the end of December 2020, the number of insured people with basic old-age insurance, unemployment insurance and employment injury insurance had reached 999 million, 217 million and 269 million respectively, more than 1.3 billion people had basic medical insurance cover, and social security card holders exceeded 1.3 billion, covering 94.6% of the total population. The housing conditions for citizens notably improved and the per capita built area of urban and rural residents was 39.9sqm and 49.6sqm in 2020 respectively.

Cultural programmes and cultural industries are developing from strength to strength. Public cultural service facilities were put into universal use. By the end of 2019, public libraries and museums nationwide amounted to 3,196 and 5,132 respectively and the coverage rate of TV programmes was 99.4%; the coverage rate of the 1,536 county (city, banner) level convergence media centres nationwide was up to 82%, the battlefield of mainstream news consensus was incessantly strengthened and cultural industries advanced fast. In 2019, the value added of cultural and related industries hit Rmb4.4363 trillion, accounting for 4.5% of GDP. The national fitness strategy was deeply carried out and the national fitness public service system was further improved. Up to 400 million Chinese people took regular physical exercise. By the end of 2019, there was an average of

25.3 sports stadiums per 10,000 people with a per capita sports venue floor area of 2.08sqm. Cultural soft power became increasingly prominent, socialist core values enjoyed popular support and the influence of Chinese culture was spread more widely.

By the 100th anniversary of the founding of the CPC, it is the goal of the CPC in the 21st century to build an all-round moderately prosperous society benefiting more than a billion Chinese people based on the basis of striving to achieve the objective of an all-round moderately prosperous society. This constitutes a solemn commitment to the people and to history. The period from the 19th National Congress of the CPC to 2020 was the decisive stage in building an all-round moderately prosperous society. The Central Committee proposed that efforts should be made to grasp the key points, make up for shortcomings, strengths and weaknesses, to be determined to win the battles to prevent and dispel major risks, to target poverty alleviation, and pollution prevention and control so that the construction of an all-round moderately prosperous society can win the people's recognition and stand the test of history. Through the continuous struggle of the whole party and the people of all ethnic groups, we have achieved the first centenary goal and built an all-round moderately prosperous society on the territory of China.

The building of an all-round moderately prosperous society has realised the wishes of the Chinese nation for thousands of years. Either in the era of backward farming civilisation or in the modern times of enduring impoverishment and longstanding debility, moderate prosperity was a wild wish beyond reach. Only under the party's leadership could this dream come true. Since its founding, the CPC has shouldered the responsibility of striving for the welfare of the Chinese people and the rejuvenation of the Chinese nation. With the continuous struggle for generations, the moderate prosperity of China finally came true. After realising this goal, the development of China and the living standards of the Chinese people have made huge strides.

Building an all-round moderately prosperous society was the key to the great rejuvenation of the Chinese nation. The 'dream for moderate prosperity' was a phased goal of the Chinese dream. Without the realisation of all-round moderate prosperity, national rejuvenation would have been impossible. Building an all-round moderately prosperous society as scheduled marked the successful completion of the first centenary goal, which laid a solid foundation for realising the second, boasted great significance in the history of Chinese civilisation, and realised a new leap from falling behind the times to keeping pace with the times.

Building an all-round moderately prosperous society, delivered significant contributions to human society, largely boosted the overall development level of human society, and enabled socialist China to tower over the east of the world in a more stately posture. The per capita GDP of about 2.8 billion people in 69 countries and regions worldwide, including about 1.4 billion Chinese, exceeded US$10,000 in 2019, according to IMF statistics. Building China into an all-round moderately prosperous society doubled the world's population with a per capita GDP exceeding US$10,000, sufficiently displaying the great vitality and superiority of socialism with Chinese characteristics. The theory and practice of building an all-round moderately prosperous society deepened recognition and understanding of the essence of socialism, opened up a new realm of socialist development and reinvigorated scientific socialism in China in the 21st century. The successful exploration into building an all-round moderately prosperous society opened up the path for developing countries towards modernisation, provided new choice for countries and nations in other parts of the world hoping to accelerate their development while maintaining their own independence, and contributed Chinese wisdom and Chinese planning to solving the problems posed to mankind.

Beijing Daxing International Airport

GRASPING THE NEW DEVELOPMENT STAGE, IMPLEMENTING NEW THINKING ON DEVELOPMENT AND BUILDING NEW DEVELOPMENT PATTERNS

With the completion of the objectives of the '13th five-year plan' and the successful realisation of building an all-round moderately prosperous society, the great rejuvenation of the Chinese nation has taken a crucial step forward, China has entered a new development stage, a significant leap of the Chinese nation into the historical process of great rejuvenation and a milestone of China's development trajectory.

The *Suggestions of the CPC Central Committee on Formulating the 14th Five-Year Plan and the 2035 Vision for National Economic and Social Development* approved at the Fifth Plenary Session of the 19th Central Committee of the CPC clarified the vision of basically realising socialist modernisation by 2035, clarified the guiding thoughts, fundamental principles and main objectives of economic and social development during the '14th five-year plan' period, narrated the key tasks of economic and social growth, and reform and opening up during this period, and made the strategic choice of the new development pattern with the domestic general cycle as the principal part, and the domestic and international dual cycles promoting each other. The *Suggestions* was the framework document for China to embark on the new journey of building a great modern socialist country and moving towards the second centenary goal, and the guide to action for China's economic and social development in the coming five years, and even beyond that.

On 11 January 2021, Xi Jinping gave an in-depth explanation of a train of major problems relating to China's economic and social growth at the opening ceremony of the themed seminar for the main leaders and cadres at ministerial and provincial levels to implement the spirit of the Fifth Plenary Session of the 19th Central Committee of the CPC. His important speech gave a penetrating reply to such major questions as the stage, patterns and methods of development, made a sensible analysis of the main basis, objectives and requirements of China's entry into the new development stage, lodged new requirements for thoroughly implementing the concept of new development, proposed the main direction to speed up construction of the new development pattern, and profoundly expounded the overall leadership of the party in the socialist modernisation drive.

Venue of the Fifth Plenary Session of the 19th CPC Central Committee

Accurately grasp the new development stage. China is standing at a new starting point in history, with the first centenary goal of building China into an all-round moderately prosperous society having been realised as scheduled, and with China entering a new development stage of building a modern socialist country. The new development stage is the one to realise the second centenary goal and promote China's great cause of national rejuvenation to a new realm. It is a phase in the primary stage of socialism and a new starting point after decades of accumulation as well as a historic leap of the Chinese people to stand up and grow rich and strong under the party's leadership. Building China into a modern socialist country and basically realising socialist modernisation are the requirements of China's development from the primary stage of socialism to the next higher stage.

Fully implement the new development concept. Development in the new stage must be complete and accurate, fully implement the new concept of innovative, coordinated, green and open development shared by all, and realise high-quality development. The new concept of development is a sound theoretical system, responds to a series of theoretical and practical issues regarding the objectives, motives, methods and path of development, and expounds the major political issues of the CPC related to development, such as the political stance, value orientation, and development modes and path. The new concept of development must serve as a baton, a traffic light throughout the development process and in all fields of development. The development modes should be practically transformed to promote quality, efficiency and serve as a force for change, and materialise development featuring higher quality and more efficiency, equality, sustainability and security. Attention must be paid to prosperity for everyone. The Fifth Plenary Session of the 19th Central Committee of the CPC set the goal of 'making significantly substantial progress in prosperity for everyone' and underscored 'solidly promoting prosperity for everyone', which was the first of its kind in the history of party sessions. We should always take satisfying people's new expectations for a better life as the starting and finishing points of development, and solve the problem of prosperity for everyone continuously and gradually on the way to modernisation. We should consciously and actively address such problems as regional disparities, the urban-rural gap and the income gap, guarantee and improve democracy in development, make overall plans for employment, income distribution, education, social security, medical treatment, housing, elderly care and baby care, implement favourable policies for rural, grassroots and less developed regions, and people in straitened circumstances in a bid to promote social equality and justice, and see that the gains of development benefit all our people in a fair way.

Speed up construction of a new development pattern. Establishing a new development pattern is the active choice of China to adapt to the stage of its economic development, the path chosen to realise its economic modernisation, a crucial strategic task relating to China's overall development, and a major strategy to blaze a trail amid turbulent circumstances, and a pivotal tactic to shape new advantages in building all-round socialist modernisation. At the Seventh Session of the 19th Central Financial and Economic Committee in April 2020, Xi Jinping proposed setting up a new development pattern with the domestic general cycle as the main part, and the domestic and international dual cycles as mutual propellers. The Fifth Plenary Session of the 19th Central Committee of the CPC launched further deployment in all respects for setting up a new development pattern. It is the strategic plan and advanced move to grasp the initiative of future development, the major historic mission to be promoted in the new stage of development, and a major move to implement a new concept of development. Setting up a new development pattern consists of domestic and international dual cycles open to the outside world rather than having a single closed domestic cycle. It is necessary to tap the potential of domestic demand, link the domestic market to better interact with the international market, leverage the domestic general cycle to attract elements of global resources, and optimise use of domestic and international markets and resources, heighten the capability for global resource allocation, strive for more strategic initiatives in opening up and development, and develop new advantages in participating in international economic cooperation and competition. Setting up a new development pattern takes the domestic general cycle based on the large national unified market rather than the local minor cycle in all regions as the main part. Its pivot is an unimpeded economic cycle and the most essential feature is to realise a high level of self-reliance.

Entering the new development stage, implementing new concepts of development and establishing a new development pattern are determined by the theoretical, historical and realistic logic of China's economic and social development, and are tightly interconnected. Entering the new development stage clarifies the historical position of China's development, implementing new concepts of development clarifies the guiding principles of China's modernisation drive, and setting up a new development pattern pinpoints the selection of China's path for its economic modernisation. Being clear about the development stage is a realistic basis on which to implement new concepts of development and establish a new development pattern. Implementing a new concept of development provides active guidance for being clear about the new development stage and setting up a new development pattern, while setting up a new development pattern is a strategic choice to address opportunities and challenges in the new development stage and implement a new concept of development.

STRIVING TO ACHIEVE A NEW VICTORY IN BUILDING A POWERFUL MODERN SOCIALIST COUNTRY IN ALL RESPECTS

Building a modern socialist country has always been the goal of the party and the state. Since the founding of new China, the CPC has diligently led the people to undertake a painstaking exploration for the development of China's modernisation. With regard to building a modern socialist country, our understanding has carried on deepening, our strategy has continued to mature, and our practice has constantly been enriched, thereby enabling us to accelerate the development of China's modernisation and to lay down the practical, theoretical and institutional foundations for comprehensively building a modern socialist country.

Socialism with Chinese characteristics has entered a new era and the CPC's understanding and grasp of comprehensively building a modern socialist country has further deepened. Xi Jinping has stressed that our country's modernisation is a modernisation of a large population, of a common prosperity for all, of a coordination of material civilisation and spiritual civilisation, of a harmonious co-existence between humans and nature, and of a peaceful development. He has also stressed that Chinese-style modernisation is either tailored to Chinese conditions, or embodies the law of socialist construction and the law of development of human society; he has further stressed that China has upheld and developed socialism with Chinese characteristics and driven coordinated progress in material, political, spiritual, cultural-ethical, social and ecological terms, has pioneered a new and unique Chinese path to modernisation, and created a new model for human advancement. These important expositions of Xi Jinping's expound the distinguished characteristics and rich connotation of Chinese-style modernisation, and provide fundamental compliance for continuing to win new victories in building a powerful modern socialist country in all respects.

China will basically realise socialist modernisation by 2035. By then, China will have made large strides in economic strength, scientific and technological strength, overall strength, economic aggregate and per capita personal income of urban and rural residents, major breakthroughs in key and core technologies and top ranking among innovative countries; basically realise a new type of industrialisation, IT application, urbanisation and agricultural modernisation, and set up a modern economic system; basically realise the national governance system and modernisation of its governance capacity, fully guarantee people's rights of equal participation and development, and basically build a country, government and society ruled by law; build a powerful state with advanced culture, education, talent, sports and good health, raise to new heights the people's cultivation and the degree of social civilisation, and noticeably improve its national cultural soft power; widely develop green production methods and life style, steadily lower carbon dioxide emissions from their peak, fundamentally improve its ecological environment, and basically realise the goal of making China beautiful; develop new patterns of opening to the outside world and form new advantages in participating in international economic cooperation and competition; raise per capita GDP to the level of a moderately developed country, obviously expand the middle-income group, basically realise equalisation of public services. and significantly narrow the gap in regional development and people's living standards; push the Peaceful China initiative to a higher level and basically realise the modernisation of national defence and the army; make substantial progress in improving people's lives, accelerating all-round development of the human race and enable everyone to enjoy common prosperity.

By the middle of the 21st century, we will develop China into a great modern socialist country that is prosperous, strong, democratic, culturally advanced, harmonious, and beautiful. By the end of this stage, the following goals will have been met: new heights will have been reached in every dimension of material, political, cultural and ethical, social, and ecological progress. Modernisation of China's system and governance capability will have been achieved. China will have become a global leader in terms of comprehensive national strength and international influence. Common prosperity for everyone will basically have been achieved. The Chinese people will enjoy happier, safer and healthier lives. The Chinese nation will become a proud and active member of the community of nations.

Bringing about the great rejuvenation of the Chinese nation, like a relay race, can only be won with the painstaking efforts of generations of Chinese people with each generation passing the baton to the next, and each generation running a good race. Everything began long ago but is far from being finished. Standing at the historic intersection of the 'two centenary' goals, China has embarked on its new journey of building a comprehensive modern socialist country. On our new journey, despite torrents along the way, the CPC will always take a people-centred approach, not forget the original aspirations, bear the mission firmly in mind, persevere by struggling day and night, push forward step-by-step the unprecedentedly great cause, and create a new and bigger miracle that will make the world stand and take notice.

GRAND CELEBRATION OF THE 100TH ANNIVERSARY OF THE FOUNDING OF THE CPC

The year 2021 marked the centenary of the founding of the CPC. During the year the party held grand, warm and solemn activities to celebrate the occasion.

A party history study and education campaign was launched among all party members. On 15 February, the CPC Central Committee issued the *Notice on Carrying out Party History Study and Education in the Whole Party* and arrangements were made for the campaign. On 20 February a mobilisation meeting was held in Beijing. Xi Jinping attended the meeting and delivered an important speech, which pointed out, "Carrying out party history study and education throughout the party is a new starting point for the Party Central Committee based on the party's century-old history, coordinating the overall strategy of the great rejuvenation of the Chinese nation and major changes in the world that have not been seen in a century, and making major decisions to mobilise the entire party and the country to confidently contribute to fully building a modern socialist country." The speech stressed that throughout the party the members must learn from history to understand the truth, to increase confidence, to respect morality, and to be proactive, and learn from the party's history to enlighten the mind, to undertake practical tasks, and to open up new prospects. Soon afterwards, all regions and ministries earnestly implemented the decisions and arrangements of the Party Central Committee and they effectively carried out the campaign of party history study and education in depth and in a down-to-earth manner. As the 'highlight' of the celebration, the campaign ran throughout 2021.

On 18 June, the opening ceremony for the *Remain True to Our Original Aspiration and Keep Our Mission Firmly in Mind – the CPC History Exhibition* was held in the Museum of the CPC which was inaugurated on that day. Construction work on the museum began on 10 September 2018 and was completed on 5 May 2021. Taking CPC history as the principal line, the museum is a site devoted to permanent and panorama-like comprehensive exhibitions of the persistent road of struggle taken by the CPC. On the afternoon of the 18th, Xi Jinping arrived at the museum and visited the themed exhibition. He led party members and leaders to review the party admission oath. For the first time, in an all-encompassing, total process, in a panoramic and epic way, the exhibition displayed the magnificent, extraordinary one-hundred-year course of the CPC's struggle, splendidly reflected the history of the party's unremitting struggle, of fearing no sacrifice, of theoretical exploration, and of bringing benefits to the people and self-construction.

On 28 June, a theatrical performance entitled *The Great Journey* was held in the National Stadium in Beijing to celebrate the 100th anniversary of the founding of the CPC. In the style of a large-scale theatre production, combining multiple means, the performance vividly displayed magnificent images of the CPC leading the people in pursuing revolution, construction and reform, and enthusiastically eulogised that since the 18th National Congress of the CPC, under the leadership of the Party Central Committee with Xi Jinping at its core, socialism with Chinese characteristics entered a new era, and the Chinese people strode proudly forward on the journey of comprehensively realising a modern socialist country. On the same day, the national commendation meeting of 'Two Excellences and One Advanced' (excellent party members and party workers, and advanced grassroots party organisations) was held in the Great Hall of the People in Beijing.

On 29 June, the 'July 1st Medal' award ceremony to celebrate the centenary of the founding of the CPC was held in the Great Hall of the People in Beijing. Xi Jinping awarded medals to 29 winners of the 'July 1st Medal' and delivered an important speech. He pointed out that the winners of the 'July 1st Medal' are all from the people and rooted in the people, they are ordinary heroes who stand by their own duties and practice silent dedication. They vividly embody the noble quality and spirit of the Chinese

Communists' firm belief, purposeful practice, hard work and dedication, and integrity. He stressed that China must vigorously publicise the touching deeds and noble morals of the 'July 1st Medal' winners and create a strong atmosphere of advocating advanced and talented people in the whole party and society, and inspiring the general public.

On the morning of 1 July, a grand gathering to celebrate the 100th anniversary of the founding of the CPC was held in Tiananmen Square in Beijing. About 70,000 people from all walks of life used the grand ceremony to celebrate the centenary of the birth of the CPC. The democratic parties, the Association of Industry and Commerce, and people without party affiliation jointly delivered speeches, paying the highest respect and expressing the most sincere congratulations to the strong leadership core of China's revolution, construction and reform - the great CPC. Members of the Communist Youth League and Young Pioneers collectively delivered speeches, paying youthful tribute to the party and expressing the ceremonious oath of 'Please rest assured, CPC, we are ready to build a powerful China'. On the Tiananmen Gate Tower, Xi Jinping declared solemnly in his speech that through the continued efforts of the whole party and the entire nation, China has realised the first centenary goal of building an all-round moderately prosperous society. This means that China has brought about a historic resolution of the issue of poverty in China, and is now marching on in confident strides towards the second centenary goal of building China into an all-round great modern socialist country. The speech systematically recalled that over a hundred years the CPC has united and led the Chinese people in opening a great path, creating a great cause and achieving great success, profoundly pointed out that all struggles, sacrifice, and creation through which the party has united and led the Chinese people over the past hundred years have been tied together by one ultimate theme – bringing about the great rejuvenation of the Chinese nation. The speech clearly raised the great founding spirit of the party, which includes the following principles: upholding truth and ideals, staying true to the original aspiration and founding mission, fighting bravely without fear of sacrifice, and remaining loyal to the party and faithful to the people, and stressed that this spirit is the party's source of strength. With regard to putting effort into learning from history to create a bright future, the speech vividly put forward the fundamental requirement of 'Nine Musts', stressing that on the new journey that lies ahead of us, we must uphold the firm leadership of the party, must unite and lead the Chinese people in working unceasingly for a better life, must continue to promote the Sinicisation of Marxism, must uphold and develop socialism with Chinese characteristics, must accelerate the modernisation of national defence and the armed forces, must continue working to promote the building of a community with a shared future for mankind, must carry out a great struggle with many contemporary features, must strengthen the great unity of the Chinese people, and must continue to advance the great new project of party building. The speech called on all party members to stay true to the party's founding mission and stand firm in our ideals and convictions, acting on the purpose of the party, we should always maintain close ties with the people, feel at one and work with them, stand with them through thick and thin, share their comforts and hardships, and continue working tirelessly to realise our aspirations for a better life and to bring still greater glory to the party and the people! Xi Jinping's important speech is a programmatic document of Marxism, a political declaration by the Chinese Communists to stay true to our original mission and stand firm in our ideals and convictions in the new era, and is the guide to action of the CPC in uniting and leading the Chinese people to learn from history to create a bright future, which further points us in the right direction and provides the fundamental prerequisite for future advancement in the new era and the journey ahead.

The celebration of the centenary of the founding of the CPC is a major ceremony of a great party and a great country based on socialism with Chinese characteristics. It was grand, solemn, magnificent, in perfect order, full of ritual, participation and modernity, in Chinese style, manner and splendour, being a grand ceremony of the party, and a festive occasion for the people. It fully displayed the vigour, vitality and high spirit of the one-hundred-year old great party, greatly strengthened the determination and confidence of the people of all ethnic groups to firmly listen to the party's words, to unswervingly follow the party, greatly inspired the lofty sentiments and aspirations of the whole party and the people of all ethnic groups in the country to strive for the realisation of the great rejuvenation of the Chinese nation, playing the role of unifying ideology, gathering strength, inspiring people and boosting morale.

The realisation of the great rejuvenation of the Chinese nation is a relay race, in which the baton needs to be passed from one competitor to another, and each generation must achieve a good result for the next generation. Everything has already begun while everything is far from over. Standing at the historical crossroads of 'two centenary goals', we have started a new journey of comprehensively building a modern socialist country. Despite the complexities and difficulties we may face on the road ahead, we shall always uphold the people-centred concept, stay true to our original aspiration and keep our mission firmly in mind, with rock-solid confidence, the spirit of racing against time, and unwavering determination, we will carry forward our unprecedented great cause one resolute step after another, and leave enduring footprints behind us, to create new and great miracles that the world will marvel at.

---

1. 'Bringing in' and 'going out' (going outside China or 'going global') are two sides of the same coin, and refer to China's reform efforts over several decades to 'bring in' or introduce advanced technology and industrial knowhow from abroad while also encouraging Chinese firms to venture outside China's boundaries to conduct business abroad.
2. 'Negative list', is an internationally accepted foreign investment management method refering to the fact that 'anything can be done regardless of law or prohibition' except for areas where foreign investment is specifically prohibited; all other areas not on the 'negative list' or 'blacklist' are open to foreign investment.
3. Engel's coefficient — the proportion of money spent on food in household expenses — is seen as an indicator of a nation's standard of living. The figure falls as a country's economic growth makes its people wealthier, and tends to rise when they get poorer.

CONCLUSION

The founding of the CPC in 1921 was an epoch-making event, which profoundly changed the course of Chinese history in modern times, the future and fate of the Chinese people and nation, and the trend and pattern of world development. From that moment on, the long-suffering Chinese people began to be masters of their own destiny and had, in the CPC, a backbone and leader for their pursuit of national independence and liberation, a stronger and more prosperous country and their own happiness.

Since the very first day of its founding, the CPC has made realising communism its highest ideal and its ultimate goal, and without hesitation shouldered the original aspiration and mission of seeking happiness for the Chinese people and rejuvenation for the Chinese nation. Over the past hundred years, all the struggles, sacrifices, and creations through which the party has united and led the Chinese people have been tied together by one ultimate theme – bringing about the great rejuvenation of the Chinese nation.

To realise national rejuvenation, the CPC united and led the Chinese people in fighting bloody battles with unyielding determination and achieved great success in the new-democratic revolution. Through the Northern Expedition, the Agrarian Revolutionary War, the War of Resistance Against Japanese Aggression, and the War of Liberation, we fought armed counterrevolution with armed revolution, toppling the three mountains of imperialism, feudalism, and bureaucrat capitalism and establishing the PRC, which made the people masters of the country. This is how we secured our nation's independence and liberated our people. The victory of the new-democratic revolution put an end to China's history as a semi-colonial, semi-feudal society, to the state of total disunity that existed in old China, and to all the unequal treaties imposed on China by foreign powers and all the privileges that imperialist powers enjoyed in China. It created the fundamental social conditions for realising the rejuvenation of the Chinese nation. Through tenacious struggle, the CPC and the Chinese people solemnly declared to the world that the Chinese people had stood up, and the time when the Chinese nation could be bullied and abused by others was gone forever!

To realise national rejuvenation, the CPC united and led the Chinese people in endeavouring to build a stronger China with a spirit of self-reliance, achieving great success in socialist revolution and construction. By carrying out socialist revolution, we eliminated the exploitative and repressive feudal system that had persisted in China for thousands of years, and established socialism as our basic system. In the process of socialist construction, we overcame subversion, sabotage, and armed provocation by imperialist and hegemonic powers, and brought about the most extensive and profound social changes in the history of the Chinese nation. This great transformation of China from a poor and backward country in the East with a large population into a socialist country laid down the fundamental political conditions and the institutional foundations necessary to realise national rejuvenation. Through tenacious struggle, the CPC and the Chinese people solemnly declared to the world that the Chinese people were capable of not only dismantling the old world, but also building a new one, that only socialism could save China, and that only socialism could develop China!

To realise national rejuvenation, the CPC united and led the Chinese people in freeing the mind and forging ahead, achieving great success in reform, opening up and socialist modernisation. We realised the great turning point of far-reaching significance in the history of the party since the founding of the PRC, established the party's basic line for the primary stage of socialism, resolutely advanced reform and opening up, overcame risks and challenges from every direction, and founded, upheld, safeguarded, and developed socialism with Chinese characteristics. It enabled us to realise the historical transformation from a highly centralised planned economy to a socialist market economy brimming with vitality, and from a country that was closed and semi-closed to one that is open to the outside world across the board. It also enabled us to achieve the historical breakthrough from a country with relatively backward productive forces to the world's second largest economy, and to make the historical leap of raising the living standards of its people from bare subsistence to an overall moderately prosperous level, and ultimately to moderate prosperity in all respects. These achievements fuelled the push toward national rejuvenation by providing institutional guarantees imbued with new energy as well as the material conditions for rapid development. Through tenacious struggle, the CPC and the Chinese people solemnly declared to the world that by pursuing reform and opening up, a crucial move in making China what it is today, China had taken great strides to catch up with the times!

To realise national rejuvenation, the CPC has united and led the Chinese people in pursuing a great struggle, a great project, a great cause, and a great dream through a spirit of self-confidence, self-reliance and innovation, achieving great success for socialism with Chinese characteristics in the new era. Following the 18th National Congress of the CPC, socialism with Chinese characteristics entered a new era. In this new era, we have upheld and strengthened the party's overall leadership, ensured coordinated implementation of the 'Five in One' programme and the 'Four Comprehensives' strategy, upheld and improved the system of socialism with Chinese characteristics, modernised China's system and capacity for governance, remained committed to exercising rule-based governance over the party, and developed a sound system of intraparty regulations. We have overcome a series of major risks and challenges, fulfilled the first centenary goal, and set out strategic steps for achieving the second centenary goal. All these historical achievements and changes in the cause of the party and the country have provided the cause of national rejuvenation with more robust institutions, stronger material foundations, and a source of inspiration for greater initiative. Through tenacious struggle, the CPC and the Chinese people have solemnly declared to the world that the Chinese nation has achieved the tremendous transformation from standing up to growing prosperous to becoming strong, and that China's national rejuvenation has become a historical inevitability!

Over the past hundred years, the CPC has united and led the Chinese people in writing the most magnificent chapter in the millennia-long history of the Chinese nation, embodying the dauntless spirit that Mao Zedong expressed when he wrote, "Martyrs' sacrifice strengthens bold resolve which dares to make the sun and the moon shine in a new sky." The great path we have pioneered, the great cause we have undertaken, the great achievements we have made over the past century will go down in the annals of the development of the Chinese nation and of human civilisation.

A century ago, at the time of its founding, the CPC had only about 50 members. Today, with more than 95 million members in a country of more than 1.4 billion people, it is the largest governing party in the world and enjoys tremendous international influence.

A century ago, China was in decline and withering away in the eyes of the world. Today, the image it presents to the world is one of a thriving nation that is advancing with unstoppable momentum toward rejuvenation.

Over the past century, the CPC has secured extraordinary historical achievements on behalf of the people. Today, it is rallying and leading the Chinese people on a new journey toward the realisation of the second centenary goal.

Today, a hundred years on from its founding, the CPC is still in its prime, and remains as determined as ever to achieve lasting greatness for the Chinese nation. Looking back on the path we have travelled, we are extremely proud of ourselves; looking forward to the journey that lies ahead, we are full of confidence. In the new journey, the whole party and the Chinese people of all ethnic groups must rally closely around the Party Central Committee with Comrade Xi Jinping at its core, and uphold Xi Jinping Thought on Socialism with Chinese Characteristics in the New Era as the guiding ideology, hold high the banner of socialism with Chinese characteristics, stay true to our original aspiration and keep our mission firmly in mind, learn from history to create a bright future, strive for the realisation of building an all-round great modern socialist country, and the Chinese Dream of national rejuvenation!